The front cover title "Mohegan" is a facsimile of the hand-written header in the *Agreement and Account of Crew* for the final voyage to New York (see Appendix 5, p. 438). Its background shows the stricken steamship *Mohegan* impaled on the Manacle Rocks.

———————————————

The spine of this book represents the *Mohegan*'s funnel, featuring the Atlantic Transport Line red and black colours: that being its distinctive marque.

MOHEGAN

The Cornish Titanic

Christopher Holwill

Tothill • Publications

Copyright © 2013 Christopher Holwill.

ISBN: 978-0-9575683-0-3

All rights reserved. No part of this book shall be reproduced or transmitted in any form or by any means, electronic or mechanical, including photocopying, recording, or by any information retrieval system without written permission of the publisher.

First published in the United Kingdom in 2013 by Tothill Publications.

Printed and set in Great Britain

by Latimer Trend and Company Ltd.

Estover Road, Plymouth, PL6 7PY

sales@latimertrend.co.uk

Although every precaution has been taken in the preparation of this book, the publisher and author assume no responsibility for errors or omissions. Neither is any liability assumed for damages resulting from the use of this information contained herein. While the author has made every effort to provide accurate Internet addresses and the contact information at the time of publication, neither the publisher nor the author assumes any responsibility for the errors, or for any changes that occur after publication. Further, the publisher does not have any control over and does not assume any responsibility for authors or third-party websites or their content.

This book is dedicated to: those aboard the Mohegan, in particular, the passengers and crew who perished in the disaster; the brave men who saved those who had endured the horror of that night; and to the good folk of St. Keverne, Coverack, Porthoustock, and Falmouth, who gave their unstinting help and comfort to those in need.

Contents

Chapters

List of Illustrations

The Royal Cornwall Sailors' Home

SS Mohegan – Salvaged Material

Key Players in the *Mohegan* Story

Ships and Views of the Wreck Sites

Scenes of the Interment and Burial Sites

A Selection of Rocks from the Manacles

Tables

INTRODUCTION

The rocks and submerged reefs that surround our island have caused innumerable maritime disasters and with tragic loss of life. In the south-west, the sea floor is carpeted with shipwreck and many communities around those shores share in their sad memories of lives lost and with family fortune forever changed, at the whim of shifting tides and storms at sea.

The southern shore of the County of Cornwall has rocks that lie in patient wait for the unwary vessel: the Scilly Isles, the Seven Stones, Wolf Rock, Land's End, the Runnelstone, and the Stags.[1] These cruel rocks have witnessed many shipwreck tragedies. But none are more infamous than the dreaded Manacle Rocks.

The very name evokes fear; ill-fated visitors are hopelessly entrapped, 'manacled' and unable to escape its clutches. The sharp granite rocks, like giant's teeth, rip the bottom out of a hapless vessel: scattering its sails, rigging, machinery, and baggage into a foaming tempest: a hellish mix of a ship's paraphernalia and humankind.

Over the centuries, the surrounding villages have been alerted by mournful cries, shrieks and the prayers of terrified crew and passengers, and were helpless witness to the shipwreck dramas that have been relentlessly visited upon these rocks.

This book is the story of the wreck of the steamship *Mohegan*, a transatlantic liner. She was, on her second only trip, and crossing the Atlantic. Aboard, were mainly rich American passengers, all travelling by first-class passage. The crew were, in the main, English and most were living in London. The ship's master was Capt. Richard Griffith, a Welshman and the commodore of the fleet, operated by the Atlantic Transport Line: an American, Baltimore-based company, with its main operation within the UK. Capt. Griffith was a well-liked man but with a surprising history that is uniquely revealed here for the first time, and with a unexpected turn of events that has been uncovered, after remaining secret for one hundred and fifteen years.

This book also offered an opportunity to bring together under the one cover, not just the story of the *Mohegan,* but also the associated areas of local and national interests, previously only available in miscellaneous publications. It is hoped that by publishing this data, as an adjunct to main story, the prevailing spirit and generosity of that age is accorded a rightful record for posterity. The sacrifice and devotion to duty, as evidenced here in times of crisis, display the very best of human spirit.

Family papers and anecdotes that eventually surface, demand that their guardians preserve those ephemeral data for future historians, and so to add to the rich story, which is our shared maritime history.

---

[1] The Stags is the generic name for the rocks extending for half a mile south of the Lizard. Each rock has its individual name: Carligga, Carnvel, Ennach, Man o' War, Dales Rocks, Maenheere (furthest south), and the Mulvin (furthest west).

Where text from contemporary newspapers and other publications are included, they are transcribed as close to the original as possible—in terms of its archaic spelling and syntax—endeavouring to preserve the character of a period publication.

In addition, it would be unforgivable (in my view) not to include the vernacular of the period. Such phrases, as for the description for death: "when it was found the vital spark had fled"; "died by the visitation of God"; "paid the debt of nature"; and, "died in the full measure of a blessed immortality" are simply too evocative of the period to ignore.

And here, a rather sentimentalised depiction of a death from the year 1875, exemplifies that very point:

> But she seemed to slumber peacefully and quietly until evening, when without a struggle, or the move of a muscle of her marble-like features, her spirit left its earthly tenement for a blessed immortality.
> So imperceptibly was it that no one in the room knew the precise moment she ceased to breathe. Calm and resigned in life under her afflictions, she passed away silently as the falling of an autumn leaf. [2]

The poor unfortunates who perished in the *Mohegan* disaster, had no such idealized exit from this world. Their deaths were sudden and brutal, in the darkness of night and in an unforgiving environment: the deep, dark, and deadly waters that swirl around the Manacle Rocks.

Not on account of the nearness of time does the *Mohegan* disaster stand prominently amongst the Manacles' victims, but because of the dreadful loss of life associated with it.

> The Manacle bell will toll on and express something of the desolation of homes in England and America and of the sorrow of a thousand broken hearts. [3]

Chris Holwill. [4]

---

[2] *Richland Shield and Banner;* Mansfield, Ohio, USA, 1875.

[3] *Cornish Magazine – "Around the Manacles"* 1898, Vol. 1, 403 - 416; Bluett, Albert.
The 'Manacles' is the inclusive title of a number of rocks that stand between a quarter of a mile and a mile from the shore: the scene of the *Mohegan* and other notable disasters.

[4] The author and a previous British Sub-Aqua Club (BSAC) Regional Coach for the South-West.

Acknowledgments

Without the help and expertise that is represented in the following list, this publication would not have been possible. I was most encouraged by their response, the unstinting attention to detail, and with the obvious pleasure shown in supplying the information. I do hope that this book reflects the quality of their response and will act as incentive for future authors—and that they are as fortunate in their selection of contributors, as I have been.

———————————————

Axford, David; *HMS Ganges* Association.

Bass, Jane; Archive Assistant; Essex Record Office.

Bastcock, David; C. Bastock (Funeral Directors) Ltd., Olton, Solihull.

Bate, Paula; a Gallaway family member.

Berners-Lee, Sir Timothy John; OM, KBE, FRS, FREng, FRSA – inventor: World-Wide-Web.

Bevan, Bob; Deputy Churchwarden at St. Akeveranus Church, St. Keverne.

Binney, Ann; Administrator for Budock and Mawnan Churches.

Boote, David; Leyton and Leytonstone Historical Society.

Bosustow, Henry; Chairman of the Porthoustock Village-hall.

Bradley, David; Maritime History Archive; Memorial University of Newfoundland (MUN).

Brown, Tobey; Plymouth College of Art.

Carlyon, Mr Edward; Assistant deputy Coroner for Cornwall [2011].

Carlyon, Dr Emma E.; Coroner for Cornwall [2012].

Caronwen Samuel; The National Library of Wales, Aberystwyth.

Chainey, Elise; Heritage Administrator; R.N.L.I.

Charles, David; Editor of the *BBKA News;* President 1992–1993 (British Beekeepers Association).

Colsell, Rob; West of England Quarry, Porthoustock, Cornwall.

Contractor, Carla; a Unitarian, local historian, and Trustee of the Arnos Vale Cemetery.

Cox, Barry; Honarary Librarian R.N.L.I.

Elsey, Lyndon; Assistant Registrar of Cemeteries and Crematorium, City and County of Swansea.

Gearon, Gerry; Press Officer; Falmouth Lifeboat R.N.L.I.

Gilson, Vikki; Communications Manager, Trinity House.

Gosling, Rick; Plymouth College of Art.

Haines, Sarah; Careers & Employer Engagement Officer, Plymouth College of Art.

Hart, Cyril; Author.

Hawker, Robert J.; *British Bee Keeping Association* – BBKA.

Hodges, Alastair; Trago Mills Company, Falmouth.

Hudol, Bryn; Abersoch, Pwllheli.

Hughes, Beti Isabel; Abersoch, Pwllheli.

Hunt, Margaret; President, St. Keverne Local History Society.

Jewell, Adrian; Boatman at Porthoustock.

Jones, Dewi Pritchard; HM Coroner, North West Wales District.

Kinghorn, Jonathan; Author; Lexington, Massachusetts.

Kinley, Martin; Photographer; Isle of Man.

Kennerley, Alston – BA (Lampeter), Dip Ed (Wales), MA (Exon), PhD (CNAA/Plymouth), Master Mariner, FNI. Honorary Researcher and Historian of the Plymouth University.

Kitchen, Eugenie Victoria; a Griffith family member.

Kneale, John; Charlestown Shipwreck and Heritage Centre.

Larn, Richard; OBE; Author.

Measure, Maureen; Leyton and Leytonstone Historical Society.

Middleditch, Emily; Administration Officer & Mayor's Secretary, Falmouth.

Mitchell, Lee Alan; Sexton at the Falmouth (Old) Cemetery.

Moyle, Terry; Author; St. Keverne Local History Society.

Owston, Timothy J.; York, England.

Parker, Jo; Archivist; Vestry House Museum – Walthamstow, London.

Potter, Alan; Lancashire [contributor: RootsWeb – Ancestry.Com].

Prettejohn, Edward.

Quigley, Elaine B.A. Hons. M.BIG (Dip); The British Institute of Graphologists past Chairman and current Administrator and Journal Editor.

Rheinberg, Nicholas; Archivist, Coroners' Society, UK.

Richards, Karen; Secretary, St. Keverne Local History Society.

Roskilly, Rachel and Joe; Tregellast Barton Farm, St. Keverne.

Russell, Nicholas; Science Communication Group; Imperial College, London.

Scott, Beri; Information Officer, Norwegian Embassy.

Silcock-Longden, Dena; Wardle and Smallbridge History Group.

Spry-Leverton, Peter and Harry; Leverton-Spry family members.

Thingsrud, Leif; Archivist for *Riksarkivet*; The National Archives of Norway.

Thomas, David; Archivist, Cornwall Record Office, Cornwall Council.

Weaver, Anne; Churchwarden; Parish of Par, Cornwall.

Whitaker, Tony; former Vicar; St. Akeveranus Church, St. Keverne.

Whiteside, D. Thomas: Gwynedd Council; Archives, Museums and Arts Service.

Wilson, Peter; Walthamstow Cemetery.

Worth, Penny; Researcher; Ditchling Local History Group.

CHAPTER 1

A Town and Villages: Adjacent to the Disaster

Falmouth Town

Falmouth, with a long tradition of maritime trade and transportation, provides a safe haven for ships and for those who depend on the sea for their livelihood. Falmouth town is situated on a deep-water channel that is the estuary to the River Fal. It is the deepest natural harbour in Western Europe and the third such deepest in the world. The Manacle Rocks are located at the south-western entrance to Falmouth Bay.

The town has given not only a safe anchorage over the centuries but also a convenient embarkation point for continental Europe and the Americas.

There is archaeological evidence for Neolithic man, together with the permanent imprints of Roman, Norman and Saxon occupation in the surrounding area. The Roman conquerors were particularly interested in tin metal: a valuable component in the manufacture of bronze. Lead, copper and tin metals, were mined in this area.[5]

Falmouth was depicted in a map (c. 1540) which showed only one building in that area; the important towns at that time were Truro and Penryn, both situated inland and with access to the Fal river. The Killigrew family created Falmouth, and by 1613, a plan had been drawn up to build a whole town. By the year 1664, the town boasted 200 houses, and a new large church. Falmouth's importance as a point of embarkation during the 17–20th centuries is reflected in the unusually high number of sombre accounts of young lives lost at sea.

The Post Office Packet Service was established in 1689, and carried mail and bullion to Corunna, in Spain. The packets were sleek and fast brigantines, with a crew of some 30 men, designed to cut and run, rather than fight and risk capture. They were a huge success, and did much to establish Falmouth as an important maritime centre. Whilst Falmouth grew wealthy on the back of this service and with ships entering the harbour to collect directions from the ships' owners for their next destination, the number of houses grew to 1,252 by the year 1861.

However, this golden era was brought to a close when the railway connection was made between Southampton and London. This, combined with the Lloyds signal station being established on the Lizard, in 1872, brought about the collapse for the packet service in Falmouth, as there was no need to put into port for instructions, and the goods were more easily taken on to Southampton, for distribution by rail. In response, Falmouth built a series of dry docks, and turned her hand to shipbuilding, repairs, and maintenance: becoming an important centre for these activities.

---

[5] Cornwall has the remnants of industrial heritage dating back to the period when the Celts traded gold, lead and tin with the Phoenicians and the Romans.

Little wonder then, that the Falmouth area held a strong attraction for maritime activity, since early man recognized it as a perfect access point for the fishing grounds, just off the shore. It is now easy to forget how prolific the fish stocks once were, before the modern fishing fleets had almost decimated them. Pilchard, mackerel, and crustacea, were there for the taking, in almost unimaginable numbers.[6] This unlimited bounty from the sea certainly helped develop trade with other communities and in establishing an early settlement in this area, serving to promote Falmouth as a major seaport.

But, as with every silver lining, inevitably there is a darker side. The town and surrounding villages have the misfortune in sharing its coastline with the Manacle Rocks. The rocks had (and still have) an insatiable appetite for the unwary mariner.

St. Keverne Village

This small village has been referred to, over the years, as: St. Achebrannus of Lannachebrann – 1085; St. Akeveranus – 1201; St. Akevranus 1278; St. Akeferan – 1295; St. Kaveran – 1236; St. Kyeran – 1240; St. Kyeran – 1265; St. Kieran – 1280; St. Keveren – 1580.

The true form for the name of the patron Saint of St. Keverne appears to have been Akeveran. In the 13th century an attempt was made to identify him with the better known Irish Saint, Kierian. This attempt was, perhaps, due to the Cistercians of Beaulieu who acquired the Church (circa 1230), and whose sister houses in Southern Ireland would have made them well acquainted with St. Ciaran or Kieran. At the Reformation, however, the popular and more correct spelling, Keveran or Keverne, came back again. A local modern-day historian gives his account:

> Sometime between 500 and 600 A.D., a man came to St. Keverne, who eventually gave his name to the place. KIERAN or KEV RAN came from Cape Clear in the district of Kerry, Ireland and was probably the first Christian to live in this parish.
> On the present site of the parish church[7] he built himself a hut to live in, and another close by, to serve as a church the entrance of which he would have placed a wooden Cross.
>
> It is not known whether he died here, but if he did, he would have certainly been buried near his two huts. Later, when other Christians died, they would have been buried near him. Thus the church and churchyard had begun, in the small hamlet of St. Keverne.
>
> The more permanent building which followed survived the Saxon invasion, it is mentioned in Saxon Charters in 911 A.D., and there is no doubt it was collegiate: a centre of religious learning and education. The church and lands were seized by Robert, Earl of Mortain soon after the Norman Conquest, and it was then that the collegiate character of the Church was lost, and it became the Parish Church of the largest parochial area in West Cornwall (10,158 acres).

---

[6] In the year 1832, 1,400 hogsheads (a large cask or barrel, of indefinite contents, that contains from 100 to 140 gallons) of pilchards were landed in one day, on Porthallow beach. However, this bounty had been known to fail. In the years 1786 and 1787 not a single pilchard appeared on the Cornish Coast.

[7] Datum point: SW 72 SE 73. See http://www.panoramicearth.com/4698/Lizard_Peninsula/St_Akeveranus_Church for a panaoramic view.

St. Keverne is mentioned in the Domesday Book [8] of 1085, as LANNACHEBRANN, i.e. the Church of St. Kebran, and reads: 'The Canons have one Manor called LANNACHEBRANN, which the same Saint held T.R.E. (Time of Edward) therein are eleven acres of land. Seven teams can plough this. The Canons have eight beasts, thirty sheep and twenty acres of pastures. Worth five shillings, when Count received it worth forty shillings.'

King John founded the Cistercian Abbey of Beaulieu in 1204, his son Richard Earl of Cornwall, presented the Manor of Lannachebrann with the Church of St.Acheveran to the Abbot of Beaulieu in 1235. Thus from that date until the dissolution of the Monasteries by Henry VIII in 1538, the Abbotts of Beaulieu were Patrons of St. Keverne. [9]

The church was built in about the year 1200 and its four sides of the church tower directly face the main cardinal compass points and is now named, St. Akeveranus, but it is known colloquially as the St. Keverne Church. It has been inextricably linked for over 1,300 years with the local fraternity, who have come to this place to worship. To see this beautiful little church, set to one side of an archetypal village square, it is difficult to imagine the grief and despair that has been witness to this place. The parchment pages of the parish register teem with the entries of the burial of unknown bodies, washed ashore on St. Keverne's long coastline.

Norman architecture is still to be seen in the north-west corner of the Church, but most of the present building is of 15th century origin. The Church spire was built in the year 1450 of granite ashlar—21 feet square, of two stages, 60 feet in height, battlement and showing the bases of the four angle pinnacles of the original design. These four pinnacles were probably destroyed when the tower was struck by lightning in 1770. This led to the re-building of the well-proportioned, octagonal ribbed spire, 38 feet high, which has been a landmark and a guide to ships for many generations.

The ancient priory church at St. Keverne [10] has played a significant role in the day-to-day life of the villager: a focus point for worship naturally, as well as a noted landmark on the eastern side of the Lizard for the local fishermen and as a warning for the grimly named Manacle Rocks. So when it was destroyed by lightning in 1770, it was an obligation to rebuild as soon as possible.

A proximity of the Manacle Rocks (the village is situated but a mile inland from the shoreline) imposed a sad duty on the local villagers, with its constant source of dead for burial in their old churchyard: a last resting place for the hundreds of shipwreck victims over the centuries.

In the 19th century, the village had been associated with three great shipping disasters: the wrecks of the sailing ship *John*[11] in 1855; the transport ship *Dispatch* at Coverack Cove, in 1809; and the *Mohegan*, in 1898.

---

[8] *Domesday Book* is the record of the great survey of England, completed in 1086, executed for William I of England, or William the Conqueror.

[9] Frank Curnow (Churchwarden for 29 years); *The History of St. Keverne Church;* St. Keverne Local History Society.

[10] Its OS map reference is SW 72 SE 73 and a 360° view of the church and graveyard may be seen at the website; http://panoramicearth.com/4697/Lizard_Peninsula/St_Akeveranus_GraveyardKeverne.

[11] The largest internment in the churchyard is marked by a relatively small slate headstone. On the top of the stone and roughly hewn is a vessel depicted as in distress on a stormy sea. A few words tell of the 120 victims resting there from the wreck of the *John* in May, 1855. The ship was a 468 ton, three-masted sailing ship that traded primarily between the South West of England and the United States and Canada during the mid 1800s. On board were 154 adult passengers, 98 children, and 16 infants, together with a crew of 19, making the total of 287 souls on board.

from these three disasters alone, 297 lives were lost, and the majority is interred in the St. Keverne churchyard.[12]

The fine reputation of the good folk of St. Keverne, and surrounding district is noted far and wide, as described in this extract from the records of the local history society:

> The interments arising from shipwrecks are, of course, largely responsible for the rapid filling up of the churchyard, and this has put a strain on the resources of the parish, which the hospitable folk of the locality would not have been called upon to meet had they not chanced to live near such a deadly coast. The responsibilities of their position have been cheerfully faced by the parishioners, and many have been the testimonies to their sympathy and generosity.[13]

Only two other wrecks have resulted in a greater loss of life, on the Cornish coast. The wreck of the transport ship *Queen,* on Trefusis Point, Falmouth, on January 14th 1814, resulted in the loss of nearly two hundred soldiers invalided home from the Peninsular War, and the foundering of the *Schiller,* a German Atlantic liner lost off the Isles of Scilly on May 7th 1875, where three hundred and thirty men, women, and children were lost.

One good turn deserves another.

> Wrecked sailors have acknowledged with gratitude the bravery of their rescuers, who dwell in the cove [Porthoustock] by the sea and the village above, and bereaved relatives have borne witness to the reverence and care with which the people have treated the remains of those who perished. Kindness of this character often brings its own reward. This is illustrated in a striking manner by a story related by Hals, the historian.[14] An ancestor in the family of Sandys, noted in the parish, with seven other persons of St. Keverne, were driven to sea in an open boat by a gale in the year 1702, and after being exposed to the tempest for four days and three nights reached the coast of Normandy. They were captured and made prisoners, but a gentleman who saw Sandys remembered him, and exclaimed, "I know your person, and well remember the kindness you shewed me in my distress many years ago at your house when my ship was cast away and lost on the coast of St. Keverne." The narrative tells how they embraced each other, and on the circumstances coming to the knowledge of the King, Louis XIV, the Englishmen were released and allowed to return to their own country. This is a romantic proof of the value of kindness but the parishioners do not find such ready results in these prosaic days.
>
> One would regard it as obvious that St. Keverne is entitled to some help from outside sources, in bearing the burden of providing for the misfortunes of those who go down to the sea in ships, but the days of romance are gone, and an unsentiment shrugs its shoulders and tells the incumbent vicar[15] that it has no funds at its disposal with which to assist in such matters. It is to be hoped that some, out of the many with whom the claim should have some weight, will be found willing to bear a share of the cost. If there is a sufficiency of funds the vicar hopes to make an adequate extension of the

---

[12] There are a total of 300 known interments in this churchyard, from shipwrecks on the Manacles and the adjoining coastline.

[13] Courtesy: St. Keverne Local History Society.

[14] William Hals (1655–1737?) was a noted British historian who compiled a *History of Cornwall.*

[15] The Reverend Canon William Arthur Diggens, the vicar at St. Keverne, in a correspondence with the Board of Trade.

churchyard, to provide a proper mortuary and possibly to place headstones on unmarked graves, and by so doing, repair the neglect of a former generation. [16]

The local history here is of course sombre, but as you walk in the churchyard and study the lines of headstones which tell of memorable catastrophes, or stand within the spacious interior of the church and gaze upon the outstanding *Mohegan* memorial window, [17] one comes under the power of a pitiable and touching spell, and with a tragic fascination for this setting.

A notable resident here was the village blacksmith Michael Joseph (An Gof – or the 'smith' in Cornish). He was the co-leader for the first of two Cornish rebellions, one in 1497, the other in 1547, that had their roots in St. Keverne. In the church wall, facing the square, there's a memorial stone to this man of. He led a protest against the punitive taxes levied by King Henry VIII and ultimately paid for his insurrection with his life.

For bells are the voice of the church.

When listening to the church bells ring out, some old villagers remember that bell number-7 was placed in the tower by William Neil King, of Ohio.[18] It was donated in memory of his brother Worthington King who perished with his family in the *Mohegan* disaster.

Porthoustock Village

The village, when referred to by the locals, is pronounced as 'Prowstock'.

It is a small village, almost a hamlet, certainly in the 19th century [19] and is situated just to the north of the Manacles. Its inhabitants were mainly agricultural workers and fishermen and some were employed by the local rock quarrying company.[20]

The Porthoustock cove is a much indented coastal feature, surrounded by high hills. The only view that is available from its shoreline is open water and with no direct sighting of the Manacles, which are just around the corner from the cove. As the cove afforded the nearest embarkation point for the Manacles, the lifeboat station[21] was duly erected here in the year 1872, and was responsible for the saving of many lives. The lifeboat is now no longer operational, though the lifeboat house still stands to this day, and serves as the local village-hall.

---

[16] Courtesy: St. Keverne Local History Society.

[17] A beautiful image of this window is seen here: http://stkeverne.com/treleague/mohegan_window.php.

[18] The inscription on the bell reads: *In Memory Of The Family Of Thomas Worthington King / Formerly Of Cincinnati Ohio. U.S.A. / All Lost On The Mohegan. October 14, 1898. / "God's Word Receive, His Truth Believe".*

[19] In 1898 there were 16 cottages here, in total.

[20] There has been quarrying activity in Porthoustock since the late 19th century.

[21] The Porthoustock lifeboat station was built in the typical nineteenth-century style, of the Early English tradition of Gothic architecture, having a distinct ecclesiastical appearance. It is one of few in this architectural style, that still remains standing.

Cornishmen though blessed with the riches afforded by the sea and the land, have mixed fortunes; for such riches demand the most dangerous of occupations: that of mining and of seafaring—a very mixed blessing indeed.

The cove allows for the docking of small vessels that are able to load rock from a purpose-built quay. The rock is excavated from a huge mining operation, alongside Porthoustock, that is still in working to this day. It has blighted the area to some extent and is responsible for raising the beach so that the sea no longer reaches the lifeboat house, as it did in earlier times (see fig. 55). The quarry company was warned by the local fishermen that, repeated dumping of quarry-spoil in the cove could eventually fill it in: the tides and storms duly obliged, in no small measure. The drastically altered shoreline in the cove led to an increasing difficulty in launching the lifeboat; thus sealing its fate. The RNLI service was eventually withdrawn in the year 1945.

Notable residents of Porthoustock include the *SS Titanic* survivor Mrs Annie Margaret Hold (1884–1960)[22] who was born in this hamlet in and also buried here. Another Porthoustock resident, 58 year old Margaret James was jailed for 20 years in July 2006 for the murder of a former parish councillor, Peter Solheim. His mutilated corpse was found floating at sea off Porthoustock in June 2004, and the murder was thought at that time to be associated with pagan rites. Sir Henry Irving (1838–1905), the renowned Shakespearean actor, made Porthoustock his holiday retreat.

Porthallow Village

From the Cornish, meaning 'port at the end of the moor' and the village, when referred to by the locals, is pronounced as *Pralla* or, as some say, *Pray-ler*. The dialect here is probably based on the original nameplace of Porthalla, as depicted on early maps.[23]

Porthallow's history has always been inseparably linked with the sea. A former thriving pilchard port, small fishing boats are still hauled onto the beach to this day. A number of buildings in the village also exhibit tell-tale signs of the industry, if a little less obvious to the casual observer. The village Association's Institute building is sited over a former pilchard cellar.

Within living memory, much of village life was more self-contained than it is now. Shops, religion and education were all available within its confines. School swimming-classes were conducted in the sea.

A wartime convoy from Montreal, Canada, disembarked at Barry, South Wales in early December, 1917. Then the captain, following orders, took the 4609 ton *SS Volnay* and a lethal load of 18-pounder shrapnel shells, together with a cargo of: tinned meats; butter; jam; coffee; tea; cigarettes; peanuts; and potato crisps, round Land's End, en-route for Plymouth City.

---

[22] See reference: http://encyclopedia-titanica.org/family-information-11.htm.

[23] First edition of the one-inch Ordnance Survey, Sheet 96 – *Truro & Lizard Head;* published in 1813.

Zigzagging a course, as the Admiralty had ordered, he kept well inside the mine-swept Channel. Even so when two miles east by south of the Manacles, at 12.45 a.m. on Friday 14th, the *Volnay* hit a mine laid by a German U-boat.

The mine had blown a hole into No. 1 hold on the starboard side, but the shells stacked in there did not explode. In the dark it was difficult to see how bad the damage was but the engines were still running, so the captain set course for Falmouth. He soon realised he would not make it. The bow was dipping further and further down. He headed for the nearest land, but was less than half a mile away in Porthallow Bay when the *Volnay* lurched to port, came upright again and then started going down by the bow. Happily, all aboard the ship abandoned her safely.

Next day the weather worsened and an easterly gale finished the job of dismantling the vessel. Cases of coffee and tea, tins of meat, butter and jam and cartons of cigarettes were piled 2 metres high on Porthallow beach. The residents of the Lizard had a wonderful Christmas that year. Today, the wreck, at 18-22 metres depth, is a popular sub-aqua dive, despite the war-time armaments that still litter the seabed.

Coverack Village

The name Coverack means 'hidden cove.' This village is situated to the south-west of the Manacles, and its inhabitants shared a similar employment pattern to that of Porthoustock. It too had a lifeboat station and it too is no longer operational.

The Coverack rocket-brigade had to take the rocket equipment from Coverack to Manacle Point, on the night of the *Mohegan* disaster. The road leading out of Coverack is precipitous and the splendid service on that night by the brigade team, manhandling the heavy equipment, was extremely arduous and they were to be much commended for their endeavour.

The lifeboat station was opened in 1901 after two major incidents: the passenger vessels *Mohegan* in October 1898 when 106 lives were lost and 44 saved, and eight months later, the *SS Paris* grounded off Dolor Point when all 750 lives were saved.

The *Constance Melanie* was a 12-oared, Liverpool Class lifeboat and was brought to Coverack in January 1901. The last lifeboat was withdrawn from service in 1971, as the newer and faster boats stationed at Falmouth and the Lizard could now safely cover the same area. Thereafter, an inshore inflatable-boat was stationed in the lifeboat house. The station was eventually completely closed on March 27th 1980.

The Lizard

The Lizard is not named after some legendary creature, its name being derived from the Cornish 'lezou', or headland. '*Lesard'*, one of the most common historic spellings for The Lizard, is French for "lizard". Such animal names are common around the Cornish coast for the naming of rocks and headlands. It might just be hat the long, regular shape of the peninsula, as seen from the sea, was likened to that of a lizard's tail. Another account is that the peninsula derives its curious name from the old Cornish *Lis-ardh,* meaning a fortress. The name 'Lizard' is also defined as a corruption of the Cornish name *Lys Ardh,* meaning 'high court'.

The Spanish Armada was first spotted from here in 1588. Sir John Killigrew, a philanthropic Cornishman from the Arwennack family of Falmouth, erected the first lighthouse on the Lizard in 1620. [24] Ship owners refused to support the venture, believing that Killigrew had ulterior motives in erecting the lighthouse, and so that venture eventually collapsed.

When approaching the UK from the Atlantic, the first landfall encountered is Land's End, followed by the most southern tip of the UK, the Lizard Peninsula; itself known as the, "Graveyard of Ships". This formidable land mass is 14 miles by 14 miles, and stretches into the English Channel, presenting a significant hazard to shipping. The Lizard is, in fact, a peninsula, whose cliffs support the moorland plateau of Goonhilly [25] Downs, some 90 metres (300 feet) above sea level.

Being in a ship is being in a jail, with the chance of being drowned.

On the 10th November 1721, thirty years before the lighthouse was built, 182 of the 185 crew of the *Royal Anne Galley* [26] lost their lives when it was destroyed in a storm, by being broken up against the Stags rocks. They are buried in a mass grave on the grass slope, just west of the old lifeboat slipway.

The dead soldiers were buried over a period of several days in pits in the nearby meadow, dug by local residents, but not before a pack of hungry dogs disposed of the remains, to the horror of all. For many years from that time, not a single dog was to be found in the region: for they were all shunned because of the gruesome scene they had enacted.

Eventually in 1752, a regular lighthouse was established at the Lizard and it was taken over in 1790 by the Trinity House. [27] This renowned lighthouse has been a traditional landfall for ships arriving in England for more than 250 years. Structural alterations were made in 1812, which left the station much as it is today.

The western tower was dispensed with after 1903 and a single flashing light remained in the eastern tower. The powerful beam of today's light can be seen at a distance of 26 nautical miles.

---

[24] The Cornish inhabitants of the neighbourhood complained that, "he was taking away 'God's grace' from them". Even if the srories of "Cornish wreckers" are exaggerated, it is certain that they regarded a wreck as a windfall and were not desirous of preventing its occurrence – Susan Gay; *Old Falmouth* – 1903, Tom Weller, 1912.

[25] Goonhilly is derived from an earlier medieval description for a *hilly hethe* [heath].

[26] The *Royal Anne Galley*, a fifth rate of 127ft in length by 31ft breadth and weighing 511 tons (builder's measurement), was built by Richard Stacey at Woolwich Dockyard and launched in 1709 from a design by Marquis Carmarthen. Her Pay List at the time of her loss shows 185 men onboard, of whom only three survived the wreck. It is known that at the time of her trials, the Royal Anne could be rowed with 66 oars and was allowed 60 men over her establishment on this account and carried 48 guns of bronze and iron.

[27] *The Corporation of Trinity House of Deptford Strond* is the official General Lighthouse Authority for England, Wales and other British territorial waters (with the exception of Scotland, the Isle of Man, Northern Ireland). It is responsible for the provision and maintenance of navigational aids such as lighthouses, light vessels and buoys and maritime radio/satellite communication systems. Trinity House is also the official deep sea pilotage authority providing expert navigators for ships trading in Northern European waters. It is a non-departmental public body

The signal station nearby was built by Lloyd's of London in 1872: to report ship arrivals and to convey by signal the owners' instructions to their shipmasters.

CHAPTER 2

The SS *Cleopatra:* also known as the SS *Mohegan*

A Specification:

Ship Builder: Earle's Shipbuilding and Engineering Company of Hull [28]

Yard Number: 415

Ship's Specification: 475 ft, Beam: 52 ft., Depth: 33 ft. A single iron screw attaining 13 knots with a triple expansion engine and with cylinders of 32", 54", and 90", with a stroke of 66". Four boilers each operating at 200 p.s.i. Two steel decks and eight watertight bulkheads with a steam pump capable of pumping out each compartment in turn.

Gross Tonnage: 6,889 [29]

Nominal Horsepower of Engines: 750

Registered Tonnage Gross: 6889

Registered Tonnage Net: 4510

Load-Line and Draught of Water:

> The centre of the disc is placed at 7 feet 8 inches below the ??aly deck
>
> Line marked under the provision of the Merchant Shipping Act.
>
> Maximum load-line in fresh water 6 inches above the centre of the disc.
>
> Maximum load-line in Indian summer 6 inches above the centre of the disc.
>
> Maximum load-line in summer the centre of the disc.
>
> Maximum load-line in winter 6 inches below the centre of the disc
>
> Maximum load-line in North Atlantic winter 12 inches below the centre of the disc.
>
> Her mean draft, after she had taken in some fresh ballast, was 20ft. 8½" [6.3m]
>
> that gave her a freeboard of 13ft. 8½" [4.2m].

Launch Date: 6th April 1898

Port of registry: Hull. Port No.: 48

Official Number: 109043

Maiden Voyage: Under the flag of the Atlantic Transport Line (ATL: July – October, 1898).

Sister ships: *Maitou* (Great Spirit); *Marquette* [30] (a city in USA); *Menominee* (a nation of Native Americans living in Wisconsin) and the *Mesaba*. (Ojibwa Native American name for "soaring eagle")

---

[28] Earle's Shipbuilding and Engineering Co. was the largest yard building the biggest ships on the Humber in Hull. The company was started in Hull in 1845 by two brothers from York, Charles and William Earle, who set themselves up as engineers and ship builders. At times, as many as two or three thousand men were employed in shipbuilding and repair activities, including the construction of many Wilson Line vessels. The company was reconstituted as Earle's Shipbuilding and Engineering Company Limited in 1871 following the death of Charles and with the illness of William Earle. Serious problems in the 1890s eventually led to the voluntary liquidation of the firm, which was then bought by Charles Wilson of the Wilson Line. The firm retained its name, but was wholly owned by members of the Wilson family for the rest of its existence. The trade slump of the 1920s and early 1930s led to prolonged short-time working. The yard was finally closed in 1932 when it was acquired by the National Shipbuilders Securities Limited, under the national shipyard rationalisation scheme, which precluded its use as a shipbuilding yard for the next 40 years. Nearly 700 ships had been built by the company between 1853 and 1931.

[29] At that time, this had been the largest vessel ever constructed by the Earle's Shipbuilding and Engineering Company of Hull.

[30] Mr Hawley Harvey Crippen, (11th September 1862–November 1910) usually known as Dr. Crippen, was an American physician hanged in Pentonville Prison, London, England, on 23rd November 1910, for the murder of his wife. He has gone down in history as the first criminal to be captured with the aid of wireless communication. He was a passenger aboard the *SS Marquette* and was apprehended on arrival at New York.

Renaming: as the *Mohegan,* sometime between September and October, 1898.

Wrecked: October 14th 1898 on the Manacle Rocks, Cornwall.

Wreck position: N 50 02 38; W 05 02 26.

The newly constructed vessel left the shipyard in Hull and sailed for London in July 1898, and made ready to embark on her maiden voyage to New York. Aboard was Robert McLaren, one of the engineers appointed by the ship's builder. Known as a "guarantee engineer," his role was to monitor performance of the ship's machinery, on their behalf.

The ship had started life as the *Cleopatra* (subsequently re-named as the *Mohegan*), a mixed passenger liner and animal carrier. She had been built alongside four other vessels at Earle's Shipbuilding and Engine Company, Hull and all were destined for the Wilson & Furness-Leyland Line. [31] She was one of the five new and almost identical ships purchased on the 29th July 1898, by the American Transport Line (ATL) from the Wilson & Furness-Leyland Line, to replace vessels requisitioned by the USA Government in the summer of 1898 for use as transport, in the Spanish American War.

The other ships acquired by the American Transport Line, in this sensational deal, were the *Alexandria, Boadicea, Victoria* and the *Winfreda,* each bought for an average price of £140,000. These other steamers were already in service; indeed, two of them had been sailing for the American Transport Line (presumably under charter) since February. At that time, the *Cleopatra,* the only one of these ships built in Hull, was the youngest of the sisters and she was still in the builder's yard when she was purchased by the ATL.

The *Cleopatra* was rated A1 at Lloyd's, a top classification in the Lloyd's Register of London, and was built for 'safety at sea'. The liner was equipped with: eight watertight bulkheads; failsafe lighting and pumping systems; eight lifeboats, capable of carrying 59 passengers each; and three compasses. Fitting-out and finishing touches were made to the ship by the Rait and Gardiner Company [32] at London, with Capt. Richard Griffith (her eventual master) travelling to Hull to oversee this work, prior to its completion. The ship was designed to carry 120 first-class passengers with no steerage, and with enough stalls for 700 cattle. The vessel also boasted, "An improved system of sanitation rendering the cattle carrying quite free from annoyance to passengers."

The passengers were travelling in absolute luxury, so it is surprising that the *Cleopatra* had a large area set aside for the co-transportation of livestock. It seems incongruous that animals should be shipped alongside the cream of metropolitan American society, but the owners of the shipping company were at pains to point out that, by using modern shipbuilding techniques and design, the passengers would be unaware of their

---

[31] The other ships acquired by the ATL in this sensational deal were the steamships *Alexandria, Boadicea, Victoria* and the *Winfreda,* each bought for an average price of £140,000. These other steamers were already in service, and indeed two of them had been sailing for the ATL (presumably under charter) since February—but *Cleopatra,* the only one of these ships built in Hull, was the youngest of the sisters. These purchases were to replace the ships sold to the American Government, for use in the Spanish American War.

[32] Rait and Gardiner Company were engineers and ship repairers who had premises at Millwall on the Thames, London.

ravelling companions. Bearing in mind, this was at the time when the principal means for everyday transport was by horse and carriage, the sights, sounds and smells would generally go unnoticed by its citizens, as being a part of everyday life. And nervous passengers might even have been comforted by the smells that would remind them of the terra-firma.

On its completion, the *Cleopatra* was described by a local newspaper, the *Hull Daily Mail*, as: 'The longest vessel ever built at Hull . . . she boasted a large handsome dining saloon in polished oak with carved panels and pilasters being situated under the bridge deck' and, 'In the house are a large music room, decorated in ivory colour and gold, a smoking room in polished oak, and a considerable number of state-rooms. The ceremony of naming the vessel was carried out by Miss Enid Wilson,[33] in 1897.'

The ship catered for a predominately-American market, and was a relatively slower means of transport and not being in competition with the faster postal steamers, which were engaged in a more competitive passenger market that vied for supplying a superior postal delivery system.[34]

The *Cleopatra* was officially recorded in the formal *Agreement and Account of Crew*[35] as, 'being able to sail from Hull to London and thence to New York and/or any ports or places within the limits of 70 degrees North and 70 degrees South latitudes, trading to and from, for any period not exceeding twelve months, and back to the port of final discharge in the United Kingdom.'[36]

The *Cleopatra* sailed on her maiden voyage from London to New York on the 31st July and arriving at her destination on 12th August, 1898. This voyage revealed some worrying defects in the ship's performance and safety. The conditions leading up to and during the maiden voyage of the *Cleopatra* are well described here, in an address to American newspaper reporters, given by Mr Philip A. S. Franklin, the general manager of the New York Shipping Company:

Regarding the condition of the *Mohegan,* Mr. Franklin said that when she came out on her first trip, arriving here [New York] on August 12, her pumps and boilers were found to be somewhat leaky. All bookings for passage on her were cancelled and the steamer started back for London, going at half speed. She was twenty-one days making the passage, but the 600 head of cattle aboard when landed, not one sick or missing. Then the vessel was laid up in London for a complete overhauling, covering a period of forty-one days. She was then subjected to a trial run, which was reported as entirely satisfactory. Lloyds passed her and rated her A1. Six days later she sailed from London on her second and ill-fated trip.

[33] Miss Enid Wilson was the daughter and fourth child of Charles Henry Wilson, 1st Baron Nunburnholme and Florence Jane Helen Wellesley, and was born 10th September 1878 at Marske Hall in Yorkshire. On the 15th February 1900 at the age of 21 she married Edwyn Francis Scudmore-Stanhope, 10th Earl of Chesterfield. Her father was selected as Liberal Member of Parliament, for the Hull constituency, He was a member of the family firm — the largest ship-building company in Hull, as well as the being the largest private fleet company. It generated immense wealth for the family and the City.

[34] The *SS Paris* was such a postal steamer and on her stranding on Lowland Point, Cornwall in 1899, criticism surfaced that she was cutting corners, in an attempt to shave off valuable distance and time; this being the master's prime commercial objective. Many passengers on such vessels complained of the bad conditions aboard, when the ship's master insisted in maintaining top speed in adverse sea conditions; again, motivated by commercial considerations. The result was a spectacular failure for the steamship *Paris.*

[35] Courtesy of: Maritime History Archives at the Memorial University of Newfoundland. This is a record of a formal contract between the shipping company and its crew members. An example of such a contract, for the *Mohegan* voyage, is shown in Appendix 5, p. 477.

[36] The agreement was signed off by Capt. Griffith on 28th July, 1898.

On her first voyage the vessel sailed under the name given to her by the Wilsons and Furness-Leyland Line, for whom she was built. That is as the *Cleopatra*. She was sold to the Atlantic Transport Line while she was still in the hands of her builders, and on her first trip her engines were run by the builders' engineers and assistants, known as "guaranteed engineers"

According to a passenger who came over on that trip, her boiler tubes leaked, her flues did not work right, and her pumps were deranged. Her plumbing was also leaky and some of the staterooms became flooded. She had to lay to half the day the third day out. She was a staunch and steady vessel, this passenger said, as shown by her conduct on two or three days when the seas were very rough, and her cabins were unusually comfortable and were handsomely furnished but there was something radically wrong in the engine department. She made the trip in eleven days, but her crew had to work like beavers to keep her in right shape. The passengers got up a protest to the line on the vessel's condition and at the same time a testimonial to the splendid conduct of officers and crew.

Regarding this story, Manager Franklin said yesterday that he had never received any protest, but he added that all initial trips were unsatisfactory [*sic*]. Mr. Franklin denied another report that the vessel had made her first trip without any preliminary trial. [37]

Mr Harrison, a passenger on the *Cleopatra*, stated in reply to questions at the subsequent Board of Trade (BoT) inquiry into the *Mohegan* affair, that on one occasion, all the lights went out. On another occasion, something happened to the steering gear, where the ship described a semi-circle and at some stage, steered in a different direction from that of New York. This evidence was confirmed by another passenger, Mr Cecil De Caterat. He thought this change in direction took place whilst something was being done to the ship's steam whistle: this provoked laughter in the court.

No news is good news.

As the vessel's return voyage was taken at half-speed, this much delayed her arrival in London. Some misgivings were raised as the *Cleopatra* failed to show, until these welcome messages were relayed to the anxious authorities:

The Overdue Cleopatra Sighted

Special Cable Despatch to THE SUN

LONDON, Aug. 30.—A despatch to Lloyd's from the Lizard says that the German tank steamer *Helios,* from New York Aug. 18 for Flushing, signalled in passing that point this afternoon that she had passed the Atlantic Transport line steamer *Cleopatra,* from New York Aug. 15 for London, on Aug. 25 in longitude 48° 36′ west. The *Cleopatra* was making a daily average speed of 170 knots. [38]

And another such sighting was reported to the world:

---

[37] The *New York Times;* 16th October 1898.

[38] *The Sun;* August 31st 1898.

Special Cable Despatch to THE SUN

LONDON, Sept. 1.—The Atlantic Transport line steamer *Cleopatra,* from New York Aug. 15 for London, and several days overdue, was spoken, on Aug. 26, which arrived here to-day. The *Cleopatra* reported all well aboard. [39]

On arrival on September 4th, she was taken in tow to the London Docks: an ignominious end for any vessel, but particularly for one on its maiden voyage. Here, in the shipyard, an extensive overhaul was undertaken. Repairs to her engines and boilers were carried out under guarantee by Rait and Gardiner of London, working for the ship's builders but under the supervision of the Atlantic Transport Line's engineering superintendent, Mr Robert McLaren, as the builders' agent. Whilst the ship was in dock, all her boats were lifted for the purpose of caulking the deck. [40]

The maiden voyage for the *Cleopatra* should have been a celebration for a new ship's arrival on the scene; instead, it was a debacle and an embarrassment for the Atlantic Transport Line company. Captain Richard Griffith, having signed off the vessel as ready for service, must have been less than delighted at the outcome.

A review of the Agreement and Account of Crew reveals an interesting mix of a ship's company:

Total crew complement: 117

Novice crew on first ship appointment: 14

Desertion from ship, in New York: 7

Crew who were discharged in London, yet failed to sign off: 32 [41]

Crew transferred from the *Cleopatra* to the *Mohegan*: 17.

One can imagine the severe disappointment created by this affair, for the ship's owner and to her builder, the Earle's Shipbuilding and Engineering Company of Hull. Criticism was soon directed at the latter, who was accused of accelerating her construction, driven by the need to avoid large penalty payments being incurred for late delivery, following a shipyard labour dispute. As a result, the accelerated marine construction was below the usual standard, and the defects were made all too apparent on her maiden voyage.

After the shipyard repairs were completed and pronounced satisfactory, the *Cleopatra* was sent for trials in the North Sea, on October 5th and under full steam. In these workouts, she achieved 12½ to 13 knots and was pronounced satisfactory. She was then rigorously re-inspected by the Board of Trade and was issued with

---

[39] *The Sun;* September 2nd 1898.

[40] In riveted steel or iron ship construction, caulking was a process of rendering seams watertight by driving a thick, blunt chisel-like tool into the plating adjacent to the seam. This had the effect of displacing the metal into a close fit with the adjoining piece—WikiPedia. Quite obviously, her sub-standard construction in the shipyard contributed to her leaking problems, and the re-caulking was one such corrective procedure adopted.

[41] This probably denotes members of the crew being re-hired, immediately following their discharge.

a new certificate. [42] During this time, the Atlantic Transport Line company renamed her as the *SS Mohegan*. [43] There is an old maritime tradition that states that, bad luck befalls a vessel that is re-named:

SAILORS' SUPERSTITIONS AND THE MOHEGAN DISASTER

The terrible disaster to the *Mohegan* will serve to revive an old superstition among sailors that it is unlucky to change a ship's name. The *Mohegan* was christened *Cleopatra*, and only changed her name after her first voyage. It will be remembered that the *Victoria* [44] went to sea under another name from that which she was originally intended to bear. [45]

The Atlantic Transport Line's funnel consisted of a red coloured stack and with a black top. Its house flag was red, white and blue horizontal stripes with stars of alternate colours. This latter insignia may be discerned on the cap of the *Mohegan*'s master, Capt. Griffith (see fig. 86).

---

[42] A typical Board of Trade inspection of the time is described in this book (see Appendix 3, p. 434).

[43] Definitions for the name Mohegan: (1) a member of an American Indian people of East Connecticut. (2) an extinct Eastern Algonquian language of the Mohegan (3) a "good canoe man".

[44] *HMS Victoria* was constructed at a time of innovation and development in ship design. She was originally to have been named *Renown*, but the name was changed before launching to celebrate Queen Victoria's Golden Jubilee, which occurred the year that the ship was launched. The ship was the lead ship in her class of two battleships of the Royal Navy. On 22 June 1893, she collided with Camperdown near Tripoli, Lebanon during manoeuvres and quickly sank, taking 358 crew with her, including the commander of the British Mediterranean Fleet, Vice-Admiral Sir George Tryon—*WikiPedia*.

[45] *Nottinghamshire Guardian;* Saturday 22nd 1898.

CHAPTER 3

The Wreck of the *SS Mohegan*

When you are at sea, keep clear of the land.

One of the most notable and catastrophic shipwrecks in modern times was that of the *Mohegan*. The ship managed to find itself inside the Manacle Rocks buoy, on a clear night of the 14th of October, 1898.

She now lies on the easternmost edge of the reef at 75 feet (23 metres) depth, a great mass: in all, 7,000 tons of steel. Her senior officers and the greater number of passengers and crew perished in the disaster[46] on a scale not equaled here since the wreck of the emigrant ship *John* that sank on striking the Manacles in 1855, with the loss of 190 lives.[47]

The modern day navigational aids has markedly reduced the likelihood of further wrecks occurring on these rocks. But there still remains the not insignificant matter of human error: certainly a factor here, in the *Mohegan* disaster.

She was carrying ninety-seven crew, who were almost all British. Many of them had sailed with Capt. Richard Griffith on previous occasions. At the Board of Trade inquiry, following the disaster, Mr Alfred Williams, the manager of the Atlantic Transport Company, stated that, "Twenty-three of the crew had sailed on the *Mohegan* (as the *Cleopatra*) on the voyage previous to her being lost. Sixty more had been in different vessels belonging to the firm." According to the *Agreement and Account of Crew* records,[48] only 17 of the crew transferred from the *Cleopatra* to the *Mohegan*.

In addition, there were six cattlemen,[49] and one horseman.[50] According to the above crew records, some of those were American employees, and came across on the return trip of the *Cleopatra*, in order to tend to the animals aboard the ship. On the *Mohegan*'s outward trip, some of the American cattlemen were returning home, with free passage.

---

[46] Of the officers and crew 62% perished, along with 79% of the passengers.

[47] After the wreck of the *John* in 1855 followed the wrecks of the *Envoy* 1858, *John & Rebecca* 1867, *Aura* 1869, *Cabinet* 1872, *Puck* 1874, *Sultana Southdown* 1876 *Dunloe* and *Naiad*, both in 1879, *Georgina* 1881, *Medina* 1883, and the *Lady Dalhousie* 1884. During this time, a lifeboat station was opened at Porthoustock in 1872. Turning to the Life Boat records, it seems that the Porthoustock boat has, since the year 1872 been on active service 16 times, and has effected the rescue of 112 persons. The same records show that 119 lives were lost from the vessels to which the Life Boat went out. There were at least 16 other wrecks during that period resulting in the loss of 44 lives to which the Life Boat could render no assistance. Four wrecks alone in the last 90 years have resulted in the drowning of no less than 470 persons.

[48] *Agreement and Account of Crew* (see Appendix 5 p. 438).

[49] Cattlemen were very lowly paid crew who were largely concerned with working their passage to Europe in return for taking care of the cattle aboard. They were known as the 'cowboys of the sea'. Men of all positions, including noblemen, sons of noblemen, ex-army officers, and lawyers have been known to work their way across the Atlantic as cattlemen, sometimes of necessity, and others for the love of adventure.

[50] The shipping-line was renowned for the transportation of horses, and each year, 12,000 to 15,000 horses were carried across the Atlantic.

There is a Reaper, whose name is Death.

On her first and final trip as the *Mohegan,* she left the Royal Albert Dock for New York, at 2:30 p.m. on Thursday, October 13th 1898. Down the River Thames, the *Mohegan* had to come alongside once again, in order to collect an additional fifty-three passengers. It is tempting to think that Death stepped aboard with those passengers, at that grimly named embarkation port: Gravesend Reach.

The start of a journey should never be mistaken for success.

Captain Griffith expected the Board of Trade officer to come aboard his ship at Gravesend; however, in a handwritten note, Griffith recorded the following outcome:

> "Mohegan"
> October 13th 1898.
> Board of Trade officer did not come aboard off Gravesend, probably too busy.
> R. Griffith – Master.

The *Mohegan* steamed on to Dover, where she briefly anchored and dropped her Trinity House pilot, Mr David Thomas Mulley, at 7:30 p.m. on the same day. A letter was given to Mr G. Pottie (see fig.79),[51] the Engineering Superintendent of the Atlantic Transport Line, by the assistant engineer William Kinley (see fig. 20), who was on board as a supernumerary, on behalf of the owners, to monitor her mechanical performance. He reported minor teething troubles but no major issues with the ship, other than a shortage of steam caused by the new team of firemen, described as, "not being up to the mark". The ship's plates had a few minor leaks, a bearing was running hot, and on the first night out a fuse had blown: plunging the dining saloon into darkness just as dinner was being served. Mr Kinley's letter was written, during the short period the ship was anchored here, and placed in the hand of the pilot to take ashore with him, and with the instruction to convey the message to the shipping company in London. Here is a transcription of the letter:

> Dover, Oct 13th 1898.
>
> Dear Sir,
>
> We left Gravesend at 2.30 P.M. & arrived at Dover at 7.30. The firemen are not quite up to the mark just yet so that we have been kept for steam. I am pleased to say that there is no sign of leaks in the backend, but there are a few rivets & parts of the shell plating leaking & 1 check valve cover slightly.
>
> We have been making 62 revolutions on 175 lbs steam. The HP crank pin has been working warm & have had water on but getting her away again now. Have just come of [*sic*] the boiler tops & find all right except Port Main Stop Valve has a

---

[51] Mr Jonathan Kinghorn of Lexington, Massachusetts, is the great-grandson of the engineering superintendent for the Atlantic Transport Line—Mr George Pottie—and has an extensive history for the Atlantic Transport Line Company, recorded on his current website: http://atlantictransportline.us/index.htm.

pump on the spindle. I hope this will disappear on a full head of steam. We have had three engineers on watch in the Channel keeping 4H [4 hour] watches.

Just as the dinner was about to be served all the light went out owing to a fuse burning out.

On the whole I think things are satisfactory.

I sent the drawings you wired me on of by Mr. Melvin:

Trusting that this will find you better & that we shall have a good voyage.

I am Dear Sir

Yours most respecting

W. Kinley

G. Pottie esq.[52]

London.[53]

The captain also placed a note in the hand of the Trinity House pilot, to pass on to his shipping company, which conveyed the message, "Everything is working satisfactory in the engine-room."

At the subsequent Board of Trade inquiry, evidence was given as to the operational state of the *Mohegan*'s engines:

Mr. Geo. Pottie, superintendent engineer to the London agents of the Atlantic Transport Company, gave evidence regarding the condition of the *Mohegan* on her last trial trip during her voyage from Gravesend to Dover.

Mr. William Kinley, appointed to report on the engines, found that they worked alright, and that a slight leakage at the back of the boilers could be put right in a few minutes. Mr. Pottie added there was no priming [54] of the boilers during the trial trip.

Mr. John McEwan, engineer and surveyor to the Board of Trade, who surveyed the *Mohegan* during construction, deposed that both the hull and boilers were in good condition and fit for the service intended.

Mr. Thomas Kendal, another Board of Trade surveyor, who completed the *Mohegan*'s survey in July, stated that for New York she was in a fit and proper condition. He could say nothing of the priming of the boilers. Witnesses added that the dirty state of the boilers, the constant use of salt water, and irregular firing would cause them to leak. Evidence was then given by passengers who travelled by the *Mohegan* on her maiden voyage [as the *Cleopatra*] to New York, and two of them stated that on one occasion in mid-Atlantic the vessel described a semi-circle.

Mr. James Balloch, Board of Trade surveyor, stated that the tests of the vessel, after she had been fitted with a crown to the combustion chamber, the old one having collapsed, were satisfactory. There was no priming and no leaking. [55]

It would seem the ship was not as yet free from mechanical problems, but that did not preclude her continuing her voyage to New York.

---

[52] Mr George Pottie (see fig. 79) – UK census, 1901; 42 Mansfield Road, Ilford, Greater London.

[53] Personal communication: Mr Alston Kennerley; BA (Lampeter), Dip Ed (Wales), MA (Exon), PhD (CNAA/Plymouth), Master Mariner, FNI, Plymouth University (2011) – who has now fully interpreted the text in this letter; in part, previously deemed to be illegible.

[54] Priming is a carryover of water with the steam flow into the engines; which can affect the turbine blade, break cylinder heads, piston, and valves, due to the incompressibility of water under pressure.

[55] *The Belfast News-Letter* (Belfast, Ireland); Friday, 11th November 1898.

The practice of the shipping company was to have three officers on each watch, in going down the Channel: two quartermasters, one at the wheel and the other on the deck; two lookouts; and a man in the crow's nest, about 50 feet above the deck.[56] There would also be three engineers on each watch.

The pilot, Mr David Thomas Mulley, said in his evidence given at the Board of Trade inquiry, that he had piloted the *Mohegan* from Gravesend to Dover, having left Gravesend at 2.30 p.m. There was a moderate east-south-east breeze. He had steered the vessel both by the compass,[57] and objects. He recorded a slight deviation on the southerly course, but did not note any error in the westerly course. According to Mulley, the captain was off and on the bridge all the time. As to Capt. Griffith, Mulley said that he had known him for some years and that he considered him a strong man, in every sense of the word, and in good health at that time. The steering gear was in good order and the engines appeared to be working without a hitch. There were never less than two officers on the bridge and he did not think that more careful officers than those of the *Mohegan* could have been selected. The quartermasters and crew seemed equally satisfactory. Having discharged his duties, he had no reason to complain of the steering.

Passing through the Strait-of-Dover, the *Mohegan* steamed down the English Channel, heading for New York, at 12–13 knots. On this occasion, the ship's master was determined to put the bad experience of the ship's maiden voyage behind him. The company was anxious that having renamed this vessel, all the past problems would now fade away. The weather fair, and with New York but twelve or so days away, the *Mohegan* would prove to be a ship of which they could all be proud.

The ship's course would have been set as she left Dover [58] and having entered the English Channel. There is no record of the heading taken, as would have appeared in the ship's log at that time, as the logbooks were never recovered, following the disaster.

Ships that pass in the night.

Later that morning, a bizarre incident came to light, when the *Mohegan* encountered another vessel, as recorded in this newspaper report:

> During the morning [of the 14th] the *Mohegan* was in company with the steamer *Scottish King*,[59] and for a period, each ship maintained a parallel course down the Channel. The steamer's [*Scottish King*] log records this meeting of the two ships, and

---

[56] Since the crow's nest is a point far away from the ship's centre of mass, any small movement of the ship is amplified and could lead to severe seasickness, even in accustomed sailors. Therefore, being sent to the crow's nest was also considered a punishment—*WikiPedia*.

[57] At the Board of Trade Enquiry, Mr A. S. Williams, manager of the Atlantic Transport Company stated that, the ship was steered by the Thompson compass, on the bridge, and not by the Standard compass.

[58] Personal communication: Mr Alston Kennerley, Plymouth University (2011)—There is a real issue with the course quoted and the language used at the time. Gradually during the twentieth century, practice changed from using points to degrees in quadrants, and finally to the full circle. There is also the question of which compass rose was in standard use: measuring from true geographical north, or from magnetic north at that date, from the north by the ship's compass which was influenced by the ship's magnetic field. The helmsman had to steer by the latter; navigation by chart in my day was always from true, i.e. geographical north. But ships in that period may have navigated on the chart from magnetic north.

that at 4 a.m. there was "a moderate south-east breeze; cloudy and showery". The *Mohegan* eventually overhauled the *Scottish King* during the morning watch,[60] after which they steamed close to each other through the afternoon. At 8 a.m. the weather record in the *Scottish King*'s log was identical to the former entry. There was some surprise expressed, by the officers and crew aboard the *Scottish King* that the *Mohegan* remained close at hand for some while, considering she was a much faster ship. The *Mohegan* was recorded as being on its port bow, the *Scottish King* thus being between her and the shore. Eventually, the *Mohegan* pulled ahead, at her usual cruising speed, and sailed directly across the course of the *Scottish King*, and now appearing on her starboard bow, and was thus placed in the position the *Scottish King* had previously occupied, now being in-shore. This was the last time the *Scottish King* paid any attention to the *Mohegan*.[61]

Prior to the disaster, the next recorded sighting of the *Mohegan* was off Prawle Point, South Devon, at 2.40 p.m. Her distance from the shore was estimated as three miles, and she signalled to the Lloyds Signal Station lookout, "All well, report me." [62] This would then have been relayed to her agents, presumably to allay any fears that they may have had, concerning previous problems with the ship's performance. So far: so encouraging.

Just after nine o'clock in the evening of the same day, the *Scottish King* steamed past the Lizard, with its bearing being about four miles on her starboard side. The weather recorded in the log at 8.00 p.m. was, 'light south, south-east wind, overcast and clear.' No further sighting of the *Mohegan* or signals of distress were encountered that evening; however, the disaster had already overtaken the fated ship. Indeed, she was now lying on the seabed, and her surviving passengers and crew were engaged in a desperate struggle for their own lives.

Lose an hour in the morning, chase it all day.

It is somewhat ironic that Capt. Griffith had interrupted the voyage in order to signal at Prawle Point, as to the well-being of his ship, as this delayed his arrival (and in failing light) in the dangerous waters of Falmouth Bay and the nearby Manacle Rocks.

The *Mohegan* was next observed by the Rame Head signalman,[63] and estimated to be ten miles offshore, and he would later comment that, ". . . this position was about seven miles less than a liner would ordinarily

---

[59] The *Scottish King,* of the Puritan Line, and in the charge of Capt. James, was a trader between Antwerp, Bolton, and Baltimore. The vessel was next reported off the Lizard, on November 13rd 1898. Her next voyage on November 20th, again from Antwerp, ended in the vessel going ashore at Seal Cove, near Cape Race (Newfoundland), on November 30th, in a thick fog. The Cape is, on average, shrouded in fog on 158 days of the year. 'She was broadside on to the beach, badly holed, bumping heavily and with ten feet with water in her hold. It is feared that she is a total loss. The crew was saved.'—*The Belfast News-Letter* (Belfast, Ireland), Thursday, December 1, 1898.

[60] The Morning Watch period was assumed to be 4 A.M. to 8 A.M. (see Appendix 14, p. 461)

[61] *Royal Cornwall Gazette;* November 24th 1898.

[62] This event had been reported as at 2.50 p.m.

[63] Mr Joseph Burnfield (elsewhere named as James Bamfield) was a retired quartermaster, R.N. and a signalman at Rame Head (Cornish: Penn Dinhir, meaning head of a long fort), which is at the western approaches to Plymouth Sound.

expected to be".[64] This sighting occurred at 4.30 p.m. and west of the Eddystone Light.[65] Such was his interest in the vessel, with her unusual positioning, that he continued to monitor her progress, until she disappeared from view.

At this point, the Mohegan's log register showed that they had completed fifty-five miles since noon and with the Eddystone now bearing broad on the starboard bow. After passing the Eddystone Light a ship would normally be set on a heading west-by-south-west, in order to clear the Lizard; however, the ship's course was set at this point as, west-by-north. We shall never know whether this was either an error in plotting the course on the navigational chart, a faulty compass reading, or a misheard command. In any event, it had clearly been erroneous (for whatever reason), as the *Mohegan* ended up on the Manacle Rocks, which was almost inevitable, having adopted a west-by-north heading.

So near and yet so far.

In support of the Rame Head coastguard comments, there is on record, an observation made by some officers and crew of the *Mohegan*, that the Eddystone Light was "too far away from its expected position" and that, "the coast seemed too close". It does depend on the interpretation of the phrase "too far away from its expected position" in that it might not mean being too distant, but in fact, unusually close. The proximity of the coast was also remarked on, among others, by a woman passenger, Mrs Compton Swift, and that observation was given by her in evidence at the subsequent Board of Trade inquiry.

Experienced officers would surely, at some stage, have raised the question with Capt. Griffith, as to the vessel's unusual positioning? However, being a strict disciplinarian and taciturn by nature, he most probably would have viewed any such interference in his command of the vessel, as impertinence.

There was evidence given that Capt. Griffith had taken to lying down, during the whole of the first day of the voyage. No reason had been given for this unusual state of affairs, and it implies that he was not in full physical command, on the bridge. According to a newspaper report, two passengers, Messrs. A. E. L. Smith and W. J. Bloomingdale, said that Captain Griffith had, "appeared very ill all day".[66]

Water is the only drink for a wise man.

Was his illness a result from an over-indulgence at the pre-sailing reception? A bar steward made a statement at the Board of Trade inquiry as having, ". . . served Captain Griffith a glass of champagne, topped-up with

---

[64] This would place her just 3 miles, south of the Eddystone. As close as this position seems to be, evidence given later would not have seen this as being too close, given the state of the weather, visual condition, and tides, at that time. Unlike the extensive distribution of the reef found at the Manacle Rocks, the Eddystone Reef is a more singular and discreet group of rocks.

[65] The Eddystone Light is a lighthouse that stands on the Eddystone Rocks; another notorious shipping hazard that is sited 14 miles due S. S. W. of Plymouth and is itself responsible for many shipwrecks.

[66] *New York Times;* 17th October 1898.

soda-water". And yet Mr Williams (an ATL company manager) was at pains to point out the abstemiousness nature of the captain. So, did alcohol play a part in his apparent illness, on the following day? It might also have been the reason the captain failed to appear at dinner, on the evening of the disaster. Of course, the real reason for Captain Griffith's apparent illness could have been more prosaic: simply due to sea-sickness, being no respecter of a man's status or experience.[67]

Where there is light, there is hope.

It is certain that, if the twin lights of the Lizard Lighthouse had been seen from the *Mohegan*, the vessel could have lined-up on them, passing three and a half miles south of the Manacle Rocks and so set to clear the Lizard and the same distance southward, clear of the Wolf Rock.[68] The navigational chart, *Approaches to Falmouth*,[69] shows a straight dotted line which began at a point due south of Fowey,[70] and ending at the red 'blob' on the Lizard. This endpoint was clearly printed, *'two Lights F'*, indicating two lights that were steady or fixed, and not flashing. The dotted line has the clear advice, *'lights in one'* printed on the eastern or Fowey end of the line. This warning could hardly have been missed by a navigator, who would have plotted a bearing off Start Point and then again off the Eddystone Lighthouse on that same chart. In reality, this instruction would have been more relevant for sailing in coastal waters, in which the *Mohegan* had no place: the more usual position being some 15 miles further south at this point. Not surprisingly, the local information regarding the Lizard light, contained in that coastal-chart, is not duplicated on the *English Channel* chart, dated 1882 (*et seq.*). This latter chart would have been the more relevant one (and most likely used) for the *Mohegan*'s track in the English Channel.

On pricking-off a new track, as she passed by the Eddystone, the captain inexplicably followed the west-by-north heading. Instead of making for the clear water south of the Lizard Peninsula, she eventually steamed across Falmouth Bay, towards the Helford River estuary (see fig. 93). At almost the last moment, she apparently turned to the south. Tragically, while her new course avoided the immediate shoreline, it also led her directly towards the most dangerous rocks in the area.

It is interesting to compare this generally accepted account of events with that of an able-seaman, who at that time was busy in cleaning the ship's deck. He stated, at the Board of Trade inquiry, that he had not noticed any change in the ship's course. If this were true, this would suggest that the *Mohegan* had sailed in a straight line from the Eddystone directly on to the Manacles, and that the ship's officers were oblivious to the impending disaster, until it was too late.

---

[67] A more detailed medical assessment for Capt. Griffith is disclosed later in this book.

[68] To use the twin Lizard lights for this purpose, one would have had to get sight of them in the ship's lower rigging, at a height of 30 feet above the sea.

[69] *Approaches to Falmouth;* Published 6th May, 1862.

[70] Fowey is a small town, civil parish and cargo port at the mouth of the River Fowey in south Cornwall, United Kingdom

The ship that will not obey the helm will have to obey the rocks.

If the ship had been on the correct heading, the Lizard lights would have been visible, sometime after leaving the Eddystone, subject to the weather and ambient light conditions. In fact, these coasts are not that ill-lighted, having the Eddystone, the St. Anthony's and the Lizard lights, forming a remarkable triangular display for the guidance of the mariner. But it should be noted, that the last half-hour of daylight may be especially dangerous. The lighthouses have already lit their warning beams, but they are only faintly to be seen in the still radiant western sky, and only gather strength when that afterglow has died away and darkness falls.[71] There was a steady swell on the sea, but this did not affect the ship sufficiently to discommode a passenger's appetite for the dining-saloon: though some children were apparently suffering from sea-sickness and resting in their cabins.

With the ship's eventual position in Falmouth Bay, the Lizard would have been occluded by the land mass ahead of her. This in itself should have alerted the ship's officers to the mistaken course on which they were headed, as by now on dead reckoning alone, the Lizard Light should have been clearly visible and on the starboard bow. A light had been noted by the ship's crew and this was almost certainly the St. Anthony's Light.[72] Travelling at full speed and with a comparatively short distance on entering Falmouth Bay before encountering its western shore, they seemingly remained oblivious as to their hazardous situation.

It was put about that the two officers on the bridge were taking it in turn to go below for dinner. If so, that meant a single officer was on watch duty on the bridge, at the time the St. Anthony light came into view and having been misinterpreted as the Lizard light.[73]

When the wind is in the east, 'tis neither good for man nor beast.

Warning rockets were sent aloft by an incredulous onshore coastguard, who had now recognised the ship's perilous position. It must have been at this point that the *Mohegan* crew were left in no doubt as to their appalling predicament: whether by the rocket signals from land or a sudden realization that the shore-line was directly ahead, is not known. A strong south-easterly wind was blowing and at such times, the bell buoy, on the southern ledge of the Manacle Rocks, rings loudly but no one on board appears to have heard its warning,

---

[71] Some leeway, however, must be given; in that, the view from the bridge towards the Lizard would be into the sun, as it sank in the western sky. This could make the Lizard Light difficult to see. However, normally the distance this light could be seen well within a ship's view, once past the Eddystone, having a throw of 21 miles and depending on the aforementioned caveats.

[72] 'The light on St. Anthony's Point is not seen by vessels coming from the east, until you are close to it, being shut in under the point.'–*The English Channel. Pilot, for the South and South-West Coasts of England, the South Coast of Ireland, and part of the North Coast of France, etc.* (Charles Wilson – 1878) The British Library Historical Collection.

[73] Had it indeed been the Lizard light and they were on a correct heading, then at some stage, the twin lights would have been seen 'in one'. This might have been mistakenly interpreted as being the St. Anthony light; which is itself a single light. However, the St. Anthony's is a revolving light, whereas the Lizard lights are fixed.

as no mention was ever made of it. It was but an academic point, as the warning bell was of little use to them by now, and its message would merely have served to herald as a death knell for the vessel.

The engines were stopped at 6.50 p.m., never to fire-up again. The *Mohegan* slammed on to the Manacles, on the north-western side of the *Vase* rock,[74] ripping her massive steel rudder clean off.[75] Her unstoppable forward motion then saw the hapless ship after ploughing into the *Voces Rock*, tearing her hull wide open. Though the *Mohegan*'s engines were stopped, the ship's momentum then carried her forward a further 450 feet, to the inner Manacle Rocks: which then closed ranks, allowing no escape. She was not yet finished, as the vessel relentlessly continued on towards the three peaks of the Maen Varses,[76] where, ripping out the starboard side,[77] her huge mass shuddered to a halt. The ship's fate was sealed and the situation for those on board was now bleak.

Where misfortune befalls, injuries follow.

During that horrendous encounter of steel and rock, the ship was totally turned round, so that to this day her stern points towards the shoreline and with the bow towards open water: as though desperately seeking escape.

She struck the easternmost edge of the Manacle Rocks as daylight faded, at a quarter-to-seven, and as dinner was being served. Immediately, the ship's captain made his way to the bridge, and the crew to their stations. Miss Roudebush, a survivor of the disaster, commented that, "Having left the dining-room and making for the deck, I noted that it was getting dark. Suddenly there was an awful sound as though the ship's bottom was being torn out." Indeed it was, with astonishing ease, as if with a butter-curler. She continued, "But, for the moment no one seemed to know what the matter was and the stewards continued to serve dinner. It was only when Charles Duncan,[78] shouted out, "To the life preservers" that we realized a serious accident

---

[74] Is also known as the *Voces* and this rock once stood several metres proud of the surface; until that is, the *Mohegan* struck the rock. From that point, the Vase Rock is now just a few metres below the surface on low water, spring-tide. The Vase Rock and the Maen Voces are the two outer eastern rocks of the triangular-shaped formation, which has the Carn-du at its northern point and the Mistrel Rock at the southern end of the triangle.

[75] Another report has her rudder placed on the Penwin (also known as the Pen Vin) rock, where to this day, it is said to remain embedded. Today, the Penwin rock has a minimum of 12 feet of water over it, at any one time.

[76] It is also locally known as the *Maen*: a Cornish word meaning a rock or stone. A futher reference is made to the Maen Voces (the *Voices*).

[77] Her hull has collapsed towards the open sea, but her huge boilers emerge through all the collapsed wreckage, which stands 8 metres proud in places, one of which is split wide open. Close by are the lifeboat davits. The boilers, on the western end of the wreckage, are one of the shallowest parts at 20 metres. Her bow is slightly shallower at 18 metres. The forepart lies to the south and is supported by rocks. From the boilers to the north is the propellor shaft. The north-east is the deepest part, dropping down to over 30 metres, where layers of steel plate lie amid the sand-floored gullies.

[78] The father to Isadora Duncan (1877–1927): she being a famous American, avant-garde dancer. Tragedy seemed to stalk the Duncan family; as not only did Charles Duncan perish in the *Mohegan* disaster, but his third wife, and their daughter, perished with him. Isadora Duncan's two children, along with their nanny, drowned in a car accident, by plunging into the River Seine, in Paris (1913). A third child died shortly after birth. As to Isadora herself, she died in Nice, by strangulation. Apparently, her last words were 'Adieu, mes amis, je vais à la gloire!' Other accounts give her the more likely line as: "Je vais à l'amour" (I go to love). Her flowing silk scarf around her neck, caught in the wheel spokes of a *Bugatti* automobile in which she was seated. The car moved forward and the scarf took her life.

had happened." And yet, many of the passengers still remained seated in the dining-room, seemingly oblivious to the danger they were in.

The engine room was immediately flooded to a depth of three feet, forcing the engine-room crew to rush up on deck. The ship was then suddenly plunged into darkness, following a failure of the ship's generators, thereby accentuating the horror.[79] The loss of power followed the ominous grating sound that had alarmed the ship's passengers and prompted a rush in the darkness from the dining-room to the deck. Here, they were witness to the desperate attempts being made to launch the lifeboats.[80]

One can imagine the incredulity that hit both the crew and the passengers. But minutes ago, the passengers were in the convivial setting of the dining-room, enjoying a leisurely meal in good company. Now, in the enormity of the situation in which they found themselves, it was simply a question of survival.
On deck, the mournful sound of the Manacle bell was heard above the wind and waves, presaging the funereal bell toll in the St. Keverne churchyard, a few days later.

Women and children first!

The alarming sea swell that engulfed the ship coupled with the failure of the electric lights, should have made for a general panic, but for the commanding voice of Chief Officer Couch, as he barked orders that, "women and children are to be saved first" and, "get the lifeboats away" stemmed any uncontrollable panic from taking hold—at least for the moment. The Captain was said to have remained calm, and actively put immediate survival tactics into action. But events were rapidly overtaking the situation. The *Mohegan* was doomed and her fate was soon to force the dictate, "Every man for himself! 106 "

An additional complicating factor was encountered in the launching of lifeboats. Captain Griffith had ordered the fitting of a high second rail inboard of the lifeboats, to prevent them being rushed at, in the event of an emergency and ensuing panic. But this fixture now seriously hampered the launching of the boats.[81] Further problems were encountered, when the ship listed to port, then heavily to starboard and with the deck now alarmingly sloped at 45 degrees. Only two lifeboats were eventually launched, with one immediately capsizing in the rough seas. Two passengers—Messrs. Smith and Bloomberg—stated that, "there was the greatest difficulty in launching the boats. The ropes were new and stiff, and blocks would not work ... in fact, [it needed] four or five times the number of sailors who ought to have sufficed at each boat, [in order] to get

---

[79] This had revealed a design fault in her construction. Her generators were located on the deck plates of the engine-room, and were flooded before the water level had reached the boiler fires. This shorted-out the electric lighting system, thus plunging the vessel into darkness: *The Belfast News-Letter,* Monday, 17th October 1898.

[80] The *Mohegan* carried six steel lifeboats and two of wood, and these could accommodate 284 persons, almost twice the number of people on board that night. But because of the severe list of the ship, the rough sea and the speed with which she went down, only two boats were ever launched.

[81] This was the only ship of the line that had this particular feature, and was expressly ordered by Capt. Griffith, during the vessel's fitting-out. It was subsequently blamed for the difficulty experienced, in the emergency launching of the lifeboats. Miss Roudebush (a passenger survivor) described these rails as being, "almost as high as one's chin", but a witness at the official Board of Trade inquiry stated that, they were only about three and a half feet high.

the women away."[82] Those same gentlemen felt that because the sailors were over-chivalrous in filling a vessel with women and with only four men to manage a large boat in such conditions, it inevitably capsized.

A newspaper report further highlighted the difficulty in launching the lifeboats:

SOMETHING UNSATISFACTORY – The want of promptitude in getting the lifeboats out was due to the inexperience of some of the crew, many of whom were fresh for this voyage. One of them stated that they were ignorant of the boat stations, and did not know how to set about the work of launching the boats. But in justice to the crew and some of the officers, it must be stated that several survivors credit them with coolness and courage in the time of peril. Primary attention was paid to the women and children, who were, as far as possible, got into the lifeboat first. There is some ambiguity as to the movements of the captain but he was stated to have given his orders clearly, and to have paid special heed to the despatch of the lifeboats. He was last seen jumping overboard with the others at the time of the fatal lurch which sent everybody into the water. Prior to this another lifeboat cleared with a good load of people. It was swamped and capsized, only two or three of its occupants being rescue, other being discovered dead under the overturned craft. Better fortune attended the movements of the other lifeboat. By dint of the arduous exertion, she was kept afloat, and clear of the wreckage, and her load of human beings was safely transferred to the Porthoustock lifeboat.[83]

As well as the difficulties encountered with the lifeboats, there was a question over the availability of lifebelts:

What could have been avoided was the unworkable condition of the tackle of the ship's boats. Lifebelts should have been accessible on deck, not stored away, as appears to have been the case, in lockers, hard to open, in the cabins below. It is no excuse to say that the boat appliances were new. Whether they were new or old, they should have been in a state of which would permit of easy handling, and the quick lowering of the craft. The *Mohegan*, as an American-owned vessel, would not be subject to the stringent laws to which British ships have to conform in respect of life-saving facilities. Ship-owners sometimes complain that they are harassed by legislation and over-much Board of Trade inspection, though it is only fair to say that the majority of them are easily solicitous thoroughly to equip their vessels with boats, life-belts, and the like. The story of this lamentable affair shows that the law can scarcely be too strict or the inspection too painstaking.[84]

Better to light a candle than to curse the darkness.

The reason so few distress signals were discharged was that the rocket-socket was on the port-side and the ship had listed heavily to that same side. As to the reason for the oil lamps not being got out: when the electric light was extinguished the forepart of the vessel (where the lamps were stored) was under water and the locker was rendered inaccessible.

William Moore, an able-seaman, was quoted as saying that, "The ship struck at either the No. 1 or No. 2 [hold] forward on the starboard, and sank head first, her stern being right up in the air." The ship rolled and sank, twelve minutes after hitting the rocks, with a loss of 105 lives. Captain Griffith, Assistant Engineer

---

[82] *The New York Times;* 17th October 1898.

[83] *Royal Cornwall Gazette;* 20th October 1898.

[84] *The Standard* (London, England); Monday, 17th October 1898.

William Kinley and all the bridge navigating officers went down with the ship. At first light, only her funnel and four masts remained visible above the waves.

Then shrieked the timid, and stood still the brave.

As the rocket apparatus was being hurriedly installed on Manacle Point in the charge of Mr Jeffers,[85] the terrible shrieks of anguish echoing to the shore carried on the easterly wind, would remain in the collective memory of the villagers of Porthoustock and Rosenithon, for the rest of their lives.[86]

A local resident of Porthoustock, Mrs Tripconey, was reported as having visited her outhouse to fetch some fuelling and was astonished to see the little cove of Porthoustock brightly illuminated. She rushed indoors and described the scene to her husband as, "like day". Mr Tripconey realized that it was most probably a large vessel in a perilous position, and almost certainly a wreck by now.[87] He quickly made his way to the local lifeboat station, shouting for help in manning the vessel, in order to make for the Manacle Rocks.

A maroon rocket fired from Tommy Noye's [88] field reverberated above St. Keverne, rattling the cottage windows and signaling other lifeboat crew to their station.

Meanwhile, Charley Tripconey and Joseph Bryant (a local shoemaker) had commandeered a small boat, owned by Dr Leverton-Spry[89] of St. Keverne, and they had bravely put to sea. They were anxious to ascertain what caused the bright lights in the sky. Sure enough, as feared, it was a large vessel come to grief on the Manacles and as yet, unidentified. In relaying this information to the crew, the *Charlotte* lifeboat embarked on the second of two trips to the wreck area. The coxswain James Hill,[90] despite his age of sixty-four years, actively commanded the lifeboat throughout the night. This heroic response by the local men from Porthoustock saved many lives, as a result of their speedy reaction to the, 'lights in the sky'.

---

[85] Mr Alfred J. Jeffers, chief of the coastguard at Coverack and his brave fellows, had pushed their heavy rocket apparatus to the top of Coverack-hill before horses could be procured. This was a physically demanding operation, and would later lead to voices suggesting a more suitable siting for that equipment: St. Keverne, being the most obvious place—an elevated location that would best serve both sides of the Manacle Point.

[86] In the *Mohegan Tapes* (St. Keverne Local History Society), a resident of the nearby hamlet of Rosenithon, Joe Rogers, said that, screams and cries for help were heard from the doorway of his cottage.

[87] From Porthoustock beach, it is not possible to see the Manacle Rocks, and so the 'sighting' of the *Mohegan* was probably the blaze of illuminating electric lights, filling the sky above, south of Porthoustock.

[88] Thomas H. Noye, a farmer residing at Chyneen, St. Keverne – UK census for 1891.

[89] Edward James Leverton-Spry M.R.C.S. Eng., – L.S.A. [Licentiate of Society of Apothecaries, London–1868] Kenwyn, Cornwall, England, 1844–1912. Information supplied by Jeffrey Carveth Spry Spry-Leverton 20th June, 1975: Medical Practitioner St.Keverne. Married Harriet Maria Kezby [30 Jan 1879]. Changed name from Leverton to Leverton-Spry by Deed Poll in 1888. He died in Newquay.and was buried 18th Oct. 1912 at St.Keverne. He was known as "Ebbie" to his close family. (see fig. 24)
http://yelland.info/LEVERTON/TNG/getperson.php?personID=I2836&tree=LEVERTON.
Clive Carter; *The Blizzard of '91* – ISBN 0 7153 5137 0, 164 – Dr. Leverton-Spry present at Board of Trade inquiry held at the Coverack Coastguard House on 14 May 1891, in connection with the loss of the 'Bay of Panama' in the great blizzard of 9/10 March 1891.

[90] In the UK census for 1891, James Hill's occupation was recorded as both a fisherman and a farmer.

A passenger's account.

On arrival in New York, on the evening of October 29th, Miss Roudebush,[91] dressed in deep mourning and showing marked traces of the awful strain of which she had been victim, had brought her mother's body back for burial. Questioned by waiting journalists, she gave an account of her experience:

"I am alive today, simply through the fact that my voice had been trained, and I understand how to make my cries for help heard. My mother and I reached the head of the stairs, where our stateroom was, where we met two stewards. We had in the meantime secured life preservers, but we were unable to put them on. As we stood there bewildered the stewards offered to assist us up stairs. There was no panic at the time, for as I looked back into the dining saloon I saw a number of persons still seated at the table. I think it must have been about four minutes after the ship struck when without warning every light went out. I shall never forget the scene as we went out onto the deck. There appeared to be absolutely no panic, and yet everyone that we could see was working with desperation to save himself or herself. It was growing dark. I saw no officers and heard no orders given. Two boats had been swung out to be launched. One was filled with sailors, but at the last minute before it was launched, Mr. Pemberton threw his wife and child into the boat, following himself. Then their maid jumped and fell into the boat almost by a miracle, and she too was saved." [92]

Miss Roudebush continued her tale, with details of her and her mother being helped into a lifeboat, by the two stewards, who then promptly proceeded to get out of the boat saying, "My God! We can't die like this; we must try something else."

Miss Roudebush decided to follow, and requested the stewards to help her and her mother to alight on to the deck once more. She noted that, "The shrouds [93] were filled with men; who I learned next day, were sailors." Miss Roudebush also noted that, "Many boats remained unfastened, and there seemed to be no attempt to launch them."

All four of them attempted to climb the rigging but then were persuaded to try and board another lifeboat. In the boat with them were: Mrs Compton Swift, Dr Fallows, Mr Duncan and a number of others, whose names she could not remember. She stated that, "For a few minutes we sat there terrified, and then the question arose, as to what we should do to save ourselves."

That decision was taken for them: as the steamer settled, it created a large wave that then hit them broadside-on. Her next recollection was that the lifeboat had capsized. All were thrown into the sea, and she found herself under the upturned boat. She continued, "I felt as though I had gone to the bottom of the sea. Consciousness had almost left me, when I came up and found myself imprisoned under the boat, only my head above water, and scarcely room enough to breathe. I think if I live to be a thousand years old, I shall

---

[91] Miss Roudebush had sailed from Liverpool, on the *SS Etruria*, on October 22nd 1898, from the port of Liverpool. Also on board was, the United States Senator, Redfield Proctor.

[92] *New York Times;* 30th October 1898.

[93] Here, shrouds do not denote burial sheets (though such items would feature heavily later in this story) but pieces of standing rigging which hold the mast up from side to side.

never forget the hour that followed, and I owe my rescue only to the fact that I was able to throw my voice [94] and kept it up. Tossed about and unable to see anything, I clung to the seat of the overturned boat and screamed. Close beside me was old Mr [Charles] Duncan, and he shouted as loudly as he was able. But his shouts became weaker, and then they stopped. I didn't dare to think what became of him. My mother I knew had been in the boat, but that was all. I did not know where she was now. You can imagine the horror of the situation when I felt the head of a drowned man bumping against me. I was in despair when suddenly the boat was turned violently over, and I fell exhausted in the bottom, still clinging to the seat. The next moment, I was grasped by strong hands and thrown violently into the lifeboat." [95]

She and her mother, together with Mrs Compton Swift, found themselves in the Porthoustock lifeboat *Charlotte*, saved by the grace of God. But regrettably, Miss Roudebush's mother, who had been trapped beneath one of the seats in the lifeboat, bled to death in the *Charlotte*, after one of its crew, Mr Frank Tripp,[96] accidentally cut off her foot with an axe while trying to free another trapped passenger. Not entirely surprising, given the appalling conditions that prevailed, with the lack of adequate lighting, and with a rough sea.

Miss Roudebush claimed that, "My mother was either caught in the wreckage, or was held fast under one of the seats, for the men in trying to release her, chopped off one of her feet. I believe she would be alive today if medical aid reached her at once, for she was a vigorous woman, not yet forty-five years of age. We were carried ashore at St. Keverne [*sic*], and I remained there three days. My mother died from shock and injuries."

Miss Roudebush continued her interview with the *New York Times* reporters, by saying, "Both my mother and myself believed that the *Cleopatra* was not a good boat, and we would have refused to have sailed had we known that her name had just been changed to *Mohegan*. I went to the inquest [at St. Keverne] but was told I was not wanted, and I do not know to this day what caused the disaster."

In reply to further questions, she said, "The opinion of John Hyslop[97] that the lifeboats were difficult of access, I believe is true, and I can say myself, they were double-railed as has been stated, and that the rail was

---

[94] She was a professionally trained opera singer, and was the protégé of Mrs Agnes Ethel Tracy, of New York. On November 6th 1898, Miss Roudebush was reported to be en-route to the Maurice Grau Theatre Company in New York, for her first professional engagement, following the disaster. A report in the *Chicago Eagle* [December 3rd 1898] stated that, "Maude evidently had had experience with high Cs before"—a weak joke and in extreme bad taste, considering what the poor woman had endured.

[95] According to George Martin Tripp, who was a stroke-oarsman in the Porthoustock lifeboat, he recalled that, on the evening of 14th October 1898 the sea was moderating with a heavy swell. When the lifeboat *Charlotte* was about half way to the Manacles by *Maen Garrick* (the rocks due east of Manacle Point) it came across an upturned lifeboat from the *Mohegan*. A couple of people were rescued from the keel, and according to Bentley Tripp's [a local fisherman] version, there were twenty-four dead people underneath it. They went on in darkness towards the cries and screams coming from the vicinity of the Manacles and came across the second *Mohegan* lifeboat–Courtesy of: St. Keverne Local History Society.

[96] The last person to be interviewed in 1966 was George Lory of St. Keverne, the village carpenter and undertaker. He was aged 18 at the time of the disaster and recalled the story of how Mrs Grandin had died in the Porthoustock lifeboat as a result of, "having her leg cut off accidentally". He too believed that the *Mohegan* had been wrecked deliberately. He referred to the embalming of some of the bodies in the house where St. Keverne garage now stands and supported the story that Captain Griffith had been rescued and then had disappeared.

[97] Mr John S. Hyslop was a passenger on the *Mohegan* and a professional yacht-measurer, living in New York.

almost as high as one's chin. They were chained down. If Capt. Griffith was responsible for the wreck, he had certainly gone out of his mind."

Miss Roudebush had lost twelve trunks in the wreck, two of which contained music, as well as curios gathered during her six years excursion abroad. She says she expects to put in a claim to the Atlantic Transport Line, for the damage. The interview now over, Miss Roudebush left for the home of Mrs Agnes Ethel Tracy,[98] at 80 Irving Place, New York.

The Porthoustock lifeboat crew, having now made contact with the one successfully launched *Mohegan* lifeboat, found twenty-seven survivors sitting in a boat filled to three-quarters with seawater, taken on from its haphazard launch. Had there been some form of adequate illumination,[99] undoubtedly many more lives would have been saved. As it was, the Porthoustock men had only the cries of distress to guide them towards the survivors, in the darkness. The local boatmen always treat the Manacle Rocks with great respect. At night, the visual marks they used to navigate themselves to safety in daylight hours were not available to them. This made their own position precarious, and they would have been understandably reluctant to venture deep into the reef, for fear of themselves becoming casualties.

Mr. George Maule, a shipper of horses, and an employee of the Atlantic Transport Line, said:

"The steamer immediately began to settle by the head. Orders were given to immediately to lower the boats, and the crew behaved like heroes. The captain stood on the bridge, and the greatest order prevailed among the officers and crew. Two boats were launched. The women were sent away in the first boat but whether these boats reached land or not, I do not know. I managed to secure a lifebelt and jumped overboard, in company with the Chief Officer of the *Mohegan*, Mr Couch[100]. He made me take off my coat and shoes. Soon after that we were parted from each other. When I was leaving the vessel, a little girl begged piteously that I try to save her, as she did not want to die yet, but I was powerless to help her. Eventually I caught hold of a plank that was floating on the water, and I clung to it for seven and a half hours. At the expiration of that time I was picked up by a tug. I could not have lasted much longer". [101]

One of the passengers rescued by the Porthoustock lifeboat said that, just prior to the disaster, he thought the steamer was nearer land than usual. All the passengers were at dinner, though some of the children, who were suffering seasickness, were in their bunks. Suddenly the vessel struck, with a grating noise. At first, the engineers thought this was caused by coal falling down in the bunkers. But a second shock followed, and the vessel began to settle.

[98] Agnes Ethel Tracy (1853 – May 26th 1903) was a Broadway actress of the late 19th century. She performed in New York City from 1868 – 1871. Ethel married Francis W. Tracy, a millionaire from Buffalo, New York in October 1873. Tracy died in 1886. His will was contested by his first wife on behalf of her daughter. The entire fortune was awarded to Ethel after it was contested in court. In 1890 she married Clive Roudenbush. She obtained a divorce from him in 1901—*WikiPedia.*

[99] The moon on that evening was a waning crescent and was a one-percentage of luminosity of a full moon. A total new-moon would have occurred on the night following the disaster: *QuickPhase Pro*; developed by CalculatorCat.com.

[100] Maule had conversed with first officer Couch, but not as a cause to the wreck, which he was unable even to conjecture, as the night was clear, and the captain knew the coast; *Illustrated London News*, Oct 22nd 1898.

[101] *Manchester Times* (Manchester, England); Friday, October 21, 1898.

A steward, on duty in the dining-room on the evening of the disaster, firmly established that the captain was not present in the dining-room:

A STEWARD'S NARRATIVE

THE CAPTAIN ON DUTY

Mr. F. Necklin [*sic*], one of the stewards of the *Mohegan*, said—I could not state at what rate we were travelling. The ship rolled very heavily. I was forward of the mainmast. The first shock was very slight, but the second was heavier, and the ship heeled over very much on the starboard side. There was no panic. The captain was not in the saloon at the time. He was on duty as far as I know. When the horn blew for dinner he was in the dining-room. I asked the question whether the captain was coming down to dinner, and immediately after we struck, so evidently the captain was on duty at the time. The order was given to the stewards' department to clear the boat lashings and covers. This we did. I assisted in launching a lifeboat from the port side. There were all together eight boats in the ship. All seemed

RESIGNED TO THEIR FATE.

Passengers were sitting down on the deck huddled together. Everybody did his duty and could do no more. We helped in rescuing as many children and families as we could. Just as the ship was settling down we cut the lashings of the boat, which contained 20 passengers, and I sprang overboard. After being dashed several times along the side of the vessel I was dragged on board the boat. Two others were picked up, and we just managed to get clear with great difficulty. The boat was half-filled with water, and those who could not row laid hold of anything available and baled for their lives. We pulled desperately away from the wreck, but the water gained on us, and, when we were about three-parts full of water, the Porthoustock lifeboat picked us up, and took us all on board. On the way to Porthoustock we picked up a lady passenger, who proved to be Miss Noble. We ultimately

LANDED WITH 28 PERSONS.

All on the sinking vessel worked for their lives up to the last moment. Captain Griffith, Mr. L. Couch, Chief Officer Coles, and the second, the third and the fourth officers were all drowned, so far as I know. I believe three or four of the ship's lifeboats were launched, but ours was the only one which weathered the storm.[102]

The following narrative describes an experience aboard the *Mohegan* at the point of the disaster. One can only imagine the reality of the even, a horrifying experience for those aboard:

THE CAPSIZED BOAT.

STATEMENT BY THE LADY WHO WAS RESCUED

Mrs. Compton Swift, an American lady, who was a passenger on board the *Mohegan,* said she had made six [transatlantic] passages before. The first night out, Oct. 13, the electric lights went out, and were out for a considerable time. She had gone up and down Channel by daylight, and she remarked on this occasion that she had never seen the coast of England for so long a time and she spoke to Dr. Fallows about the ship being so near shore. She was sitting down to dinner when the crash came. An engineer officer was opposite her at table, and she noticed his face at that moment; he got up at once and went on deck. She did not, however, then think there was danger. She went on deck, and someone suggested that they should go back and finish dinner. She went down, but returned to the deck, and heard a cry for the boats, as she was going up the stairs the lights all went out. Dr. Fallows went down to get lifebelts. The waves were coming over, and fearing that she would be swept away she went to look for Dr. Fallows. She found him down two flights of stairs. He had got the lifebelts

---

[102] *The Dundee Courier and Argus;* Monday, October 17th 1898.

and assisting each other to the deck they put these on. They went again to the port side where many men were trying to launch a boat without success. The captain, who was on the bridge, then ordered everybody to the starboard side. They all rushed over, and she got over the rail which separated the deck from the lifeboats with great difficulty, and reached up and clung to one of the hanging lifeboats. As the ship went down witness saw the captain slide off the bridge into the sea. The lifeboat, with about 25 persons in her, filled with water when it reached the sea. Dr. Fallows got out his knife and she passed it down to cut one of the ropes by which it was suspended. The boat shortly afterwards capsized. On coming to the surface she found herself underneath the boat, with her chin on one of the seats and a foot caught in a plank. She heard another woman call out. Then a little child called for some time, and then its voice was silenced. The man called, and his voice was silenced. She lay some time in this position when she suddenly felt the boat jerk over, and saw the lights of the shore lifeboat over her. Two men tried to lift her but could not, until they brought an axe, and cut the plank. Then she was thrown into the bottom of the shore lifeboat, and taken to land. The other lady was also saved.[103] There was plenty of time to have lowered the ship's boats and saved everybody if these boats had been manageable. She believes that 20 or 25 minutes elapsed between striking and going down.[104]

Another surviving passenger, Mr A. E. L. Smith, said that, as the ship sank, he saw Capt. Griffith run along the side and then, "sprang overboard". The vessel lurched, and the passengers all seemed to be thrown in the water at the same moment. The ship sank by the head and the stern, "rose right up in the air".

The lifeboat *Charlotte* reached the wreck in total darkness. Unable to see either the vessel or the rocks, the coxswain was attracted in the direction of cries for help. Bodies were found floating in the vicinity of the wreck. Working now only by the light from hand-held torches, in otherwise complete darkness, the enormity of this disaster was now made apparent to the lifeboat crew. Harrowing scenes, particularly where children were found clutched in the arms of their mothers, must have been difficult for the crew, even though hardened by encounters with the aftermath of previous shipwrecks on this malignant coastline, to which they were well accustomed.

We may have come on different ships but we're in the same boat now.

The *Charlotte* encountered an upturned ship's lifeboat, to which were clinging, with great difficulty, four or five men. They were taken on board. On hearing shouting from within the upturned lifeboat, the crew got out their grapnels and proceeded to right the boat. Inside, they found a woman and two or three men alive. The woman was so tightly jammed in the wreckage that the lifeboat men had to cut away the thwarts of the small boat, before they could extricate her. One of the lifeboat's crew, at great risk to his own life, jumped on to the steamer's boat when it was righted, and pulled Mrs Grandin from her perilous position. But she was landed in a dying condition, and all the efforts made to revive her were unsuccessful.

---

[103] This is most probably the incident where Mrs Grandin's foot was accidentally severed, whilst the axe was employed in releasing Mrs Compton-Swift. As a result, Mrs Grandin died of her injury through the resulting haemorrhage and shock.

[104] *The North-Eastern Daily Gazette* (Middlesbrough, England); Saturday 12th November 1898.

The lifeboat continued to pass several dead bodies of men and women, and picked up a couple of men floating on wreckage. It then encountered a ship's lifeboat having on board twenty-two passengers and crew, who would have been speedily lost if not rescued at that time, as the boat was rapidly filling with water and drifting on to the rocks. The occupants were taken on to the *Charlotte* lifeboat. While the latter was beating homeward, it picked up Miss Noble of Baltimore, adrift and clinging to a piece of wreckage.

Miss Noble had removed her dress and shoes, on the advice of the fourth officer, that otherwise would have restricted her movements in the water. With a lifebelt fastened around her waist by a crew member, she clung to a hatchway, before a wave washed her off the ship and into the foaming sea below. "She was the pluckiest woman I ever saw in my life," said Mr James Hill from the lifeboat crew. "She shouted, 'don't shove me an oar: give me a rope.' The sea then swept her towards us, and we caught her hands and got her safely on board, in as good a state as could be expected. She was plucky to the last. We then had forty-eight persons on board the lifeboat, including the crew, and could hear shouting from the steamer."

Though the *Charlotte* crew had heard the continuing cries for help from the direction of the wreck and with their boat filled with its crew and survivors, it was not possible to further continue securing persons or retrieving bodies. Of course, the coxswain at this time would not have been aware that the *Mohegan*'s masts were still above water and that desperate survivors were clinging to the rigging. He had already concluded that those cries came from victims in the water, and that by the time he returned, it would simply be a task of gathering bodies for burial.

A few hours later, having deposited the survivors on the shore, James Hill returned to the wreck. He must have been surprised at still hearing voices imploring for help, as he edged out of the cove and again headed towards the Manacles. A greater surprise awaited him on encountering the scene, in the growing morning light. As the lifeboat approached the broken vessel, the amazing scene unfolded: the *Mohegan* had slipped off the Manacle Rocks, and had sunk into deep water. Astonishingly, the funnel and all four masts were still standing above the surface, enabling survivors to cling on precariously to the rigging (see fig. 54).

The coxswain skillfully approached the vessel, but fearing a catastrophe, should they become entangled in the wreck, he laid to at some distance. It was at this point that the brave quartermaster Juddery leapt into the water from the ship's rigging and swam towards the lifeboat. Retrieving a rope, he returned to the wreck and so commenced the process of saving each individual from their perilous situation. All this occupied several hours, as the *Charlotte* crew retrieved a further sixteen survivors;[105] before making for the welcoming arms of those already on Porthoustock Beach.[106]

---

[105] See Table 19, p. 412/413; Passengers / Crew List: Saved from the *Mohegan*'s Rigging.

[106] No doubt with great difficulty. At that time, the sea came almost up to the lifeboat station; the modern-day position of the shoreline is as a result of back-fill with spoil from the local quarry. The beach would have been packed with helpers and onlookers from the surrounding area, and with an easterly wind, would have experienced heavy seas running onshore.

There were only two of the ship's lifeboats launched that night. One of them was all but swamped in the process and the other overturned completely. Unable to take to the boats, many passengers and crew went astern to the taffrail,[107] and were eventually washed overboard. Mr Ferguson, one of the engineers who was thrown into the sea, managed to swim back and climb the ship's funnel: badly scalding his hands on the steam pipe, as he did so. Robert Barrows, one of the greasers, even managed to swim the three miles to Coverack, having divested himself of his outer clothing and swimming only in his 'drawers and singlet'. Mr John Smith (fifth engineer) was a strong swimmer and managed to pass through the mass of people in the water, evading those who clutched at him, in desperation. He swam for three and a half hours, before reaching the shore. Two-thirds of those on board were not so lucky: they went down with the wreck and with the sea folding over them as a watery shroud.

To the boats, lads! To the boats!

At the following Board of Trade inquiry, the Falmouth lifeboat crew expressed their view of events:

> Mr Henry Fooks, Customs Officer and Receiver of Wrecks[108] at Falmouth, gave evidence as to the launching of the lifeboat, there in connection with the wreck. In giving evidence at the subsequent Board of Trade inquiry, Mr. Henry Fooks, stated that he had heard a sound of the mortar about 25 minutes to ten p.m. and five or six minutes later, he was informed by the coastguard that a vessel was on the Manacles. Believing it was a passenger steamer, he urged the expediency of getting the lifeboat out as quickly as possible. In being got out, the boat went on the [mud] bank in the docks, and grounded for some time, this having caused some delay in heading off to the wreck site. From the time when the mortar was fired to the time when the boat was got out would be about 45 minutes, and but for the grounding, the natural difficulties of the station, and the lowness of the water, the boat might have been got out in half an hour.[109]

Charles May, boatman to the Coverack Coastguard also helped raise the alarm. Even so, 105 men, women, and children perished that night, despite their best endeavor.

The *Mohegan* had the misfortune to crash on to the Manacle Rocks during an easterly half-gale, with the tidal stream set south-westerly and described by a life-boatman as, "a very nasty sea". This combination of wind and tide[110] gave no leeway for all those on board the crippled liner.

The following letter had been forwarded to a newspaper by Mrs Mary Besant, of 39, Craven Road, Lancaster Gate, London W2. The author of this note was her brother, Mr Bentley More[111] who was a member of the Porthoustock lifeboat crew, on the night of the disaster:

---

[107] The aftermost positioning of railing around the stern of a ship; often, but not always, ornately carved.

[108] Henry Fooks is named as Fookes in many records relating to the *Mohegan* disaster. The 1891 [Paignton, S, Devon] and 1901 [Falmouth] UK census unequivocally record his name as Fooks. The Fookes variant is used here where it appears in any contemporary account.

[109] *Royal Cornwall Gazette;* Thursday, 17th November 1898.

[110] Approximately 2½ hours after HW (an ebb tide, direction: south-by-west).

"Trenance", St. Keverne, R.S.O., Cornwall.

We were really in no danger in the lifeboat as long as we kept clear of the rocks, it was intensely dark, and we could see nothing. We were out for four hours, and came home with a 'boatload of dead and living, most of the living were injured— broken fingers, cut and crushed hands, &c. It took a long time to patch me up on Saturday. I am bruised all over, and the skin is knocked off my hands and wrists. The lifeboat was launched again directly we got the people out, but all had to be carried out. The first shipload we came to was capsized, bottom up, but we threw a grapnel and righted her. One man jumped into the boat (a smart man, he ought to be rewarded), and the boat was full of water. I and one or two others caught hold of the boat then, and the man in the boat got one woman out, but she died soon afterwards. The next boat was all right but the people were terribly soaked: we took them all in, women and children and men. One woman threw her arms round my neck; they were mad with joy. Then we picked up all we could, some on lifebelts and some on wreckage. The last was Miss Noble, a girl on a piece of wreckage. She had been in the sea three hours and, mind you, a very nasty sea. All she said was, "Just chuck me a rope," and we hauled her on board and she just shook the water off her and sat down in the most unconcerned way. We got ashore after a devil of a pull; we had so many in the boat and we took two hours rowing home. She went out again. I got into her to go again, but I was ordered out, and very properly, as a fresh man was better than a tired one; so went ashore (not at all sorry). I went home and changed my clothes: we were well wet through, and then went down again to help haul the lifeboat in as she came back. She had this time found the wreck and saved the man [*sic*] from the rigging. It was much lighter than when we were out; we could not see the wreck at all. From the time the first rocket was fired to the time the boat was launched was 20 minutes—a smart piece of work we think.[112]

When your mind says give up, hope whispers one more try.

Miss Noble gave an account of hearing others in the water going down all around her. She thought of letting go, but a recollection of the length of time that a young woman from the steamship *Elbe*[113] disaster was in the water encouraged her to hang on, and she felt she would be saved for the sake of her mother. After three hours drifting in the water, she was rescued by the Porthoustock lifeboat.

Bodies were swept away from the scene, by the tide. Allegedly, the ship's captain, Richard Griffith, was found some three months later, in Caernarfon Bay, near Anglesey. Headless, and still dressed in his uniform, he was identified by his captain's tunic; in particular, by its distinctive buttons (see fig. 74). Considering the location of the wreck site, it is hard to believe that his body could have washed up over 250 miles distance from the wreck site. It would have needed to navigate itself around the land mass of the Lizard, Land's End, then across the Bristol Channel to the Pembrokeshire coast, traversing Cardigan Bay, around the

---

[111] Mr Bently More—UK census 1901; aged 39 years, 'living on own means' with his wife Annie and their three children.

[112] *The Times;* 20th October 1898.

[113] During the night of 30 January 1895 North Sea conditions were freezing and there were huge seas. *SS Elbe* had left Bremerhaven for New York earlier in the day with 354 passengers aboard. Also out at sea on this rough night was the steamship *Crathie*, sailing from Aberdeen in Scotland, heading for Rotterdam. As conditions grew worse the *Elbe* discharged warning rockets to alert other ships of her presence. The *Crathie* either did not see the warning rockets or chose to ignore them. She did not alter her course, with such disastrous consequences, that she struck the liner on her port side with such force that whole compartments of the *Elbe* were immediately flooded. The collision happened at 5.30 a.m. and most of the passengers were still asleep; *Royal Cornwall Gazette*, October 20th 1898.

Lleyn Peninsula and eventually arriving at its final destination of Caernarvon Bay. It is worth noting that, not one other body was knowingly recovered west of the Lizard.

There were other reports by the Porthoustock locals, that the captain had been rescued and taken by lifeboat to shore; believed to be a man dressed in evening clothes.[114] This in turn led to a belief that the whole *Mohegan* episode was deliberately staged by the captain,[115] as he was rumoured to be in financial trouble, and being a shareholder in the shipping company, was made eligible for a substantial insurance payout. But this seems a far-fetched claim, and indeed, the insurance payment made to the company was for a sum of £112,000 pounds sterling, some £28,000 less than the cost of £140,000 for its initial purchase; Atlantic Transport Line having elected to carry the £28,000 shortfall, as a company liability.

It had been asserted that Griffith did not want command of this particular ship, had had a row with the company, who then had summarily stripped the captain of his rank as commodore of the line. As a result, he had developed a grudge and so deliberately ran the *Mohegan* on to the Manacles.

Such popular conspiracy theories are not just a modern phenomenon.

A Bounty is Raised for Victims.

As an incentive, Messrs. G. C. Fox & Co.,[116] Falmouth agent for the Atlantic Transport Company, had promised a bounty of £10 reward, to the finder of victims of the wreck.

The dead were now continually brought ashore, amid scenes of immense grief, with the local rescuers ably dealing with the situation, as only they could. This was not the first time that they had rallied around and generously dealt with an aftermath of a shipwreck, as hundreds of such disasters had been thrown up by the Manacle Rocks, on their very doorstep–such is their destiny.

It was a time for frantic cabling, interviewing, identifying victims, and with arranging shelter and hospitality to the hapless survivors. From the Squire at Lanarth to the humblest cottager, all opened their doors to the survivors and did what they could for those in need with their customary generosity.

Little did the good people of St. Keverne and surrounding hamlets imagine that history would tap them on the shoulder that night, and so forever irrevocably link them with the *Mohegan* tragedy.

---

[114] As the disaster occurred at dinner time, it is not surprising that at least one such man in evening clothes (though another witness said that the man was dressed in crew overalls). However, it was later reported that a man had taken a boat and rowed himself across the Helford River. The local view was that this man was Captain Griffith, seen alighting on Porthoustock beach that evening, and running from the scene. No doubt, whoever it was, his likely destination was Falmouth, accessible only on the opposite bank of the Helford River, and some miles distant. Even so, it would have been difficult (but not impossible) in making one's way from Porthoustock to the Helford River, given the night's events, the darkness and the difficult terrain. Also, a knowledge of the area would have been required, in order to navigate one's way to Falmouth, from this rather remote location.

[115] High profile events that are, in some ways, inexplicable, often attract conspiracy theories and such stories about the *Mohegan* can be traced back to within weeks of the disaster.

[116] Messrs. Fox, G. C. & Co. The company office was located at 48 Arwenack Street, Falmouth and is still in business to this day, at Falmouth Docks.

The Bitter End.

By every rail train, family members, who had scraped together the rail fare to Falmouth,[117] were arriving to seek out their loved ones, or to attend their funeral service. They were horrified to find that St. Keverne was a further twenty miles by road, and the cost of the hire of a carriage was as much again as the long rail journey from London. Their pitiable plight was duly recorded in the local newspaper:

Cases of Real Destitution At Falmouth

The wives of some members of the crew who are dead scraped enough money together to get to Falmouth in order to see the last of their loved ones. Having done this, and finding that the bodies they are seeking are not yet found, they are in a condition of absolute want. Any help for them would be received with gratitude by Mr. H. Toulson, the superintendent of the Cornwall Sailors' Home, Falmouth, whose name is a sufficient guarantee for the discreet distribution of any funds forthcoming.[118]

As all but two of the passenger victims of the disaster were American,[119] it is not surprising then that the American Press showed a particular interest in the affair, giving a rather imprecise account of the event:

ATLANTIC LINER MOHEGAN LOST

Wrecked Off the Lizard on Her Way to New York

PROBABLY 169 DROWNED

Only 31 Saved Out of 50 Passengers and a Crew of 150

LIFE SAVERS AT WORK

Several Persons Washed From Boats and Bodies of Others Dashed Ashore by the Waves

LONDON, October 14.—The Atlantic Transport Company's steamer *Mohegan*, formerly the *Cleopatra* of the Wilson-Furness Leyland Line, which left London for New York yesterday with 50 passengers and a crew numbering 150, is ashore off the Lizard, between the Manacle Rocks and The Lowlands. It is thought that there has been a great loss of life. According to a dispatch just received from Falmouth, out of the 200 persons constituting the passengers and crew of the *Mohegan*, only 31 have been saved.

A coastguard message reports that, "passengers are drowning like rats".

Another account says: "Bodies are washing ashore, one being of a lady lashed to a plank, with both legs severed".

Lifeboats put off from the Lizard and Falmouth, one returning with passengers. Several were drowned however it is reported, on the passage of the lifeboat to the shore.

The boat landed thirty of the *Mohegan*'s passengers, and returned for more. One lady died after she was brought ashore. Another lifeboat saved six persons.

---

[117] Falmouth was linked to Truro by rail, in 1863. The rail trip, from Paddington to Falmouth was (at that time) of eight hours duration.

[118] *Royal Cornwall Gazette;* 24th October 1898.

[119] Of those 49 saved, 36 were members of the crew. The disproportionate number was probably as a result of all passengers being below deck: either in their cabins, or in the dining-saloon, and coupled with their naivety as to the ship's layout and shipboard protocol, in the event of a disaster.

Particulars as to the disaster are difficult to obtain. It appears that when the *Mohegan* struck a gale was blowing and the sea running high.

A dispatch from Falmouth said the *Mohegan* foundered and was probably blown ashore by the heavy east wind after her machinery was disabled. All the Falmouth tugs went out, but were unable to approach the vessel.

The coast at that point is extremely dangerous, and has been the scene of numerous wrecks. Some years ago there was a movement set on foot to get a lightship placed there, but it failed.

The *Mohegan*, as the *Cleopatra*, was the last addition to the fleet of passenger and freight steamships built by the Wilson-Furness Leyland Line for its newly inaugurated passenger service, between London and New York. She was built at Hull and made her maiden trip here last summer. In fact, her present trip would have been only her second westward voyage.

Shortly afterward the Atlantic Transport Line, which has sold the *Massachusetts, Michigan, Mohawk* and sister ships to the government for transport service, brought out the Wilson's new fleet. The sum of $5,000,000 was paid for the *Cleopatra, Winifreda, Alexandra, Boadicea,* and *Victoria* the terms providing also that the Wilsons should not operate a rival line between New York and London for seven years. Though built at various yards, these vessels are about all of same size and character. The *Cleopatra* became the *Mohegan,* the *Winifreda* is the *Mesaba,* sailing today from this port; the *Victoria* has become the *Manitou,* the *Boadecia* the *Marquette,* and the *Alexandra* the *Menominee,* the names of all vessels of the Atlantic Transport Line beginning with the letter "M".

The *Mohegan* was 480 feet long, 52 feet beam, and 36 feet deep, with a carrying capacity of 8,500 tons dead weight, and of 13,500 tons measurement. She had stalls for 700 cattle, with an improved system for sanitation rendering the cattle carrying quite free from annoyance to passengers. Accommodation for passengers was provided by an amidships superstructure in which there were staterooms for 125 first cabin passengers, no second cabin or steerage passengers being carried.

Lizard Head, near which the *Mohegan* was wrecked, is a bold headland on the southern coast of Cornwall, and is the southernmost point of England. Its longitude is 5 degrees twelve minutes west. The lighthouse situated there is visible for twenty-one miles, its altitude being 186 feet. The coast from the Lizard to northeast to Manacle Point, a distance of more than 10 miles by water, is a particularly dangerous menace to navigation.

The *Mohegan* was a single-screw steamer, and made about 14 knots an hour. The distance to the Lizard is about 375 miles [from London], and she had therefore been out probably a little over twenty-four hours when she struck on the rock. The *Mohegan* was in the command of Capt. Richard Griffiths, formerly of the steamship *Manitoba*.[120]

The only person who was at the company's pier, at the foot of King Street, North River, last night was the receiving clerk. The names of the passengers who sailed on the *Mohegan* were not yet known, he said, at the offices here. He said the only names he knew aboard the steamer were Chief Officer Couch and Purser Fennington [*sic*].[121] Both they and the Captain lived in London. No news was received by the company last night in regard to the disaster.[122]

Death is the port where all may refuge find.

Reports of the funerals for the victims of the disaster, started to appear in the national newspapers:

---

[120] It was during this period of command of the *Manitoba* (official number 91998) that an accident occurred whilst uploading cases of primers, at the Royal Albert Docks, London. William Woodham, an employee of the Atlantic Transport Line company, and another man were killed. A case was held at the Bow County Court [July 6th 1898] for compensation, for his widow and others injured in the same incident: compensation was awarded.

[121] Edward Sennington was his true name.

[122] *New York Times;* 15th October 1898.

The body of Barnes, one of the stewards of the *Mohegan*, was interred at Falmouth yesterday [18th October] amid general signs of mourning. In the harbour the vessels had their flags at half-mast, as also did the public institutions of the town; whilst during the afternoon when the funeral was being performed all the shops remained partially closed. The deceased's father and brother and Maule, one of the survivors, a New York cattleman, were the principal mourners. Among many wreaths were those sent by the Mayor and Mayoress. By the mid-day train several of the survivors left Falmouth for London. Most of them had received injuries, their arms and heads being bandaged. The same train also conveyed two bodies of victims to the metropolis.

The work of identification being still incomplete many persons continue to arrive from various parts for the purpose of identifying the unclaimed bodies lying at the Falmouth Sailors' Home and at St. Keverne. The gratifying information was received yesterday at the London offices of the Atlantic Transport Company that two more of the passengers were safe: Mr. John Hyslop and O'Rorke, the valet to Mr. King, who perished in the disaster with his wife and two sons. Rumours were current both on Monday and Tuesday respecting the safety of Mr. Hyslop, but they were not confirmed until yesterday. The number of those saved passengers and crew is thus increased to 52. Telegrams were also received at Fenchurch Street [ATL London headquarters] during yesterday notifying the recovery of the bodies of the following passengers :– Mrs T. P. Firing, Mrs Fenton, Mr. and Mrs Charles Duncan, Miss Roza Duncan, Mrs L. M. Luke, Mrs. J. L. Le Lacheur, Miss Elliott (Mrs King's maid), and Mrs Weller. The body of another member of the crew, named Brownjohn, was also recovered. The number of bodies recovered and identified down to yesterday is thus increased to 44—namely, 21 passengers and 23 of the crew. Of the 156 persons known to have been on board, 96 are thus accounted for, and no hope is entertained as to the safety of anyone else who embarked on the ill-fated vessel. Messrs. Williams, Torrey, and Feild (Limited), the managers of the Atlantic Transport Company, have received several telegrams from relatives of those who lost their lives to send their bodies to America. Relatives of the deceased members of the ship's company, some of whom have just got together the railway fare and have but a small sum in their pockets remaining, have been horrified to find on reaching Falmouth that they have a 20 miles road journey before them, a journey which would cost them nearly as much as the long railway journey from London. Efforts are being made to assist them, but the horses of Falmouth have been run almost off their legs lately. The little post-office at St. Keverne, with its primitive instruments, is practically closed against Press messages. The friends of some of the drowned passengers are having bills posted offering large rewards for the recovery of these bodies. In one large grave a few feet from the north gable of St. Keverne Church a score of the ship-wrecked crew of the *Mohegan* were buried yesterday afternoon. The funeral was attended by the whole neighbourhood.[123] Squires and farmers, artisans and labourers, fishermen and Coastguard men crowded the church during the service there and afterwards surrounded the grave. There were also there some of the survivors. The vicar of the parish read the service, the vicars of the neighbouring parishes of Manaccan and St. Martins giving the responses. The service was solemnly impressive and the church portion was closed with the beautiful old hymn "Forever with the Lord". The bodies were then carried out in slings by surviving sailors, life-boatmen, and villagers. The chief cook [John Edge] and boatswain [John Cruikshank] helped to carry the bodies of their dead messmates. The chief [Agnes Piggot] stewardess stood weeping as her assistant's coffin was lowered at her feet. Coffin was piled on coffin in three tiers that room might be left in the deep and wide grave for those still remaining in the church and for the bodies expected to be cast up from the sea. The committal sentences were read over each, and a few simple wreaths were laid on the coffins. Apart from these members of the crew some of the deceased passengers were buried in separate graves further down the churchyard slope. The bodies of a number of the passengers have been taken away for burial in the United States and more are to follow. The doubts about identity have now been solved. They arose partly from a rule of the Coastguard that all valuables should be taken off the bodies of persons found drowned and inventories made of them to prevent their being subsequently stolen. Twenty-four of the surviving

[123] The funeral took place on Wednesday 19th October.

sailors were sent off from the Falmouth Sailors' Home to London yesterday. They included one or two who were really not fit to travel, but they wished to go and would not be hindered. One or two injured men still remain at the home. The Falmouth Chamber of Commerce yesterday evening decided to write to the corporation and the harbour board, in order that they might, appoint three members each to serve with three members of the chamber on a committee with a view to inviting the Board of Trade to hold an inquiry, through the Trinity Brethren, as to the best means of making navigation between the Deadman [Dodman Point] and the Lizard safer. It was also resolved that the secretary should draw the attention of the Board of Trade to the danger of allowing electric light to be used as a mast-head light. The matter had been prominently brought forward in connection with the wreck of the *Mohegan* as, owing to the electric light being extinguished, the lifeboats were unable to find the wreck. Admiral Sir E. R. Freemantle, naval commander-in-chief at Plymouth, visited the Manacle Rocks yesterday in the yacht *Vivid* and steamed round the scene of the wreck of the *Mohegan*. Naval officers and men do not favour the theory advanced at the inquest that the captain of the *Mohegan* mistook the Falmouth light for the Lizard, as the two are entirely dissimilar.[124]

A second report, relating to the funeral at St. Keverne, gave a empathetic account of the proceedings:

THE LOST LINER
FUNERAL OF THE VICTIMS
TOUCHING SCENES

Twenty of the shipwrecked crew of the *Mohegan* were yesterday afternoon laid to rest in one huge grave a few feet from the north gable of St. Keverne Church. Many most affecting scenes were witnessed. Some of the deceased passengers, whose bodies were encased in polished elm coffins with heavy mountings, were buried in separate graves. Rain fell very heavily during the sorrowful ceremony, and the scene was of the most woebegone description. The fifty remaining bodies are expected to float in the next few days, and they will be buried as they are recovered. A number of those recovered have been taken away for entombment in the United States. Twenty-four of the survivors left the Sailors' Home, Falmouth, for London yesterday.[125]

Believe none of what you hear, and half of what you see.

At this time, the company was at a loss as to the cause of the disaster and already its representatives were at pains to persuade everyone that, all was well aboard the vessel. The outcome of the vessel's short trip, however, belied that fact. A company spokesman was quick off the mark:

WILL "EVER REMAIN A MYSTERY

An interview was obtained with Mr. Torrie, one of the firm of the Atlantic Transport Line, who stated that he was afraid it would be quite impossible to issue a formal statement. He had received a letter from his partner, Mr. Williams, who was in Falmouth, who had interviewed the ship's doctor [Arthur Herbert Trevor],[126] some of the engineers, passengers, cattlemen, and they all agreed on the following points:—

---

[124] *The Times;* 19th October 1898.

[125] *The Dundee Courier & Argus* (Dundee, Scotland); Wednesday 19th October 1898.

[126] The duties of a ship surgeon while at sea are a combination of those of a doctor and a sanitary inspector. As a health officer he must visit every part of the ship to see that everything is clean; disinfect, if that is necessary; watch the food that is prepared for the crew, steerage and cabin passengers. All

(1) That there was no derangement of the machinery or anything else.

(2) The night was clear, but dark.

(3) The vessel was going at eleven knots when she struck.

(4) The captain and third officer were on the bridge when she struck.

(5) That there was no panic. The officers and men worked hard to launch the boats, and the women and children were put into them first.

(6) The officers also distributed lifebelts to those unable to get into boats.

Mr. Torrie concluded by expressing his regret at not being able to throw more light upon the cause of the disaster and expressed the fear that it would ever remain a mystery.[127]

The result for both the Cornish coroner's inquest and the Board of Trade inquiry was unequivocal. Before those deliberations became public however, the shipping industry was not reticent in giving *its* interpretation for a most likely cause of the accident:

THE CAUSE OF THE DISASTER

The Central News says in shipping circles the loss of the *Mohegan* cannot be satisfactorily accounted for. An hour before the ship struck the land must have been perceptible to the officer in charge of the bridge, as the westerly course would give an addition of twenty minutes to the daylight.[128] The course of a ship bound as the *Mohegan* was bound should have placed the Lizard several miles to the starboard but instead of this the course taken practically placed the Lizard to the left, and, in fact, the ship headed directly for the land. The assumption that the *Mohegan* had broken down or would not steer accurately is not admitted by the seamen, because in such an event her captain would have borne directly for Falmouth Harbour. It is also pointed out that after passing the Eddystone the ship must have trended towards the Cornish coast instead of keeping it well on the starboard side, and giving the Lizard a wide offing. Assuming thick weather, there must have been a serious miscalculation after passing the Eddystone which would give the course even if it had been lost. Moreover, from the position of the *Mohegan* at 6.30 [p.m.] the lights of Falmouth ought to have been an intelligent warning[129]

Invariably, a disaster develops from a combination of factors that come together in a particular sequence, each factor amplifying the effect of the other, and so resulting in a breakdown for a process. Events, aboard the *Mohegan,* may well have caused a loss of *situational awareness*, brought on by a dysfunctional team management.[130] The *Mohegan* disaster, may have exhibited this particular phenomenon.

---

the steerage passengers pass before the ship surgeon as they go on board. If there is any just cause why they should not be tolerated they are sent back—Hoyt, John C.; *Old Ocean's Ferry; the Log of the Modern Mariner, the Trans-Atlantic Traveler, and Quaint Facts of Neptune's Realm (1900).*

[127] *The Royal Cornwall Gazette Falmouth Packet, Cornish Weekly News, & General Advertiser;* Thursday, 20th October 1898.

[128] The sun set at nine minutes past five on the evening of the disaster and it was normally quite light for an hour later. *The Cornish Coast (South) – And The Isles Of Scilly:* Charles G. Harper; London: Chapman & Hall, Ltd. 1910; 137.

[129] *The Dundee Courier and Argus;* Monday, 17th October 1898.

[130] A current U.S. Coast Guard training publication defines this age-old problem: *"Situational Awareness* is the ability to identify, process, and comprehend … what is going on around you". The Coast Guard has estimated that at least 40 percent of accidents involving its cutters and boats are

There was a strong rumour abroad, that Captain Griffith and his company had a difference of opinion, over some matter or other, just before the sailing. In a letter, written by the first mate Llewellyn Couch, to his brother at Swansea [131] he sounded a note of dissatisfaction about the vessel, "... the re-naming was not lucky, and she only did thirteen knots on her trial". This letter would have been sent to Swansea between October 10th and the 14th, with the *Mohegan* sailing on that latter date. The same letter hints at continuing trouble with the *Mohegan*'s engines and could have been the reason for the dispute between Capt. Griffith and the ATL management (denied by the company) and arising from his insistence on further engineering work to be carried out, and with a costly delay in sailing.

Who laughs at others' ills, has his own behind the door.

The pressure Griffith was subjected to can be imagined, but with the shipping-line wanting an immediate return on their investment it would be no surprise that the captain would have been ordered to do what he had been paid to do. It was also suggested that the Griffith had been stripped of the title of 'Commodore' following this confrontation. Griffith, a proud man, having already suffered the humiliation of the *Cleopatra* debacle, would have been determined that his reputation was to suffer no further damage. The Port of London transatlantic shipping community was a small and competitive world. Its members had ringside seats for the unfolding twists and turns for a career of a ship's master, so exposed and providing much schadenfreude for its spectators. The Commodore would have been acutely aware of this.

Then, there is the puzzling incident of an encounter with the vessel *Scottish King*. The *Mohegan*, for no apparent good reason, matched her speed to that of her companion's slower progress down the Channel; then, sometime later, speeding ahead and crossing her path. A further (and unnecessary) delay was embarked on by an unscheduled stop at Prawle Point [132] in order to inform the company that, "All is well," [133] a rather pointless and ironic message to have sent, as later events would prove. Was this a deliberate ploy on his part: designed to show the company that he remained the loyal and consummate commodore, and anxious to downplay any discord between them, that had occurred the day before?

---

linked to the loss of *situational awareness*. The International Maritime Organization now issues guidelines that require member nations to train merchant mariners in the dangers of losing awareness. Copyright © 2005 David G. Brown, all rights reserved. It was originally published in the *Professional Mariner Magazine* (June/July 2005).
A good overview of the theoretical model is to be found here, in a paper: Endsley, M. R. and Garland D. J. (Eds) (2000); *Situation Awareness Analysis and Measurements*. Mahwah, N J: Lawrence Erlbuaum Association;
http://zonecours.hec.ca/documents/A2007-1-1399574.TheoricalUnderpinningsofSituationAwareness_ACriticalReview.pdf.
and also at this website; http://maritimesun.com/portal/wp-content/uploads/2011/02/BTM-and-figures.pdf.

[131] *Western Mail* (Cardiff, Wales); Monday, 17th October 1898.

[132] Prawle Point is Devon's southernmost extremity. Projecting into the English Channel between Bolt Head to the west and Start Point to the east, its lofty promontory has served as a vantage point since ancient times and, appropriately enough, the word 'Prawle' is Old English for 'lookout.'

[133] Signal Station 1882–1956. The present building is believed to have been erected by the Admiralty as a Coast Guard Lookout in the 1860s. It became a Lloyds Signal Station in 1882 and from here signalmen telegraphed details of passing ships to Lloyd's of London for the benefit of anxious owners and underwriters. Between 1903 and 1951 the lookout served as a Royal Naval Shore Signal Station with both Lloyd's and Admiralty signalling undertaken by naval personnel who also carried out coastguard functions. [Lloyd's signalling continued here until 1956]. ©National Coastwatch Institution.

Following the engagement at Prawle Point and on setting a course to the Eddystone Lighthouse, the vessel continued its progress down the Channel. That course now placed the ship at three miles south of the Eddystone, (instead of the more usual 10 miles) at around 4.30 p.m., as recorded by the lookout at Rame Head. It had been at this point that a further course was set: but on the wrong heading, west-by-north, instead of west-by-south. The ship's fate was now sealed.

With a cumulative delay in the ship's progress thus far, and in delaying the ship's arrival in Falmouth Bay, valuable daylight had been needlessly squandered, that could otherwise have given the officer crew an earlier indication of the ship's perilous position.

Another peculiarity relating to the remaining voyage was the persistent and proximity of the Cornish coastline, from the Eddystone onwards; even remarked on by the passengers.[134] Surely, if the passengers had noticed this anomaly, why on earth did the ship's officers not see this for themselves? It is almost certain that one or more of the officers *had* been alerted to this unfamiliar sailing pattern; after all, they were seasoned officers with many transatlantic voyages under their lifebelts. The captain himself had accomplished at least three hundred such voyages during his career, and ought to have been aware that not all was as it should be.

In the kingdom of the blind the one eyed man is king.

There is a question of Capt. Griffith's clarity or sharpness of vision. We now know he had lost his right eye, as a result of a violent shipboard incident some years previously, and so we must ask the question: was he visually impaired in his remaining eye? Did Griffith wear spectacles, or perhaps chose not to because of personal vanity? If so, this could have affected his ability to accurately read the charts and the compass, or even to discern the nearness of the coastline. Coupled with the character of the man—in that he was deemed unapproachable by his officers—he would have certainly judged it impertinent: their questioning his navigational skills. This would no doubt have dissuaded an officer in raising the matter with his captain and so to risk damaging a career progression. The officers' reticence in challenging their Captain, and in turning *their* blind eye, would cost them their lives a few hours later.

Each man for himself.

Several persons aboard the *Mohegan,* as well as those not aboard the vessel, gave their personal account of the disaster:

A MAN IN THE RIGGING

Mr. Hyslop, of New York, well known in the yachting world as the measurer for the New York Yacht Club, said in an interview this morning :—"When I went on deck I saw the ship was lost. Rocks rose out of the water close by us. I knew that if the boats were got clear before the ship sank, the men could not probably get more boats afloat than the women

---

[134] This is further evidence that the weather was clear, leading up to the encounter with the Manacles.

would fill. I therefore thought I would take my chance in the mizzen rigging. While putting my resolve into execution the stern settled, so that the water overtook me and went over my head. I managed to scramble up, however, until I was clear".

"The vessel struck at about quarter to seven, and her stern remained above water not more than twelve minutes, I should think the bottom was ripped up forward right aft as far as the centre. I don't think there was any deficiency of lifebelts. There were people all about me with them on. I did not see a single man who was not doing everything he could. When I got into the rigging the sea surged well up to those in the lower part of the rigging. Then the sea swept right over us. I could hear the screams of the poor women and children swept into the darkness close at hand and yet hopelessly out of reach. The voice of the perishing people will be in my ears for a long time. All the lights were electric, and when the vessel struck all were extinguished. Had there been an ordinary oil-lamp at the masthead it would have been of the greatest value [135]

The Pemberton family was spared:

A SERIOUS STATEMENT:

Mr. F. R. Pemberton, a banker of Wall-Street, New York, described how he jumped into a boat that was being lowered, and called to his wife to throw their two children down. They were safely caught and his wife and maid also jumped in. They were in the boat for about three hours. The boat was half filled with water; they had no rudder, and only a small bailer. When they saw the rockets from the [Porthoustock] lifeboat they all yelled, and the lifeboat bore down upon them. The crew of the lifeboat behaved splendidly, and although they had no officer in the ship's boat, he says that all of the sailors remained especially calm. The two children were in their night clothes, and Mrs Pemberton, who was ill, was only in a nightdress and wrapper, and she had not even any shoes on, and her feet were trampled upon dreadfully. "I was impressed with the apparent lack of discipline and order aboard," adds Mr. Pemberton. "Only on Friday morning Mrs Pemberton and I discussed this apparent lack of discipline and order, my wife remarking that in case of accident there would be little possibility of passengers being saved. Officers were smoking at all hours. I propose to inquire into the whole matter. When the boats were out of the davits they could not be detached easily from the ship. The boat I was in was within an ace of being overturned, when a knife was produced and the rope cut. The boat went up and down thirty feet or so, and bumped against the ship. It was a fine night—not only lights, but the land itself was plainly within view of the naked eye. It could be seen that we were but a hundred yards from the shore". [136]

The Look-out at Rame Head gave his account:

Joseph Barnfield, retired Quartermaster R.N., and now signalman at Rame Head, said he reported the ship at 3.20 p.m., on the 14th, when she was about eight miles south of that point. There was rather a thick haze at the time. The nearest point South, at which the vessel passed him, about twenty minutes to four, was less than ten miles. He judged that she would be four of five miles westward of the Eddystone Lighthouse. It appeared to him that she was much nearer than was usual with the ordinary run of liners. [137]

[135] *The Pall Mall Gazette* (London, England); Monday, 17th October 1898.

[136] *The Royal Cornwall Gazette Falmouth Packet, Cornish Weekly News, & General Advertiser*; Thursday, 20th October 1898. Mr Pemberton's view of the shoreline is probably mistaken and he was more likely looking at the extensive sweep of the Manacle reef itself, exposed by a low tide.

[137] *The Morning Post* (London, England), Saturday, November 12, 1898. Barnfield (in another version of this report) thought that, as the liner was as close as it was, it was probably bound for Falmouth.

The Lighthouse Keeper at St. Anthony's Head gave his account:

Richard Nelson, one of the keepers at Falmouth Lighthouse [St. Anthony] said that from 4 p.m. to 7 p.m. on the day of the disaster the weather was clouded. At a quarter to six o'clock the wind was East-south-east, and it blew a moderate gale from that quarter during the remainder of that evening. The evening was dark, but clear in the sense that the lights could be seen as far as it was ever possible to see them. He saw nothing of the *Mohegan*. She would have been visible if he had been outside but he had been inside. The Falmouth revolving light – there was also a fixed light [138] – would be visible at the distance of some fifteen or sixteen miles. The lights were working well at the time. [139]

The Lighthouse Keeper at the Lizard gave his account of weather conditions at the time:

Alfred Lewis, light keeper at the Lizard, stated that at the time in question the weather was so clear that it was not thought necessary to sound the syren [*sic*]. [140]

The Collector of Customs at Falmouth and some passengers, gave their accounts at the Board of Trade inquiry:

. . . Mr Henry Fookes, collector of Customs and Receiver of Wrecks at Falmouth, gave evidence as to the launching of the lifeboat on the banks in the docks and grounded for some time, this necessarily causing some delay. From the time when the mortar was fired to the time when the boat was got out was about forty-five minutes, and but for the grounding, the natural difficulties of the station, and the lowness of the water, the boat might have been out in half-an-hour. Previously, whist walking on the cliffs, he had seen a large steamer apparently making for Falmouth Harbour, but she passed, and seemed to be steering straight for the Manacles. Then she apparently altered her course and he thought she had gone clear of the rocks. The tug was ready before the lifeboat, and had to wait for her about ten minutes.

By Mr. Pyke [for the owners, master and officers]—His impression was that those on board the steamer saw their danger and altered their course so as to avoid it. This was not an uncommon occurrence there, and the Coastguard always warned off vessels that they saw running into danger.

Mrs. C. Smith [*sic*], [141] one of the passenger on board the *Mohegan* at the time of the disaster said, she had crossed the Atlantic six times previously. She remarked to a friend that she had never before seen the land so close going down the Channel. At about twilight they had seen a light going down the Channel, and spoke of the strangeness of the occurrence. Just as she was sitting down to dinner the crash came. At first there was no alarm, but presently there was a cry, and they rushed on deck the electric light went out. The passengers run aft and the witness stood on the port side while Dr. Fallows, a fellow passenger, went to get the life-belts. Meanwhile the vessel heeled over, and seas began to break over her. The doctor returned with the life-belts, and the Captain from the bridge directed them to go to the starboard side. Eventually witness and others got to the life-boat, which was cut away and capsized. Witness and others were under the boat for some time, and they were almost suffocated, until suddenly there was a jerk the boat righted and she saw the [Porthoustock] lifeboat

---

[138] The fixed light, being 37 feet below the revolving light, is exhibited to clear the Manacle rocks; it is only seen between the bearings of N.N.E. ½ E. and N. by E. ½ E.

[139] *The Royal Cornwall Gazette Falmouth Packet, Cornish Weekly News, & General Advertiser*; Thursday, 20th October 1898.

[140] Ibid.

[141] This report was attributed to Mrs. Amelia Compton Swift: a veteran of six transatlantic voyages.

above her and a man with a torch. It was then found that her foot was jammed by something in the boat, and the man could not extricate her. She asked for an axe and one was brought, with which a man chopped at a plank that held her. Before she got under the boat she heard a slight explosion and saw the Captain go overboard as the steamer heeled over still further. Miss Catherine [sic] Noble, another passenger said she was one of those who, by direction of the fourth mate [Stanley Browning], took to the rigging. They were washed down first, but the officer placed her higher up in a place of safety. He then went away. Presently she felt herself going under water, but she rose to the surface and swam to a piece of wreckage, to which she clung until rescued by a lifeboat. While in the water she saw the fourth mate clinging to another piece of wreckage, but they were separated by a [heavy] sea, and she saw him no more.[142]

Of Mrs Compton Swift's observation, on the, "strange light close by", this was almost certainly the St. Anthony Light. A rough calculation, based on the reported speed of the *Mohegan* just prior to impact, and her position in Falmouth Bay at a point when the St. Anthony's light would have first been visible, suggests a time-frame of approximately 10 minutes between the two events.[143] This would probably have been a sufficient interval for Mrs Compton Swift to have seen the St. Anthony's light, having reached the dining room below, and in seating herself at the table, at which point the ship collided with the Manacle Rocks.

First impressions are the most lasting.

In October 1966, an electronic tape-recording was made of interviews with three St. Keverne people who had witnessed the tragedy, or who had heard firsthand accounts of it, from within their respective families.[144]

John (Joe) Rogers was born at Treglohan Farm, in Rosenithon,[145] in October 1893, overlooking the Manacle Rocks. He had lived all his life in the parish. Some of his recollections are his own and others are from members of his family who were personally involved both during and after the events of October 14th 1898.

John Rogers remembered being disturbed by the rocket which was fired from Tommy Noye's field above St. Keverne, because the noise reverberated to such an extent that the windows rattled. His sister, Dora, heard screams from the direction of the Manacles from the front steps of the Rogers' family home in Rosenithon. His mother and Janie Tripp immediately took off for Porthoustock, to offer their help. They were the first two women on the scene.

John Rogers also recalled that: "The first thing I remember at all is standing with my father at the doorway of the farmhouse, looking out at the four-masted *Mohegan*. I was two years old. It was probably because of

---

[142] *Morning Post* (London, England; Saturday, 12th November 1898.

[143] The calculation was based on the navigational chart of the period – *Approaches to Falmouth* – surveyed 1853–55; corrected in 1890.

[144] These recordings are available via the St. Keverne Local History Society website; http://st-keverne.com/History/mohegan/index.html.

[145] An alternative spelling—"Rosenython" appears occasionally. The different spellings of "Rosenython" and "Rosenithon" are because the farm name comes from old Cornish meaning "Nest in the Moors". That is the name of the farm. When this was explained to the ordnance survey map-makers, the reply was that the village (hamlet, settlement,) has been spelled with an "I" for so long that it must remain so—Courtesy of: St. Keverne Local History Society.

the great and sensational tragedy of this ship's loss that the scene had been sketched [*sic*] on my mind all my life."

Next morning Joe was taken to the shore by his father and he vividly remembered seeing the *Mohegan*'s four masts and red funnel sticking up above the water.

John Rogers' grandfather, William Matthews,[146] and his great uncle, Captain John Matthews, both of Porthoustock, saw a man jump off the prow of the Porthoustock lifeboat as it grounded on to the beach, and disappear through the hamlet and up the valley. Tradition has it that this was Captain Griffith of the *Mohegan* and was quoted in supporting the story that the vessel had been deliberately wrecked.

Joe also recalled that four survivors stayed with his grandparents at Porthoustock, including the boy John (Jimmy) MacFarlane who was best remembered for his swearing and for playing the mouth organ. He had two broken legs and remained at Porthoustock for about six months.

Joe was out with his father the day after the wreck and they found a body washed ashore which they took by cart to St. Keverne. He again recalled the story of Miss Noble who stayed at Rosenithon with the Rogers family after the loss of the *Mohegan*, Miss Noble commented to Joe's parents about the chaos on board because the lights went out on the *Mohegan* so soon after striking the Manacle Rocks.[147]

John Rogers died in 1977, aged 81 years.

The second person interviewed was Bentley Tripp who was born in 1901, the son of George Martin and Ellen Jane (née Peters) Tripp.

Bentley had been brought up on stories of shipwrecks and the sea as his father was a fisherman and a lifeboat crew member at Porthoustock. Bentley himself was a fisherman with firsthand experience of the coastal waters off St. Keverne and he knew the Manacle Rocks, "like the back of his hand".

Bentley Tripp recalled his father (George Martin Tripp, a stroke-oarsman aboard the lifeboat that night[148]) relating that the *Mohegan* was seen steaming into Falmouth Bay, from an easterly direction, lights ablaze, and looking like a floating town and then, suddenly turning and taking a course straight for the Manacles.[149]

Mr Tripp related the following from memory, "I was born at Halwyn Farm [150] in 1890. My school days began at Porthallow in a small room immediately below a shoemaker's shop. There were about twelve scholars, boys and girls, and we were taught the three 'Rs' by Miss Bryant, for which my parents paid two pence a week. At the age of eight, I was one of the first pupils to attend the new school. I can remember

---

[146] William Matthews, a retired naval pensioner (Greenwich).

[147] Miss Noble later sent, from America, a photograph (see fig. 19) of herself to the family. Courtesy of the Rogers family, Rosenithon.

[148] *Cornish Magazine* – *"Around the Manacles"* 1898, 408; Bluett, Albert. It is remarkable that among the men who did noble work in the lifeboat, five were named Tripp.

[149] These events would not have been seen from Porthoustock. However, the 1901 UK census shows the Tripp family lived at Porthallow, from where the whole event of the *Mohegan*'s approach to the Helford River estuary and her sudden turn towards the Manacles would have clearly been witnessed.

[150] Halwyn is an old Cornish farmstead, with the farmhouse believed to be around 250 years old and is situated at Manaccan.

seeing the *Mohegan* on the Manacle Rocks with her funnel and four masts showing above the water. My father was a member of the Porthoustock Lifeboat crew that saved so many lives, from this unfortunate ship."

On the evening of the 14th October 1898 the sea was moderating with a heavy swell. When the *Charlotte* was about half way to the Manacle Rocks by Maen Garrick (the rocks due east of Manacle Point) it came across an upturned lifeboat from the *Mohegan*. One or two people were rescued from the keel, but, according to Bentley's version, there were twenty-four people found dead underneath it. They went on in darkness towards the cries and screams coming from the vicinity of the Manacle Rocks and came upon the second *Mohegan* lifeboat.

George Tripp had told Bentley that there was one young lady, about twenty-eight years of age, in a *Mohegan* lifeboat. She had long hair which had become entangled with ropes at the bottom of the lifeboat. Frank Tripp, a crew member of the *Charlotte*, who was, "a good man on land and sea" took an axe and cut her hair to free her.[151] However, as he was wielding the axe to cut the hair, the *Charlotte* rolled and the axe blade struck the leg of another passenger and badly cut it. The result of this incident is that this unfortunate person, Mrs Lizzie Small Grandin, bled to death in the Porthoustock lifeboat, before reaching shore.

Bentley's mother Janie Tripp and Margaret Ann Rogers had rushed to Porthoustock as soon as the rocket had been fired and witnessed the scene on the shore. They remembered the distress on the beach as the lifeboat landed because families had been split up and some were still missing.

The local doctor, Edward James Leverton-Spry, had rendered help to the victims and had instructed Janie Tripp to escort two elderly male survivors up to a cottage in Porthoustock village, but in the darkness, she took fright and returned to the beach.

Bentley recalled that the next morning bodies from the wreck came ashore on all the beaches between Lowlands and Godrevy [*sic*] and that they were carried in farm carts, up to the St. Keverne village. The bodies were laid out in the church, although some of the more affluent Americans were embalmed and taken back to the USA. A firm of embalmers came from London to St. Keverne, as this practice was not carried out by any local firm of undertakers.[152]

He remembered that his father had said that, after the *Charlotte* had landed on Porthoustock beach, a person dressed in brown fireman's overall jumped off the side and ran up through Porthoustock village as, "if fired from a gun".

The next morning, allegedly, a man was seen taking a boat and rowing across the Helford River estuary. Was this person Captain Griffith? Rumour had it that he knew the area well and had deliberately lost the ship

---

[151] This is a very similar account to that of the rescue of Mrs Compton Swift except that in the other version she had been trapped by her foot.

[152] The eight bodies were transported in lead-lined and hermetically sealed caskets, and returned to America on the *SS Menominee* from London. An agent of the Atlantic Transport Line was at the pier, and made the necessary arrangements with the health authorities for the transit of the bodies through the city, to where their relatives took them within their care.—*New York Times* – November 8, 1898.
Bodies of Mohegan Victims Here—On the Atlantic transport steamship *Menominee*, which arrived yesterday from London, were the bodies of the following persons lost in the wreck of the steamship *Mohegan* off the Lizard: Mrs. King and her boy, Mrs. Weller. Mr. and Mrs. Luke, Mrs Grumbrecht, Mrs. Granden and Mrs. Crane—*The Sun* (New York); November 08, 1898

in order to be eligible for (as a shareholder of the Atlantic Transport Line) an insurance pay-out. However, if Captain Griffith had local knowledge, the question is: why did he run the *Mohegan* on to the Vase Rock when he could have run her inside the Voices or on to the Lowlands without loss of life?

The last person to be interviewed on the tape in October 1966 was George Lory of St. Keverne, the village carpenter and undertaker. He had been born at Trevalso in 1881 and was eighteen years of age at the time of the disaster. He recalled the story of how Mrs Grandin had died in the Porthoustock lifeboat as a result of having her, "leg cut off accidentally by Frank Tripp's axe". He too believed that the *Mohegan* had been wrecked deliberately. He also confirmed the embalming of some of the bodies in the house where the St. Keverne garage now stands, and supported the tradition that Captain Griffith had been rescued and then disappeared. George told how the last victim's body was picked up some seven or eight weeks after the disaster.

He recounted that there had been a lot of ale on board the *Mohegan* and that some of this was washed ashore. Mr Lory concluded that this ale was of good quality, and was much enjoyed by the locals.

James Austen Pengilly was born in St. Keverne [153] and lived there all his life, and died there in January, 1983. In his written account of the *Mohegan* disaster,[154] he recalled:

"I was four and a half years of age and I was watching my mother skimming cream off pans of scalded milk.[155] A light east wind was coming through the window which faced the Manacle Rocks. Mother said,'Tell your father to come in and listen to the shrieks and cries for help.' Then a man shouted from our gate that there was a great liner on the Manacle Rocks, and that he was off to Porthoustock to help the rescue boats off the beach. That man was Frank Curnow's grandfather [Charles Curnow], and he and my father left immediately for Porthoustock, and remained there throughout the weekend".

"When my father arrived at Porthoustock, it was pouring with rain. Both the living and the dead were being landed on the beach and the lifeboat house. The survivors were wrapped in blankets and clothes given by the local people, and were given hot drinks. Our local doctor, Dr. Spry, was rendering first-aid to those people who were injured. Several bodies were taken to a little thatched cottage where St. Keverne garage now stands, and these bodies were embalmed and sent home to New York".

"All night long, and throughout the weekend, bodies were being brought up to the church. Meanwhile, several men were digging a great grave [13 feet x 20 feet x 10 feet] at the north side of the church. Here were laid over forty coffins, with some smaller ones elsewhere in the churchyard".

In the intervening years, the *Mohegan* oral history was inevitably distorted by time and with the re-telling. When electronic recording mechanisms became widely available, those with tales to tell were quite advanced in age. In addition, they would have been very young and impressionable in 1898 and this could have given a further, but unintentional twist to their story.

---

[153] Born in the year 1894 at Trebarwath Farm, St. Keverne; UK census 1901.

[154] James Austen Pengilly; *A Night to Remember.*

[155] This describes the making of traditional Cornish clotted cream—a well known local delicacy.

However, an overall truth seems to permeate the recordings and we are privileged to hear those first-hand accounts of that terrible night's events, now preserved for posterity.

CHAPTER 4

The Cause of the SS *Mohegan* Disaster

All the waters in the ocean could never sink a ship, unless it gets inside.

The so-called 'local emissions' from the Manacle Rocks (of which more later) and with the rocks themselves purporting to affect a ship's compass, was hotly debated over, as a cause for the disaster.

A more likely cause was that of human error. In a professionally run ship, as was the *Mohegan*, the disaster must have resulted from either: bad communication, navigational skills, or in an execution of duty. A simple miscalculation of the ship's intended course down the English Channel is a distinct possibility, and a degree or two of error to the north in a bearing set at the Eddystone Light, would be sufficient to ensure a collision with the Manacle Rocks, over a projected distance of 45 nautical miles. In the absence of modern-day navigational aids, a ship relied solely on the stars, compass bearing, log of the ship (speed relative to the water), the lead, and landmarks. In poor visibility or in the open ocan, landmark facilities would not be available to a navigator, leaving a reliance on soundings (with bottom types) and 'taking the log' together with following an established compass heading. A ship's course is plotted on the navigational chart and is recorded in the ship's log. Unfortunately, no logbook was ever recovered from the *Mohegan*.

An article here, speculates on the mind of its master Capt. Griffith, leading up to the disaster:

No one has a critical word for Capt. Griffiths. The inference is inevitable, Capt. Griffiths either intended to wreck his vessel, which is impossible and absurd, and which we mention only to exhaust the theories, or his mind for some unknown reason, some overwhelming grief, or thought, or preoccupation, or it may be some hallucination as to the point he had reached, had temporarily had failed him, and he gave orders the import of which he did not perceive. The moment the catastrophe had occurred he was himself again, a calm resolved officer who gave the right orders clearly, who was obeyed by his men to the last moment, and who inspired such confidence that, as all the witnesses testify, under the horrible circumstances, with lights all out, and the women on board all screaming so that they were heard four miles away, with immediate death staring everybody in the face, there was no panic. He made no effort to save himself till he had done his duty to the last, and then he failed, and was drowned like any passenger. Subject always to fresh evidence, which is conceivable though improbable, we can hardly doubt that this is the explanation. The Captain, the General, or the engine-driver "loses his head," not through drink, or by cowardice or by reason of incompetence, or a temporary failure of brain power, akin to the momentary failure of power that will sometime paralyse a man's limbs.

The Captain mistakes a sea road, that he knows as well as the way to his cabin, the General forgets utterly some cardinal piece of information or topographical fact, the engine-driver does not see the signal which should stop him, the catastrophe occurs, and no one of the three, if he survives, can ever remember clearly what it was went wrong. Usually it is [due to] a tired brain which has given out, but intense anxiety will produce the same effect, so will an excessive absorption in one subject, and sometimes there is no explanation at all, a truth of which great chess players, among others, are curiously well aware.

Make your vessel the most marvelous of structures, but if her Captain is momentarily confused for any reason, and fails to distinguish between the Manacles and the Lizard, the marvel of her structure will not save her or her passengers from instantaneous ruin". [156]

Further *Mohegan* related stories appeared in the newspapers, such as this intriguing account:

Extraordinary stories are in circulation owing to the non-recovery of the captain's body. It will be remembered that someone stated that Captain Griffiths was seen to jump from the ship with one lifebelt around his body under his arms, and another on the lower part of his body. The inference was that he desired to drown and put on the second lifebelt to throw his head under water. Now another, and more extraordinary story, is in circulation. It was said that the captain knew that he could not sink if he had on two lifebelts, and that he managed to get ashore, obtain a suit of clothes, and leave the locality. This absurd tale is believed by scores of persons, who say it is proved by the fact that inquiries have been made by relatives for the captain's body. It appears however, that two ladies from Huntingdonshire [157] were at St. Keverne on Friday [November 4th] asking anxiously if the Captain's body had been picked up. Many bodies are still missing, and this is not surprising, when it is recollected that bodies from the *John*, wrecked in May, were picked up in the following July, and that one was found in September. Not a few of the people who reside near the scene of the disaster have become full of fear since they have heard of bodies being found or deposited near to their homes, and nothing would persuade some of them to go out after sunset. The able-seaman, whose body was brought from the wreck to St. Keverne in a serious condition, is progressing slowly. The only other survivor in the immediate locality is a youth [J. Macfarlane], who had both his legs broken. He is doing well at Porthoustock.

On all hands, praise is given to the owners for the way in which they have endeavoured to meet the wishes of all who have suffered by the terrible calamity. It is probable that some memorial will be erected to those who lost their lives, and the Rev. Canon Diggens, who has proved a friend to many survivors and to the friends of the drowned, suggests that it should take the form of a coloured window in the church. [158]

The Canon's suggestion did in fact meet with general approval, and with the window thus installed, [159] it serves as a poignant memorial to this day (see fig. 40):

The stained-glass window which has been placed in the east end of St. Keverne Church, Cornwall, to the memory of the victims of the *Mohegan* disaster was unveiled on Wednesday by Mr. A. S. Williams, manager of the Atlantic Transport Company, and was dedicated by Archdeacon Cornish. It bears the inscription, "To the glory of God, and in memory of the 106 persons who perished in the wreck of the s.s. *Mohegan* on the Manacle Rocks, October 14th, 1898. This window was dedicated by the Atlantic Transport Company, owners of the vessel". At a meeting of the parishioners afterwards the vicar

---

[156] *The New York Times;* 2nd November 1898 – originally published in the *London Spectator.*

[157] Huntingdon is approximately 40 miles due North, of London. The two women might well have been previous passengers, aboard a ship with Griffith as its captain. It was not unknown for women to change their itinerary, in order that they travel with their preferred ship's master.

[158] *The Royal Cornwall Gazette Falmouth Packet, Cornish Weekly News, & General Advertiser;* Thursday, November 10th 1898

[159] The glass window was created and installed by the firm of Messrs. Burlison and Grylls—*The Graphic;* April 29th 1899. The company was founded in 1868. Both John Burlison (1843–91) and Thomas Grylls (1845–1913) had trained in the studios of Clayton and Bell [London]. Good examples of the company's work can be found at St Chrysostom's Manchester and some windows in Truro Cathedral.

of St. Keverne moved that the Atlantic Transport Company be heartily thanked for their gift of the window. He said that, after the wreck, the company did their best to make provision for the care of the dead and the comfort of the living. Mr. Williams, in reply, said that the disaster to the *Mohegan* showed not only the bravery of the men who served the lifeboat on the coast, but also the charity of the people on shore. Nothing could have been better than the feeling shown by the whole neighbourhood to the poor people who came ashore after exposure to terrible suffering. He wished the company could have done more. The fund for the relief of the families of the crew amounted to about £4,000, and had been expended in giving donations for immediate relief and small annuities to the widows, and children.[160]

A report in a local newspaper described an entirely credible scenario, leading-up to this tragic accident. It was made public on the completion of the Board of Trade inquiry, and so would not have been available to the authority, at that time:

A SOLUTION

I have heard of circumstances associated with the wreck of the *Mohegan* which may throw light on the question as to her position when she struck the Manacles on the night of the 13th inst. [*sic*]. There is always a pilot boat on guard between Falmouth and the Manacles between sunset and sunrise. Probably to escape the swell of the channel, she was at slip anchor off St. Anthony on the night in question, when her crew saw a large vessel steaming for Helford River. At first she was supposed to be one of the large torpedo boats, but was soon after discovered to be too large, and her presence in such a dangerous position at once called forth a flare-up from the pilot boat (No. 10). At this time, I am informed, the vessel was actually in the act of signalling to St. Anthony,[161] and this would indicate that the officer in charge believed he was off the Lizard, and was unaware of his terrible proximity to the most dangerous point along this treacherous coast. After the flare-up the vessel seems to have altered her course, the helm being to all appearances put round and the vessel's head pointed S.E. By this means she was brought clear of the first line of rocks, and the officer in charge, probably desirous of covering up his mistake before his chief could discover it, instead of keeping her bow to mid-channel by which means he could have cleared the reef, made for the nearest course for the Lizard and had his vessel's side gored by the hidden rocks where she now lies.

CONFIRMATORY TESTIMONY.

That this is a solution of the disaster is borne out by a person who was walking on Falmouth Castle Drive at the time of the disaster [Mr. Henry Fooks]. He stated that he saw a large vessel making straight for Helford, and expected every minute she would founder but suddenly she altered her course and apparently cleared the Manacles. He watched her lights till they disappeared, thinking at the time that she had vanished in the distance, and had no thought that her lights disappeared in consequence of a disaster. If the captain of the *Mohegan,* when he passed Start Point, left the vessel in charge of another officer, with the course set and instructions that the next light passed would be the Lizard, it is easily conceivable that if he were inexperienced in the navigation of the channel he might have mistaken St. Anthony's for the Lizard light, and when the flare up came seeing land ahead and on either side, hastily consulted the chart and discovered his fatal error. The position in which the wreck lies is confirmatory of the fact that she must have altered her course after discovering her dangerous position off Helford. Had the engines been reversed and proper bearings taken, the *Mohegan* could, in all

---

[160] *The Times; 21st April 1899.* The sum of £4,000 would be the equivalent in today's currency to £230,000.

[161] Richard Nelson, one of the keepers for the St. Anthony Light, stated that he had not seen the *Mohegan,* as he had been inside at the time she had passed them by.

probability, have been saved. Since this note was written the same solution of the problem has been discussed at Truro Mercantile Association [162]

The local crew aboard pilot boats were entirely familiar with the Falmouth estuary and the surrounding approaches. Their job was to identify vessels that were approaching Falmouth Port, particularly at night, and requiring their local knowledge and expertise in offering a safe passage and mooring, within the port itself. The pilots afforded a most reliable account of the events of that night of the disaster, with a very credible assessment of the *Mohegan*'s final moments, towards her nemesis: the Manacle Rocks. An essential part of this expertise was in their ability in interpreting a ship's navigational lights signature, at night: the lights inform of a ship's orientation, and its directional course. Intriguingly, at this point, the *Mohegan* was allegedly engaged in signaling the St. Anthony's Lighthouse.[163] The keepers failed to remark on this at any subsequent hearing. A pity, as the message itself could have revealed the thinking aboard the vessel, as to its assumed position and intent.

Regrettably, it would seem the Board of Trade inquiry panel was not acquainted with this revealing account of events: a missed opportunity perhaps.

The best laid schemes of men and mice.

The Board of Trade, in its conclusion, was not moved to comment on the situation on the *Mohegan*'s bridge and with its officers' actions, at the time just prior to the wrecking. Presumably as there were no survivors, such conjecture would remain just that. The only point, at which the captain and officers' movements were addressed, is after the foundering: when their heroic actions were highlighted as an exemplar of English bravery and stoicism, and was much lauded as such.

A report appeared in a newspaper that suggested that, at the time leading up to the event, the first and third mate (Llewellyn Couch and William Logan Hindmarsh) were both on the final watch and that, as it was dinnertime, they had taken turns in going below for a meal, leaving just the one officer on the bridge.[164] Both officers had no notion that every revolution of the engines was hurrying the ship and her human freight on to their final port of call: the Manacle Rocks.

At some point, Couch had gone below for his meal, leaving Hindmarsh (the junior officer) alone on the bridge and in command. It is unlikely that Capt. Griffith would have agreed to this arrangement, unless of course he was on the bridge throughout, as he was certainly not in the dining room at that time.

---

[162] *The Royal Cornwall Gazette Falmouth Packet, Cornish Weekly News, & General Advertiser;* Thursday, October 27th 1898.

[163] The Keeper at St. Anthony stated at the Board of Trade inquiry that he had not seen the *Mohegan* and that, "she would have been visible if he had been outside".

[164] *The Belfast News-Letter;* Monday, 17th October 1898.

At the Board of Trade inquiry, Mrs Compton Swift stated that just before she had left the deck, at about 6.20 p.m. and it being about twilight, she had noticed the land. When sitting down to dinner and on the point of turning her chair, she heard a crash; the chief engineer and first and fourth officers rushed on deck, followed by some anxious passengers. By chance, her testimony unequivocally placed both first officer Llewellyn Couch and fourth officer Browning at the dinner table. This was also confirmed by Mr Arthur Herbert Trevor, the ship's doctor, in his evidence given at the same inquiry.

On arrival at New York, the passenger Miss Roudebush had proclaimed to the American press, that, "If Capt. Griffith was responsible for the wreck he had certainly gone out of his mind." She continued, "As I remember it, he [Griffith] at 4 o'clock left the chief officer [Llewellyn Couch] in command. The chief officer was relieved at 6 o'clock by the third officer [Hindmarsh], who I understand, was young and inexperienced. The fact remains the boat went on the rock, and despite the fact that those on shore saw her course of danger, and sent up rockets of warning. I saw no officers who were apparently in authority during the excitement."

Absent without leave.

As officer Couch had left the bridge to attend dinner, and in leaving the third officer in charge, to face a terrible dilemma. With a warning flare shooting skyward and an indistinct land mass looming ahead out of the darkness, the young officer was now solely responsible for saving the ship from its deadly track. Did Cole give the order to the helmsman, (Quartermaster August – drowned) in taking evasive action? It would seem not, as a member of the crew, who was working on the deck at the time, later testified that he was unaware of any change in the ship's direction. Had the ship gone hard over to port, everyone aboard would have been made aware of a sudden change in heading, as the ship would have heeled over. It is assumed that had the Captain been on the bridge, he would have certainly opted for that more aggressive response, in facing the danger ahead. If this was indeed the case, then Cole's faint-hearted response helped assure the wrecking of the *Mohegan*.

Another possibility is that the *Mohegan* had sailed in an unwavering straight course from the Eddystone to the Manacle Rocks. However, this is not supported by the various witnesses' accounts given from either on the shore, or on the pilot boat at slip-anchor, off the St. Anthony's Light.

Concerning the dead, people should say nothing except good.

Passengers had remarked on the fact that the captain was not present in the dining room that evening. There was an accusation, levelled at him, that he had been entertaining a woman in a cabin at the time. Miss Noble later made this assertion to the assembled journalists on the New York pier, "It seems singular, that he permitted to direct three sane men to steer the Mohegan on to the rocks … such was the fact however, and lack of discipline was responsible for the terrible loss of life. It was suppertime; Capt. Griffiths was not in the [dining] saloon. My seat was next to his was empty. I was told that he was in another cabin with some woman."[165]

We shall probably never know if the above scenario had truly been enacted, but there must have been other members of the crew who had survived the event and who perhaps knew more than they were saying at subsequent inquiries. That the captain set his ship on the wrong heading at the Eddystone is not in dispute, and there is no defence at all for this appalling lack of judgment. With the demise of key witnesses and with a careful selection of the surviving members of the crew in giving evidence, the domestic arrangements on the bridge, (in breach of the company's standing-orders) ensured the matter was not given a more forensic examination at the Board of Trade inquiry.

What makes this event so appalling, is that the ship was at its most hazardous point in traversing the Channel and the more so, as it was in the wrong position to start with. Whatever the case, it was a gross negligence on the part of the captain, and his officers.

Steam is no stronger now than it was a hundred years ago but it is put to better use.

At the turn of the century, ships wrecked at sea were a common occurrence (see Tables: 2, p. 162 and 3, p. 164). Steamships were still a relatively new form of transport, and ships (whether by steam or the more traditional sail) were the only means of intercontinental travel. The wreck of the *SS Titanic* would occur in the year 1912, some fourteen years later, and the much-vaunted invincibility claims for that liner being cruelly dismissed by a rogue iceberg. As with the *Mohegan*, the *Titanic* had a series of watertight compartments that should have prevented her sinking, in the event of a strike. In both ships, too many of those compartments were breached, and so both vessels were mortally wounded. The only element missing in the *Mohegan* tragedy was that of an iceberg. However, the Vase rock was a formidable substitute, and it proved equally unforgiving.

Words that weep, and tears that speak.

The journalists of the day could not have imagined that their copy would be of lasting interest and still commented on, here in the 21st century. The story of the *Mohegan* was a shared tragedy between the two greatest English speaking countries in the world: having close economic, social, and political ties. The story, so full of sadness and huge loss, struck a chord with our two peoples. It shocked everyone, and the fact that the newspaper media could react so quickly and disseminate the information, on both sides of the Atlantic, by means of the new media of cablegram and telegraphic technologies,[166] further strengthened the story, by its immediacy. Such communication was a novel experience then, which nowadays we take for granted.

---

[165] *New York Times;* 20th November 1898.

[166] The effort to lay a transatlantic cable in 1858 met with problems, but they were overcome and on August 5th 1858, it was possible to send a message from Newfoundland to Ireland via the cable. On August 16th Queen Victoria sent a congratulatory message to President James Buchanan. But soon, the

CHAPTER 5

A Theory of Magnetic Attraction

Opposites attract.

Whenever an event takes place that is largely inexplicable, such as that of the *Mohegan* disaster, it is usual to see a flurry of newspaper letter-writing, offering theories as to its cause. This particular event did not disappoint in that area.

How could this have possibly happened? It was a new ship, with all the modern aids to navigation and with every safety measure, available at that time. However, no safety aid in the world could have helped save this ship from her fate, when human error took a hand at the wheel. Natural magnetism is known to abound in the rocks along the shoreline of south Cornwall and the Manacle Rocks themselves show this particular phenomenon. There are those who state that the Manacle Rocks give off, 'emissions' that affect the compasses aboard passing ships. This phenomenon becomes much stronger, following a storm from an easterly quarter: as was indeed the case at the time of the *Mohegan* stranding.

This was an era of profound change in marine technologies. Passenger ships were now constructed using iron and steel;[167] and with regular use of generated electricity, for both lighting and communication.[168]

The *Mohegan* underwent extensive trials, following her re-fit, after her maiden voyage. During this time Mr Charles Chappelle of Messrs. Hughes & Sons, of Fenchurch Street, undertook the task of preparing a deviation-chart for the working compasses aboard the ship [169] and a minimal deviation was encountered on an east-west heading; with a fairly significant deviation in the north-south heading. This deviation calculation had originally been carried out on the *Cleopatra* but, following her re-fit, it had to be repeated once more, to take account of the ship's altered magnetic pattern.[170]

cable went dead. After perfecting the cable construction and at the end of the American Civil War, it was then possible to arrange further financing. A subsequent attempt to lay cable in 1865 failed when the cable snapped, just 600 miles from Newfoundland. An improved cable was successfully put in place in 1866. Messages were soon flowing between the United States and Europe. And the cable which had snapped the previous year was located and repaired, so two functional cables were operating. In the years following, underwater cables connected the Middle East with India, and Singapore with Australia. By the end of the 19th century, much of the globe was wired for communication, and those destined for the UK came ashore at Porthcurno beach, South Cornwall; as they still do to this day.

[167] This metal structure has a marked effect on a ship's compass, and so techniques to negate its inherent magnetic signature were adopted. With the additional effect of electrical cabling within its superstructure, it is more vitally important in this regard.

[168] The first electric lighting was first introduced aboard the steamer *City of Berlin* in November, 1879 – Magginis, John, *The Atlantic Ferry: Its Ships, Men, And Working* (London, UK: Whitaker & Co.1893), 47.

[169] These charts were recovered from the sea, following the catastrophe, and were still legible.

[170] The direction of permanent magnetism of hard iron is related to the direction that the ship was facing when it was built; the compass needle will be attracted to the part of the ship that was south of it during construction. Archibald Smith (1813–1872), held that an iron ship should be built with its head in a north-south direction, and preferably south. The effect is due to the alignment of magnetic domains in the iron with the external magnetic field of the Earth while being worked and pounded. In fact, Gilbert had created magnets by hammering iron rods laid in a north-south direction as part of his demonstration that the Earth acts as a mostly dipole magnet. But this initial permanent magnetism doesn't last, and in some cases over half of a ship's

A local scientist, Mr Thomas Clark of Truro,[171] maintained that all rocks from Porthallow to the Lizard were strongly magnetic and that his suspicions had been confirmed by personal experiments. A supporting article was published in an American newspaper:

The local scientist, Thomas Clark, of Truro, England, whose study on the basic Rocks of Cornwall has attracted much attention and has been discussed by several scientific institutions, said the other day that the *Paris*, like the *Mohegan* was drawn out of her course by magnetic influence. He said: "I have made this a particular study. Generally it is believed that there are no Rocks on the British Isles whose power over the bar magnet or needle equals that of the Compass Rocks at the apex of the island of Canna in the Hebrides. This is wrong, for I have obtained stones from the Botallack mine near St. Just in Cornwall and from a quarry at Launceston, whose magnetic powers surpasses that of the Canna stone. The Rocks along the coast of Cornwall, from Porthallow along the Lizard, are all more all less magnetic. In the case of those miles of basic rock along the Cornish cliffs, where thousands of pounds of magnetic material are brought into motion by a storm, there must at times be an enormous increase of magnetic power. Of this power the sea would be no barrier, water being a conductor of magnetism." [172]

Further evidence was forwarded, in support of this theory:

MAGNETIC ATTRACTION THEORY

The following has been put forward by a local seafaring expert as the cause of the loss of the *Mohegan*:—There exists at the Manacles an uncertain but at times a very powerful magnetic attraction, and vessels are often quite unaccountably drawn miles out of their course. The case, on March 14th, 1885, of the *Palmyra*, 2,000 tons burden, belonging to Bath [Maine Sagadahoc County], U.S.A., goes to prove this. Captain Minoff was steering, as he believed, due west after passing the Eddystone, and thought he was 12 or 13 miles from the Manacles and four or five [south of] from the Lizard when his ship struck the Manacle Rocks. Trinity House and the Board of Trade have repeatedly been memorialised to afford further protection to passing ships, but without result. Falmouth, Newlyn, Penzance, and other places have memorialised, but without effect. Local seamen believe it is the duty of Trinity House to place a lightship with a powerful siren there until, at all events, the disturbing elements in and about the Manacles are scientifically determined.[173]

But such theories had never been officially supported, and faulty navigation alone is held to be responsible for all recorded disasters on and around the Manacles.

---

original permanent magnetism is lost in the course of its first year of use. And while the permanent magnetism of a ship is fairly constant after that point, any collision or repair of the ship will alter that permanent magnetism, requiring a new set of measurements and corrections to be applied. www.myreckonings.com/wordpress/2009/04/18/magnetic-deviation-comprehension-compensation-and-computation-part-i/

[171] The Council of the *Royal Institution of Cornwall*—VOLUME XII. 1893–4/5 ; "The papers by Mr. Thomas Clark on "*The Magnetic Rocks of Cornwall*" were also highly commended, and it is proposed that he be elected an Associate of the Institution". A full scientific report for the geographic magnetic anomaly, as found at Manacle Point and surrounding area, is to be found here;
http://archive.org/stream/journalofroyalin11189193roya/journalofroyalin11189193roya_djvu.txt.

[172] *L'Abeille, De La Nouvelle-Orleans*; Wednesday 9th August 1899.

[173] *Nottinghamshire Guardian* (London, England); Saturday 22nd October 1898.

An interesting point here relates to the night-time use of electrical lighting, aboard a ship. [174] This could well exert an untoward effect on a compass, and one wonders whether or not this was taken into account during the adjustment for the *Mohegan*'s compasses, with nearby live electrical equipment:

CALM ARGUMENT

Captain E. E. Wilson, of Hull, writes to the *Shipping Gazette:*

Sir—I cannot help thinking that the cause of the disaster at first to the *Mohegan* and then to the *Paris* may be attributed in some measure to electricity affecting the compasses. These two vessels have come to grief during the night, when they have been fully charged with electricity used for lighting purposes and here is an enemy to the mariner in the disguise of a friend. When these vessels' compasses were adjusted they were not under this charge, but in a normal condition. I have known an electric cloud passing over a vessel at sea cause compasses to spin round like a cartwheel, and of no use whatever till the cloud had passed, while their deviation was affected for two or three days afterwards. I think experiments should be made regarding this matter, for it seems, as far as I can learn, that no one has given any thought to this theory. I may be wrong, but I should like to hear the opinion of experts on this subject. I place no trust in the theory of the Rocks and cliffs of Cornwall affecting the compasses, and the flood tide placing these ships in the position they get into. I have navigated the Channel both in sail and steam, and have never felt any of these. The tide in that part of the Channel sets half round the compass during the flood. [175]

The theory was now gaining ground in the American Press:

COMPASS FALLIBILITY
The Possible Cause of the Loss of the Mohegan

London Shipping World: The very fact that the mariner's compass is above all things a supersensitive instrument renders it particularly liable to those sudden and capricious changes of which many navigators can speak from experience and to their sorrow.

The compass of today is perhaps as perfect a production as the highest scientific skill and the most delicate mechanical manipulation can attain to, and yet at a critical moment, and by causes beyond human foresight, the vagaries of its readings may lead the most experienced seamen into utter disaster.

If, as has been said there should exist in the vicinity of the Manacles a powerful and uncertain magnetic field by whose influence vessels have at times been inexplicably drawn miles out their course, then the terrible loss of the *Mohegan* might well be explained by this hypothesis alone. And it should be borne in mind that its suggested solution of the mystery is strengthened by a reference to the *Palmyra,* lost [*sic*] on the Manacles on March 14, 1885. Here the commander, Capt. Minoff, was steering as he believed, due west after passing the Eddystone, and thought he was some dozen miles of the Manacles and four or five off the Lizard when his ship struck the fatal rocks.

But there are other causes which may separately or conjointly with the supposed magnetic field in the vicinity of the *Mohegan*'s loss, have contributed to disturb her compasses. For instance, we are told that the vessel had recently undergone

---

[174] Deviation is the problem of compass error owing to the structure of the vessel, proximity of metal objects, magnetic fields or electrical equipment. Deviation also varies with a vessel's heading as this may change the position of the magnetic field in a boat relative to the earth's magnetic field. In 1820 Hans Christian Oersted discovered a relationship between electricity and magnetism. If an electric current flows through a wire, it creates a magnetic field. Oersted demonstrated this by placing a compass near a wire that carrying that electric current, the compass needle would swing around to match the direction of the electric current.

[175] *The Royal Cornwall Gazette Falmouth Packet, Cornish Weekly News, & General Advertiser;* Thursday, 1st June 1899.

extensive alterations. If in the course of carrying out these any considerable hammering of the beams or plating were necessary, then that part of the metallic structure may have had its magnetic polarity interfered with, even to the point of reversal. If such were the case, it would be interesting to know whether the compasses were readjusted to meet the altered conditions before the vessel proceeded on the last and, as it proved, calamitous voyage. Again, there is the possibility of compass deviation due to the presence of the dynamo, whose large external magnetic field would probably be lying dormant until the lights were switched on, perhaps only some hour or less before the *Mohegan* struck. Such a deflection would, of course, vary steadily—that is, without oscillation of the needle—directly as the number of lights turned on. In the experiments on the [*HMS*] *Royalist* one wire from the dynamo was led under the standard compass at a distance of thirteen feet, the return being separated only five feet from it. With these conditions it was observed that a current of about 100 amperes caused a deflection of eight degrees in the compass, which indeed, resolved itself into an excellent dead-beat galvanometer, the inflection increasing and decreasing, without oscillation, for every variation of the current.

That such exaggerated condition existed on the *Mohegan* we do not for a moment suggest, but that these disturbing influences may well have been produced on a minor scale is well within the bounds of probability. We have seen a sensitive needle "jump" to the influence of the magnetised ribs of an otherwise inoffensive and innocent-looking umbrella, and many of us have suffered the inconvenience of a magnetised watch—a small mass of metal, truly, but perhaps in the pocket of an officer near a binnacle all sufficient to deviate the sensitively poised compass card. Hitherto, with one exception, we have dealt with only with possible and unforeseen disturbing causes that may have existed within the ship and baffles even so experienced a navigator as Capt. Griffiths. Of disturbing influences beyond the ship, probably the most troublesome of all is the "subpermanent" source of error due to the constant action of the earth endeavouring to form in that part of the ship nearest north a pole repellent to the north point of the compass—a source of error the peculiar danger of which arises from the fact that as it accumulates it produces no visible effect on the compass while the vessel is steering a steady course. Thus, to exaggerate the *Mohegan*'s course, if Capt. Griffiths had been steering west for some days, and then altered his course at right angles to south the greatest effect would have been produced, as in every case this error causes the vessel to err in the direction of the course previously steered. An error of half a point in the long stretch of sixty-two miles from the Start to the Lizard would have been sufficient to cause the disaster, and from any one of the causes we have enumerated this slight fallibility of the compass, with its terribly disastrous consequences, may have been [enough to bring about the disaster]. [176]

The local magnetic variation being cited for the wreck of the steamship *Palmyra*,[177] referred to in the above correspondence, is again reported here:

Its master, Capt. Mindee [*sic*], was steering what he believed to be on a course due west, after passing the Eddystone, and calculated he was some 12 or 13 miles distant from the Manacles, when his vessel struck these dreaded rocks; this is in spite of having a Channel pilot aboard. The vessel commenced taking in water, but managed to come off the rocks and limp towards Falmouth Port. She foundered short of her destination and became embayed at the port entrance. Two tugs went to assist her and brought her into a safe berth.[178]

---

[176] *The Appeal* (St. Paul and Minneapolis. Minn.); Saturday June 24th 1899. Courtesy of the Minnesota Historical Society.

[177] An American vessel of 1,359 tons, owned by Mr Reed of Bath, Maine County – on March 14th 1885 from Hartlepool and in ballast for Cardiff.

[178] *The Dundee Courier & Argus* (Dundee, Scotland); Monday, March 16th 1885.

However, not all were supportive of this theory, as to the effects of magnetic rock on a ship's compass:

TO THE EDITOR OF THE STANDARD

Sir,—Will the "local seafaring expert," to whom you refer in the *Standard* of today, furnish data to bear out his assertion as to the powerful magnetic attraction of the Manacle Rocks, and thereby enlighten his nautical brethren? Even assuming such a magnetic power to exist, it appears to possess a fickle character, and to use its influence at periods of long and uncertain intervals. But, as a master mariner, with some slight knowledge of compasses, and their behaviour in so-called magnetic areas, I treat these assertions as absolutely worthless, and a means of bluffing seamen into believing in what has no existence. Rocks of exceptional power may be safely approached to within a mile without danger of attraction, and I thought every modern seaman was conversant with this established fact.

I presume the "local seafaring expert" is aware that every iron or steel ship is in itself a powerful magnet, yet by the suspension of a compass, say, fifty feet above the hull, the compass is removed beyond the influence of the ship's magnetism. The local expert must, I opine, seek other causes for the loss of the ill-fated *Mohegan* and so many valuable lives, and I can assure him that many will refrain from giving an opinion out of British respect for those who are no more, and therefore unable to defend themselves.

I am Sir, your obedient servant.

GEO. HARVEY.

Wivenhoe [179] Essex, October 1998. [180]

Some little spat took place in the readers' correspondence section of *The Times* newspaper, following the grounding of the steamship *Paris*. A distinguished admiral roundly dismissed the question of the magnetic theory, raised by a previous correspondent. Those two letters follow, in chronological order:

Sir, —In your issue of date (24th inst.). Admiral Algernon de Horsey animadverts [181] on the unfortunate stranding of the American mail steamer *Paris*, and he seems most unreasonably to infer that the misadventure was the result of wilful default. He asks as why such losses as the *Drummond Castle*, the *Mohegan* and the *Stella* have not been followed by, "conviction for manslaughter and consequent sentence of penal servitude". The answer is obvious — such losses never occur by wilful default; they are the result of human fallibility, in the same as the loss of her Majesty's ship *Serpent* with all hands on Cape Finisterre or her Majesty's ship the *Victoria* in the Mediterranean with fearful sacrifice of life. These latter vessels were not, "fully insured" and there was no "shareholder's profit" to be considered. Why import any unworthy sentiments in any case? The principal actors in these sad dramas paid the penalty for error of judgment with the loss of their lives.

[179] Wivenhoe was the home town of the *Mohegan*'s second officer – Benjamin Cole. One wonders if the correspondent's plea that there were those 'unable to defend themselves,' was as a result of some social or professional standing between the two men, prompting this support.

[180] *The Standard* (London, England); Thursday 20th October 1898—Admiral Sir Algernon Frederick Rous de Horsey KCB (25th July 1827 – 22nd October 1922) was a Royal Navy officer who served in the nineteenth century—*WikiPedia*.

[181] Animadvert: a rather old-fashioned term that means, to comment critically or unfavourably.

The gallant admiral forgets that he is a very old sailor, and things are not the same now as 60 years ago, when it would be thought good seamanship in a three-decker bound for New York to blunder out into the Atlantic on a mid-Channel course. That, however, was not the problem before the commander of the *Paris*; he would be probably be steering for the Atlantic mail steamer route, which starts for $10°$ west longitude, at about 20 to 30 miles south of the Irish coast. A direct line from Cherbourg to that point would cut through Cornwall, twenty miles inland. The problem, therefore, was how to round the Lizard or Scilly Isles at a safe distance.

Whether miscalculations of tidal currents or magnetic influences has caused the disaster may surely be left to the American court of enquiry, without imputing in advance unworthy motives either to the managers of the line or to the unfortunate commander of the vessel.

Yours &tc.,

London, May 24.

G. A. L.[182]

With the reply to this letter:

To the Editor of *The Times*. Sir, — Your correspondent, "G.A.L". in *The Times* of today, misquotes me. The captains of the *Drummond Castle*, *Mohegan*, and *Stella* gallantly died at their posts, thus paying with their lives the penalty of whatever default was attributable to them. It is, therefore, evident that I could not have referred to them when asking where to find that an enquiry has been followed by conviction and punishment for manslaughter. "G.A.L". discounts the value of my opinion. He is quite justified in taking it for what it is worth — perhaps, little. But his reference to my views — of a very old sailor in a three-decker bound for New York sixty years ago — is not a happy hit. I plead guilty to age, but the command of steamships and squadrons of (no sailing ships) from 1853 to a recent date does not bear out his strictures about blundering in three-deckers.

"G.A.L.'s" assertion that the losses of the *Drummond Castle*, *Mohegan*, and *Stella*, as those of her Majesty's ships *Serpent* [183] and *Victoria*, did not occur by default, or, to quote his own words, "such losses never occur by wilful default" but, "are the result of human fallibility," involves the absurd theory that a person in charge of a ship is never in fault unless he intentionally produces the disaster.

With one sentence, and only one, in "G.A.L.'s" letter, I thoroughly agree — the problem therefore, was how to round the Lizard or the Scilly Isles at a safe distance". This is precisely the simple problem that the *Paris* did not accomplish. From Cherbourg breakwater (giving Cape La Hague a berth of five miles) the distance of Long Island, New York, is only seven-and-a-half miles more, if passing even as much as twenty miles of St. Agnes, Scilly, than it is by passing Land's End and Scilly. In the former case there are no possible dangers. In the latter, the Runnelstone, the Wolf Rock [184] and the Seven Stones are perils to navigation unless the weather is clear. "G.A.L". suggests that the captain of the *Paris* was "steering for the Atlantic mail steam route that starts from 10 [degrees] west longitude, at about 20 or 30 miles south of the Irish coast". It may, if so, be inferred that possibly such were his orders from his board of directors. If this be true, it is quite time that the Merchant Shipping Act — and a similar statute in America — contained a clause to the effect that, "No regulations issued by the owners or by the directors of a company shall be held to justify the master of a passenger ship in proceeding by a

---

[182] *The Times*; Friday 26th May 1899.

[183] In 1890, an English ship, carrying 300 naval cadets, set out on her voyage to Spain. Reaching the coast of Galicia in a raging storm at night, it appears that the lighthouse of Cabo Vilan was manually operated and misled the sailors. The *Serpent* crashed on the treacherous rocks half submerged under the towering waves and 298 of the cadets lost their lives.

[184] The Wolf Rock lighthouse entered service in January 1870.

route which he considers dangerous, and which is not absolutely necessary for the prosecution of the voyage to the port of destination".

With regard to the magnetic attraction theory, it is hardly worth contradicting. The same pretended excuse has been put forward in the case of the *Serpent* at Finisterre and other vessels wantonly lost. The scientific and responsible officers of the Admiralty will tell "G.A.L". that, "there is no magnetic attraction at the Manacles". But, if it did exist, one may ask why it should be reserved for the *Paris* and *Mohegan*, when thousands of iron and steel ships navigate that part of the coast of Cornwall in safety?

I am, Sir, your obedient servant.

Cowes, May 26.

ALGERNON DE HORSEY.[185]

Again, the theory was given short shrift in an earlier article in the New York Times, some years prior to the *Mohegan* calamity:

On this matter of the magnetic attraction, of the land which has local interest from the fact that it has been offered as a reason for some of the shipwrecks on the south shore of the Long Island, nothing better can be offered that the words of one of the best living authorities on navigation, Capt. S. T. S. Lecky.[186] He says: "The proximity of the vessel to land of volcanic origin is supposed by some seamen to influence the compass. It is true that many masses of rock are intensely magnetic, and affect the compass most powerfully if placed sufficiently near to them but it has been ascertained beyond a doubt that such land causes no disturbance to compasses aboard ship, as they are entirely beyond its influence at the distance vessels are usually navigated from the shore. From time to time one hears extremely foolish accounts of vessels being wrecked through the attraction of land. The writer recollects one in particular—loss some years ago of a steamer near Cape Santa Maria, in the River Plate—which was attributed by some sage newspaper correspondent to the effect of a magnetic hill in the vicinity of the wreck. As a matter of fact the vessel was lost through ignorance of the northeasterly current, which invariably runs on that coast with great strength during a pampero". [187]

So much for the magnetic mountain theory. The heeling error had doubtless much more to do with the loss of the *Serpent*. This error has been known to amount to as much as 2 degrees for every degree of heel. A vessel that rolls from 10 degrees port to 10 degrees starboard may change the deviation of her compass by 40 degrees. It cannot be denied that this is a very serious matter and as any adjustment to compensate for heeling error is only good for magnetic latitude for which it is made. It is easy to see that even under expert navigators, bad mistakes as to the course may be made where heeling error is aided by treacherous current in heavy weather.[188]

A reference here to the locality of interest, is worthy of our further attention:

---

[185] *The Times;* 29th May 1899. Admiral Sir Algernon Frederick Rous de Horsey KCB (25 July 1827–1922) was a Royal Navy officer who served in the nineteenth century. He was appointed KCB in 1903 and lived at Melcombe House in Cowes. He frequently contributed letters to The Times and wrote *An African Pilot* and *The Rule of the Road at Sea*. He died on 22 October 1922 and was described by *The Times* as a "Doyen of the Navy".

[186] Captain Squire Thorton Stratford Lecky, the famous author of the hugely popular: *Wrinkles in Practical Navigation*.

[187] The Pampero is a burst of cold polar air from the west, southwest or south on the pampas in the south of Brazil, Argentina and Uruguay. This wind (often violently) picks up during the passage of a cold front of an active low passing by. It takes the form of a squall line and there is a marked drop in temperature after its passing. The Pampero is most common at winter in the southern hemisphere (principally between May and August) – *WikiPedia.*

[188] *The New York Times;* 4th December 1890.

Sir,—As the suggestion of the wreck of the *Mohegan* may have be due to a local deviation of the compass is again referred to in a letter which appears in your columns to-day, you will perhaps allow me to point out that such deviations are more likely to occur on land, where the needle may be within a few feet of the disturbing cause, than at sea, where they must be separated by a greater or less depth of non-magnetic water.

During the magnetic survey of the United Kingdom, carried out by Dr. Thorpe [189] and myself, observations were made at 12 places in Cornwall. Of these Lizard Down, Porthallow, and Falmouth were the nearest to the scene of the disaster, and at all of them the deviation of the compass from the normal magnetic meridian was extremely small. The largest disturbance of this kind which was observed in Cornwall occurred at St. Levan, near the Land's End, and only amounted to 11 minutes of arc or less than two-tenths of a degree. The largest disturbance of the dipping needle was at Mullion, and was only 14 minutes.

It is true that it is not impossible that the compass of a ship in relatively deep water might be appreciably affected for a distance of three or four miles by a concealed centre of magnetic disturbance. The best known case of this sort is that of Port Walcott in North-West Australia, which was fully described by Captain Creak in the, "Philosophical Transactions" for 1896. In that case, however, a compass on the neighbouring coast was affected, not as in Cornwall to the extent of a few minutes of arc, but through a range of 10 deg.

To the improbability of such a source of danger as that suggested having escaped the notice of naval surveyors in a district so well known as the neighbourhood of the Manacles, we must, therefore, add the improbability of a great magnetic focus existing near land on which the magnetic disturbance are as small as they are in Cornwall.

It is, of course, possible that here and there in that county there may be centres of magnetic disturbance greater than we discovered, but from evidence collected in districts, such as the West of Scotland, where magnetic rocks abound, I have no hesitation is saying that in general such causes could not affect the compass of a ship at a distance of a couple of hundred yards, and that though cases, such as that above referred to, are known to which this generalization does not apply their number is small.

I am Sir, your obedient servant, October 22.
ARTHUR W. RUCKER. [190]

Despite the various rebuttals that the more learned members of the maritime fraternity make, the following observation does seem to add credence to the theory:

THE MANACLE ROCKS:—At the time of the loss of *Mohegan* on the Manacles, and still more strongly on the recent occasion of the stranding of the *Paris*, the suggestion was put forward that there was some magnetic attraction in the neighbourhood which had drawn the ships out of their course, or had affected their compasses. The idea, however, of a ship being drawn bodily so far out of her course was generally scouted, as it would have required a mountain of lodestone to accomplish the feat, and it was said by those who ought to know, that there was no magnetic ore nearer than the Northern part of Portugal. The theory of any magnetic influence having been exerted on the compasses by local causes was also generally received with ridicule, but, strange to say, the experience of the Channel Fleet when leaving England on its last cruise appears to lend

---

[189] The last half of the 19th century showed a large increase in the number of observatories taking magnetic observations. After 1890 there was an increased interest in magnetic work. One of the contributory causes was the magnetic survey of the British Isles made by Sir A. Rucker and Sir T. E. Thorpe, which served as a stimulus to similar work elsewhere; *The 1911 Classic Encyclopedia*.

[190] *The Times;* Monday, Oct. 24th 1898.

some countenance to it. When at no great distance from the English coast a number of the ships noticed the needles of their compasses jumping in the most lively manner for some seconds, and of this occurrence no explanation has been forthcoming. A special report on the subject was made to the Hydrographical Department, and more will be perhaps heard of it. Meanwhile, the *Army and Navy Gazette* [191] tells the story of an occurrence that seems to bear on the subject. A coasting steamer on arriving at Brisbane reported that in passing through Torres Straits [192] he had discovered a shoal which affected her compass. A local surveyor proceeded to the spot, and his incomplete examination appeared to confirm the statement. A Naval surveying vessel was then sent, but did not satisfactorily determine the position of the shoal, and the officers rather pooh-poohed the notion of its existence. Thereupon the local surveyor started again with a proper equipment, and eventually verified the original reports both as to the existence of the shoal and as to its magnetic attraction. [193] It seems worthy of investigation whether masses of magnetic ore in shoal water are capable of exercising a dangerous influence on compasses. [194]

Being a relatively new science, there was still a lack of an in-depth knowledge and experience around the question of electricity and magnetism. [195] Therefore, exotic theories continued to be offered as an explanation for the shipwrecking events, that otherwise defied any other logical principle of marine science and practicality.

Such theories continued to proliferate in yet another letter to *The Times*: where the recent stranding of the *Paris* suggested it had taken on the characteristics of an anode, as part of a gigantic natural battery:

Sir, there are Rocks in different parts of the world on which magnificent steamships are occasionally wrecked, without any satisfactory explanation being given as to why they were so far out of well-known courses as to steam to destruction.

In the case of the *Paris* the sea was calm, the weather was thick, the vessel was pursuing a well-known course, steered to points by an experienced hand, — and yet she ran on dangerous and well known Rocks, at high tide, and at high speed.

I have long thought that what is commonly thought a magnetic attraction has been the cause of these inexplicable disasters, occurring at the times when the circumstances for its development have been favourable.

A morning paper has mentioned, "that the Brixham fishermen state when passing up and down the Channel, they invariably observe variation in their compasses, consequently they allow two points each way on the proper course".

Permit me to offer an explanation which is so simple as to carry convictions to the minds to most scientific men as to the cause of this magnetic attraction. If I have discovered this and can fix the source of the danger I hope I may have prevented for the future of these unfortunate occurrences, with their attendant losses of life and property, which are painful to us all.

---

[191] *Army and Navy Gazette*: Journal of the Militia and Volunteer Forces; London – 7th January 1860 - 26th November 1921.

[192] The Torres Strait is a body of water which lies between Australia and the Melanesian island of New Guinea – *WikiPedia*.

[193] Interestingly, there is an island—*Magnetic Island*—named by Captain Cook (7th November 1728 – 14th February 1779; a British explorer, navigator and cartographer) because of the apparent "magnetic" effect it had on the ship's compass as he passed the island when sailing up the east coast of Australia in 1770.

[194] *The Morning Post* (London, England); Thursday, 29th June 1899.

[195] Between 1861 and 1865, James Clerk Maxwell developed and published a set of Maxwell's equations which explained and united all of classical electricity and magnetism. The first set of these equations was published in a paper entitled *On Physical Lines of Force* in 1861. The mechanism that Maxwell proposed to underlie these equations in this paper was fundamentally incorrect, which is not surprising since it predated the modern understanding even of the atom. Yet, the equations were valid although incomplete; *WikiPedia*.

Taking the *Paris* as 500 ft. in length, with 25 ft. below her water line, we have one side of the ship one enormous submerged plate of a galvanic battery of 12,500 square feet, surface over a quarter of an acre! Taking the Manacle Rocks, going perpendicular in the water in several places, that have been washed bare of every atom of earthly matter below the water-line, it is fairly certain these Rocks contain strata of metallic ores, the outer sections of which are covered by the sea, and more would be covered at high water than at low, while some of the Rocks might be masses of ore.

We have for the battery on one side a vast plate of 12,500 square feet in extent; on the other we have the areas of the section of the metallic veins below the water, and the masses of metalliferous rock. These are many thousand square feet in extent.

But these two enormous metallic surfaces were connected by the exciting medium of salt water! The day was perfectly calm and the water was high; there was thus every facility for the production of galvanic force to the fullest possible extent.

Is it not probable that this affected most seriously the compasses of the *Paris*?

Referring to the fishing boats, the bottoms were probably sheathed in metal; the owners met the effect of the galvanic force, generated as in the larger example, by allowing two points each way on the proper course. This is a grave fact.

When we consider the distance of the magnetic pole from the ship *Paris* and the Manacles, we cannot fairly expect the needle of the compass to have pointed steadily towards it, when we remember that the ship and the Rocks formed together a powerful galvanic battery which probably deflected the needle.

It is a melancholy thing to reflect that iron ships and wooden vessels with metal sheathed bottoms carry with them possible causes of their own destruction, should they approach Rocks that have metallic strata below under water-mark.

The observations I have made as to the *Paris* and the Manacles apply to most of the unexplained wrecks on Cape Finisterre and other rocky coasts.

It is in the hope of doing an important service to the world that I wish the great principle set out in this letter acknowledged and acted on. The side of a ship under the water-line is one "plate" of the battery, the clean edges of the metallic strata under the water-mark are the other "plate" and the salt water connecting the two "plates" is the exciting medium. Galvanic action is therefore generated and this is a serious danger to the true action of the needle of a compass on board of the ship.

The subject is of very high importance to the naval and mercantile marines of all the nations of the world.

The limits of this letter do not permit me to enter into the possibilities of making iron ships non-conducting or of isolating compasses from external magnetic influence.

May I say I have tried to avoid the use of scientific terms as much as possible, as I wish all should understand my meaning?

I have the honour to be yours faithfully,

Henry BENTINCK COATHUPE, Late captain 72nd Highlanders and passed Staff College, &c.[196]

The theory continued to attract yet more discussion:

To The Editor of *The Times*.

Within the last few months no less than three fine steamers have been cast away in the English Channel. And in all three the proximate cause was the same—ship off her course. One is naturally apt to enquire how or why fine modern ships, with every appliance and careful and experienced captains and officers, should get so woefully out of their reckoning and in such short distance from their port of departure. I would suggest the compass as a probable culprit. I have travelled over

---

[196] *The Times;* Saturday, 27th May 1899.

100,000 miles in iron and steel vessels, both sail and steam, and, taking a great interest in all matter appertaining to navigation, have had much conversations on such subjects with the masters and navigating officers on the vessels on which I have travelled, to which I may add my own observations. There seems a pretty general agreement that on the huge steel ships now in vogue the compass, even with all the modern improvements in the way of "correctors," &c., is a comparatively unreliable instrument. In fact, that its main use nowadays is to act as a guide to the helmsman, but that as far as actually directing the ship is concerned it is not to be trusted, unless its indications are incessantly checked by "aximuth" observations, taken at every possible opportunity. "Deviation Cards" however accurately calculated by, "swinging the ship" in harbour seems of little use at sea. Without going into the scientific question, it may be suggested that it is not so much the ship's magnetism—which can be in great part be neutralized by, "Kelvin's spheres" and other corrections—as a fact of a huge mass of metal being interposed between the needle and the "earth's magnetic field," which seems to have a "numbing" effect on the compass, especially on certain bearings. In fact, quartermasters have told me that in some cases the needle showed a tendency to "follow the ship" on the helm being shifted.

Now, it is well known that, in the cloudy Channel, opportunities in checking the eccentricities of the compass by "aximuth" are by as no means as frequent as they might be. For want of them, the most careful of captains might easily, at the high speeds of modern ships, get many miles out of his course, without knowing it, merely by the erratic behaviour of his standard compass, and in a few hours. In the open sea he would soon discover his error by observation, and, at worst, it would only mean a slightly longer passage but in close quarters like the Channel it might well mean the Manacles. Buoys and beacons are apt to be a warning too late to be much use to a fast steamer, even if the too constant fog allowed them to be seen. Except decreased speed and due vigilance, it is difficult to see what more can be done, if a compass is proved to be an uncertain guide— and all the facts point that way. The divergence necessary to put a ship bound from Cherbourg to New York [the *Paris*] so far out of her way as to be near the Manacles is far too great to be due to a careless helmsman, or to escape the notice of any officer who looked at the standard compass on the bridge—if that compass was doing its duty. There are strong and torturous currents in the bay and around the reefs, but, in the proper Channel course, miles south of the Lizard, there are only the well-understood Channel tide-streams to contend with. As to "magnetic rocks," "magnetic shoals," &c., (such things do exist), they can hardly be expected to act on compasses miles away on the open sea, though, on the north-west coast of Australia, I have seen the needle swing completely round and back again in a few minutes, sailing over a "magnetic shoal," well known to survey ships.

C. M.[197]

In taking a modern-day view of this magnetic theory, the following observation is of particular interest:

The Lecky's *Wrinkles* [*Wrinkles In Practical Navigation*] is a highly respected book written by a very experienced late 19th century navigator for navigators serving at sea. But it is of its time. By the early 20th century, ship's masters were examined on their understanding of the magnetic compass and the magnetic effects of the ship and of the earth's magnetic field but probably not to the detail of local magnetic anomalies. And it may only have been included in the oral examination. By my time we had to answer written questions on the principles and carry out the process of correcting a magnetic compass in a practical test during the series of examinations for master.

In 1910 there was certainly awareness of local attraction, as it was called, and locations where this was known to occur were labelled, "magnetic anomaly" on charts, as is still the case. The text book I used in the 1950s—Charles H. Brown; *Deviation and the Deviascope* (Glasgow, 6th ed. 1954)—gives some examples: Shetland Isles, West Coast of Scotland,

---

[197] *The Times;* Tuesday, 30th May 1899.

Lough Larne approach, and I also remember areas in the Baltic. It quotes an Admiralty warning: "In some parts of the world there are depths of water sufficient for the largest ships to navigate in safety where the bottom is sufficiently magnetic and close enough to affect their compasses. Increased vigilance should be exercised". It goes on to ask for [newly identified] positions, and reports to be sent in. I should expect that if the Manacles or nearby had a magnetic ore composition, for it to be well known by 1910 and so marked on the charts of the area, as well as described in the appropriate volume in the *Channel Pilot*.

There are also irregular magnetic disturbances. These may be due to electrical currents in the earth and in the atmosphere, and mostly associated with the Aurora Borealis, which may, "sensibly deflect" the compass card, especially in high latitudes. Lat. 50 degrees North is very much at the limit of seeing the Aurora Borealis though. Thunder storms nearby can in theory also affect the compass.

The algebraic sum of the influences on the ship's magnetic compass changes with each change: of ships heading, changes with change of position, and changes in the earth over time. Ships also have a permanent magnetism as a massive magnetic bar, which is caused during building, long lay-up or by hammering and by exposure to the earth's magnetic field.

After each alteration of course, the real compass error should be observed through a convenient transit of land objects or by calculation of the true bearing of a star or the sun, and that error then applied. This error should then be recorded in a deviation book with position, so that in poor visibility the error used when recently on that course and in that position may be applied. In the end the whole business of applying the error (earth's magnetic variation for the date and location, and the effect of the ship's magnetism called deviation), is a mix of art and science, and always something to be wary of.[198]

It is perhaps easy with hindsight to see why this particular matter caused much concern and discussion. Electricity aboard a ship was a relatively new development, particularly in combination with the adoption of a steel construction for ships.[199] It is not surprising that the old-guard would use this new technology as a contributory factor in a current batch of shipwreck. In fact, the number of shipwrecks overall had not altered that much (see Tables, 2: p. 162 and 3: p. 164). The use of iron and steel construction gave the capability for a construction of larger-sized ships and with increased number of persons aboard them; therefore, with such ships being wrecked and with inevitable huge loss of life, these events would attract a much greater volume of comment.

It would suggest that this theory, involving magnetic attraction, offered a convenient excuse for poor navigational skills. In the case of the *Mohegan,* perhaps the theory should not place the blame on geological factors, but rather much closer to the *Mohegan*'s compass itself.

Mr. Richard Benney—Trinity Pilot attached to the Falmouth District—stated that, "The idea of magnetic attraction at the Manacles I consider to be all moonshine."[200]

Perhaps on that note, the 'magnetic theory' needs trouble us no further.

---

[198] Personal communication: Mr Alston Kennerley, Plymouth University (2011).

[199] Steel was not used in the construction of merchant ships' hulls until 1859. "As wood in the construction of ships was gradually replaced by iron, so iron, in its turn, has practically given way to steel. The tougher metal better stands the tremendous wear and tear of quick voyages. As to comparative safety in collisions with other vessels or with icebergs, the shock can be sustained with less damage to steel than to iron—Hoyt, John C.; *Old Ocean's Ferry; the Log of the Modern Mariner, the Trans-Atlantic Traveler, and Quaint Facts of Neptune's Realm* (1900).

[200] *The Royal Cornwall Gazette Falmouth Packet, Cornish Weekly News, & General Advertiser*; Thursday, 1st June 1899.

CHAPTER 6

An Aftermath of the Wreck

A safe pair of hands.

The entrepreneurial, hands-on attitude of an American businessman of the day, is well illustrated by this newspaper report. It describes a rather dramatic means by which the Chairman for the Atlantic Transport Line made his way to New York to board a ship bound for the UK, in order to oversee the *Mohegan* crisis. He had paid the owners of this vessel £200 an hour in order to delay her sailing, until he had arrived at New York:

> Mr. B. M. Baker has the reputation of not only being a great financier, but a "hustler" as well. When the *Mohegan* struck on the Manacle Rocks, he received the news by telephone, at his country home, ten miles from Baltimore. He at once determined to make his way to the scene of the disaster. Packing a few things he ordered his carriage and was in Baltimore at two o'clock in the morning. There he chartered a special train to take him to New York, where he arrived at 8 o'clock and at nine, was aboard a steamer for England.[201]

When money speaks the truth is silent?

Mr. Baker had decided to attend the lead-up to the inquiry into the disaster, in order to manage the *Mohegan* affair and to minimise its impact on his company's standing. A top-flight legal team would help minimise liabilities and present a more favourable version of events leading up to the disaster, with the assistance of a judicious choice of witnesses (see Appendix 17, page 466).

Where Mr Baker had the advantage, was in his being adept in public relations. He would have sanctioned the payment of a gold half-sovereign to each of the surviving members of the crew and in paying the bill for the burial of those of the crew and passengers who had lost their lives. The installation of a memorial window in the St. Keverne church; the impressive granite cross, marking the mass grave; taking an active role in the national appeal for funds, to help those families affected by the loss of their loved ones; . . . the list goes on.

In a final analysis, his company was paid handsome dividends. Mr Baker's deft handling of the aftermath of the disaster resulted in a reasonable outcome: in terms of a public perception. He would have returned to Baltimore, safe in the knowledge that his company's reputation remained relatively intact, and not adversely affected by events.

Following the disaster, it was business as usual for the Atlantic Transport Line and this announcement was typical for an advertisement, as it would have appeared in the national newspapers of the time:

---

[201] *Freeman's Journal and Daily Commercial Advertiser;* Friday, 15th December 1899.

SHIPPING

---●---

ATLANTIC TRANSPORT LINE.

EVERY THURSDAY, LONDON to NEW YORK

All Twin-screw Steamers.

No Steerage or second-cabin passengers carried. All staterooms amidships. Electric light through the ship. Surgeon and Stewardess. Fare strictly first-class.[202] Average time London to New York, ten to eleven days. For particulars apply to Managers,

WILLIAMS, TORREY and FEILD (Limited),

108, Fenchurch-street, E.C.

Absence sharpens love: presence strengthens it.

A report of the situation at the New York shipping office recorded the distressing scenes, as friends and families awaited news from Falmouth:

All day long an anxious crowd of people besieged the offices of the *Atlantic Transport Line* at 1 Broadway [New York] inquiring for missing friends and relatives, and there were some painful scenes enacted, intensified by the fact that information from the other side was coming in slowly, and this served in large measure to increase, the anxiety of the inquiring friends. The joy of those that could be assured that their loved ones were safe was in striking contrast to the grief to the bereaved, and the latter looked enviously at their more favoured brethren as they received good news.

The office of the line usually closes at noon on Saturday, but remained open until 5 o'clock yesterday to answer queries and to give what information it was possible to impart.

One of the first persons to arrive was Henry Morrison, retired lawyer of 223 West Seventy-Eighth Street, who inquired for his son, Henry Morrison Jr., and his stepdaughter Ann Hart [both unaccounted for, at this time]. He asked the clerk if the *Manitou* had sailed on Oct. 13, and when told it had not the father said he was then sure that his son and daughter must have taken passage on the *Mohegan*. Their names were on the list that came in later, and when no word came of their safety, the grief of the old gentleman was pitiable. Finally a friend led him from the office, the clerks promising to send him any good news that might be received later. Mrs John Hyslop and daughter called at the office to enquire for Mr. John Hyslop the yacht measurer of the New York and other yacht clubs, whose name had figured in international races for years. As in the case of Mr. Morrison, Mr. Hyslop had written to his wife that he would leave on the *Manitou*. When the name of Mr. Hyslop was found on the list, Mrs. Hyslop fainted, but was brought around by her daughter, who begged that she should not give way until all hope was gone.

---

[202] The company had developed a niche market, in retricting itself to the exclusive carriage of first-class passengers as well as cattle and, most importantly, race-horses; this remained the case until well after 1909.

For three hours the weeping woman and her daughter remained in the office of the company, and they had just about decided to go home, and that there was no hope, when there came a ring on the telephone, and Capt. Tuzo of Tuzo, Corbett and Co., Custom House Brokers at 44 Exchange Place, at the other end of the wire, said that he had just received a cablegram saying simply, "Hyslop saved". After some further conversation Capt. Tuzo said he was positive that the cable was correct, as Mr. Hyslop was the only person abroad at present who was acquainted with his secret cable address. Mrs. Hyslop was told of the good news, and after a fervently muttered, "Thank God," went home with her daughter.[203]

An unlucky choice of a ship results in tragedy for one family, whereas another family survives against the odds: such are the vagaries encountered in life. Here, Fate was resolute, in that the Fireng family would lose their lives in one shipwreck or other:

A STRANGE FATALITY

John Phelps Firing, chief clerk in the office of the Paymaster in the navy, in the Stewart building, was one of the anxious inquirers at the office. His wife and daughter, Bessie May Firing, were reported as among the missing. The Firings lived in Glen Ridge, N. J. and there is a strange fatality connected with their selecting the *Mohegan* for their return voyage. Mrs. and Miss Firing [*sic*] had been abroad for some months on a pleasure trip, and had purchased tickets for home on the ill-fated French Line steamer *La Bourgogne*.[204] Some articles of apparel that they had ordered were not finished to permit of their sailing on the date set, and they were about to have their tickets transferred to another French Line boat, when Mr. Firing cabled them, advising against such a course.

The line, it is said, refused to return the passage money, and Mrs. Firing was content to lose it. They elected to remain abroad for some time longer and finally selected the *Mohegan* for their return trip. Mr. Firing is prostrated over the news of his loss, and there is much sympathy for him in Glen Ridge, where his wife and daughter were well known and beloved.

Later in the afternoon a relative of W. J. Bloomingdale called at the office with word that he had received a cable from Mr. Bloomingdale announcing the fact that he had been saved.

A woman who said she was a sister of Mr. William Baker,[205] a steward on the *Mohegan*, haunted the office all day for news. She said that she had had a presentiment that something would happen to her brother on this voyage, and tearfully told that he had invested his savings with her lately in a small lunchroom in Bond Street [New York], which she at present was running.

Word was sent to the office by Miss Osborne Moore of 965 Fifth Avenue that she had received a cablegram from Mrs. Compton Swift announcing Mrs. Swift's escape. Mrs. Swift is a resident of Columbus, Ga., and had been an invalid for some years. She went abroad with her physician, Dr. Fallows, who is reported among the missing.

John J. Le Lacheur, wife and son, who are reported among the missing, were on their way from the Island of Guernsey to spend the Winter with Mr. Le Lacheur's nephew, C. W. Gavey, at Grand-View-on-the-Hudson, near Nyack.[206]

---

[203] *The New York Times;* 18th October 1898.

[204] The French passenger liner *La Bourgogne*, from the Compagnie Generale Transatlantique, sank after a collision with the British ship *Cromartyshire*, in dense fog, 60 miles south of Sable Island near Nova Scotia, in the Atlantic, on 4th July 1898. Of 711 passengers and crewmen, only 165 survived, thus recording a terrible death toll of 546 lives. Reliable evidence attested that ignorant, undisciplined, and unfeeling crewmen had taken possession of the ship's lifeboats and rafts, to the exclusion of the passenger's rights. In addition, it was felt that in the forty minutes interval between the collision and the sinking of the French liner, more lives should have been saved. The outcome of the disaster was considered a disgrace to the officers of the ship, her owners and the French merchant marine in general.

[205] A mistaken reference here: this is almost certainly meant to be the steward, Mr William Barnes, who lost his life in the disaster.

[206] Nyack is a village, primarily in the towns of Orangetown and Clarkstown in Rockland County, New York.

Mr. Le Lacheur was in charge of the Gille Alles [Guille Alles] Library, at Guernsey, and formerly lived in Mount Vernon, N. Y. His son's health had been poor for some time and it was thought that the change in climate might benefit him.

THE PEMBERTON FAMILY

F. R. Pemberton, who with his wife and two sons, was saved, is a member of the banking firm of Pemberton & McAdoo at 15 Wall Street. Mr. McAdoo received two cablegrams during the day, the first announcing his partner and family were safe, and a latter one asking that money be cabled at once, as everything had been lost. The cable stated that Mr. Pemberton and a governess had escaped in one boat and Mrs. Pemberton and her two sons, Francis, aged five years and John Clifford, aged four years, escaped in another. The family lived at 24 West Eighty-Fifth Street.

F. W. Lockwood and Mrs. Gumbrecht, whose names appear on the list of missing, were father and daughter. Mr. Lockwood was a member of the Standard Oil Company, and had for some years acted as its foreign representative. He was one of the best known citizens of Stamford, Conn., and his wife yesterday morning received a letter from him, stating that he and his daughter would leave on the *Mohegan*. Almost simultaneously with the receipt of the letter Mrs. Lockwood read of the disaster, and the shock has prostrated her. Mr. Lockwood's office in this city was at 81 New Street and prior to his connection with the Standard Oil Company he was associated with his brother, George Lockwood, in the oil business here. He was the inventor of several valuable appliances for the transportation of oil in tropical countries. Mr. Lockwood was sixty-five years old.

Richard A. Kipling, one of the passengers reported drowned, was a diamond merchant in Paris, where he went from Elizabeth, N. J. nearly fifty years ago, and succeeded his father, Richard Kipling, who lives with his wife and family in Roselle, a suburb of Elizabeth. Mr. Kipling was well known in Elizabeth, and was coming on a visit to his parents. He has a wife and family in France. He visited his parents in the Spring of last year. They are distracted at his reported death.

Mr. and Mrs. Loren M. Luke, who are also on the list of missing, were residents of Kingston, Penn., where they were prominently known. Mr. Luke was a graduate of Princeton, in the class of '93.

A telegram signed, "Lawrence" from Plainfield, N. J., was received at the office of the company inquiring about R. A. Baxter, who at one time was a prominent surgeon at that place, but who lately had been living in Surrey, England. It was stated that he was coming to this country on a visit to the Lawrences. He is reported to be among the drowned.

Miss Shepherd, who is missing, is thought to be the only sister of Beaumont Shepherd, a prominent citizen of Montreal, where he is manager for Greenshields and Greenshields.[207] Miss Shepherd was accompanied by her niece, Miss Fraser, who is also thought to have been lost. Miss Shepherd lived in Woodstock and had been in Germany for some time studying music, in which she had taken many honors.

Miss H. L. Mershon of 34 West Thirty-Second Street said yesterday afternoon that she very much doubted whether her niece, Miss Louise H. Warner, was the Miss L. H. Warner whose name appears on the passenger list of the *Mohegan*. Her niece had left Scotland, where she had been visiting some relatives, on Sept. 26, and the latest news that has been received is a letter dated Sept. 28, and sent from Stratford-on-Avon. She had planned to sail from Rotterdam after a short stay on the Continent. Miss Mershon said that, whilst her niece may have altered her plans and taken passage on the *Mohegan*, she would not credit the report that the Miss Warner on board was her niece until she received further information.[208]

MAUDE ROUDEZ

Miss Maude Roudebush, who was saved, is professionally known to the music world as Maude Roudez. She was engaged last Summer in London [Covent Garden] by Maurice Grau to sing small soprano roles during his season in this city, at the Metropolitan Opera House, and in various cities he expects to visit through the country. She was born in Meadville Penn.,

[207] The Greenshields family was quite prominent in business and artistic circles in Montreal during the late 19th and early 20th centuries. The family firm, begun in 1833 as S. Greenshields and Son, flourished in the dry goods trade until 1933 as Greenshields Limited.

[208] Unfortunately her niece, Miss Warner, was a victim of the shipwreck.

but after the death of her father the family moved to Buffalo, where Miss Roudebush was married to J. J. Grandin. It was in Buffalo that Miss Roudebush developed her musical talents by singing in one of the churches. She held the position of leading soloist for a short period, when a desire to extend her education in the art prompted her to come to this city and place herself in the hands of a competent vocal professor. She afterwards went to Paris, studied at the Conservatoire for several months, and then returned to this city, where she appeared in various concerts, one of which was a Sunday night concert given at the Metropolitan Opera House two years ago. At the termination of that season she returned to Paris and resumed her studies. She also sang in London and Brussels.

The Rev, David J. O'Neill, who is missing, was a young Presbyterian clergyman living in Georgetown, *Penn.* who had been with a friend on a three months trip in Europe. He was about thirty-five years of age, and had been ordained four years, but had never had a charge [stipendary]. He was sometime assistant to the Rev. C. Calhoun of the Somerville church, and also occasionally assisted at the First Presbyterian Church, of which he was a member. He was a graduate of Princeton University. He was popular in Germantown, especially among the members of the Young Men's Christian Society, in which he took an active part. Mr. O'Neill was unmarried and lived with his mother.[209]

This telling account in the New York Times, of the aftermath of the *Mohegan* disaster, builds on a human kinship for both the casualties and the survivors of this wreck. The tragedy with its heartbreaking stories, and the suffering of the families and friends, are starkly reported. Each survivor had a story to tell, and this lucky man relayed his own account of the wreck:

JOHN HYSLOP ARRIVES

He Tells of the Wreck of the *Mohegan*

Improvements in Life-Saving Appliances Needed

Among the passengers who arrived yesterday on the steamship *Umbria* was John Hyslop,[210] official measurer of the New York Yacht Club, who is one of the survivors of the ill-fated steamship *Mohegan*. Mr. Hyslop was met by his daughters. Despite his experience, Mr. Hyslop looked well and consented to speak of the wreck.

"It is beyond human reason", said he, "to conceive the cause of the *Mohegan*. The only person who could make an explanation of the disaster perished with the vessel. It will remain forever a mystery. When the steamer struck I was below, but I immediately went on deck and saw Capt. Griffiths on the deck giving orders to clear away the boats. I did not see a man not doing all that he could in such an emergency. The first officer was the last to dive from the stern of the ship as she went down. The night was perfectly clear and the shore was visible from the deck of the steamer. The Manacle Rocks were close at hand. I knew that the men were not likely to get more boats afloat than the women would fill, so I decided to take my chances in the mizzen rigging.[211] While there, the *Mohegan*'s stern settled so that water overtook me, and went over my head. Gradually I climbed higher, and sometimes I had to stand on one foot to keep my head above water".

"The *Mohegan*'s stern did not remain above water more than twelve minutes. The darkness, the heavy listing of the steamer one way and another and the presence of the inner set of rails all hampered the men getting the boats away. I do not think there was a deficiency of lifebelts, as there were people all about me wearing them. It was high tide when I got into the rigging, and the sea surged well up towards those in the lower part of it. As the sea swept over us and rolled away,

---

[209] *New York Times;* October 16th 1898.

[210] He was a well-known and respected man in the world of American yacht racing.

[211] A term referring to the stern-most mast on a three-masted vessel that supported a triangular shaped sail, called the mizzen sail. A vessel with less than three masts would have no mizzen-mast at all.

I could hear the screams of the women and children who were almost within reach yet not visible in the darkness. As the ship went down the wave which made it swept a score or two of the passengers into eternity".

"It was wrong that all the ship's lights were electric. As soon as the engines stopped and the fire room was flooded all the lights went out. A lamp [oil-fuelled] at the masthead would have served as a beacon to the life savers and more of the passengers might have been rescued. I was in the water at 7 'o clock at night until 2 'o clock next morning. Then help came. My own sufferings I can willingly forget, but to have seen the others perishing about me is an experience that will always remain in my memory".

"The inner railings about the lifeboats retarded their launching, and it was useless for people who were in New York at the time to say they did not. There has been disaster after disaster at sea, and yet none of them had led to any improvement in lifesaving methods. The lifeboats of ten years ago are the same style as those used today".

"When the sudden call comes and the ship is listing the tackle or something else is out of order and the boats cannot be set free. There has been advancement in everything else. A few years ago it took ten minutes to load and fire an eight-inch gun. Now the same work can be done in one minute and a quarter. I only hope that the terrible loss of life on the *Mohegan* will lead to improvements in life-saving appliances".[212]

Another passenger on the *Umbria* was J.P. Fireng, the naval paymaster of Bloomfield, N.J., who brought back with him the bodies of his wife and daughter, two of the victims of the *Mohegan* disaster. Their bodies will be taken to Bloomfield, where memorial services are to be held a week from to-day. Mr. Fireng was accompanied on his trip by George A. Oakes, a friend of the family.[213]

A sudden influx of destitute crew members in the area attracted the attention of a national society whose purpose was to help shipwrecked mariners:

SHIPWRECKED FISHERMEN AND MARINERS' ROYAL BENEVOLENT SOCIETY.

This society carries out the most needful and valuable work in an unostentatious and quiet manner, and on that account the public hardly realise what an immense amount of distress is annually relieved. Last year the sum of £20,000 was disbursed in relieving 11,000 sailors, fishermen their widows, orphans and dependent parents, and during the society's existence over half a million persons have been assisted by this institution and its 1,000 honorary representatives located in all ports and fishing towns. All shipwrecked men are instantly cared for on the spot, clothed and sent home. All widows and chidren of men lost at sea are immediately sought out and succoured. All distressed seafarers are at once assisted. Mariners and fishermen are directly encouraged in self-help, by the advantages gained by membership of the society, which include substantial benefits to their dependants; nearly 40,000 men are enrolled at the annual payment of 3s [shillings]. As examples of how relief is administered:—ss. Mohegan, lost on the Manacles Rocks, when the local agent expended £81 in lodging and clothing 50 survivors.[214]

---

[212] Mr Hyslop was still 'banging the drum' for this topic in the year 1912, as no real progress in the adoption of improved lifeboat launching technology by the shipping lines had occurred, even after all this time. A letter to *The New York Times,* highlighting this lamentable state of affairs appears later in this book (see page 214).

[213] *The New York Times;* 13rd Wednesday, November 1898.

[214] *The Belfast News-Letter* (Belfast, Ireland), Tuesday, May 23, 1899.

What can't be cured must be endured.

Life goes on. Following the recent tragedy on their shore, the local newspaper recorded that a concert was performed in St. Keverne village. No doubt, simple pleasures, but a necessary event that helped provide the glue that binds a small community together. After the upheaval and the sorrow witnessed by the villagers, this event re-affirmed life for that community and celebrated those who had risked their own in saving the few, in that tragedy. It is likely that one or two of those saved from the wreck may have been in the audience that evening:

Note from St. Keverne

A successful miscellaneous concert was given by the church choir and friends on Thursday the 5th [January, 1899].

A large audience appreciated the solos, and considerable diversion was caused by a farce, the characters in which were ably taken by five ladies and one gentleman, Mrs. Dale, Miss A. Roskruge, Miss M. Roskruge, Miss E. Roskruge, Miss Phillips of Falmouth, and Mr. Noel Diggens.[215]

Tuesday the 10th was the anniversary of the old St. Keverne Fair, once an important fair for the sale of livestock. Only a poor show was made, leading one to look upon this as a thing of the past.

Dr. Leverton-Spry has very kindly gone to the expense of presenting each member of the lifeboat crew with a framed print illustrating the saving of the *Mohegan* passengers and crew.[216]

To this day, the village of St. Keverne is still remembered for its generous care and comfort afforded to the victims of the *Mohegan,* and with a constant reminder of other associated maritime disasters, in the churchyard at the centre of their village. And as a poignant irony to this story, the Manacle Rocks are eternally visible from that last resting place, for all those who came to grief on its cruel ledges.

People who like this sort of thing will find this is the sort of thing they like.

The disaster attracted the attention of an infamous Scottish tragedian, WilliamTopaz McGonagall (1830–1902),[217] which let loose his bathetic poem, *The Wreck of the Steamer Mohegan* (see Appendix 18, p. 467). He was a self-educated hand-loom weaver from Dundee and after discovering his muse in 1877 he embarked upon a twenty-five year long career as a working poet; delighting and appalling audiences across Scotland and beyond with his **doggerel**. His output was prolific, and the poems were littered with calamities and disasters of every conceivable type: those particular topics being his stock-in-trade.

---

[215] Noel Diggens was the son of the Rev. W. A. Diggens; the vicar of St. Keverne.

[216] *The Royal Cornwall Gazette Falmouth Packet, Cornish Weekly News, & General Advertiser;* Thursday 12th January 1899. The framed print would almost certainly have been the illustration in the supplement of *The Graphic* magazine (see fig. 54).

[217] See http://mcgonagall-online.org.uk/.

CHAPTER 7

Claims and Counter-claims for Damages

Bag and baggage.

Naturally, legal claims would follow the disaster, brought by the survivors and the families of the deceased. Here, such a claim is reported in a newspaper:

> Mr Pemberton, a passenger of the ill-fated liner *Mohegan*, who is suing the company for the value of baggage, claims damages to the amount of $5,000.[218] He alleges that the steamer was unseaworthy, that the officers were incompetent, and that the crew were both insufficient and disorderly.[219]

Based on the observations, made by other passengers, Mr Pemberton seemed to have been travelling on another ship. According to some passengers, the officers were exemplary, and to be commended. In such a tightly run ship, as evidenced by its master Capt. Griffith, it is highly unlikely that the crew would have behaved in any other way.

Miss Roudebush had intimated that she would be lodging a claim for her baggage and personal effects, and no doubt others would be pursuing claims for their own loss and damages.

A further lawsuit was embarked upon, as recorded here:

> The Loss of the *Mohegan*—Threatened Litigation. By the last mail news has been received that Mr. Horace Noble, of Baltimore, U.S., father of Miss Katherine B. Noble, the courageous young woman who was one of the eleven persons saved from the wreck of the steamer *Mohegan* off the coast of Cornwall on October 14th last, may enter suit on behalf of his daughter against the Atlantic Transport Steamship Company for damages. Mr. Noble has retained several Baltimore attorneys and a noted Admiralty lawyer of Boston as advisory counsel. Correspondence between the attorneys of Mr. Noble and those of the Transport Company was in course, with a view to a settlement. It was understood, however, that a compromise was improbable. If the suit is brought, it will be filed in the United States Court of Admiralty. Miss Noble's loss is roughly estimated at about 3,000 dollars. The only things she carried out of the disaster were the rings on her fingers and a stick pin. Twenty-seven costly gowns, all her jewels, and silver she was bringing from an extended trip abroad, and other articles, adjuncts of an up-to-date young woman's wardrobe, which filled twelve trunks, were lost. The suit will be for 5,000 dollars or more.[220]

---

[218] When using the CPI/RPI, the (average) value in 2010 of $5000 from 1898 is £98,900.00 http://www.measuringworth.com/exchange/.

[219] *Trewman's Exeter Flying Post or Plymouth and Cornish Advertiser;* 4th January 1899.

[220] *The Royal Cornwall Gazette Falmouth Packet, Cornish Weekly News, & General Advertiser;* Thursday 12th January 1899.

The question of insurance recovery, on the ship and its cargo, quite naturally became of more than a passing interest; not only for the company, but also for the insurance market:

INSURANCE ON THE VESSEL

[Mr. A. S. Franklin – New York agents for the company]—The hull of the *Mohegan* was valued at about $350,000, and was insured abroad, a large proportion of the line being written at Lloyds, London. The insurance on the cargo was placed partly in Boston, partly in Philadelphia, and partly in this city. As it was covered by open policies, its value cannot be definitely determined before the arrival of the invoices, but it is generally estimated at about $200,000.[221]

The wreck did have an impact on the global insurance market, but payments by the insurance underwriters were not as generous as first calculated by Mr A. S. Franklin, off the top of his head, as can be seen here:

COSTLY RESCUE WORK

The wreck of the *Mohegan* on October 14 near where the *Paris* went ashore is fresh in the minds of all. She left London for New York on the 18th with fifty passengers and a crew of 150. She went ashore off the Lizard, between Manacles and Lowlands, in a fog, and 116 of those on board were lost. It cost the underwriters nearly £70,000 to pay for the wreck.[222]

The true ship is the ship builder.

The Atlantic Transport Line now sued the builders of the *Cleopatra*, claiming a series of defects in its construction had caused a loss of confidence in the vessel, incurring a substantial loss of income: with the ship's temporary docking and extensive repair work. This complex case eventually appeared in court:

Before Mr Justice Bigham, in the Queen's Bench Division yesterday, Earle's Shipbuilding Company *v.* the Atlantic Transport Company was an action which came before his lordship before the long vacation, when the point raised then by the plaintiff company was disposed of, and the matter then came before the court in respect of the counter-claim by the defendant company, a claim amounting to some £15,000. At the hearing in June last, his lordship held that the claim for the damages on the contract between Messrs. Wilson and Messrs. Earle's was assignable, and that the defendant company were entitled to recovery from the plaintiff company damages, which Messrs. Wilson were entitled to recover under an assignment to them of a contract of the 15th September, 1896, between Wilson and Earle's in respect of building the building of a steel screw steamer, 492 feet in length, 52 feet beam, and 34 feet 6 inches in depth, first named the *Cleopatra*, and subsequently altered to the *Mohegan* and which was eventually wrecked on the Manacle Rocks, when over 170 lives [*sic*] were lost. The vessel was to be equipped with two double-ended and two single-ended boilers, with a steam pressure of 190 lb. to the square inch. The total cost of the vessel was to be £105,000. Owing to strikes and other causes, the delivery over the vessel was very greatly delayed.

At the time of hostilities between America and Spain, the United States Government purchased a large number of defendant's company's vessels. The result of that was that, to carry on their own business it was necessary for the defendant company to purchase this particular ship. Certain alterations had to be made, and arrangements were made with the plaintiff

---

[221] *New York Times;* 16th October, 1898. When using the CPI/RPI, the (average) value in 2010 of $200,000 from 1898 is £3,960000.

[222] *The Dundee Courier & Argus* (Dundee, Scotland); Thursday, July 20th 1899.

company that they would become directly responsible for them. A large proportion of the purchase money was paid, and the vessel left Hull for London on her trial trip, when certain defects were discovered, such as priming and leakage of the boilers. Minor defects having been put right, the vessel sailed for New York, on which occasion the voyage occupied a period of eleven days, and during that time much priming and leakage was discovered. The result was that the engineers were continually repairing, so that they became exhausted and prostrated with overwork. In consequence of these matters, the defendant company counter-claimed. The plaintiff company's case was that the boilers, etc., were of good and sound workmanship. that the priming and leakage must have occurred through improper firing, shortness of water, use of salt feed water, owing to the evaporator not being used, and, finally, that the engine and boiler-room staff with few exceptions, were a demoralised, drunken, and incapable body of men.

Mr Justice Bigham, in giving judgment on the main question, said that the action was brought by the plaintiff company to recover the costs of certain work which they did to the steamer *Mohegan*, afterwards lost on the Manacle Rocks. There was no defence to that action, and he entered judgment for the plaintiffs some time ago. But the defendants put on record a counterclaim for breach of contract entered into between the plaintiffs and Messrs. Wilson. The defendants alleged the contract had been assigned to them, on behalf of the plaintiff, and it was suggested that the claim for breach of contract was not such a claim as could be assigned under the Judicature Act. He was of opinion the claim could be assigned, and under the circumstances he came to the conclusion that the boilers were subjected to grossly improper treatment both going to New York and coming back, and that the condition in which the *Mohegan* arrived in London was entirely due to the treatment it was subjected to by some of the men engaged. His conclusion was that the faults of the boilers were due to mismanagement of the vessel, that the defendants subjected the boilers to improper straining by irregular firing—that this caused priming, which caused shortness of water, and that the defendant's servants had failed to observe proper precautions to prevent the results. Therefore, the condition of things was due solely to the negligence of defendants' servants, and not in any way to faults of construction.

After some discussion Mr. Hurst said that the plaintiffs had agreed to allow £850 on the claim for unfinished work. Mr. Justice Bigham said judgment would be for the plaintiffs on the claim and the counterclaim, with costs on the counterclaim. The plaintiffs must have the money out of court, then the costs would be taxed, and when it was found what the amount of costs were the £850 could be allowed from that account.[223]

Following the Board of Trade inquiry; the final phase of the coroner's inquest; and the various legal claims and counter-claims; the world moved on to other events, and the *Mohegan* affair gradually faded from view.[224]

---

[223] *Daily News* (London, England); Saturday, January 27th 1900.

[224] Further research for this publication revealed that the 'Mohegan' name was repositioned in the newspapers, by a persistent reporting of a popular and eponymously named racehorse.

C H A P T E R 8

An Extraordinary Libel Case

The greater the truth: the greater the libel.

In December 1898 a charge of defamatory libel against the Atlantic Transport Line's managers, by Robins Purdy (aged 54 years) was brought before the courts, by the Williams, Torrey, and Feild (Limited) company. It had its first hearing at the Justice Room, of the Mansion House, London.

It was a bizarre case and the proceedings attracted a deal of attention, and were widely reported in the national newspapers:

> At the Justice Room, of the Mansion-house, yesterday, Robins Purdy, of Norfolk-house, Caulfield-road, East Ham, was summoned before Mr. Alderman Newton for having on October 31 unlawfully and maliciously published a certain defamatory libel of and concerning Messrs. Williams, Torrey, and Feild (Limited). Mr. Horace Avory was counsel for the prosecution. In opening the case, Mr. Avory said the prosecution was instituted by Williams, Torrey, and Feild (Limited), the managers in London of the Atlantic Transport Company. The Atlantic Transport Company were the owners of the *Mohegan*, which was wrecked recently off the Cornish coast in very distressing circumstances. Mr. Williams, who was the managing director of Williams, Torrey, and Feild (Limited), was registered under the Merchant Shipping Act as managing owner of that steamship. On October 31 his company received a letter which constituted the alleged libel. The letter was as follows:—

> MANSION HOUSE
> COURTROOM

> Norfolk-house, Caulfield-road, East Ham, Essex, Oct. 20, 1898.

> To the survivors, relatives, and friends of those who perished in the *Mohegan*   Atlantic Transport Line:—

> I am a ship captain, and taught Captain R. Griffith, the late captain of the "Mohegan", navigation in 1877, and have his handwriting to vouch for the fact. In August, 1893, I was given a cheque for £110 and letter of commendation. This was given to me by underwriters after accusing a ship-owner in their presence of offering me a bribe to wreck a ship. I know that ships are put away [deliberately wrecked], and if I know anything the *Mohegan* was, and why? For a consideration. And who should offer the captain, that consideration, but the owners who are a set of rogues, and have got other ships put away. I know that I shall have trouble over this, and call for help from those who have relatives and friends to avenge, and from honest seamen, who will give evidence against dishonest ones.

> Very truly yours, Robins Purdy.
> Please copy and Distribute R.P.[225]

---

[225] Exhibits, concerning the wreck of the *Mohegan*: CLA/004/09/004 – File CLA/004/09 – London Metropolitan Archives.

Mr. Avory, continuing, said that the prosecutors on receiving the letter thought that it was the production of some lunatic [226] and took no notice of it but they soon discovered that documents in the same wording were being sent broadcast over London, and they received a copy from the underwriters at Lloyd's, who were the underwriters of the ship, to whom a copy had been sent. A clerk was sent down to see the defendant at East Ham, and he admitted that he was the author of the document, which he described as a pamphlet. At that interview the defendant made a statement which showed that by the words "owners of the *Mohegan*" he meant Williams, Torrey, and Feild (Limited), and not the Atlantic Transport Company. The defendant said he had sent copies of the document to Lloyd's and had been down at the docks giving them away, and he was still at work on them. The defendant further said, "I know Messrs. Williams Torrey, and Feild. They are a set of liars, rogues, and thieves. Mr. Williams, the present manager of the line, put the *Suffolk* [227] away, and had his certificate suspended by the Board of Trade for six months.

Mr. Williams, who was the head of the company, was never a captain and never commanded the *Suffolk*, and the defendant might be confusing some other person or ship of which they knew nothing. It was clear by the libel that the defendant intended to say that Williams, Torrey, and Feild (Limited), as owners of the steamship, caused the ship to be wrecked. The moment Williams, Torrey and Feild (Limited) found that this statement was being issued broadcast over London they thought it their duty to take these proceedings against the defendant. There was no foundation for the allegation made by the defendant. Since the summons was granted against the defendant similar documents had been sent to the acting manager of the Gaiety Theatre [228] and to Messrs. Thomas Cook and Son, the tourist agents. He should ask for the committal of the defendant for trial, and then proper steps must be taken to see that if he was not in his senses he must be controlled. Witnesses were then called for the prosecution. Mr. A. S. Williams, director of Williams, Torrey, and Feild (Limited), deposed that he was never a ship captain, and, therefore, never had his certificate suspended. There was no foundation at all for the suggestion that his company were responsible in any way for the disaster. They knew nothing of the defendant by name or otherwise. In cross-examination by the defendant, witness said that they had a captain in their employment named Williams, but he was not a relation of witness's. He commanded the *Suffolk*, which witness thought was lost 12 years ago. Captain Williams had his certificate suspended for 3 or 12 months. Witness thought the ship was insured for £32,000. Mr. Avory here interposed, and said that the defendant must clearly understand that at this Court there could be no inquiry into the truth of this libel. If the defendant wanted to take such a foolish course as to suggest that there was any truth in it, he must wait until his trial and plead a plea of justification. The defendant said he did not deny writing the letters, but he believed them to be true. Mr. Weight, clerk to Messrs. Pritebard and Sons, solicitors, Gracechurch-street, said that, acting upon instructions which be received, he went to East Ham on November 1, and there saw the defendant. Witness was on his way to Norfolk-house, and met the defendant in Caulfield-road. The defendant came across the road and asked him whom he wanted to see. Witness replied that he was looking for Norfolk-house, and wanted to see Captain Purdy. The defendant replied, "I am your man," and he accompanied witness to Norfolk-house. Witness said he was a friend of the late chief officer of the *Mohegan*, which was the fact. The defendant said, "You have one of my pamphlets," and then handed him a copy of the pamphlet on which was written, "Please copy and distribute". There were other similar documents on the table in the course of preparation. The defendant said that he had sent the pamphlets to Lloyd's, to the underwriters, and to

[226] The doctor who examined the prisoner noted: "I conversed with him about the loss of this steamship—he had a great deal to say about her being scuttled—he said that the captain's certificate had been suspended and the ship had been wilfully wrecked—he seemed to think that he had a mission to put before the public". Mr Horace Avory, for the prosecution, said:"there was no doubt he was decidedly 'cracked' on the one subject of wrecking vessels".

[227] The *SS Suffolk* (of London) Owners: Messrs. Hooper, Mundell & Co. London. Carrying cattle (8 bullocks saved) bound from Baltimore to London. She was wrecked under the Old Lizard Head. The crew were all saved. *The Times;* Sept. 30th 1886.

[228] The Gaiety Theatre, London was a West End theatre in London, England, located on Aldwych at the eastern end of the Strand. The theatre was established as the Strand Musick Hall [*sic*], in 1864 on the former site of the Lyceum Theatre; *WikiPedia*.

several other people, and that he had been round the docks distributing them, and he went on to say, "I know Messrs. Williams, Torrey and Feild. They are a set of liars, rogues, and thieves. Mr. Williams, the present manager of the line, put the *Suffolk* away, and had his certificate suspended by the Board of Trade for six months. They have black-listed me, and I will black-list them unless they make it worth my while to keep quiet. "Witness said to the defendant :– " Don't you think you are acting very foolishly? You will get yourself into trouble". The defendant immediately flew into a passion, and ordered him out of his house and called to a man downstairs to put him out. Witness left of his own free will. Since that interview two of the members of the crew of the *Mohegan* had handed witness a letter and postcard which they had received, the wording of which was similar to the wording of the libel. Mr. Avory said that that concluded the evidence for the prosecution. It would be for Mr. Alderman Newton to consider whether, having regard for the statement made by the defendant, "They have black-listed me and I will black-list them unless they make it worth my while to keep quiet," the defendant should not be committed for trial for publishing the libel with intent to extort money as well as for publishing a defamatory libel. His view was that if the defendant was sane, then his object was to extort money. It was not for this Court to say whether he was sane or not. He asked for the committal of the defendant for trial for publishing the libel with intent to extort money, and for publishing a defamatory libel. Mr. Alderman Newton intimated that he should commit the defendant for trial upon both those charges. The defendant said he wrote the letters believing them to be true. He did say that he believed some class of ship-owners had black-listed him. He did say that he wanted to get at the owners of the *Mohegan* in the law Courts, but he did not ask for any money to hush up the case. Mr. Avory asked that the defendant should be put under substantial sureties for his appearance at his trial, because he was still continuing the annoyance by circulating the pamphlet. He hoped that the defendant would understand that any continuance of the conduct pending his trial would certainly be taken notice of by the Judge. Mr. Alderman Newton said he should require substantial bail for the defendant's appearance at his trial He committed the defendant for trial, admitting him to bail in two sureties in £ 250 each.[229]

Calumny is only the noise of madmen.

An example given for the 'putting away' of a vessel, put forward by the defendant Purdy at his trial, was the steamship *Suffolk*. He accused Mr Alfred Strover Williams as being its master and in collusion with his company, deliberately ran the vessel aground. This was completely denied by the prosecution, with some justification, as this following piece shows:

> The *Suffolk* was an iron screw steamship, belonging to the Port of London, of 2,923 tons gross, and 1,923 tons net register, and was fitted with engines of 275 horse power. She was built at Blackwall in the year 1883, and at the time of her loss was the property of "The Suffolk Steamship Company, Limited," Mr. Alfred Strover Williams of No. 31, Lombard Street, London, being the manager.
>
> The *Suffolk* entered service in 1882 and for a year was chartered by the Royal Netherlands Steamship Company to augment its new Amsterdam to New York passenger/cargo service. She then spent most of her career sailing on the London to Baltimore line under the command of Captain William Henry Williams.[230]

---

[229] *The Times;* 16th November 1898. And the bail was indeed substantial: £14,000 in each of the two sureties.

[230] Purdy had quite obviously confused this captain with Mr Alfred Strover Williams.

London-bound, "on one of her regular runs" the *Suffolk* ran aground in fog right under the lighthouse on the Old Lizard Head on September 28, 1886. In addition to her cargo she was carrying two passengers, who were not regular fare paying travellers but, "young gentlemen, friends of the owners". The crew of 38 and both of the passengers took to the lifeboats but they were unable to find a landing place and returned to the ship. Fortunately the local lifeboats had put to sea and were able to lead them safely to shore.

The ship and her cargo were abandoned. The *Suffolk* was carrying a general cargo consisting mostly of tobacco, wheat, and flour. In addition her decks were stacked with walnut logs, and 161 steers were penned on the foredeck. A salvage operation designed to recover the cargo began almost immediately but much of it was washed ashore and very few of the cattle survived.[231] The stranded hulk of the *Suffolk* broke up, capsized, and sank in October 1886.

The formal Board of Trade investigation into the incident determined that responsibility lay entirely with the master, and that the opinion that the certificate of the master, Captain William Henry Williams, should be dealt with. In that opinion we entirely concur. It is true that Captain Williams has received a very high character from the owner, as well as from the officers who have served under him. Here, however, is a vessel worth, we are told, some £46,000, with a cargo probably worth as much more, making a total sum of about £100,000, which has been lost by the reckless way in which he has navigated this vessel. It is not, as has been contended by the learned counsel, a case of error of judgment, it is a case of gross negligence, and we shall therefore suspend this gentleman's certificate for six months.

The Court further, on the application of the counsel for the master, agreed to recommend to the Board of Trade that during the suspension of his master's certificate be should be allowed a first mate's certificate.[232]

Purdy's trial resumed, following an earlier adjournment:

The absence of evidence is not the evidence of absence.

At the following trial, at the Central Criminal Court, London – December 12th 1898 – before the Recorder, Mr. Horace Avory, for the prosecution, in the case of Robins Purdy, a ship's master, indicted for libelling Messrs. Williams, Torrey, and Field (Limited), the owners of the *Mohegan*, lost recently off the Cornish coast, pointed out that the case was postponed from the last Session in order to give the Defendant, as he wished, an opportunity of putting in a plea of justification. He was warned that a plea of justification was a very technical matter, and advised to seek legal aid. That advice the Defendant had not paid any heed to. He had drawn up by himself what he put forward as a "plea of justification" to libel, the substance of which was "I plead that I have made the accusation firmly believing it to be true. So help me God". This was no plea at all, and, on behalf of the Crown, he asked for judgment on demurrer.[233]

The Recorder (to the Defendant).—Your plea is clearly bad; you have not pleaded it in proper form.

Mr. Avory.—I ask for judgment on demurrer.

The Recorder.—I give you judgment on demurrer.

The Defendant asked for a further postponement to enable him to get a lawyer.

---

[231] Out of 161 cattle on board, 8 were put on board a hulk, which had been brought from Falmouth for the purpose, and 41 were thrown overboard and reached the shore. Of these some had to be killed on the rocks, but 26 were got up through a gulley to the top of the cliffs.

[232] Board of Trade Wreck Report for the vessel *Suffolk*, 1886.

[233] A demurrer is a pleading in a lawsuit that objects to or challenges a pleading filed by an opposing party. The word demur means "to object"; a demurrer is the document that makes the objection. Lawyers informally define a demurrer as the court saying "so what" to the pleading; *WikiPedia*.

The Recorder.—I cannot allow you to go about libelling firms in a wholesale way.

Mr. Avory said the Defendant was warned by the Common Serjeant, [234] before the case came last Sessions, with respect to the obtaining of legal advice with reference to the obtaining of legal advice with reference to the preparing of the plea.

The Recorder suggested that the case had better be put into the Common Serjeant's list for him to dispose of. This was done.

The Common Serjeant upheld the decision of the Recorder, and advised the Prisoner, as his plea stood for nothing, to plead guilty. The Defendant declined to accept this advice.

Mr. Avory thereupon elected to proceed with the case, and evidence was called to prove publication of the libel which was contained in a pamphlet addressed by the Prisoner to the relatives and survivors of the *Mohegan*, and was sent to a member of the prosecuting firm. The Prisoner not only suggested that the *Mohegan* had been wrecked wilfully, but that the owners were, "liars, rogues, and thieves," and he added that Captain Williams, who was an entire stranger to the Prisoner, had had his master's certificate suspended for six months in respect of the loss of a vessel called the *Suffolk*. There were no grounds for this statement.

Mr. Weight, from the office of Messrs. Pritchard and Sons, 9, Gracechurch–street, solicitors to Messrs. Williams, Torrey, and Field (Limited), said he visited Prisoner with reference to the libellous pamphlets, and when he told him he was acting in a very foolish manner in making these accusations he flew into a most violent temper and ordered him out of the house. He said that the Prosecutors had black-listed him, and that he would black-list them unless they made it worth his while. The Prisoner at the interview made reference to a letter written to him by the late Captain Griffiths, the master of the *Mohegan*, who perished, and allowed the Witness to make a copy of it.[235]

Mr. Avory said this letter, which he read, appeared to have been in reply to one from the Prisoner, apparently asking for money or something of the sort.

The Prisoner.—That is not true.

The Common Serjeant said the letter of Captain Griffiths' had nothing to do with the issue before the Jury, and he could not allow any questions to be put in regard to it.

The statement of the Prisoner, when before the Magistrate, was put in, and in this he denied having had any intent to extort money from the Prosecutors. "He wanted to get the owners of the *Mohegan* into the Law Courts".

The Common Serjeant.—Mr. Avory, are you not going to call the prison doctor?

Mr. Avory.—I do not like to raise the issue as to the Prisoner's mind. I do not want to send him to Broadmoor for life.

The Common Serjeant thought it right that medical evidence should be given as to the Prisoner's mental state.

Dr. Scott (of Holloway Prison) said he could not certify the Prisoner as legally insane. He was of weak mind, and took exaggerated and distorted views of nautical matters. He seemed to have a delusion that vessels had been wilfully wrecked, and he had a mission to expose this to the relatives of the lost.

The Prisoner, who when called upon for his defence, produced a large sea-chart, when asked for a Mr. Juddery, quartermaster of the *Mohegan*, and one of the survivors of the wreck.

The Witness was called.

Prisoner.—I want, my Lord, to ask the Witness what course the *Mohegan* steered after she left Start Point.

The Common Serjeant.—I cannot allow the question, it has nothing to do with the issue before the Jury.

---

[234] The Common Serjeant of London (full title The Serjeant-at-Law in the Common Hall) is an ancient British legal office, first recorded in 1317, and is the second most senior permanent judge of the Central Criminal Court after the Recorder of London, acting as deputy to that office, and sitting as a judge in the trial of criminal offences. – *WikiPedia*.

[235] A transcription for this letter (most likely referred to) is shown below and appeared in the court records.

The Prisoner was found guilty of publishing the libel, but not with the intent to extort money.

A Juryman.—We think that he is hardly responsible for his actions.

The Common Serjeant.—I hardly think he is.

Mr. Avory said the prosecution would be satisfied if the Common Serjeant could make the prisoner understand clearly that he must not repeat these libels, either by writing, orally, or printing.

The Prisoner.—I will give up writing, but I still believe what I do.

The Common Serjeant.—You are in a free country, and can believe what you like but keep your opinions to the bosom of your family (laughter).

The Prisoner undertook not to repeat the libels, and was accordingly released on entering into a recognisance in £100 to come up for sentence if called upon.[236]

There is in existence a letter, written in the hand of Capt. Richard Griffith and addressed to Capt. Robins Purdy. The letter in question is held in a file[237] that also contains a handwritten copy of the libelous letter distributed by Purdy:

Manhattan Queens Road Leytonstone

Queens Road

Leytonstone Essex

> Captain R. Purdy
>
> Managing Director of the Norfolk Steamship Co. Ltd.

D^r [Dear] Sir, I am in receipt of favour dated Feb^y [February] 26 with sundry enclosures re: the above named Coy [company]. I also note you ~~cannot~~ comment on my last letter, i.e. scornful. In reply I beg to state that I can not now call to mind when or what I wrote in my last. I note also your reference to your having taught me once upon a time which fact I do not dispute. It would however be in order to mention in this connection that for this teaching a fee was charged and if my memory serves me aright paid in advance without terms or discount, therefore I feel justified in crying quits on that score.

With ref^n [reference] to any future mat^s [matters] you may deem necessary to cram into my neglected cranium you have omitted to men^t [mention] the fee in your ??? unless indeed the $foll^g$ [following] words copied from your letter viz; another ??? knowing something in with me refers to it this however is very indefinite seeing there is no specified amount mentioned.

Your ref^{ce} [reference] to to the Mgg B [?] shipowners I am not in any sort of position to reply and feel just in leaving the matter ent^{ly} [entirely] in the hd^s [hands] of the S^d Mg^r [?Manager] If however as you infer they the Mg^{rs} [Managers] have succeeded [?] in keeping shipmasters and seamen from becoming too saucy as you style they have done one very malicious deed. Sea^n [seamen] are not $just^d$ [justified] in being saucy to their employers. I think if I may be personal; [?] the

---

[236] *The Times;* Tuesday, Dec 13th 1898.

[237] Exhibits, re-wreck of *Mohegan* : CLA/004/09/004 – File CLA/004/09 – London Metropolitan Archives.

remark that you w^d [would] have leave neog^d [negotiated?] this fact had you pass as my ??? of y^r [your] life on the P????
??? as I have, for instance, aye or even half of that time.

The result of the deeds [?] of these very terrible money grabbers I am in no way responsible (?) for??? neither have I the very smallest fear of the dire consq^{ces} [consequences] you predict for us. I have no remark to offer on your ref^{ce} [reference] to the Military Marine and the unreasonable Marine [?] problem. I am content to leave it entirely in the care of those whose business in life is to give and guard it. I am q^{te} [quite] sats^f [satisfied] I am not capable of ?? implying that ??? and ??? this branch of particular offence ??? ??? ??? of your ability therefore let us jointly descend to things more in keeping with our nautical capability such things for instance that might bring us our Daily Bread and a little baccy [tobacco].

Yours Truly

R. Griffith.[238]

A full interpretation for this letter is made that more difficult by its missing text, and the thread of the story lacks a certain coherence because of this. The fact that this letter appears in the court papers (note the official stamp at the head of both above letters) would suggest it was a copy made by Capt. Griffith, with the permission of the prosecuting counsel, as supporting evidence. This is further confirmed by the use of shorthand words that would not likely have been used in the original.

The letter is in poor condition and as a consequence, some text is illegible. Nonetheless, it is included here for the sake of completeness, and it gives us something of an insight into the characters of the two men involved, as well as the dynamics of that relationship.

Only a spoon knows what is stirring in the pot.

It was indeed, a most peculiar case. Some would say: 'no smoke without fire', others would say: 'that the man Purdy was deluded and was rightly made to recompense for his damaging claims, which had no substance whatsoever.' Whatever the situation, Williams, Torrey, and Feild Ltd., and the Atlantic Transport Line management team, could well have done without this distraction and with possible damaging consequences; particularly at such a sensitive time—the Board of Trade inquiry for the *Mohegan* affair. The published details of this case most likely fuelled the persistent rumour that Capt. Griffith had deliberately run the *Mohegan* on to the Manacle Rocks, for his own pecuniary advantage.

The Purdy file.

The first official record for this man Purdy was in the UK census for 1851 where his birth year was recorded as 1845 (see page 452). He was resident in Yarmouth, Norfolk, at that time, with his parents and four sisters. His father was employed as a spirit-merchant (see page 452).

---

[238] Ibid.

The UK census for 1861 reveals him, at the age of 16 years, as a 'boy' aboard the vessel *Thomas Rising,* one of a six-man crew. At the time of the census, the vessel was docked at Devoran, in Cornwall.

Both UK census records for 1901 and 1911 record him as being self-employed and living at Norfolk. His death was recorded at the age of 87 years, in his home town of Yarmouth, Norfolk, in the year 1932.[239]

---

[239] GRO/BMD: 1932 Q4 – Yarmouth 4b, 16.

CHAPTER 9

Pilfering: Beggars Can't Be Choosers

Opportunity makes a thief.

There are two popular misconceptions about shipwrecks in Cornwall. The first is that most wrecks were caused by wreckers shining misleading lights from the cliffs, in the hope of bringing vessels laden with bounty onto the rocks. This was never required, as nature had—with its strong winds, heavy seas and unforgiving rocks—a deadly combination of reserve, ensuring a constant stream of wrecked vessels.

The second misconception is that the wreckers deliberately killed survivors of shipwrecks to ensure they could carry off the hapless ships' cargo, unchallenged.

Though there were inevitable occasions when violence was used, far more wreckers were have likely to have drowned than the possibility of sailors being murdered. A combination of poor wages and valuable cargo was too much to resist, with wreckers often taken by the same treacherous seas that had caused the original occupants to abandon ship.

Cornwall, though rich in natural wealth, had its fair share of poor, who scraped a living from the land or the sea to feed their families and keep the wolf from the door. This local economy was made worse by the natural fluctuations of the market:

> With the whims of the markets and policies, Cornwall's mineral and maritime trade economy received severe blows in the mid-nineteenth century which affected the living conditions of those involved, and hence had an impact on wrecking activity. Agricultural depression also periodically hit the population culminating with the 'Hungry Forties' potato blight. Cornwall's lack of large centres of population that are needed for markets allowed other mega-ports: Liverpool, Bristol, and London to emerge as the preferred options. Cornwall was plunged into a prolonged economic depression. Thus, in the beginning of the 1830s, one of Cornwall's heaviest exports was its own people.[240]

Cornishmen and their families now inhabit the world over: having transferred their skills and talents to those countries that had sufficiently buoyant economies, to support them.

---

[240] Catharine J. Pearce; *Cornish Wrecking 1700 – 1860 Reality and Popular Myth;* Woodbridge: Boydell, 2010.

"A billowy sea and a shattering wind,
The cliffs before, and the gale behind". [241]

Against this economic backdrop, there should be little surprise that the stranding of a ship on a shore was seen as a gift from God, and an opportunity not to be missed. Abject poverty, a hard life, and primitive medicine at unaffordable cost: those were willing foot-soldiers for Death, to wage its war on the poor.

Shipwrecks were thought to be fair game across all strata of society with sometimes hundreds of people following a troubled ship along the coast in anticipation of a rich harvest.[242] This is perhaps best summed up by the local version of the saying, "it's an ill wind that blows no good to Cornwall."

Cornwall had a fearsome reputation for shipwrecks among seafarers, all the more so in the days of sail. The curved shape of many sections of a protruding coast were an absolute death-trap for sailing vessels which, if blown into them and embayed, had no means of escape.

Shipwrecks often occurred through no fault of the vessel's Master, but rather through the simple fact that in those days a ship could only manoeuvre according to the limitations of the wind and tide. In heavy seas and strong winds, safety could only be partly assured by a ship having enough sea-room to ride the storm out, drifting or being blown where the wind took it, and regaining position and course once the weather calmed. In the case of the waters around Cornwall's coast, there simply isn't enough sea-room for this to work and if ships failed to find shelter, or were caught by surprise, they soon found themselves in a difficult situation. There were many unseaworthy vessels, with rotten wood and with rotten owners, who had a concern only for a quick return on a shipment, and with total disregard for the safety of their crews, that added to the relentless toll of wreck around our shores.

Under the legal umbrella of what was known as 'dead-wrecks' [243] this being the basis of the persistent myth of the Cornish being engaged in wrecking activities and with survivors murdered in order to ensure a legal [*sic*] claim on salvage.

Although Cornwall's name is synonymous with the idea of a deliberate wrecking of ships, in fact Cornwall has a long and noble tradition of rendering assistance to those in distress which continues to this day. The coastline is dotted with Royal National Lifeboat Institution (RNLI) stations, still manned by volunteers, many of which have a long and proud history, though a dangerous undertaking, even in modern

---

[241] Said to be the Cornish wrecker's toast in byegone days – Sabine Baring-Gould; *The Vicar of Morwenstowe.* London: King, 1876; New York: T. Whittaker, 1876.

[242] In all fairness, some of those people were motivated more by a need to help those aboard an unfortunate vessel, in perilous conditions.

[243] Catharine J. Pearce, *Cornish Wrecking 1700 – 1860 Reality and Popular Myth.*
The most quoted definition of wreck rights comes from Edward I's Statute of Westminster (1275), where it stated that 'where a man, a Dog or a Cat escape quick out of a Ship, that such a Ship nor Barge, nor any Thing within them, shall be judged wreck'. In other words, if there were any survivors, shipwrecked goods could not be claimed as 'wreck'. The ship or cargo was defined as wreck, eligible to be claimed by those holding wreck rights, *only* when there were no survivors – in other words, a 'dead-wreck'. Thus, the popular belief that the country people had claim to 'dead-wrecks' had its genesis in the legal definition of 'wreck'.

times. The bravery and skill of those who set out in all weathers in an open-top rowing boat is quite humbling and it is a shame that this tradition is overshadowed by the "wrecking" identity.[244]

The looting of cargo washed ashore is quite different to wrecking however; given both the poverty in Cornwall and the number of wrecks, it should come as no surprise that locals would regard items from ships as "fair game". This reflects an objective reality for poor people rather than any particular degree of callousness. After all, many Cornish families had members at sea of their own, and would have been acutely aware of the dangers and would naturally have had sympathy for those lost in wrecks around their shores.

What cannot be ignored, in the story of the *Mohegan*, are some well documented instances of pilfering small items of jewellery and monies, from the bodies of some victims. The greater majority of those who were involved in the rescue or recovery of the passengers and crew were above reproach and were motivated solely by humanitarian needs. However, there will always be a small minority who care not so much for their fellow man, but for their personal gain. It can never be condoned, yet it must be viewed in the context of the time. Grinding poverty within a family is a powerful motivator for a man to commit those crimes in the guise of a gift from God. But in some cases perhaps, needs must.

As far as these 'traditional' events are concerned, not one person was convicted of an offence, over the disappearance of valuables; the only involvement in a magistrate's court, arising from the *Mohegan* event, was an alleged assault involving a dispute in the claim for reward, in a recovery of a corpse.

Shrouds have no pockets.

Disquieting local rumour, in the matter of pilfering from bodies, prompted a public announcement in a local newspaper:

IDLE RUMOURS

The wreck of the *Mohegan* like many similar catastrophes, has given rise to a great many stories which will not bear investigation. Among these may safely be classified all allegations or insinuations of the pilfering or robbery from bodies, and on the other hand of services being rendered without recognition. Not a single case under the former category has been substantiated, and several have been proved to be entirely baseless. The unstinted and ready help of all classes in St. Keverne and neighbourhood is free from all shadow of suspicion under this head. It is equally satisfactory to know that the passengers and their friends have joined with the owners in recognising what has been done, and where payments would be accepted it has been made or will be made. Messrs. J. C. Fox have been instructed, as will be seen by a letter elsewhere, to receive and deal with all claims for services, and therefore there is no warrant for stories of fishermen labouring without reward. The owners have under consideration the placing of some permanent memorial in St. Keverne Church to all who lost their lives in this disastrous wreck.[245]

---

[244] The Penlee lifeboat, *Solomon Browne*, disaster occurred on 19 December 1981 off the coast of Cornwall, in England, UK. The Penlee Lifeboat went to the aid of the coaster *Union Star* after its engines failed in heavy seas. After the lifeboat had managed to rescue four people both vessels were lost with all hands; sixteen people died including eight volunteer lifeboatmen; *WikiPedia*.

[245] *The Royal Cornwall Gazette Falmouth Packet, Cornish Weekly News & General Advertiser;* 3rd November 1898.

This instruction to Messrs. J. C. Fox had an immediate effect, in that there was a promise made that for any individual, in securing a body from the wrecking, would receive recompense for their humane act. In response, a confirmatory letter was duly published to that effect:

To the Editor of the Royal Cornwall Gazette–The Mohegan Disaster.

Sir,—As charges have been made in the public Press that fishermen helping to bring in bodies and take care of them are not being properly compensated for their labours, permit us to say that the owners of this steamer instructed us immediately after the wreck, to remunerate all who have rendered any service to the living survivors or to the dead bodies, and no one who has applied for same has been refused, and we shall be glad to receive particulars of any services that have not yet been sent in.

We are, yours truly,
C. G. Fox & Co.
Falmouth, 1st Nov., 1898.[246]

A passenger, who had placed some money and other valuables in the care of her physician, a travelling companion, described the outcome on the recovery of his body:

There appears to be no foundation for the report of a robbery of one of the bodies. In information from an official source shows that among the *Mohegan*'s passengers was Mrs. Compton Swift, an invalid lady, who was accompanied by Dr. John Fellows [*sic*]. Mrs. Swift escaped with her life, but Dr. Fellows was drowned. According to Mrs. Swift's statement, when the vessel struck the Manacle Rocks she handed to the doctor something like £100, with other valuables, which was made into a parcel. What became of that parcel no one knows, but it is quite likely that it was lost in the confusion. At any rate, when the body of Dr. Fellows was recovered at Durgan [247] none of Mrs. Swift's property was found on it, but there was something like £50 worth of doctor's own belongings in his clothes, and those are now in the possession of the Falmouth police. Among the papers in his pockets were the passage tickets for Mrs. Swift and himself.[248]

The same story had a different slant placed upon it, which must have given some welcome respite for the local population, who had to endure those persistent and objectionable accusations:

THE LOST LINER.

AN UNFOUDED SCANDAL

(From our Special Correspondent)

FALMOUTH, Thursday Night.

---

[246] *The Royal Cornwall Gazette Falmouth Packet, Cornish Weekly News & General Advertiser;* 3rd November 1898.

[247] Durgan is a small fishing village on the north shore of the Helford River and is now owned by the National Trust. It lies midway between Porth Navas to the west and Mawnan to the east.

[248] *The Royal Cornwall Gazette Falmouth Packet, Cornish Weekly News, & General Advertiser;* Thursday 27th October 1898.

Unpleasant stories of the robbing of corpses as they were thrown up by the sea have been current in the neighbourhood of St. Keverne, but I am glad to able to state that there is no truth whatever in them as far as can be ascertained. Among the passengers on the *Mohegan* was a Mrs. Compton Swift, an invalid, who was accompanied by Dr. John Fallow, on whom were subsequently found both tickets. Mrs. Swift has stated that when the vessel struck she passed to the doctor a quantity of valuables worth about £100. These were made into a parcel and of that parcel nothing has since been heard. This is not surprising, in view of the confusion which must have prevailed, and the drowning of the doctor. When the doctor's body was found none of the lady's property was discovered on him, but, Police-Superintendent Beare now has in his possession about £50 worth of the doctor's personal belongings taken from his clothes. It seems clear that no charge of robbery can be evolved from these circumstances.[249]

More support for the local inhabitants of the villages surrounding the Manacles, came in a welcome piece in the local newspaper, though the report chose to play-down the apparent circulation of banknotes in Durgan that had been recorded three days earlier:

The Plymouth "Mercury"[250] says:—The allegations that one of the victims of the Mohegan was robbed of a bundle of banknotes is generally discredited in West Cornwall, though it is not considered improbable that if the notes were washed ashore the finders put them into circulation. In connection with this phase, it may be mentioned that when two strangers to St. Keverne were having tea in one of the most comfortable houses in the village on Sunday, a lady who had spent all her life in the village remarked. "I daresay a good many people will have money after this," suggesting at the time that they would not come by it honestly. But most people will refuse to believe on anything short of absolute proof that those who have been so kind to the living robbed the dead.[251]

When it comes to divide an estate; the politest men quarrel.

In addition to those unwelcome stories of alleged pilfering, an unseemly dispute ended up at the Magistrates' Court at Helston:

The Wreck Of The Mohegan—A Gruesome Sequel

At Helston, yesterday, Thomas Smitheram, of St. Keverne, was summoned for assaulting Mark Trebilcock on November 11th. Two days after the wreck of the *Mohegan* the body of a young lady came in near St. Keverne, and he, the defendant, and a man called Beer got it on the cliff, where Mr. Rogers took charge of it, and carried it to the parish church to await identification. Witness was not paid his share of the money given for removing the body, although the defendant admitted that they had the money [a payment made by the shipping agent in lieu of recovery]. On November 11th he was at his house when the defendant sent word by Beer that he wanted to see him in the public-house. Complainant replied if he wanted to see him he must come to his house. The same night Smitheram came, forced him against the wall and threatened to knock his and his wife's brains out (complainant's wife corroborated). Defendant said on 9th November Trebilcock

[249] *Daily News* (London, England); Friday 21st October 1898.

[250] Commenced publishing on June 2nd 1860. It was first known as the Daily Western Mercury. From issue number 79, published on September 26th 1860, it was renamed the *Western Daily Mercury* and is more usually referred to as such.

[251] *The Royal Cornwall Gazette Falmouth Packet, Cornish Weekly News, & General Advertiser*; Thursday, October 27th 1898.

demanded *1s 8d.*,[252] his share for removing the body. They had agreed that Trebilcock should help them but he picked up the body by the feet in such a manner that he told them to let it down. He still kept hold of the feet while they carried it twenty yards on to the green grass. That man never did anything, and defendant told him two men were quite enough to carry a body any time. A day or two afterwards complainant again asked him about the money, and he told him if the rest were agreeable he would have his share. In regard to the assault, he said complainant came out to him in a threatening manner, and defendant merely pushed him back in order that he would not strike him. Francis Beer swore to seeing Trebilcock with his hand on Smitheram's collar. Smitheram then put up his hand and pushed him against the wall. The Bench fined Smitheram *5s.* and *18s. 6d.*[253] costs.[254]

That such pilfering took place is undeniable; indeed, based on reports from other wrecks over the years, it is almost inconceivable that such activities were not prevalent, in some degree or other. The reports relating to the victims Mr Edward Sennington and Mrs Amelia Gumbrecht strongly suggest this as having been the case.

Again, it must be stressed that the above incidents be viewed in the situation that prevailed at the time. There was abject poverty in the county, and every opportunity to improve a well-being for a poor family, was to be seized at. Little wonder then that small incidents involving money became blown out of all proportion, as in the case that ended up in the Helston Court.

To this day, the general public still flock to the scene of a shipwreck and openly flout the law, by carrying off flotsam, jetsam, lagan, and where possible, derelict.[255] The viewpoint of the common man on the beach is that, it is providence and a gift from God. It's as though these actions are an ingrained part of the human psyche: a primitive desire for survival and the protection of the family.

From the historical perspective and in its reporting here, it is necessary to record these events for posterity, as it is an integral part of the story—even though most would prefer to ignore it. In this unforeseen event of such savagery, all human emotions and desires surface alongside the wreckage and the outcomes are not always as one would hope. Such misery acquaints a man with strange bedfellows.

---

[252] This sum of of 1s. 8d. equates to approximately £5 in today's currency.

[253] These sums in today's currency would equate to £14 and £53 respectively; sizeable sums of money and entirely out of proportion to the small amount of cash payment that was the subject of dispute.

[254] *The Royal Cornwall Gazette Falmouth Packet, Cornish Weekly News, & General Advertiser;* Thursday, 17th November 1898.

[255] *Flotsam*: floating wreckage of a ship or its cargo; broadly speaking, floating debris. *Jetsam*: the part of a ship, its equipment, or its cargo that is purposefully cast overboard or jettisoned to lighten the load in time of distress and that sinks or is washed ashore. *Lagan*: is cargo that is lying on the bottom of the ocean, sometimes marked by a buoy, which can be later reclaimed, and *Derelict*: is cargo that is also on the bottom of the ocean, but which no one has any hope of reclaiming; *WikiPedia*.

CHAPTER 10

Mr Edmund Laurence Carylon: Cornwall County Coroner.

In the midst of life we are in death.

Mr. E. Laurence Carlyon (see fig. 21) was installed as the Coroner for Cornwall in the year 1893 and was destined to be the coroner at the inquest, relating to the steamship *Mohegan* disaster.

A summary of Mr Carlyon's life events appeared in a local newspaper, as a background to a forthcoming election for the position as the Cornwall County Coroner, following the death of the previous incumbent, Dr John Carlyon:

> Mr. Laurence Carlyon was appointed by the Cornwall County Finance Committee as provisional coroner for the Truro district until February 7th when the County Council will meet to settle the matter. Mr. Laurence Carlyon comes of an old and honoured Cornish family, and is a young and rising solicitor. He was born at Stoodleigh, North Devon, and is the son of the Rev. Frederick Carlyon, now resident in Truro, and who was rector of Mevagissey during the cholera epidemic of 1849: burying at that time not less than 100 of his parishioners.
>
> Mr. Laurence Carlyon is a grandson of Dr. Clement Carlyon, a bust of whom now adorns the Truro Council Chamber. Dr. Clement Carlyon was five times Mayor of Truro, and associated with all the public institutions of the city. Mr. Laurence Carlyon's maternal grandfather was Mr. Edmund Turner, M.P. for Truro for eleven years, and once Mayor of the borough. The provisional coroner was educated at Felstead, Essex, and was afterwards articled to his uncle, the late Mr. Edward Trewbody Carlyon, of Truro, completing his legal education with Mr. J. W. Tolvert, solicitor, Doctors' Common, London.[256] After leaving Dr. Commons, Mr. Carlyon proceeded to St. Austell, where he remained with Messrs. Coode, Shilson, and Co., for nearly three years. He then came to Truro on his own account, where he has been in practice over two years.
>
> Since April, 1892, he has acted as deputy to the late coroner, Mr. John Carlyon, and the citizens of Truro have testified their confidence in Mr. Carlyon by appointing him honorary secretary of the Truro Central Schools and the local branch of the Society for the Prevention of Cruelty to Children, as well as selecting him to one of the honorary managerships of the Truro Savings Bank.[257]

The election for the new coroner, to replace Dr John Carlyon[258] took place on the 7th February, 1893, at the Cornwall County Council meeting at Truro, with the Lord Mount Edgcumbe as its Chairman. Mr E. Laurence Carlyon won the vote by a majority of the Council, and was declared elected and duly appointed.[259]

---

[256] Doctors' Commons, also called the College of Civilians, was a society of lawyers practising civil law in London. Like the Inns of Court of the common lawyers, the society had buildings with rooms where its members lived and worked and a large library. Court proceedings of the civil law courts were also held in Doctors' *Commons;WikiPedia.*

[257] *The Royal Cornwall Gazette Falmouth Packet, Cornish Weekly News, & General Advertiser;* Thursday, 12th January 1893.

[258] He died aged 87 years, on December 30th 1892, at Strangways Terrace, Truro, whilst still in office as County Coroner. He had conducted an inquest at Truro, just four days prior to his death. *The Royal Cornwall Gazette Falmouth Packet, Cornish Weekly News, & General Advertiser;* Thursday 5 January 1893.

What is remarkable, is that this family has continued to provide a Cornwall County coroner until the present day—one hundred and seventy-six years in an unbroken line:

Dr John Carlyon 1837 – 1892 [December]

Mr E. Laurence Carlyon. 1893 – 1935 [appointed deputy coroner in April 5th, 1892]

Mr Laurence Jago Carlyon, 1935 – 1971

Mr Edward T. Carlyon, 1971 – 2003 [currently assistant deputy coroner – 2012]

Dr Emma E. Carlyon 2003 – [2013]

His appointment in 1893 would ensure Mr E. Laurence Carlyon was in place, as coroner at the *Mohegan* inquest. His compassion, diplomacy and professionalism would all be to the fore, in dealing with this complex and shocking disaster.

A Coroner's Inquest for the Mohegan Disaster

The coroner, Mr E. Laurence Carlyon, must have heard of the *Mohegan* disaster on the following day, Saturday 16th October. He would have contacted his office and worked through that weekend in preparation for the largest case he would ever have adjudicated for.

The inquest was to have commenced on the following Tuesday and that required his presence in the village of St. Keverne. The weather was difficult, with incessant rain and high winds. The roads were sodden and the going difficult: nevertheless, he had prepared himself and set off from Truro for the sad task ahead of him.

The Coroner, having been installed in the year of 1896, this was indeed a testing ordeal for a relatively new incumbent of that office. Mr Carlyon now tasked with the unraveling of events, with identifying a huge number of the deceased, and with setting up a formal inquest that was to commence almost immediately.

The Press Association had installed correspondents in St. Keverne, who telegraphed their reports to the outside world:

The Coroner (Mr Carlyon) opened the inquest at St. Keverne on Monday [October 17th]. The proceedings were confined to taking evidence respecting the identity of the 40 bodies at St. Keverne. He would then adjourn the enquiry for a week in order that the Board of Trade might, if it thought fit, furnish him with a nautical assessor to assist in dealing with expert questions about navigation..[260]

---

[259] *The Royal Cornwall Gazette Falmouth Packet, Cornish Weekly News, & General Advertiser*; Thursday 9th February 1893.

[260] *Nottinghamshire Guardian* (London, England); Saturday, 2nd October 1898.

Mr. Carlyon was used to death and its aftermath, but one wonders if he had prepared himself for that overwhelming spectacle that greeted him, in the melancholy surroundings of the gloomy church, off the square at St. Keverne:

HEARTRENDING SCENES

The inquest on the pitiable ranks of the dead, which crowd the end of the aisle of St. Keverne's Church, was opened yesterday. The work of the identification necessitated the abandonment of the design to hold the inquiry at Falmouth; but it is of the necessity involved taken back along the steep and miry twenty miles of road the poor sailors who had escaped, and whose testimony was wanted. This distance seemed incredible to anyone not acquainted with the conformation of this wild country. The Manacle Rocks, the scene of the shipwreck, lie only six miles from Falmouth by sea, but to get to St. Keverne, the village opposite to them, by road it is necessary to go far inland until a bridge can be found to cross Helford Creek up which the sea runs widely, and then returns seaward to reach the village. Such a journey was a trying ordeal for some of these men—two of whom wounded and carrying their arms in slings, and the rest of them more or less battered by the terrible struggle of that night of disaster. While they were on the road the sad preliminaries of identification were being completed at St. Keverne. Several of the relatives have an exceedingly sad tale to tell. One poor lad of seventeen, who came to identify his mother, spoke of her as the last relative he had in the world. Parents came looking for children and sisters for brothers. Heartrending were the scenes that occurred within the screen which closed in the end of the church where the rows of dead were lying. The linen that veiled the faces of the dead was removed as the weeping searchers passed along the rows, making their dreadful examination, and then if the loved one was found, there was a sob of anguish which almost choked the utterance, "That is he," or "That is she". The women and children had been decently shrouded in white nightdresses, with bands tied neatly around their waists. The men were clothed very much as they had been in life. The sailors especially looked as if they had been lain down in a tired sleep. Their pallid features showed no contraction, but the mouths of all were open as if they sought to breathe through them. Outside the screen coffin was piled on coffin in great stacks. It was a spectacle of woe which must have smitten the heart of the most callous. The Coroner, Mr. Carlyon, swore in a jury of sixteen, in order that to secure that he should be sure of having at the end of what promises to be a protracted inquiry, the necessary number to deliver a legal verdict. The Coroner expressed profound distress at the calamity and keen sympathy with the sorrowing relatives. No doubt the disaster would raise again the question of a light being put on the Manacles. Some differences of opinion existed as to whether a light there would not cause disaster as well as prevent it.[261]

Distance leads enchantment.

Cases of Real Destitution At Falmouth

The wives of some members of the crew who are dead scraped enough money together to get to Falmouth in order to see the last of their loved ones. Having done this, and find that the bodies they are seeking are not yet found, they are in a condition of absolute want. Any help for them would be received with gratitude by Mr. H. Toulson, the superintendent of the Cornwall Sailors' Home, Falmouth, whose name is a sufficient guarantee for the discreet distribution of any funds forthcoming.[262]

---

[261] *The North-Eastern Daily Gazette* (Middlesbrough, England); Tuesday, 18th October 1898.

[262] *The Royal Cornwall Gazette Falmouth Packet, Cornish Weekly News, & General Advertiser*;Thursday, October 27, 1898.

Efforts were made to assist these poor unfortunates, but the local horses had been almost run off their legs recently.[263] It had been raining by day and night since the disaster, and the primitive roads were exceedingly heavy going.

One can imagine the distressing scene, as an identification of the dead was established. In one instance, two families claimed the same woman's body: quite obviously a case of mistaken identity.

Some among those that managed to reach the village of St. Keverne had the pitiable task of meeting with their loved ones, laid out the floor of the belfry,[264] in St. Keverne church (see fig. 39):

WRECK ON THE MANACLES.

A HEARTRENDING SCENE.

Such demonstrations of human hearts in dire bereavement as have been witnessed within the walls of St. Keverne Church are happily rare. There was a most distressing incident on Tuesday morning [October 18th]. A poor woman dressed in black was in search of her dead husband, [David] Robb, a steward. His body had been placed in a coffin, and the lid was removed as the woman was led weeping into the church. Directly she caught sight of the dead face she fell down and kissed it saying, "My God! And he is to be taken from me? How can I live alone?" For a long time she lovingly stroked his hands and kissed all over the face of her dead husband, and then composing herself by a violent effort, got up and walked away. In a minute or so, however, she returned for one more inexpressibly sad and wistful gaze upon the dead, and then the coffin lid was fastened down. Equally painful scenes were enacted alongside other coffins. Under the superintendence of Mr. Orme Fox,[265] a number of men were busily occupied all Tuesday morning in placing bodies in the plain stained wood coffins which nearly covered the floor of the belfry end of the church.

THE GRAVES

From Sunday afternoon until Tuesday several men were engaged in digging a great grave within ten feet of the north wall of the church which faces Falmouth Bay. Night and day the gravediggers pushed their work, until Tuesday morning a pit thirteen feet across, nineteen feet long and ten feet deep, was excavated. It is situated in the older part of the churchyard, not twenty yards from the little headstone which records one of the most direful disasters which has ever happened, even on this fateful coast. This is the stone indicating the internment of one hundred and twenty persons drowned in the wreck of the *John*, in 1855. It was expected that about fourteen separate graves would be required, but on Tuesday morning only two were prepared, and these in the more modern section of the churchyard, This part, however, has but little room itself to spare. For the reception of the remains of young [John] Marshall a grave was dug between two others, where there was barely room for it. Just over the pathway was the grave for another deceased passenger. Of the great common grave a plan has been prepared, on which will be shown the exact position of all the bodies buried in it, so that if it is desired to exhume any particular bodies at the request of those who have a right to claim them or erect headstones no difficulty will be found in locating them.[266]

[263] There is a reference to horse-drawn buses being available in the year 1891: *The Great Blizzard 1891; the wreck of the Panama.*—The National Maritime Museum, Cornwall.

[264] The caretaker for the St. Keverne church, Mrs Mary Frances Perrow, received much thanks for the way in which she had prepared the bodies for burial.

[265] Mr Orme Fox of Fox and Co., Falmouth

[266] *The Royal Cornwall Gazette Falmouth Packet, Cornish Weekly News & General Advertiser;* October 20th 1898.

Unused to national attention, and with a sudden influx of people, the little post-office at St. Keverne, with its primitive telegraphic instruments, had practically closed against further Press messages.[267]

Several survivors were transported from Falmouth, some twenty miles in distance, in great discomfort, having sustained injuries from the event, and some with arms in slings. The journey called for travel over rough and primitive roads, to attend the coroner's inquest. One wonders, did the survivors actually see the Manacle Rocks, with the *Mohegan*'s masts and funnel still visible, as they entered the village and looking out over the disaster area? If so, then a more dispiriting start to a sad day's business cannot be imagined.

The inquest commenced on October 17th in the St. Keverne village school hall.[268] The Coroner Mr E. Laurence Carlyon presided and the elected foreman of the jury was Mr John Coad.[269] A formal identification of those who had perished, had previously taken place in the St. Keverne Church.

This report gave an account of the Coroner's opening address:

> The calling of the death roll at the inquest was deeply pathetic. As names were mentioned friend after friend rose and claimed kinship. In some cases, however, no one claimed kindred or possessed knowledge respecting the corpse, and they simply had to be passed over with a number attached as to the to the particulars of sex, apparent age, features marks and dress. In one case a man identified a ring, probably taken off his wife's finger, and yet the body from which it had to be taken from was claimed by a lady of quite another name. These doubtful cases had to be passed over also, for further and more private inquiry to determine identity. In still other cases the doctor, who had been saved [Dr Arthur Herbert Trevor] had to be sent back to the church to see if he could assist identification. It was a long and sad, though quite necessary formality. The Coroner expressed very kindly to some of the American friends the formalities of English law in these respects, but assured them they would immediately be provided with certificates, which would enable them to have the bodies at once removed, if they were not content that they should be buried there. Arrangements have been, in fact made, for some of the bodies partially embalmed in some fashion and enclosed in leaden shells to the United States.[270]

In attendance was the London manager for the Atlantic Transport Line company, Mr Alfred Strover Williams. He gave evidence as to the state of the ship as being, "in the finest condition". He made mention of the ship's maiden voyage (as the *Cleopatra*) and of problems with the ship's boilers, leading to a temporary withdrawal from service. He described the necessary repair to the ship's machinery and taking several weeks before re-

---

[267] At a meeting of the Institute of Journalists, held on Monday, 16th January, 1899, at the Stationers' Hall, Ludgate-hill, the following resolution was made: 'Arising out the delay which occurred when the *Mohegan* was wrecked off the Cornish coast, it was resolved that a letter should be addressed to the Postmaster-General with a view to securing the provision of improved telegraph facilities in out of way districts.'—*Daily News;* January 16th 1899. The arrival for the electric telegraph at Arwenack, Falmouth, was in the year 1857.

[268] The school hall [built in 1876] was commandeered for the inquest. The local school children were given impromptu leave, for its duration. It is still in use as the local primary school to this day.

[269] Mr John Coad—UK census 1901: a farmer and auctioneer (employer) / aged 60 years / resident at Treleague, St. Keverene.

[270] *The Royal Cornwall Gazette Falmouth Packet, Cornish Weekly News, & General Advertiser;* 20th October 1989.

entering service (now named as the *Mohegan*). He continued to affirm the high standing of the ship's crew, and in particular, stressing the abstemiousness of the ship's commander, Captain Richard Griffith.

When identification had, as far as possible, been completed, evidence was called. Mr Alfred Strover Williams [Witness] – 108, Fenchurch-street, London, was sworn in and asked by the Coroner to give evidence to the Court:

The Witness: I am the representative of the registered owner of the steamship *Mohegan*. Her tonnage was 4,500 net and nearly 7,700 gross. Her crew numbered 97. She had accommodation for a little over 100 passengers. She was a new vessel, this being only her second voyage. Her speed was 12 and a half to 13 knots. The captain was Richard Griffiths, who had been in our employ about 12 years. He first joined as second mate, but had been seven years master, and was now senior captain and commodore. He was on the vessel during her first voyage, and had travelled to Hull to fit her out prior to her completion.

The Coroner: Did she prove satisfactory during her first voyage?

The Witness: No we had some trouble with her boilers. We therefore allowed her to miss a trip, and during the six weeks interval we had everything perfectly adjusted in London.

The Coroner: When did she leave London?

The Witness: She left the Royal Albert Dock at noon on Thursday [October 13th], and took 53 passengers on board at Gravesend.

The Coroner: She had her full complement of crew?

The Witness: Yes, she had the 97 men, but besides that had six cattlemen on board.

The Coroner: Had she not a stowaway

The Witness: Yes, one but he has been included in the crew. The total number on board was therefore 156.

The Coroner: Do you produce any list of the passengers and crew?

The Witness: Yes, it has not yet come from London.

The Coroner: You know nothing about her after she left London?

The Witness: I know that everything went right as far as Prawle Point, because the captain at 2.50 p.m. signalled there, "All well".

The Coroner: I shall leave questions of navigation until the arrival of the nautical assessor but you may possibly desire to give to the jury your opinion of the officers. Take the captain.

The Witness: Captain Griffiths was in the prime of life, about 42 years of age [actually, 46 years] and a perfectly sober man. I know that because I have made a voyage with him and noticed that he was very abstemious. He was a man of good nerve, a strict disciplinarian, and altogether a most capable commander. He was, indeed, our commodore; always took command of a new boat as the biggest and best.

The Coroner: What about the other officers?

The Witness: The first officer was named Llewellyn Couch. He was about 30 years of age.

The Coroner: Had you every confidence in him?

The Witness: Yes; he was a splendid man, who had been in our employment eight years.

The Coroner: Then the second officer?

The Witness: His name was Ernest Cole, who had been with us a comparatively short time. Of him I have little personal acquaintance. Hindmarsh was the third, and Browning the fourth officer.

The Coroner: In all those officers you had the utmost confidence?

The Witness: Yes; they were first-class men.

The Coroner: Would anybody like to ask any questions?

A Juror: Was the captain in good health?

The Witness: I saw him just before starting and he seemed perfectly well.

A Juror: Is it not a fact that the captain was lying down on a couch most of the first day?

The Witness: I should be extremely surprised to hear that. The ship's doctor is one of the survivors he could tell you.

A Juror: I had this from a lady passenger.

The Witness: How could she tell? Was she in his room?

The Juror: She says she knows.

The Witness: Unfortunately there is no officer living to tell the tale, but we know they did all they could along with the crew to get out the boats and save the passengers.

Mr. Richard Kelly [a passenger]: There was not an officer on deck when the crew were trying to get out the boats. The only officers I saw were the officer on the bridge and the captain, who had gone up to join him there.

The Witness: That is only negative evidence. I can bring positive evidence that the officers were all on deck aiding to get out the boats.

The Coroner [to Mr Kelly]: You will have an opportunity of giving evidence afterwards.

The Vicar of St. Keverne: Was the vessel well loaded?

The Witness: It had about 1,500 tons of general cargo and about two or three thousand tons of water ballast. We have only to provide for a small cargo going over the Atlantic. She was in splendid running order.

The Vicar of St. Keverne: What about the compasses.

The Witness: After we completed the overhaul I spoke of, we had a trial run out for a day and a night[271] and the compasses were adjusted by a professional adjuster, and any error noted on the card for guidance in steering. I should be delighted to produce this professional adjuster.

The Vicar of St. Keverne: The quartermaster, who was on duty till 6 o'clock, has been saved; he [Frederick Butt] can be asked.

The Witness: We are getting on ground a little difficult now. Had we not better wait for the nautical assessor?

The Vicar of St. Keverne: The coastguard says that when the ship struck the electric lights went out, and there was not a single light to show the locality of the vessel. Would an oil lamp at the masthead not have been of assistance to the lifeboats?

The Witness: Quite possibly. The vessel was fitted out in accordance with the regulations of the Board of Trade.

A Juror: How do you account for the disaster?

The Witness: To me it is inexplicable.

The Juror: They only launched four [*sic*] boats. Was the vessel in proper trim in case of accident?

The Witness: Unfortunately when the vessel struck she took a strong list to one side. That would hinder the getting out of the boats but they got out four in 20 minutes. The officers and crew are told off to the boats at boat drill.

Mr. Richard Kelly: The boats were not slung out on the davits as I have always seen them in other steamers in the Channel. These boats were all sticking in the chocks, and not one was fit to launch. They had to be lifted out of the chocks.

The Witness: Our rule is to have one boat on each side lifted out of the chocks and swung out on the davits.

The Vicar of St. Keverne: I have been told there was great difficulty in getting the boats out in consequence of a rail that hampered the work.

---

[271] It suggests that the compasses were being adjusted while the dynamos were running and feeding the electrical system, at nighttime.

The Witness: It was possible the rail may have hampered the work a bit, but if the rail you allude to were not there children would be very apt to be lost overboard. The rail is also placed there as a protection to the crew.

Mr. Richard Kelly: The men could not get boats over the rail

The Coroner: These things had better be left to the Board of Trade.

The Witness: It may be from what some of the crew have said that it did hinder the launching.

A Juror: We also hear that the new ropes would not run through the blocks. How long was it before the boats were got out?

The Coroner: You must not ask Mr. Williams that; he was not there.

The Juror: I had it from a lady passenger that the crew worked heroically, but that they could not move the boats for a long time.

The Witness: You will have evidence that the vessel went down in 20 minutes, and four boats were got out. That is not bad work.

Mr. Richard Kelly: Aye, but the real question is, were your boats hung out on their davits in the way they ought to have been?

The Coroner: We must adjourn this inquiry, and these questions will all be fully gone into under competent guidance.

The Coroner, now informed of the Board of Trade's intention to hold an inquiry, had decided not to resume the inquest until after the inquiry had completed its course. The Board's authority stated that they would be happy to grant the Coroner the assistance of a nautical assessor, for the purpose of his inquest. The inquest was accordingly adjourned for a week and the witnesses bound over.

Speak as you find.

It is clear from the above transcript, that the inquest was a prickly affair. Understandably, feelings were running high and Mr Kelly, a witness to the disaster, was not backward in coming forward. He raised some pertinent points, and yet the Coroner was clearly anxious to bring the inquest to a close, rather than pursue the matter to any conclusion.

Having adjourned the inquest, in order that an expert witness could be secured from the Board of Trade, this prompted Mr Kelly to complain that, "up to this point, only members of the crew had been summoned to give evidence." The Coroner replied that he would be happy to hear experience of the passengers. When Mr Kelly suggested that the Coroner should hear that evidence now, the Coroner ruled this as, "out of the question". The Coroner must have realised, that the passengers would most probably be returning to their homes and not attending at St. Keverne, at some unspecified time in the future.

Between a rock and a hard place.

The parish authorities —and not least, the villagers—were anxious at the increasing number of bodies that now occupied a corner of their church. The sexton was told to instruct grave diggers to prepare a grave, in the St. Keverne churchyard. The plan did not go well:

After the inquest it was intended to bury some of the dead and many persons waited to see the sad ceremony, but at the spot where the graves were begun rock was encountered at too little depth, and the design had to be abandoned. Many of the sailors to whom reference had been made, and many other persons whose duties of various kinds had them taken to this remote village, had then another road journey and 20 miles to make in vehicles of all kinds to get back to Falmouth. The weather throughout was wretched, rain falling in torrents. The roads were exceedingly heavy.[272]

There was a suggestion of foul play; whether true or not, is now unlikely ever to be established. The affair of Capt. Griffith having colluded in the 'accident' for financial gain and that he had survived and had made a speedy exit from Porthoustock beach, on alighting from the lifeboat *Charlotte*, further angered the fraught passengers and the families of the deceased. Some attendees at the inquest were in a foreign country; some having lost members of their own family, or friends; suffering the deprivations of an arduous journey from Falmouth; having lost all their possessions and suffering from severe shock; little wonder that the atmosphere in the St. Keverne Church was, to say the least, tense.

It would be interesting to know how Mr A. S. Williams, the company representative, was received. His role was to represent the interests of his company, and would have strived to put the best possible spin on things. There were some wealthy passengers on board the *Mohegan*, and the company would be facing protracted legal claims on several fronts. Mr Williams would have been anxious in dispelling any suggestion that his company, the ship, or its crew, were in any way deficient. He was most indignant, at the accusations levelled at Capt. Griffith.

The performance of the ship is well documented, and showed a long list of faults and untoward events, in its short history, leading up to the disaster. He also pointed out the general policy was that a crew had constant boat practice: not, however, borne out by the evidence given by some passengers for this trip. His statement was possibly true, for *other* vessels, and at *other* times. In truth, it is likely that no lifeboat practice was carried out on the *Mohegan*. Some passengers also noted that during the desperate situation, the launching of the lifeboats was made more difficult by the new and unworked ropes being too stiff and the blocks in not running smoothly. The launching was further complicated by the installation of double-rails, installed at the insistence of Capt. Griffith, to prevent panicking passengers from uncontrolled access. A missed opportunity as it happened, as a lifeboat trial would have alerted the crew to a difficulty in launching the boats.

Mr Williams had been assigned a challenging task, in persuading everyone that the ship and his company were of the highest standard expected of British maritime practice. He had no other option than in offering unwavering support for the brave Capt. Griffith and his officers; as this was, in effect, the only means of shoring-up the company's reputation, before the official Board of Trade inquiry had completed its business.

Capt. Griffith was an old hand at the transatlantic run, having made many such previous trips, as commander on ships of the line. It is almost inconceivable that he would not have noted how close his ship was to the coast. And yet he failed to navigate his vessel with the necessary skill and with absolute regard for

---

[272] *Nottinghamshire Guardian* (London, England); Saturday, 22nd October 1898.

the wellbeing of his crew and passengers. Following, a minor adjustment in to the ship's heading, carried out on passing the Eddystone Lighthouse, the ship commenced on its catastrophic course. What was in his mind? If only a member of the officer crew had survived, what evidence would *then* have emerged for public scrutiny?

The irrefutable facts are that: Capt. Griffiths was the senior officer, with the final word in all things nautical; he was responsible for the safety of his crew and passengers; that the *Mohegan* had signalled to Prawle Point (an unplanned and unnecessary diversion); and that the ship was set on the wrong heading, and so having placed the vessel on its calamitous course.

In support of Capt. Griffith and his crew, Mr N. A. Cross, the superintending officer for the Atlantic Transport Line, swiftly set sail for the UK from New York, on the *SS St. Paul*, to represent the company and to give evidence at the Board of Trade inquiry. However, his first action was to find out what had happened to his eldest son, Arthur Cross,[273] who was a junior engineer on the *Mohegan*. Interestingly, Mr Cross (senior) had previously made sixty-eight trips as chief engineer, under Capt. Griffith,[274] on the *SS Manitoba*.[275]

Religion gives a dignity to distress.

In what was described as a "great funeral," took place at the St. Keverne Church, on the following Wednesday, October 19th, where over 40 victims were interred, with 36 of the dead buried in a mass grave.[276]

The Vicar, the Rev. Canon Diggens, assisted by the Rev. Dr Eajar of Manaccan and the Rev. F. R. Sell, read the service. As each coffin was committed to the huge grave, the clergy intoned their eulogies. Loving hands had made wreaths for every coffin (with flowers supplied from Lanarth) [277] and lifeboat men and survivors were the coffin bearers. The following Sunday, memorial services were conducted by the Archdeacon Cornish (afterwards Bishop of St. Germans) and Canon Diggens.

A memorial stone was to be erected at the mass grave site, enabled by public subscription, and its installation was much anticipated:

[273] Regrettably for Mr Arthur Cross, his son did not survive the disaster.

[274] An article in the *New York Times* records that: "Letters to her captain published with the official record of the of Trade's inquiry into the loss of *the Mohegan* indicate that in September 1894 and February 1895 *SS Manitoba* was commanded by Richard Griffiths, the commodore of the line, who lost his life in the *Mohegan* disaster in 1898. Five men were killed when a case of safety cartridges they were unloading from *Manitoba* exploded at the Royal Albert Docks on July 6th, 1898".

[275] *SS Manitoba*: Tonnage: 5,670, Length: 445', Beam: 49.2', Builder: Harland & Wolff, Belfast, Launch Date: January 7, 1892, Maiden Voyage: April 15, 1892, Destruction: Scrapped 1926, AKA: Logan, Candler, Operated by ATL: 1892 – 1924. Notes: One funnel, four masts. Twin screws, triple expansion engines by builder with cylinders of 22 1/2", 36 1/2" and 60", stroke 48", 611 n.h.p. Steam pressure 175 lbs, speed 13 knots. Accommodation was available for 80 first class passengers.

[276] Its dimensions were: 13 feet by 19 feet, and 10 feet deep (4m x 5.8m x 3m). In addition, eight unknown persons were buried at St. Keverne, five of whom were definitely crew members. The unknown crew members were buried on the 29th October and the 1st November. The remaining unknown persons were buried on the 5th, 9th, and the 11th, of November. Of the crew members who lost their lives, twenty-eight were never recovered from the sea.

[277] A hamlet, situated near to the village of St. Keverne.

The memorial-stone for the grave containing the "Mohegan" victims will be erected in the course of a few days. It has been designed by the well-known architect, Mr, Edmund Sedding.[278] of Plymouth. There is naturally much curiosity as to the design of the monument for which the public so generously contributed.[279]

Eventually, a granite monolith, in the form of a traditional Cornish cross, was unveiled and with the simple epitaph that marks this communal grave.[280]

M O H E G A N

A single word is all that is needed to record this terrible tragedy, still resonant after all these years. There will never be a time when somebody, in the future, looks at this marker that bears silent testimony to the disaster and asks, "What is the *Mohegan*?"

Many hands make light work.

The weekend, following the disaster, saw an unprecedented flurry of activity for the villagers for anyone with a useful skill. From the quarryman with a shovel; to an old woman who would care for the injured and give temporary shelter; to a farmer who loaned his cart to transport human cargo, disgorged by the sea; children told to search the shoreline for victims of the wreck; all volunteering to help. This concentration of local activity would help heal, not only the suffering of the survivors, but their own kinsfolk, so brutally confronted with this horror, washed up on their own shoreline.

Following the adjournment of the Coroner's inquest, a letter appeared in the press. It criticised the Coroner for ignoring the requests of passengers present, to be able to give evidence, before leaving the area. On the part of the Coroner, it seemed an omission, in his not taking advantage of this offer, which, on the face of it appears entirely reasonable. However, a thinly-veiled accusation that the crew members may well be not so forthcoming in giving evidence, because of their allegiance to the shipping company, did cause some misgivings. A local newspaper took up this point:

> It is much to be regretted that the Coroner refused to take the depositions of Mr. Kelly and other surviving passengers who were ready, and offered to give evidence before the adjournment of the inquest. The ends of justice may be defeated, and the impartiality of the inquiry destroyed, by depriving the passengers of this opportunity of giving their independent testimony about the facts that occurred, and by only accepting the evidence of the crew—the paid servants of the company.

---

[278] Edmund Harold Sedding (1863 – 1921), son of Edmund Sedding (1836 – 1868) was an architect active in the late 19th and early 20th centuries. He was articled to his uncle, John Dando Sedding (1838 – 1891) and inherited the practice on his uncle's death. He was involved in some design aspects of St. Paul's Cathedral, Dunedin, New Zealand. Perhaps as a result of their paths having crossed over the cathedral project in Dunedin, Sedding was recommended by Canon Diggens for the design of the *Mohegan*'s memorial cross.

[279] *The Royal Cornwall Gazette Falmouth Packet, Cornish Weekly News, & General Advertiser*; Thursday, 24th August 1899.

[280] This memorial cross was erected by donations, for the most part from St. Keverne, and the surrounding neighbourhood, and is set in the churchyard of St. Keverne Church, whose spire was re-built in 1770 to act as a seamark to prevent such calamities.

The attendance of members of the crew at the adjourned inquest is compulsory, that of the passengers is optional, and their expenses are not paid. In the case of a national disaster such as this, justice and humanity alike demand that the inquiry should not be one-sided only, but as searching and exhaustive as possible, and that the Coroner should be compelled, at the commencement of the inquest, to take the depositions of surviving passengers, who are unable to be present as witnesses after the adjournment.

Your obedient servant.

W. Arnold Burgess.[281]

It is surprising that he did not pursue the matter. Perhaps the Coroner was overwhelmed by the event, and was anxious to bring this inquest to a close—mindful that the Board of Trade inquiry was imminent, and that that forum would likely provide a definitive judgment. Thus may have been the argument in persuading himself to adjourn the inquest. Nonetheless, there is a nagging suspicion that, not only was valuable local evidence now being lost by the imposed delay, but also that some pressure was being applied from either a political or commercial direction. Perhaps Mr Carlyon was mindful that uncorroborated evidence or hearsay, made public in his court, could have compromised the forthcoming Board of Trade inquiry. In this context, evidence should perhaps have been taken *in-camera,* or by formal deposition. However, that was not to be. Whatever was in the mind of the Coroner, the proceedings came to an abrupt halt, at that point.

Too little: too late.

A report of the outcome of the inquest appeared in a New York newspaper, in which further criticism of the Coroner was made, as to his conduct. It is rather more outspoken than the more usual and circumspect British newspaper view of such events:

> The British Coroner of the present day shows no improvement over the Coroner of SHAKESPEARE'S time, if we may judge at all from the conduct of the magistrate [coroner] who is presiding at Falmouth [*sic*] over the inquest on the bodies of the dead passengers and crew of the wrecked steamship *Mohegan* of the Atlantic Transport line. In the course of the proceedings before that officer on Monday it became evident that the passengers in attendance entertained very different views in regard to the condition of the steamer and the conduct of the officers at the time of the disaster from those presented by the members of the crew who had been summoned to testify. The London manager of the line was present and insisted that everything about the ship was all right and that the officers did all they could under the circumstances. Some of the jurymen, however, had evidently received intimations to the contrary, for one of the jurors asked whether it was not a fact that the Captain was so ill when he started on the voyage that he was obliged to remain lying on a couch throughout most of the first day, and Mr. Richard Kelly, a passenger, declared that on the deck while the crew were trying to get out the boats there was not an officer [in command].
>
> But the coroner did not take testimony of the passengers present ready and anxious to testify. He adjourned the inquest for a week so that a nautical expert representing the Board of Trade might attend as witness. "Mr. Kelly

[281] *The Royal Cornwall Gazette Falmouth Packet, Cornish Weekly News, & General Advertiser*; Thursday, 17th November 1898.

complained that only members of the crew had been summoned to testify," says the cable dispatch. "The Coroner replied that he would be glad to hear the experiences of the passengers. In response Mr. Kelly with others protested inability to remain for an adjourned hearing a week later, offering to testify immediately. The Coroner declared that this was out of the question". [282]

By his refusal to hear the story of the passengers at once the Coroner belied his professed willingness to listen to their side of the case. In other words, he deliberately pursued a course which he knew would prevent them from testifying at all. The *Mohegan* inquest is not any more creditable to British justice than the *Mohegan* wreck is to British seamanship. We are surprised at both.[283]

The event *did* affect the Coroner, Mr E. Laurence Carlyon, as he recalled many years later:

He said he had had many unpleasant experiences but none more distressing than that in connection with the wreck of the *Mohegan* on the Manacle Rocks, involving a heavy loss of life. The sight of about 100 bodies laid out in rows in the belfry of St. Keverne Church and an equal number of coffins piled up in the church, was one never to be forgotten.[284]

When he retired from his coronership, he gave the same local newspaper an interesting account of his professional life:

At the time of his appointment the custom was to hold inquests on licensed premises and many of the jurymen used to spend their "bob"[285] before they left. In those days the inquest was a notable event in a village. It was a common occurrence to find that practically half of the jurymen and witnesses could not write, and were what was known as "marksmen".[286] The position of foreman of the jury was generally allotted to the same person, every town having its favourite foreman.

Many changes took place during his occupancy of the coronership. There used to be few mortuaries, and those that did exist were a perfect disgrace, being poorly lighted, with no water supply or towels and other necessary things. Mr. Carlyon was determined to alter this state of affairs and by degrees, with the help of juries. This was remedied after repeated representations had been made to local authorities. Frequently it was necessary to conduct post-mortem examinations in the homes of dead persons. This was a disagreeable experience, and it was no wonder that coroners were reluntant to order post-mortem examinations in those circumstances if it could be possibly avoided.[287]

Within a few weeks, a majority of victims were by now interred in the mass grave, in the St. Keverne churchyard; however, more bodies were expected as they rose to the surface from their former entrapment, and demanding a final resting place:

[282] It is most likely that this criticism never reached the ear of a British audience and in particular the Coroner, Mr E. Laurence Carlyon, as no reference to it has been found in researching the UK newspaper records covering the event.

[283] *The Sun* (New York); October 19th 1898.

[284] *West Briton;* Tuesday, 18th January 1940.

[285] "Bob" was an informal term used to describe a shilling piece – twelve pence in the pre-decimalisation coinage.

[286] The term "marksmen" most likely refer to those illiterates using their mark (**X**) as their signature.

[287] *West Briton;* Tuesday, 18th January 1940.

The great grave close to the church is not yet completely filled in, a small pit being reserved for further use if required. Altogether 50 bodies have been brought on shore in the parish of St. Keverne of which six are registered as unknown. The *Mohegan* carried 104 officers and crew and 53 passengers, of whom 66 of the former and 40 of the latter were drowned. The schoolmaster (Mr. R. M. Clayton) has received from the Atlantic Transport Company a large watercolour painting of the *Mohegan*, attended by a tug, evidently in some part of the Thames.[288] It is a fine representation of the majestic liner, and an inscription records that the picture was presented by the company, "in grateful recognition of kind services rendered to the lost and saved". The company have also offered to pay for a large photograph of the submerged vessel, as she appeared shortly after the wreck, to accompany the picture on the walls of the village school.[289]

A commencement of the Board of Trade inquiry was heralded, thus:

The Merchant Shipping Act, 1894—In the matter of a formal investigation held at the Guildhall, Westminster, on the 10th, 11th, 24th and 25th and at the Town Hall, Westminster, on the 12th and 26th days of November, 1898, before R. H. R. Marsham Esq., assisted by Captain RONALDSON, Mr. HALLETT C.E., and Captain DYER R.N. into the circumstances attending the stranding and total loss of the British *SS* "MOHEGAN" on the Manacle Rocks near the Lizard on the 14th October last, whereby loss of life ensued.[290]

Now, the full story will emerge. Perhaps!

---

[288] This painting now hangs the the Roskilly's tea-room in the Tregellast Barton Farm, St Keverne.

[289] *The Royal Cornwall Gazette Falmouth Packet, Cornish Weekly News, & General Advertiser*; Wednesday 29 December 1898. For the percentages distribution of deaths between the officers and crew: see Table 17, p. 412/413; *Mohegan* Survival for Crew by Class.

[290] See http://atlantictransportline.us/content/PDFfiles/24BOTreport.pdf

CHAPTER 11

The Board of Trade Inquiry for the Steamship *Mohegan*

When the ship has sunk everyone knows how she might have been saved.

The Board of Trade inquiry was witness to a sobering account of the fateful moment at which the *Mohegan* struck the Manacles. It is worthy of inclusion here, as it conveys the story of the ship's progress down the Channel, and with the events immediately leading up to the disaster.

The inquiry into the circumstances of the wreck of the steamship *Mohegan* on the Cornish Coast was continued yesterday at the Guildhall, Westminster [11th November], by Mr. Mayham, Stipendiary Magistrate; Captain Dwyer, R.N.; Captain Ronaldson, and Mr J. H. Hallett C.E; Mr. Mansell Jones and Mr. Butler Aspinall appeared for the Board of Trade, Mr. Pike and Mr A Pritchard for the owners (Messrs. Williams, Torrey and Field), Mr. Nelson for relatives of the deceased captain [Griffith] and third officer [Hindmarsh], and Mr. C. C. Graham for the National Lifeboat Institution.

Mr Alfred Williams, one of the owners, continued his evidence. He said that of the crew of 96, 23 had been with the vessel on its first voyage, but 60 of the men had been with the line at various times in other boats. Bonuses were given for length of service. Of the total crew of 96, 38 were saved and 58 lost. Of the 53 passengers, 13 were saved and 40 lost. Of the six cattlemen, three were saved and three lost.

In reply to questions put by Mr. Pike, the witness said that there were 30 stewards amongst the crew, and of these stewards only two were saved. The company had a special insurance fund, and ran a large risk on each of their vessels. Witness was on board the *Mohegan*. Nothing had been spared in her repairs. The helmsman would steer by the Thompson compass[291] on the bridge. It was not usual to report vessels going down the Channel beyond Dover, but with a new ship the captain would be perfectly justified in reporting at Prawle Point. It was not the practice of any vessel to call into Falmouth to report. It had only been done once, and that was in a case of fire. The company issued special printed instructions for boat drill, and one of Captain Griffiths' letters showed that he was in the habit of going through this drill. The captain had an absolute clean record in respect to obedience to the company's instructions. On the fatal voyage he reported off Dover— "Everything is working satisfactory so far; the weather is fine and clear". Witness went now and again [on] a voyage with one of the ships. He had been with Captain Griffiths a voyage on the *Manitoba*. He was in good health, and there was not the slightest ground to doubt his sobriety. He was a good disciplinarian. A boat drill was undergone during that voyage. Witness had gone to the scene of the wreck, and had done everything possible for the survivors in sending them across the Atlantic by any other line they chose free of cost. The bodies recovered had either been sent to America by the company or had been buried in the neighbourhood.

Re-examined by Mr. Mansell Jones the witness said that in boat drill the boats were not lowered into the water except when the vessel was in port. While in London the vessel was so crowded by other craft that boat drill could not be carried

---

[291] This being a most sensitive form of navigational compass, the Thompson or mirror galvanometer was invented by William Thomson (Lord Kelvin) and patented by him in 1858. Instead of a compass needle, it used tiny magnets attached to a small lightweight mirror, suspended by a thread; the deflection of a beam of light greatly magnified the deflection due to small currents. Alternatively the deflection of the suspended magnets could be observed directly through a microscope.

out. As far as he was aware, there was no reason whatever for this vessel going into Falmouth Bay. In the company's instructions to captains, they were told to keep well clear of all promontories.

Captain Robinson, marine superintendent to Messrs. William, Torrey and Field, examined by Mr. Aspinall, said he was perfectly satisfied with the seaworthiness of this vessel when she started on her second voyage. He had not seen the act of hoisting, but when they were up. The falls were made of Manila.[292] It was not more apt than hemp to kink. He perfectly agreed with the high estimate expressed of the captain and the officers. He had himself engaged them, and consequently had made full investigation into their antecedents. There was no bad mark made against any one of them in the books of the company. He saw the captain on the day the vessel sailed, and bade him goodbye at the dock gate. The captain was in perfect health. As to the boat stations, general instructions were given to the captains as to setting them, but he could not say that this would be done within 24 hours of the commencement of a voyage. He had been down to see the wreck, and produced photographs which represented her position. She was heading, south by east and lay about 450 feet, from the main rock of the Manacles [Carn-du]. She had a strong list to port. He believed she had swung round, the helm being hard a starboard. He thought she must have torn her bottom out.

Examined by Mr. Pike, the witness, in company with a diver, said that he had visited the wreck. Her list to port was from 25 to 30 degrees. She lay on a pretty even keel. They got one sounding on the starboard side of 11 fathoms [66 feet/20 metres]. Pulling a few feet away, they struck and the boat filled. Consequently they had to take to the ship's rigging, and were rescued by a Trinity boat. Though it was a fine day there was a strong swirl of water in the neighbourhood of the rocks. From his experience of the list of the rigging, he was surprised that so many persons were saved out of it. So great was the list of the ship that that launching of boats would be, almost impossible, and he believed the only chance of saving life was to get the passengers into them and cut away the falls, so as to let the boats float when the vessel sank. There were no boats now on the wreck. The vessels mean draft was 20ft. 7½ in. [6 metres, approx.] laden as she was, and she had consequently a freeboard of 13ft 8½ in. [4.2 metres]. The gear of the lifeboats was effective and simple. The Board of Trade had certified it all. The vessel must have struck on a two and a-half hours' ebb tide, the wind being from the south east.

Replying to Mr. C. C. Graham, the witness said that he believed that with a strong tide and numerous rocks the place was a difficult one for lifeboats to work.

John Downing, fisherman, Durgan, near Falmouth, was called to identify a card of compass deviations he had picked up at the Helford River, about seven miles from the scene of the wreck, in a north-westerly direction. He found some other papers floating up the river. He gave them up to the coastguard officer.

Mr Chappell, compass adjuster, recognised the card as having been made out by himself, framed, and sent to the *Mohegan* to be hung up in the wheel-room. He has adjusted the compasses during the trial trip early in October. The captain assisted in the adjustment, and thoroughly informed himself of the deviations. The standard compass was on the upper bridge, so that the man at the wheel could see it. There was also a light needle compass in the wheelhouse, and he supplied a card of deviation for that also. He did not think the electric lighting system would have any effect on the compass.[293]

---

[292] Manila rope is made from Manila hemp, which is a type of fibre obtained from the leaves of the abacá. It is very durable, flexible and resistant to salt water damage, allowing its use in rope, hawsers, ships' lines, and fishing nets. Manila rope shrinks when it becomes wet. Since shrinkage is more pronounced the first time the rope becomes wet, new rope is usually immersed into water and put to dry before use so that the shrinkage is less than it would be if the rope had never been wet. A major disadvantage in this shrinkage is that many knots made with manila rope became harder and more difficult to untie when wet, thus becoming subject to increased stress.

[293] The first use of the electric light was made aboard the steamship *The City of Berlin*, November 1879 – four years after she was built. Magginis, John; *The Atlantic Ferry: Its Ships, Men, And Working* (London, UK: Whitaker & Co.1893), 47.

Examined by Mr. Nelson, the witness said that he adjusted the wheelhouse compass as carefully as the standard compass.

Examined by Mr. Mansell Jones, the witness said that if the helmsman was steering by the wheelhouse compass a west by north course, the true course would be west three-quarters north. If he was steering by the standard compass west by north he would be steering west by north magnetic.

Captain Robinson,[294] recalled, described the ship's lifeboats. They were steel with air tanks and were as efficient as and easily handled as wooden boats. A steel boat would bend, whereas wood would break with a heavy blow.

In answer to Captain Dwyer, the witness said that they had always found the disengaging apparatus fitted on the *Mohegan* worked well.

A former shipbuilding witness said, in answer to the Court, that the steel boats compared with wooden boats cost about 20 per cent more and weighed about 10 per cent more.

Joseph Barfield, retired quartermaster of the Royal Navy, and now signalman at Rame Head, said the *Mohegan* passed about 3.40 in the afternoon of the 14th October. He thought that she passed two miles outside, or inside, the Eddystone. As she proceeded westward he thought she was much nearer the land than was usual.[295] She was not out so far in the Channel as was usual with big liners. His signal station was nine or ten miles from the Eddystone. When he first saw the vessel to the south-east the weather was clear, but when he last saw her, about five o'clock, it was getting thick, and she seemed to be going 11 or 12 knots speed. In answer to Mr. Nelson: the witness said it was a dirty afternoon, with squalls from the south-east and east-south-east. It was getting dark when he lost sight of her. The Eddystone light was then burning. When the *Mohegan* passed Prawle Point she had good offing and appeared steering the usual course. The weather report of the Eddystone Lighthouse keepers on the 14th October was read. It was that there was a moderate gale, E.S.E.

Richard Wilson, assistant keeper to St. Anthony Lighthouse,[296] Falmouth, said that on the evening of the 14th October a moderate gale was blowing from six o'clock. It was very clear and lights were visible as far as it was possible to see them at any time. He saw nothing of this vessel. There was a fog bell at the lighthouse. It was not sounded at all that night. It would have been their duty to have sounded it if the weather had been thick.

Alfred Lewis, lighthouse keeper at the Lizard, said that this was the official report of the weather there for the night of the 14th October—"Very dark and cloudy – Vessels' lights seen bright and clear at a distance of five or six miles – Fresh breeze, varying from E.S.E. to E".

Cross examined—he believed the wind rose to a moderate gale after nine o'clock.

Mr. Fooks, Collector of Customs, Falmouth, said the mortar was fired to summon the crew of the lifeboat there at 25 minutes to 10 on the night of the 14th October. About 45 minutes elapsed before the boat was got away. Some of the delay was due to the bad position of the boathouse and the low tide. About six o'clock witness was walking with his daughter near Pendennis Point.[297] He saw a bright masthead light of a steamer about four of five miles off, and a bunch of

---

[294] Captain Robert M. Robinson, marine superintendent to Messrs. Williams, Torrey and Field, the Company's London agents.

[295] He could not have been watching the *Mohegan* continuously. Otherwise he would have noted her passage either in front of, or behind the Eddystone Light. Later, during cross-examination, he did mention that his attention was drawn elsewhere, during this period.

[296] St. Anthony's Lighthouse is located on St Anthony Head on the eastern coast of the entrance to the harbour of Falmouth, Cornwall. St. Anthony's Lighthouse was designed by James Walker and built by two Cornish brothers, Jacob & Thomas Olver for Trinity House, between the years 1834–35. The light originally came from eight Argand oil lamps. The light source was changed to pressure vapour and later to electricity when electricity was connected in 1954. Today the light is automated, flashing every 15 seconds, with a red sector for The Manacle Rocks and a range of 22 miles. The lighthouse once had the largest bell in Cornwall, hung outside the structure, until it was replaced by a fog horn in 1954. When the fog bell was dismantled in 1954 which hung from the gallery at the front of the tower it was donated to a local church but, after many years of sitting on the church front lawn it was taken away to be melted down; *The InfoRapid Knowledge Portal – The Manacles*.

[297] Pendennis Point is situated on the western arm of the entrance to Falmouth. It rises 233 feet above high water and has the most spectacular panoramic view across Falmouth Bay, from St. Anthony's Lighthouse to the east, towards the Lizard to the west, and including the *Manacles*, at six

lights, as if on deck, below. The vessel seemed to be at first making towards Falmouth Harbour, then across the bay westward and next as if it was going in the direction of the Helford River. He was much puzzled by all this. Then she seemed to steer away and take a southerly course towards the Manacles. It was a sharp, clear night, though overcast. He went home when he thought the vessel had cleared the Manacles. Afterwards, when he heard the mortar, he feared the vessel he had seen had gone ashore. The lifeboat had not to wait for a tug. A tug had to wait for the lifeboat, and then towed it out to the wreck.

By Mr. Pike—Have you any nautical experience?—No.

Perhaps you will be able to tell us this – did this vessel appear to be trying to get out of a difficulty she had suddenly found herself in?—It struck me that was so.

Does that sometimes happen in this bay?—I believe it does.

And the coastguard warned them when they see them?—Yes, I believe they have done so on many occasions.

Mrs. Compton Swift said she left London on the 13th October in the *Mohegan*. She had made six trips before. On this evening the electric lights went out half an hour after they were lit. A candle was then given to her. On the following night she remarked that they were a long time near the land compared with her former experience. They were very close to land. When twilight came on, just before going below, she remarked about the nearness of the shore lights. She was just taking a chair at the dining table when the crash came. She and her physician, Dr. Fallows, went on deck, when they heard the cry of "The lifeboats". Just as they got up the electric lights went out. They went to the port [side].

James Hill, boatswain of the Porthoustock lifeboat, said he saw the *Mohegan* come into Falmouth Bay and approach within a quarter of a mile of the shore before she altered her course outwards. As she turned her cabin windows were sideways on to him, [lit up] like a street in London. When she turned he feared she would strike on the Manacles, and as he saw her stop he went and summoned his crew, as he believed she would become a total wreck. There were not enough fishermen at Porthoustock to man the lifeboats. They had, therefore, a mixed crew, some of whom had to come from St. Keverne, a mile off. The boat was launched without delay, and they did their best in the saving of life. The Manacle Rocks were very hard and jagged rocks.

The Court then adjourned until today.[298]

The darkest hour is just before the dawn

A terrifying time for sixteen persons, who had to endure their clinging to the ship's rigging all night, before being saved by the *Charlotte* lifeboat, at first light. The bravery of a member of the *Mohegan*'s crew, quartermaster Juddery, was relayed to the assembled judiciary at the Board of Trade inquiry, on Thursday, Nov 24th 1898. The evidence was heard in complete silence, in the austere surroundings of the Westminster Guildhall, as the chilling events were recounted:

THE LOSS OF THE MOHEGAN.

INQUIRY RESUMED

LIGHT STILL WANTED ON THE DISASTER.

miles. distance.. Mr Fooks' statement gives further evidence that the weather was clear, leading up to the encounter with the Manacles. The distance from Pendennis Point to the Helford River is about 4 miles.

[298] *Glasgow Herald* (Glasgow, Scotland); Saturday, 12th November 1898.

Yesterday morning at Westminster Guildhall, the official inquiry into the circumstances attending the loss of the steamship *Mohegan* was resumed from November 12th.

A BRAVE QUARTERMASTER'S STORY

Mr. J. W. Juddery, a quartermaster of the *Mohegan*, said he had a certificate as chief mate. The vessel was in every respect in a proper condition to go to sea. Witness steered by the standard compass on the upper bridge. The ship steered well. He took the wheel between the Isle of Wight and Portland, and his course was W. three-quarters N. until noon,[299] when he went below, giving the same course to the man who succeeded him. When the wheel was changed, an officer stood by to hear the course given. At four o'clock, he came on deck again, but did not take the wheel. He had an order to check the log, and later he checked it again. The captain called one of the officers on the bridge, and they spoke about the log. Witness judged that the Eddystone was passed at a distance of three miles or a little over. He went below at six o'clock. The wind was south-east, at half a gale, and there was a high sea. At half-past six he was on deck for a short time. The second and third officers [Cole and Hindmarsh] were on the watch, and a man named [William] Daniels was in the crow's nest. Land was on the starboard. The weather was threatening, with rain showers. He went below, and was in the quartermaster's berth when the vessel struck. The side lights were lighted by electricity; the oil-lamps were in the lamp room, trimmed, not lighted, but ready for fixing and could have been fixed in a couple of minutes. He went on the saloon deck when the ship struck, but it was too dark then to see whether the captain was on the bridge; shortly afterwards he heard him giving orders to clear away the boats. At that time the crew had not had boat stations allotted. Witness went to the first lifeboat on the starboard side, but the men could not push the boat put on account of a heavy list to port, which was increasing— practically, it was pushing the boat uphill. He saw all the officers at the boats. He went to the port side, on the call of the fourth officer. The electric lights were then out. He heard no order given to light the oil lamps, but it could not have been practicable, as the ship was going down by the head, and the lamp room was under water. He assisted to get one port boat out. The captain was urging the men on, and he said the women and children were to be put first in the boats. The angle of the deck was quite 45 degrees. Witness went back to the starboard boat, but women and children got in, and the weight was too great for the men to push the boat out. Some of the people got out of the boat, and this happened several times. Then the falls were cut and the passengers got into the boats, as they were, ready to float off when the ship sank. The boats were on the chocks, not swung out, all the way down the Channel. Had the boats been swung out the passengers must have jumped for them, and they were better off with the boats on the chocks. Witness had seen the stewards serving out life-belts. There was nothing like a panic, not even among the passengers; everybody was cool—much cooler than he should have expected. The list of the ship was constantly increasing, and witness had to crawl along by the rail. The captain ordered that as many women and children as possible should get into the jigger rigging. Witness went down on with the ship, but came up and got on the mizzen rigging. Before that the chief officer [Llwellyn Couch] told witness that they had done all they could, and that everyone must do their best he could do for himself. Witness agreed that everything was done that could been done. It was inside of fifteen minutes from the time of striking the vessel sank. Witness who had not a life-belt, swam from the rigging to the lifeboat in the morning, and got a line, as the lifeboat could not approach the wreck, and by this means all in the mizzen were saved. Witness had not heard any intention to put into Falmouth, though he had heard since that the company's vessels sometimes signalled at the Lizard [only in daylight].

---

[299] This is presumed to be the heading for Prawle Point, where the *Mohegan* would signal 'All's well' to the Lloyds station there.

Mr. F. Butt, quartermaster on board the *Mohegan*, whose left hand was in a sling, said he relieved Blake at four o'clock, and received the course from him, west by north, the officer of the watch standing by and hearing the course given. About a quarter past four they passed the Eddystone, three or five miles off, and continued the same course until six o'clock, when Quartermaster August relieved witness, who gave him the course west by north. Witness then went below. At that time land was visible on the starboard. When the ship struck he went on deck, where there was a rush of passengers. The Chief Officer told them to keep cool. The witness described, like the other witnesses, the attempt to get the boats out, and he appeared to have done his best to assist passengers. He was, he said, stretched on the deck by something falling on his head, and was washed aft by the sea before he recovered himself. He got into a boat which was full of people, and seeing it was swamping he swam off to the mizzen rigging. A woman called out, "Save me," and he saw her below him, and he went down and held her in his arm. It was Mrs. Piggott, the second stewardess. While on deck his finger was crushed by a boat : he afterwards found the finger hanging by a piece of flesh, but he did not feel it at the time the accident happened. Discipline was well preserved throughout.

EVIDENCE OF SEAMEN

Geo. Wood, a seaman serving on the *Mohegan,* said he was on deck at six o'clock, and then ten minutes or a quarter of an hour later, he heard two bells from the crow's nest. He then saw a bright light about three miles off on the starboard bow.[300] It was a fixed light, and he took it to be a shore light. When the ship struck he went on to the boat deck, and, with others, got a starboard boat out, the cutter, with people in her, but she capsized. Witness was on the mizzen rigging until three in the morning.

By Mr. Pyke : Everything was done that could be done to save life, both by the officers and by the crew. He could not be sure what kind of light it was that he saw. When the bell rang from the crow's nest, one of the officers called out, "All right".

William Moore, seaman, said he was the lookout from four to six o'clock. At six o'clock he went below, land then being on the starboard beam. He heard the two bells that meant, "light being on the starboard bow". The witness stated what was done with the boats, much the same as the previous witnesses, and said that he thought the ship was going to turn over he threw himself into the sea, and was carried away by the tide. When he came up he could not see the ship. He swam about and, and saw a ship's lifeboat with water in it, but no people. He got into the boat, and afterwards helped a shipmate into it, but this man could do nothing, as his collar-bone was broken, he was injured internally, and his legs were hurt. The sea washed all the loose gear out of the boat. Witness and mate got on to some rocks on the low land [Lowland]. Discipline was maintained on board after the ship struck, and there was no panic; one or two gentlemen were rather frightened, but all the ladies were very calm.

By Mr. Pyke : On the previous voyages on the company's boats, there had been boat drill. The captain was in his usual health, and after the vessel had struck he gave his orders calmly and collectedly. Witness had not a lifebelt; he found one on the deck, and gave it to a lady passenger.

Thomas Nicholls, another seaman on the *Mohegan,* said that twenty-five or twenty-six persons were in the port lifeboat which got off; four of these were seamen, and there were some firemen and stewards. Witness dived off the ship to the boat, and got into it. Another man, Whitehead, did the same. Witness and the three other seamen took the oars.

---

[300] This light was almost certainly that of the fixed St. Anthony sector-light, specifically giving warning of the Manacle Rocks. With no more than a cursory glance in that direction, it is quite possible that he missed the revolving flashing white light (every 20 seconds) while during its occulted phase, as he made no mention of that occurrence.

By Mr. Pyke : Witness and Whitehead got to the boat by order of the captain.

Another seaman named Huntley, who was in the crow's nest from half-past five to six, said that after heard the two bells from the crow's nest he looked out on the starboard and saw a red light. It looked too high for a ship's light. He threw himself into the sea, and was picked up by one of the ship's boats.

By Mr. Pyke : Witness had sailed with Capt. Griffiths for some years, and he was one of the best captains he had ever seen.

Mr. Pyke called the following witnesses:

Mr. Frank Nicklin, chief saloon steward on the *Mohegan,* said that there were thirty stewards all told. The captain was a reserved man and very particular. Witness had never seen him take a drink except once, when he poured half-a-glass of champagne into a tumbler and filled up with soda-water, Witness had never seen anything wrong with any of the officers, and he had sailed with them on previous voyages. He put lifebelts on four or five passengers. The stewards were doing their best to put lifebelts on the passengers. Witness assisted with the boats. All the people worked splendidly. Finally, witness jumped off, and was taken into the only boat that was saved.

By Mr. Marsham : Only two of the whole thirty in the stewards' department were saved [Mrs Agnes Piggott and Frank Nicklin].

Mr. W. T. Pollard, holder of an extra master's certificate, said he was third officer on the *Mohegan* on her first voyage [as the *Cleopatra*]. The officers were good disciplinarians, and temperate. On the voyage the ship passed the Eddystone distant seven miles, and the course was west half north. The officer on the bridge examined the compasses from time to time to see that the course was being kept. Unless there was an obvious danger an officer would not think of altering the course laid by the captain. Coming down the Channel it was unusual to see land after passing the Eddystone until the Lizard. On the previous voyage of the *Mohegan,* out and home, there was no boat drill, the deck hands being wanted below, owing to the engines being out of order. He had been with Captain Griffiths on other voyages, and there had always been boat drill.

By Mr. Nelson : he did not think that Captain Griffiths would have given a course west by north at four miles south of the Eddystone. Had that course been given witness, he should have drawn the captain's attention to it. Witness here examined the chart and said that if the vessel was going to Falmouth, west by north would be about right. On a clear night they would pick up the Lizard light before they lost sight of the Eddystone. On a clear course from the Eddystone to the Lizard they would not see the low light at St. Anthony's at all.

The Court here adjourned until this morning.[301]

The dead cannot cry out for justice. It is a duty of the living to do so for them.

The hearing resumed and with an eagerly awaited adjudication:

The Report of the Board of Trade Inquiry into the Loss of the *Mohegan*

(No. 5803)

"Mohegan" (SS)

[301] *Daily News* (London, England); Friday, November 25th 1898.

The Merchant Shipping Act, 1894 In the matter of a formal investigation held at the Guildhall, Westminster, on the 10th, 11th, 24th and 25th, at the Guildhall at Westminster, on the 12th and 26th days of November, 1898, before R. H. R. MARSHALL ESq., assisted by Captain RONALDSON, Mr. HALLETT C. E., and Captain DYER R.N. into the circumstances attending the stranding and total loss of the British SS "Mohegan" on the Manacle Rocks near the Lizard on the 14th October last, whereby loss of life ensued.

The Court having carefully inquired into the circumstances attending the above mentioned shipping casualty finds for the reasons stated in the Annex thereto, that the cause of the stranding of the vessel was, in their opinion, that a wrong course—W by N.—was steered after passing the Eddystone after 4.17 p.m. on the 14th of October last, and that the deplorable loss of so many lives was in consequence of the vessel taking a sudden and serious list to port, of her going down in not more than a quarter of an hour of her striking, and there being no light to indicate her position through the electric light having gone out.

Dated this 30th day of November, 1898.

We concur in the above report.

A. RONALSDON

J. H. HALLETT C.E.   Assessors.

RICH^D. C. DYER

Annex to the Report:

This inquiry was held at the Guildhall, Westminster, on the 10th and 11th November, at the Town Hall, Westminster on the 12th November, at the Guildhall, Westminster on the 24th and 25th November, and was concluded at the Town Hall, Westminster, on the 26th November, 1898.

Mr. H. R. Mansell Jones, with whom was Mr. Butler Aspinall, appeared on behalf of the Board of Trade; Mr. Pike, with whom was Mr. Arthur Pritchard, represented the owners of the "Mohegan," the Atlantic Transport Limited, and the representatives of the officers not represented by Mr. Nelson; Mr. Nelson appeared on behalf of the representatives of the master and third officer of the vessel: whilst Mr. Charles Cunningham Graham of the Royal National lifeboat Institution represented it.

The "Mohegan," late "Cleopatra," official number 109043, was a steel screw steamship, built by Messrs. Earle's Shipbuilding and Engineering Company Limited at Hull, for Messrs. Thomas Wilson & Company Limited of Hull. But before she was launched she was purchased by the Atlantic Transport Steamship Company Limited of London on the 29th July, 1898, along with some other vessels from Messrs. Wilson & Leyland with the goodwill of the New York trade; Mr. Alfred Strover Williams, of 108 Fenchurch Street, London, E.C., being the designated manager, and she was registered at the port of Hull.

Her dimensions were: length 482.4 feet; breadth 52.1 feet; depth from top of beam amidships to top of keel, 35.7 feet. She had four steel masts. She was fitted with triple expansion vertical direct acting engines built by Messrs. Earle's Shipbuilding and Engineering Company Limited; she had three cylinders of the following dimensions, 32 ins., 54 ins., and 90 ins., with a stroke of 66 in. She had four boilers, built of steel, which were loaded with working pressure of 200 lbs. per square inch; with an indicated horse power of 5,500 her speed would be 14 knots. She was lighted throughout by electricity; for this purpose she was fitted with duplicate sets of dynamos, each of which was compound wound, and were capable of an output of 300 amperes at 100 volts, the motive power being a double-acting compound engine built and supplied by Messrs. Bolliss & Company Limited, of Birmingham. Each of these dynamos was capable of lighting the whole of the ship's installation, in the event of a breakdown.

The wiring was on the latest double wire distributing box system. She was fitted with the usual steam pumps to the main engines, and also a large centrifugal circulating pump, together with an auxiliary duplex pump, and an ordinary pump of large size. These were fitted so that they could be connected to each compartment, and each compartment could be pumped out either by steam or hand.

She had two steel decks below her upper deck, which was of pine, and eight water-tight bulkheads extending from the keel to the upper-deck, only one of which was pierced, and that one was fitted with a water-tight door of an approved plan.

On the upper-deck she had a Shed or deck for cattle, above this deck was an enclosed bridge extending the whole length of the engine and boiler space, somewhat aft and forward of them. This contained the state-room and passengers accommodation. Over this bridge-deck was a large steel house containing the music room, saloon, smoking room, and state-rooms. The top was extended as a deck to the ship's side and formed the boat-deck. She had eight boats, six being lifeboats built of steel, of the aggregate capacity of 2,343, cubic feet and capable of accommodating 234 persons and wooden boats of the aggregate capacity of 472 cubic feet and capable of accommodating 59 persons. They were carried on davits fitted with falls and patent disengaging gear, inboard on chocks. She had 256 lifebelts and 2 life-buoys. She was constructed under Lloyd's special survey and was registered 100 A1.

She had three compasses on deck: Lord Kelvin's patent—on the flying bridge, by which the courses were set and steered; one on the second deck, underneath the bridge and one aft. She was steered by steam.

She had only made one voyage to New York and back. Mr. Charles Henry Wilson, M.P., of the firm of Wilson Sons & Company, of Hull, stated that his firm had entered into a contract with Messrs. Earle & Company for the building of the "Cleopatra," afterwards called the "Mohegan," and four other steamers; that she was built under special survey, and that she and the other four vessels were being built for the passenger trade between London and New York. Mr. Wilson was the chairman of the Hull firm and also of the London Company of Messrs. Furness, Wilson & Leyland. During the late war the American government purchased steamers of the Atlantic Transport Company and it was to replace these that the company purchased the five steamers that were being built. For the "Cleopatra" they paid £140,000. She was insured for £112,000 at Lloyd's and other offices, the owners taking £28,000 on her themselves.

Mr. F. H. Pearson, assistant general manager of Earle's Shipbuilding Company, put in a statement including the specification of the vessel, and stated that when she was in dock in Hull before leaving, all the boats were lowered into the water in the presence of the Board of Trade officials, and that it took employing eight men-about five minutes to lower and re-hoist them. A rail was built on the boat deck for the purpose of preventing passengers falling overboard.[302]

The steamship "Mohegan" when completed left Hull on the 29th July, 1898, for London, she was then named the "Cleopatra," that being her launching name. It is worthy of notice that this steamer left the port of Hull without ballast or cargo; she arrived at Tilbury on the 30th July at about 11.30 a.m.

On this passage, through the negligence of one of the engineers, an accident happened to one of the boilers, the engineer on watch allowing the water to become low in the port double-ended boiler but upon examination of the boiler in London nothing was found wrong, and apparently no damage was done.

Having taken her passengers and cargo, she proceeded on her maiden voyage to New York on the 31st July at 7.40 a.m. It appears that on this voyage they had considerable difficulty in feeding the boilers in consequence (as the Court was informed) of the engineers not understanding the feed pumps. She arrived in New York on the 12th August after a passage of 12 days.

---

[302] Mr Pearson, the naval architect to the builders of the steamer – Messrs. Earle and Co. – also testified that: "Any damage done to the boilers on her previous voyage [as the *Cleopatra*] had been entirely repaired before she set out on the fatal voyage in question".– *Royal Cornwall Gazette;* November 17th 1998.

Upon the owners being communicated with and the condition of the boilers being made known to them they wired instructions to their agents in New York that owing to the unsatisfactory state of the boilers no passengers were to be taken on board for the return voyage. The instructions being carried out she left New York on the 15th August, arriving in London on the 4th September, thus being 20 days coming across.

The boilers having given a deal of trouble, both from priming and leaking, during the passage, on arrival in London a survey was called, and instructions given to Messrs. Rait & Gardiner to carry out the necessary repairs.

These repairs having been effected to the satisfaction of the surveyors, on the 5th October the vessel was taken to sea for the purpose of a trial trip under full steam. She had on board on this occasion the Board of Trade surveyors, Lloyd's surveyor, the owner's representative, and others, and also Mr. Charles Chappell [303] of Messrs. Hughes & Sons,[304] of Fenchurch Street, for the purpose of adjusting the compasses while at sea and he stated that there was little or no deviation on westerly course. The Court was informed that everything having proved satisfactory the vessel returned to London. Whilst in dock all the boats were lifted for the purpose of caulking the deck underneath them. She was placed on the berth for New York and it was upon this voyage that her name was changed to "Mohegan". [305]

She left London on the 14th October under command of Mr. R. Griffiths, who was the commodore of the Atlantic Transport Company's fleet, and who had been sent by the owners to superintend the finishing of the vessel before she was launched, and had made the previous voyage in her. She had a crew of 97 men, there were seven [sic] cattlemen on board, and 53 passengers were taken on at Gravesend.

Mr. D. Mulley, a licensed Trinity House Pilot, took charge of her at 2.30 p.m. to conduct her to Dover, where he was landed at 7.55 p.m. He also stated that there was no deviation on westerly courses, and that when he left her everything appeared in good order.

She has a general cargo of 1,280 tons of bunker coal, 1,180 tons of water ballast, and the other ballast tank, which held 940 tons, was filled after leaving Dover; the total dead weight of the cargo, coals, and water being 4,450 tons. She was drawing 20ft. 8 ins. mean draught, and had a freeboard of 13 ft. 8 ins.

John William Juddery, quartermaster aboard the ill-fated vessel, who had charge of the wheel between ten and noon on the day of the disaster, spoke as to the course he steered—west, three-quarters west.

All seems to have gone well, and at 2.40 p.m. of the 14th, off Prawle Point, she signalled, "All well, report me". She was then about three miles off.

She was afterwards seen by the signalman at Rame Head, Mr. Joseph Burnfield, who stated that at that time there were passing rain showers and a moderate gale. She was abeam of Rame Head at about 3.40 p.m., less than ten miles off. He also saw her about 5 p.m. some 10 or 12 miles [to the west] from the Eddystone lighthouse. Mr. Charles Robert Snell, boatman of the coastguard station at Falmouth, stated that at about 7 p.m. he noticed a coloured light ascend, but did see any more, and he did not regard it as a signal of distress; his patrol connection at the Stack,[306] also saw the light. On the way back he saw several more coloured lights in the direction of the Manacle Rocks and when he arrived at Falmouth he reported to his chief officer; this was about 8.40 p.m. he was then ordered to the telephone station, and at 9.30 he received

---

[303] The compass deviation card was later found in the sea, following the disaster, It was signed as having been adjusted by Mr Chappell. The ink was blurred but it was still clearly discernable.

[304] The Messrs. Hughes & Sons company was founded in 1828 in London as a maker of chronographic and scientific instruments.

[305] This would appear to be an on the spur-of-the-moment decision for the name change. This would support the thesis that, no "Mohegan" bell was ever cast and that the "Cleopatra" bell is the only such bell for this vessel. Indeed, if a ship's name is changed, maritime tradition is that the original bell carrying the original name will remain with the vessel.

[306] The *Stack* – a reef situated three miles south west of Pendennis Point.

a message from the Porthoustock asking for the lifeboat and tug to be sent. He sent warning by signal to the coxswain of the lifeboat and the owner of the tug to get the crew and lifeboat ready.

Mr. Fookes, Collector of Customs and Revenue of Wreck at Falmouth, said that on the evening between 6 and 7 p.m., whilst walking towards Pendennis Point with his daughter, he noticed some lights to the southward of St. Anthony's lighthouse; upon looking carefully he noticed that one was a pilot boat light, but further away from the shore he noticed a bright light, which he took to be a steamer masthead light. It appeared to him, as he described it, a bunch of lights, one overhead and some below; the steamer looked as though she were making for Falmouth harbour. A short time afterwards he looked at her again, and then observed she was going across the harbour, as if she were making for Helford River. Passing round the bay on his way home he saw the vessel nearly the whole time, his view being obscured for a short space of time only as he passed some trees. He then noticed that the vessel had altered her course to the south, and appeared to be turning round to go up the channel. At this time he could see the masthead light and the lights aft. He stated that it passed through his mind that the vessel was going on the Manacle Rocks. At 6.50 p.m. when he last saw the steamer he remarked to his daughter' "she is going all right now," she was then about seven miles distant. He said it was a clear night for seeing lights.

Mr. James Hill, coxswain of the lifeboat at Porthoustock stated that at a little before seven he was standing by the stable-door when he saw a masthead light bearing N.E. from him and thought it was the Irish boat coming out of Falmouth harbour. She appeared to be going stem [the forward part of a boat or ship's bow] on to him and only a half-mile off. She altered her course because as he believed, she saw the shore lights. He saw that she was in danger; this was about 7 p.m. He summoned his crew, by signal as some of them lived some distance off, and at 7.25 p.m. they had the lifeboat afloat and on the way to the Manacle Rocks. The tide was about 1½ hours ebb. He burnt a white light, but received no response. Shortly after, they fell in with some wreckage which was found to be an overturned boat with two men on her bottom. These were rescued and cries were heard from beneath the boat. With considerable difficulty the boat was righted and two ladies, one of whom was Mrs. Compton Swift—who gave the Court a lucid account of her experiences—and a child who was then dead, were found and rescued.

The witness then burnt three red lights as a signal that more help was required. Hearing more cries [307] he pulled in the direction they proceeded from and met with a ship's lifeboat with 14 persons in her. This boat was very much damaged and nearly full of water, had the occupants tried to land in her all would probably have perished. He transferred them to his boat and took them ashore, where he landed them about 10 p.m. Having got a fresh supply of lights he went out again and pulled in the direction of the Manacle Rocks. Hearing shrieks and cries he anchored as near the wreck as he could with safety. Quartermaster Juddery, who was in the mizzen rigging, seeing the boat could not approach any nearer to the wreck owing to the heavy tide, swam off to the lifeboat and taking a line, swam back again to the rigging, and through this prompt, brave action materially helped to save the twelve [sic] people in the rigging.[308] The anchor was then lifted and the boat allowed to drop down so as to take off the rest of the people who were in the other rigging and on the funnel. The rocks all around were searched but no other persons were found, and they stayed there, burning lights at intervals, till reaching the shore between 4 and 5 a.m.

---

[307] About twenty minutes at the most elapsed between the striking of the vessel on the rocks and her foundering. During that time scenes of the most poignant pathos occurred on the sinking ship although there was an absence of anything like panic. Mothers' agonized entreaties for the safety of the children, the heartbreaking separation of members of families and the severance of comrades, are incidents which have burnt themselves into the memories of all who witnessed and have lived to narrate them. – *Royal Cornwall Gazette*, 20th October 1898.

[308] The committee at Lloyd's have decided to bestow the silver medal of the Society of Lloyd's upon Quartermaster J. W. H. Juddery, of the steamship *Mohegan*, as an honorary acknowledgment of his extraordinary exertions in contributing to the saving of life on the occasion of the loss of that vessel on the Manacle Rocks, near the Lizard, in October last. *The Times*, March 2nd 1899.

It is most unfortunate that there was no light displayed to indicate the position of the steamer, this being solely due to the electric light having gone out. Had a light been visible, the Court agrees with the assertion of the lifeboat people that probably more lives would have been saved. So much time was lost in consequence of the position of the wreck not being located.

Mr. Charles John May, boatman of the coastguard stationed at Coverack, being on duty at 6 p.m. saw a steamer's masthead and port light a little to the N. and eastward of his station. He reported it to his chief officer because he thought the vessel was too close to the Manacle Rocks. He lost sight of her for about five minutes, and when he saw her again she had turned round; when he first saw her he thought she was heading for Falmouth; when she was coming out he thought she was in a dangerous position. He fired a rocket to warn her, upon lighting his blue light he stuck it in the ground; he gave the alarm to the villagers and summoned the rocket brigade, who immediately started off in the direction of the Manacle Rocks. On the way he saw three rockets fired from the wreck; when they reached there the chief officer gave him directions to proceed to Porthoustock to take charge of the telephone, and to get all the information he could as to the wreck. He then sent a message to Cadgwith [309] as follows "inform district officer and collector of Customs supposed wreck on the Manacle Rocks". This message was repeated to Falmouth about 8.45 p.m. The Porthoustock lifeboat had gone out before he arrived at this station. [310] Signals from the lifeboat for more help were reported to him and he immediately sent instructions to Falmouth for them to send their lifeboat and tug. When the Porthoustock lifeboat came back he assisted the people that were saved; most of them were very exhausted and had life-belts on. He assisted them into the fishermen's cottages and he was also present when this lifeboat came back with the remaining survivors. After this he went along the beach and picked up four dead bodies; three of these had life-belts on. About midnight he found a wooden boat near the Lowland Point; this was all broken to pieces and quite unseaworthy. He afterwards found four or five steel lifeboats, there were all dented but only one had a hole in it, and they all could have been rendered seaworthy. The whole of the channel where the wreck was is a veritable wasp's nest of rocks.

Mr. A. J. Jeffrey [sic], chief officer of the coastguard at Coverack stated that the last witness called his attention to the "Mohegan"; he soon lost sight of her and thought she had gone into Falmouth. About ten minutes after this he heard a rocket fired and went to the telephone and learned that the Porthoustock lifeboat was telephoned for. From there he went to the rocket house and found that the rocket apparatus had already left and the lamps lighted. He followed it but on reaching Manacle Point could see nothing. He ordered two signal rockets to be fired off and ordered a boatman to the Lowland Point with a blue light which he was to show if he discovered the wreck. This man picked up three persons on the rocks. [311] He reached Manacle Point at 8.30 p.m., and there heard that a lifeboat had brought off some people from the wreck. He then fired some more rockets as a signal to any people who might still be on the waters, and also as a signal to the lifeboat he saw down to leeward.

Around midnight, finding that the rocket apparatus was of no further use he sent it back to the station and remained at the Point until next day, giving instructions to the men, sending some of them round the coast with lamps. He stated that had he known that the vessel was on the main rocks he could not have done any good with the rocket apparatus as it would not reach that spot. He saw three red lights from the lifeboat but did not know it was a signal for more help. This witness also confirmed Mr. Charles John May as to the condition of the lifeboats and the condition of the broken wooden lifeboat.

[309] Cadgwith is a fishing-port in Cornwall and is situated on the Lizard Peninsula between The Lizard and Coverack.

[310] It was about seven o'clock that the assembly rocket from the Porthoustock lifeboat station gave the alarm to the district that a shipping disaster had occurred in the immediate vicinity. Porthoustock of itself does not contain a sufficiency of men capable of managing the lifeboat, and the crew has had consequently to be drawn from the village of St. Keverne, a mile and a half away, and from the surrounding places. By half-past seven the boat was launched, and there can be little doubt but by this time the worst of the trouble had happened, and many live had been sacrificed. *Royal Cornwall Gazette,* October 20th, 1898.

[311] This information suggests his finding the crew members: Robert Barrow, George Hill, and William Moore.

Mr. Francis Jose,[312] coxswain of the Falmouth lifeboat, heard the mortar fired about 10 p.m. At 10.30 p.m. he got his lifeboat off, but in getting her into the water she slid too far and it being low water she had to be hauled back that she might be turned round to get her into deep water. This delayed them about 10 minutes. The tug "Penguin" took her in tow and proceeded in the direction of the Manacle Rocks. About midnight they fell in with the Cadgwith lifeboat and were told that they—the Cadgwith lifeboat men—had seen nothing of the wreck. They then cast off from the tug and rowed towards Porthoustock, as they could see lights there. He was informed that a steamer was on the Manacle Rocks, and proceeded back there. They picked up the dead body of a lady. They waited near the wreck until near daylight, between 5 and 6 a.m., and could then plainly see the four masts and the funnel. As they could do no further good they returned to Falmouth.

Mr. Benjamin Williams, master of the tug "Penguin," stated that he was called at 10 p.m. and ordered to tow the lifeboat; he was ready in half an hour. He confirmed the coxswain regarding what transpired while towing her. After casting off he picked up a man [George Maule] and the dead body of a [Le Lacheur, John Guille] boy; the man had a life-belt on. He was of opinion that the Falmouth lifeboat could not have done any more.

Mr. Thomas Jane, coxswain of the [Cadgwith] lifeboat,[313] received instructions to launch his boat at 10 p.m. In 12 minutes the boat was in the water, and they rowed towards the Manacle Rocks; they remained there, pulling about all night returning at 8 a.m. of the next day. This witness was very strong in his expression of regret that his boat had not been called out when the Porthoustock lifeboat was summoned.

Mr. James Ross, chief officer of the coastguard station at the Lizard stated that at about 7.23 p.m. he received information that a ship was on the Manacle Rocks; he immediately ordered a man to the telephone, and was himself to the instrument in his office, but it was not until 9.37 p.m. that he had a message to send to Falmouth for their lifeboat and tug. He wired instructions and then saw the coxswain of the Lizard lifeboat. About an hour and three-quarters after this, while he was speaking to the coxswain of the Lizard lifeboat, he received a message, "Go at once". He at once communicated to the Lizard lifeboat coxswain, who immediately summoned his crew, and the lifeboat was got into the water by midnight.

Mr. E. Matthews, coxswain of the Lizard lifeboat, stated that at about 11.20 p.m. he was instructed to get his lifeboat launched; he summoned his crew by means of the rocket, they being scattered about, and it took some little time to collect them. At about midnight the lifeboat was launched; owing to the ebb tide they could not proceed straight to the Manacle Rocks, but went to the southward and set sail to weather the Black Head;[314] they reached the Manacle Rocks around 2 a.m. and remained in the vicinity of the wreck until 4 a.m. They did not pick anyone up, and the coxswain was of the opinion that everything possible had been done by the other lifeboats. As it was impossible for them to beat back against the flood tide, they proceeded to Falmouth. He stated that they were burning signals all the way up from Black Head. This witness expressed his regret that he had not been summoned earlier as he felt sure that had he started about 7.30 p.m. he might have been instrumental in saving some of the unfortunate people but he also stated that he had never been summoned to the Manacle Rocks during the 33 years he had been coxswain of the Lizard lifeboat.

Lieutenant Keppel Foote R.N., at present district inspector to the Royal National Lifeboat Institution, stated that it was his duty to attend to the exercising of the lifeboats in the district. Falmouth, he stated, was a station that had not done much work, and he gave a description of the station. He pointed out that at dead low-water Spring tide it was more difficult to launch the lifeboat, because she had to turn round at right angles at the foot of the slip. He also stated that he had attended a meeting convened by the Local Committee a few days before the deplorable casualty, and the conclusion the meeting

---

[312] Mr Francis Jose—aged 56 years / Occupation: Boatman (employer); 1901 UK census.

[313] The delightfully named: *Minnie Moon.* In 1898, this new lifeboat arrived in Cadgwith. She was 39 ft long (12 m) and 9 ft 6 in (2.90 m) wide, with twelve oars and fifteen crew. She cost £798 and was built at Thames Ironworks, Blackwall. She holds the record for the greatest number of lives saved from one rescue: 227 lives were saved from the SS *Suevic* on the night of 17/18th March 1907.

[314] Black Head is a promontory, south of Coverack village.

arrived at was that to render the station capable of launching a boat at any moment a new slip would have to be purchased, and that it would cost from £1,200 to £1,500, an expense he did not feel justified in recommending.

Mr. William Ferguson, auxiliary second engineer on the "Mohegan," who has been in the company's service seven years, and who has worked his way up from fifth engineer to his present position, was in charge of the engines with the fifth and sixth engineers on the night of the wreck. He went on duty at 6 p.m., the engines were working well, the pointer on the telegraph was standing at full speed, making 68 revolutions with a pressure of steam of 197 lbs. At about 6.50 p.m. he was startled by a slight shock as if the cable were running out; simultaneously the telegraph rang stop, which was accordingly done. Water poured into the stoke-hole in great volumes, lifting up the floor plates; he remained in the engine-room about half a minute, called out to the men to ease all the valves; there was no explosion, but a slight noise was heard owing to the gauge glasses breaking. All hands rushed on deck from the engine-room and stoke-hole and about three minutes after this all the lights went out. This was caused by water at this time rising to the dynamo and drowning it out, the water at this time being about 14 feet from the floor, proving how rapidly it was rising. Upon leaving the engine-room he rushed to his cabin and got a life-belt; from there he rushed to the lifeboat on the port side, which was filled with people. He saw it launched and leave the vessel's side, but did not see any officer in the boat, they being all busy trying to launch the other boats, the chief officer, having his coat and waistcoat off, not only giving instructions but assistance as well. He saw the fourth officer at this time discharge three rockets on the port side. The steamer was sinking rapidly, she having a list of about 45 degrees to port and the waves were washing over the starboard side. He did not see anyone washed overboard. He saw the captain on the bridge and heard him call out to the men to hurry up with the boats. When the steamer went down he was standing by the side of one of the starboard lifeboats, was taken down with it, and remained under water about half a minute. When he got free he found himself among a lot of wreckage, which made it very hard to swim; he could see the masts and funnel above water, and as he could not swim to the shore he turned round and swam to the funnel, which he reached and remained upon until about 4 a.m., when he was taken off by the Porthoustock lifeboat. He was the only person on the funnel.

This witness described the cause of the electric light going out on the passage down channel. The masthead and side-lights were on a separate circuit to the lights used for the purpose of lighting the vessel, the latter being those which went out in consequence of the safety fuse going round. The electrical installation was under his charge and he stated that the wiring was well and carefully set up, the dynamos and engines were of the highest class and had given no trouble. The witness also stated that the main engines and boilers worked well till she struck, and this was confirmed by Mr. M. E. Gray, fourth engineer and, Mr. J. C. Smith, fifth engineer.

Mr. M. E. Gray, fourth engineer, stated that he was on watch at the time the ship struck; he heard the telegraph ring and saw Mr. Ferguson stop the engines; he had charge of the boilers. He rushed on deck and heard one of the officers calling out, "Now Lads! Remember the passengers; look out after the women and children first!" He went to the port lifeboat; the captain, who was on the bridge, called out, "There are too many at that boat, spread yourselves". He jumped out and went to the next boat, this got jammed. He then went to the third boat and assisted to get it into the water. Having heard an order to go to the starboard boats, and whilst helping to get one out, he was washed overboard and the steamer at this moment went down. The sea washed him back to the mizzen rigging into which he got, 14 or 16 other persons being there also. He stated that quartermaster Juddery swam from the rigging to the lifeboat and then back with a line and attached to the mast; by means of this brave action they were all taken off by the lifeboat. Everyone on the "Mohegan" behaved most coolly, the officers and crew were doing their best to get the boats out to save the passengers. The captain was directing the men from the bridge and the crew were doing their best to carry out the orders. This witness further stated that from the time he left the engine-room until the vessel sank it would be about ten or twelve minutes.

Mr. J. C. Smith, fifth engineer, was on watch with the last two witnesses, and corroborates their statements. He stated that shortly before the vessel struck he was standing by the telegraph. When he came out of the engine-room he met the chief engineer, who asked what the telegraph was standing at, and upon being told, "Stop," shouted to them to get the life-belts on. They did this, and he saw several of the passengers with life-belts in their hands, and some of the crew were trying life-belts on to the passengers; he himself tied on two or three life-belts. He was at the after end of one of the starboard boats when she foundered; he swam from the vessel and got hold of a plank on which he remained until picked up by the lifeboat and he was landed with the others. He stated that he did not think anything else could have been done, owing to the darkness, the position of the vessel, and the weather. The night was very dark, but clear overhead. The officers and crew did all they could to save life.

Mr. Arthur Herbert Trevor, the ship's doctor, stated that he had been in her the previous voyage, and consequently knew the captain well. He always enjoyed good health, and there was nothing the matter with him; he was talking with him on deck about one hour before the disaster. When the vessel struck he was at dinner in the saloon, the chief [Couch] and fourth officers [Browning], the chief [McLaren] and one other engineer were also there; the captain, second [Cole] and third officers [Hindmarsh] were on the bridge. He felt a shock and heard a grinding, tearing sort of noise. The vessel suddenly took a list to starboard, sending everything off the table. He did not leave the saloon, as he thought it was his duty to stay with the ladies, some of whom were in a fainting condition. The fourth officer [Browning] came down and told everyone to get their life-belts on and go on the top deck; the stewards assisted the passengers in doing so, the latter being much more cool and collected than when the vessel first struck. He then went in search of Mrs. Lakes [*sic*], who was ill, but could not find her. Then he went on deck and found the officers busily engaged with the boats, and heard the captain giving his orders in a clear and collected manner. The electric light went out when he got on the deck, and some 15 minutes after she struck the vessel foundered. He, together with 12 other men, and the stewardess Mrs. Pigott, had got into the mizzen rigging, and were rescued by the lifeboat. This witness also corroborated the statement of quartermaster Juddery's pluck in swimming off to the lifeboat.

Mr. John Cruickshank, who has been five years in the service of the company, was in his berth when the vessel struck. He went onto the boat deck and the chief officer told him to get the boats clear, to cut the covers off, not to stop to unlace them. He went forward to get the men up and saw the carpenter's mate, who told him he was ordered to sound the wells. He again went onto the boat-deck and assisted at the boats; the chief officer was then quite cool and the captain was on the bridge giving orders. Some of the crew were at the port lifeboats; in consequence of the heavy list they could not get the starboard lifeboats out. The chief officer then ordered all the boat falls to be cut, the davits swung out, and everything cleared that when the vessel went down they might float off from her. The steamer had at this time a list of 45 degrees to port, and was all down by the head so that it was impossible to get to the lamp room which was in his charge, it being under water. Shortly before the vessel went down he went aft to cut ladders adrift and the chief officer called out to all to get into the rigging.

Just previously the second officer shook hands with him saying. "Goodbye, we have done all we can". He then went aft to the taffrail. The vessel has such a list that the men were outside the rail and the starboard quarter stuck up like a spire. Neither the chief nor second officers had life-belts on. When the vessel went down he was sucked down with her; when he came up he was struck by a bucket rack; he seized hold of it and then got hold of a life-buoy; he saw the vessel's mast, which surprised him. He thought she had gone down on her beam ends. He swam to the mainmast, where he remained until he was rescued, with the cook, by the lifeboat. He has heard the captain call out, "Hurry up with the boats my lads! Keep cool!"

Mr. John W. H. Juddery, quartermaster, who holds a first mate's certificate, stated that this was his first voyage in the *Mohegan*, and that she was in a fit and good condition, and in every respect a very fine vessel. He was in the chief officer's watch and on duty on the 14th October from 8 a.m. to noon; when at the wheel from 10 a.m. to noon the course was W. by N. He had received the course from Quartermaster Butt at 10 a.m., the chief officer standing by whilst the wheel was relieved in order to see that the right course was given, the company's orders being that an officer is always to be there at the reliefs. The same thing was done at noon when he was relieved. He came on deck at 4 p.m., at 4.03 he received orders to take the log and he reported 55 miles on it and saw the Eddystone broad on the starboard bow [Bearing 045° relative]. At 4.17 p.m. he was again told to take the log; it registered 57¾ miles, which he reported; the Eddystone was then abeam, distance about 2 ¾ miles N. he did not notice the course being steered, her speed was about 12 ¾ knots.[315] He then went into the chart room to put the flags away as they had been used for signalling. The captain came into the chart-room and called the fourth officer from the bridge and questioned him as to the distance the vessel was off the Eddystone, to which he replied that he thought it was three miles. At 6 p.m. he went below, the wind was about half a gale from the S.E., clear generally, but with an appearance of dirty weather. Land was visible on the starboard side, high, bold land. He saw [William] Daniels in the crow's nest. About 6.30 he came on deck but went below again and remained there until she struck. Upon coming on deck he found the men were carrying out the orders, to get out the boats, given by the captain who was on the flying bridge. All the officers were engaged with the lifeboats, and almost immediately the lights went out. The vessel had a list of about 45 degrees to port, and was all down by the head. He saw some of the stewards serving out life-belts to passengers. The port lifeboat was got away; the captain was on the bridge cheering on the men and telling them to keep cool. The list was gradually increasing, and he heard the captain calling, and on crawling towards him he found his orders were to get the women and children into the jigger-rigging;[316] then the vessel took her final plunge; the doctor and 11 others were there; the steamer went down bodily, not by the head. Shortly before the vessel went down the chief officer shook him by the hand and said, "good bye, we have done all we can, look out for yourself".

On the arrival of the lifeboat [*Charlotte*] the anchor was let go near them, and seeing she could not come closer he swam towards the funnel[317] on account of the strong tide running, and eventually got to the lifeboat; having got a line he swam back with it, by which means they were all enabled to get to the lifeboat.

Frederick Butt, quartermaster, stated that he was at the wheel from 4 p.m. to 6 p.m., he relieved quartermaster Blake, who gave him the course of west-by-north, the chief officer standing by in accordance with the Company's orders. He was given the distance of the Eddystone as three or four miles off. The chief officer looked repeatedly into the standard compass by which he was steering. The captain came up about 5 p.m. and looked into the compass and had a conversation with the officers. At 6 p.m. he was relieved by quartermaster August and he gave the course W. by N. in the presence of the second officer.

George Wood, who took over on the six o'clock watch, at a quarter past six, just before the disaster took place, heard two strokes of the crow's-nest bell: indicating a "Light on the starboard bow". Looking in that direction, he saw a bright shore-light about three miles off. The signal from the crow's-nest was answered—"All right" from the bridge.

After the vessel struck they tried all they could to get the lifeboats out; he was knocked down by something falling from aloft, and a sea washed him along the deck. On recovering he got into the starboard lifeboat; the sea lifted her up and she was swamped. He swam to the mizzen-rigging, and when he got there he found one of his fingers hanging by the flesh. He was eventually taken off by the lifeboat.

Frank Nicklin, chief steward, stated that he was in the vessel on her previous voyage; there were 30 stewards and stewardesses under him. He assisted with the others in putting life-belts on the passengers, and he also assisted in getting out one of the lifeboats. He spoke most highly of the captain and officers.

---

[315] Based on Juddery's stated log parameters, this equates to a ship's speed of 13.6 knots.

[316] The jigger rigging is positioned at the shortest, aft-most mast on vessels with more than three masts.

[317] Given the orientation of the wreck relative to the rocks, the location of the jigger mast, and the set of the tide; Juddery's description of swimming towards the funnel to reach the lifeboat is entirely authentic, with the lifeboat being anchored upstream and as close to the wreck, as was considered safe.

Mr. William Pollard,[318] who holds an extra master's certificate, stated that he was the third officer of the "Mohegan" on her previous voyage. He spoke most highly of Captain Griffiths. All the A.Bs.[319] who were examined also spoke most highly of the captain; they said he was a strict disciplinarian, but they could not wish to sail with a better man. He also said that, if the captain was well, it was his duty to lay down the course and give it to the officer of the watch, who in turn gave it to the quartermaster. Unless the vessel was running into immediate danger, the officer would not alter the course, without first consulting the captain. It was, he said, usual to pass the Eddystone five miles off. On passing the Eddystone, it was not usual to see the land until the Lizard was approached. He could not conceive of the captain giving a course west by north, after passing the Eddystone, to clear the Lizard. On a clear night, the vessel should pick up the Lizard Light before she dropped the Eddystone.[320]

In answer to a question by Mr. Pyke (Board of Trade inquiry) as to whether officers could inspect the charts which were in the wheelhouse, Mr. Pollard stated that Captain Griffiths generally looked at the charts himself.[321]

Mrs. Compton Swift, one of the lady passengers, who was fortunately saved, gave a very lucid account of her experience. She stated that she had made several [6 in total] voyages across the Atlantic before in the Company's steamers, but never with Captain Griffiths. On the way down channel she remarked to her physician how close they were hugging the land.[322] The witness also stated that: "In passing the Eddystone Lighthouse we seemed nearer to it than I had ever been before".

On the evening of the casualty, and just before she left the deck, at about 6.20 p.m., she noticed the land, it being about twilight.[323] When sitting down to dinner, and on the point of turning her chair she heard a crash; the chief engineer and first and fourth officers rushed on deck, followed by the passengers, Mr. Kelly told her the steamer was aground. Not feeling any alarm she suggested to her doctor that they should go back and finish their dinner; when going below they heard orders given to man the lifeboats and, on rushing to the stairway, the lights went out. At this time there was a heavy list to port. She heard the captain from the bridge give orders; she never at any time felt nervous. The lifeboat which had turned over was thrown out into the water, but as soon as it reached the water it righted itself. There would be, she stated, about 25 or more persons in the boat, of whom she was one; after she had been in the boat about two minutes a wave struck it and turned it bottom upwards. Putting up her hands she thought she was under the bottom of the wreck, but upon realizing her position she tried to extricate herself, but was unable to do so as she was jammed between the thwart and the boat. When the boat was righted by the lifeboat men one of them, by cutting away the wood with an axe, succeeded in getting her free; she never lost consciousness, and was taken ashore. There was another lady under the boat with her and a little child which was dead. The lady subsequently died, and proved to be a Miss Roudebush.[324] Personally she felt perfectly sure that there was plenty of time for lowering the boats, and saving the passengers. She saw the captain on the bridge and saw him washed overboard. She did not see any other officer on the bridge.

---

[318] As stated, he was the third officer on the ship's previous voyage (as the *Cleopatra*). On that trip, the vessel passed the Eddystone at 7 miles and the course was west-half-north. Unless there was an obvious danger, an officer would not think of altering a course laid by the captain. On coming down the Channel, it was unusual to see land after passing the Eddystone, until the Lizard. He had been on other trips with Capt. Griffith, and boat drills were always carried out; however on the trip in question, there was no such drill carried out: the deck hands being wanted below, as the engines were constantly in need of attention.

[319] An Able Bodied (A.B.) seaman is of higher rank and is more experienced than an Ordinary Seaman (O.S.).

[320] *Glasgow Herald* (Glasgow, Scotland); Friday, 25th November 1898.

[321] *Daily News* (London, England); Saturday 26th November 1898.

[322] *Royal Cornwall Gazette;* 17th November 1898.

[323] On this day, the following times are relevant: sunset at 1713 hrs. and nautical twilight at 1823 hrs.

[324] This is a case of mistaken reporting, as the unfortunate woman was, in fact, Miss Roudebush's mother Mrs Grandin.

Miss Katherine Noble, one of the fortunate survivors of the disaster, said that she sat at the captain's table and next to him. He only came down to dinner [only] on the first night. On the afternoon of the 14th she was on deck; she did not notice the land, although she remained on deck until 6.15 p.m. She heard a crash and rushed on deck, being the first passenger to reach it. She was told to keep calm as the ship had grazed something; the crew were all rushing to the boats and she heard someone shout, "Get out the boats!" She returned to the cabin to get some wraps, and when she again reached the deck she was horrified to learn than no boats were launched; the crew were going from one boat to another. Eventually she stepped over the rail to a boat and got in; she heard the captain call out, "Hurry with the boats!" and asked the men why they could not get them out. The men complained that the boats were too full, and the people were ordered to get out, but the crew were then unable to get the boats out. The waves at this time were washing over the vessel. The fourth officer came along and tried to get her into the rigging, but the seas washing over prevented her doing so. He then told her to get behind one of the lifeboats. The fourth officer then went to the assistance of some other of the lady passengers; immediately after she was washed overboard and seized hold of some wreckage. She had a life-belt on, the fourth officer had not; he was clinging to a hatch close by her for nearly an hour, then a wave washed him away. She was ultimately rescued by the lifeboat and taken on shore. In her judgment she was sure the officers and crew did all they could to save the passengers.

Mr. George L. Dashwood, of Trade Inquiry of 1, Fleet street, London, stated to the Court that he was a passenger on the first voyage of the *Mohegan*—then known as the "Cleopatra"—on her first voyage to New York and that her engines and boilers broke down on several occasions during the voyage. He did not remember any boat drill being carried out.[325] He returned home in the same Company's steamer *Victoria*, the sister ship of the *Mohegan*; this steamer overtook the *Cleopatra* when about five days out and arrived home some time before her.

The captain and officers being all drowned, the Court is utterly unable to arrive at any conclusion as to why the course W. by N. was set and steered.[326] They can only suggest that it was done inadvertently by the captain and from overconfidence on his part he did not discover it in time to avert the calamity.

The Court wishes to throw out that if one of the officers has a strong opinion that a wrong course is being steered it becomes his duty to bring the matter to the attention of the master, and the master's duty to examine the question. The Court, in conclusion, wishes to express its deep sympathy with the relatives and friends of all passengers—American and British—and of the master, officers, and members of the crew who lost their lives in this dreadful calamity.

Although there was such serious loss of life it is worthy of notice that none of the officers were saved, proving without doubt the bravery and unselfishness displayed by the master, officers, and crew.

These were the facts of the case and on the conclusion of the evidence, Mr. Mansell Jones, on behalf of the Board of Trade, put to the court the following questions:

1. Was the vessel in good and seaworthy condition when she left the Thames on the 14th October last, and was she sufficiently ballasted?

2. What number of compasses were on board; were they in good order and sufficient for the safe navigation of the vessel; when and by whom were they last adjusted, and by which compass was the vessel steered?

3. Was the vessel wired on the double wire system, and could the compasses have been affected by the electric current?

---

[325] Another passenger on that maiden voyage (Mr. Carteret) also confirmed the lack of any boat drill, during the voyage.

[326] Mr Nelson, appearing for the relatives of some of the officers, produced log-books of the *Mohegan* on previous voyages (as the *Cleopatra*, and on her single Atlantic voyage, earlier that year). These showed that her course after leaving the Eddystone was about W. by ½ N. On the day of her wreck she was steering W. by N. at this point.

4. Was the vessel supplied with the boats and life saving apparatus required by the Statute, and were the boats so carried as to be at all times fit and ready for use?

5. Was the vessel supplied with lamps independently of the electric lamps, and were they kept trimmed and ready for use, and accessible?

6. Was the vessel supplied with proper and sufficient signals of distress?

7. Was the vessel efficiently officered and manned?

8. Was the master in good health, and did he give proper personal attention to the navigation after leaving the Thames?

9. At what distance was the Eddystone lighthouse passed about 4.15 p.m. on the 14th October, and what was the course steered after passing the lighthouse?

10. Was a light seen and reported shortly after 6 p.m., and if so, was this St. Anthony's light?

11. Was a good and proper look-out kept?

12. What was the cause of the stranding of the vessel?

13. What were the circumstances in which so few distress signals and no lamps were exhibited after the stranding of the vessel?

14. What were the circumstances in which only one boat with passengers successfully left the vessel?

15. Was every effort possible made by the late master, officers, and crew to save life, and was good discipline maintained after the casualty?

16. Were good and prompt measures taken by the coastguard at Coverack and by the coxswain of the lifeboat at Porthoustock to render assistance?

17. What were the circumstances in which the Porthoustock lifeboat did not rescue those in the rigging until about midnight on the 14th–15th October?

18. What were the circumstances in which the services of the Falmouth lifeboat were not requested until 9.15 p.m., the services of the Cadgwith were not requested until 9.55 p.m., and the services of the Lizard lifeboat were not requested until 11.20 p.m. of the 14th October? Were the respective lifeboats promptly launched, and what were the circumstances in which they failed to rescue any of the passengers and crew?

19. What were the circumstances in which this casualty was attended with the loss of so many lives?

Mr. Pike, Mr Nelson, Mr Cunningham Graham and Mr Mansell Jones then respectively addressed the court, and judgment was given as follows:—

1. The vessel was in good and seaworthy condition when she left the Thames on the 13th October last, and she was sufficiently ballasted.

2. She had five compasses on board, not including boat compasses. One, the standard Lord Kelvin's patent, by which the vessel was steered by as on the upper bridge; one was in the wheel-house and one aft. They were in good order and sufficient for the safe navigation of the vessel. They were last adjusted by Mr Charles Chappell of Messrs. Hughes & Son, Fenchurch Street, E.C., on the 5th October last.

3. She was wired on the double wire system, and the dynamo being places 100ft. from the compasses, the Court is of opinion the compasses could not have been affected by the electric current.

4. The vessel was supplied with the boats and life-saving apparatus required by the Statute. They were so carried as to be at all times fit and ready for use but the Court is strongly of opinion that a lifeboat should be swung out on each side of a passenger vessel when navigating the English Channel.

5. The vessel was supplied with lamps independently of the electric lamps. There were two sets of copper signalling lamps, one set being kept trimmed and ready for use and accessible under ordinary circumstances. She had also other oil lamps for general use.

6. The vessel was supplied with proper and efficient signals of distress.

7. The vessel was efficiently officered and manned.

8. The master was in good health. Dr Trevor, the ship's doctor, stated the master enjoyed very good health and that there was nothing in the world the matter with him. He also stated that about an hour before the casualty he had had a conversation with the master, when he expressed himself well satisfied with the behaviour of the vessel. The master gave personal attention to the navigation after leaving the Thames.

9. The Court is of opinion the vessel passed the Eddystone lighthouse about 4.15 [p.m.] at not a greater distance than three miles, and that the course steered was W. by N.

10. A light was seen and reported shortly after 6 p.m., and in the opinion of the Court, it was St. Anthony's light. The Lizard lights were not seen on account of the vessel never having come within the arc illuminated by the light.

11. There were two officers—the second and third—on the bridge, an A.B. in the crow's nest, another A.B. forward and the Court considers that a proper look-out was kept.

12. Quartermaster August, who was at the helm when the vessel struck, was drowned. Quartermaster Butt, who took the helm from 4 to 6, stated that he received the course W. by N. from Quartermaster Blake, who was also drowned, and that he steered that course until he was relieved at 6 [p.m.] by August, to whom he gave the same course. Both changes at the helm were made in the hearing of an officer in accordance with the usual practice of the ship. Butt also stated that the captain looked in the binnacle about 5 [p.m.], and that the chief officer, who was in charge from 4 to 6 [p.m.], looked in the binnacle continually and the Court is of opinion that the cause of the stranding of the vessel was that a wrong course– W by N.–was steered after passing the Eddystone lighthouse at 4.17 p.m.

13. The reason so few distress signals were discharged was that the rocket-socket was on the port side, and the vessel took a list of about 45 degrees to port within a few minutes after she struck, which made it very difficult to discharge them.

14. The foremost boat on the port side—a wooden cutter—became jammed; the first boat on the port side was launched and saved 24 persons. An unsuccessful attempt was made to launch the other two lifeboats on that side, but from the great list to port and the heavy sea washing over the side it was found impossible to do so. On the starboard side efforts were made to launch the boats, but the heavy list prevented their being got out. The difficulty was increased by some of the passengers crowding into the boats, but the Court is of opinion that the boats could not have been launched if no crowding had taken place.

15. Every possible effort appears to have been made by the late master, officers, and crew to save life, and good discipline was maintained after the casualty.

16. and **17.** Prompt and proper measures were taken by the coastguard at Coverack and by the coxswain of the lifeboat at Porthoustock to render assistance. Hill, the coxswain of the Porthoustock lifeboat was standing outside his stable door and saw the "Mohegan" apparently less than a mile from the shore; she altered her helm and as she was running into danger he at once summoned his crew and launched his boat at 7.25 p.m. He went in the direction of the Manacle Rocks and on approaching them he heard cries in the water; then he fell in with a boat, bottom up, on which were two men, whom he took off. Then, hearing cries underneath the boat he righted her, and found Mrs. Compton Swift, another lady, and a child who was dead. He had to cut one of the thwarts to release Mrs. Swift, and he took her and the other lady into the boat; the latter died on shore shortly after being landed.

Mrs. Swift, who was rescued, gave at the inquiry a very lucid account of the "Mohegan's" proximity to the land and the Eddystone, and of her subsequent experiences.

Hill [coxswain] then burnt signals for further assistance from shore, and shortly after he fell in with the ship's lifeboat with 24 persons on board; he took them all into his boat, thinking the ship's boat, having a good deal of water in her, was not fit to carry them through the heavy surf and between the rocks and safely to shore. He landed the persons at 10 [p.m.], and about 10.30 put off again and reached the wreck, which he found to be on the Manacle Rocks, and rescued 16 persons from the rigging and funnel.

When the lifeboat arrived at the wreck the coxswain did not deem it safe to go down to it for fear of being damaged by the wreck, and let go her anchor as near as he could with safety. He could not venture to throw his loaded cane and line [327] towards the wreck for fear of injuring some of the persons in the rigging.

Quartermaster John William Henry Juddery swam from the wreck to the lifeboat, procured a line and swam back with it, and another line being drawn from the boat 12 persons were hauled into the boat from the mizzen-rigging. The lifeboat subsequently took off four more persons from the main and jigger rigging and the funnel.

The rocks were searched, but no other persons were found, and the lifeboat returned to Porthoustock.

18. The services of the Falmouth lifeboat were not requested until 9.15 p.m. because the Porthoustock lifeboat had gone out and it was not known on shore that further assistance was required until signals from the Porthoustock lifeboat for more help were seen around 9 p.m. The services of the Cadgwith lifeboat were not requested until 9.55 p.m. because it is stationed at a further distance from the Manacle Rocks and because the Falmouth boat has a tug and the Cadgwith boat does not.

The services of the Lizard lifeboat were not requested until 11.20 [p.m.] because it is stationed at a much greater distance from the Manacle Rocks, is a smaller boat than any one of the other three, and in consequence of the ebb tide could not have reached the wreck until after the other boats. The boat at the Lizard is intended only to service the coast and rocks in its immediate vicinity, and is practically never summoned to wrecks in the vicinity of the Manacle Rocks, that coast being well protected by three larger lifeboats.

The respective lifeboats were promptly launched; they failed to rescue any passengers and crew because there were no lights to indicate the position of the wreck, which caused much loss of time in searching for her and because before their arrival at the wreck, all the survivors on it had been taken off by the Porthoustock lifeboat. One person was picked up by the "Penguin," the tug of the Falmouth lifeboat.

19. The deplorable loss of so many lives, amounting to 106, 51 only being saved, was in consequence of the vessel taking a sudden and very serious list to port, her going down in not more than a quarter of an hour from the time of striking, and there being no light to indicate her position through the electric light having gone out.

This Court is strongly of opinion that where a vessel is lighted with electric light she ought at night always to have lighted, and in an easily accessible position, oil lamps, to take the place of the ship's lamps in case of failure of the electric light.

The Court wishes to express its great approbation of the conduct of Mr. Juddery, who at considerable personal risk, swam from the wreck to the lifeboat, and swam back with a line, and materially aided in saving those in the mizzen-rigging.

The court also wishes to speak with approval of the promptness and skill of the coxswain of the Porthoustock lifeboat, Mr. Hill, and his crew.

R. H. B. MARSHALL, Judge

We concur.

A. RONALSDON
J. H. HALLETT C.E.   Assessors.[328]
RICH^D. C. DYER

---

[327] The weighted cane and the line attached to it are the means adopted for getting into first communication with a wreck. An elliptical lump of lead, almost as large as the fist and weighing two pounds, is fastened to the end of a springy cane some 24 inches in length. This is thrown by hand, and it is wonderful to what a distance it will travel when propelled by an experienced man. A light heaving-line is made fast to the cane, the slack of which is loosely but neatly coiled in a round bucket. The bowman of the boat takes a few fakes [single loops or windings] of the coil in his left hand and throws with his right. He seldom fails to reach his mark, and, if he does, he can try again without a moment's delay. By means of the light heaving-line the shipwrecked crew are enabled to draw out a block through which is rove [passed through] a stout rope. To the latter a life-buoy is attached, and the men are placed in it and drawn to the life-boat one by one. The whole method is simple in the extreme, and, on that account, it is well suited for the particular emergency. Anything more complicated would quickly foul and be put out of action—Noel T. Methley, *The Lifeboat and its Story*, London Sidgwick & Jackson Ltd., 1912

[328] PORTCITIES Southampton – Wreck Report for 'Mohegan', 1898.

The Court here inserts some extracts from the sailing directions for this coast, with notes bearing on the casualty.

The land generally between Rame Head and the Lizard is moderately high on or near the coast, being backed by still higher ground at more or less remote distances inland, and presents a variety of aspects to vessels in the offing as they vary their position. The Gribben head, westward of Fowey, is a remarkable object, having a beacon tower 84 feet high, its base being 250 feet above high water. Nearly midway between the Eddystone and the Lizard, the Dodman stands out boldly seaward, being a precipitous bluff 363 feet above the sea, with a steep face towards the East, and is a very conspicuous landmark for the neighbourhood.

The "Mohegan" must, by the course steered and the distance run from the Eddystone, have been some eight or nine miles off this point at about 5.30 p.m., when there was still good daylight, and it should have been distinctly visible at that time, the weather being then described as clear. The Lizard lights, or the Head, ought also to have been seen, but the evidence does not show that any directions were given to look out for them. The fact that the Lizard lights were not seen at the time they were lighted ought to have shown the vessel was within the line of arc.

When the light was reported at 6.15 p.m. two points on the starboard bow three or four miles distant it was probably St. Anthony's light, as the course and distance from the Eddystone would put her in that position.

It is high water full and change at the Lizard at 5 p.m.; springs rise 14 ½ ft., and neaps 10 ½ ft., and off the Manacle Rocks the stream runs westward from 1 to 1 ½ knots, until nearly half flood by the shore.

Of the three lights bearing on the "Mohegan's" case, the Eddystone is a bright flashing light, visible on a clear night 17 miles. St. Anthony's is a revolving white light with bright face every 20 seconds, visible 14 miles, and to a vessel approaching from the eastward the light first opens out on a North West bearing; the Lizard has two fixed electric lights distinct from each other 74 yards, and are visible 21 miles. When in line from the eastward they lead 3¾ miles southward of the Manacle Rocks.

Some questions arose as to the steel boats that were fitted; the Court desires to express its opinion as to the strength and quality of them. The two wooden boats that were on board were broken into matchwood, and notwithstanding that the steel boats were battered about on the rocks; there was a hole in only one of them. This proves their efficiency and superiority over the wooden boats.

The Company have formulated instructions as to boat drill and they have been satisfied that this should take place when the vessels are at sea. But in the opinion of the Court, there is no reason why this should not be carried out on the crew signing on their articles, when their numbers and stations should be allotted them, and that boat and fire drill should be practiced before the vessel leaves the dock. They do not consider it necessary that the boats should be lowered into the water for this purpose, but that the crew should all know their stations.

Extract from printed instructions issued to captains and officers of the Atlantic Transport Company:

GENERAL

All commanders and officers are specially requested to make themselves acquainted with the rules and regulations of the Company and adhere to them strictly.

September 1st, 1894

Captain Griffiths,

SS "Manitoba"

Sir,

Please note that no passengers, under any consideration, are to be allowed on the bridge. This is by order of the President.

Yours (signed)

R. ROBINSON, Marine Superintendent

February 20th, 1895

Captain Griffiths,

SS "Manitoba"

Dear Sir,

Since the sad disaster to the *ss* "Elbe" it becomes a matter of paying strict attention to the boats. Please, in order to meet any such emergency, either before leaving the dock, after leaving the dock, or before leaving Gravesend, to have all your boats hung to the davits ready for swinging out, and keep them there until your steamer has cleared the Channel. Of course, in passing down Channel you will quite understand you will be guided according to the weather. On approaching the Channel on your return passage carry out the same operations. I take it for granted that the fittings and gear of your boats are in constant readiness.

(signed)

R. ROBINSON,

Marine Superintendent.

August 4th, 1898

To the captain *ss* "Manitoba"

Sir, Please note that at least once during each round voyage one of your boats is to be lowered into the water and manned. A note to this effect is to be inserted in the log book. You are not to inform the officers which boat is to be lowered until the actual time of giving the order, and then you will select the boat yourself.—Yours

(signed)

R. M. ROBINSON,

Marine Superintendent.

During the course of the Board of Trade inquiry on the 24th November, 1898, particularly during the periods of cross-examination and in the concluding summing-up by both legal teams, some interesting points were made:

Mr. Juddery held a mate's certificate, but he had never been on a liner before. He served on this particular voyage as the chief officer's watch, and he was steering at the wheel on the bridge from 10 to twelve in the morning, using the standard compass (which from previous evidence had proved to have been accurately adjusted and corrected). The vessel, at 10 o'clock in the morning, the *Mohegan,* was between the Isle of Wight and Portland, and her course was W. ¾ N. The officer stood by and heard him pass the course along to the next man who took the wheel. The witness [Juddery] went on duty again at 4 o'clock [p.m.] when he stood on the bridge to transmit orders to the wheel-house. When Butt, another quartermaster, went to the wheel, he [Juddery] did not hear what course was given. The log register showed that they had done fifty-five miles from noon, and at that time the Eddystone was bearing broad on the on the starboard bow. When the Eddystone was astern, the register showed fifty-seven and three-quarter miles, and they about three miles south of the lighthouse just previously – that is, at 4.17 [p.m.]. The ship was then going at a rate of thirteen and a quarter knots an hour.

Mr. Jones [for the Board of Trade] expressed the wish that Butt might be called, so that it might be shown that the course was W. by N., but Mr. Pyke [for the company] said he might take it that the course was W. by N., and that the *Mohegan* was a little to the north of the Manacle Rocks.

The witness, continuing his narrative, said that about six in the evening [almost an hour from the disaster] the wind was blowing half a gale from the south east, and half an hour later he described land on the starboard but he could see no lights. The weather was overcast, and there were signs of raining coming on. When the shock came, not long after this, he had gone below. He heard the fourth officer announce that they were four miles off the Eddystone at 4.30, and the captain, who was repeatedly on the bridge, shouted out: "All right". A man named Davids [*sic*] [329] was in the crow's nest.

Mr. Juddery continued at this point to describe the confusion aboard the vessel, as it lurched to port and disabling the launching of all but two lifeboats. He went on to say that he managed to get into the rigging, after the vessel sank, and that he assisted several others up with him, and then, after waiting several hours, the lifeboat appeared and came leeward to the wreck. The rocks were visible, and he felt pretty certain that if the starboard boats had got off, which he believed they did, they would have struck on those rocks. Nobody was washed off the rigging. The lifeboat could not come up to windward and anchored.

Mr. Jones: You jumped off and swam to it?

Witness : Yes, although a flood tide was running strongly against me. I got a line and swam back to the mizzen rigging, and made it fast.

Mr. Jones: And by means of that act of yours all the people clinging to that rigging were saved?

Witness : Yes. They were ultimately got off into the lifeboat. Having done all they could in the immediate region of the wreck, they, in the lifeboat, cruised round the Manacle Rocks but could not see a soul on the rocks. They arrived in harbour [Porthoustock] at about nine o'clock in the morning.

Mr. Jones : Can you tell me whether there was an intention to put into Falmouth?

Witness : I don't see why there should be.

Mr. Jones : Do you know whether it was the captain's intention to signal the Lizard?

Witness : I have heard since that that is sometimes done.

Mr. Jones : Was all the tackle of the boats ready?

Witness : Yes, all ready for launching and fully equipped.

Mr. Jones : And if it had not been for the list there would have been no difficulty in launching the starboard boats?

Witness : None at all.

Witness : I have never before seen a ship go to sea with such a sober crew.

Mr. Jones : Was there no difficulty with the lifeboats owing to the tackle being new?

Witness : No difficulty whatever.

Cross-examined by Mr. Pyke [for the company] Juddery said it certainly would not have been a prudent thing to have had their boats swung out in such weather, Asked whether the captain was cool throughout the proceedings, he confirmed the

---

[329] A little confusion here, as there was no crew member so named; however, William Daniels *was* in the crow's nest at that time.

many previous statements of former witnesses that he was, and asked that he was whether he was a good disciplinarian, he answered: "Well, he struck me as being a bit of a martinet [strict, and in demanding that people obey their orders]".

Mr. Pyke, in concluding his brief cross-examination, expressed to Juddery on behalf of the owners, their thanks and appreciation for services he had rendered.

Following further questioning from Mr. Nelson [for some relatives of the deceased] and Mr. Graham [for the Royal Lifeboat Institution] Mr. Jones then proceeded to ask him some pointed questions:

Mr. Jones : If you had been told when you took the wheel that the course was W. by N., would you have accepted it?

Witness : Yes, I should in a general way. Had I known that the vessel was steering for the Lizard I should not have accepted it.

Mr. Jones : But steering down Channel, three mile south of the Eddystone, if you had that course given to you at that time?

Witness : It would not be for me to know where the vessel was going.

Mr. Jones : You knew where you were bound for?

Witness : Yes, but I did not know but that there might be some reason for putting in for Falmouth.

Mr. Jones : Was there any reason for that?

Witness : It is all supposition. The engineer and captain might have had a private consultation in consequence of something going wrong with the machinery, and have decided to put into port.

Mr. Jones : Then if you had the course W. by N. given you, you would have supposed that you were putting into Falmouth?

Mr. Pyke : You had no reason for thinking that anything was wrong with the engines?

Witness : None whatsoever.

That concluded Mr. Juddery's cross-examination, and the President of the Court proceeded to praise him for his courage and his part in saving those who found themselves in the ship's rigging.

The next witness was Frederick Butt, another quartermaster, who appeared in court with his left hand in a sling.

He gave a statement similar to that of Mr. Juddery. During the whole of the time he was at the wheel the course was W. by N., and that course he passed to Quartermaster Orris [*sic*],[330] who relieved him at six o'clock, and the second officer [Mr. Benjamin Cole, drowned in the wreck] heard it. He could see land on the starboard bow as he was going below, and he was below till the boat struck. He confirmed the testimony of Mr. Juddery, as to the captain being on the upper bridge, and giving orders about tending to the women and children.

The cross-examination continued:

Mr. Pyke : The captain was a thorough seaman and a good one to sail under?

Witness : He was a strict captain, but a good one.

Mr. Butt went on to say that he did not know of anything of the course of the vessel after six o'clock. If she had kept an even keel he believed they would have all got out.

---

[330] A misidentification in the newspaper report of the proceedings, as this named person was not aboard the *Mohegan*. The only possibility is that it was either Mr G. August or Mr L. A. Blake (most likely the former), both of whom perished in the wreck.

At the inquiry on behalf of the Board of Trade, written evidence proffered on behalf of two American passengers was not pursued:

Mr. Jones proposed to read the two depositions of two passengers who had left for America. One was made before a Lancashire magistrate, and the other before the American Consul at Southampton. [331]

The President of the Court said that the latter was clearly inadmissible.

Mr. Pyke strongly objected to the evidence of any passenger who was not there to be cross-examined, and the point was not pressed.[332]

It would have been most interesting to have seen these documents, but unfortunately they are not available at the present time.

The outcome of the Board of Trade inquiry was generally along the lines as expected. There was no ignoring the appalling lack of seamanship on the part of the master of the ship, and so Captain Richard Griffith must take the responsibility for this catastrophe.

His name will always be said in the same breath as the phrase '*Mohegan* disaster' and he has joined that list of inglorious individuals who took it upon themselves to pursue a course of action, that eventually was their undoing:

The Loss of the *Mohegan*

"The cause of the stranding of the *Mohegan* was that the wrong course for the Lizard was steered—west by north—after passing the Eddystone lighthouse". That was the chief finding of the Court that conducted the Board of Trade inquiry into the loss of that new steamship with 106 lives. Captain Griffiths, who, with all his officers, went down among the Manacle Rocks, in Falmouth Bay, gave that course; the officers of the watches heard it passed to the new helmsman, and no question was raised by any of them. The log could have been consulted as to the distance run if there had been the least doubt as to the correctness of the course. Passengers who had made the voyage between the Thames and New York before remarked on the closeness of the ship to the Eddystone lighthouse, and further on to the Devon and Cornish coast. But no misgiving disturbed the sense of the security entertained by the captain and his officers. The course was steered unflinchingly, truly, and accurately in a perfect spirit of discipline. The appalling disaster was the result. The captain was described by a petty officer as a good seaman and all that, but he was "a martinet"—a man not likely to tolerate suggestions from subordinates. His professional record was in his favour. He was very strict, reserved, and carried not only a sober, but a most abstentious man. But the wrong course was steered for all that. When Admiral Tryon [333] was informed by an officer that the

---

[331] The former passenger was Mr John Hyslop and the latter being Mr Francis W. Pemberton.

[332] *The Royal Cornwall Gazette Falmouth Packet, Cornish Weekly News, & General Advertiser*; Thursday, December 1st 1898.

[333] *HMS Victoria*, a 10,000-ton, iron-plated leviathan with 16¼ in. guns—the largest in the world at the time—was launched in 1887. She became the flagship in the Mediterranean of Vice-Admiral Sir George Tryon, regarded as a brilliant yet fearsome naval officer whose domineering character ultimately caused the tragedy that cost him his life. The fleet, consisting of ten battleships, prepared a complicated manoeuvre on June 23, 1893, before dropping anchor off Tripoli. It was drawn up in two columns of five ships, steaming parallel to each other about 1,200 yards apart. The columns were meant to turn towards each other in single file so that when completed they would be sailing 400 yards apart in the opposite direction to the previous course. The final move was to turn the entire fleet 90 degrees to port then drop anchor, making a dramatic spectacle to those watching from the shore. Two of Admiral Tryon's officers told him that 1,200 yards was not far enough for the two leading ships, the *Victoria* and *HMS Camperdown*, to turn towards each other without colliding. They recommended that the columns be at least 1,600 yards apart. The admiral agreed, but inexplicably later gave instructions to close the columns to the original 1,200 yards. The *Camperdown* struck the *Victoria* on the starboard side below the waterline; 13 minutes later the flagship sank below the surface, bows first with the propellers still spinning. There were only 357 survivors. Admiral Tryon, who remained on the bridge, is reputed to have said, "It's all my fault"—*The Times,* September 2nd., 2004.

H.M.S. Victoria could not turn within six cables, and was asked should the signal be for eight, his answer was "Let it be six". To this day the nation deplores that colossal catastrophe.[334]

The American Press printed a suprisingly brief account of the Board of Trade ruling:

THE MOHEGAN WRECK INQUIRY.
British Board of Trade Commission Expresses
Admiration of the Efforts Made to Safe Life

LONDON, Nov. 26.—The Board of Trade inquiry into the Atlantic Transport Company's steamer *Mohegan*, which was totally wrecked off The Lizard, between The Manacle Rocks and The Lowlands, on Oct. 14 last, while in command of Capt. Richard Griffith, was concluded to-day.

The judgment of the Board was that the ship was in good seaworthy condition, and that Capt. Griffiths was in good health at the time the disaster occurred, the stranding of the vessel being caused by a wrong course being steered after the *Mohegan* had passed Eddystone Light.

The commission, in addition, expressed admirations of the efforts that had been made to save those on board the steamer.

The commission also found that the great loss of life was due to the extinction of the electric lights on the steamer after she went ashore.[335]

A leap in the dark.

The failure of the *Mohegan*'s electric lights, moments after colliding with the Manacles, caused much confusion in the darkness. It was difficult to perform the prescribed manoeuvres that would normally be undertaken in such an event. On sinking, and in the darkness, passengers and crew had no idea in which direction to jump and swim towards safety. Again, the darkness prevented the assisting lifeboats in seeing the survivors and also dissuaded the coxswains from venturing too close to the rocks and the sunken vessel, for fear of joining in her fate.

Needless to say, there would have been a chorus of cries for help but the temptation to pluck the poor souls from the sea was resisted—difficult though to ignore. They would have to wait for first-light. Apart from those lucky few who found a precarious sanctuary in the ship's rigging, no living persons were recovered in the morning.

A sorry sight.

A commercial photographer of the time was offering salacious photographs of the disaster victims, in their last days before burial,[336] and the fact that pictures were on general sale had reached the ear of the Board of Trade inquiry, causing not a little disquiet:

[334] *The Belfast News-Letter* (Belfast, Ireland); Monday, 28th November 1898.

[335] *The New York Times;* 27th November 1898.

Mr. Pyke on behalf of the owners of the *Mohegan* complained of a photograph, which was being exhibited for sale in Penzance. He thought it was highly objectionable, and would give pain to the relatives of the persons photographed, and he asked for the censure of the Courts upon it. The owners had done all they could with reference to the unfortunate victims of the catastrophe, and they felt that this was unfair to them, as well as painful to the friends. (The photograph, that was understood to represent a large number of dead bodies, was handed up to the Court).

Mr. Marshall said the Court had no jurisdiction in this matter but the photograph was a very painful one to see, it would hurt the feelings of the friends of the deceased, and it ought not to have been shown.[337]

That concluded the Board of Trade inquiry, into the affair of the wrecking of the *S.S.Mohegan*.

[336] An example of such image is seen in Fig. 39. No doubt more than one photographer had access to the victims laid out in the church, and it is not assumed that this was the particular photograph under criticism.

[337] *Daily News*, (London, England); Saturday, 26th November 1898.

CHAPTER 12

A Resumption of the Coroner's Inquest

The Board of Trade inquiry completed and its findings now made public, the coroner's inquest re-convened, after two months in abeyance.

A coroner has a remarkable degree of autonomy, in the matter of inquests. He (exclusively male at this time) is empowered to call any witness he deems pertinent to a case, in order to arrive at a cause of death, and to apportion any blame, based on the evidence and the law of the land. However, it would be a brave man, who would challenge the might of the courts of London and turn their judgment on its head; unless, that is, there is irrefutable evidence to support such an outcome. Mr Carlyon had no such evidence, but many rumours, suppositions, and accusations were awash in the wake of the disaster and would need careful handling; in this, the closing chapter of the inquest. It would certainly test the coroner's ability to maintain discipline and legal rectitude:

THE MOHEGAN DISASTER INQUEST.
Verdict of Carelessness and Irregular Navigation.

The inquest on the victims of the wreck of the *Mohegan* on the Manacles on October 14th last, was resumed by Mr E. L. Carlyon, county Coroner, at St. Keverne on Thursday [December 23rd]. Nobody was present except those immediately concerned.

The Coroner said he communicated with the Board of Trade on the day after the opening of the inquest suggesting they might send a representative to help them. In reply, the Board stated they would be pleased to send a nautical assessor, but an inquiry was to be held in London, and they suggested it might [send an assessor] should the inquest take place after that. A Coroner's inquest was held chiefly for finding out the cause of death, and if anybody was to blame. In this particular case, even if criminal neglect could have been proved against some people in authority onboard, and all those persons had been drowned, so it was perfectly impossible to bring in a verdict of murder or manslaughter against them. Therefore, it seemed unnecessary to hold a further inquest until the Board of Trade inquiry had taken place. He and the jury were in possession of the report of the Board of Trade inquiry, which was most exhaustive and elicited some very important facts. Upon the most important fact, however, they could throw really no light, and he was afraid it would never be found out how the officer in charge at the time the *Mohegan* left the Eddystone caused the vessel to be steered west by north. This steering of the wrong course was reported as the cause of the wreck, and the great loss of life was attributed to the bad list of the vessel to port almost immediately after striking the rocks, preventing the majority of the boats being got into use. The inquiry elicited the important fact that the vessel was in every way well-founded, complying in every respect with the Board of Trade requirements. She was manned and officered by a perfectly competent crew. Directly the vessel struck the second and third officers were on the bridge, and the captain was there immediately after. Those who were actually on the scene stated that everything that could be done was done to save the passengers. They must agree with the gentlemen who held the inquiry that the conduct of the officers and crew after the vessel struck was most commendable. From the report they further gathered that the lifeboat crew were on the spot as soon as possible, and did everything in their power to save life. They joined in praising the crew, who could not be praised too much for the heroic services they rendered. The report contained nothing much about what happened to the survivors after they were on shore. The inhabitants of that locality were too modest to say anything about this, but he thought a word of praise was due to them for the grand way in which they rallied to the assistance of the unfortunate people brought on shore in a wet and helpless condition. This report also referred to lifeboat drills on vessels, and boats being swung out going down Channel. No question was raised at the inquiry as to the desirability of having a lighthouse on the Manacles, but that question had not escaped the notice of the authorities. The Trinity Board and the Board of Trade had given very careful consideration to the matter, he had no doubt and they had come to the conclusion that a lighthouse or a lightship was not necessary on those rocks. Indeed it would appear that even if there were a lighthouse every four of five miles down the coast some accidents would happen in a most unaccountable way. They had only to remember the recent wreck of the *Bluejacket*, which ran right up under a lighthouse.[338] If a vessel could do that in clear weather she could do anything. They could only suppose that it was owing to some gross carelessness on somebody's part that the *Mohegan* got into the position she did. It seemed utterly inexcusable, but on the Manacles she went and on a perfectly clear night. If she had gone the course vessels usually went she must have seen the Lizard lights after leaving the Eddystone, for those lights were very bright and were visible for 21 miles. It seemed almost incredible that a vessel so well founded and so well manned could get into the position she did. It might be perfectly possible that some officers in charge did notice that the vessel was not going on her right course and were afraid to speak to Captain Griffiths, who seemed to be, though a very good officer, rather a severe man and a man who could not be very well approached. In the report it was suggested that in future officers that saw that a vessel was out of her course should be in bounden duty to report to the captain for inquiry. These were very useful and proper suggestions by the Board of Trade. There was no evidence that he (the Coroner) could bring to help the jury any further, The Atlantic Transport Company were perfectly willing to send their witnesses down and be legally represented. But he told them he thought it would be unnecessary. He suggested that the jury should return an open verdict.[339]

There follows a transcript of the resumed inquest: [340]

Mr. W. Boaden said that what they really wanted to know was the cause of the wrong course being steered.

Mr. W. James said most people were agreed that the cause was neglect. He called it manslaughter for a man to cause the wreck of a ship in sight of land, as it was the case with the *Mohegan*. He was aware it was a fearful thing to say.

Mr. W. Boaden: It is a bad thing to say, but we are here to do our duty.

The Coroner: You cannot bring in a verdict of manslaughter unless you bring it against somebody.

Mr. James: The captain—

The Coroner: He has paid the penalty.

A Juror thought it very wrong that so many of the witnesses were officers and men in the company's employ. No passenger was there to give a contradictory message.

Mr. Boaden pointed out that the captain quite disobeyed the regulations that captains should keep the bridge coming down the Channel.

The Coroner: We must all agree that the wrong course was steered, but why we shall never find out.

---

[338] The steam ship *'Bluejacket'* was wrecked on rocks near the lighthouse on a clear night in 1898, and nearly demolishing the lighthouse in the process.

[339] *The Royal Cornwall Gazette Falmouth Packet, Cornish Weekly News, & General Advertise;* Wednesday, December 29, 1898.

[340] The venue for this resumed inquest was in the Boy's Schoolroom, Churchtown St. Keverne.

A Juror: Any man who used his eyes could see the vessel was going wrong.

Mr. J. Coad (foreman of the jury) said that had captain and officers been living they would have been brought to book.

A Juror: It is useless to ask questions because there is nobody here to answer.

Mr. Boaden said they could not help coming to an unfavourable opinion upon the matter.

Someone made a remark about the captain willfully running the ship on the rocks, but the Coroner said there was absolutely no evidence in support of such a statement.

Mr. W. Matthews: A great many people think the captain is still alive. If he escaped hanging he did not ought to. I think the Board of Trade surveyor should inspect vessels just before sailing in order to see if the boats are in a serviceable condition.

Mr. Coad observed that there did not appear to have been any attempt to conceal anything in the investigation.

The Coroner: I do not see the smallest reason for any supposition of that kind.

Mr. Boaden said in his opinion the vessel was lost through culpable negligence.

The jury agreed, concerning the forty victims upon whom the inquest was held, that they were found dead, having met their death by drowning through the wreck of the *Mohegan*.

Mr. Rogers moved that, and Mr. Pengelly seconded, the rider, "We consider that the disaster took place in consequence of the gross carelessness of the captain".

A second rider was moved by Mr. R. M. Clayton, and seconded by Mr. T. J. Joyce, that, "the disaster was the result of carelessness and irregular navigation".

Eight voted for each rider, and the foreman gave his casting vote in favour of the second.

Mr. Coad said it was thought the time had now arrived when some steps should be taken to better protect the Manacles and warn mariners from that dangerous spot. It was understood that a coastguard station was to be built at Porthoustock. That station, instead of being built at an indented place in the coast where it would not have much value, should be erected on the most dangerous point. He suggested they should endeavour to get it built near the projecting rocks, so that proper appliances for avoiding disaster should be ready at the most convenient spot. The cost could not be much greater.

Mr. Joyce concurred, and thought the coastguard cottages might be built on Watchhouse Point,[341] whence those in charge could command the coast from Dodman nearly to the Lizard.

It was decided to write to Falmouth Chamber of Commerce urging this point

Look here upon this picture.

Altogether 50 bodies have been brought on shore in the parish of St. Keverne, of which six are registered as unknown. The *Mohegan* carried 104 officers and crew and 53 passengers, of whom 66 of the former and 40 of the latter were drowned. The schoolmaster (Mr. R. M. Clayton) has received from the Atlantic Transport Company a large water colour painting of the *Mohegan* attended by a tug, evidently in some part of the Thames.[342] It is a fine representation of the majestic liner, and an inscription records that the picture was presented by the company, "in grateful recognition of kind services rendered to the lost and saved". The company have also offered to pay for a large photograph of the submerged vessel as she appeared shortly after the wreck, to accompany the picture on the wall of the village school.[343]

[341] Interestingly, on a navigation chart for the Manacles, dated 1863, there is the symbol '*CG Watch H*' already located on *Manacle Point*. This could well be the origin of that particular location.

[342] The background image is a water colour painting commissioned by the Atlantic Transport Line for display in the St. Keverne schoolhouse. The picture is signed by Sidney John Roberts and is currently on display at the Roskilly's tea-room in the Tregellast Barton Farm, St Keverne.

[343] *The Royal Cornwall Gazette Falmouth Packet, Cornish Weekly News, & General Advertiser*; Wednesday 29th December 1898.

The proceedings at this resumed inquest were rather low key in nature. Perhaps the Board of Trade inquiry overshadowed a more parochial inquiry at St. Keverne. Nevertheless, there was the occasional clash of views, and the coroner was obliged to keep the proceedings on course and under control. There were rumours awash within the local community: mainly hearsay, and in some cases, bordering on the scandalous. The vocal Mr Richard Kelly (a passenger present at the original inquest) was not present and his cogent views, expressed earlier, were absent here.

An account, at the completion of the coroner's inquest, duly appeared in the Press:

INQUEST AND VERDICT

The inquest on the bodies of the *Mohegan* victims was concluded at St. Keverne yesterday. The Coroner remarked that after the exhaustive inquiry by the Board of Trade, it had not been thought necessary to produce further witnesses before the Jury, or to call upon the Atlantic Transport Company, who owned the *Mohegan*, to be legally represented at these adjourned proceedings. The principal duty of the Jury was to ascertain if anybody was to blame criminally for the disaster. Even if criminal neglect were proved, it could only have been proved against some of the people in authority on board, and such persons had been drowned, so it was perfectly impossible to return a verdict of manslaughter against them. Although the Board of Trade investigation had elicited certain very important facts, it really threw no light on the most important of all, namely, how the officer in charge at the time the ship left the Eddystone caused her to be steered west by north. He was afraid there never would be much found out on that point. There had been raised a question as to the desirability of placing a light house on the Manacle Rocks.

It seemed utterly inexcusable, and it was almost incredible that a vessel so well founded and manned could have been lost under such circumstances. Perfectly possible was it that some of the officers in charge did notice that the *Mohegan* was not going on the right course, and were afraid to speak to Captain Griffith, who seems to have been thought a very good officer, but was rather a severe man, a man one could not approach very well. The Board of Trade suggested that in future if officers did see that a vessel was out of her course, it was their bounden duty to report the matter to the Captain that it might be enquired into, He advised the Jury to return a verdict that the deceased met their death by drowning, owing to the wreck of the *Mohegan*.

One of the Jurors was inclined to attribute the disaster to culpable negligence, while another went so far as to describe the affair as manslaughter.

The Coroner explained that any verdict of manslaughter must be brought against somebody, and such a charge could not be preferred against the Captain, as he had already paid the penalty.

A Juryman alleged that the Captain was guilty of disobedience to rules by not keeping on deck when near land.—The Coroner observed they never would find out the reason why the wrong course was steered.—The foreman advised his colleagues that they must deal with the case as it was submitted to them. If the Captain and officers had been living, of course they would have been brought to book.—The Coroner suggested that the verdict should be an open one, and eventually that suggestion was acted upon.—In the opinion of the Coroner, there was absolutely nothing to show that Captain Griffith wilfully put his ship on the rocks.—A Juror: Supposing the Captain is alive—and a great many people think he is (laughter)—if he escapes hanging he ought not to (renewed laughter).—Two riders to the verdict were proposed–first, "That the Jury consider the cause of the disaster was due to the gross negligence of the Captain"; and, secondly, "That the disaster was the result of carelessness and irregular navigation". Eight Jurymen having voted for each rider, the Foreman gave his casting vote for the second one, which was declared adopted. It was decided to ask the

Falmouth Chamber of Commerce to approach Trinity House or the Board of Trade with the object of having a Coastguard look-out placed on a prominent point near the Manacles.[344]

The coastguard lookout was eventually built on Manacle Point, looking out over the Manacle Rocks. Commonsense had prevailed: this being the most obvious place to position the lookout station. There is a picture of this building on the Manacle Point (see fig. 63) but sadly the building itself no longer exists. The associated coastguard cottages were built to accommodate three coastguards and their families, in the village of Porthoustock.[345]

Essentially, the Coroner's inquest came to much the same conclusion as that of the Board of Trade inquiry. The latter investigation was carefully orchestrated. Rumours, personal views, and interpretations, not based on facts or corroborative evidence, were not given a voice at the proceedings. In comparison, the Coroner's inquest was not as rigidly controlled, and enabled both the jury and onlookers to contribute their views, almost at will. The Coroner's task was difficult and an unenviable one. However, to his credit, he managed to gently direct the court towards the same conclusion as with the Board of Trade, with minimal damage to reputations or local sensibilities.

A local belief refuses to go away.

To this day, Capt. Richard Griffith, master of the ill-fated *Mohegan*, is thought to have survived the catastrophe, and that he had been involved in a deliberate wrecking of his vessel, for his own pecuniary gain. That a so well-known a person was not recognised by either a member of the crew or a passenger at Porthoustock, is difficult to imagine. But this is not entirely impossible, given the circumstances that prevailed on that night. Griffith received much opprobrium by the survivors and families of those affected by his action. He no doubt assumed the role of a bogeyman, and children would have been afraid to venture out into the night, or set foot on the quiet shore, for fear of meeting up with the 'captain of death' —a suitable model for instilling fear and making obedient, any wayward Victorian child.

That his body was found in North Wales, some three months after the disaster, is as much a part of this myth that now surrounds the man and this point will be re-visited, later in this book.

Whatever his previous success and reputation had achieved, 105 persons would curse the day they stepped aboard the *Mohegan*: a ship under his command.

---

[344] *The Standard* (London, England); Friday, 23rd December 1898.

[345] They still exist [2013] and are currently available as rented holiday accomodation.

CHAPTER 13

Salvaging the *SS Mohegan.*

Pride would be a lot easier to swallow if it didn't taste so bad.

An embarrassing moment for an inspection party, who had visited the *Mohegan* wreck site, resulted in a repeat of the scramble for the ship's rigging that had occurred on the night of the disaster. An alarming incident that could so easily have claimed yet more victims, ended happily with no more than wet feet and a bruised pride.

It was a fine day on October the 19th and the tide was set at about low water. Captain Robert M. Robinson, marine superintendent to Messrs. Williams, Torrey and Feild, the ATL Company's London agent, had been down to the wreck and photographs taken there were to have been produced in court at the Board of Trade inquiry, showing the location of the ship. The trip to the wreck was made in a tug from Falmouth, in company with the salvage officer and a diver. Leaving the tug, the men approached the wreck in a rowing boat. On the starboard side, near the foremast, they recorded a sounding of eleven fathoms, and found the vessel on a pretty even keel. Capt. Robinson then got the men to pull the boat further aft, in order to take another sounding: but in the manoeuvring, the boat got close to the mizzen rigging, the bow struck on the steamer and was holed. With the sudden inrush of water, they all hurriedly took to the safety of the ship's rigging:

THE WRECK OF THE MOHEGAN

An unpleasant experience befell the inspecting party who visited the scene of the wreck yesterday. Their tug lay off the wreck some distance, and they rowed around the *Mohegan* in a small boat. One of the steamer's awning stanchions [346] penetrated the bottom of the rowing boat, and she quickly filled with water. The occupants had to seek safety in the rigging of the sunken liner. They made known their plight by shouting and waving handkerchiefs, and were quickly relieved from their uncomfortable position by one or two rowing boats which were fortunately handy at the time. Happily the mishap did not involve the party in anything more serious than wet feet. While rowing around the *Mohegan's* masts a quantity of woman's hair and a cloth band were noticed clinging to the mizzen. These must have been severed from the body of some poor creature who was washed away from the rigging. The hair, which was auburn was fixed to the mast at a spot which would be covered by the sea at high tide. It will be remembered that the only woman saved from the rigging was the assistant stewardess. [347]

---

[346] Awning stanchions are the support poles for fabric sunshades set up temporarily over open deck areas.

[347] *The Pall Mall Gazette* (London, England); Thursday October 20th 1898. This would refer to Mrs. Piggot; however, she was saved from the rigging and the 'poor unfortunate' may well have been another woman, who had been swept away. The cloth could have been from Mrs Piggott, as she had ripped up her apron to provide a head-bandage for Quartermaster Butt, while both were in the mizzen rigging.

In describing the state of the tide, a member of the party said: "I only wonder how a boat could ever have got out of there." Asked how the tide was, in the neighbourhood of the wreck, he said: "There was a sort of whirl—the tide was not steady at all, although it was a fine day. The top of the bridge was gone. I did not notice any direction of the tide towards the Voces Rocks; it did not seem steady in one way."

A report appeared in a newspaper, which gave some additional information on the situation, leading up to the disaster:

The Sunday following the disaster, a tug from Falmouth visited the wreck, that morning, despite the very dirty weather. The vessel was found to have settled even deeper in the water. Her masts and funnel were still visible above the water, and her bow was facing seaward, and her stern towards the land. She must have, therefore swung around after striking, for there was no fact ascertainable to support a theory propounded by some persons that the officer on the bridge having discovered he was in Falmouth Bay had the ship's course so completely altered as to stand out to sea on the port side at an angle that would bring him to the Manacle Rocks. The two engineers who have been saved declare that there never was any slackening of speed, which would certainly have occurred, had suspicion arisen on the bridge that the steamer was out of her course and in dangerous water. Only one man in that watch had been saved, an A.B., who was busy in cleaning work on the deck. He never noticed any change in the ship's course. If any was made it must have been a very gradual one, and would point back to an error begun after leaving the Eddystone.[348]

Another report described a preliminary inspection, prior to the salvage operation being undertaken:

The representative of the London Salvage Association and some divers during the day surveyed the wreck, the position of which has not altered. An inspection of the sunken ship was made yesterday by Captain Ridge, representing the London Salvage Association, who are acting for the underwriters. It was accompanied by local divers and salvors. At a safe distance from the Manacle Rocks buoy was anchored the Trinity boat *Mermaid*, which came to see if the wreck was any impediment to navigation. Situated right among the rocks, the *Mohegan* is away from the track of all passing vessels. Captain Ridge reported that it was quite possible to save the cargo, but the saving of the vessel was very uncertain. The ship's gear and passengers' belongings might also, he thought, be recovered. Around the wreck was a depth of water of about 11 fathoms. The list to the port is about 30deg. Divers would have to be employed for the salving of the cargo, but it would be a very hazardous operation. Joseph Breen,[349] a Penzance diver and salvor, accompanied the party, and he declared that the danger of diving work on the *Mohegan*, in consequence of the strong tide, would be so great that it would be difficult to find anyone to tender to take it. Just at this place the tide at the full had a velocity of six knots. The *Mohegan* had a general cargo of about 1,000 tons, comprising Manchester goods, bales of hemp, and such valuable material as antimony and other things which would not be damaged much by water. The wreck lies about three-quarters of a mile from the mainland in a rocky archipelago. About a quarter of a mile outside of the wreck is the *Manacle* buoy with its warning bell. On the outward side the *Mohegan* is considerably deeper in the water than on the shore side, owing to a heavy list to port, and in consequence the davits and ventilating shafts can be seen on the starboard, whereas the corresponding fittings on the other side are beneath the waves. At half tide the greater part of the red funnel and the masts show above the water. The covered part of

---

[348] *The Belfast News–letter;* Monday 17th October, 1898.

[349] Joseph Breen was the owner of the steamship salvage boat *Chase*, which was wrecked on the Longships while salving the *Bluejacket*. All the crew were saved. *The Royal Cornwall Gazette Falmouth Packet, Cornish Weekly News, & General Advertiser;* Thursday, February 15, 1900.

the bridge deck is just washed at low water. There has been no change in the position of the ship since the disaster. Except for a little broken planking there is no wreckage floating in the vicinity. Captain Ridge's report will be considered by the underwriters.[350]

Even before the funeral of the *Mohegan*'s victims had taken place, salvage of her cargo had already commenced: linoleum, jute, tin, furniture, lace and church ornaments were raised. Some of the cargo, most memorably casks of good quality ale, washed ashore and fell into the hands of appreciative locals; a small reward perhaps for their unstinting generosity following the disaster (see Table 1, p. 146).

It was no surprise that the forward part of the wreck was greatly damaged, as she sank by her head, with the tremendous weight of the vessel settling on the seabed, causing most of the damage. The additional corkscrewing forces, generated by the rough seas and vicious tides helped further disassemble the wreck, for the salvors. As can be deduced from this report, only four weeks after the wrecking, the *Mohegan* was now rapidly breaking up:

> Captain Ridge, of the London Salvage Association, has obtained the services of a second diver, being desirous of doing all he possibly can do to save the passengers' baggage. The one diver engaged has been the means of bringing to the surface a lady's travelling basket, belonging to the late Miss Bushnell, and a trunk, the property of the late Mr. Lacheur. There is every hope of doing more in the direction of salving personal property. The cabins are in such a confused state, caused by the debris and other obstacles, that the work of a diver in them is one of no little difficulty. Captain Pomeroy, of the Liverpool Salvage Association, whose chief concern is the recovery of the tin on board, is also to receive the aid of a second diver. The *Mohegan*'s cargo included 1,500 slabs of tin, weighing seventy-five tons, and representing a value of £6,000. Thus far, there have been salved 131 slabs, of the value of £500. With the extraordinary power of the sea around the Manacles the position of the liner has changed, and she is undergoing a great strain. The charthouse has been completely washed away, the promenade deck has "started," and the ship's funnel has gone.[351]

Whilst the ship was relatively intact, the salvage company embarked on this difficult operation:

> Under the direction of Capt. Pomeroy, of The Liverpool Salvage Association (who is acting in accord with Capt. Ridge, of the London Salvage Association), a diver has been down into No 1 hold and salved 31 bales of gunnies.[352] The ship's bell and a reel of wire rope have also been recovered. The whole matter of salving the passengers' baggage and cargo, other than in No 1 hold, is entirely in the hands of the London Salvage Association. Arrangements are being made to carry on these operations as quickly as possible. The position of the ship remains the same. She is in a fairly easy position for getting at the cargo, but the salving of the liner herself would be a matter of considerable difficulty.[353]

---

[350] *The Times;* 20th October 1898.

[351] *The Royal Cornwall Gazette Falmouth Packet, Cornish Weekly News, & General Advertiser;* Thursday, November 10th 1898.

[352] A gunny sack is an inexpensive bag made of burlap [a coarse canvas woven from jute, hemp, or a similar fibre], also known as a 'gunny shoe'. Gunny sacks are traditionally used for transporting grains, potatoes, and other agricultural products.—*WikiPedia.*

[353] *The Royal Cornwall Gazette Falmouth Packet, Cornish Weekly News, & General Advertiser;* Thursday, November 3rd 1898.

The salvage vessel *Mallard* and a number of tugs were soon on the scene with standard divers, salvaging her cargo. Nearly 3000 blocks of tin were recovered by the Western Marine Salvage Company of Penzance. With the winter months approaching and while the weather remained favourable, the salvage work continued unabated:

> The weather on Friday was more favourable for salving operations on the Manacle Rocks than it had been since the *Mohegan* foundered. Two divers went down to the wreck. The steamship's cargo included £6,000 worth of tin,[354] and the diver[355] who had undertaken to do his best to salve sent up several tons. Very little was done by the other diver, who is to explore the cabins, and to obtain some of the passengers' luggage and valuables. His idea was to make explorations in order to see how best he and his party can work. He visited the saloon, where the passengers were sitting at the commencement of dinner when the *Mohegan* struck, and found the things on the tables apparently just as they were left, although the vessel had a considerable list. There were no bodies in the saloon or in the chart room. The cabins could not be entered without forcing the doors, which the diver was not prepared to do then. While the divers were at work, a few Porthallow fishermen found a body, in an advanced stage of decomposition, floating nearby. From the clothes it appeared that this was one of the crew of the *Mohegan*—probably a fireman, and he was buried on Saturday at one o'clock in the large grave containing several other victims of the *Mohegan* disaster. In this grave the remains of the stewardess, Mrs. Bowles, were interred, with others, a fortnight ago, and now the relatives or friends are anxious to have her body exhumed.[356]

In salving the wreck the divers had many problems to contend with, making the task difficult and dangerous. The operations were still underway, when the steamship *ss Paris* went aground on the 21st May 1899, at Lowland Point:

The Mohegan and the Paris

> Two important salvages are in progress at the Manacles. For nearly nine months, the London Salvage Association has had in hand the work of recovering property from the wreck of the *Mohegan*, whilst for several weeks a foreign combination of salvors has been expending its energies on the steamship *Paris*. The character of the respective undertakings differs to a considerable extent in two ways. The *Paris*, so to speak, above water; the *Mohegan* lies deep down among the rocks, with only the upper portions of her masts peering above the surface of the sea. Then, in the case of the *Paris*, the effort is to save the ship bodily, but the position of the ship *Mohegan* allows only piecemeal salvage. After the south-easterly gales of a whole winter, in an exposed situation like the Manacles, it is not surprising to find that the *Mohegan* is tumbling to pieces. The promenade deck over the saloon is gone entirely; the saloon fittings on the higher side—the boat is heavily listing— have broken adrift and fallen to leeward, thereby confronting the divers with a great obstacle forcing their way over the vessel. As yet the whole of the ship has not been explored. From time to time a considerable quantity of general cargo has been hauled up from the holds, and not a little still remains in the ship. The handling of perishable merchandise and general effects of the passengers has been by no means a pleasant task, their state after so long an immersion being most objectionable to the nasal organs. In the third hold operations have been much impeded by an enormous mass of loose and

---

[354] In today's currency, this would have a value of £342,000.

[355] One diver engaged with the salvaging was the Falmouth man, Mr Cecil Albany Chard. He had also worked on the salvaging of the scuttled vessel *SMS Libau*, in retrieving evidence for the trial of Sir Roger Casement – the Irish revolutionary traitor – *Ellesmere Guardian; 23 Feb 1932. His fellow citizens elected Mr Chard as the mayor of Falmouth (1935–36). Mr Chard was featured in a book entitled, *Don't Forget the Diver* –1958, Chambers.

[356] The *Royal Cornwall Gazette; 10th November 1898.

decomposed rice, cheese, currants, and articles of general grocery, reaching to above the knees of the three divers. Now the *Mohegan* has a covering of seaweed of 12ft. and when lowered the divers are lost in the "forest". That alone is sufficient to indicate the extent of the many difficulties that beset the workers. To bring up all the winches—nine in number—without the least damage from the deck was a pretty heavy job. Nor was it an easy matter to raise four massive bar anchors as well as 240 fathoms of two-and-a-half-inch cable. A little while ago a hunt of the ship resulted in the discovery of the captain's safe, containing the *Mohegan*'s papers. There was still another safe which the salvors were anxious to alight on, that belonging to the purser—and a long search met its reward on Thursday afternoon. It was in the saloon, and on Friday a more suitable resting place was found for it in Falmouth.

Until the fastening has been released the contents of this particular safe cannot be known; possibly there are a good many valuables in it. Future operations will entail a good deal of heavy labour. In the course of a day or two, there will be what is known as a big "blow" on the propeller to get it off, and for the purpose of the salvage, a 15lb charge of dynamite will be employed. The shaft is of solid steel, about 2ft. in thickness, and to achieve the object in view has to be cut clean through. The removal of the propeller, if successfully carried out, will form a significant part of the salvage, inasmuch as it is a special one of manganese bronze and worth something like £150.[357] After the recovery of the propeller and the most valuable portions of the cargo, it is intending to begin the salving of the engines and boilers. Captain Corner, representing the London Association, superintends the salvage work. By a singular coincidence the stern of the *Mohegan* rests upon the wreck of another vessel, thought to be a Greek [Spyridion Vagliano–1890].[358]

The matter of retrieving the safes from the interior of the wreck was of great importance, for obvious reasons:

THE SAFE OF THE MOHEGAN

Salvors of the steamship *Mohegan* wrecked on the Manacles, have found on the rocks surrounding the ship her safe, which was conveyed to the Falmouth branch of the Cornish Bank.[359]

As regards the *Mohegan* relics, a report in a local newspaper covered an interesting artifact, the ship's bell:

MOHEGAN RELIC
Coverack Home for Bell of ill-fated Ship

Brought ashore 52 years ago from the liner *Mohegan*, lost with 106 lives on the dreaded Manacle Rocks on her maiden voyage [as the *Mohegan*] to New York, the ship's bell, after lying for many years in the now defunct Falmouth Museum, has once again returned to the scene of the historic wreck. When the museum was closed and most of the exhibits were sold by auction some months ago, the bell was purchased by Mr. S. James, of *Parc Behan*,[360] Coverack, and is being cleaned and polished to take its place among other mementos of the disaster.

After the *Mohegan* was wrecked, Mr. W. ["Billy"] May, aged 91, Coverack's oldest resident, and harbourmaster for many years, was appointed by Lloyd's as receiver of salvage, and all material recovered from the steamer was brought into Coverack. Mr. May accompanied Mr. James to Falmouth when he purchased the bell at the museum auction, and

---

[357] In today's currency, this would equate to £8,600. In the specification for the *Cleopatra*, the propeller was reported as made of iron (see page 10).

[358] *Royal Cornwall Gazette Falmouth Packet, Cornish Weekly News, & General Advertiser*; Thursday, 13rd July 1899.

[359] *Royal Cornwall Gazette Falmouth Packet, Cornish Weekly News, & General Advertiser*; Thursday, 8th June 1899

[360] A private house at that time and now is used as accommodation by the Youth Hostel Association. The address is: School Hill, Coverack, Helston, Cornwall, TR12 6SA; coverack@yha.org.uk. The *Mohegan*'s staircase had been installed here (see fig. 9).

recognised it instantly as the one which was handed to him at the scene of the wreck by the late Mr. J. ["Jim"] H. Cliff, of *Manacle View*, St. Keverne.

The words "Cleopatra Hull 1898" inscribed on the bell, have been explained in a letter which Mr. James has recently received from Lloyds. It is pointed out the *Mohegan* was originally named *Cleopatra*, but the name on the ship's bell had not been changed.[361]

The bell found itself an unusual new home, far from its typical maritime setting:

The ship's bell [362] salved from the *Mohegan* has been hung in the bell turret of the Mission-room on the Moor [363] at Falmouth, and will in future do duty in a new capacity. It has a full and musical sound and can be heard much further than the old one, the fittings of which were very much worn.[364]

The Bell from the wreck was sold in the 1950s, and is currently in the ownership of the Roskilly family. [365] Over five decades later, the *Mohegan* and the history of its bell, continues to generate interest:

THE MOHEGAN BELL

Sir,—I was interested to read in last week's issue an account of the *Mohegan* Bell. I was an officer in the Atlantic Transport Line (the owners of the *Mohegan*) from 1906 – 1914. The *Mohegan* was laid down by the builders as the *Cleopatra*, by order of the Wilson, Furness, Leyland line. She was purchased before launching by the Atlantic Transport Line and renamed *Mohegan*. Presumably the bell was cast with the name [*Cleopatra*] on before the purchase, The *Mohegan* had four sister ships: the *Menominee*, *Mesaba*, *Manitou*, and *Marquette*, owned by the Atlantic Transport Line, I was first officer of the *Menominee* in 1914 before joining the Royal Navy as Lieut. R.N.R. in 1912, when first officer of *Montana*, one of our quartermasters, named Huntley, told me he was a quartermaster on the *Mohegan* at the time of her stranding on the Manacles. He was taken off by the lifeboat from the fore rigging. The *Meseba* was torpedoed off the Tuskar Rock whilst in convoy in September, of 1918. All hands were lost as she sank in three minutes. I was in command of one of the gunboats, *H.M.P.G. Kilkeel*. We carried out, with the other escorts, the depth charge attack on the enemy submarine, which torpedoed her. The submarine was sunk.

J. T. ROWE, Lieut.-Com., D.S.C. R.N.R. Situel Bungalow, Mawgan, Helston.[366]

---

[361] *West Briton;* c. 1950
There appears to be two bells in circulation: one named as the *Cleopatra* and another for the *Mohegan*. The latter bell is thought to be a fake. The *Cleopatra* bell is currently owned by the Roskilly family in St. Keverne, and is on current display in the National Maritime Museum, Falmouth (2011).

[362] Personal Communication – Terry Moyle: "My cousins (Edna and Sinclair James, now deceased) bought the Cleopatra Bell at an auction and it was in Parc Behan (YHA – Coverack, since 1977) for many years until they retired when Joe [Roskilly] bought it. I am sure that their bell is the original bell and I am almost certain that the '*Mohegan*' bell is a fake. I do not think that there would have been time for a new bell to be made. Would a vessel have two bells on board?"

[363] The Moor is an open area in the centre of the town of Falmouth that is used as an open-air market.

[364] *The Royal Cornwall Gazette Falmouth Packet, Cornish Weekly News, & General Advertiser;* Thursday 25th May 1899.

[365] The Roskilly family is still at Tregellast Barton, St. Keverne and is nationally famous for its locally produced ice-cream.

[366] *West Briton;* c. 1950. A letter detailing the quartermaster Huntley, aboard the *Mohegan*, appears on p. 177.

Unusual items were retrieved from the wreck:

The salving of the cargo of the *Mohegan* is being actively prosecuted, the weather being favourable. Two life-size figures intended for a Roman Catholic Church in Chicago, recently recovered, have been bought by Mr. John Burton,[367] of the Old Curiosity Shop, Falmouth.[368]

An astonishing variety of ship's manifest was also recovered:

100 bales of hemp, wool and skins	Casks of dye	6 cases of candles
Straw plaits	Eno's Fruit Salts [369]	3 cases druggist's sundries
Pepper and Rice	Mirbane [370]	Golf balls
Gelatin	Barrels of pitch	7 cases of vinegar
Sticklac [371]	Wax vestas [372]	Nutmeg, cinnamon and nutmeg
Gin, wine, rum	Old rope	Allsop's beer 16 /Ale 6 barrels
Steel hawsers / Chains and cable	India rubber	One case of hare's tails
Cheese	Furniture	Creosote and Paint
Ink	Ship's secure safe	160 cases of oilmen's stores
Lace and Clothing	Shellac	Cases of boots and shoes
Nails	Dundee (Jute)	The *Mohegan*'s anchor
Tin ingots	Church ornaments	The *Cleopatra*'s bell

Table 1: *Mohegan:* A List of Salvaged Items

The subsequent stranding of the *Paris*, within sight of the *Mohegan* wreck, gave a useful platform for the salvage items from the *Mohegan*, and in offering increased efficiency as a combined operation:

SPOIL FROM THE MOHEGAN

The temporary repairs to the *Paris* are almost completed, and she will probably leave this week for Glasgow. The *Mohegan* provides an ever-changing supply of interest. Divers are constantly busy bringing away her contents.

The huge manganese bronze propellers, valued at hundreds of pounds, have been torn away by dynamite and deposited near the rescued *Paris*. The *Mohegan*'s stores and cargo have been salved and visitors eagerly buy mementoes of the wreck.

---

[367] One of 19th-century Falmouth's most memorable inhabitants was John Burton (1839–1907) who, with little education but much spirit and "flair," in 1862 set up in a china business in Falmouth. Burton offered £500 for Smeaton's Lighthouse when the new Eddystone lighthouse was erected, and the offer was seriously considered by the Trinity Brethren. His attempted purchase prompted the City Fathers of Plymouth into action to retain it for the Hoe. Ultimately the Lighthouse was given to Plymouth on condition that the town paid the cost, estimated at £1,600, of removing it and re-erecting it upon the Plymouth Hoe, where it stands to this day—Newquay Old Cornwall Society.

[368] *Royal Cornwall Gazette Falmouth Packet, Cornish Weekly News, & General Advertiser*; Thursday, February 2nd 1899.

[369] Jonathan E. Eno, a London chemist was responsible for a formula of bicarbonate of soda, tartaric acid and Rochelle Salt and was marketed as an aid for ailments of the liver, fever, indigestion and rheumatic conditions. Marketing of the Fruit Salt began in about 1880. It was advertised as being made from sound ripe fruit made into a health-giving, invigorating beverage and was prepared by Eno's Fruit Salt Works, Hatcham, London, S. E.

[370] This is an exotic name, under which nitrobenzol is sold as oil of mirbane or essence of mirbane.

[371] A resinous exudation from the bodies of females of a species of scale insect (Tachardia lacca), from which liquid shellac – a solution of lac in alcohol or acetone is prepared. India is the chief source of shellac, although some is obtained from other areas in Southeast Asia. The insects feed on the sap of the twigs of certain tropical trees, some of which are cultivated for this purpose. The resinous secretion hardens upon exposure to air and forms a protective incrustation around the female and young, which are thus held fast to the twigs. The twigs are scraped to remove the incrustation; this crude lac material is known as *stick lac*.

[372] The wax vesta was made like a small wax taper and was exactly like the wax vestas of today, although very few of them are now produced, having been almost entirely superseded by the wood vestas.

They may purchase dining chairs in which the passengers were sitting when the *Mohegan* struck the Manacles; may secure the theatrical costumes of Miss Noble [actually, belonging to Maude Roudez], the plucky American lady who was rescued after clinging four hours to an oar; or they may actually feast on bottles of pickles, sauce, tins of preserved meat and fruit recently brought up from the *Mohegan*'s interior, and wash the same down with a bottle of *Mohegan* beer.[373]

A public announcement had been made for the sale of damaged goods from the salvage of the *Mohegan:*

> Two Day's Sale of Damaged Goods, ex *Mohegan* S.s., *Bohemia* S.s., and *City of Agra* S.s.[374] also Fire Salvages.—By Order of the London and Glasgow Salvage Associations and the Fire Insurance Companies.
> Robert Lyon and Co. will SELL by PUBLIC AUCTION, on Wednesday and Thursday. Nov 23 and 24, at Noon each day, at 72 Leo-street, Old Kent-road, London.[375]

Many items floated away from the wreck, particularly as the gales and high seas dislodged structures washing out their contents.

> As may be imagined, articles of every description are constantly washed ashore, and many little things are preserved by local residents as mementos of the calamity. If in years gone by the inhabitants have been industrious in collecting relics of wrecks the houses in the neighbourhood of St. Keverne must, in many cases, be museums on a small scale.[376]

During the duration of the salvage work, carried out on the *Mohegan,* one of the divers from Falmouth had lost his life in the process. Finally, she was worked by a local salvage operator, Mr Sandover,[377] who in 1904 raised the ship's sixteen and a half ton condenser.

You don't need to pray to God when there are storms in the sky, but you do have to be insured.

The insurance underwriters were to meet their obligations arising from their cover for the *Mohegan*:

COSTLY RESCUE WORK

> The wreck of the *Mohegan* on October 14 near the *Paris* went ashore is fresh in the minds of all, She left London for New York on the 18th [*sic*] with fifty passengers and a crew of 150. She went ashore off the Lizard, between Manacles and Lowlands, in a fog, and 116 [*sic*] of those on board were lost. It cost the underwriters nearly £70,000 [£3,999,440 in today's money] to pay for the wreck.[378]

---

[373] *The Dundee Courier & Argus* (Dundee, Scotland); Wednesday, 2nd August 1899.

[374] *City of Alga* – wrecked in a gale near Finisterre; loss of 31 lives in 1897.

[375] *The Standard* (London, England); Friday, November 18th 1898.

[376] *The Royal Cornwall Gazette Falmouth Packet, Cornish Weekly News, & General Advertiser*; Wednesday 29th December 1898.

[377] Mr Sandover ran his operation from his steamboat *Mallard*, out of Falmouth. He was said to have, "salvaged his own grandmother for the sake of the stoppings (fillings) in her teeth"; C. A. Chard, *Don't Forget the Diver* –1958, Chambers.

[378] *The Dundee Courier & Argus* (Dundee, Scotland); Thursday, 20th July 1899.

The Manacles had claimed the *Mohegan;* the salvors had claimed their share of the wreck; now the sea was intent on claiming all last traces of the event:

Last Saturday was the first anniversary of the wreck of the *Mohegan*. She has stood the stress of wind and tide well, and it was only on the day following the anniversary of her disastrous voyage that her mainmast fell and she began to break up. This was due to the easterly gale which prevailed, the first since the 14th October, 1898. Quantities of wreckage from her have been washed ashore.

The south-easterly gale on Sunday last gave a finishing stroke to the wreck of the *SS Mohegan*, which has stood so well for twelve months and proved such a source of attraction to visitors. The beaches around Swanpool were strewn with pieces of wood from the decks and cabins, and one at least of the masts has disappeared. And soon there will be no trace of the great disaster which created such an impression last October, except the graves in St. Keverne Churchyard and the memorial cross there.[379]

A wreck on shore is a beacon at sea.

The heavy seas, relentlessly pounding on the Manacle Rocks, continued to break up of the *Mohegan*. Three masts and her funnel had now been swept away, leaving a solitary mast as a forlorn beacon to passing ships:

A very heavy gale from the east blew at St. Keverne, accompanied by a heavy sea. Rain and sleet fell almost continuously. In the evening the wind veered to the E.N.E., and by seven o'clock a blizzard was raging. Only one mast is now left of the steamer *Mohegan*.[380]

The sea had almost claimed the entire ship. In a few short months, evidence of the wreck would no longer be seen above the waves.

Every cloud has a silver lining.

This was certainly the case for the people of Falmouth, who profited from the unfortunate wrecking of ships around this dangerous coast. This is not meant as a criticism, as salvage work was (and still is) a necessity following any wreck, and the good people of Falmouth have always shown an abundant generosity to those poor unfortunates, whose disabled ships have come their way:

---

[379] *The Royal Cornwall Gazette Falmouth Packet, Cornish Weekly News, & General Advertiser;* Thursday, 19th October 1899.

[380] *The Royal Cornwall Gazette Falmouth Packet, Cornish Weekly News, & General Advertiser;* Thursday, February 22nd 1999.

While Falmouth's over-sea connection has dwindled in the regular run of things, a good deal of activity has [been] obtained in local channels. The foundering of the liner *Mohegan* at the Manacles, followed by the stranding of the steamship *Paris* in that vicinity, has established a notable record of salvage work. The *Mohegan* operations were successful in more ways than one : the recovery of cargo provided a great deal of labour in the town, while the goods themselves commanded a satisfactory market. The latter consideration was especially noteworthy in regard to tin and kindred properties hauled out of the *Mohegan,* for those metals would be brought to the surface at a time when prices for them had an upward tendency. The mishap to the *Paris* created a considerable amount of business in the transport of cargo and the floating of the ship. As one result of these undertakings there are now two good companies engaged in salvage operations, with every likelihood of regular occupation.[381]

Over time, the *Mohegan* faded from memory: only 'surfacing' again[382] with the advent of scuba-diving.

The wreck was re-discovered in 1967 by the local divers, Roy Davis and Bernard Rogers. Unsurprisingly, after 69 years immersion, all they found was a well-broken up vessel; her hull collapsed and with the four boilers still standing impressively behind her two 100-volt generators.

The divers estimated the position of the *Mohegan* using old photographs that showed her mast and funnels among the easily recognised group of rocks surrounding her.[383] The wreck was located by Roy Davis, who was being towed behind Mr Roger's boat, using a hand-made aquaplane, at about 100 feet. They located the wreck in 75 feet of water off the Vase rock, north of the group called the Varses (Voices). The wreck site was littered with floor tiles and crockery bearing the name and crest of the shipping line: "Thomas Wilson Sons and Co. Ltd, Hull". As far as is known, only one intact plate has been recovered.[384]

Since that time, the wreck has become a magnet for sports divers, eagerly searching for a piece of history: hopefully, in the form of non-ferrous metal!

---

[381] *The Royal Cornwall Gazette Falmouth Packet, Cornish Weekly News, & General Advertiser;* Thursday, January 4th 1900.

[382] The salvage diver on the *Mohegan*, Cecil Albany Chard, had already dived on her, 30 or so years after the disaster – *Ellesmere Guardian;* 23 Feb 1932 – "Diver's Perilous Work".

[383] The most likely photograph that had assisted the two divers in locating the wreck site, is used as this book's front cover (also, see Fig. 48). They had alighted on this image in the 1960s., in a copy of the *Coastguard Magazine.*

[384] This dinner-plate is now in the possession of Mr Terry Moyle (see fig. 8).

CHAPTER 14

The Navigation of the Day

The winds and waves are always on the side of the ablest navigators.

'Navigating is locating oneself accurately and guiding oneself efficiently and safely from one location to another. It's easy on land because there are so many natural and man-made reference points to use. On the high seas, there are few so permanent and obvious.' [385]

There had been a longstanding and widespread view, that there was a dearth of navigational aids in the area around the treacherous rocks that are the Manacles, forewarning this much feared hazard. The only such aid was an inadequate bell buoy, which had been described as, 'worse than useless'. A generous offer of funding for a lighthouse from a millionaire philanthropist, Mr Passmore Edwards,[386] had already been declined by the Trinity House Brethren as an unnecessary undertaking, given the adequate warnings already in place: the St. Anthony's and the Lizard Light. Now, following the *Mohegan* affair, the clamour for a lighthouse or lightship, drowned out the puny sound of the bell-buoy, and much regret was expressed at the Trinity House Brethren's previous decision. Indeed, some have speculated that the Brethren were perhaps more concerned with the ongoing costs of such an enterprise, rather than the safety of mariners in these waters. The Falmouth Chamber of Commerce had petitioned the Trinity House for the installation of a lightship and foghorn at the Manacles, in the year 1885 and so this already had a longstanding history, associated with it.[387]

The Manacles had been responsible for innumerable disasters, and near misses, over the centuries. A reflection by a local mariner, recalls its dreadful history:

> What is the record of the Manacles? The "Times" has printed an interesting article from a correspondent who has collected valuable information on the point. He says one fisherman, who is still in middle life, recalls thirty-six casualties within two or three miles of the reef. But his list is incomplete, for more than fifty have happened during the past thirty years, of which considerably more than half may be classed as total wrecks. Turning to the lifeboat records, Porthoustock boat, which was sent to the hamlet consequent upon three quickly ensuing wrecks, has since the year 1872 been on active service sixteen times and has rescued one hundred and twelve persons. The same records show that one hundred and nineteen lives were lost from the vessels to which the lifeboat went out, while there were at least sixteen other wrecks during that period, resulting in the loss of forty-four lives, to which the lifeboat could render no assistance. When one looks at this terrible

---

[385] *The Captain Speaks about "Old Ironsides" Her Crews – Her Times.* A Timonier Publication, 1990, 1997, TGM

[386] John Passmore Edwards (24 March 1823 – 22 April 1911) was a Victorian journalist, newspaper owner and philanthropist (*par excellence*). He was born in Blackwater, a small village, situated between Redruth and Truro, in Cornwall, the son of a carpenter. A life-long champion of the working classes, Passmore Edwards is remembered as a generous benefactor. Over the space of 14 years, 70 major buildings were established as a direct result of his bequests. These included hospitals, 11 drinking fountains, 32 marble busts, 24 libraries, schools, convalescence homes and art galleries and the Passmore Edwards Settlement in Tavistock House, Bloomsbury London. He was also a generous donor to the Workers' Educational Association.

[387] *The Royal Cornwall Gazette Falmouth Packet, Cornish Weekly News, & General Advertiser;* Friday, January 30th 1885.

array of facts, says the "Times" correspondent, it may appropriately be asked if the means of averting disaster and saving lives are adequate in the neighbourhood. Four wrecks alone in the last ninety years have resulted in the drowning of no fewer than four hundred and seventy persons and having discussed the present modes of warning and rendering assistance to distressed vessels, the writer concludes that perhaps if the proposed coastguard station were established on Manacles Point, instead of Porthoustock Cove, if the rocket apparatus were removed to St. Keverne, and if a lifeboat were sent to Coverack, the force of the plea for a lightship at the Manacles would be greatly diminished. Time will show what the force of public opinion can do. If the public make up their mind that the warning at the Manacles is inadequate, and that even an automatic gas-buoy is entirely beside the mark, the Trinity Board will have to abdicate their position, or the public will have to "know the reason why". [388]

A pertinent argument was made as to the malign effect the Manacles had on shipping, even by proxy:

Mr. Duckham [389] points out that many vessels when disabled in N.W. gales, instead of coming into Falmouth when off the Lizard, are afraid to attempt that port on account of the Manacles, and rather than do so encounter all the risk of going to Plymouth. And it is only fair to assume that some of these vessels never reach Plymouth, and these add to the calamities of which the Manacles are either the immediate or indirect cause. [390]

The discussion around the stranding of the steamship *Paris* [391] inevitably drew comparison with the *Mohegan* event. Again, the state of the navigational lights around this part of the coast was brought into question, and the Trinity House Authority was being pressed to place a lighthouse or lightship at the Manacles; because of a perceived ambiguity of the existing lights, at St. Anthony's and the Lizard. Such a point was raised in this item from a local newspaper, and it does serve to show the general opinion around this issue, particularly in the response by the Trinity Brethren:

HUGGING THE SHORE TOO CLOSELY

To discover how the *Paris* came so far out of her proper course is as difficult a problem as in the case of the *Mohegan*. But as in the case of the *Mohegan*, one is compelled to come to the conclusion that even apart from navigation the look-out was not as effective as it might have been. The theory that the officers of the *Paris* mistook the light of the St. Anthony lighthouse for that of the Lizard, and thereupon steered a north-westerly course, is too absurd for consideration. It is impossible to mistake the lights even in hazy weather. The Lizard lights are two powerful shafts of electric lights situated on high cliffs, and visible to vessels proceeding eastward or westward; they are also fixed lights. The St. Anthony lights are produced by oil lamps, are revolving, and are situated low down under a hill, and are opened up to ships coming from the east, when they are abreast of Falmouth Harbour. No two lights in the United Kingdom are so dissimilar as those of St. Anthony and the Lizard. [392]

---

[388] *The Royal Cornwall Gazette Falmouth Packet, Cornish Weekly News, & General Advertiser*; Thursday, 25th May 1899.

[389] Alfred Benjamin Duckham (1811–1894) was the Secretary and Superintendent for the Royal Cornwall Sailors' Home, Falmouth (UK census, 1891). He was recorded in the UK census for 1861 as: resident at 2 Arwennack Street / aged 51 / occupation: Agent & Chart Seller.

[390] *The Royal Cornwall Gazette Falmouth Packet, Cornish Weekly News, & General Advertiser*; Friday, February 6th 1885.

[391] The *Paris* went aground on Lowland Point, seven months after the *Mohegan* was lost, and within view of the earlier wreck.

[392] *The Royal Cornwall Gazette Falmouth Packet, Cornish Weekly News, & General Advertiser*; Thursday, 25th May 1899.

A seemingly well-reasoned letter, from a sea-captain to a local newspaper, dwells on the tidal streams that affect this area of the Channel. His calculation for the *Mohegan*'s actual position, taken in consideration with the tidal streams at the time, gives further credence to the mistaking of the St. Anthony's Light for the Lizard:

Sir, There have been several letters in your newspaper giving so-called reasons for the *Mohegan* getting on the Manacle Rocks. Not a word has been said about the tides, which are a very important factor in navigating the English Channel. The magnetic variation of the compass is well known in this part of the Channel, and the annual decrease of the same is shown on all modern charts. If the ship passed the Eddystone at 4 p.m. it was then slack water with the shore, and the ebb tide made about 4.30 in shore but the flood was running its strongest where the ship was; consequently they had a three-knot tide against them until about 6.30 p.m., and the logs and engines might indicate the ship to be going 13 knots through the water, whereas she was only going 10 knots over the ground. If the ebb tide had been running they would have been abreast of the Lizard at 6.30 p.m., which would account for the ship being off Falmouth.

The only conclusion I can come to is that they thought they were abreast of the Lizard, and shaped a course for the Wolf, there being a white haze over the land and the Lizard lights being electric, they might possibly have been obscured about that time. Outside the line of points the tide runs three hours after it is high water with the shore, and being top of the springs there was a good three-knot tide running. The course from the Eddystone to the Lizard as the crow flies is W¼N magnetic, 39 miles. At seven p.m., allowing for the tide, the ship would be nine miles to the eastward of the Lizard.

What was it that put the torpedo boats on shore at the Dodman [Point]? [393] Not making allowance for the tide. Until the Board of Trade inquiry takes place, it would be out of place to say anything about course.

Yours Etc. (Capt.) H. Nicholls.

Sea View, Ruan Minor.[394]

Following the *Mohegan* disaster, public opinion was now asserting itself in the national newspapers, as evidenced in the following letter:

A petition is being sent to the committee of Lloyd's urging them to use their influence to induce the Trinity Brethren to provide a lightship off the Manacle Rocks, which would become a Channel light and lessen the yearly wrecks on and around these dreaded reefs, and would also tend to safeguard the Stags under the Lizard. A leading member of the House of Commons has expressed his opinion that the matter requires immediate attention, and hopes that something will be done. The following is a list of some of the more recent disasters on these rocks and in their neighbourhood :- 1836, *Port Chalmers, City of Venice,* and *Suffolk,* s.; 1888, *Godolphin,* s., *Lady Dufferin,* barque, *Nettlesworth,* s.; 1890, *Spiridion Vagliani,* s.; 1891, *Bay of Panama,* four-masted ship; 1893, *Gustab Bitters,* s., *Clifton Grove,* s., and *Auric,* s.; 1895, *Andola,* 1,966 tons; 1836, *Liffe,* s., and *Metana,* s.; 1897, *Plantagenet,* s.; 1898, *Abernyle* and *Mohegan,* s.; 1899, *Paris;* 1902, *Glenbervie,* barque. About all of these proved total wrecks. Since February 22 last we have had four narrow escapes and another total wreck the schooner *Isabella.* Now, as approximately 11,000 vessels pass the Lizard eastward and 15,000

---

[393] A corruption of dead-man, so called because it once had a gibbet (gallows) placed there.

[394] *The West Briton;* 10th November 1898. Ruan Minor is a small village on the Lizard peninsular.

westward annually, this is not a matter of local interest alone, but affects the shipping of the world using this part of the English Channel.[395]

As regards the pattern of navigational lights, that mark the westerly progression of the Channel, in the vicinity of Falmouth and the Lizard; a correspondent was made to 'see red', and in letter to a local newspaper made the following observation:

> The Wreck of the *Mohegan*—Sir. Having reference to the remarks made at the recent County Council meeting and the statement by Mr. Pedarven Vivian, "There is no red light on the coast," this is an error. The next two lights to the westward are red. The Wolf [Rock] shows red and white alternately, the Longships [at Land's End] show red between certain bearings, red towards the land. There is also a red light on Round Island—one of the Scilly Isles. In the opinion of men who are well acquainted with the coast, another red light would not be desirable. It is, however, a question that should be thoroughly thrashed out.
>
> T. W.[396]

Again, not all were supportive of additional red navigational lights being installed in the vicinity of the Manacles:

TO THE EDITOR OF THE TIMES

Sir, most of the unfriendly critics of the Manacles do not seem to be aware that these rocks are only about eight miles from the Falmouth [St. Anthony's] Lighthouse and (about) eight miles from the Lizard Lights.

A ship steering for them down Channel would not see the Lizard Lights but it would have the Falmouth Lighthouse in full view; in fact, the [Manacle] rocks are "covered" by the latter.

To establish lightships, as suggested by your America Correspondent, between the Lizard and Eddystone, would probably only increase the danger (assuming any danger exists) for properly navigated vessels.

No! If Americans really wish to decrease the danger they should insist on the various steamship lines abandoning their growing custom of trying to "cut time" in transatlantic voyages.

I am yours obediently, S. M. Fox[397]

Arts Club, 40 Dover Street, Piccadilly, West London.[398]

On another important point, there was no formal set of signals that would warn a vessel of its immediate running into danger, either by ship-to-ship or shore-to-ship communications. The following proposal seemed eminently sensible:

---

[395] Mr William Kirkness, *The Times;* 1st April 1902 – a retired mariner of the *Haven*, Falmouth.

[396] *The West Briton;* 10th November 1898.

[397] Samuel Middleton Fox (1856 – 1941) was an amateur writer and dramatist, who also documented the life of the wealthy Quaker Fox family of Falmouth during the latter years of the 19th century.

[398] *The Times;* Saturday, 27th May 1899. The Arts Club is a London private members club founded in 1863 by, amongst others, Charles Dickens, Anthony Trollope, and Lord Leighton. Today it is a meeting place for men and women involved in the creative arts either professionally or as patrons— *WikiPedia.*

Sir,—Through the medium of your paper may I be allowed to point out the necessary and long felt want of a night signal (under the present rule of the road), whereby a ship seeing another running into danger can at least warn her of her course or of any approximate peril by adopting such a signal as will be inexpensive and at the same time handy for use? This warning signal, "Proceed with caution," might be made by six successive long and short blasts on the steam whistle or siren, or such number of blasts as would not interfere with the present signals for alteration of course—"proceeding ahead", "going astern"—and at the same time convey the required meaning to the ship in danger.

In making this suggestion I would remind the public of the wreck of the *Drummond Castle*. When a vessel called the *Werfa* [399] saw this ill-fated steamer steering towards the rocks the officer on watch remarked, "If that ship continues on her present course she will be piled up," or words to that effect. Still nothing could be done owing to the present system of night signals.

Now we have yet another case on May 21 last, when the pilot cutter seeing the *Paris* steering direct on the Manacles could do nothing except burn a blue light, which means "Do you want a pilot?" A signal which must have seen almost ironical to the officers.

Surely it is time something must be done to enable a warning to be given to those in charge of so much life and property when steering a dangerous course, and so ensure that such an answer as that vouchsafed by the men of the pilot cutter No. 13 should not be repeated. When asked why a rocket signal was not adopted these sailors replied, "We do not carry rockets and even if we did fire one it would not be construed as a signal of distress and would summon the lifeboat," and consequently convey nothing to the ship in danger.

I am, Sir, yours faithfully, W. G. W. [400]

The question of introducing a standardised form of warning signals between ships, when one or other is sailing into danger, received yet more support:

THE STRANDING OF THE PARIS

Sir,—The letter of Admiral de Horsey, which I have only just seen, on the stranding of the *Drummond Castle*, the *Stella* and the *Paris* deserves serious consideration at the hands of the Board of Trade, especially as the stranding of the *Paris* could have been avoided had the Board of Trade authorised some warning signal to be given by a passing vessel by day and by night when a ship is known to be on a dangerous course.

It cannot surely have been forgotten that had such a signal been in use the *Wertha* would have warned the *Drummond Castle* that she was on a dangerous course, and the pilot cutter from Falmouth could have given the *Paris* a real and effective danger warning. The Board of Trade were appealed to after the *Drummond Castle* disaster but nothing has been done in the meantime and now the bloodless wreck of the *Paris* occurs practically through the lack of such definite and ready signal. The admiral is very severe upon the counsel engaged in recent enquiries; had he been present he might have realised that they secured a fuller exposure to the recklessness than otherwise might have been officially attained. With regards to the evidence of captains of traders to which the admiral so properly calls attention, the findings of the Court was very clear and positive, but all such findings and condemnations are useless unless the Board of Trade will enforce a new rule, and above all, connect all the lighthouses and lightships with the coast.

---

[399] The ship *Werfa* was passing round Ushant within a few hours of the time at which the *Drummond Castle* was lost. Those on board were probably the last to see her, before she met her end.

[400] *The Times;* May 26th 1899.

I have the honour to be your obedient servant,

Amsterdam, May 26.

H. C. Richards.[401]

Today of course, such signals have been universally adopted as an unequivocal aid to safety at sea. But still the Trinity Brethren seemed reluctant to engage in public enquiry, over the matter of safety at the Manacles. This recorded debate proposed a gas-lighted buoy, to replace the old bell buoy, and the dismantling of the St. Anthony's Lighthouse, and rebuilding it at the top of the cliff. A rather extraordinary move, which would never see the light of day (or night, for that matter):

THE MANACLES

Although the Trinity Brethren do not consider it advisable to hold the public enquiry asked for with regard to the dangers of navigation between the Lizard and the Eddystone, it is satisfactory to find that they are giving some attention to the numerous representations to them on the subject, and intend taking action very shortly. Mr. T. Webber, the chairman of the committee, had an interview last week with some of the principal officials, and learned that it is intended to replace the Manacle Buoy by an improved Gas-lighted Automatic Sound-producing buoy, with the latest fittings. This announcement will be read with satisfaction by those who have interested themselves in the matter, and shows that the efforts of the various public bodies who have taken up the subject are bearing fruit. At Falmouth Chamber of Commerce meeting very general satisfaction was expressed, though there are several members who urge that while this change is very well as far as it goes, yet what is also required is that St. Anthony Lighthouse should be removed to the top of the hill. There seems no prospect of this change being entertained, and they must therefore be content for the present with what is promised.— SCRURATOR [402]

The question of a light vessel to guard the Manacles was put to the Elder Brethren at the Trinity House. As can be seen in the report, the authority was not keen to take on the additional expenditure, for such an undertaking:

The Manacle Rocks.—A Trinity House View

Falmouth Board of Guardians received from Mr. Kent, of Trinity House, the following letter:—

"Having laid before the Board a resolution passed by the Guardians of the Falmouth Union, suggesting the establishment of a light-vessel and fog signal to mark the Manacle Rocks, I am directed to acquaint you that seeing that navigation from the Start [Point] to Scilly [Isles] is as simple as possible, that the powerful lights of the Lizard are visible for a distance of twenty-one miles, that the revolving light at St. Anthony's affords an additional aid for verifying the position of a vessel, the white fixed light of 8,000 candle power (which is as good as the North Foreland light) [403] shown therefrom clears the rocks, and that the Manacles bell buoy is placed outside

---

[401] *The Times;* 31st May 1899.

[402] *The Royal Cornwall Gazette Falmouth Packet, Cornish Weekly News, & General Advertiser;* Thursday, 18th May 1899.

[403] North Foreland is a chalk headland on the Kent coast of southeast England. North Foreland forms the eastern end of the Isle of Thanet. This report confirms that the light that covers the Manacles was fixed and white in colour.

the rocks, which are only seven and a half cable distant [0.75 nautical miles] from the shore. The Elder Brethren do not consider that a light-ship and fog signal, as suggested, are required for the purpose of general navigation, and they are unable to recommend that the cost of lighting the rocks should be charged to the Mercantile Marine Fund".

The CHAIRMAN (Mr, T. Webber) understood a letter had also come from the Board of Trade declining in any way to be responsible for a light at the Manacles and saying it was entirely a matter for Trinity House.—Mr. WILLIAMS asked if Trinity House and the Board of Trade had come to a mutual arrangement (laughter).—The CHAIRMAN said the subject would again come before the Chamber of Commerce next week. Neither Trinity House nor the Board of Trade thought themselves responsible, and there appeared to be a great difficulty in shewing that they were.—Mr. C. PEARCE said Falmouth Harbour Board had a like reply from the authorities concerned a few years ago.—The CHAIRMAN intimated that the question would not end here.[404]

Such was the intensity of discussion around the topic of the Manacles that inevitably an outlandish proposal or two would soon emerge. Such a far-fetched plan was put forward: that the Manacle Rocks should be blasted out of existence by high explosives, at an estimated cost of 2 million pounds. Such a huge expenditure would in itself have simply blown this project out of the water.

Meanwhile, the Trinity Brethren attracts more criticism for an apparent disregard for the improvement of safety measures at the Manacles:

The Deadly Manacles

Sir,—From the Trinity House letter read at the County Council meeting as reported, it is apparent that the Trinity Brthren do not really grasp the situation. In clear weather the lights they quote are doubtless visible, as they state; but the danger arises in thick or foggy weather, when those lights are valueless to warn mariners of those terrible rocks. That these rocks are a danger is best proved by the fact (entirely apart from the "Mohegan") of the number of wrecks which have occurred in the neighbourhood within the last ten years. To quote (as that letter does) the Manacles Bell Buoy as being a warning, is a further proof of the want of a practical knowledge by the Trinity Brethren. As a warning it is worse than useless, as was I believe, publically stated when the matter was discussed by the County Council. That the bell cannot be heard when most needed, ie., with an onshore wind, is notorious in the neighbourhood. A muffin bell would almost do as well.[405]

When one remembers (1) that large area covered by these rocks, (2) how comparatively close they are to Lloyd's Signal Station, where thousands of vessels approach in the year for the purpose of signalling, (3) how unprotected from the Manacles are vessels approaching from the south and east in thick weather if they miss the Lizard, and are to the east of it, (4) how these rocks lie in the fairway (from the south and west) to Falmouth, where vessels of a total of 600,000 tons, roughly, call annually, one sees the necessity of of providing efficient protection against these deadly rocks, and I trust our public authorities, including the Cornish M.P.'s, and those interested in shipping, and also our Western Press, will not weary in their efforts to obtain it. In my humble opinion what would best meet the case would be the provision of a lightship with a powerful foghorn, as a lightship would least interfere with the main Channel lights, and would not,

---

[404] *The Royal Cornwall Gazette Falmouth Packet, Cornish Weekly News, & General Advertiser*; Thursday, 22nd December 1898.

[405] An amusing analogy is used here: a 19th Century muffin sellers' hand bell has two half dome bells, a swinging double clapper within and a turned with a wood handle and with a steel suspension ring on the end. This bell gives a delightful double ring if handled properly and with a good resonance. Used at street corners by the muffin seller to drum up business.

therefore, complicate matters in that direction, the nearest lightship, I believe, being at the Seven Stones, away to the north of the Scillies.

Yours, &c.,

REGINALD N. ROGERS.

Falmouth, February 8th, 1899.[406]

Left hand doesn't know what the right hand is doing.

In another letter, a question of port and starboard as a course to be steered, is deemed confusing, to the point that the helmsman should be carefully watched, to check that he had correctly interpreted an officer's true intent. A proposed system for a more logical process, is made:

TO THE EDITOR OF THE DAILY NEWS

Sir,—although probably nothing will ever be known as to the real cause of the terrible disaster on the Manacles, I venture the following as a feasible explanation—in fact, the only one in my opinion which will hold water. It is a well-known fact that a master taking his ship along a coast does not always give the actual course to be steered by name, but given an order to port a point, or starboard a point, as the case may be. It is also well known to masters and officers that time after time even the best of helmsmen will on receiving such an order, say, "Starboard a point," promptly put the wheel to starboard which is exactly the opposite of what he should have done, instead of casting the ship's head to port—or left—casts it to starboard—or right. Probably every master afloat will bear me out in this, and knows the importance of either himself or a junior officer actually watching the helmsman when shifting the wheel on such an order being given. In the case of the *Mohegan,* my idea that having passed the Eddystone, the captain gave the order to the helmsman to "Starboard a point," thereby intending to bring his ship out to the Lizards—that is, to the left. Instead of that being done, the man put about the wheel to starboard, thereby bringing the ship's head to the right or inside the Lizards, and consequently heading on to the rocks, shutting out the Lizard lights, which in all possibility Captain Griffiths was anxiously looking out for when the ship struck. I am not defending (or otherwise) that captain's action on this occasion, but simply stating a case that must have happened to numbers of ship masters.

Yours truly

.

THOS. WHITE, Master Mariner (Retired).

Walsall, Oct. 19.[407]

Not wholly conversant with 19th century seamanship and navigation, an expert view of the points raised in the preceding letter, helps clarify:

It is of course perfectly possible that one or more helm orders were misunderstood by the man at the wheel and he did the opposite of what the order had intended. It is easy enough to speculate.

---

[406] *The West Briton;* February 16th 1899.

[407] *Daily News* (London, England); Friday, 21st October 1898.

First we need to understand the conventions; there may be something on that to be found in the seamanship text books, though it is likely not the kind of thing that would get into published books. However it is the kind of thing that Lecky in his *Wrinkles* might have addressed and for naval practice it might have been mentioned in the Admiralty volume on, *Seamanship for Boy Seamen*.

A key problem is that orders continued to be given as though the man at the helm was handling a tiller,[408] as is still the case when steering whalers, cutters and dinghies. To turn the vessel to port or left the tiller has to be put over to starboard or right, and vice versa. But all vessels of any size were by the twentieth-century, steered using wheels, and it was perfectly possible to arrange the mechanism so that rotating the wheel, upper half, to port (left) would cause the vessel to turn to port, and vice versa. Usually the helmsman stood abaft the wheel, even if at the stern of the vessel, but larger vessels—such as the *Mohegan*—were steered from the bridge amidships, and the linkage to the rudder head was by rod and chain; or wire cable, in steamers assisted by steam steering engines.

My understanding is that the convention in British ships of ordering starboard in order to turn the ship to port persisted until the 1920s, when the stupidity of that convention was recognised and the Board of Trade issued a statutory instrument, or a shipping notice, cancelling that convention and decreeing that an order to port the helm, would cause the ship to turn to port.

In fact there are two ways in which the helmsman can be ordered to change the direction of the ships head. In open water a change of course can be effected by naming the new heading. In my day we used 360 degrees, thus the order might be simply: 'steer 274 degrees.' But there were still ships using quarter points 100 years ago, and degrees were introduced via quadrantal notation, up to 90 degrees: hence an order such as steer 'N–35 degrees–E.' The other type of order used in an emergency, especially would be 'hard-a-port'—'hard-a-starboard,' or perhaps some intermediate term to indicate the amount of helm or rudder angle to use. At 'hard over,' the rudder angle would be about 35 degrees; so intermediate positions might be 10 or 15 or 20 degrees so as to slow the turn. To stop a turn, opposite helm had to be employed, and an order to that effect be given.

We do not know what the practice was on the *Mohegan*, unless it had turned up in evidence to the enquiry. Further, practice aboard vessels belonging to other countries, such as Germany, may have been different, and the US has long persisted with left and right.

Passenger ships of the period usually carried superior able seamen, who were called quartermasters, and paid a few shillings more than ordinary able seamen, and had special duties connected with steering, and other tasks on the bridge. They were men of experience, tried and tested and could be expected to be fully conversant with the helm order conventions aboard their ship.

I have no comment on the letter content [see previous correspondence, T. White; p. 157] as it does not distinguish between a course order and an order to swing the ship to port or starboard.

In fact, even with helm steering, commands to helmsmen followed the tiller steering convention, until approximately 1937, when the commands were reversed. Thus, in 1912, a turn to port was done by instructing the helmsman: "hard-a-starboard". [409]

---

[408] In steering a boat, the tiller is always moved in the direction opposite of which the bow of the boat is to move. If the tiller is moved to port side (left), the bow will turn to starboard (right). If the tiller is moved to starboard (right), the bow will turn port (left). Sailing students often learn the alliterative phrase, "Tiller towards trouble" to remind them of how to steer—*WikiPedia*.

[409] Personal communication: Mr Alston Kennerley, Plymouth University (2011).

For whom the bell tolls.

In a letter concerning the useless bell buoy, stationed at the Manacles, the writer takes the opportunity to include a sideswipe at the self-elected body, the guardians of our buoys and lighthouses—the Trinity Brethren:

THE MANACLE REEF

TO THE EDITOR OF THE TIMES

Sir, Yesterday, in this yacht, I passed close to the Manacles Reef, where one of the masts of the ill-fated *Mohican* [*sic*] bears grim testimony to the dangers of the place. That wreck took place in October, 1898. In June, 1899, the *Paris* went ashore at the same spot, but luckily without the same fatal results. Shortly afterwards the Trinity Brethren, yielding unwilling to public opinion, promised to replace the ridiculous bell buoy which marks the rocks by a gas buoy. Nearly sixteen months have now elapsed, but the bell buoy still remains.

When approaching it yesterday at a rate of eight knots in a sailing yacht with no noise of engines, and all hands straining their ears to catch the sound of it, no one heard it until less than half a minute before we passed, and we passed it within three yards and the bell was ringing so violently as such an inefficient one can do.

Such a "warning" is worse than useless, because it encourages the inexperienced to rely upon it. I am informed by residents here that only a few weeks ago a large mail steamer was only saved from stranding on the reef by reason of the fog lifting. We shall say how many lives would have been sacrificed to the inertness of the Trinity Brethren but for that occurrence?

I have just arrived here from a cruise extending from Carlingford Lough to Valencia, and have been much impressed by the striking contrast afforded by the lights and buoys managed by the Commissioners of Irish Lights to those in the care of our English self-elected body. For instance, off Carlingford Lough there is an automatic whistling buoy which can be heard for miles. I heard it constanly at Greenane, some three and a half miles away. Such a buoy is of some use, whereas bell buoys (unless of very large dimensions) carry their sound a very short distance, even to leeward. I know that the contention of the Trinity Brethren is that no mariner ought to be near the Manacles in thick weather, but the same excuse would do away with the block system on railways.[410] The fact is that these systems are required for the safety of the travelling public, and not merely for the benefit of the extra careful shipmaster.

Another dangerous place near here is the "Stags" off the Lizard. If it were in Ireland, a buoy or beacon would be placed on the outer rock, which covers at three-quarters flood. Here, as a matter of course, there is nothing.

I am Sir. &c. ARTHUR UNDERHILL. Yacht *Wulfuca*, Falmouth, Sept. 28.[411]

In a reply to this letter, the Trinity Brethren came in for yet more stinging criticism, from its author:

THE REEF OF DEATH

MANACLE ROCKS STILL INSUFFICIENTLY PROTECTED

It will be unpleasant news to the public that the promises made nearly sixteen months ago by the Trinity Brethren to establish adequate warning at the Manacles Reef has not yet been fulfilled.

---

[410] Block system on railways, a system by which the track is divided into sections of three or four miles, and trains are so run by the guidance of electric signals that no train enters a section or block before the preceding train has left it.

[411] *The Times;* Saturday, September, 29th, 1900.

Attention is drawn to the matter in a letter published in the *Times*, on Saturday in which the correspondent refers to the ridiculously inefficient bell buoy, which in spite of several disasters and many protests, still marks the dangerous group of rocks upon which the *Mohegan* and the *Paris* came to grief.

In view of the experience of all who have personally proved the utter worthlessness of the bell buoy as a means of warning, the apathy of the Trinity Brethren is inexplicable.

It is admitted by those who are well acquainted with the subject that the coast from Falmouth to the Lizard is one of the most dangerous portions of our shores, and for further proof of the fact one has but to read the melancholy testimony on the headstones in the little graveyard of St. Keverne's.

The most conclusive evidence of the uselessness of the bell buoy is given by the correspondent of the *Times*, who states that he and his companions on a sailing-yacht never heard a sound until they were passing within three yards of the "warning," when they saw the bell ringing violently on the heave and insuck of the sea.

Personal experience of the spot establishes the fact that with an off-sea wind, which of course creates a lee-shore for passing ships, not the faintest sound of the bell is audible twenty yards away, and even with the wind one has to creep up almost above the spires of the reef to catch the muffled clang. When the weather is thick and the sea is restful the bell is a dumb delusion and a snare.

With these facts in view, and with the additional argument of the recent narrow escape of a mail steamer from disaster at the Manacles, [the *Paris*] another attempt will be made to get the Trinity Brethren to fulfil their sixteen-month's old promise.[412]

Let there be light.

On the question of gas-lit buoys replacing the traditional and now discredited bell buoy, there was also a move to have replaced the electric lights in lighthouses to a gas-fuelled system. One notes that the following correspondent had a vested interest, in a promotion of gas-lit illumination:

THE STRANDING OF THE PARIS

TO THE EDITOR OF THE TIMES

Sir,—Shortly after the loss of the *Mohegan* and a 100 lives, the *Liverpool Journal of Commerce* suggested that one of my continuous buoy lights, to which attention had been called in the columns of *The* Times, should be established in the neighbourhood of the Manacles, and at that time I wrote to the Trinity House asking that they should place one of these buoys there, but they did not do so. These lamps, which are lighted by petroleum, are very simple in construction, and whistling apparatus can be attached to them, so that both sound and light may be brought into the service to the mariner. They show their light continuously for months together without requiring any attention whatever.

This system of guarding the rocky dangers of our coast is very inexpensive, and therefore the question of cost, which deters lighthouse authorities carrying out many useful works, would not have been an objection, and one might suppose that so obvious an improvement would have been carried out forthwith. Had such been done the probability is that the *Paris* would be safely on her way to New York, instead of lying hopelessly stranded on the Manacles. But useful as that system has proved itself to be, in the various places it has been adopted, it is useful only at close quarters. The great sea lights round the coast should be sufficient to deter vessels from approaching danger, but to do this it is necessary that they should be efficient. In my mind, the great cause of the stranding of the *Paris* was the inefficiency of the Lizard light. This light is

---

[412] *The Courier and Argus* (Dundee, Scotland); Wednesday, 2nd October 1900.

electric, and I have over and over again pointed out to the lighthouse authorities that electric lights such as that at the Lizard are worse than useless in fog or mist. I remember giving my reasons for this opinion 20 years ago at a meeting of the Institute of Civil Engineers, when the late Sir James Douglass [413] read a paper respecting the establishment of these lights. Since that time nautical people have almost unanimously come to the conclusion that the electric light is useless in foggy weather. Let me quote one example. Captain Wilson Boyd, of the British and Irish Steam Packet Company, who passes and re-passes the Lizard lights continually, says:—"With regard to the electric light, I quite agree with what the shipmasters say. I have often passed quite close to the electric lights on the South Coast of England in hazy weather and found them invisible. In fact, to my mind, as a lighthouse light the electric light is quite useless".

I trust the Board of Trade will see it right to call upon the Trinity House to substitute for the dangerous electric lights on the Lizard large gas flames, such as are used in Irish lighthouses, notably that of Tory Island,[414] respecting which the late Dr. Tyndall, writing in the *New Review*,[415] said:—

"No wonder, then, that Captain Park, who has been in all parts of the world, declares that he 'is quite certain that he has seen no light which at all approaches in brilliancy the new Wigham gas lights on Tory. Captain Carruthers saw the light plainly at 21 miles and its glare at 30 miles.' Captain Brown states that 'in the showers we never lost sight of the light and could clearly count the flashes; its great illuminating power seemed to light up the mist and to make a great glare.' Captain Wilson has seen 'the halo of the light three-quarters of an hour before seeing the light itself.' He pronounces it is the finest in the kingdom. Captain Meiklereid says that 'vessels can now pick up the light 20 or 30 miles off. The new illuminate is so powerful that the halo could be seen for four or five miles off through fog.' The last letter on this subject contains the exclamation, 'What a pity it is that you cannot get one of the English Channel stations and fit up permanently there your lanterns and burners ! You would soon get the credit which is certainly your due, and it would come from the best of all authorities—the thousands of shipmasters who have to thrash their vessels round the coasts of the United Kingdom in all weathers".

I am, Sir, your obedient servant, JOHN R. WIGHAM

33 to 36, Capel-street, Dublin, May 23.[416]

It is always wise to look ahead, but difficult to look further than you can see.

From a layman's point of view, it is difficult to see why electric lights are 'worse than useless in fog or mist,' as compared to gas-light; when the Lizard light is able to throw illumination a distance of 21 miles, on a clear night. And one assumes any form of light is compromised by mist and fog; .[417]

In the meanwhile, business is still business:

[413] Sir James Nicholas Douglass, FRS, (16 October 1826 – 19 June 1898), was an English civil engineer, a prolific lighthouse builder and designer, most famous for the design and construction of the fourth Eddystone Lighthouse, still standing to this day on the Eddystone Rocks.

[414] Tory Island is situated off the coast of Ireland, located 14.5 km (9 miles) north-west of the coast of County Donegal.

[415] The *New Review* was a Victorian periodical, 1824–1900.

[416] *The Times;* Friday, 26th May 1899.

[417] Hoyt, John C.; *Old Ocean's Ferry; the Log of the Modern Mariner, the Trans-Atlantic Traveler, and Quaint Facts of Neptune's Realm:* The electric arc lamp, apparently very powerful, is found to be very unsatisfactory in fogs, owing to its slight penatatrive power.

Wigham had a long-standing rivalry with the Engineer-in-Chief of Trinity House, James Nicholas Douglass, which erupted over trials of rival gas, oil and electric illumination systems conducted at South Foreland Lighthouse, Dover, in 1884–5. Tyndall, still acting as a scientific consultant, accused Douglass of using his position to influence the trials' outcome and ensure the adoption of his own patents over those of Wigham. Wigham also stated that Douglass had used elements of one of his rejected designs. As a result of the dispute, Tyndall resigned, while Wigham was eventually paid £2,500 [418] by the Board of Trade for patent infringement. [419]

The Quick and the Dead.

To put the annual total of vessels and lives lost into context, here is an annual report from a Board of Trade publication:

THE WRECK REGISTER AND CHART FOR 1899

The people of a great maritime nation like Great Britain attach, it may be safely assumed, a special importance to everything connected with the sea, and will therefore be interested in perusing the following digest of the latest valuable table of statistics issued by the Board of Trade in their well-arranged Blue-Book,[420] relative to shipping casualties on or near our coasts during the year ending 30th June of last year [1899] and in doing so we feel sure that it must be evident to everyone how important a matter it is that the fullest and strongest support should be given to any work, the intention and result of which is to minimise, and as far as possible prevent the loss of life in connection with shipping casualties on our rock-bound shores.

It is shown that the total number of shipping casualties which occurred on or near the coasts of the United Kingdom in the year 1898–9 was (5,040) 4,434 befel British and Colonial – 606 of which were foreign vessels, this total being unfortunately an increase of 76 as compared with the preceding 12 months. The total number of lives lost as a result of these casualties was 520, no less than 225 more than in the year 1897–8. On examination, however, it is found that nearly half of this large increase was due to the sad wreck of the *Mohegan* on the Manacles (Cornwall), on the 14th October, 1898, when 106 souls perished. [421]

An interpretation of these figures is better illustrated in the following table:

UK COAST LOCATION	Year: 1897–8 (Vessels)	Year: 1897–8 (Loss of Life)	Year: 1898–9 (Vessels)	Year: 1898–9 (Loss of Life)
East Coast	924	89	763	93
South Coast	570	32	560	148 (Including *Mohegan*)

[418] This sum of £2,500 equates to £150,000 in modern day currency.

[419] *WikiPedia.*

[420] Blue book or Bluebook is a term often referring to an almanac or other compilation of statistics and information. The term dates back to the 15th century, when large blue velvet-covered books were used for record-keeping by the Parliament of the United Kingdom.

[421] *The Huddersfield Daily Chronicle* (West Yorkshire, England); Tuesday, 23rd October 1900.

West Coast of England, Scotland and the East Coast of Ireland	1,195	59	1,357	118
North Coast of Scotland	157	36	105	14
East Coast of Scotland	162	1	272	55
Other Parts	248	—	268	92
Grand Total:	**3,256**	**217**	**3,325**	**520**

Table 2: Wrecks–Derived from the Board of Trade Blue Book (1899)

The number of vessels meeting with casualties during the period of 46 years, (1864 – 1899) was 144,964. And in the same period, the number of lives lost in these incidents, were 29,790. A further extract from the above publication, allows us to examine the role of the lifesaving organisations:

It is consoling to know that, had it not been for the work done by the lifeboat and crews of the institutions, etc., the number of lives lost would have been considerably doubled, the total number of lives rescued by these means in the same period being 32,039, so the lives thus saved exceeded those that were lost by 2,249.

The Institution granted rewards in 1899 for saving 609 lives from shipwreck and landing of 67 other persons, by means of lifeboat, from apparently perilous positions.

The 313 rocket apparatus, and other stations, that are so well managed by the Board of Trade, and admirably worked by the coastguard and rocket brigades, perseveringly carry on their life saving duties, and were instrumental in the year 1898–9 in rescuing 223 persons from a watery grave. This total was an increase of 92 as compared with that of the previous year.

The total number of lives, for the saving of which the institution has granted rewards, has exceeded 42,200.

We may add that the contributions to the lifeboat fund will be thankfully received by all bankers in the United Kingdom, and by the secretary, Charles Dibdin, Esq.,[422] at the institution, John-street, Adelphi, London.[423]

Man proposes: God disposes.

As regards the transatlantic maritime trade, from the year 1840 to 1893, the number of lives lost was recorded at 7,523 of which 6,923 were as a direct result of steamship disasters.[424] An interesting picture emerges, as to a cause for maritime disaster during this particular period:

---

[422] Oliver Warner; *The Lifeboat Service – A History of the Royal National Life-boat Institution 1824–1974.* Charles Dibdin – Secretary (at the head of the full-time administrative staff) 1883–1910, 275, 57. He came to the RNLI from the Post Office service, which was then under the control of the Civil Service.

[423] *The Huddersfield Daily Chronicle* (West Yorkshire, England); Tuesday 23rd October 1900.

[424] Magginis, John: *The Atlantic Ferry: Its Ships, Men, And Working* (London, UK: Whitaker & Co.1893), Table-7.

Cause of Shipping Disaster:	Number in Category	Percentage of Total Incidents
Wrecked	40	33.6
Never heard of [again]	26	21.8
Collision	16	13.5
Foundered	15	12.6
Burned	9	7.6
Stranded	7	5.9
Collision with iceberg	5	4.2
Lost in Fog	1	0.8
Total:	**119**	

Table 3: Steamships Lost In the Atlantic Trade: 1840–1893.[425]

Any shipping disaster is a matter for sad regret, but the most chilling phrase listed here is the *Never heard of* category, that denotes, "a noble vessel and her living freight being suddenly engulfed in eternity." [426]

Lightning never strikes the same place twice?

An astonishing maritime incident was that of the International Navigation Company's steamship *Paris*. A mere seven months after the *Mohegan* disaster, that vessel went ashore at Lowland Point, a half a mile along the coast from the *Mohegan* wreck site and, amazingly, within view of her four masts that still protruded above the waves. This once again raised the issue of a lack of navigational markers in this area:

TO THE EDITOR OF THE TIMES

Sir,—Once more we are confronted with a serious stranding in the vicinity of the Manacle Rocks. This time happily without loss of life. The lethargic British public is at last awakening to the fact that something has not been done which obviously should have been done long ago—viz., the instalment on the Manacles of a warning light and an efficient fog signal.

Whose fault is this? Surely an ancient corporation such as the Trinity House, with an honourable line of engineers who have not been daunted by such reefs as the Bishop, Wolf, and Eddystone, would consider a work such as I have mentioned one of no difficulty from an engineering point of view, although of deepest and most urgent import where the safety of human life is at stake.

Is nothing to be done? The world is informed that a whistling and gas-lit buoy is to take the place of the present bell buoy. It is common knowledge that for the situation the one is no better than the other. The next question is how long is this state of things to continue and again, what should be done to press the point home to those in authority?

May I offer the suggestion that the low power light at St. Anthony's—at the entrance to Falmouth Harbour—of 7,000 candles is totally inadequate to guard the outlying dangers, even with the addition of a whistling and gas-lit buoy?

[425] Ibid.

[426] Ibid.

The constant recurrence of disasters on this part of the coast proves this without a doubt, and calls for the erection of a first class light and fog signal on the Manacle Rocks.

Yours obediently, ONE WHO KNOWS THE COAST.[427]

The public clamour for additional navigational aid for this notorious coast line had now reached a new level of intensity. No doubt the hapless shipping company for the *Paris* vessel was grateful for this diversion; as *any* change in navigational aid would not have prevented this latest near-disaster. The master of the *Paris* appeared more concerned with cutting corners (in an attempt to shave off travelling time) than for the safety of his vessel.

The Elder Brethren of the Trinity House must have made a collective sigh of relief, when the cause of both the *Mohegan* and *Paris* events was deemed as due to, 'errors in navigation', rather than a lack of navigational infrastructure. As a result, public opinion became less demanding, as reported here:

FROM ALL QUARTERS

The Elder Brethren of the Trinity House have under consideration the desirability of erecting a lighthouse or placing a lightship to mark the position of the Manacles. Immediately after the disasters of the *Mohegan* and the *Paris* there was a great outcry for such provision to be made, but when it was shown by the subsequent official inquiry that the disaster was due to errors in navigation the demand became less pronounced.

It is still the opinion of many competent navigators that something might be done with advantage in the way of indicating more definitely the position of the rocks. It may be true that ordinary precautions are quite sufficient to prevent collision with the Manacle Rocks, lying as they do, quite out of the course of ordinary navigation. But that it cannot be forgotten that within a very short period of time the two appalling disasters referred to did take place.[428]

A quid pro quo.

TO THE EDITOR OF THE TIMES

Sir,—In a letter on May 24 Mr. Haviland asks, "Is England wholly without blame?" "Are there a sufficient number of lights between the Eddystone and the Lizard?" "Does England require vessels to employ Channel pilots?"

Admiral de Horsey's letter on May 23 is sufficient answer to some of the questions. As to the insufficiency of lights on the English coast, suppose the *Paris* had left New York for Southampton, and run on rocks near Coruña, would the disaster have been caused by neglect in the Spanish Government to provide sufficient lights on the coast of Spain? In such case the *Paris* would have been south of her true course, but the deviation would not have been much greater than that by which she was going north of her course at the time she ran ashore at the Manacles.

I am Sir, your obedient servant,

Melksham, May 29. E. Kingston.[429]

---

[427] *The Times;* Tuesday, 23rd May 1899.

[428] *Isle of Wight Observer* (Ryde, England); Saturday, 7th April 1900.

[429] *The Times;* Wednesday, 31st May 1899.

If you don't know where you are going, you will probably end up somewhere else

As was highlighted at the Board of Trade inquiry; one witness was asked, "Why, if he felt the course was wrong, he did not call the attention of the officers?" A rather obvious reason for that, was reported thus:

When the *Mohegan* reached the Eddystone Lights the course set for the Lizard was "west by north". One or two witnesses said the course was "west three quarters north". It was given by Captain Griffiths himself, and without authority to vary it to "west by south," it had to be steered, as one witness after the other stated. "West by north" was, therefore, steered almost to half a point for the thirty miles that landed the new ship among the Manacles—a "wasp's nest of rocks" westward of Falmouth. The course given, if steered, was bound to land her on the Bell-rock of the Manacles. But, as often happens, the mistake of the wrong course was augmented by circumstances, for there was a half-gale from the south-east, and the tide set in to Falmouth Bay, rendering the escape of the vessel impossible. One witness was asked, why, if he felt the course was wrong, he did not call the attention of the officers of the watch to the fact. "I was not to know," was the reply, "that the captain did not intend to call in at Falmouth". Another witness described the captain as a good seaman, and an excellent officer, but," he added, "He was a martinet". A suggestion to the captain, modestly put and rightfully received, might have saved 106 lives and a valuable ship. But what quartermaster or able seaman would presume to hint at an error on the course set by the captain? The men at the wheel were bound to steer the course set, although it landed them among shoals of rocks. The facts are not in dispute even by the owners of the vessel, and tomorrow afternoon we shall know what a court [BoT] of four experienced gentlemen consider led to a calamity unfortunately not infrequent along the British coast.[430]

Two heads are better than one.

However, the heart of this matter is not arriving at a point, where it is thought necessary to question a ship's course, but more in having a consensus, between a captain and his senior officers, as to a correct course to adopt, in the first place. This would seem to be obvious and a valuable safeguard for a ship's wellbeing; however, not every vessel had such a regime in place and that seemingly would include the *Mohegan*. To be sailing so close to shore and with no knowledge as to whether or not the captain intends to call in at Falmouth, speaks for itself.

The experts were again promoting in favour of an open and transparent dialogue, between a captain and his officers, as being an essential safety measure:

TO THE EDITOR OF THE TIMES

Sir,—Would you kindly insert the following letter?

I have been many years an officer in steamships of the largest lines afloat and in steamers really not much better than the ordinary "tramp". [431] My experience differs from "Steamship Director" as regards an officer's opportunity for verifying his course.

---

[430] *The Belfast News-Letter* (Belfast, Ireland); Saturday, 26th November 1898.

[431] A "Tramp" was a commercial steamer for hire; one having no regular schedule.

In all the big lines I have served in, the officers have a distinct set of charts from the captain. Instead of resenting (as "Steamship Director" says "many masters would do") an officer's wish to check the course, the captain will very often order him to do so, and wait on the bridge meanwhile; if he did not do this, he would certainly take for granted that his officer would satisfy himself and also lay off as many bearings as possible to get fresh positions. The more careful you are to report any discrepancy (or what you consider a discrepancy) the more your commander would like it.

In the case of the ordinary "tramp" the captain's cabin is always open to the officers with the chart on the table.

I do not think any captain afloat would be so unreasonable as to resent his officer wishing to see the ship's position on the chart in the "English Channel," or, as far as my experience goes, anywhere else.

Yours faithfully.

October 19.—STEAMSHIP OFFICER.[432]

In another letter to a provincial newspaper, the role of a master and his officers, in the matter of a safe navigation for a ship, was again discussed:

GOSSIP OF THE WEEK:—I learn from New York that the Atlantic Transport Company are issuing instructions to their Captains that their ship's courses are in future to be worked out by their officers, and checked by the Captains themselves. I am glad of this. This is the precise method that I have more than once advocated to keep the *Mohegan* and other ships off the Manacles and other rocks. Certainly the *Mohegan* could hardly have gone ashore as she did if her Captain's calculation had been checked and found wanting, while the Captain of the *Paris* had himself stated that his own unaccountable error was the cause of the ship's stranding.

As for a Captain's dignity, that can go hang. If a Captain do not like the interference of his officers in a matter of this kind he had better leave his ship. A Captain's dignity is not to be pitted against one passenger's life–let alone five hundred lives.

Anyway, I would rather swing any Captain over the side than let him sink the ship.[433]

This would suggest that, within the Atlantic Transport Line company, it was not common practice for ships' officers to have a role in the laying-off a course for their vessel. As a result of the ensuing internal inquiry and aware that their own commodore was disinclined to involve his officers in this task, this prompted the company to make it a mandatory duty, on the part of a master of a vessel to allow his officers to work out a ship's course and then to check and verify their calculation. Not only did this provide a confirmation of a ship's true course ahead, but also as a valuable learning exercise, that allowed an officer to make his mistakes in a safe environment and not wait until he had become a ship's master, to demonstrate any deficiencies. In addition: a collective and mutually agreed heading of, say W-by-S would not likely and casually translate to that of W-by-N.

An article written by a *Mohegan* passenger, Mr John Hyslop, appeared in *Harper*'s *Magazine*,[434] during June, 1899. It speculated on the mindset for Capt. Griffith and how that might have influenced his actions

---

[432] *The Times*; Thursday, 20th October 1898.

[433] *Hampshire Telegraph and Sussex Chronicle* etc. (Portsmouth, England); Saturday, 12th August 1899.

aboard the *Mohegan*. Mr Hyslop was professionally engaged in maritime matters[435] and it is worth quoting this here, as it is a thoughtful treatise based on his unenviable experience, on the deck of the *Mohegan* itself:

THE STRAIN OF THE CAPTAIN.

NEEDED PRECAUTIONS FOR THE SAFE
NAVIGATION OF OCEAN-GOING VESSELS.

Two questions arise. Given a due complement of competent officers for the proper navigation of a ship, do existing methods give full effect to their combined skill, care and direction, or is it a fact that in important respects the captain is not only supreme, as he ought to be and must necessarily, but that he is practically left without systemized help or check? The other question is, is it sufficient to merely provide for vessels' boats of a sufficient number or size, even though the means of launching them are so utterly crude and inadequate that under conditions of any difficulty and where many boats would need to be launched together or within a limited time, miserable failure could be the only result?

It should be understood that the *Mohegan* was lost by striking the Manacle Rocks, near to Falmouth and Land's End, shortly after dark and two and a half hours after passing three miles southward of the Eddytone Lighthouse.

She had on deck the second and third officer, and, it is believed, the captain also. It is known that he had observed the course and the compass shortly before the ship struck. A course west by north—the course she was being steered—extended on the chart to thirty sea miles [from the Eddystone] would run just inside of the Manacles, as would be plainly apparent to anyone with a chart before him. The course was half a point more northerly, and more into the land, than the same vessel under the same captain had been steered on the next preceding voyage from a position four miles further off shore.

That the captain was a sober, careful and capable man, with an excellent record, I fully believe. What the particular debility, and it does not seem to have been apparent to others but I cannot believe that this brave and unfortunate man had a mind clear and in its normal working condition. Various conditions and statements have appeared in print bearing on this point, and whatever may or may not have been the nature of Captain Griffith's misfortune. It cannot be doubted that shipmasters as a class are subjected from time to time to the most severe trials of physical hardship, to responsibility, care and exhaustive effort, to sleepless nights, and, added to these, to the ordinary ills and cares of men, to consequent periods of reduced mental vigor, to preoccupation and errors of perception and calculation. The system which is so large an extent depends on the healthy and vigorous working of one mind for the direction of affairs has (it is only a truism to state) not yet attained to the most desirable condition, or to a maximum of safety, if consistently and properly needed checks and safeguards can be introduced.

It is the opinion of the writer that to no single man should be left unaided and unchecked the control and direction of the course of a passenger vessel to the extent which he now obtains, and it appears quite practicable to devise a method and routine by which added safeguards may be had without injury to discipline and without, by the method, questioning that supreme and ultimate control which must always properly remain with the captain. As the custom now is, when a vessel is out at sea, and it becomes necessary to take an observation with the sextant and to work out by calculations a knowledge of the vessel's position, the captain will do this, but it will also be done independently by one, and perhaps two, of his officers, and the results of the calculations, when these have been completed, will be compared. If, in consequence of a

---

[434] HARPER'S BAZAAR, was an American weekly women's fashion magazine that began publication in 1867 in the large newspaper format design of *Harper's Weekly*. The publication, based in New York, was intended for the women of the middle and upper socio-economic classes of the second half of the 19th century.

[435] Mr Hyslop was yacht-measurer for the prestigious New York Club; a post he held for 17 years.

lack of such check, a considerable error were made, there would be (so long as the vessel was far from land) no immediate danger.

If, however, during night or day the vessel were moving along a coast line and near to rocks and other dangers, and on a course set by the captain, and if an officer saw danger in it, or failed to see why such a course was set, he would, I think, in most cases be chary about asking questions or in offering suggestions and he would be especially so if, not having a chart open before him, or if for any other reason, such as the captain's own experience and carefulness, he entertained the least doubt of his own correctness.

In any case he would probably be willing to run close to danger, in the hope and expectation that the captain might detect his own error. This matter of the relations of officers to the captain receives some light from the evidence given before the court of inquiry by Captain Pollard, who had formerly sailed with Captain Griffith as third officer. In reply to the question as to whether the captain "would have been extremely pleased if he had seen any of the officers looking at the charts going down channel," he said: "No, I do not think he would; he generally looked after that sort of thing himself".

I find that among sea captains and officers there is a common opinion that any examination of charts or questioning of correctness of a course given by a captain would in the majority of cases be resented, and would be too risky undertaken. So that while we see under present conditions a vessel's position is most carefully taken and checked off when she is in open water, where a large error would bring no peril, when she is close to land, and when the smallest deviation from a correct course may make all the difference between safety and destruction a ship's safety is practically wholly in charge of one man, and a headache or a fit of forgetfulness may determine things the wrong way and send the ship to the bottom.

The subject of an improvement on present methods is well deserving of consideration and discussion by all men interested in it. It may, however, be said suggestively that if, instead of the captain laying the vessel's course, it was made to be the ordinary routine that this should be done be by an officer under him, subject of course, to the captain's concurrence, a new and valuable check would be provided, and without any entrenching on the dignity of the captain's position or on discipline an understanding would be had of purposes which might otherwise be unknown excepting to the captain himself and which might quite possibly be unsafe. In cases of error, or of differences of opinion, these would naturally lead to comparison. With the officers there would be a new responsibility and a call of increased watchfulness. Due warrant to look at and examine the charts would then exist, and these would be referred to whenever there was occasion for it. If, in addition to this regulation, there was a further one that when a vessel was within a distance from shore, to be defined—say, for instance, fifty miles—a chart or charts of the locality should be spread open in the chartroom, and when the officer of the deck was relieved he should mark the vessel's position and course, and this should be checked by his successor.[436]

A correspondent discarded the misinterpretation of the St. Anthony's and Lizard lighthouses as a causal factor, and so navigated one's attention back to the wheelhouse of the *Mohegan*:

THE MOHEGAN DISASTER

Sir,—The lamentable catastrophe on the Manacles will, I think, remain a mystery, unless it can be shown that the steering compass had at least a full point of easterly deviation, and that, too, without the knowledge of the captain. This, if it should be surmised, cannot be sustained. Had the deviation mentioned existed without the knowledge of the officers of Mohegan, she would not have cleared the "Start Point". Another theory set forth is the possibility of the officers in charge having mistaken St. Anthony's Light for the Lizard Lights. This too, cannot be believed by, I am sure, by most of nautical man,

[436] *New York Herald-Tribune;* May 27, 1899

since there is so great a difference between the lights. "St. Anthony" being single revolving, while the "Lizard" is double fixed. Perhaps, therefore, I may be permitted to express my opinion upon the matter. At six or six and a-half miles south of the Eddystone (which is the general track) a fresh course in all probability was being pricked off in order to give the Lizard a decent berth. Now from the position stated, the course would be W½N., but on delivering this new order to the helmsman if he understood it to be W by N½N., instead of the former (the mention of the ½ being the cause), then the latter course would bring the *Mohegan* exactly to the place where she unfortunately came to grief.

I am &c.

NEPTUNE.[437]

In a vintage publication are described some pertinent navigational marks of interest to those who frequented these local coastal waters:

St Anthony's Point, Falmouth.—on eastern side of the Falmouth entrance. The lighthouse is an octagonal white tower, exhibiting a revolving light at an elevation of 72 feet above sea level. The light [438] is first visible in coming from the eastward on a N.W.½N. bearing, round seaward, and up to the harbour of Falmouth; appearing in a quick but regular succession of brilliant flashes every 20 seconds, and may be seen for more than 13 miles off. A fixed light, 37 feet below the revolving light, is exhibited to clear the Manacle Rocks; it is seen only between the bearing of N.N.E.½E. and E.¼E., and when in sight leads 2 cables [1,200 feet] eastward of the rocks and buoy of the Manacles.

Eddystone Light.—This lighthouse is 89 feet high, and is coloured red-and-white in alternate horizontal bands, and built upon a rock, bearing from Prawl [sic] Point W.N.W. ½W., about 21 miles, and from Rame Head S.W. by S., southerly, 8 miles. It bears a fixed Light, 72 feet above high-water, and is brilliantly lighted with lamps and reflectors, visible 13 miles.

The Manacles.—Lie 5 ½ miles S.S.W., from Pendennis Point, and are 3 miles, S. by E. from the entrance of Helford Sound; they require a good offing, and lie nearly a mile from the shore. These rocks are high, and not a bad object, to confirm the situation of Falmouth, and are dangerous in sailing from Falmouth with easterly winds and ebb-tides, the latter setting strongly upon them.

About N.E. by E. from the outer Manacle Rock, distant ½ a mile is a small rock, under water, having only 5 feet over it; this lies with the only slated house in Porthoustoc [sic], nearly N.W. ½ W.

Buoy—A bell buoy, painted black, with staff and globe, and marked with the word, "Manacles" upon its head, is placed in 18½ fathoms [111 feet] at low water, spring tides, 56 fathoms [336 feet] S.E. from the outer sunken rock [Penvin] at the eastern extremity of the Manacles Ridge.[439]

The Manacle buoy light was about 5½ miles distant from St. Anthony's Point, and is approximately 10 feet above sea level, flashing every 2 seconds and of the usual type of buoy light.

---

[437] *Glasgow Herald* (Glasgow, Scotland); Monday, 24th October 1898.

[438] The power of the main revolving light at St. Anthony's was equivalent to 7,000 candles and the single fixed light at 8,000 candles.

[439] *The English Channel Pilot for the South and South West Coasts of England, the South Coast of Ireland and Part of the North Coast of France*; Published by – Charles Wilson.

The LIZARD and Dangers Adjacent.—The Lizard Head is a bold and precipitous headland, and is well known in the English Channel navigation as a point of departure, and is frequently made when homeward bound. It may be seen when the weather is clear at a distance of 24 miles, and is easily recognised by the two white lighthouses upon it. With the assistance of these light-houses either in day-light or at night, you may approach the head with confidence, bearing in mind that the dangers extend nearly half a mile off the point in the vicinity.

LIGHTS,—The light-houses erected on the Lizard are each 61 feet high, and the buildings are octagonal, white, bearing W. by N.. northerly, and E. by S., southerly, 74 yards apart; they are respectively 229 and 232 feet above high water, and exhibit fixed lights, visible 21 miles. When in one these lights lead 3½ miles to the southward of the Manacles, and the same distance southward of the Wolf Rock, but you must get a sight of them from the lower rigging, 30 feet above the sea, if you desire to use them for such dangers.[440]

Most of the references in this publication describe passages designed for close coastal navigation. Ordinarily, this would not be of intrinsic interest to a captain of the *Mohegan*; though on reflection, it might have proved of some value, considering the *Mohegan*'s persistent proximity to the Cornish coastline.

Based on the distance at which the Lizard lights were thrown, it is assumed that the lighthouse was relatively unchanged between the years of 1878–1903; thus, the same lights characteristics prevailed at the time of the *Mohegan* disaster. The twin lights were converted to a single fixed light in 1903, when one of the towers was dispensed with. In 1932, the Lizard lighthouse was said to have the most powerful lights in the world and were visible at a distance of 21 miles.

The quality of lighting, available for 19th century navigation was not on a par with modern-day lighting technologies. The 'throw' of a light, as described above, is based on optimal atmospheric and sea conditions. A comparison for the lighting technologies available, at that time, is described here:

Shore and floating lights established to aid navigation, i.e. designed to be seen from seaward, are of three types: flashing (the period of the visible flash being of small duration in the cycle such as every ten seconds, and can be multiple short flashes, for example: two, three, four, every ten seconds; occulting) the light is on continuously but interrupted by one or two short periods of darkness, and fixed: that is, on continuously.

The quality of the white light depends on the method of illumination and could be yellowish to white depending on the fuel. But as a general rule so called white lights are visible at much greater distances than coloured lights. The rules with coloured lights are that red sectors mark bearings where there are dangers to ships and green lights mark safe areas. Red is more visible than green, but distance erodes the precise perception of colour. The ability to project colour in 1898 was probably not very effective. The range quoted for lights, such as 21 miles is for a dark night with a clear atmosphere, and is related to the height of the light above mean high water springs at the source and a height of observer of 15 feet (geographical range); the geographical range may be reduced when printed on charts if the power of the light is low (luminous range). However it might be necessary to establish the definitions in use in 1898. On a clear relatively calm night lights may be seen at much greater distances from an observer at a greater height than (say) 15 feet. The loom of the light (reflected by the clouds/atmosphere) may in the clearest conditions be seen at even greater distances. So, 30 or

[440] Ibid.

40 nautical miles might be possible for a strong light, aided with some height but only at night. Usually in clear condition, lights were turned off during the day.

If the wind was blowing at say force five on the run from Start Point and the Eddystone, there would have been some reduction in the visibility by the water droplets churned up by the wind.

In a paper, I have recently discussed signalling Lloyds signal stations from seaward. By day signal flags, semaphore or Morse code light could have been used in such a modern vessel [*Mohegan*]. For all three, the international code of signals might have been used or the message spelled out letter by letter.

By night Morse code only was possible, and could have been seen at three miles. But there was also a less precise method; shipping companies had personalised rocket signals they could send up; these identified a ship of the company but not the name of the ship.[441] However the signal station would be able to distinguish east bound from west bound.[442]

Every legitimate authority should respect its extent and its limits.

But why did the officers not question the course the *Mohegan?* Well, perhaps this observation may help explain:

> The question will naturally arise as to why the first officer [Llewellyn Couch] of the *Mohegan,* on seeing the extraordinary course which the captain was steering, did not venture to remonstrate and to realize that something had gone wrong with his commander. This is easy to explain. The discipline on the big ocean liners, especially on board those flying the English flag, is almost as strict as that on a man-of-war. As a general rule, the skipper does not invite familiarity on the part of his subaltern officers, and for the latter to remonstrate if they saw anything that they did not quite understand, or which in their opinion was an error of judgment, would in nine cases out of ten result in sharp censure, possibly discharge, and extreme difficulty in finding another ship, berths on an ocean liner being at a premium among officers of the merchant navy. Moreover, it is doubtful whether any one of the officers on board the *Mohegan* realised at the time that so sound a brain as that of the commander could possibly have thus suddenly and unaccountably got out of gear.[443]

Land, Ho!

Inevitably, the question of the *Mohegan*'s proximity to shore prompted some discourse in the national papers. This piece suggests the adoption of known scientific principles, in giving some forewarning of a ship's hazardous position at sea:

THE DISTANCE FROM LAND

Methods of Reckoning Is Suggested Apropos of the *Mohegan* Disaster

Letter to the Editor of the *Pall Mall Gazette.*

---

[441] Atlantic Transport Line: A Roman candle throwing six balls of the following colours—viz., one Green, one White and one Red, to be repeated once in the same order. These are recognised within British jurisdiction and on the high seas. http://www.kellscraft.com/ShipsandShipping/ShipsandShippingCh10.html

[442] Personal communication: Mr Alston Kennerley, Plymouth University (2011).

[443] *New-York Tribune*; November 27th 1898.

With your kind permission I will continue my remarks in support of the theory developed in my last letter. It will take years of observations and record before we have charts marked with standards of obscuration in various conditions of wind and tide, as charts are now marked with the bottom. But I do not despair of seeing the time when the proudest boast of a rich yachtsman will be, not that he has won a silver cup for covering twenty miles ten seconds faster than somebody else, but that he has sent to the Admiralty the best obscuration chart of the year, and so done something to make poor Jack's life a little more secure. Years ago, Proctor [444] printed in *Knowledge* my suggestion to use the thermopile in air to detect the presence of icebergs. But there is another mode in which, I believe, science can help in this matter, and that is by making use thermo-electric pile [445] to ascertain the temperature of the water in which the vessel is floating. It is quite clear that (other things being equal) water that has been beaten by the wind upon the rocks or shore must be considerably warmer than that which is only beaten against other yielding water; the friction of a fluid against a solid must develop more heat than the friction of a fluid against a fluid, though this difference may be unfelt by our senses, the thermopile galvanometer could measure and record it. Again the sea water will take up and hold air in comparatively large quantities—surely the measure of this can be easily effected—and a continued increase in the quantity would indicate to the careful observer that some of the conditions surrounding him had changed to give a warning that a cause must exist for the change, and the cause would be known to be the presence of the shore or rocks breaking up the waves and so continually mixing the air and water that the excess of the former was easily detected. The objections that these tests could not be applied in a rapid current are a strong one but if they can only be applied in a proportion of cases, the stake is so great as to make it worth using them.

There is, however, another means of ascertaining the neighbourhood of rocks and shore and also of approaching vessels, and that is by sound in the air.

A man viewing a row of lights along the beach of a sea coast town sees only a line of light, but he can with a telescope examine any point of this and cut out of view the rest because the rays of light move in regular lines, but so also do the waves of sound, and with a phonoscope, if I may coin a word, and a microphone, it would be possible to cut off all other vibrations than those proceeding from a certain point in the horizon and magnify them, and attention being exclusively fixed on these, their character might be discovered with ease. The dashing of waves on rocks, the grinding of the shingle on the beach, the beating of a screw of a steamer are sounds that only want isolating to be at once identified, and the direction from which they originate ought to be at once known from the position of the narrow mouth of the instrument. In nature the mobile ears of the ass, the horse, and the hare are example of the use of the phonoscope for localizing the origin of sounds.

In cases of vessels in fog using fog-horns or whistles, or bells, the indication of their exact whereabouts is vital, and this can be ascertained within a few points, either by the wearer and the hand phonoscope or by means of a membrane in a larger instrument vibrating a pendulum and this making an electric connection with a small bell which sounds only when the mouth of the instrument is pointing dead [ahead] at the source of the sound waves. With a pair of flattened ear trumpets of tin, about 10 inches long, and with a mouth about 4 inches by ¾ of an inch, covered all over with fur on the outside and 3 inches down the inside, I could blindfold, determine the position of voices and footsteps within two or three points of the compass, (this was a trial for military purposes to detect the approach of the enemy in night attacks).

But in the water itself we find a still further help to safety. At the Folkstone baths in Winter, the water is heated by steam blown in from pipes on the bottom of the swimming bath. On one occasion some years ago I found that, while the

---

[444] 'Richard Proctor's magazine *Knowledge* was designed for the free interchange of views between the scientific profession and the public, an attempt to keep scientific practice and direction firmly rooted in public concerns. But this was bucking what turned out to be the successful professionalizing trend; *Knowledge* folded while *Nature* survived to this day.'— *Thomas Hardy, Richard Proctor and the dialogue of the deaf–How scientists evolved to be resistant to public accountability*; Nicholas Russell; Imperial College London. 18 February 2006.

[445] A thermopile or a thermal telescope is an instrument designed to measure the force of radiant energy. It consists of a thermoelectric pile and a voltage indicator.

sound of the steam in the air was a mere dull crepitation, on plunging in and immersing the ears there was experienced a series of deafening blows, absolutely unendurable. In 1826 some experiments were made on one of the Swiss lakes, and it was found that the blows on a bell in the water nine miles away were heard distinctly by a listener, with an immersed tube with a diaphragm turned in its direction. A combination of telephone and microphone properly immersed would convey to the ear vibrations in the water as distinctively as the sounds of various voices are conveyed by the telephone every day. The throb of the screw of an approaching vessel, say, a torpedo boat; the thunder of waves against rock or iceberg; the grinding of gravel on a beach, could be all distinguished one from the other by an experienced listener, and thus, with a simple instrument of this kind, half an hour's warning might be obtained of the neighbourhood of rocks, icebergs, or shore, and a quarter of an hour's of the approach of the fastest vessels.

It is of the most remarkable facts in connection with marine progress that while speed and power have so enormously increased, the means of guiding and controlling this increase remain what they were in the days of the old wooden ships. The dropping of a lead with a piece of string overboard seems to be the only method of ascertaining the whereabouts of the land, and to do this with a vessel going fifteen knots an hour is impossible. If the vessel is stopped for the purpose in the twenty minutes required for the work she will nearly roll the masts out of her and drive half her passengers frantic with sheer fright. It is time surely that all this was changed, and that some rational method should be adopted for lessening of the dangers of the sea. Such methods I have indicated, and a grave responsibility rests upon those whose duty it is to attend to these matters, if they longer remain un-investigated and untried.

That more than 600 men professing an earnest desire for the welfare of their country should meet year after year without attempting to do something to remedy such glaring and conspicuous evils will in the time to come be one of the gravest reproaches of the age that boastfully claims to be the most humane and the most enlightened of any that the world has seen.

I am, Sir, yours. &c.,

Stewart Harrison. Lieutenant Colonel. V.D. 26 College Street, Dowgate Hill, E. C., Oct. 18.[446]

The day has eyes; the night has ears.

This being a point of conjecture: as to whether half the passengers would be, "frantic with sheer fright" at the prospect of a ship's masts rolling out of her, or by certain members of the ship's company wandering the deck, dressed as a hare with long fur-lined ears, particularly during the month of March.

To be fair, the correspondent makes some pertinent points in his scientific application and some aspects of his 'thesis' had been adopted in the twentieth century, whereby, submariners 'listen out' for other approaching vessels, from many miles off; even identifying a type of vessel in question, by its sound signatures in using a new technology of ASDIC.[447]

---

[446] *New York Times;* November 8th 1898.

[447] ASDIC, developed through the work of the Anti-Submarine Detection Investigation Committee from which its name is derived, was the primary underwater detection device used by Allied escorts throughout the war. The ASDIC, known to the Americans as Sonar, was basically a transmitter-receiver sending out a highly directional sound wave through the water. If the sound wave struck a submerged object it was reflected back and picked up by the receiver. The length of the time from transmission until the echo was received was used to measure the range, which was shown as a flickering light on the range scale. By mounting the transmitter head so that it could be directed almost like a searchlight, the bearing of the target could be read from the compass receiver. © Gudmunder Hegason.

During the First World War, large concrete dishes[448] were constructed and strategically positioned, around our coastline. Their purpose was to concentrate and amplify the sounds of German aircraft, as they approached the UK. This gave the English Command a valuable advanced warning, in enabling the aircrew to get aloft, and in taking a proactive engagement with the enemy.

A Company's strategy.

An obvious strategy for the Atlantic Transport Line was to show the Board of Trade Court that the *Mohegan* was in the best possible mechanical state and fit for purpose. Several witnesses were presented to confirm that point, and included the following maritime experts:

> Mr. Pearson, naval architect to the builders of the steamer–Messrs. Earle and Co.– said that any damage done to her boilers on her previous voyage [as the *Cleopatra*] had been entirely repaired before she set out on the fatal voyage in question.

> Mr. George Potter [*sic*], engineer to Messrs. Williams, Torrey and Field, London agents for the Company, also testified to the satisfactory condition of the boilers, before the *Mohegan* sailed on her last voyage.

> Mr. John M'Ewen, an engineer and surveyor to the Board of Trade, stated that he surveyed the ship in April: the he had surveyed her during the time of her construction and that he had issued the usual declarations in the Board of Trade form.

> Mr. Thomas Kendall, a surveyor to the Board of Trade, who had completed the survey of the vessel in the latter part of July, also said he issued the usual declaration.

> Mr. Andrew, to whose firm the *Mohegan* came for repairs after the first voyage, bore testimony to her satisfactory condition after the repairs had been carried out.

> Mr. Ballock considered that everything about the ship was satisfactory before she set out on her last voyage.[449]

With no dissenting voice to be heard, the *Mohegan* was accepted by the Court as an exemplar, for the finest traditions of British shipbuilding.

In addition, the Atlantic Transport Line's regulations, issued to all its masters and crew members, decreed that:

> The company had laid down detailed regulations: not to secure speed at the risk of accidents, to use the lead [to establish a sea depth and a seabed composition] whether it involved delay or not, to pay close attention to the compasses, to practice

---

[448] 'Sound mirrors' – acoustic early-warning system. A forerunner of RADAR, acoustic mirrors were built on the south and northeast coasts of England between about 1916 and the 1930s. The 'listening ears' were intended to provide early warning of incoming enemy aircraft and airships about to attack coastal towns. With the development of faster aircraft the sound mirrors became less useful, as an aircraft would be within sight by the time it had been located, and radar finally rendered the mirrors obsolete; http://andrewgrantham.co.uk/soundmirrors/.

[449] *The Standard* (London, England); Friday, 11th November 1898.

the getting out of the lifeboats. "Above all," the company said, "we desire you to make safe passages, and to secure the latter we will not allow you to run any risk." [450]

In essence, the defence offered at the Board of Trade inquiry was that: the ship, its master and crew, the overall management and an adherence to maritime best practice, were all above reproach. The only point at odds, despite this level of excellence, was that the *Mohegan* ended up wrecked on the Cornish coast. The company was left with no option, other than to attempt to explain *that* unpalatable fact.

In the absence of the ship's logbook, a total reliance on the evidence given by the survivors of the catastrophe was presented at the Board of Trade inquiry.

In this report, a detailed timeline was constructed by the various crew members involved in navigation:

[BoT Court proceedings] . . . that officer survived, and would be called to give evidence. He would state from ten to twelve o'clock the course given him was "west by three-quarters north," and that at 2.40 p.m. the ship passed Prawle Point at about three miles distance, and reported there, "All right; report me". Further evidence will be given by surviving officers as to the Eddystone having been passed at about half-past four. At four o'clock Juddery was on deck, and at three minutes past four he received an order from the fourth officer [S. Browning] to read the log, which gave a distance of 55 miles. At that time the Eddystone Lighthouse appeared at about four points from the starboard bow. At 4.17 he was sent again to read the log, which showed 57¾ miles, giving a distance from the Eddystone at that time of 2¾ miles. Quartermaster Blake was at the wheel from 2 to 4 o'clock, when he was relieved by Butt, who received from the former the course of west by north. At five o'clock, the Master looked at the compass himself, and, the learned counsel believed, spoke to the officer on the watch afterwards. There was no change of course up to five o'clock, when Butt gave up the wheel to a quartermaster named August. During the whole time he was at the wheel, it appeared, the loom of the land was visible. Shortly after six o'clock the man in the crow's nest, named Daniels, twice struck his bell, for giving signals, and also hailed, "Light about 2 points to the starboard bow". He was answered from the bridge, "All right". At 6.50 Perks [*sic*], the third engineer,[451] who was then at that time in charge of the engines, suddenly got the order to "Stop her". That order was carried out, but in half a minute the vessel struck.[452]

He that pays the piper calls the tune.

The detail of the evidence that each witness gave, appears well-rehearsed. Timelines as to exact minutes past the hour at which certain manoeuvres were carried out just seemed a little glib. Of course, a seaman's life is orchestrated by an exact timetable, especially that of changes of the watch, and so perhaps it is not unreasonable for a witness to give a precise account of himself, against the clock. Nevertheless, as reported elsewhere, the 'story' of the wrecking among the crew was said to have been 'checked and corrected among themselves' whilst recovering at the Royal Sailors' Home in Falmouth. Also present was Mr A. S. Williams, a

---

[450] Ibid.

[451] There was no person aboard with this name. The third-engineer was, in fact, John Marshall; he did not survive the disaster.

[452] *Standard* (London, England); Friday, November 11th 1898.

company man. How much coercion, suggestion, and with a reminder of the implications for a career, was employed, will never now be known. But, with the arrival of the company owner, Mr Baker from Baltimore, and in immediate consultation with a legal team in London, it would be no surprise that a 'strategy' would have been concocted that presented the company's position in the best possible light. That would certainly have involved the main witnesses—the crew members aboard the *Mohegan*—and they would have been expected to support the company line.

Fourteen years later, the steamship *Titanic* disaster occurred, in the mid-Atlantic. The story needs no elaboration here, as it is the world's most well-known shipwreck. There is now overwhelming evidence that a cover-up was perpetrated at the subsequent investigations, both in America and at the London Board of Trade inquiries:

Birds of a feather flock together.

> *Titanic* Second Officer Charles Lightoller was the top-ranking survivor of the *Titanic* sinking other than the company chairman.[453] The public looked to Lightoller to tell the world what happened. Lady Patten [author] says the only person Lightoller told the truth about why the *Titanic* sunk was to his wife Sylvia. He, other officers and owners of White Star Line lied at both the American and British inquests held after the sinking to protect themselves from criminal charges, ruining their careers and bankrupting the company. In the end, all they all avoided was criminal charges.[454]

It doesn't take a great deal of imagination to suspect there was some cover-up employed in the *Mohegan* affair. Granted, not to the same extent and as blatant as in the future *Titanic* inquiry, but nonetheless, one does get a feeling that there that there had been some massaging of information, in order to present the best possible case for the company.

Interestingly, in a letter from Lieut. Commander J. T. Rowe to Mr Frank Strike,[455] at Helston, Cornwall, the Lt. Commander relayed a story told him by Mr F. Huntley, who was aboard the *Mohegan*. The letter is reproduced here and it contains additional facts of general interest, as well as the quartermaster Huntley's recollections:

To His Worship
The Mayor of Helston

Skyburriowe Mill,
Helston,
Cornwall.
February 12th, 1958.

Dear Mr. Strike,

[453] Joseph Bruce Ismay – After the disaster, Ismay was savaged by both the American and the British Press for deserting the ship while women and children were still on board. Some papers called him the, "Coward Of The Titanic" or "J. Brute Ismay"—*WikiPedia*.

[454] Lady Louise Patten; *Good As Gold*. Lady Patten is the granddaughter of the *SS Titanic*'s second officer, Charles Lightoller.

[455] Mr Frank Strike B.E.M. was the Mayor of Helston, Cornwall; from 1957–1958. His award of the Medal of the Order of the British Empire for Meritorious Service was announced in the Supplement to The London Gazette, 1 January, 1958: *Frank Edyvean Strike, Member, Coast Life Saving Corps, Porthleven L.S.A. Company, (Helston, Cornwall)*.

I am writing in reference to a lecture you gave at Townsend [456] on the 7th instant, "Wrecks on the Cornish Coast". I was one of the audience and enjoyed the talk and the slides were very good. I did not speak with you afterwards, as I was with my brother-in-law and sister, who live in Townsend, and I was visiting them. As you will see from my paper heading, I was at sea for 25 years, 10 years in sail, 15 years in steam, with an extra Master's square rigged certificate, which I obtained in 1907.

The matter I am writing about is the loss of the *Mohegan*. I joined the Atlantic Transport Line in 1907, about eight years after the *Mohegan* was lost on the Manacle Rocks. I sailed in four of her sister ships. They were as follows:- *Mesaba*,[457] *Naniton, Magutre, Monomince*.

As you stated, the *Mohegan* was built for the Wilson Furness, Leyland Line and named *Cleopatra*. The Atlantic Line bought her on the stocks, when she was being built at one of the Tyne shipyards, and renamed her *Mohegan*. Whilst building, a strike occurred at the yard and there was a "No Strike" clause in the contract. The Atlantic Transport probably, perhaps, demanded delivery on the finishing date. Apparently insufficient labour was called in to finish the ship. The penalty for non-delivery was high, so I heard they rushed the job and delivered her. She leaked like a basket on her first voyage. They docked her in New York and she came back much better. She went back to the Tyne and was re-conditioned, and the end came on her next voyage, at the Manacle Rocks. This was all told to me eight years after her loss, when I was sailing as Third, Second and First Officer of the four sister ships.

Re: Captain Griffiths

I never knew him, but the story of his death in the Atlantic Transport Line was as follows:—A headless body was washed ashore in Caernarvon Bay about three months after the loss of the *Mohegan*. The uniform had four stripes (Captain's uniform of the A.T.L). The button under coat lapel was ATL, so that it was therefore supposed to be Captain Griffiths. The Chief Officer (Couch) and the Second (Cole) were not re-claimed; [458] at least that is my information.

I was going down the Channel in 1908 in *Menominee*.[459] We passed Start Point and steering the usual course, W. by S. ½ S. about S. 82 West. That course will take you five miles off Beachy Head, five miles off St. Catherines Point, five off Start [Point] and five off Lizard [Point], also five off Bishop's Rock; of course an allowance for wind, perhaps a degree or two degrees. When off Start Point on this occasion in the *Menominee*, I sighted a number of fishing vessels from Plymouth, and altered course to the Southward to clear them. I was the First Officer and in charge of the bridge. When we had cleared them, I steadied her back on course, and in so doing the Quartermaster, in the wheelhouse, who was steering by wheelhouse compass, said to me: "Another such night as the *Mohegan* went". His name was Huntley.[460] I said: "What do you know about that?" He said: "I was one of her Quartermasters". I then asked him when he left the wheel, and he said: "Just off Start [Point]". I was curious and asked him what course he had been steering, and he said: "W. x S. ½ S., the same as now". The

---

[456] Townsend is a small village approximately 10 miles from Helston.

[457] The *Meseba* was torpedoed of the Tuskar Rock [a group of rocks surmounted by a lighthouse off shore of the south east coast of County Wexford, Ireland] while in convoy in September of 1918. All hands were lost as she sank in three minutes. Lieut.-Commander. Rowe was in command of the gunboats H.M.P.G. *Kilkeel*. He carried out with other escorts, the depth-charge attack on the enemy submarine which torpedoed her. The submarine was sunk.

[458] In fact, both the bodies of Llewllyn Couch and that of Ernest Benjamin Cole were recovered.

[459] Menominee started out as Wilson & Furness-Leyland Line's *Alexandra*. Built by A. Stephen & Sons of Glasgow, she was launched in 1897 and made her maiden voyage from Glasgow to New York on 8 October 1897. She was sold to Atlantic Transport Line in 1908 and made one London-New York roundtrip for ATL under her old name before being renamed *Menominee*. She remained on ATL's London-New York route until 1905, when she was switched to Red Star Line service. (ATL had become part of J. P. Morgan's International Mercantile Marine combine in 1902. Red Star was one of IMM's original lines). For Red Star, she served on the Antwerp-Philadelphia route until Antwerp was occupied in 1914. She then made one London-New York sailing for Red Star before returning to ATL while remaining on the same route. *Menominee* was taken over as a British transport in 1915, and returned to ATL service as a cargo carrier in 1920. She was scrapped in 1926.

[460] Mr Frank Huntley was an able-seaman aboard the *Mohegan*.

standard compass is the one on the bridge; the steering compass is the one in the wheelhouse. In this case there was only one degree difference in the two compasses.

I said to the Third Officer, who was on the bridge with me: "Keep a sharp look-out. I am going down to the chart room". I put the parallel ruler on the chart, "West Sheet of English Channel," and laid a course to the Manacle Buoy. It read W. x N. ½ N. What I mean by that is: from Huntley's statement they were on course alright to Start Point, but the course from Start Point was 23 degrees out from that position off Start.

My finding, therefore, was this: the Quartermaster steered the wrong course, W. x N. ½ N., instead of W. x S. ½ S. The Officer on the watch did not check the course by standard compass. I take you have been to sea, Mr. Strike, and will follow my reasoning?

The Company did all that was necessary or all they could do. A window in St. Keverne Church. The *Mohegan* grave. They embalmed about sixty bodies and took them back to America for burial and free passage to any relatives to visit those in St. Keverne. B. M. [*sic*] Baker, the President, was in Baltimore at the time, and when he received the news he called New York and held up the Cunarder, *Lucania*, [*sic*] at £200 per hour, so that he could come to England. I refer by that they were a first-class company.

Unhappily, they are now out of business. They went into Atlantic Combine with the White Star in 1910, "Pierpoint Morgan" Combine, and that was not a success.

I have written at length because I felt a correction might be necessary in reference to [Capt.] Griffiths. In any case, you can take it the Captain and Officers were to blame, as the course should have been checked, and was not. Quartermaster Huntley, of whom I spoke, said the water poured in after striking and he scrambled out of Quartermaster's room, which was forward, and into the rigging. It was all over very quickly. The dynamos went under water and she was in darkness.

Yours very sincerely.

(Signed) J. T. Rowe.

(Lieut.-Commander J. T. Rowe, D.S.C., R.N.R.) [461]

The *Mohegan* passed Prawle Point at 2.40 p.m., as established at the Board of Trade inquiry. Huntley's name was never mentioned in the enquiry, and if he did have the wheel at the time he said, then this would have been an omission of fact. It would leave the crucial period for the navigation of the ship, in the hands of quartermaster Blake, who perished in the disaster and so not available as a witness. The Board of Trade inquiry established that Blake (having commenced his role as helmsman at 2.00 p.m.) was replaced at the wheel by quartermaster Butt at 4.00 p.m.

The confirmed turns at the wheel are shown here, arising from the facts assembled in the report by the Board of Trade inquiry:

Ship's Position:	Time Period:	Helmsman:	Course Set:
Isle of Wight to Portland:	10.00 – 12.00 a.m.	Juddery, John	W. x ¾ N. [462]
Portland to Start Point	12.00 – 2.00 p.m.	Huntley, Frank [463]	W. x S. ½ S.

---

[461] Frank Strike, B.E.M.; *Cornish Shipwrecks*; (Published by F. L. Strike, Porthleven, Cornwall 1965).

[462] Huntley gave the same course to his successor (unnamed). At half-past six, he saw land to starboard—*The Pall Mall Gazette* (London, England); Thursday, November 24th 1898.

[463] This is according to Huntley's statement made in the above letter from Lt. Cdr. Rowe to Mr Strike.

Signalled to Prawle at 2.40 p.m.	2.00 – 4.00 p.m.	Blake, Leslie	(not known)
Arrival at Eddystone at 4.30 p.m.	4.00 – 6.00 p.m.	Butt, Frederick	W. x N.
Arrival at Falmouth Bay/Manacles	6.00 – 6.50 p.m.	August, George	W. x N.

Table 4: Helmsmens' Turn at the *Mohegan*'s Wheel: 14th October, 1898.

There is an apparent gap in the timeline between the engagement of the quartermasters Juddery and Blake on the wheel. If Huntley *was* a helmsman aboard the *Mohegan* on that day, it would have to have been during this unaccounted-for period: namely, 12.00–2.00 p.m. This would fit in with his account of being relieved of his post by quartermaster Blake, as Prawle Point was but three miles distance after passing Start Point. However, Huntley relayed his account of the voyage to Lt. Commander Rowe, as having steered a course of W. x S. ½ S. This seems at odds with Juddery's account of handing over the instruction for the W. x ¾ N. heading. The question is, was Blake given the course as W. x S. ½ S., as stated by Huntley?

A comparison between the *Mohegan*'s course and the *Menominee*'s must be viewed in the context of their respective objectives. The *Mohegan* was deliberately heading for Prawle Point, in order to engage with the Lloyd's signal station there. It is assumed the *Menominee* [464] was at the more usual distance off, for a routine transatlantic route: that is, seven to ten miles.

Huntley also detailed a watch as look-out in the *Mohegan*'s crow's nest and then handing over to William Daniels, who shortly after six o'clock, rang two bells from his vantage point and hailed, "Light about two points to the starboard bow." Daniels presided over the wrecking from the crow's nest and subsequently lost his life during the mishap:

> Another seaman named Huntley, who was in the crow's nest from the half-past five to six, said that after he heard the two bells from the crow's nest he looked out on the starboard and saw a red light.[465] He threw himself into the sea, and was picked up by one of the ship's boats.[466]

The actual time at which the *Mohegan* struck the Manacles and in establishing the remaining daylight available at that point, is dependent on the whether local or Greenwich Mean Time (GMT) was in use, aboard ship. The following observation would imply that GMT was used, at this time:

> With respect to time and longitude, the use of the Greenwich meridian was agreed internationally at the Washington Conference in 1884. I don't have at my fingertips when the UK adopted summer time, though World War I might be a possibility; certainly in World War II double summertime was in use. My guess is that summertime was not in use in 1898

---

[464] It is interesting to note that the *Menominee* had been sold to the Atlantic Transport Line who promptly renamed her. The fate of the *Mohegan* following her renaming, appeared not have given any cause for concern. One assumes that the need to name their ships beginning with the letter 'M' overcame any inhibition they might have had.

[465] A red light did not feature as part of the St. Anthony's light pattern. The Falmouth pilot boat No. 10 was at slip anchor off St. Anthony lighthouse at the time. The red light in question could possibly have been her port-side light.

[466] Daily News (London, England); Friday, November 25th 1898.

and the ship would have been keeping GMT. As a passenger ship there would have been many clocks to wind up, but these would have taken their time from the ship's chronometers probably in the charthouse abaft the wheelhouse, and might have been a duty for the quartermasters. The chronometers ought to have been rated (that is, their rate of gaining or losing time) by the appointed nautical optician while in London or on board using the mechanical time signals, such as that at the Royal Observatory at Greenwich.

With 5 hours for the clocks to be put back before arrival in the USA, this would have been done to ships' clocks, in approximately 30 minute groups, usually during the night (related to predicted longitude the following noon). Chronometers were never altered during the voyage at all: that is, they always kept GMT plus or minus a few seconds or minutes error, of which a record was kept. It is unlikely that clocks would have been retarded before clearing the Channel.

One other complication was that the ship's day and date started at noon, whilst at sea, until the 1920s. It is thought that ships kept the day half a day ahead of the civil date. In port, ships reverted to civil usage.[467]

There is a question of which ship's course was the more usual one, for exiting the English Channel and on entering the Atlantic Ocean. The following view gives an interesting take on the usual course adopted, and with its associated safety aspects:

There is general guidance in the sailing directions (viz. Channel Pilots) about entering the Channel from the Atlantic and some general pointers about leaving but nothing detailed for specific types of vessels [at that time]. However it is clear that there is advice to avoid the French coast owing to its dangers, and to keep a reasonable distance clear of the Scilly Islands. There is also warning about an intermittent north trending current across the mouth of the Channel and plenty of advice about tides and tidal streams, and about lights and other fixed marks. The longstanding lore about taking departure from and making landfall at the Lizard is still there. As for the passage between the Scilly Isles and Cornwall with its danger (Wolf Rock, Seven Stones, etc.), vessels for the Irish Sea certainly saved time and distance, but the conditions were by no means easy. Vessels headed for the Mediterranean, for example, certainly passed well to the south of the Scillies, and vessels headed for North America added hardly any distance by passing south of the Scillies, and gave themselves much extra complex navigation trying to pass north of the Scillies. There is little doubt in my mind that the normal plan of passage was to take vessels to the south of the Scillies, and to plan a distance south sufficient to allow for the unknowns tending to push the vessel to the north.

Ship-owners (or their nautical advisors) gave its masters specific guidance about many things including navigation, and I should not be surprised if such happened in the case of *Mohegan* and with her master. But they might have been verbal or in manuscript form. In my time, my company had a printed company's navigation guidance book on the bridge. With respect to Ushant and the Scillies it ships were expected to pass 20 miles away, and the charts were inspected on arrival in Liverpool or London by the nautical advisers' staff to see if this had been complied with. Such guidance suggests a measure of safety which the master of the *Mohegan* might have planned for.

From one mile off Prawle Point to 2 miles off the Lizard, the true course is about S. 75 W. (255 degrees) and from two miles off the Lizard to two miles off Bishop Rock the true course is about S. 84 W. (264 degrees).[468] But that is for yachts: larger steamers would be wise to plan to be further off.

From off Dover it is not possible to plan [from this point] a straight track out of the mouth of the Channel. It would take a vessel too close to France. So there will be alterations of course off Dungeness and Beachy Head, but from Beachy

---

[467] Personal communication: Mr Alston Kennerley, Plymouth University (2011).

[468] See Table 7 p. 187; Compass Points and with their Headings.

Head a straight track to the middle of the mouth of the Channel is possible, in planning terms. There was no provision for traffic separation in the Channel until the 1970s. Vessels went where they chose, and there are famous cases of collision where steamers misjudged the speed of sailing vessels and of course many groundings.[469]

A more usual distance off the Lizard for a transatlantic vessel, would have been about fifteen miles. At this distance, the obvious exit point from the Channel would be the track south of the Scillies. The heading the *Mohegan* had adopted at the Eddystone, could have suggested that she was destined for the more hazardous exit corridor, north of the Scilly Isles; whether by intent or unfortunate happenstance, remains unclear.

Perhaps the final judgment, as to the reason why the *Mohegan* met her end on the Manacle Rocks, should be left in the words of Mr A. S. Williams, head of the firm of Williams, Torrey, and Field, London agents for the Atlantic Transport Company:

"It is absolutely impossible to account for the catastrophe. If I did not know Captain Griffith so well, and had not known how excellent a navigator he was, I might explain the fact of his being where he was. As it stands it is absolutely inexplicable. No one knows the English Channel better than he. I am as completely at a loss to understand his being where he was as you can be. It seems the Eddystone Lighthouse was passed at four o'clock, when the vessel was steaming eleven knots. From this point, the bearing is usually west-south-west, which takes the ship clear of the Lizard. For some reason, which will probably never be explained, the course was altered to west-by-north compass-bearing. The vessel was thus headed in almost a direct line for the inner side of the large group of rocks known as the Manacles". [470]

Better late than never.

Eventually, a decision was delivered regarding the navigation lights on the Manacles. After due consideration, the Elder Brethren of Trinity House informed the Cornwall County Council officers, who had petitioned them for additional navigational cover over the Manacles, that, "they consider the Manacle Rocks sufficiently marked for general navigation".[471]

However, the Trinity Brethren, as a result of a persistent criticism of their lack of signposting at the Manacles, introduced a new technology to supplement the old bell buoy:

Since the wreck of the liner *Mohegan* in fact, the Trinity Brethren have frequently been urged to place a light on the Manacles, but it has been contended by the Commissioners that any additional light would interfere with the navigation of the Channel. Recently, however, the authorities altered their opinion on the matter, for at a meeting of the Falmouth Harbour Board on May 10, Mr. T. Webber informed the members that he had laid the evidence prepared by the Cornwall County Council and the Committee appointed to deal with the subject before the Trinity Brethren, and had been accorded a personal interview with them. After hearing the arguments in favour of the additional light, the Trinity House authorities

---

[469] Personal communication: Mr Alston Kennerley, Plymouth University (2011).

[470] *The Royal Cornwall Gazette Falmouth Packet, Cornish Weekly News, & General Advertiser*; Thursday, 20th October 1898.

[471] *Aberdeen Weekly Journal*; 15th February 1899.

decided to erect, during the ensuing summer, a gas-lighted automatic sound-producing buoy at the spot. The present bell buoy is almost useless for any practical purpose, and the new light will not interfere with other lights in the Channel. In this connection it may be stated that the lighting of coast-buoys by means of compressed gas has been of late successfully attempted. Experiment proved that buoys 5 feet by 3 feet could contain enough of gas (made from shale oil [472] refuse, or the like) to keep up a brilliant light.[473]

Eventually, a lookout was established on Manacle Point, at the very heart of the issue:

> Probably as a result of the loss of the *ss* Mohegan in 1898 it was decided to build a coastguard station at Porthoustock as soon as possible. A coastguard lookout building ("the watch-house") was constructed by Edwin Nicholls [474] at Manacle Point, a position overlooking the Manacles and the Lowlands. With the station in operation, it was necessary to build coastguard houses and these were duly built at the top of Porthoustock Hill. In the 1901 census, three coastguard families lived in these new purpose built houses.[475]

Then was established, a telephone link at the Watch-House:

> The new watch-house on the Manacle Points [*sic*] is now connected by telephone with Porthoustock Coastguard station, so the in the event of a wreck occurring both the lifeboat at Porthoustock and the Rocket Brigade at Coverack will have timely warning.[476]

Order! Order!

After two years, following the *Mohegan* disaster, questions were still being asked in Parliament, regarding the emplacement of warning vessels to prevent further catastrophes occurring in this area: as is shown in the following extract from the Hansard[477] parliamentary record:

HANSARD 1803–2005—QUESTIONS.

LIGHTS ON THE MANACLE ROCKS. HC Dec 29 March 1900 vol. 81 cc699-700 699

§ MR. LOUGH (Islington, W.): I beg to ask the President of the Board of '* See The Parliamentary Debates [Fourth Series], Vol. LXXIX, page 798.' 700 Trade whether, in view of the casualties that have recently occurred, steps can be taken to provide a lighthouse or lightship on the Manacle Rocks, off the south coast of Cornwall and whether either the Trinity House or the Board of Trade are doing anything in the matter.

§ THE PRESIDENT OF THE BOARD OF TRADE (Mr. RITCHIE) Croydon: Although the matter has been fully considered, no action is being taken by the Trinity House at present. The Manacle Rocks and adjacent coast lie well out of the ordinary

---

[472] Shale oil has currently become the latest potential source of energy for the UK. Its extraction is being undertaken by a controversial 'hydrofracking' process that is thought to be associated with increased local earthquake activity (2012).

[473] *Daily News;* Monday, 22nd May 1899.

[474] UK census 1901: Edwin Nicholls; Age: 28; Employer (Building Contractor) – Tregaminion, St. Keverne.

[475] Communication: *Moyle, Billy* – Courtesy of: St. Keverne Local History Society.

[476] *The Royal Cornwall Gazette Falmouth Packet, Cornish Weekly News, & General Advertiser;* Thursday, November 29th 1900.

[477] *Hansard* is the traditional name for the published transcripts of parliamentary debates in the Westminster system of government.

Channel track. The casualties which have given notoriety to this part of the coast have occurred to outward bound vessels which had just left known points of departure. The expenditure involved would not be justifiable in view of the demands at this time for new lighthouses and sea marks in many much more urgent cases.

The response to Mr Lough's question, Mr Ritchie seemingly implied that the only danger was for outward bound vessels that had just left a known point of departure. On the face of it, his remark seems to make sense but even so, the Manacle buoy had been placed on-station by Trinity House in 1838,[478] sixty years before the *Mihegan* disaster, and it still did not prevent this or many other catastrophes from happening here.

Agree to disagree.

As a consequence of the recent wrecks on the Cornish coast, the shipping lines had decided to establish 'rules of the road' for vessels crossing the Atlantic:

OCEAN LINERS IN DANGER

City of Rome is Travelling Eastward on the West-Bound Track

REPORTED BY A GERMAN SHIP

Agent of the Anchor Line Says Captain of Vessel Was Ordered to Take Course on Account of Ice.

The navigation of ocean liners is now being carefully watched in view of the recent disasters to the *Paris* and the *Mohegan*, now lying on the rocks of the Cornish Coast. Consequently the report made by Capt. Walter of the German steamship *Prinz Regent Luitpold,* which arrived yesterday from Bremen, occasioned no little surprise and some alarm in shipping circles. On the log of the incoming vessel was the following:

> "June 5, in latitude 41.30, longitude 60.35, passed steamship *City of Rome* was steaming east on the western track of transatlantic vessels".

Shipping men upon reading this entry recalled the fact that on Jan. 15 last a conference of representatives of nearly every passenger steamship line crossing the Atlantic was held in London, and with a view of minimizing the dangers of collisions of vessels and of vessels with icebergs, established certain routes or lanes to be travelled at various seasons of the year. The companies adopting the rules were the American Line, Atlantic Transport Company, Compagnie Générale Transatlantique, Cunard Line, Elder Dempster & Co., Furness Line, Hamsburg-American Line, Holland-America Line, W. Johnstone & Co., Limited: National Steamship Company, Red Star Line, White Star Line, and Wilson Line.

The routes agreed upon were fixed definitely, and along these lanes more than two-score of fast passenger vessels are constantly passing. For a vessel to deliberately steam eastward on a west-bound route is therefore suggestive of a passenger train running westward on an east-bound track. The fact that nearly every one of the big passenger steamers are supposed to under the agreement to adhere closely to this track, largely increases in the estimation of shipping men the danger of a vessel steaming on the wrong path, and places the lives hundreds of passengers in danger.

When the entry was brought to the attention of the New York agents of the Anchor Line, to which the *City of Rome* belongs, the first reply was that, "it is no one's business but that of the Anchor Line what course the vessel takes". Agent

---

[478] Courtesy of: Vikki Gilson—Communications Manager, Trinity House; www.trinityhouse.co.U.K.

William Coverly, finally explained that the course was being taken to avoid the drift ice, which it was feared existed further to the northward.

"Capt. Young of the *City of Rome*," said Mr. Coverly, "is a careful navigator, and took this course according to orders received from this office. Before sailing he was instructed not to cross longitude 50 west or go north of latitude 43, because we do not believe a more northerly course is yet free from drift ice. Beyond longitude 50 our route turns to the northward towards Glasgow. In giving Capt. Young these instructions, the safety of the vessel was considered".

Mr. Coverly admitted that the *City of Rome*'s course to longitude 50 was directly in the line of westward-bound steamships, but denied that he had ever heard of any general agreement between the principal lines as to ocean lanes. He said the Anchor Line was not a party to any ocean lane agreement and that the steamers of the line took whatever course at the time of their departure from New York or Glasgow was considered the safest. The *City of Rome* sailed last Saturday with 230 passengers.

The agents of the lines in the ocean lane agreement were astonished and considerably alarmed when they learned that the *City of Rome* is being run across the Atlantic directly in the path of their west-bound vessels.[479]

It is assumed that under pressure from passengers, this eventually changed the minds of those obdurate shipping lines who resented any interference in the way they operated their ships.

Today, the coastline still presents a formidable hazard, but shipwrecks, though very infrequent, still occur from time to time. These are, in the main, small coasters that suffer engine failure, or are caught up in gales or fog. The last sizeable disaster was that of the of the supertanker *SS Torrey Canyon,* in the year 1967 on the Seven Stones reef, between the Cornish mainland and the Scilly Isles. That wreck caused an unprecedented oil spillage and ecological damage to the beaches and wildlife of the south-west approaches.

Time and tide wait for no man.

The state of tides on the day of the wrecking of the *Mohegan* are listed here:

Location Point	Predictive Time of High Water (hours)	Time Difference From Devonport (minutes)	Predictive Height of Tide metres (feet)
Devonport (Plymouth)	16:54	n/a	5.3 (17.7)
Mevagissey	16:34	– 20	5.2 (17.2)
Truro	16:29	– 25	3.3 (10.9)
Falmouth	16:20	– 34	5.2 (17.2)
Helford	16:19	– 35	5.1 (16.8)
Coverack	16:20	– 34	5.1 (16.6)
Greenwich	18.30	+ 96	n/k
Dover	09:51 / 22:10	n/a	n/a

Table 5: Tide Tables for 14th October, 1898.

Lunar Tide Interval: at almost full spring tide.

---

[479] *The New York Times;* 8th June, 1899.

Tidal state on the Manacles at the time of the *Mohegan* disaster:

Approximately 2½ hours after HW (the ebb tide – direction: South-by-West).

Tidal directions and flows, that generally prevail on the Manacle Rocks:

> 1 hour ebb to 1 hour flood – South by West [236.25°]
> 1 hour flood – South [180.00°]
> 1½ hour flood – S.E. [135.00°]
> Half hour ebb – East [90.00°]
> 2 hours flood and from 4 hours flood to H.W. – E.N.E. [67.50°]
> 2½ hours flood – N.E. [45.00°]
> 3 to 4 hours flood – N.N.E. [22.50°] [480]

Tidal Streams

At the *Manacles* the stream begins to run to the S.West two hours ebb by the shore: when meeting with the stream out of the bight [481] between Cadgwith and Black Head, (which sets to the eastward from half Ebb till 5 hours Flood) they unite, and both set to the south east but at 2 hours Flood the stream at the Manacles again begins to turn, and to the S.E. line of direction is warped [482] more easterly until high water, when it ceases altogether.

Off the Manacles, the Stream runs to the west-ward until nearly half flood by the shore, at from 1 to 1½ knots an hour. [483]

The Night walked down the Sky with the Moon in her hand.

The moon on the evening of the disaster, was a waning crescent and displaying a one percentage of full-moon luminosity. A maximum new moon phase was on the 15th October, the day following the disaster.

You do the maths

The following may prove to be a useful conversion table, for those who may wish to do their own navigational calculations, on the track of the *Mohegan:*

	m/s	km/h	mph	knot	ft/s
1 m/s =	1	3.6	2.236936	1.943844	3.280840
1 km/h =	0.277778	1	0.621371	0.539957	0.911344
1 mph =	0.44704	1.609344	1	0.868976	1.466667
1 knot =	0.514444	1.852	1.150779	1	1.687810
1 ft/s =	0.3048	1.09728	0.681818	0.592484	1

Table 6: Conversion Table for Common Units of Speed. (Values in **bold** are exact)

---

[480] England – South Coast SEVENSTONES, LONGSHIPS, MANACLE and RUNNELSTONE ROCKS. – Surveyed by Captain G. Williams and Mr J. Wells, Master 1851…52 and 1863.

[481] Bight: A curve or recess in a coastline, river, or other geographical feature.

[482] Warped – distorting effect of.

[483] Navigation chart – Notice to Mariners: 'Approaches to Falmouth' published 1872.

The following table shows the compass points and with their interpretation:

No.	Compass point	Abbreviation	Heading	Heading Range
1	**North**	N	0.00°	0.00 – 5.62°
2	North by east	N by E	11.25°	5.63 – 16.87°
3	North-northeast	NNE	22.50°	16.88 – 28.12°
4	Northeast by north	NE by N	33.75°	28.13 – 39.37°
5	**Northeast**	NE	45.00°	39.38 – 50.62°
6	Northeast by east	NE by E	56.25°	50.63 – 61.87°
7	East-northeast	ENE	67.50°	61.88 – 73.12°
8	East by north	E by N	78.75°	73.13 – 84.37°
9	**East**	E	90.00°	84.38 – 95.62°
10	East by south	E by S	101.25°	95.6 – 106.87°
11	East-southeast	ESE	112.50°	106.88 – 118.12°
12	Southeast by east	SE by E	123.75°	118.13 – 129.37°
13	**Southeast**	SE	135.00°	129.38 – 140.62°
14	Southeast by south	SE by S	146.25°	140.63 – 151.87°
15	South-southeast	SSE	157.50°	151.88 – 163.12°
16	South by east	S by E	168.75°	163.13 – 174.37°
17	**South**	S	180.00°	174.38 – 185.62°
18	South by west	S by W	191.25°	185.63 – 196.87°
19	South-southwest	SSW	202.50°	196.88 – 208.12°
20	Southwest by south	SW by S	213.75°	208.13 – 219.37°
21	**Southwest**	SW	225.00°	219.38 – 230.62°
22	Southwest by west	SW by W	236.25°	230.63 – 241.87°
23	West-southwest	WSW	247.50°	241.88 – 253.12°
24	West by south	W by S	258.75°	253.13 – 264.37°
25	**West**	W	270.00°	264.38 – 275.62°
26	West by north	W by N	281.25°	275.63 – 286.87°
27	West-northwest	WNW	292.50°	286.88 – 298.12°
28	Northwest by west	NW by W	303.75°	298.13 – 309.37°
29	**Northwest**	NW	315.00°	309.38 – 320.62°
30	Northwest by north	NW by N	326.25°	320.63 – 331.87°
31	North-northwest	NNW	337.50°	331.88 – 343.12°
32	North by west	N by W	348.75°	343.13 – 354.37°
1	**North**	N	360.00°	354.38 – 360.00°

Table 7: Compass Points and with their Headings.

A simple algorithm can be used to convert a heading to an approximate compass point:

1. Divide the heading in degrees by 11.25 (360/32) to get to the case of 32 named points.

2. Add 1.5 to center the named points in their respective sectors on the circle, since north is **1** in the table instead of **0**. If the result is 33 or more, subtract 32 to keep within the 32–point set.

3. Now look up the contents of the result in the table: column 1.

For example: a heading of 75° divided by 11.25 gives 6.67, added to 1.5 gives 8.17, truncated to give 8 and this figure corresponds in column 1 to east by north.

The longest mile is the last mile home.

The distance in sea miles from London to New York, showing the intervening sea miles between significant coastal lights, are shown in the following table:

Port of London to Gravesend	30
Gravesend to Nore [484]	191
Nore to North Foreland	20
North Foreland to Dover	25
Dover to Dungeness	24
Dungeness to Beachy Head	30
Beachy Head to St. Catherine's	60
St. Catherine's to Portland Bill	55
Portland Bill to Start Point	50
Start Point to Eddystone	22
Eddystone to Lizard	40
Lizard to Bishop Rock	28
Bishop Rock to Fire Island	2,919
Total Distance	3,494

Table 8: London (Thames) to New York: Distance in Sea Miles.

---

[484] The Nore is a sandbank at the mouth of the Thames Estuary, England. It marks the point where the River Thames meets the North Sea, roughly halfway between Havengore Creek in Essex and Warden Point in Kent.

CHAPTER 15

The Stranding of the *SS Paris*

More haste less speed.

The year following the *Mohegan* disaster, on the 21st May 1899, the International Navigation Company's [485] steamship, *Paris* ran aground on Lowland Point, offering its passengers an unscheduled view of the masts of the *Mohegan*.[486]

This was a major public relations disaster for the company, with the memory of the *Mohegan* still fresh in the mind of the general public, both here and in America.

TOPIC OF THE TIMES

According to a published interview, Mr. BERNARD N. BAKER, President of the Atlantic Transport Company, calls the wreck of the *Paris* an "impenetrable mystery," and declares his inability to understand how the vessel came to approach the English coast, since she had started from the coast of France and had a perfectly clear and straight course out into the open sea. The impenetrability of the mystery, it may fairly be assumed from the developments in the case of the *Mohegan*, is simply the result of the present refusal of Capt. [Frederic] WATKINS and his officers to reveal the circumstances that preceded and caused the disaster. As for the reason why the *Paris* was close to the northern shore instead of in the middle of the Channel, Mr. BAKER can materially assist his understanding by a little deliberation on where the steamer was going. The "clear and straight" course was a long course; at least, it was longer by a good many miles than another course, equally straight but far from equally clear, that just shaved the extension known as the Lizard. The longer course that might have been taken and the shorter course which it was intended to take were in one sense equally safe, from slight deviations from the first would have been inconsequential, while a slight deviation from the second was known to be, and, as a matter of fact, was fatal. So in another sense, the two courses were not equally safe. The *Paris* like the *Mohegan*, went ashore, and whatever desire there may have been to save time—and coal—resulted in a large expenditure of both those precious articles. There is no mystery as to why the *Mohegan* struck the rocks instead of skirting them. Her Captain gave the steersman orders that took her there. The mystery is why he did it, and about the impenetrability of that no question can be raised. At least until after Capt. WATKINS takes the stand the two disasters must stand together in the public mind. And one of them, it has been conclusively demonstrated, was a direct result of allowing the fate of a ship to depend upon the perfect action of a single brain.[487]

In a further interview with Mr Bernard Baker, he suggested that the wrecking of the *Paris* was possibly brought about by, "a wrong manipulation of the big lights on the Lizard". However, he conceded that, even if

---

[485] In 1899, its chairman – Clement Griscom – became acquainted with J. P. Morgan, an investment banker who was responsible for many of the large mergers during the period. With financing from Morgan's syndicate, in 1902 Griscom and Morgan expanded International Navigation by acquiring the Atlantic Transport Line, the Leyland Line, the White Star Line, the Dominion Line and half of Holland America. International Navigation was renamed International Mercantile Marine—*WikiPedia*.

[486] The funnel had collapsed in the winter gales but the four masts remained above water for some time afterwards.

[487] *The New York Times;* May 30th 1899.

this was true, it would be difficult to prove. He described there being two big fixed white lights, and a red revolving light [488] on the Lizard Point, and if one of the white lights had been inoperative, and the other one being taken as the one further out, the boat might have run on the rocks, thinking all danger had passed. He was not suggesting this same circumstance contributed to the *Mohegan* disaster, as she was wrecked at dusk, when the lights would be just appearing, and the *Paris* was wrecked at about 2 o'clock in the morning, which in England is very close to daylight, and about the time the lights would disappear. These suggestions would imply that Mr Baker thought that this was why both the *Mohegan* and the *Paris* came to grief. In reality, the *Paris* was too far north of her correct position, even before she was able to have seen the Lizard Light, and the *Mohegan* had simply not been in a position in order to see the Lizard headland.

Mr Baker seems to have got his facts wrong here, regarding the Lizard Light configuration. Was he suggesting that one of the lights had failed on the night of the *Paris* grounding (not so) and that there was was a red light showing (not so) and in mistaking it as being the St. Anthony's Light (not possible)?

Indeed, there was never a lighthouse nor a lightship placed here to warn off mariners from the Manacles. A news item following the stranding of the *Paris* recalled a generous private offer, for a lighthouse to be erected to overlook the Manacles:

> Whatever the cause, the fact is the same—the Manacles are a menace to the safe navigation of the Channel even with the most experienced masters on the bridge. This must be rectified. It is no good of the Elder Brethren of the Trinity Board setting up their wise theories against such facts as these. Within six months two large liners have come to grief here in spite of the assertion of the Trinity Board that the bell-buoy is sufficient. Supposing there had been a repetition of the appalling loss of life on Sunday [the stranding of the *Paris*] that happened in October [*Mohegan*], to whom would the blame have been attributable, as far as human understanding can judge from present events, but to the Trinity Board? Whatever the conflict of opinion on the point as to whether more definite means of warning to passing vessels is needed here or not, no more practical demonstration of the fact that they are wanting could be found than the loss of the *Mohegan* and the stranding of the *Paris*. There seems an idea in some quarters that a light on the Manacles would be confusing but if we are to believe Mr. James Tucker of East Looe, who has been at sea forty-four years, and master in sail and steam over thirty years, safety in dangerous places such as the Manacles alone lies in their being distinctly marked. The argument that a multitude of lights would be confusing he dismissed as absurd, and points to the Estuary of the Thames, where lights are very numerous, but by their distinctive character they give navigators confidence in their position and in the safety of their ships. There is no need for a light here which would be confusing. It need only be visible from the open Channel, and if on the flare-up principle, or in marked contrast to the other lights, there is every indication that disasters such as those of the past few months would never recur. I deeply regret that the Trinity Board thought fit to reject the munificent offer of Mr. Passmore Edwards [489] to build a lighthouse here years ago. Had the scheme been entertained the probability is that the

---

[488] There was never a red-coloured revolving light at the Lizard.

[489] Mr Passmore Edwards writes:—"I certainly offered to build a lighthouse at the Manacles, to the memory of Adams, the distinguished Cornish astronomer, and joint discoverer with Leverrier of the planet Neptune but after some discussion at Falmouth it was thought that a hospital and a free library could be more acceptable and useful. I accepted the decision and provided the hospital and free library. I hoped, and expressed the hope at the time, to erect one lighthouse in Cornwall and another to the memory of Leverrier on the coast of France, so that both should acknowledge with luminous nods the dominant claims of commerce and brotherhood of nations"; *Falmouth Packet Archives; 1680–1850.*
http://www.falmouth.packet.archives.dial.pipex.com/id116.htm

Mohegan would never been wrecked with the appalling accompaniment of loss of life, and the *Paris* might now have been on the point of carrying her passengers into New York harbour safely and happily.[490]

Interestingly, a few years later (1903) one of the two light towers at the Lizard—the western light—was dispensed with, leaving the eastern tower with a single flashing light, signaling to this day.[491] Given the previous protestations by the Trinity House Brethren, on the benefits of a twin light at the Lizard (in order to distinguish it from the St. Anthony's Light) it is difficult to make sense of their subsequent decision to remove this distinctive feature.

A great attraction for all ages – and free.

Huge interest was generated by this giant ocean liner on the rocks at Lowland Point, giving a much appreciated boost to the local economy:

> The interest in the *Paris* shows little sign of waning, Sunday last being a record day. Over a thousand cyclists and the occupants of four hundred vehicles wended their way to St. Keverne. It was enough to make some of the astonished rustics on the Helston road imagine that this had suddenly become the hub of the universe. Everybody was a "Parisian" and bound for Lowland Point. Even the staid old natives were seized with the epidemic. "I've never been down there for twenty years," said one. But she went.
>
> Johnny with his camera was much in evidence.
>
> The representatives of the London Mutoscope and Biograph [492] have been down, and Londoners will soon, in all probability, be able on putting a penny in the slot machine to see the launching of the *Charlotte* at Porthoustock,[493] and tugging of the *Paris*, rescuing from the *Mohegan* masts, &c., whilst visitors to the famous London Palace Theatre [494] will revel in the delightful biograph pictures of the same scenes.[495]

Pleasure-boat trips were very popular with the locals and visitors alike (see fig. 90):

---

[490] *The Royal Cornwall Gazette Falmouth Packet, Cornish Weekly News, & General Advertiser;* Thursday, 25th May 1899.

[491] Peter Jefferson; *And Now the Shipping Forecast.*

[492] The K.M.C.D. syndicate – comprising Koopman, Marvin, Casler and Dickson – became the American Mutoscope and Biograph Company, major film producers, (and eventually 'Biograph', home of major stars such as Mary Pickford, and the director D. W. Griffith). Companies were set up in many countries. Dickson returned to Britain and became a roving filmmaker for the British Mutoscope Company. In 1898 he filmed Pope Leo XIII at the Vatican. The Biograph ran at London's Palace Theatre for five years. Biograph eventually dropped the use of wide film, and conformed to using 35mm.

[493] The original productions are available from the IDMb Pro; www.imdb.com/company/co0103009/: *The Wreck of the Mohican* [sic] (1899); *Launch of the Porthonstock* [sic] *Lifeboat* (1899); *Wreck of the* s.s. *Paris* (1899).

[494] The Palace Theatre, London, is an imposing red-brick building that dominates the west side of Cambridge Circus. The foundation stone was laid in 1888. It is still in business to this day.

[495] *The Royal Cornwall Gazette Falmouth Packet, Cornish Weekly News, & General Advertiser;* Thursday, 1st June 1899.

TO VIEW THE WRECKS OF THE "MOHEGAN" AND "PARIS"

Per

S.S. Resolute,

FROM TRURO QUAY

(weather and circumstances permitting).

On FRIDAY, June 16th [1899] leave Truro at 10.30 a.m., and Malpas and Falmouth for the above at 11.30 a.m., for Falmouth. Leave MALPAS at 11.30 a.m., and Falmouth for the above at 3 p.m. Fare 2s. Passengers by first boat each day can land at Porthoustock for St. Keverne, to view the Church. Return to Falmouth. Leave Falmouth to return to Truro Quay at 5.30 or 7 p.m. Passengers by first boat can land at St. Keverne three hours, and return by second trip if they wish. Fare 2s.[496]

As to this day, the Cornish are ever vigilant in exploiting a commercial opportunity, if and when it arises.

He maketh the deep to boil like a pot.

The Manacle Rocks seem to have a capacity to surprise those who venture near them. In the re-floating of the liner *Paris* from Lowland Point and in tow to the Falmouth Docks, an unexpected anomaly was encountered, in which the currents around the reef took control of the *Paris*, causing some concern for her salvage team:

ANOTHER REMARKABLE THEORY

It is not generally known that a somewhat expected risk was experienced during the towage of the *Paris* to Falmouth. A northerly wind, with the tide ebbing, ought to have taken the vessel southerly. Instead of that, however, those in charge of the *Paris*, though they allowed more than ordinary room to clear the Manacles, found themselves but four hundred yards or so from the big Manacle Rock [Carn-Du], and for a while the circumstances produced a little uneasiness in the official mind. It is the firm conviction of one holding a position which enables him to speak with authority that there prevails in the region of the Manacles some mysterious current which brings vessels towards the reef. The magnetic theory he regards as nonsense. To illustrate his meaning of a mysterious current, he likens the position to a hole in the earth. Somewhere through the hole the sea rushes and comes out near the Manacles, causing an enormous current.[497]

Over the years, the tidal streams around the Manacles have been misinterpreted, unexpected, and frankly, not that well understood, in detail. They defy the usual and more accurately forecast tides in the surrounding area, and seem to have a track of their own. Little wonder that the rocks are treated with the utmost respect, when approached by a vessel. Indeed, apart from local fishermen, sub-aqua divers, and lifesaving agencies, there is no possible justification for any visitation, and the rocks should remain strictly off-limits.

The *Paris* incident prompted a memorable turn of phrase, in a letter to a newspaper:

---

[496] *The Royal Cornwall Gazette Falmouth Packet, Cornish Weekly News, & General Advertiser*, Thursday, June 15th, 1899.

[497] *The Royal Cornwall Gazette Falmouth Packet, Cornish Weekly News, & General Advertiser*; Thursday, July 20th 1899.

"A navigator who cannot take a well-founded steamship from Cherbourg to the Atlantic (bar collisions) without running on to the Cornish coast cannot be fit to be trusted to command a walnut shell". [498]

Quite!

[498] *The Times;* 22nd May 1899.

C H A P T E R   16

The Lifeboat Service

A Lifeline.

The Royal National Lifeboat Institution was founded on the 4th March, 1824. It was originally named as the *National Institution for the Preservation of Life from Shipwreck* (which didn't exactly trip off the tongue) adopting the name of the *National Lifeboat Institution* in 1854, and then receiving Royal Patronage from King George IV of England and Ireland, shortly thereafter. It now operates as a national service to the peoples of the UK and Ireland and enjoys an official charity status in each nation.

Porthoustock Lifeboat and its Role in the Mohegan disaster.

The role of the local lifeboat and rocket-men are well drawn here in a report for the *Mohegan* disaster:

THE WRECK OF THE MOHEGAN
GREAT LOSS OF LIFE

She was seen by the lifeboat coxswain at Porthoustock to be in danger at about 6.30 p.m. A P. and O. [499] officer, staying at Porthoustock ran round the cliff to watch her movement. He saw two or three rockets fired, then the electric lights became suddenly extinguished and all was darkness. Meanwhile, James Hill, the lifeboat coxswain had fired a mortar to summon the crew and helpers. Other people two or three miles to the southward had also noted the vessel's danger. Mr. Jeffers, chief of the coastguard [Coverack], saw the port and masthead lights of the steamer as she ran to the inhospitable shores and sent up a warning rocket.[500] The signal was answered, but only when the great vessel lay at the mercy of the rough sea embedded on sunken rocks. By this time the whole parish of St. Keverne was in a state of excitement, and hundreds of men, women and children were hastening towards the sea. The lifeboat at Porthoustock was quickly launched and was soon ploughing the heavy sea. Presently the coastguard with their rocket apparatus arrived. The brave fellows had pushed the heavy machine right up the Coverack-hill before horses could be procured. As shouts continued to come from the sea towards the north-east the vicar of St. Keverne suggested to Mr. Jeffers that rockets should be fired in order to acquaint the crew of the large boat with the presumed position of the large wreck. This was done, and so accurate was the aim that the second rocket, after travelling over a mile, passed right between two masts of the vessel. It did not carry a line as the Mohegan was evidently too far from the shore to be reached by such means, but it had the effect of bearing a message of hope and encouragement to the people who were clinging to the masts and shrouds and who up to this time thought that their cries were not heard. The lifeboat crew, however, had ample work to hand. When the rockets had been fired an answering cry came back from the north-east, and a proposal was made to launch the old lifeboat [*Mary Ann Storey*].

---

[499] The Peninsular and Oriental Steam Navigation Company.

[500] From the positioning of the coastguard lookout at Coverack and its view towards the Manacles, and in identifying the *Mohegan*'s masthead and port-side lights, the vessel would appear to have been on a direct run from the Eddystone, with no deviation from that course. This would seem to confirm the observation made by an able-seaman, aboard the *Mohegan* engaged in deck cleaning duties, in that: he did not notice any change in the ship's direction of travel, just prior to the disaster.

Several men volunteered to man her, and their determination was strengthened by the fact that the Porthoustock lifeboat had signalled for further help. Their good intentions were, however, frustrated by the fact that the old lifeboat was utterly unfit for sea and possessed no equipment.[501]

A small boat was launched, but could hardly live in the sea, much less attempt to save life. About midnight the Porthoustock lifeboat reached the cove, bearing the precious freight of human lives. All the rescued were drenched to the skin and were exhausted by long exposure. They were lifted out of the boat and conveyed to the surrounding cottages. The people spared themselves no trouble to make provision for the sufferers; they literally turned their cottages inside out to find clothes and accommodation for their guests, while Mr. Edward Roskruge saw to the refreshments of the lifeboat crew. Dr. Leverton-Spry[502] was setting broken limbs, and the vicar, with many assistants, were ministering to the needs of the rescued. Again, the lifeboat went out to return shortly before daylight with the 16 persons who for seven hours had been holding on to the ship's rigging. Their condition was pitiable, and only by long and unceasing efforts were life and warmth brought back to almost inanimate bodies. On Saturday morning the business of providing clothes was set about. Mr. Pengelly, agent to the Shipwrecked Mariners' Society,[503] came to the aid of Mrs. Diggens, Mr. W. Roskruge, and others by promising in the name of the society to pay for any wearing apparel required. The St. Keverne shops had been exhausted of their stock of clothes before the rescued had been habited. Yesterday bodies had been washed ashore, and these were conveyed to the fine old church of St. Keverne, where they were arranged at the west end. About 40 are now in the sacred edifice, where they are screened off by curtains from the rest of the building. St. Keverne all through Sunday was crowded with visitors. Many had come out of mere curiosity, but others had arrived to identify the bodies. The inquest is to be held today. All the survivors expressed the greatest admiration of the skill and daring displayed by the lifeboat crew. The fact ought not to be omitted that from the squire to the humblest villagers all parishioners have done their utmost to minister to the needs of the survivors, who have practically lost all their belongings.[504]

The man responsible for the commandeering of a local boat belong to Dr Leverton-Spry, together with a volunteer group of four,[505] was the second coxswain of the *Charlotte*, James Henry Treloar Tripp. He had been in St. Keverne and had missed the signal to 'all stations' on Porthoustock Beach.[506] His action allowed him to approach the *Mohegan* towards the direction in which the cries of distress were heard. They came across the wreck on the Maen Varses (Voices) whereupon he signalled a reassurance to the victims by setting fire to his own neck-tie and shouting that they would, "return with reinforcements". On arrival at

---

[501] This referred to the *Mary Ann Storey* (the predecessor to the *Charlotte*) that had been replaced in the year 1886, and, at the time of the disaster, was still lying at Porthoustock. Eventually, the best boat in the cove was commandeered, that belonging to Dr Edward James Leverton-Spry.

[502] Dr Edward James Leverton-Spry M.R.C.S. Eng., L.S.A. Lond., St. Keverne R.S.O., Helston, Cornwall.

[503] In February 1839 the Shipwrecked Mariners' Society was founded in London. The first President was Admiral Sir George Cockburn who had the distinction of capturing Washington in 1814 and burning the White House and the Capitol Building. He was also Napoleon's gaoler on St Helena. Incorporated by Act of Parliament in 1850, Queen Victoria became the first Patron and that Royal connection has continued ever since.—*Association of Royal Navy Officers* (ARNO).

[504] *The Times;* 17th October 1898.

[505] The group of four comprised: James Bastian, Porthallow; Charlie Tripp; Joseph Bryant, Porthallow; and William Pengelly, Coverack. – *Down to the Sea in Ships, The Memoirs of James Henry Treloar Cliff,* 116: Published by Dyllansow Truran – Truan Publications.

[506] James Henry Treloar Cliff (1858–1938) a cousin of Sir William Purdie Treloar (Lord Mayor of London; 1906–1907), was thirteen years as Second Coxswain of the Porthoustock lifeboat, and succeeded the late James Hill as Coxswain in 1907. Mr Cliff's home, 'Manacle View', looked out over its namesake. The house still stands to this day.

Porthoustock, James Henry Treloar Tripp then transferred to the *Charlotte* (which had already returned from her first foray to the wreck site) and was able to then direct her coxswain to the *Mohegan*'s exact location.

They could not approach the wreck, as on her starboard side was the Maen Varses rocks with a heavy sea breaking over them and on the other side, the ship's derricks were projecting out of the water. Eventually, the impasse was overcome by the brave action of one of the crew in the ship's rigging, Quartermaster W. H. J. Juddery—of which more, later.

Courage is simply the willingness to be afraid and act anyway.

One cannot underestimate the pivotal role played in this disaster, by the lifeboat service; in particular, the Porthoustock lifeboat and its crew, under the splendid command of the coxswain, Mr James Hill.[507] It is as a result of his endeavour, as well as that of the magnificent crew,[508] that forty-five lives were saved on that fearful night. Other lifeboats—from The Lizard, and Falmouth stations—eventually attended the wreck; however, as Porthoustock was within a mile of the scene of the disaster, inevitably it gained the greater credit for its timely achievement. It was also a question of a delay in the relaying of messages and with standing orders that hindered the more distant lifeboats in achieving a more prompt action.

The Board of Trade inquiry asked some awkward questions to the attending lifeboat crews. To their credit, given the circumstances, they gave a reasonable account of themselves:

> The Board of Trade Inquiry into the loss of the *Mohegan* on the Manacle Rocks, off Falmouth, on Oct. 14, it was resumed at Westminster Town Hall on Saturday [12th November].
>
> The first witness called was Charles May, Coastguard boatman at Coverack, about three miles southwest of the Manacles. On October 14, at 6 p.m., witness was on duty, and saw the masthead and red light of a steamer. He thought she was rather close in, and called the chief officer's attention to her.
>
> Alfred Jefferies [*sic*], Chief Coastguard officer at Coverack, had his attention drawn to the vessel by May, and detailed the steps he took after seeing rockets fired from her.
>
> Francis Jose, coxswain of the Falmouth lifeboat, Benjamin Williams, master of the tug *Penguin*,[509] of Falmouth, and James Ross, chief officer of Coastguard at the Lizard, gave evidence as to the steps taken when the wreck became known. The latter, in answer to Mr. Pyke, said he sent his chief boatman to assist the patrol in case any message had to be transmitted through the telephone.
>
> Mr. Pyke—You did nothing else?—Witness replied that he could get no further information till 9.27, when a message came "Wire Falmouth for lifeboat and tug".
>
> Mr. Pyke—But why did you not summon the lifeboat? Witness—Because it is not my duty.

---

[507] James Hill (1835–1919) was still the coxswain of the Porthoustock lifeboat in July of 1900 and was 62 years of age, at that time – *The Royal Cornwall Gazette Falmouth Packet, Cornish Weekly News, & General Advertiser*; Thursday, May 25, 1899.
James Hill was coxswain for 27 years and 2nd coxswain for 9 years. He retired as coxswain in 1905.

[508] The crews in attendance at the *Mohegan* incident appear in Appendix 20 (See page 473).

[509] The tug *Penguin* was a two-funnelled vessel and a familiar sight around the harbour, until about 1914 (see fig. 28).

Mr. Pyke—Then when you hear there is a wreck on the Manacles it is your duty to do nothing? Witness explained that there were other lifeboats much nearer than the Lizard, and unless specially called he was not to suppose that their boat which was only a small one, was required, Further questioned, witness expressed the belief that if the boat had been sent off earlier she would never have reached the Manacles at all against the wind and tide.[510]

Edward Mathews, coxswain of the Lizard lifeboat, said he was first called at 11.20 [p.m.]. They got the boat out and reached the Manacles in two hours . . . The inquiry was adjourned.[511]

The accounts highlight a delay in attendance for the Lizard and Falmouth lifeboats at the scene of the disaster. It is debatable, whether or not more lives may have been saved, had the lifeboats been launched at or about the time the Porthoustock boat made headway. In the conditions that prevailed, not least the lack of light available to the crews and with the predominating tidal stream and wind directions, a congregation of lifeboats could have, in itself, caused a danger—a classic case of 'too many cooks' perhaps. Nevertheless, it was maybe a risk worth taking. The timely attendance for additional lifeboats might well have by chance come upon desperate souls, who had drifted away from the wreck site and, fortuitously, in crossing their tracks.

That night, provided lessons for all. There was a demand that this remote coastline have a telegraphic system installed there, where it was most needed. The petty regulations that hitherto restricted any existing telegraphic line used as a shared service were nonsensical. It took a major disaster to get things moving, but at least discussions were now instigated, over a control of the local lines of inter-communication:

FALMOUTH CORPORATION AND INCIDENTS OF THE WEEK

At Falmouth Corporation, upon the invitation of the Chamber of Commerce, the Mayor, Messrs. Fox and Banks were appointed to represent the Corporation on a joint committee to urge the Board of Trade to hold an inquiry as to the special dangers of navigation between the Dodman and the Lizard—Mr. Fox drew attention to the fact that policemen are not allowed to use the railway or telegraph for certain purposes. There was only one policeman in St. Keverne and when the *Mohegan* was wrecked he had to walk to the nearest policeman at Mawnan. This man had to walk to Perranwell, and the man there walked to Truro, where the coroner's office was. How much more convenient it would be if the policemen were permitted to use the rail and telegraph, (hear, hear). Then the coast-guard had the monopoly of the telephonic service along the coast. That service was provided at the national expense, and if it were open for more general use in time of emergency it would be a very valuable means of communication. He moved that these matters be referred to the Joint Committee for consideration.—The Town Clerk : No.—Mr. Bowles said there was a case at the Docks a few years ago where the effect of the police regulations was most ludicrous. If the police wanted to arrest a thief they could use the telegraph, but not in communicating with the coroner.—Dr. Harris : Crowner's Quest law is very ridiculous, almost in its entirety.—The motion was agreed to.[512]

---

[510] The tide and the wind were determinedly set against the lifeboat and its crew; so the assertion is entirely correct.

[511] *The Bristol Mercury and Daily Post* (Bristol, England); Monday, November 14th 1898.

[512] *The Royal Cornwall Gazette Falmouth Packet, Cornish Weekly News, & General Advertiser;* Thursday, November 3rd 1898.

This situation was intolerable, particularly where the saving of lives was concerned. The three police message-takers, described in the above report, had to walk from St. Keverne to Mawnan, then to Perranwell, and then finally onward to Truro; many miles in difficult conditions.

Commonsense did prevail in the end, and a telegraph wire was duly installed: but only covering a short distance. However, it was to be sited at the most contentious part of this fearsome coastline:

THE NEWS OF THE COUNTY

Helston Rural District Council has consented to poles being erected to carry a telegraph wire from Manacle Point (near where the *Mohegan* went ashore) to Porthoustock.[513]

Praise where praise is due.

Nevertheless, acclaim for the actions carried out on that night of the disaster by the lifeboat service was fully deserved, and was immediately forthcoming:

Remembering the Porthoustock Lifeboat Crew

Meetings of the committee of the Royal National Lifeboat Institution [R.N.L.I.] have been held at the home of the institution, John-street, Adelphi. The General Committee on Thursday was presided over by Col. Fitz Roy Clayton. The silver medal and a framed copy of the vote on vellum were voted to Mr. James Hill, coxswain of the Porthoustock lifeboat, and extra pecuniary rewards to the crew, in recognition of their services on the occasion of the wreck of the *Mohegan* on the Manacle Rocks on the night of Oct. 14.[514]

An American passenger expressed a warm appreciation, to the crew of the Porthoustock lifeboat, *Charlotte*:

Mohegan Passengers and Porthoustock Lifeboat
A New York Gentleman's Recognition

It will be remembered that Mr. F. R. Pemberton, of New York, the story of whose rescue from the ill-fated *Mohegan* was told at the time, sent Porthoustock lifeboat crew a presentation of £50. The crew, in acknowledging his kindness, forwarded to him photographs of themselves and their boat, and they have now received from Mr. Pemberton the following interesting reply:—

15, Wall-street, New York, May 16th, 1899.

To the members of the crew of the Life-saving Station, Porthoustock, St. Keverne, Cornwall, England.
My good friends,—I have received with very great pleasure photographs of the lifeboat and of the members of its crew, which photographs, appropriately framed, now adorn the wall of my library.

---

[513] *The Royal Cornwall Gazette Falmouth Packet, Cornish Weekly News, & General Advertiser;* Thursday, September 6th 1900.

[514] *The Royal Cornwall Gazette Falmouth Packet, Cornish Weekly News, & General Advertiser;* Thursday, November 17th 1898.

I appreciate more than I can say to you the kindly feeling evidenced for my family and for me in thus remembering us, and I shall carefully preserve the pictures as mementoes of the melancholy occasion when so many lives were lost, and when those of my family and myself were saved only by your bravery and heroism.

Your manly acts will afford a lesson which I shall delight to teach my sons, whose lives you saved, and will be an inspiration to your children to like deeds of heroism.

If it shall ever be my good fortune to visit England, I shall surely go amongst you at Porthoustock, when I sincerely hope I may find each member of the life-saving crew in good health and surrounded by those comforts which comes to those whose lives are placed so constantly in jeopardy in the interest of their unfortunate brethren.

Mrs. Pemberton desires to join with me in again extending to each of you our sincere good wishes.

I am your friend,

F. R. Pemberton.[515]

The £50 gratuity was distributed between the two sets of lifeboat crew. Mrs Piggot (a stewardess who was rescued by the lifeboat, after being many hours clinging to the rigging) sent packets of tobacco for the crew.[516]

The brave men—including Henry Treloar Tripp (the second coxswain, who attempted an early reconnaissance of the *Mohegan*, in a small boat owned by the local doctor) were also remembered:

I understand that several persons have sent donations to the Porthoustock lifeboat crew in acknowledgment of their plucky efforts to save life. One gentleman has sent five pounds for the five men who went out in Dr. Leverton-Spry's boat.[517]

It is believed that the Royal National Lifeboat Institution had made an extraordinary grant, in addition to the ordinary allowance, to those who crewed the *Charlotte* lifeboat.

Charity sees the need, not the cause.

The body of the officially recognised stowaway was given a Christian burial:

Messrs. Fox and Co., Falmouth, agents for the Atlantic Transport Line, being in possession of information that the body of Mr. Le Lacheur, a passenger, was at Kingsbridge [a South Devon town near Salcombe]. Mr. Orme Fox proceeded to take the matter in hand. On Saturday, the remains of the stowaway, who had a Hungarian wife living in New York, were discovered at Porthallow, near the scene of the wreck, and identified by a member of the crew. The representatives of the *Mohegan*'s owners had seen to the proper burial of this victim as though he was a member of the ship's company.[518]

[515] *The Royal Cornwall Gazette Falmouth Packet, Cornish Weekly News, & General Advertiser;* Thursday, June 1st 1899.

[516] *The Morning Post* (London, England), Monday, December 19th 1898

[517] *The Royal Cornwall Gazette Falmouth Packet, Cornish Weekly News, & General Advertiser;* Thursday, November 3rd 1898.

[518] *The Royal Cornwall Gazette Falmouth Packet, Cornish Weekly News, & General Advertiser;* Thursday, November 10th 1898.

The local Member of Parliament, Edwin During-Lawrence,[519] conveyed his effusive praise to the Porthoustock crew, through the Hon. Secretary for the Porthoustock institution, Mr Edward Pearce Roskruge:

King's Ride, Ascot, Berks. Oct. 19th, 1898.

Dear Mr. Roskruge,—May I ask you to convey to the coxswain of the Porthoustock Lifeboat Lady Durning-Lawrence's and my own warm congratulations on the gallant conduct which has brought credit not only upon themselves but upon the county, and indeed upon the country at large. As member of the division, I feel proud that it is our men who behaved so nobly when duty called them to risk their lives. Further words would be useless. I only desire to repeat that Lady Durning-Lawrence desires to join with me in expressions of high appreciation of their heroic conduct.
Believe me, yours faithfully,
EDWIN DURNING-LAWRENCE.[520]

The story of the disaster and the heroic saving of lives, gripped the country and the Porthoustock crew became overnight national heros:

LITERARY NOTES

The Royal Magazine for June maintains the high standard of excellence attained by the preliminary numbers, and contains a wealth of bright literary matters and attractive illustrations. Of special interest to Cornishmen is the article on "Heroes of the Lifeboat," for amongst those who have the proud distinction of men is James Hill, the brave coxswain of the Porthoustock lifeboat, a portrait of whom, taken by the Rev. W. Diggens, is reproduced (see fig. 61). The writer says:— "James Hill has been a coxswain of the Porthoustock lifeboat for 29 years, and has saved 94 lives. The silver medal of the Institution was voted to him for pulling off twice and rescuing 44 persons for the wreck of the ill-fated *Mohegan* on the Manacle Rocks, on the 14th October, 1898. Had it not been for the brave and persevering efforts of Coxswain Hill and his crew, few if any, of the 106 persons on board would have lived to tell the tale".[521] (C. Arthur Pearson,[522] Ltd., London, W.C.)

Praise from across the Atlantic continued much in the same vein, but more directed towards the officers and crew of the *Mohegan*:

The New York newspapers, pending the official investigation into the cause of the *Mohegan* disaster, refrain from attempting to fix the responsibility, although they intimate that somebody had blundered. All unite in praising the coolness and bravery of the officers and crew. The journal said that the conduct of the crew was in striking contrast with that of the

---

[519] Sir Edwin Durning-Lawrence, 1st Baronet (1837–1914) was the Liberal Unionist MP for Truro in 1895.

[520] *The Royal Cornwall Gazette Falmouth Packet, Cornish Weekly News, & General Advertiser;* Thursday, December 22nd 1898.

[521] *The Royal Cornwall Gazette Falmouth Packet, Cornish Weekly News, & General Advertiser;* Thursday, May 25th 1899.

[522] Cyril Arthur Pearson, proprietor of the London halfpenny newspaper, *The Daily Express*, and of, a score of weekly and monthly publications, including the *The Royal Magazine*, a monthly British literary magazine that was published between 1898 and 1939.

cowards who manned the *La Bourgogne*. They obeyed their orders implicitly, and they made no attempts to crowd into the boats, and they rendered every assistance possible to the panic stricken passengers. They died like heroes.[523]

Mr. James Hill had been a member of the Porthoustock lifeboat team for twenty-nine years and the universal accolades were well deserved: a high point in his lifeboat career, of diligent service.

Saved by the Bell.

The perennial argument was raised, yet again, as to the suitability of the Manacles bell buoy as a warning of the local danger. A call for additional lifeboat cover in the area, stating a lack of adequate coastguard service and the inappropriate siting of the rocket apparatus equipment, also featured:

Shipwrecks At The Manacles
(From A Correspondent)

I have been at some pains to collect information as to the number of casualties that have taken place latterly within two or three miles of the Manacles. One fisherman who is still in his middle life recalls 36. His list, however, is incomplete, for more than 50 have happened during the past 30 years. Of these considerably more than half may be classed as total wrecks. To turn to the lifeboat records, it seems that the Porthoustock boat, which by the way was sent to the hamlet in consequence of three quickly ensuing wrecks, has since the year 1872 been on active service 16 times and has affected the rescue of 112 persons. The same record shows that 119 lives were lost from the vessels to which the lifeboat went out. There were at least 16 other wrecks during that period, resulting in the loss of 44 lives, to which the lifeboat could render no assistance. In some instances the crew rowed ashore in their own boats. In others a hurricane from the east made a launch impossible. When one looks at this terrible array of facts, it may be appropriately asked if the means of averting disaster and of saving life are adequate in the neighbourhood. A bell buoy certainly exists at the Manacles, but it is of so little use that it hardly deserves to be mentioned. Next, there exists at Coverack, two-and-a-half miles from the Manacles, a very good Coastguard station. The men attached to this station have by their untiring vigilance saved many ships from destruction. Only a single Coastguard is stationed at Porthoustock, but previous to the wreck of the *Mohegan* it was decided to increase the number to three and to erect cottages for them in the cove. It may be pointed out, however, that from Porthoustock only a limited view of the sea is to be obtained and none at all of the Manacles. Persons thoroughly acquainted of the situation are most strongly convinced of the eminent desirability of stationing these men on Manacle Point. Had they been there last October they would probably have been able to signal the *Mohegan* in time to prevent her from being stranded,

Next, the fact that on the night of the wreck of the *Mohegan* the rocket apparatus at Coverack had to be laboriously pushed up a great hill directs attention to the unfavourable position in which the machine is placed. Save in the actual cove itself there is no road along the shore from Coverack in either direction. In fully nine cases out of ten a steep ascent has to be made with the apparatus before it can be conveyed to any point outside a half-mile radius. As horses are a scarce commodity in Coverack human labour must be employed. Obviously the best place for the apparatus is St. Keverne, where horses are always to be had, whence by an easy descent any part of the neighbouring coast may be reached. In the great blizzard of 1891, when four vessels were wrecked in two days, the delay in getting the rocket apparatus to the scenes of the catastrophes is locally held to be responsible for much unnecessary loss of life. Finally, it might be suggested to the Lifeboat Institution

---

[523] *Western Mail;* Wednesday, October 19th 1898.

that a boat stationed at Coverack would be likely to prove useful.[524] Occasionally very serious wrecks indeed, accompanied by great loss of life, occur at St. Keverne. Four wrecks alone within the last 90 years have resulted in the drowning of no fewer than 470 persons. In such cases one lifeboat is manifestly insufficient. Boats coming from a distance, however brave and skilful their crews may be, cannot render much service. It is not possible for men who have no intimate knowledge of the Manacles to take their craft safely at night through all the intricacies of the treacherous waters. At Coverack there are enough experienced fishermen, acquainted with, by reason of their avocations, with every rock and cove and shoal and headland in the neighbourhood, to man a boat. These men in a lifeboat might have been able to save many of the unfortunate passengers and crew of the *Mohegan*, who for a time were kept afloat by lifebelts only to be dashed finally against the cliffs and boulders of the inhospitable coast.

Perhaps if the proposed Coastguard station were established on Manacle Point instead of in Porthoustock Cove, if the rocket apparatus were removed to St. Keverne and if a lifeboat were sent to Coverack the force of the plea for a lightship at the Manacles would be greatly diminished.[525]

Better lose the anchor than the whole ship.

The *Charlotte* coxswain had some pertinent points that he raised at the Board of Trade inquiry, including a missed opportunity for the use of the *Mohegan*'s anchor:

THE LIFEBOATMAN COXSWAIN'S STORY

Mr. James Hill, coxswain of the lifeboat at Porthoustock, which rescued the persons who were saved, said that on the evening of the 14th October, his attention was called to a masthead light of a vessel that was coming stem on. He said, "Why you seem coming on to my stable". She next altered her course, and at that time she was about a quarter of a mile from shore. She ought to have dropped her anchor then, and everybody would have been saved. When the lifeboat started he could not see any light from the vessel, which has struck on the Maen Voces Rock. On his way to the Manacles he burnt a white light, but there was no response. He heard cries, and picked up two persons from the keel of a boat that was bottom upwards. There were cries of "Under," and he and his men turned the boat over, with difficulty, and found people in it. He burnt red lights to show that he wanted more help from shore, and then went on and found a boatful of people, and took them on board, as it would have been a great risk for that boat to go on by itself. After landing the people the crew went out again over the same course, and heard cries from time to time, and so found the wreck. A sailor [Juddery] swam out from the rigging and took a line back. And the people on the rigging were taken off.

By Mr. Pike: Before the mortar was discharged to summons the crew he had seen a rocket or two from the ship, and caused him to hurry with the lifeboat. From the Manacles he could see the [St.] Anthony's Light plainly.[526]

It is not surprising that some rivalry would have existed between the local lifeboat stations and their respective crews; even though they all had the same objective: that of saving lives at sea and bringing home the poor unfortunates who had lost the struggle.

---

[524] The Royal National Lifeboat Institution stationed a lifeboat at Coverack in 1901 following the wreck of the *Mohegan*. A boat house with a slipway was built on the harbour. The station was closed in October 1978 following the allocation of a faster boat to Falmouth Lifeboat Station.—*WikiPedia*. It was, in part, as a result of Canon Diggens lobbying the Board of Trade, and others. The first lifeboat on station was the "Constance Melanie". She was a 12-oared 'Liverpool' Class lifeboat and was built at a cost of £906, and was brought to Coverack in January 1901.

[525] *The Times;* Monday May 22nd 1899.

[526] *Daily News* (London, England); Saturday, November 12th 1898.

Geographically, the Porthoustock lifeboat was well placed to attend the Manacle Rocks and would have inevitably been first on the scene, for any untoward incident in this place. The Falmouth lifeboat would routinely have been towed the long distance to the Manacles, by a tug-boat. In addition, the causeway from the lifeboat station to open water at low tide, was a difficult manoeuvre, and indeed caused a significant delay on the night of the disaster.

Only the man who isn't rowing has time to rock the boat.

During the callout for the *Mohegan* incident, the Falmouth station was involved in an unseemly train of events, at the point where the lifeboat [527] was launched. The background to this affair was made public at the next annual general meeting of the Royal Lifeboat Institution at Falmouth:

FALMOUTH

The attendance at the annual general meeting of the Lifeboat Institution would no doubt have been larger had it been known what was going to happen. Too often the business on such occasions is of a purely formal character, interspersed with the inevitable appeal for more funds. The collector of customs, who was the chairman on this occasion, gave a special turn, however, to the proceedings by inviting a discussion as to the behaviour of some of the crew on the evening of the wreck of the *Mohegan*, and an unexpected discussion took place. There can be no doubt that there are very many who share Mr. Fookes' idea as to the necessity of some alteration in the personnel of the crew, but it was impossible to avoid the reflection that the remarks made did not apply to those members who were present and would not have too much effect upon the absent. It is understood that the committee are dealing with the matter, and we should all hope that next time there is a sudden call the launch will be carried out with due order and decorum, and the boat prove more successful in life-saving than it has hitherto done.

In the case of the *Mohegan* it is right to remember that the information available on the night of the wreck was of a very insufficient and misleading character, and no one realised what a terrible tragedy was taking place. The unfortunate consequences of the mast-head lights being electric, and thus extinguished when most wanted, threw a great difficulty in the way of ascertaining the exact position of the ship, and whatever lack of discipline there may have been on board the Falmouth boat, it is doubtful if she could have done more than she did under all the circumstances. [528]

Reading between the lines, in the above account, it would seem that discussions had already taken place, regarding this affair, and that those responsible had deemed it prudent to stay away from the proceedings. A more detailed account of this meeting, and with its disturbing revelations, is reported here:

FALMOUTH LIFEBOAT AND THE MOHEGAN WRECK
Stringent Criticism

---

[527] Named the *Bob Newbon* and on station from 1894 to1922 and was a twelve-oared, self-righting vessel. This vessel saved 58 lives over her 28-year service.

[528] *The Royal Cornwall Gazette Falmouth Packet, Cornish Weekly News, & General Advertiser*; Thursday, May 4th 1899.

The annual meeting of the Falmouth branch of the Royal National Lifeboat Institution was held on Friday evening, under the presidency of Mr. H. Fooks, collector of Customs, who remarked that he filled the position with great reluctance, because since last October, when the *Mohegan* was lost, he had nothing to do with the branch. In reality he formed the intention of having nothing more to do with the institution, and his idea in being present that evening was to give the secretary some little assistance in a new work.—The HON. SECRETARY, Mr. E. T. Oliver, stated that Mr. Cavendish-Bentinick retired from the presidency and Mr. Horniman, M.P.,[529] had consented to be vice-president. The minutes of the last meeting recorded that practical suggestions were made by Mr. Fooks, and the CHAIRMAN observed that he made

THREE SUGGESTIONS.

One was the possibility of charging against all ships for orders one shilling each, half to go towards the lifeboat and half towards the Royal Cornwall Sailors' Home. He and others waited on the shipping agents, and unfortunately found the idea impracticable. In other places with which he had been connected, the scheme worked well. Another suggestion was that they should have a Lifeboat Saturday or Sunday. Owing to the illness and death of Mr. Carter, the late secretary, that fell through. The third suggestion was that the subscription boxes should be placed on tugs fitted out in the summer as pleasure boats, and this had been partially carried out with a certain amount of success. He thought with a new secretary, who was taking a lively interest in the work, and was anxious to bring the branch up to its proper level, they would be able to work more successfully, provided he received support from the public and the committee, and encouragement from the crew. He could not say that such encouragement had been received up to the present.

THE REPORT.

Arrangement had been made with the coastguard by which immediate communication would be made with the lifeboat officials when distress signals were observed at any of the adjoining stations, and this would be greatly facilitated by the complete telephonic connection between Falmouth, Maenporth, Helford Passage, and Gillian Creek. The difficulty of launching at the slipway at low water was still a matter for serious considerations, in consequence of the unavoidable delay resulting from it. In order to obviate this in cases of emergency the parent institution had intimated that when information was received of a wreck as being in such a position as to possibly require assistance the lifeboat might be launched forthwith, so as to be ready for starting when necessary. The wreck of the *Mohegan* was known in Falmouth at seven o'clock in the evening, and the crew were assembled, but no definite application for assistance was received until 9.30. Owing to this and the inconvenience of launching at low water the boat although in tow of a tug,[530] did not reach the scene until about eleven o'clock. At that time the Porthoustock boat had done much of the work, and owing to the darkness and consequent difficulty of ascertaining where assistance was required the Falmouth boat was only enabled to bring back one body, while the tug secured one passenger [the horseman, George Maule] and the body of a child [Le Lacheur, John Guille]. The cost for these services was £37 10s. for the boat, defrayed by the parent institution, and £10 for the tug. The subscriptions received during 1898 were under £20, and £28 was received from the institution. £38 was paid to the coxswain and crew and £6 in incidentals.

THE WRECK OF THE MOHEGAN

He had heard a great many unpleasant remarks respecting Falmouth lifeboat, and he would like to hear some expressions of opinion. No one responding, the Chairman said he felt compelled to refer to the matter himself, although he would rather not have done so. He was surprised to see that £37 10s. had been paid for services, seeing that the boat did practically nothing. He witnessed the launch, and had no fault to find as the getting of the lifeboat into the water, but he did complain

---

[529] Frederick John Horniman; M.P. (Liberal) Falmouth and Penryn from 1895. Engaged in the tea trade, and became chairman of W. H. & J. Horniman & Co. Ltd.; for 40 years. Collector of curios – natural history, arts and manufacturers throughout the world – which are accumulated in the Horniman Free Museum, Forest Hill, open to the public; travelled throughout Canada, U.S., Japan, Ceylon, Burma and India, and visited China, and wrote notes of his travels. Address: Falmouth House, 20 Hyde Park Terrace W. London.
http://www.horniman.ac.uk/media/_file/the_horniman_family_history.pdf.

[530] This was the Falmouth tugboat *Penguin.*

of the disgusting language and horrible noise. He heard of this afterwards from many genteel and respectable people, who told him that they were shocked at such conduct on the part of the men going on an errand of mercy, and they had no faith in the men and did not believe the crew were going to do any more that they did. A great many people who witnessed the launch went away sick at heart and felt the same as he did. Namely that

THE CREW WERE NOT GOING TO DO JUSTICE

Complaints were made to the Institution and to the Board of Trade. It was not for him to say what the boat did or did not do at the wreck. Probably they did the best they could. But a small shore boat from Porthoustock ascertained the exact position of the wreck, and thus rendered most valuable service. He had always maintained that the Manacles was the position where the Falmouth boat should be of real service, and the Falmouth men professed to know all about the scene of the wreck. That being so, he could not understand how it was the boat did so little. From his official position he knew all the evidence that had been adduced in this matter, and understood the Falmouth boat made a tour of the rocks and went to Porthoustock and Porthallow. He learned that at the former place they were told to go on to the wreck. He was in hopes that these matters would have been investigated privately, and but for the unnecessary interference of the deputy chief inspection of the Institution, who shut him and others up and snuffed them out entirely, they would not have been brought forward now. The subject would otherwise have been discussed, and probably if any of the crew were at fault they would have been weeded out. He believed now it was the intention of the committee to

WEED OUT ANY INCOMPETENT MEMBERS OF THE CREW

There were some very good men in the crew, he believed, and he would stand by them but there must be some very bad ones, otherwise there would not have been that horrible and disgusting language. He felt that the boat might do more. What encouragement was there to the public to support the branch when it was known that although the boat had gone on service many times during the past twenty or thirty years , and although large sums of money had been paid, the record of lives saved was a blank. This was not even so much as he himself had done in a small boat. If the committee were determined henceforth to see if the crew were really worthy, the branch would improve and the inhabitants would shew greater interest in it. It was only right to explain all these things, because people who gave money were entitled to expect a return for it.—The HON. SECRETARY said that there was a strong determination on the part of the committee to maintain discipline in the crew, and to stand second to no branch in the kingdom. Men who entered the boat with

NO HIGHER AIM THAN THE GAINING OF MONEY

were the wrong men, and the sooner such were replaced by men of nobler spirit the better for the institution and the cause of humanity generally.

In reply to Mr. T. Coward, The CHAIRMAN said there were definite instructions to coxswains, who were responsible for maintenance of discipline. No talking whatever was allowed in the Porthoustock boat, and it was only when they were getting amongst dangerous rocks that any voices other than the coxswain's was heard.

Mr. A. Tonkin, a member of the crew, said he was sorry the chairman had such a bad opinion of Falmouth men. The bad language at the launching was caused mostly by the outsiders. He denied that they were told at Porthoustock to go to the wreck.—Mr. Francis Jose, the coxswain, confirmed this.—Mr. Tonkin: You blame us for not finding the *Mohegan*.—The CHAIRMAN said the owner of a tug

WAS NOT GOING TO RUN UNECESSARY RISK

but he had always understood a lifeboat was a lifeboat, and if her bottom was knocked out she would float. He, therefore, saw no reason why it should not go amongst the rocks.—Mr. Tonkin: We were amongst the rocks.—The CHAIRMAN: You went around them, I admit. Then you went to Porthoustock and Porthallow.

Mr. S. Collins, harbour-master, thought this was somewhat out of order for the annual meeting. The Porthoustock lifeboat was able to mark the position of the wreck because they saw the vessel's lights when she went there, but everything was dark when the Falmouth boat arrived. He could not see that there was any blame to be attached to the Falmouth men for not finding the wreck, or credit to the Porthoustock men for finding it.—Mr. F. J. BOWLES saw no advantage in continuing the discussion.—Commander TARGET, R.N., remarked,

IN JUSTICE TO THE FALMOUTH CREW

that he had attended several launchings for practice, and on those occasions the conduct of the men was excellent and their work seamanlike.—Mr. BOWLES said he always thought the lifeboat-house was in an unsuitable position. The site was chosen because it could be had for a nominal rent.—Mr. COLLINS said in a south-easterly wind the boat would almost knocked to pieces before it could be got out.—The report was then adopted, on the motion of Mr. COLLINS, seconded by Mr. COWARD.

OFFICERS WERE ELECTED

Mr. BOWLES, in proposing thanks to the chairman, said he had initiated a very searching discussion, and on the principle that if there were anything to be brought to the front it was desirable to have it out, they thanked him. The motion was carried, and the CHAIRMAN said he believed from now the crew would endeavour to do its best, so as not to cause censure. He was not in any way antagonistic to the crew, and always made great allowance for them.[531]

An investigation into the role played by the Falmouth lifeboat in the *Mohegan* incident, resulted in several recommendations that would have been most helpful, had they been installed before the disaster had taken place; however, that had not been the case. Of some interest perhaps, is the financial breakdown attached to the callout to the wreck, on that particular evening.

It is not immediately apparent as to the reason for this confrontation on the night of the disaster, and it was certainly regretted by the committee, and it duly became a formal agenda item at the annual general meeting. Perhaps the crew felt that the long trip to the wreck-site, so late in the day, was a superfluous undertaking and would not result in any tangible benefit: presenting a challenge to the coxswain's authority. The proximity of the Porthoustock station to the Manacles would have rendered their attendance as being rather futile. In the event, the Falmouth crew brought back one body, while its accompanying tug[532] secured one live passenger and a further body of a child.

An accusation was levelled at the coxswain that he had not located the *Mohegan* and that time was spent in Porthoustock, instead of sweeping the area to try and locate the wreck and its victims. The inference is that the Falmouth lifeboat was not prepared to enter the Manacles reef for fear of damaging the lifeboat and endangering the crew.

In truth, the Falmouth crew seemed to have adopted a rather desultory response to the whole affair, to the discredit of their organisation. To be fair, the situation on station was dangerous for the lifeboat and it being very difficult to negotiate the rocks with any confidence, in total darkness. Almost certainly the shouts of the persons, clinging to the rigging of the *Mohegan*, would have been clearly heard by the lifeboat teams but their hands were stayed, for fear of losing all in among the treacherous rocks. The Porthoustock lifeboat later saved all those crew and passengers in the rigging.

---

[531] *The Royal Cornwall Gazette Falmouth Packet, Cornish Weekly News, & General Advertiser;* Thursday, 4th May 1899.

[532] The vessel was the Falmouth-based tugboat, *Penguin.*

Either way, it was unfortunate that such bad feeling arose in response to an appalling tragedy. The annual meeting, having taken place in May of the year following the disaster, gave many months for this dispute to grow; no doubt causing increasing unease for the Institution and its stalwart supporters. But it was evidently a boil that had to be lanced, as the matter forced its way to the top of the agenda.

There was, reading between the lines, an apparent schism within the lifeboat crew: those who saw their service to the Institution as being paramount and unquestioning in their attendance, and others (of a more mercenary nature) falling below the standards one normally associates with the Royal National Lifeboat Institution. It is not known at this time what the outcome was, but it is assumed that the threat to, "weed out the more incompetent members of the crew," was vigorously embarked upon. Indeed, a report on the aid given to the liner *Paris* by the Falmouth lifeboat confirmed a reorganisation of the crew, following the stringent criticism raised at the meeting, a couple of months previously:

> The crew who manned the Falmouth lifeboat on the morning when the *Paris* stranded have been rewarded for their services. Many of them were not old "hands," severe criticism after the wreck of the *Mohegan* having created vacancies which, when the *Paris* was ashore, were filled by outsiders. For future work it is hoped to get together a good crew from the material at disposal. The local committee of the Lifeboat Institution has now a new chairman in Captain Target, the successor of Capt. G. H. B. Reed, whose health prevents him from taking part in active life.[533]

Whatever was decided, took place behind closed doors—where perhaps it should have remained from the outset.

Arising out of this rather cheerless affair was a more dedicated lifeboat service drawn from within its loyal ranks and supporters; which had quickly regained the encouragement and admiration of the public, which is still evident to this day.

At the annual meeting, the following year, a perennial problem, that of difficulty in launching the Falmouth lifeboat, was again discussed. Certain remedial measures, introduced by the Institution, seemed to have helped the situation, but a further review was called for:

FALMOUTH LIFEBOAT AND LAUNCHING DIFFICULTIES

> The Mayor of Falmouth, presiding at the local lifeboat annual meeting on Thursday, spoke of the improvements effected for the launching of the boat. He felt quite satisfied that the committee and officers of the parent society had done their very best to finds a suitable position for the lifeboat house—a matter presenting greater difficulty than at first might be supposed. While willing to admit that possibly the present position was the best that could be found, he thought a further expenditure of money on the slipway would lead to better results. He wondered, as others had, why there had not been some arrangement by which the boat might be kept on a kind of cradle, ready for launching. Each time he had witnessed a launch it had been made under very great difficulty.[534]

---

[533] *The Royal Cornwall Gazette Falmouth Packet, Cornish Weekly News, & General Advertiser*; Thursday, July 20th 1899.

[534] *The Royal Cornwall Gazette Falmouth Packet, Cornish Weekly News, & General Advertiser*; Thursday, May 10th 1900.

You take your life in your hands.

In venturing out to sea, particularly in the 19th century, there was always a threat of shipwrecking to consider. And so, a novel form of life-saving equipment would always attract attention worldwide, as reported here in a New Zealand newspaper:

The Mayor of Falmouth [UK] has had a unique experience. Shocked by the terrible loss of life through the wreck of the *Mohegan* and with a view to preventing such wholesale loss in future, he has been experimenting with various life-saving appliances. The people of Falmouth have been enabled to see their chief magistrate, dressed in heavy clothes, and with sea-boots reaching above his knees, boldly taking the water in order to test appliances submitted to him. He has now written a letter to Mr. S. Bickley, of Royal Hill, Greenwich, who is the inventor of a novel life-jacket, giving his appliance the preference. He says, "If the passengers (on the s.s.*Mohegan*) had been supplied with your jackets we should not now have to deploy the serious loss of life that occurred. I sincerely hope, for humanity's sake, that the Board of Trade will see its way clear to adopt them instead of the old-fashioned cork belts now used". The jackets in question are nothing like the one hitherto used, but are comfortable, flannel-lined garments, with a multitude of rubber compartments filled with compressed air. They can be worn as an ordinary warmth-giving jacket at sea, and may even be slept in without inconvenience. The wearer cannot sink in them in the roughest water, and the body does not get chilled, no matter how long immersed. It is understood that the Board of Trade gave its approval to Mr. Bickley's invention, but, while any sailor or passengers may buy one privately, the Board will not allow shipping companies to put them on their boats for general use, but insist on the old-fashioned cork belts being carried. This is a red tape absurdity which, when human life is at stake, should not be tolerated.[535]

A lifeboat was first installed at Porthoustock in the year of 1868—the *Mary Ann Storey*. The benefactor for her replacement, at first remained anonymous,[536] but its builders were named and the boat's latest attributes were proudly proclaimed to the maritime world:

PORTHOUSTOCK NEW LIFEBOAT.—The National Lifeboat Institution has just sent a new lifeboat to Porthoustock, near Falmouth, to take the place of the smaller lifeboat on that station. The new boat is 37 feet long, 8 feet wide, and rows 12 oars double banked; it was built by Messrs. Forrest and Son, of Limehouse, London, and possesses all the latest improvements, including the water-ballast fittings, which consists of a series of tanks amidships, one or more of which can be filled with water or emptied at will in the space of one minute. The object is to increase the ballast and immersion of the boat, and consequently her draught of water and stability, when circumstances admit of doing so, without materially increasing her fixed weight for land carriage or her draught of water when launching or in very shallow water. The lifeboat has all the other characteristics of the boats of the National Institution in the way of self-righting, self-ejecting water, &c. A new transporting and launching carriage has been provided for the boat. The cost of the new lifeboat, which is named the

---

[535] *The Star;* 7th Saturday, January 1899—New Zealand

[536] Obituary: At London, on the 12th inst., for MARY ANN STOREY, widow of Mr John Hepburn [*sic*], of the Arctic Expedition: *The Aberdeen Journal* (Aberdeen Scotland). Wednesday, March 19th 1862.
The ROYAL NATIONAL LIFEBOAT INSTITUTION—On Thursday a meeting was held at its house, Johnson street, Adelphi—and the late Mrs. Mary Ann Storey of Lensington [*sic*], £500, to pay the cost of a lifeboat—*Isle of Wight Observer* (Ryde, England), Saturday, December 15th 1866.

Charlotte, has been defrayed by, "A. F. H.," a lady living near London.[537] The Institution has now 292 lifeboats under its management, 37 of which are stationed on the coasts of Devon and Cornwall, and during the past year it contributed to the saving of 555 lives from shipwrecks on our coast. A large sum is needed annually to maintain the lifeboats in a state of thorough efficiency. Contributions in aid of their support will be gladly received by the several bankers, the honorary secretaries of the different lifeboat branches, and by the secretary of the institution, Mr. Charles Dibdin, John-street, Adelphi, London.[538]

Amidst much joy and celebration, the officials and local people gathered to witness the naming and the launching of the *Charlotte,* the replacement vessel, in the year of 1886:

LAUNCHING OF A LIFEBOAT AT PORTHOUSTOCK

The neat fishing cove of Porthoustock, St. Keverne presented a holiday appearance on Thursday, on the occasion of the launching of a new lifeboat. A luncheon given by Miss [Sarah Wills] Smedley, of Parkventon, Sithney, took place in the boathouse at half-past one, and among those present were the Rev. M. A. Smell and Mrs. Smell, of Cheltenham, the Rev. H. G. Vivian and Mrs. Vivian, the Rev. A. A. Vawdrey, the Rev, M. J. Salter and Mrs. Salter. the Rev. W. H. Bloxsome and Mrs. Bloxsome, Mr. F. V. Hill, Mr. Humphrey Hill, Mr. L. L. Haslope, Mrs. And Miss Haslope, Mr. E. J. Leverton and Mrs. Leverton, the Misses Roberts, Mr. E. P. Roskruge and Mrs. [Mary Joanna] Roskruge. After luncheon the boat, on her carriage, was drawn to the water's edge through an immense quantity of seaweed thrown on shore by the easterly gales. The Rev. M. J. Sutton, vicar of St. Keverne, offered prayer for the success of the boat, and the preservation of the crew. Miss Smedley, who had consented to name the boat by the unanimous desire of the committee, then performed the ceremony naming and christening, naming the boat the *Charlotte* at the request of the anonymous donor. The president of the local branch (Mr. W^m. Treven) then accepted the boat on behalf of the chairman (Mr. E. Leverton-Spry) and the local committee. He reminded those assembled that the Royal National Lifeboat Institution since its formation had been instrumental in saving of upwards of 30,000 lives, having at present a life-saving fleet of 292 boats, and the whole fleet being supported by voluntary contributions. He was pleased and proud to inform them that the old boat, the *Mary Ann Storey,* which Miss Smedley had the honour of naming there seventeen years ago [1869], had saved forty-three lives from shipwreck (a record of which could be seen in the boathouse), besides a valuable amount of property. He expressed the hope that the *Charlotte,* which is fitted up with water ballast tank and all the newest appliances would prove equally good or better than the old boat, and he felt confident that the crew would, as hitherto, do their duty as Englishmen and Cornishmen. The Hon. Sec. (Mr. E. P. Roskruge) asked for three cheers for the donor, which were heartily given, and the beautiful new boat, at a given signal from the coxswain, glided off her carriage through the surf amidst the acclamations of all present, the band striking up "Rule Britannia". The lifesaving apparatus under the efficient superintendence of the Mr. Gibson, chief-officer, Coverack, on the northern cliff, was put in position and a rocket fired across to the opposite shore. The ropes were smartly handled by the coastguard and Board of Trade brigade. In a few minutes all was ready to for the conveyance of persons from the supposed shipwreck. A man was first quickly drawn across the water to all appearances contained a woman and baby, the cries of which were heard from the opposite cliff. They also were landed safely, amidst cheers from the people. The cliff ladder was next thrown over, shewing the method of saving life from high

---

[537] The generous donor was eventually identified by this author as Miss Anne Francis Howis (1809–1905) Ashurst House, Trinity Road, Tulse Hill London. She was a wealthy unmarried woman, living on her own means, with four servants and a footman; UK census 1891.

[538] *The Royal Cornwall Gazette Falmouth Packet, Cornish Weekly News, & General Advertiser*; Friday, August 20th 1886.

and precipitous cliffs. The proceedings were brought to a close by the lifeboatmen jumping overboard and swimming ashore in their cork jackets. In the evening there was a display of rockets at the village of St. Keverne.[539]

The only recorded criticism of the Porthoustock lifeboat appeared in 1891, following the local wrecking of two vessels, where the lifeboat failed to show:

Some dissatisfaction was expressed that during the wrecks at Porthoustock and Porthalla [Porthallow], on March 9th,[540] when about thirty lives were lost, no life-boat had been launched, and the National Lifeboat Institution sent to St. Keverne, about a fortnight after the occurrence, Commander Biddors, R.N., who made inquiries into the matter. It appeared on investigation that some of the life-boat crew did not readily respond to the call signals, their explanation being that they did not hear or see them. When they arrived at the life-boat station the storm had increased, and it was dangerous to put to sea. A proposal for the provision of a smaller life-boat, requiring fewer oars, has been submitted to the life-boat committee.[541]

The Porthoustock lifeboat was to be involved in the *SS Paris* stranding on Lowland Point, some few months after the *Mohegan* wrecking. Following the *Paris* event, a peculiar incident occurred that was at first thought to be another disaster on the Manacle Rocks:

ALARMING REPORT AT FALMOUTH

Much excitement was caused at Falmouth on Friday night by the reception of the following message:—"Large ship on Manacles; Porthoustock lifeboat gone out. Falmouth boat not needed". It was at once assumed that another vessel had run on the dreaded Manacles, and that the Porthoustock lifeboat, which rendered such gallant service on the occasions of the wrecks of *Mohegan* and the *Paris*, had added to her already brilliant record. Falmouth shipping agents and tug owners immediately made preparations to proceed to the Manacles. After the receipt of the first startling message nothing was heard until the coastguard, just before midnight, received a telephonic message that Porthoustock lifeboat had returned, and could find no vestige of a distressed ship. This, of course, only added to the anxiety of the situation, it being assumed that the vessel, on striking the rocks, had gone down with all hands. Subsequent circumstances, however, appeared to point to the fact that the coastguard and lifeboatmen had simply mistaken signals of rejoicing for signals of distress. There can be no doubt from the facts since come to light that the crew of some homeward-bound ship on nearing land were apprised of Cronje's capitulation and the relief of Kimberley and Ladysmith, and had used all available rockets on board to signalise their joy. Certainly rockets were seen, and their variety was very puzzling.[542]

Thankfully, it was not another disaster, but was due to an inappropriate use of a ship's rockets to herald a victory in the 1899–1902 Boer War. Britain was on a heightened level of alert and the war was much glorified

---

[539] *The Royal Cornwall Gazette Falmouth Packet, Cornish Weekly News, & General Advertiser*; Friday, October 1st 1886.

[540] A blizzard, the worst for over two centuries with hurricane winds that generated mountainous waves preventing the launch of the Porthoustock lifeboat. The *Bay of Panama* was the major loss that night with the loss of 18 lives, together with three schooners; one of which went aground in Porthoustock (2 lives saved) and the other two were smashed to pieces with a loss of seven further lives. The *Charlotte* lifeboat at Porthoustock could not be launched as the seas were washing clean through the lifeboat house.

[541] Great Britain – Privy Council; Judicial Committee. The blizzard in the West: being a record and story of the disastrous storm which raged throughout Devon and Cornwall, and West Somerset, on the night of March 9th, 1891.

[542] *The Royal Cornwall Gazette Falmouth Packet, Cornish Weekly News, & General Advertiser*; Thursday, March 8th 1900.

by the national Press. Nonetheless, the ship's captain should have known better than to raise an unwarranted alarm and so endanger the lives of the lifeboatmen, on a needless callout.

Another report put the reason for that apparent outburst of joy and patriotism, closer to home:

LOCAL GOSSIP

There was no shipping mishap at the Manacles on Friday night, as recorded elsewhere. All the alarm and trouble at Falmouth, Porthoustock, and Coverack were occasioned by youths exploding dynamite in celebration of the Ladysmith achievement. That was the explanation given on Saturday. Is it usual for youths to be in possession of and allowed to explode dynamite in this way? There must be something wrong somewhere.[543]

At the end of her active service, the *Charlotte* lifeboat at Porthoustock was duly replaced, as reported here:

A New Cornish Lifeboat

The Royal National Lifeboat Institution has just replaced the boat stationed some year since at Porthoustock, near Falmouth, by a new lifeboat 36 feet long and 9 feet wide, built by the Thames Ironworks Company.[544] She rows twelve oars, double-banked, and is also provided with masts and sails. She is not a self-righting boat, but belongs to what is known as the "Liverpool" type of lifeboat. The cost of the new boat and equipment has been met from the handsome legacy received by the institution from the estate of the late Mr. James Stevens, of Birmingham, this boat being named the *James Stevens No 17*. The boat which has thus been superseded has rendered excellent services at different times, the total number of lives saved amounting to 79, besides other help rendered to vessels in distress. The institution is much indebted to Mr. E. L. Spry, Mr. E P. Roskruge, and other friends at Porthoustock for their valuable co-operation in the management of the lifeboat station. The Royal National Lifeboat Institution has now 287 boats under its management, 33 of which are stationed on the coast of Devon and Cornwall, and not a winter passes without some of those boats rendering good service in saving life from shipwreck. The expense of maintaining a lifeboat establishment in a state of thorough efficiency exceeds £100 a year, including rewards to the crew for going off to save life from shipwreck, payment for quarterly exercise, necessary repairs, &c.[545]

A bizarre story appeared in an Australian newspaper, which almost beggars belief, but for the fact that a photograph of this strange dwelling-house supports the story (see fig. 82) in which an upturned lifeboat acted as a roof for the small building, owned by a local resident—Mrs Julia Jenkin. The lifeboat's accompanying history clearly identifies this as the *Charlotte:*

A famous Cornish lifeboat, after years of service has been converted into a dwelling, and is to be let for a week. This old lifeboat has done duty at many wrecks. It was launched when the *ss Mohegan* went ashore on the Manacles with the loss of so many lives, and also at the stranding of the American liner *Paris*.[546]

---

[543] Ibid.

[544] The Thames Ironworks Company (1837–1912) notably produced iron work for Isambard Kingdom Brunel's Royal Albert Bridge over the River Tamar (spanning the Devon/Cornwall boundary) in the 1850s, and for the world's first all-iron warship, *HMS Warrior*, launched in 1860.

[545] *The Royal Cornwall Gazette Falmouth Packet, Cornish Weekly News, & General Advertiser*; Thursday, October 25th 1900.

[546] *Evelyn Observer and Bourke East Record (Vic.: 1902–1917)* Friday December 11th 1914.

The lifeboat *Charlotte* was based at Porthoustock from 1886–1900, and then placed on the reserve fleet. She was eventually condemned and sold in November 1912. This date would concur with the above story that appeared in the Australian newspaper in 1914.[547]

The Porthoustock lifeboat had an illustrious pedigree, in its attendance on ships in distress, invariably associated with the Manacle Rocks:

Porthoustock boat has, since the year 1872 been on active service 16 times, and has effected the rescue of 112 persons. The same records show that 119 lives were lost from the vessels to which the Life Boat went out. There were at least 16 other wrecks during that period resulting in the loss of 44 lives to which the Life Boat could render no assistance. Four wrecks alone in the last 90 years have resulted in the drowning of no less than 470 persons. The RNLI closed down the station in 1942, having been established in 1869, the first lifeboat, the *Mary Ann Storey*, cost £283, and was pulled through Helston by nine horses, en-route to the cove of Porthoustock. The lifeboat men rescued over 130 people in the early years of the station's history. Today, Porthoustock has no lifeboat stationed here. The village is now best known for its quarry, from where 20,000 tons of stone per month are shipped out by large vessels, which use a purpose-built quay, which extends out to deeper water. The beach has been a great deal altered since the late 19th century, and the shoreline is now much further down the cove and removed from a somewhat isolated lifeboat house.[548]

The decision by the RNLI to withdraw the lifeboat service from Porthoustock Cove in 1945 must have caused some sadness and anxiety to the local people. However, the record for the penultimate lifeboat on station—the *Queen Victoria*—speaks for itself (see below).

The Porthoustock Lifeboat Station was built in 1869 at a cost of £170. The station was closed temporarily in 1942, due to the war with Germany and completely disbanded in 1945.

COXSWAINS	PERIOD IN POST	COXSWAINS	PERIOD IN POST
John George	1869–1878	William Henry Tripp	1908–1922
James Hill	1878–1905	George Martin Tripconey	1922–1935
James Henry Treloar Cliff	1905–1908	Joseph William Tripconey	1935–1945
HON. SECRETARIES		PERIOD IN POST	
Edward Pearce Roskruge		1869–1904	
Rev. Canon Diggens		1904–1913	
Dr. Leverton-Spry		1913–1942	

Table 9: The Porthoustock Lifeboat: Coxwains and Hon. Secretaries.

The cottage was available to let for 15s. a week – *Gippsland Times (Vic. : 186–1954)* Monday 13 March 1916. The building was eventually demolished, and the *Charlotte* lifeboat was burnt deliberately, in a fire on the beach. Today, this would be classed as cultural vandalism: then, it was not seen as such.

[547] Regrettably, the dwelling no longer exists and so a unique link with the *Mohegan* and a boat that had witnessed so much bravery, elation and misfortune, is no longer with us. If it were, it would have made a wonderful exhibit in the National Maritime Museum in Falmouth.

[548] Courtesy of: St. Keverne Local History Society.

Station Lifeboats	Period	Launches	Lives Rescued	Cost (£)
Mary Ann Storey Its donor was Mary Ann Storey, London, bequeathed in her will. The boat was named by Miss Sarah Wills Smedley – Park Venton, Sithney.	1869–1886	9	43	282
Charlotte Gift of Miss Anne F. Howis of Ashurst lodge, Trinity Road, Tulse Hill, London. Named by Miss Sarah Wills Smedley – Park Venton, Sithney.	1886–1900	11	79	373
James Stevens No. 17 She was one of 20 vessels paid for out of a £50,000 legacy left by Birmingham businessman, James Stevens, after whom all 20 were named.	1900–1923	9	8	772
Queen Victoria Provided from RNLI funds. She was already 20 years old, having seen service in Bemberidge, Isle of Wight (1887–1902). She was sent to Porthoustock in 1922.	1923–1931	1	0	920
Kate Walker Another second-hand vessel that had seen service at Lynmouth, North Devon. She had been constructed by Roberts of Mevagissey. The cost of this lifeboat was defrayed by the legacy of the late Mr John C. Walker of Ingleton, Yorkshire. She arrived at Porthoustock in 1931.	1931–46			

Table 10: The Porthoustock Lifeboats: A History.

A new lifeboat for Porthoustock, being constructed in the boatyard of Groves and Gutteridge,[549] was destroyed in an air-raid during the Second World War. However, times were changing and with the increased difficulty in getting the lifeboat to the water's edge at Porthoustock, the end was in sight. The service was temporarily suspended in 1942 and with a permanent shutdown in 1945.

The following words are indeed applicable, to the lifeboat service that had served humaity so well:

[549] The Groves and Gutteridge boatyard occupied the area now known as the Cowes Yacht Haven, Isle of Wight.

It drives on with a courage which is stronger than the storm. It drives on with a mercy which does not quail in the presence of death. It drives on as proof, a symbol, a testimony that man is created in the image of God and that valour and virtue have not perished in the British race.[550]

Shore-based lifeboats operate under a strict regime, having implemented the necessary infrastructure, training, and expertise, necessary in the saving of life. However, a ship may never experience the launching of a lifeboat in a real disaster, and only go through an unrealistic dry run: either during practice or in a vessel's Board of Trade inspection.

In a situation where persons aboard a ship are obliged to abandon their vessel, any shortcoming in the above regimes is then cruelly exposed. A few years later, the question of a safe lifeboat launch prompted this letter in the American Press:

LAUNCHING OF LIFEBOATS.
Plea for an Organisation to Study the Subject.

To the Editor of the New York Times:

The letter in THE TIMES of Monday last on the launching of ship's boats in cases of wreck most surely dealt with an important subject, strangely neglected. To any one who has stood on the deck of a foundering ship, as has the writer, when it has been necessary to launch not one, but many boats, within the few minutes that the vessel remained afloat, and has witnessed the strenuous and heroic efforts of men, continued vainly through a space of time which should have been more than ample for success . If used with properly devised apparatus; to any one who has had such an experience, and who has any knowledge of the means of launching now commonly used, it is not to any extent a question whether these means are adequate or whether they can be improved upon.

The methods most commonly in use in large passenger steamers are obviously and absurdly inadequate and inefficient for operation, excepting only under the most favourable conditions, as when a vessel is on an even keel, steady, and in smooth water. The fact that under these conditions, and with the work done by men exclusively sailors, boats have been, and may be launched in a few minutes, is apt to mislead many, but has the only saddest kind of significance for those who have seen people engulfed by scores, including men, women, and children, and the brave workers who went down at their posts after efforts continued through much longer periods of time. Of the nine or ten times different processes which must ordinarily be gone through before a lifeboat, lying on the deck of a ship and inboard of the davits, can be put afloat a number have in instances been improved and simplified, but the instances appear to be, so far as I am aware, isolated, through the adoption of some of these improvements would involve little cost and the advantages are clearly manifest. Of course, on a large ocean steamer it is impracticable to assign a full crew of seamen to every boat, perhaps the average falls short of two sailors to a boat, the complement of each being made up of stewards, firemen, and others, and for such men with a high sea and a rolling or a listed ship work difficult or perhaps doubtful for the sailor is apt to prove a blundering and hopeless task.

Much has been done within the last year or two by invention to give increased power and control to whatever skill and intelligence may be employed in launching a ship's lifeboat, and in consequence to lessen dependence on the unskilled and unreliable, and it has been shown that the most risky and difficult part of the process can be eliminated. It might appear like an interested business proceeding to further refer to what has been done in this line, (though the assumption would be

<hr>

[550] Sir Winston Churchill, speaking at the RNLI's centenary in 1924.

wholly false) but in view of such calamities as the *Mohegan* of 1898, the *Norge*[551] of this year, and others, and of similar disasters which, however lamentable, we must expect to occur in the future, and in view of the further fact that as relates to the common practice the methods of launching ship's boats is no better today than it was fifty years ago.

It does seem that an important common interest and the cause of humanity might be well and fitly served, if this subject were taken up and earnestly dealt with by some organisation, and with the aid of duly qualified men. An investigation and study of the matter by such men, which should include mechanical or civil engineers in the number, would reveal the present status of boat launching appliances, would show how defective those are which are in common use, might be advantageously employed, and how a few that have great and special merit are little known, and are not employed at all.—J. H.[552]

New York, Aug 4. 1904.[553]

Some years later, the same topic and by the same correspondent—who had been aboard the *Mohegan* and witnessed at first-hand the shambles over attempts at launching her lifeboats—points out the singular lack of any technological development over the intervening years :

LIFEBOATS ON ALL LINERS ANTIQUATED

John Hyslop, Venerable ex-Official of New York Yacht Club, Points Out Gross Negligence.

URGES IMMEDIATE REFORM

Tells Personal Experience in Lowering Small Craft in Time of Emergency—Davits at Fault.

John Hyslop, the venerable yacht owner, sailor, and writer on nautical matters, who was for seventeen years Official Measurer for the New York Yacht Club, asked the THE NEW YORK TIMES yesterday to urge that every facility to safeguard life at sea be no longer neglected. Mr. Hyslop, who, since he ceased to be the yacht club's official measurer, has been living at 4 River View Terrace, opposite East Fifty-eighth Street, is 78 years old. During his half-century of practical experience as a yachtman and sailor, he has four times found himself with the problem of quickly launching lifeboats in the open sea.

On three of these occasions he sought to save the lives of men or boys who had been swept overboard. The other attempted launching was when the steamship *Mohegan* struck the Manicle [*sic*] Rocks off Falmouth, Eng., in 1898. In the first three cases, boats could not be launched at all because of the poor facilities, and that one was damaged.

The Captains of many of the ocean liners on which Mr. Hyslop has crossed the Atlantic, have confided it to him at different times that were their ship to sink they would sooner trust to a plank than to hope to have themselves by getting out the lifeboats, because of the difficulties which the launching of the lifeboats always entail.

The reason that the *Titanic* did not have more mishaps in launching her lifeboats was not so because of the calm sea, as because she was one of the few ocean liners which had been provided with up-to-date davits. Even the davits of some of the ships which went to the *Titanic*'s are old-style Mr. Hyslop said.[554]

---

[551] The *SS Norge* was a Danish passenger liner sailing from Copenhagen, Oslo and Kristiansand to New York, mainly with emigrants, which sank off Rockall in 1904. It remained the biggest civilian maritime disaster in the Atlantic Ocean until the sinking of the *RMS Titanic* eight years later. On 28th June, 1904 the *Norge* ran aground on Hasselwood Rock, close to Rockall, on St Helen's Reef. According to the account, the final death toll was 635, among them 225 Norwegians. The 160 survivors spent up to eight days in open lifeboats before rescue—*WikiPedia*.

[552] Its author was, John Hyslop; a yacht measurer from New York and a survivor from the *Mohegan* disaster.

[553] The New York Times; 7th August, 1904.

"Any effort to force improvements must be aided by an aroused public opinion," said Mr. Hyslop yesterday. Appliances for launching lifeboats from ocean steamships are in a flint-lock stage. But the inadequancy of these appliances are discovered only when there is a big marine disaster. The survivors generally think that the mishaps in launching the lifeboats then have been due to the bad weather or the incompetent crew, or some like cause, but the survivors haven't technical knowledge enough to understand that the fault is generally with the antiquated machinery—the davits, or the falls, the chocks, &c.—by means of which the boats are lowered.

"Collision with an iceberg or a derelict on a dark night or in a fog is a constant possibility. In such an event, nothing but the speedy launching of lifeboats will save a single life. I have stood four different times on ship decks when it was necessary to launch lifeboats quickly. In none of these four cases could the boats be effectively lowered.

"During the sinking of the *Mohegan*, I cut the tarpaulin off one of the lifeboats myself in the attempt to launch her. One hundred and fifty passengers waited for ten or fifteen minutes while we tried to clear the boats. But we were all in the water before more than one of the boats could be cleared. I myself snatched a plank, and some of the leading Captains of ocean liners to-day have told me in confidence that they preferred a chance of a plank to that of clearing a lifeboat".

"Alleged experts are sometimes quoted as saying: 'I have seen boats put afloat from a ship's deck within three minutes from the time the first order was given.' This is misleading, because such tests are made in daylight in a calm river, when all conditions are favorable. The Captain of a large transatlantic liner recently told me that he could clear a lifeboat in two and a half minutes. His vessel was equipped with with the ordinary old-style davits.

"'What would you do if the vessel was rolling or listed?' I asked him.

"'We know we could not launch them at all,' he answered.

"And he was the Captain of a big modern transatlantic liner, too!

"The chief difficulty in launching lifeboats from ships equipped with the ordinary swivel davit, which most liners are equipped with is that, while it is comparatively easy to turn heavy davits and to swing heavy boats while the steamship remains horizontal, and while the boats and davits will stay out out under such circumstances, the problem is very different when the vessel is listed or rolling. The davits can't be stayed in an inboard or outboard position by ordinary guys when the boat rolls or lists. The crudity of such appliances, indeed, would be obvious to any one.

"The working of launching a lifeboat from a liner consists of removing the canvas covering, casting off the grips, throwing down the outer chocks, casting off the lanyards, or tackles of the guys, hoisting the boat clear of its seat, pushing outward the boat and davits, and securing the guys, lowering the boats evenly by the falls, unhooking the falls, and pushing clear of the ship.

"The problem seems to be to carry the boats inside the ship's lines, so that they won't be swept away, and yet at all times outside the davits, so that the difficulties of swinging and staying will be obviated. The Mallory [555] davit has much to recommend it, although it was patented in 1871. It keeps the boat inboard and yet outside the davits and has no need of guys. The davits move forward on a hinge when the boat is to be lowered. The *Titanic* was fitted with the newer Welin davits.[556] The *Carpathia*,[557] judging from the pictures which THE TIMES printed, was fitted with the old-style swivel out to a position ready for lowering,"

[554] The Board of Trade regulations had made no extra provision for larger ships, having not been changed since 1894, when the largest passenger ship under consideration was only 13,000 tons.

[555] G. W. Mallory – Boat Lowering Apparatus.

[556] A modified pattern of davit recently brought out by the Welin Quadrant Davit, of Hopetoun House, Lloyd's-avenue, E.C.

[557] The *SS Carpathia* came to the rescue of the *Titanic*'s survivors, who were adrift in their lifeboats.

Mr. Hyslop stated that he believed that if the *Titanic* had hit the iceberg head-on she would have been less damaged, and might even not have sunk at all, as only one or two of her compartments would have been damaged, instead of several being torn through, including the engine room compartment.

"In many instances, when an iceberg or rock is seen when too close ahead to clear it, the safety of the passengers and crew would be best assured by reducing speed as much as possible and striking head-on, without any attempt to clear the object," Mr. Hyslop said, "an example of this was when the *Paris* struck the English shore in May, 1899, without the loss of a life, and where the vessel was taken off and repaired. The *Paris*, unlike the *Mohegan*, struck head-on. A Captain knows the veering power of his ship and can always tell whether or not it is going to clear an object ahead".

Mr. Hyslop said that a number of new devices had been invented during the last few years for launching ship's boats, but in comparatively few cases had the steamship companies adopted these inventions.[558]

After all is said and done, more is said than done.

Clearly, the whole question of the technical development of a ship's lifeboats remained largely unaddressed and was a hit-and-miss affair for saving life, when confronted with imminent disaster.

The largest rescue in the RNLI's history took place on the 17th March 1907 when the 12,000 tonne liner *SS Suevic* hit the Maenheere Reef, a mile off Lizard Point in Cornwall. In a strong gale and dense fog, RNLI lifeboat volunteers rescued 456 passengers, including 70 babies. Crews from The Lizard, Cadgwith, Coverack and Porthleven rowed out repeatedly for 16 hours to rescue all of the people on-board. Six silver RNLI medals were later awarded to two members of the crew of the steamship *Suevic*.

You know who the good seamen are when the storm comes.

The Royal National Lifeboat Institution is still an active force in Falmouth and is on constant call-out to distressed mariners and to members of the general public, who find themselves in peril at sea. This service is in close collaboration with the Coastguard agency. The latter organization was under threat in 2011, in a cost-cutting exercise, being undertaken by the Government of the day. Commonsense prevailed, and the Falmouth Coastguard was reprieved. With this unforgiving coastline and with that malevolent group of rocks lying in wait at the entrance to Falmouth Bay, the maritime fraternity and others are much relieved to know these excellent services are still readily to hand, to preserve life and to coordinate rescue strategies.

On one occasion, a Cadgwith lifeboat coxswain was told, "You can't go out in a sea like that" to which the coxswain replied: "We have to go out; we don't *have* to come back."

As this book was being prepared for publication, a luxury 144,000-ton, Italian-owned cruise liner, the *Costa Concordia,* sailed off course and struck rocks a few hundred metres from the tiny Tuscan holiday island of Giglio, on Friday 13th January 2012. Quite quickly, she listed and in keeling over, revealed a 45 metre gash in her hull.

---

[558] *The New York Times;* 23rd April, 1912.

A massive coastguard rescue and evacuation operation was launched, and despite some panic among passengers the vast majority of more than 4,200 people on board made it to safety. As with the *Mohegan,* there was great difficulty in launching the ship's lifeboats, particularly on the port-side, due to the ship's list. Many jumped overboard and swam to shore. There were 32 deaths and the Prosecutor arrested both the captain, and the officer who was on the bridge at the time of the accident.

This disaster took place exactly 100 years after the most famous maritime disaster: the *SS Titanic.* One is led to believe that a ship, in the 21st century, could hit rocks, run aground, and *still* float, as there are so many safety measures in place that it would be practically impossible for a ship of that size to tip over.

It is indeed a salutary message that, even with the sophisticated computer-controlled maritime navigation now available to a vessel, it all comes to naught when the hand of human error rests upon the tiller.

Never respect men merely for their riches, but rather for their philanthropy.

There were many fundraising events staged, to help financially support the bereft families of the crew members who had lost their lives in the *Mohegan* disaster. One such report appeared in a London newspaper:

> The proprietors of the Queen's, Poplar,[559] Messrs. Tom Maltby, Williams, Wickes & Co., have generously granted the use of their hall for a benefit on behalf of the relief fund for the widows and orphans of those who went down in the wreck of the *Mohegan.* Dec. 6th is the date fixed.[560]

Presumably, the takings from the show on that night would have been donated to the fund. The Poplar district of London was home to many of the crew of the *Mohegan.* Another spontaneous fund-raising event was reported as having taken place in Falmouth:

> At Falmouth the amount collected in the town and neighbourhood towards the *Mohegan* Relief Fund is £129, including the receipts of the concert got up by Messrs. Spooner and Co.'s employees.[561]

If you have, give; if you lack, seek.

THE COUNTY NEWS.

The total received in aid of the *Mohegan* Fund by C. G. Fox and Co., at Falmouth, and Mr. M. A. Toulson
, at the Falmouth Sailor's Home, up to Saturday, was £68 8s.[562]

[559] The *Queen's Palace of Varieties* theatre, 275/277/279, Poplar High Street [a local amenity for many of the *Mohegan*'s crew and families]. It was originally built as a music-hall, called The New Albion Theatre, which was attached to a public house and built in 1856. The Theatre later became known as the Oriental and then the Queen's Arms Palace of Varieties and Public House. This music-hall, built at a cost of £7,000 had a capacity of 800 people. The building was entirely reconstructed in 1898 and this new purpose built theatre with an auditorium on three levels – Stalls, Circle, and Gallery – had the much larger capacity of 1,360. The theatre was demolished in 1964. Courtesy: The Music Hall And Theatre History Website; arthurlloyd.co.uk.

[560] *The Era;* London England, Saturday, 19th November 1898.

[561] *The Royal Cornwall Gazette Falmouth Packet, Cornish Weekly News, & General Advertiser*; Thursday, January 19th 1899

These events represented but a few of such activities, as the *Mohegan* tragedy gripped the country's attention and prompted a variety of charitable institutions, engaging themselves with this popular cause. The Lloyd's Gazette and Shipping List [563] detailed assistance given to the crew members and to their families. Capt. Ivey of the Relief Office of the Shipwrecked Mariners Society, of Dock Street, East London, subscribed to the immediate needs of the families of the twenty-eight men who were drowned. Most of these families lived in or around the East End of London.

The London commercial institutions were sufficiently moved to help the fundraising cause, and showed a particular generosity in this regard. Note the substantial donation made by the Atlantic Transport Line. The modern day equivalent is bracketed alongside each donation figure:

The following letter speaks for itself:

Sir,—We beg to inform you that the following gentlemen have consented to act as a committee in the distribution of this fund, to which you already have been kind enough to make reference in your columns. i.e. : Mr. John P. Hooper, 31 Lombard Street, E.C.; Mr. Alexander Howden (Messrs. Alexander Howden and Sons, Leaden-hall-street, E.C.); Mr David Wills (Messrs. Wills, Faber and Co, of Lloyd's, London, E.C.); Mr. Frank Holman (Messrs. John Holman and Sons, 50 Lime-street, E.C.); Mr. Henry Langridge, Great St. Helens, London, E.C.

Williams, Torrey and Field Ltd.,

Alfred S. Williams, Director.

100 Fenchurch-street, London, E.C., October 26, 1898.

The fund already amounts to £2,600 [£148,000]. The Atlantic Transport Line have given £2000 [£114,000]; Messrs. Williams, Torrey and Field £200 [£11,000]; Messrs. Robartes, Lubbock and Co.,[564] 50 guineas [£3,000]; the London Grain Elevator Company,[565] 50 guineas [£3,000] and Mr. J. P. Hooper £50 [£2,800].[566]

---

[562] *The Royal Cornwall Gazette Falmouth Packet, Cornish Weekly News, & General Advertiser;* Thursday, November 24th 1898.

[563] Lloyd's List is one of the world's oldest continuously-running journals, having provided weekly shipping news in London as early as 1734.

[564] This private bank was established in London in 1860 through the merger of Lubbock, Forster & Co (established in 1772) and Robarts, Curtis & Co (established in 1791). It was the last private bank to have a seat in the London Clearing House. In 1914, a year after the death of its senior partner Sir John Lubbock, later First Lord Avebury, one of the City's most influential bankers, the firm merged with Coutts & Co of London. It then had reserves of £500,000 and customer balances of well over £4 million.

[565] The London Grain Elevator Company was located in the London Docks and were principally engaged in removing grain stocks from transatlantic liners, particularly those of the Atlantic Transport Line: the *Minnehaha* and her sister ships. A newly designed grain elevator derrick, the 'Grasshopper' was designed, in collaboration with Mr. A. S. Williams of the Atlantic Transport Line: *The Sydney Mail* – July 1st 1903.

[566] *The Royal Cornwall Gazette Falmouth Packet, Cornish Weekly News, & General Advertiser;* Thursday, November 3rd 1898.

CHAPTER 17

The Royal Cornwall Sailors' Home

"Where he goes and how he fares,
No one knows and no one cares." [567]

An adoption of the *Mercantile Marine Act – 1850*, and with its further amendments, was a first step towards the establishment of a new Sailors' Home movement, and the foundational home was introduced in the United Kingdom in the same year:

SAILORS' HOMES.—The first sailors' home, under the recent Mercantile Marine Act, is to be established, it is understood, at Plymouth. The 43rd section of the (13th and 14th Victoria, cap. 93) states that it is expedient to encourage sailors' homes in the seaports of the United Kingdom. The Board of Trade, or a local marine board, appointing any person to be a superintendent or shipping master, connected with a sailors' home, may authorize the whole or any portion of the fees paid at any such office to be appropriated for the use of such home. The Board of Trade, in the Post of London may appoint any superintendent of any sailors' home, or any other person connected therewith, to be a shipping master, with such clerks and servants as may be necessary, and all shipping masters, deputies, clerks, and servants so appointed, and all shipping offices so constituted in the Port of London, are, to be subject to the immediate control of the Board of Trade, and not to the local marine board of the port. [568]

A description of the aims for encouraging a safe haven for seamen is explained in this particular address:

In one of the annual reports, Captain Elliot [569] said—"The Sailors' Home was established to preserve sailors from the temptations and depredations to which they are exposed in London on returning from sea. Sailors are often to be seen wandering about the streets in rags and this was because they had no place to go to with safety to themselves on coming ashore. A home was the very thing a sailor wanted. I heartily approve of these institutions, and if I had arguments at command I would use all I could find to induce Christian ladies and gentlemen to support them. In a national view they are incalculably advantageous to the country. The Sailors' Home is a kind of nursery for good seamen, and the country is at present very much in want of good seamen, and it is impossible to say how soon that want might be considerably increased. [570]

---

[567] *The Royal Cornwall Gazette, Falmouth Packet, and General Advertise;* Friday, September 05, 1851. This couplet was intoned by Capt. Hall, R.N. at a support meeting as the introduction for a Sailors' Home at Falmouth, to draw attention to a sailor's lot in the 19th century.

[568] *The Royal Cornwall Gazette, Falmouth Packet, and General Advertiser* (Truro, England), Friday, October 25, 1850.

[569] Sailors' Home, Well-street, was originally founded in 1828 by Captain Robert James Elliot, RN., Admiral G. C. Gambier, and Lieut. R. Justice, R.N., who, in the previous year, had successfully started the Destitute Sailors' Asylum.

[570] The website of the Anglican parish of St George-in-the-East with St Paul is: http://stgite.org.uk/floatingchurch.html.

In the year 1852, the Falmouth Sailors' Home was established, and it played a major role in caring for the victims of the many shipwrecks, as well as providing a safe haven for visiting seamen.

From its major benefactor, Barclay Fox,[571] in his journal, there is a reference to a meeting, convened to promote the establishment of the Falmouth Sailors' Home:

> Attended a very interesting meeting held by the Hon. Capt. Elliot to advocate the cause of the Sailors' Home & the Destitute Sailors Institution, twin societies & the most admirable in their working & most judicious in their management of any Benevolent Societies in the Kingdom. Elliot spoke feelingly & beautifully. Capt. Plumridge, who was in the chair, cried like a child, as did several others.[572]

Clearly, an emotional meeting!

Nailing one's flag to the mast.

An address by Mr Alfred Benjamin Duckham, Secretary for the committee, encapsulates for us the core values for the Sailors' Home movement and the reasons for its proposed inauguration at Falmouth:

AN ADDRESS
FROM THE COMMITTEE OF THE CORNWALL
SAILORS' HOME AT FALMOUTH.

The necessity of these institutions is now so obvious, that in a nation like Great Britain the claims of Seamen to general sympathy and assistance only require to be brought prominently before the public mind to ensure support. The character of Seamen possesses many striking features fitted to secure respect. They are, as a class, bold, brave, and generous; but, as their occupation excludes them so much from the rest of mankind, they are compatively totally ignorant of the social relations of a community on shore. The value of seamen may be briefly stated:—They are, under Providence, the great connecting link of the nations of the world; all countries should, therefore, be interested in their welfare. To their instrumentality we are indebted for many of the comforts and luxuries which we enjoy; how often do our tables bear the produce of the East and West Indies, and other distant countries, which have been brought to us by means of their efforts, and in accomplishing which they are exposed to storms, changes of climate, and all the various dangers incident to a seafaring life. With the extended commercial machinery of modern times, it may appear, while we are enjoying our comfortable meal, in one sense, as if we individually traded directly with those distant regions, the produce of which may be before us, and which is obtained by us without trouble, and at a comparatively small expense. We should reflect on the toil, privations and labour that are required in conveying such necessaries and luxuries to us. These considerations should, at least, induce us to sympathise with the men who devote themselves to such a hazardous profession; and surely, in addition to their hard-earned wages, we should rejoice to welcome them to port, to guide, instruct, and protect them from

---

[571] Robert Barclay Fox (1873–1934) was a Falmouth businessman and Conservative Party politician in Cornwall. He was an industrialist, Quaker, traveller and a Cornishman. Barclay Fox supported the Royal Cornwall Polytechnic Society. He was its Vice-President 1909–1912. Its Annual Report 1934 included a photographic portrait of him. Barclay Fox also followed his family in his interest in horticulture and continued his father, grandfather and great-grandfather's development of Penjerrick [garden, created 200 years ago by the Fox family]. He became the senior partner in the conglomerate business, G.C. Fox & Co (originally a Shipping Agent). He was a director of the Falmouth Dock Board and Consul for Denmark and Vice-Consul for Norway, Germany and Finland. The King of Norway awarded him a knighthood of the order of St. Olav—*WikiPedia.*

[572] Barclay Fox (Author), Professor R.L. Brett (Editor), Charles Fox; *Barclay Fox's Journal 1832 – 1854.*

those who would deceive them and plunder them, and to unite in endeavours to do them all the good in our power while they continue under our influence. In the history of our sea-girt island, seamen have never been wanting to guard our commerce, and protect our shores.

Let us for a moment reflect on the Great Exhibition of All Nations of 1851,[573] all the plans about which would be unavailing without the instrumentality of seamen. And may we ask, who conveys the Christian Missionary to his distant post? How are the blessings of Christianity and civilization to extend without their aid? By steady and persevering efforts to advance the character of the British Seamen, we tend to advance the national character of which they are, in one sense, the representatives in foreign climates. To evince our sense of their value, it is our duty and interest to have Sailors' Homes at every seaport in the United Kingdom, where seamen could be boarded at a just and reasonable charge, their property taken care of, and encouraged to preserve their earnings by means of a Savings' Bank; and where, at the same time, they themselves should be given every facility for improving their minds and advancing their professional character.

Happily the great and mighty spirits of the times, advancing in every direction and in every circle, has for the benefit of Seamen visited this county. The efforts of not a few of the most respectable and disinterested portion of the community of this neighbourhood, assisted by that philanthropic and gallant officer Capt. Hall, R.N., were early in the month directed towards consulting as to the necessity of establishing a Sailors' Home at Falmouth.

By order of the Committee,

Alfred B. Duckham, Secretary. Committee Room, Falmouth, Sept. 24, 1851.[574]

And here, yet more public discourse on this same topic:

SAILORS' HOME, FALMOUTH—A public meeting was held at the Guildhall, Helston, on Friday evening last, for the purpose of expressing approval of this Institution. The chair was taken by Mr. MOLESWORTH St. AUBYN, of Clowance, at half-past six, and the meeting was very respectably but thinly attended. Captain SKENE and Capt. HEAD attended from Falmouth, as a deputation to explain the objects of the Institution. The meeting was very ably addressed by the Rev. W. Thomas, Rev. E. BOGER, Rev. M. WILSON, and Mr. F. HILL, and Messrs. FANING and ROGERS. Resolutions were passed approving of the establishment of a sailors' home at the port of Falmouth, and pledging support to the establishment. A committee was appointed consisting of the magistrates, ministers, and gentlemen of the town and neighbourhood, for the purpose of obtaining subscriptions and donations, and otherwise advancing the objects of the Cornwall Sailors' Home.[575]

[573] History's first real World's Fair took place in the newly built Crystal Palace in London and at the glittering opening England showed their national achievements. It was the first major effort in World fairs and it was a success since it was the largest trade show the world had ever seen. The event had six million visitors. The exhibition would include 13,937 exhibitors of whom 6,556 were outside the UK.

[574] *The Royal Cornwall Gazette, Falmouth Packet, and General Advertiser*s; Friday, September 26th 1851.

[575] Ibid.

Religion is the basis of civil society, and the source of all good and of all comfort.

The establishments had evolved from a concept, adopted by religious bodies, which were ever vigilant to the wellbeing of the maritime fraternity, engaging with their spiritual as well as temporal needs. The following piece shows a typical evolution, for a sailors' home:

DESTITUTE SAILORS' ASYLUM

The Asylum opened in 1827, originally in an old warehouse in Dock Street,[576] with bread and soup in the basement and straw laid in the upper stories for sleeping quarters. A more permanent base followed at 23 Well Street. Its purpose was to provide shelter and relief, with food and clothing, for distressed seafarers of all nations who had not left their last ship more than a year, and to assist them to find work. A discharge-ticket from the *Dreadnought* Hospital Ship at Deptford was an automatic passport into the asylum. The old and infirm had their passages home paid for, and others were helped to get into hospitals and infirmaries around London. Morning and evening prayers, and the Scriptures, were regularly read, with a sermon every evening at 7pm. The Asylum helped about 1,500 men a year, and had a good track record of enabling them to find work. A contemporary commentator said its arrangements are well worth imitation in lodgings for the lowest class, such as ragged school boys, and common beggars—a description of lodging-house much needed, and which has not yet, as far as we know, entered into the plans of either of the great societies now in operation. In due course it was run in parallel with the Sailors' Home, and later changed its title to the *Destitute Sailors' Fund*, assisting those who were unable to pay for any accommodation.[577]

This extract further declared the objectives for the Falmouth venture:

The objects contemplated by this Committee comprise the following—to protect Seamen from imposition, and the evil designs of persons who are constantly on the look out for them, the moment they set foot on shore, and oftentimes before they leave their vessels; to provide for this neglected class of their fellow creatures a comfortable wholesome retreat, to afford them therein the best diet at a low price, and without profit, to have their clothes and bedding well cleansed, and mended when required; to encourage provident habits in their expenditure for a renewal of clothing by their obtainment of the shilling's worth for the shilling; to secure their hard earnings by means of the Savings Bank, in opposition to debauchery and dissapation, and, as a consequence being victimized; to prevent their month's advance notes for wages being mortgaged to appease the morbid appetites of themselves and others, who from the basest motives urge them on to depravity; to administer to the sick, by providing medical attendance, and by appropriating to each a separate and well ventilated room—there being no hospital or infirmary here, this provision is essentially requisite; to provide for the comfortless Mariner a habitation; to encourage Seamen to discipline, morality, and religion; to enable Seamen to value their individual characters, in the degree of their subordination to their superiors, and by their bearing in foreign climes; by recreation and a library to allure them from vicious propensities; to have them to join their ships in health, cleanliness and sobriety, at the hour stipulated, reversing the present and past—the prostate body, badly and dirtily clothed, in an intoxicated condition, forced out of some den of imfamy to join the ship, the delay engendering feelings, terminating in a magisterial investigation here, a foreign prison, or a muleting [a fine imposed] of wages for expenses, or for neglecting to join the vessel at the time agreed to on the articles. To admonish Seamen to avoid the course to the parochial prison,

---

[576] Dock Street is located in the London dockland.

[577] The website of the Anglican parish of St George-in-the-East with St Paul; http://stgite.org.uk/floatingchurch.html.

recently prepared for them, and also the borough jail. And as to non-residents in the Home; to provide refreshments for Sailors casually coming on shore, and a resting place when detained waiting for their Masters, to offer them a shelter from the pitiless storms and chilly dews of night, whereat Captains may find their men sober and happy. To effect so great a change from the existing state of things, is the end of the formation of the Cornwall Sailors' Home at Falmouth, in unison with those admirable Institutions already established at upwards of sixteen other Ports of the Kingdom.

Upon a moderate calculation the above necessaries might be provided for 1s. 6d. per day, per head, which would be a great saving of their hard-earned wages. No doubt comfortable Lodging Houses with unexceptional persons may be procured, but what Lodging Houses could afford the Sailor so many comforts at so low a rate? [578]

Given a challenge: rise to the occasion.

The Falmouth dignitaries took up the Sailors' Home venture as a worthy cause. They set about charitable works, in order to raise the funds for its inception:

THE CORNWALL SAILORS' HOME - The Bazaar in aid of the funds of this most valuable and benevolent institution, was held at Selley's Royal Hotel, Falmouth, on Wednesday the 6th instant and two following days, and realized upwards of £200. The spacious room was fitted up and tastefully decorated by the Bazaar committee, by whom, and the directors present, the most unremitting exertions were made to give full effect to the object in view. The deep interest felt in the welfare and prosperity of "The Cornwall Sailors' Home" was evident from the numerous and splendid contributions received, the crowded state of the room, with the elite of the county, and the ready sale of the elegant and tasteful articles exhibited, (many of which through the kindness of a lady of Falmouth, ever foremost in the promotion of all that is benevolent, were sent by kind contributors resident in London, Liverpool, and other distant parts of the kingdom). Lady RASHLEIGH, Mrs. G. C. FOX, and Mrs. W. WILLIAMS, presided at their stalls; the other Lady Patronesses were unable to be present, but magnificent contributions were received from many of those absent. The ladies of the Directors of the Home, and many others of the town and neighbourhood, presided at the remaining stalls; all of whom kindly exerted themselves to the utmost, and seemed to vie with each other in zeal for the promotion of this noble cause. [579]

From afar, subscriptions posted to the fund helped the cause:

THE CORNWALL SAILORS HOME—Among the more recent contributors to the society are MR. FREDERICK BENJAMIN and MR. JAMES ANDREW, both of Rio Janeiro, who have generously subscribed £5 each; also MR. J. K. LETHBRIDGE £2, 2s, and CAPTAIN COGHLAN, R.N., £1. 1s. We are informed that the institution will be opened on the 17th instant. The supporters, by pecuniary means, may feel an interest in knowing that LIEUT. CROKE, R.N. has undertaken, gratuitously, the office of superintendent and CAPT. HEAD, R.N., has been engaged to conduct the daily prayers at the establishment with occasional assistance. [580]

---

[578] Ibid.

[579] *West Briton and Cornwall Advertiser;* Friday, September 15th 1854.

[580] *West Briton and Cornwall Advertiser;* May 7th 1852.

Someone felt moved to put their feelings into poetry—perhaps wisely keeping their identity to a minimum. However, it does reflect the Christian sentiment of that time and with a genuine concern for a sailor's wellbeing:

SAILORS' HOME

To the Editor of the Royal Cornwall Gazette

Sir,

Having heard that it is proposed to establish a "Sailors' Home" at Falmouth, and that an appeal is being made to the public to raise funds for that purpose, perhaps the printing of the following lines in your valuable paper may forward the benevolent object, whose usefulness needs only to be generally known to ensure it abundant and cordial support.

The Tar who braves the treacherous deep
Beneath the azure dome.
In lengthen'd watch and broken sleep,
Dreams of a "Happy Home".

The voyage is o'er, the port is gained,
His native land is gloom ;
No friend to greet, his heart is pain'd,
And longs for a "Sailors' Home".

The perils of the sea are past,
The rock and angry foam,
The perils of the land still last,
But for the "Sailors' Home".

When unemployed, the haunts of crime
Entice where'er he roam ;
He flees temptation for a while
Safe in the "Sailors' Home".

The aged too, whose sins' dark stains,
Forebode the wrath to come,
May humble penitence attain
Within the "Sailors' Home".

Then lend your aid the 'Tar to save,
From sin's appalling doom ;
Shew him the Port beyond the grave,
The Christian's "Happy Home".

Truro, Dec., 1851. B. B.[581]

This concept for a Cornish Sailors' Home had attracted the great and the good, and through their hard work and commitment, the premises [582] were established, furnished, and opened for business in promoting the wellbeing of the many seamen who passed through the town:

On the occasion of the opening of the Sailors' Home, on Monday next, several of the clergy of the neighbourhood, and very many ladies residing in the locality, are expected to be present. Admiral Sulivan [583] no doubt will favour the meeting by

---

[581] *The Royal Cornwall Gazette, Falmouth Packet, and General Advertiser;* Friday, 2nd January 1852.

[582] It was established at 3, Bank Place, Falmouth (see fig. 3).

[583] Sir Bartholomew James Sulivan (1810 – 1890) was a British sailor and hydrographer, born at Tregew, Flushing, near Falmouth, Cornwall – *WikiPedia.*

presiding over the proceedings. This institution was one of the last suggested as most desirable to be formed, and through the energetic exertions of its friends, and especially of ladies, it is the first to commence its operations.[584]

Because all the sick do not recover, therefore medicine is not an art.

Given the rudimentary medical knowledge of the time, it is a credit to the Home that only 8 deaths were recorded for the year 1852. The Home was also used as a mortuary and as a venue for the coroner's inquests: where a seaman either died at the Home or was transported there from a ship in harbour:

The necessity of a Sailors' Home does not, to casual observers, appear so great at Falmouth as at the larger ports, but returns of the number of seamen who frequent this port and are known to need such accommodation lead to a different conclusion. The house is at present fitted with twenty sleeping berths. Lieut. Croke has kindly undertaken the duties as Superintendent, and medical gentlemen have volunteered their services free of charge. The directors desire to carry out all the objects contemplated by Sailors' Homes, but for these additional funds will be required, and they earnestly appeal for the necessary assistance. The past successful exerting of the ladies, interested themselves in the institution, and of the chairman of the executive committee, are gratefully acknowledged, through whom the entire contribution have reached the sum of £494 10s. 9d. of which nearly 100% has been expended in fitting up the House. In answer in application for support to Her Majesty the Queen through Lieut. Col. Phipps, Her Majesty has been pleased to require certain information, which the directors are now in a position to afford. They appeal to all who feel the importance of promoting the moral and religious improvement of our seamen to extend their aid to the Institution and congratulate its friends on the success which has already been secured.

THE RECTOR OF FALMOUTH moved the first resolution, that the report now read be received, printed and circulated under the sanction of the directors, and that this meeting tenders its heartfelt thanks to Almighty God for the success which has already attended the efforts of the county to establish a Sailors' Home at this Port. He acknowledged the compliment to his office and himself in the invitation to take part in the proceedings, and sanctify the commencement of the institution with prayer. The report they now heard was gratifying, and that the institution had commenced its operations so soon, reflected much praise on its managing officers. The objects of their solicitude were a class of men, not the least deserving our regards, yet the least cared for, and the most neglected. To them we are indebted for comforts and luxuries, for defence and security and the present undertaking is an attempt to do something in acknowledgment of the debt. Our seamen must be cared for, and not abandoned to corrupting influences leading to a moral degradation which fearfully retaliates the neglect of society. The sailor who has been accustomed to the comforts of a "Home" will not abandon himself to brutal pleasures and associations, but he will be prepared for every duty of his hazardous calling.

He congratulated the officers of the Institution on having done their duties so well, as he was enabled to judge from his inspection of the Home. He learnt that already twelve seamen had taken up their quarters in it and that its first act was the Samaritan duty of receiving a sick sailor boy. Its opening was an era for the town and neighbourhood, and he hoped that a blessing would attend it.

WILLIAM CARNE, Esq., seconded the resolution, which was carried unanimously.

The next resolution, "that this meeting feels deeply grateful to those friends who have so liberally contributed to the support of this institution," was moved by the Rev, Dr, Cope, who expressed his satisfaction that so much money had been

---

[584] *The Royal Cornwall Gazette, Falmouth Packet, and General Advertiser;* Friday, May 14th 1852.

collected, and his readiness, as it appeared more was required, to use his best exertions to increase their funds. J. Baynard, Esq., seconded the resolution.

Capt. Triscott, R.N. acknowledged the compliment to the Committee, who had worked unitedly and perseveringly, and had that day realized the first fruits of their labours.

The chairman then vacated the chair, and Capt, Triscott having taken it, J. B. Moorman Esq., moved that the full thanks of this meeting are due, and cordially tendered to Admiral Sulivan for his kindness in taking the chair, which being unanimously and heartily carried, was acknowledged by the Admiral, and the meeting separated.[585]

The above record of the meeting illustrates the Victorian attitudes, mores, and social structures, more than it intended: a mere reference to the, "ladies," and with not one of its representatives referred to by name; the attendance of the upper echelons of county life, much decorated, lauded and given due deference; and the iron grip of the instruments of Empire: the Queen, Church, and the Military. The lower orders—ordinary seaman—were patronisingly addressed as the "sinner" ever burdened by the results of a weak moral fibre and with the attractions of alcohol and loose women. That is not to disparage the intended work of the Sailors' Home: indeed, it was to be much praised in its achievement. A sailor was, without a doubt, exposed to danger; not only at sea, but equally on dry land. In a foreign port, and with no moral compass with which to steer, no friendly face or a secure place to rest his head, a Sailors' Home reached out and gave him those comforts, and in offering him a safe haven.

God Save the Queen!

Having made representation to Her Majesty the Queen, the royal response is recorded here:

FALMOUTH EXPRESS

In reply to a letter from the Directors of the Cornwall Sailors' Home, we have the highest gratification in announcing that Her Most Gracious Majesty, "being strongly impressed with the importance and beneficial effect of the establishment of the Sailors' Home," has been pleased to present the munificent donation of £50 in aid of the funds of the above Institution, at Falmouth.

—The Right Hon. The Earl Spencer has most liberally contributed £10 in aid of the funds of the Cornwall Sailors' Home. The Hon. Mrs. Agar, of Lanhydrock, has presented 10/- [10 shillings] and Mr. Robartes, M.P., 10/- as a donation, and an annual subscription of £1 1s [also known as a *guinea*—21 shillings].[586]

The curse of two-legged land-sharks.

There was much concern over the immoral behaviour of the sailor. The usual culprits, known as the four cardinal maritime vices, were: promiscuity, drunkenness, swearing and the desecration of the Lord's Day. An early argument in the favour of a London Sailors' Home had been that the outward-bound seaman seemed

---

[585] *The Royal Cornwall Gazette, Falmouth Packet, and General Advertiser;* Friday, 21st May 1852.

[586] *The Royal Cornwall Gazette, Falmouth Packet, and General Advertiser;* Friday, 18th June 1852.

predestined to go only, "from the brothels of Wapping to the brothels of Calcutta". People were only too aware of the close connection between sailortown prostitution[587] and the crimping system.

The Falmouth Sailors' Home concept had become a reality and every contribution, monetary or otherwise, helped the cause and the inauguration of the establishment duly took place. A local newspaper covered the event:

FALMOUTH EXPRESS

CORNWALL SAILORS' HOME.—The ceremony of opening the Institution, which we trust will promote the welfare of the seamen frequenting the port of Falmouth, their comfort, morals and interests both temporal and spiritual and whose necessity is the more manifest, now that the prospect of an immediate commencement of the Cornwall Railway holds out the expectation of a speedy and great increase of the trade of the Port, took place on Monday. We regret that the pressure of other matters of great importance and interest to the county, allows us to give only a condensed report of the proceedings.

The attendance was so large, as to make it necessary to adjourn to the long room of the Custom House. The Naval gentlemen present were, Rear Admiral Sulivan. C.C., Capt. Skene, inspecting commander, Capts. Griffin. Triscott, Henderson, Head. Moorman, Lieutenant Croke, Lieut. J. T. MacDougal, R.M., J. Caddy Esq., R. N., and T. Hubbard, Esq., R.N.; with the parochial clergy of Falmouth, J. Shelley, Esq., collector of the Customs, Major Wynter, Lieut. Sutton, E.I.S., Lieut, Triscott, with several gentlemen of the town, and a large attendance of the most influential ladies.

On the motion of Capt. Triscott, Rear Admiral Sulivan was called to the chair by acclamation and the Rev. the rector of Falmouth having commenced the proceedings with prayer, the chairman called on the secretary, Mr. A. B. Duckham, to read the report.

The report expressed the gratification of the manager at the meeting the friends of the institution on the completion of their work of benevolence, and congratulated them on having accomplished their undertaking within so short a time, surpassing in this respect the efforts to establish similar institutions at other ports. It is alluded to the in the origin of the present home, to which the first impulse was given by the visit of Capt. Hall,[588] about eight months since. The necessity for a Sailors' Home does not, to casual observers, appear so great at Falmouth.[589]

Nevertheless, the growing reputation of the movement attracted the attention from the highest level:

CORNWALL SAILORS HOME,—His Majesty the King of Sweden and Norway has been most graciously pleased, in consideration of the benefits which his subjects have received from the "Cornwall Sailors' Home," at Falmouth, to contribute the sum of £50, in aid of the funds of that institution.[590]

In researching the Royal Cornwall Sailors' Home, a bundle of legal documents came to light.[591] These dealt, in the main, with the leasehold for the property at either, No. 1 [sic] on the Bank, or No. 44 in Arwennack Street, Falmouth:

---

[587] A service given by the poor women, known as 'sea-harlots' or 'maritime Magdalenes' – Roald Kverndal; *Seamen's Missions: Their Origin and Early Growth.*

[588] Admiral Hall, R.N. – who was well known as Captain Hall of the *Nemesis.*

[589] *The Royal Cornwall Gazette, Falmouth Packet, and General Advertiser*; Friday, May 21st 1852.

[590] *The Morning Post* (London, England); Saturday, January 22nd, 1853.

- 1855 – Planning for a sick-ward to be installed was instigated.

- 1857 – A six months rental fee of £16 6s. 8d. was confirmed.

- 1864 – The negotiations over the leasehold from the lessor (Mr Sleeman – South Town House, Torre, Torquay) and with an alternative proposal to purchase the premises outright—the premises were purchased in October of the same year.

- 1866 – The Bank House Falmouth is formally recorded as the address for the Royal Cornwall Sailors' Home.

- 1895 – Details for alterations to the premises to accommodate a sick-ward were finalised.

Also among these papers was a pencil-drawn sketch of the three premises that go to make up Bank House complex, and showing the lessees, as at September 1868:

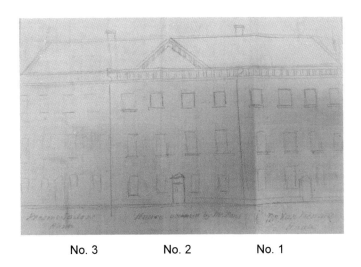

No. 3   No. 2   No. 1

No. 1   [Michael] Van Weisnen [?Welner] Huer & Co Ship & Commission Agents.

No. 2   Vos, Nathan; ship chandler and was also the keeper of the local inn – the "Marine".

No. 3   The Royal Cornwall Sailors' Home.

The Home was an exemplar of the Victorian ethos that, cleanliness is next to godliness, as intimated in this correspondent's piece:

"RAMBLER"—At the invitation of the genial Purveyor of the Sailors' Home, I recently paid that Institution a visit, and was much pleased with all I saw whilst he conducted me through the clean and well-kept premises. Beginning at the Smoking and Reading Rooms, it was gratifying to note the means adopted to allure those who resort to the Home from the many traps and snares which are so temptingly offered to unsuspecting and generous seamen in port. With some pride the portrait of Admiral Hall, K.C.B., the founder of Sailor' Homes, which was presented to the Institution by his daughter, was pointed out, as was also the library, which contains many Books suitable for the Home. Now we went 'aloft' where everything was

[591] Courtesy of: Plymouth and West Devon Record Office.

found in 'apple-pie' order—clean, sweet, and wholesome—the numerous dormitories presenting an appearance in these respects which would put to the blush the owners of many bedrooms which are not nightly occupied by 'seamen of all nations'. Thence we journeyed to the spacious Kitchen, which, like the Bedrooms in such a place, is most difficult to keep trim but here the general tidiness and good order which pervaded the whole premises were perhaps more conspicuous—brightly polished range with shining irons, dressers full of clean ware free from dust, table scrubbed almost as white as snow, mats and floors with scarce a blemish—all testified that there was a stirring somebody about who 'could not bide dirt.'—There were too many occupants of the Hospital to admit of my making a very close survey of this valuable adjunct to the Home—appliances of all sorts, comfortable cots, easy chairs for the convalescent, baths and bathrooms, with again the usual clean and tidy appearance—these must certainly be the proper features of such a place. I came away feeling that the Royal Cornwall Sailors' Home is an Institution to be proud of.

Donations and Subscriptions will be thankfully received by ALFRED B. DUCKHAM, Secretary.[592]

Indeed, it was something to be proud of. The establishment sounds a delight: cleanliness, comfort, and a stable environment; very different from the conditions usually encountered on board a ship, or in a local doss-house. The rather wholesome national operation was to be commended.

A rose by any other name would smell as sweet.

Her Majesty has pleased to approve of the name of his Royal Highness the Duke of Cornwall being announced as the patron of the Cornwall Sailors' Home. The Institution, therefore, will henceforth be designated "The Royal Cornwall Sailors' Home." [593]

Another aspect of the Home, and its service offered to the sailors, was as a hospital and all injuries or medical conditions, brought on by long voyages to foreign climes, were treated here. A sailor could be patched-up and sent on his way, either on the next voyage, or in returning him to his family home.

A gruesome story, reported here, in which a crew aboard a vessel had resorted to eating the ship's pet animals:

SHIPWRECKED CREW AT FALMOUTH.—On Friday afternoon, the steamer *Deptford*, of Sunderland, from New Orleans to Hamburg, put into Falmouth to land the captain and crew, nineteen all told, of the barque *Quebec*, of Nova Scotia. The men experienced terrible privations. The dog was killed and eaten, and the cat was being cooked when the steamer came in sight. The captain and the crew are in good health, and are now staying at the Sailors' Home. The *Deptford* took coals and sailed on the next tide.[594]

---

[592] *Falmouth and Penryn Weekly Times;* Saturday, December 20th 1879.

[593] (*Plymouth Mail*) – *The Standard* (London, England), Thursday, August 16, 1855.

[594] *The Royal Cornwall Gazette Falmouth Packet, Cornish Weekly News, & General Advertiser;* Thursday, February 9th, 1893.

The Home played an enormously helpful role in the aftermath of the *Mohegan* disaster. Indeed, one wonders how the authorities at Falmouth and surrounding area would otherwise have coped with the sudden influx of bodies, injured victims and with a significant administrative burden, that had accompanied this event. It is to the credit of the Home, its superintendent and his wife, together with the people of Falmouth, in providing the utmost care, concern, and comfort for the unfortunate victims:

THE LOST LINER

AN UNFOUDED SCANDAL

WORK AT THE SAILORS' HOME

(From our Special Correspondent)

FALMOUTH, Thursday Night.

. . . In connection with the loss of the steamship *Mohegan*, except that funerals of the dead are now of daily occurrence. This afternoon the funerals took place here of Mr. Horn [Alexander Horne], of Gateshead, who was going out in the *Mohegan* to observe the working of pumps of his own patenting, and Topham, the Texas cattle man. Both bodies were taken from the Sailors' Home, the coffins being covered with the Union Jack and wreaths supplied by local people in the absence of relatives. The Rev. C. A. Walker conducted the service at the cemetery, and there were present to see the last of the poor fellows some of the survivors of the crew, waiting at Falmouth for the adjourned inquest.

Since Saturday morning the Royal Cornwall Sailors' Home, Falmouth, has been a veritable house of refuge for people plunged into grief and misfortune by the loss of the *Mohegan*. On the morning after the wreck the survivor Maule, who was in the water for seven hours, and the corpse of the little boy Le Lacheur, both picked up near the Manacles by a tug, were taken to the home, and since then the establishment has been a scene of continual bustle and activity night and day. Altogether there have been nine bodies in the mortuary, and five injured people have been receiving medical treatment in the hospital, and these still remain. In laying out the bodies, attending to the requirements of the wounded, and in making provision for the thirty-one survivors of the crew who found lodgement in the home; Mr. H. Toulson, the superintendent, and his wife have earned the warmest thanks of the Atlantic Transport Company (specially conveyed by Mr. Williams, one of the managing owners) and all concerned.

Questions of identification and the removal of bodies have involved a vast amount of clerical work, and this has been undertaken by Mr. Bonham, secretary to the Home. Most of the crew have returned to London, where their homes are, having their fares paid by the company, and a half-sovereign presented to each. Today the bodies of Mrs. Le Lacheur and her little boy were despatched from the Sailors' Home for Jersey, via Weymouth, and that of [William] Kinley, an engineer, to London.[595]

The London Sailors' Home took it upon itself to organise help for the local families of the drowned crew of the *Mohegan*:

Capt. Ivey of the Relief Office of the Shipwrecked Mariners Society, at the Sailors' Home, Dock-street, states that he has a list supplied by the Board of Trade from the articles of the ship of twenty-eight of the men who were drowned on the

---

[595] *Daily News* (London, England); Friday, October 21st 1898. The tag-line in the sub-title, "An Unfound Scandal" refers to sories of valuables stolen from the *Mohegan*'s victims. This is dealt with elsewhere (see chapter 8; Pilfering: Beggars Can't Be Choosers).

Mohegan, and, acting for his Society, he is seeing to the immediate necessities of their families and those who have been bereaved by their deaths. The families are all living in or near to the East-end.[596]

The fall-out from the calamity was a testing time for the Royal Cornwall Sailors' Home, and almost overwhelmed the organisation and yet (rather touchingly) the superintendent and the staff of the Home were minded, and found the time, to attend the funerals for those who were many miles from their home, and with no one to mourn for them at the graveside. It was a most laudable and humanitarian act on their part.

You cannot keep out of trouble by spending more than your income.

The Home much relied on both public and private subscriptions, in order to survive. The *Mohegan* event was an opportune moment to bring the important role the Home had to play, to the attention of the general public. The help and assistance, afforded to sailors who had been overtaken by such disasters and accidents, was made available to all and with no embargo on foreign crews: all sailors were treated equally and without discrimination.

The following letter illustrates that most admirable ethos for the movement, coupled with an urgent need to replenish the Home's funds, much depleted by the *Mohegan* incident:

ROYAL CORNWALL SAILORS' HOME, FALMOUTH

Sir, —Would you kindly allow us space to urge the claims of the above institution which has for 47 years done invaluable service in the cause of humanity for our sailors by affording them a temporary home while in search of a ship, as well as to the more unfortunate ones who have been shipwrecked or have met with any misfortune whilst afloat, and who are in need of medical or nursing attention? While speaking upon the subject of shipwreck, we may call attention to the work done in the home in the case of the *Mohegan*, when this institution took the leading part in ministering to the needs of the rescued, the injured, and last, but not least, the dead—altogether nine corpses were received and prepared for identification by their friends to whom in the early days of that calamity the home was truly a "Home of Refuge"; 37 of the crew (5 of whom were injured and required medical treatment) also received the comforts of the home until they were sent to their destinations.

And here we may fairly quote the record of work done at the home in 1898, when there were received 181 Englishmen, 24 Norwegians, five Swedes, 11 Germans, three Frenchmen, 14 Italians, 10 Americans, four Russians, two Danes, one Austrian, one Greek, one Spaniard, one Maltese, making a total of 258 (quite independent of those received from the *Mohegan*, referred to above). Thirty-two of their number were shipwrecked and 55 were afforded treatment in the hospital. Our doors are open day and night and no really destitute case is refused. Who will help to carry on this excellent work? Subscriptions will be thankfully received and acknowledged by the Consolidated Bank of Cornwall, Falmouth.
Your obedient servants.
G. G. Pender, Chairman. S, Bonham, Secretary. Royal Cornwall Sailors' Home, Falmouth.[597]

Further subscriptions were forthcoming and including a welcome support from the Lords of the Admiralty:

---

[596] *The Standard* (London, England); Wednesday, October 19th 1898.

[597] *The Royal Cornwall Gazette Falmouth Packet, Cornish Weekly News, & General Advertiser*; Thursday, May 11, 1899.

THE CORNWALL SAILORS' HOME - Among the recent contributions, the directors acknowledge a donation of £10 by Messrs. TWEEDY, WILLIAMS, and co., bankers, towards the sick-ward fund, in addition to their donation and subscription for the general purposes of the establishment, - £5 from Mr. T. G. BARING, £1. 1s. from the Misses GEE, of London, who are at present making a tour of the county, and the following through the exertions of the wife of Mr. THOMAS L. STAPLETON, (late of the Customs, at Falmouth, but now the comptroller at Newport, Monmouthshire), Mr. W. C. WEBB, £1; Mr. JAMES N. KNAPP, 10s.; Capt. MAY, 10s.; and in small sums, £ 5. 7s. 6d. We understand that the Lords of the Admiralty have given instructions that in all cases of seamen invalided from her Majesty's ships, and landed at Falmouth, they be sent to the Sailors' Home.[598]

The Home had the perennial problem in seeking funds to continue its good work. Its fortunes were linked to the country's economic cycles, including an engagement in national wars:

The Sick: the Maimed and Shelterless Sailor

All the year round, at night as well as by day, the door of the Royal Cornwall Sailors' Home and Hospital, Falmouth, is open to needy seafarers of every nation. For well nigh half a century this institution has been performing its excellent work. The past twelve months have witnessed a continuation, and in some respects the completion of the plan of improvement inaugurated within comparatively recent date with the object of providing facilities for the conduct of the home. The year 1900 has, too, been marked by an increased number of cases of sickness, the excess up to the present being twenty. The incoming and outgoing of occupants is constant, and at times, often after severe weather, the demands upon the hospital are particularly heavy. Of late there has been a considerable drain on the medical, surgical, and nursing resources of the hospital. One day this week sixteen men were in the home, and eleven of them were on the sick list. Lately there had been added to the institution a new and convenient mortuary, adapted also to the requirements of post-mortem examinations, and the sanitary arrangements have received attention. The hospital wards contain ten beds. In the main building, on the ground-floor, there is a dining-room capable of seating twenty-four persons. Opposite, another apartment has been allotted to officers and those who find delight in reading. Thanks to the thoughtful friends, this room has nice bookcases and a good supply of English books. What is badly needed is suitable literature in foreign languages. Behind, a small department is set aside for the sailors' letter writing. Upstairs on the first floor, can be accommodated for sleeping or in sickness eight mercantile officers; this same provision is also available for officers or men of the Royal Navy. On the top floor are five bedrooms for twenty-four persons. If the home possessed more space in the front for dining and recreation there are occasions when it might be used to advantage. There has long existed the idea that structural extensions would be beneficial, but the way has not been cleared financially. Improvements already effected in other directions have entailed a good deal of expense. Recently Colonel Tremayne, one of the supporters, made an appeal to Cornwall—because the home has a just claim on the whole county—for monetary help towards the better equipment of the institution. That appeal was fruitful to some little extent, but doubtless the claims of the war [599] sufferers at the time limited materially the public response. By an extra effort, a considerable sum has been raised during the year in Falmouth and district towards the special outlay on very necessary objects, local friends having stood by the home well but in view of the all-national character of the work those responsible for the management naturally look further afield for contributions. This is above all seasons the one when fortunately-circumstanced people are moved by a desire to befriend those who are in very real need of assistance. And who is more deserving of practical friendship than the one rendered shelterless by shipwreck or laid low by disease or broken

[598] See http://freepages.genealogy.rootsweb.ancestry.com/~wbritonad/cornwall/1852/misc/jul.html.

[599] The Second Boer War; 1899 – 1902.

limbs? If during the festive season this institution should arrest the sympathetic thought of any west-country readers, Mr. H. Fooks, chief of the Customs at Falmouth (who acts as hon. secretary) or Mr. H. Toulson (the superintendent) would be grateful recipients of their gifts.[600]

Here, an example for a kindly donation to the Home, from a member of the British establishment:

The directors of the Royal Cornwall Sailors' Home gratefully acknowledge the charitable contribution by the Right Honourable Lady [Anna] Brassey of £5; also of conferment through Mr. Thomas Olver for the library, of the establishment, of copies of "A voyage in the Sunbeam," [601] and of "Sunshine and Storm in the East," volumes of her ladyship's composition.[602]

A fascinating insight in the setting-up, management and the day-to-day running of the Falmouth Sailors' Home, is revealed in a formal report which is based on the supplementary documentation, sent by the Home directors, in an application for the *New Order of Reward*: offered by the French Government, in association with the Paris Exhibition, of 1867.[603] Its ambition was explained in the following newspaper advertisement:

PARIS EXHIBITION.—REWARDS.

The IMPERIAL COMMISSION for the UNIVERSAL EXHIBITION of 1867, have issued the following ANNOUNCEMENT:

SPECIAL ARRANGEMENTS RESPECTING A NEW ORDER OF REWARD.

Art. 30. A distinct offer of reward is instituted in favour of the persons, establishments, or localities which by a special organization, or special institutions, have developed a spirit of harmony among all those co-operating in the same work, and have provided for the material, moral, and intellectual well-being of the workmen.

These rewards consist of 10 prizes of the total value of 100,000 francs (£4,000), and twenty honourable mentions.

One grand prize of 100,000 francs may, in addition, be awarded to the person, establishment, or locality, distinguished under the head by a very exceptional superiority.

Applicants who desire to claim the above-mentioned rewards must send in their applications and documents on or before the 1st November next, addressed to the Secretary of the British Commission for the Paris Exhibition, South Kensington Museum, London.

---

[600] *The Royal Cornwall Gazette Falmouth Packet, Cornish Weekly News, & General Advertiser*; Thursday, December 27th 1900.

[601] It describes Baroness Brassey's family voyage around the world in 1876–7 in their luxury yacht the *Sunbeam*. A guest among those aboard was Capt. Squire T. S. Lecky, a famous author whose works include *Wrinkles in Practical Navigation*; G. Philip (London) 1918. She was to die aboard the same yacht, in November 1886, from malaria, en-route to India and Australia and was buried at sea.

[602] *The Royal Cornwall Gazette Falmouth Packet, Cornish Weekly News, & General Advertiser*; Friday, October 1st, 1886.

[603] The Exposition Universelle of 1889 was a World's Fair held in Paris, France from 6th May to 31st October 1889—*WikiPedia*.

Naturally, the Falmouth Sailors' Home administrators were keen to take part in the contest, as recorded here:

> Special interest in the Sailors' Homes will be evidenced at the Paris Universal Exhibition in June; the several secretaries having been required to supply returns of varied character to contest for the new order of reward which the Imperial Commissioners have formed for establishments which have made special arrangements for promoting the welfare of particular classes. A request has been made that this "Royal Cornwall Sailors' Home and Infirmary for seamen of all nations" should be specially brought under the notice of the International jury, in connection with the new order of reward. It is believed that this Sailors' Home will take a high position on the roll.[604]

The Supplementary Documentation from the Sailors' Homes, in the United Kingdom, included the following sections:

1. Annual reports since 1852.
2. Placard showing rules and object of institution.
3. Specimen of register used.
4. Specimen of Superintendent's Journal.
5. Balance sheet for 1866.
6. Returns of Sicknesses and Nationality of Inmates, 1866.
7. Terms of Agreement with the Purveyor.
8. Terms of Agreement with the Medical Officer.

It is a happy coincidence that the Falmouth Home applied for inclusion in that contest, as it has left us with an historical document that reveals the workings of the Institution and for the Falmouth Home in particular.

The Falmouth Home return is taken as an extract from the National Homes' combined report:

STATISTICS FOR THE SAILORS' HOMES IN THE UNITED KINGDOM

The returns sent in by the Directors of several Sailors' Homes, as applicants for the New Order of Reward, will be found in the preceding pages.

As the Imperial Commission, however, expressed a special wish to receive full and precise information respecting this class of Institution, a communication was addressed to the Superintendent of every Home in this country, asking for certain details respecting it. And for copies of the reports which had been published since it was opened. The particulars in the following tables have been obtained from these reports, and by correspondence with the secretaries or superintendents, who have kindly furnished much interesting information relating to the Homes with which they are severally connected.

The Tables show that 29 Sailors' Homes have been established in seaport towns of the United Kingdom since the year 1835, when the Home in Well Street, London, the oldest and largest of these Institutions, was first opened. Many Naval Officers and others interested in the well-being of the 300,000 British seamen who are employed in the Mercantile Marine and Royal Navy, have assisted in the work of establishing and carrying on these Homes; "it were not easy in speaking of the establishment of Sailors' Homes, both in this country and abroad, to be silent as to the fact that it was to the exertions of

---

[604] *The Royal Cornwall Gazette, Falmouth Packet, and General Advertiser;* Thursday, 17th January 1867.

Admiral Hall, R.N.[605] (so long and so well known as Captain Hall of the *Nemesis*), that the success that has been hitherto attained is mainly due".

Cornwall Sailors' Home—Balance Sheet and Analysis Report – 1867 [606]

1.	Name of establishment.
	    a. Where situated.
	    b. Full postal address.
		"The Royal Sailors' Home and Infirmary for Seamen of all Nations". Falmouth, Cornwall.[607]

2.	Name of proprietor, or body of proprietors.	The premises are held in trust by a deed lodged in the Cornwall Bank on the part of Mr. William Carne and Mr. R. M. Tweedy, and the donors and subscribers of the second part.
3.	Name in full, description and address of the correspondent or secretary of the institution.	Alfred Benjamin Duckham, secretary and superintendent. [18 Arwenack Street, Falmouth]
4.	Principal object of the establishment.[608]	To promote the welfare of seamen.
5.	By whom was it formed?	On September 1st, 1851 by the following gentlemen:—Captain Hall, R.N., Captain Skeen, R.N., Lieut. Croke, R.N., Alfred Fox, Esq., Captain Miller, Thomas Hubbard, John Shelly, A. B. Duckham, Esquires.
6.	When was it established?	May 17. 1852.
7.	Have the works of the institute ever been suspended? If so, for how long, at what date and what cause.	No.

8.	State the number of persons at present employed, or received into the institution.
	    a. Adult males or females.
	    b. Young persons.
	    c. Children.
	    d. And the average numbers in each during 10 Years.
		Can board and lodge 54 seamen, each having a separate bed. Daily average throughout the year 1852–53, 11, which number has continued to be about the standing average. Notwithstanding the facility since afforded through railway transit, the average for sick occupants has increased to beyond 13 days per man; the stay of convalescents has, however, decreased.

9.	Are there any restrictions or qualifications for admission or employment in labour, namely,–
	    a. Age, and at what age? [609]
	    b. Instruction.
	    c. Apprenticeship, or other period of service.
		Admissions are unrestricted for seamen brought by their masters, and those sent by the consuls. Seamen generally applying for admission are readily received, if not deserters, or those known to have been guilty of disorderly conduct.

10.	What is the proportion of married females employed?	[No response]

---

[605] Admiral Sir William Hutcheon Hall, K.C.B., who died on 25th June, 1878; *The Times* announced that on that day he had, "Paid the debt of nature".

[606] See http://pooleygates.co.uk/wp-content/uploads/2010/09/Sailorshomes.pdf.

[607] There seems to be some debate over the Falmouth address for the institution: 3 Grove Place, 3 Bank Place, and Bank House.

[608] The London Home's response more pointedly reveals its objective prioritisation: 'To raise the character and improve the habits of seamen, by bring them under the power of religious instruction and within the influence of moral restraint, and provide them a board and lodging house.' Its hotel function, was viewed almost an afterthought.

[609] The Liverpool Home felt it necessary to state: 'Seldom admit under 14 years of age.'

11.	What regulations are made to enable them to attend to their families and domestic duties?	Inmates who are employed at daily work in refitting their ships are supplied with their dinners, which they take with them on going away each morning; or, if the vessels are in the docks, and it be so required, hot dinners are sent to them at mid-day.
13.	Has the establishment been remunerative, or otherwise?	Taken in a commercial point of view, at the prices charged to inmates, sailors' homes can never be remunerative or self-supporting.
14.	Is any pecuniary assistance received from the Government, or from any other body not participating in the profits? If so, define its nature and amount.	No pecuniary assistance is received from the Government or any other body in England. The Government of the Emperor of the French contributes £5 annually. Donations have been received from other foreign governments.
15.	Has the establishment any special privilege or monopoly of any kind, and what is its nature?	None whatever. It has to bear its burthen of local taxation in common with other properties.
15a.	Enclose a copy of all rules framed for the government of the establishment, or any information which specially refer to it, and any plans of the building.[610]	Plans of the new Home and of the newly built hospital have not been taken.
19.	During the last five years, what has been the average yearly profit per cent, and in what proportion and according to what principle has it been divided among— (1.) The partners or shareholders. (2.) The workpeople. (3.) Any other persons. (4.) Devoted to capital or other purposes?	No profit can ever be realized (see line 13). A day's bill of fare :—Breakfast, fried smoked bacon, two slices, and two eggs with bread and butter, coffee and sugar at will. Dinner :—A feed on roast beef, vegetables, plum pudding and beer. Tea :—Beef steaks and fried onions, bread and butter, and tea, sugar, and milk. At night a separate clean bed, with means for a hot or cold bath, and his clothes washed—for 2s.
20.	What are the daily number hours of work at the establishment, exclusive of meal times?	[No response]
23.	Have dwellings, at the cost of the establishment, been provided for the workpeople? a. Of what character? b. When erected? c. How many? d. At what cost?	a. Brick. b. Purchased in 1863.[611] c. Two. d. The purchase of the lease of the premises, refitting same to some extent, and the building of the hospital in its rear caused an expenditure of £1,000.
24.	What are the average weekly rents paid for such dwelling? a. By a family. b. By a single workman.	If seamen have the means they pay 14s. per week, their clothes washed (and beer) included and 16s per week if sick, which includes the day and night nursing.
25.	Are there any, and what, regulations made and enforced relative to periodical cleansing of the dwellings and workshops?	The dormitories are washed out once every week, sometimes oftener; the dining room and reading and smoking room very frequently are washed out daily by the purveyor's assistants.
26.	Is there any co-operative society, or arrangement amongst the workmen for the purchase of food or clothing, and how is the management provided and	The food for the inmates is provided by the purveyor (as per his agreement, abstract forwarded); constantly inspected by the superintendent, and from

[610] Interestingly, the Swansea Home felt that: "The committee decided upon not having any printed rules. Sailors dislike them, and feel that they are inimical to their freedom. Our rules are therefore only understood to be decent and proper conduct."

[611] An arrangement was made with the lessor of the present Sailors' Home for the purchase of the lease, but the terms were such as to be inadmissible and the premises now occupied by the Falmouth Docks' Company, having been offered to them upon highly advantageous terms, the directors had resolved to purchase the same subject to the approval of the subscribers. *The Royal Cornwall Gazette, Falmouth Packet, and General Advertiser* (Truro, England); Friday, June 26, 1863.

	paid for?	time to time by the directors.
27.	Do the employers contribute in any way?	Each of the directors contributes towards the funds. They inspect the affairs of the Home, and attend monthly meetings, and oftener if expedient, without fee or reward.
30.	State the proportion to the average of the locality of— a. The deaths of the workpeople employed. b. Their marriages. c. Births—legitimate. d. Births—illegitimate.	Average number of deaths of inmates, eight annually, seamen brought in the last stage of disease from their ships.
36.	Are any plans adopted for taking charge of the savings of the workpeople?	The superintendent receives into his charge the monies of seamen, as accounted for in his journal (as per sheet furnished). Each depositor has a voucher (as by accompanying form: (see fig. 5); each sum, when paid back, is tallied on the voucher and initialed by the depositor. Occasionally the monies are sent to inmates' mothers, sisters, or other relatives, which step is promoted by the superintendent.
37.	How long have they been in operation	From commencement of the establishment.
38.	What is the number of contributors, and the average amount of their savings?	The average amount annually in superintendent's charge fairly beyond £1,000.
39.	Are there any instances of savings invested in life assurance, and to what extent?	Inmates are induced to subscribe to the Shipwrecked Mariner's Fund. Some officers insure in the marine societies, but to what extent is not known.
41.	Have any of the workpeople joined a Trades' Union, or formed any such union among themselves?	No.
42.	Have such unions had any, and what influence upon, their hours, or modes of labour, or their rates of wages?	The rates of wages of seamen engaging by the month are on the average £3 at this port. The crews of British ships generally consist of men of all nations, which tend to avert the efforts of "Union" men as to seamen's wages. It cannot be supposed that the stamina of crews is improved by a preponderating mixture of foreign sailors.
43.	Have there been any strikes among the workpeople?	Frequently vessels put in here in consequence of the crews being dissatisfied. It is scarcely known of a native born crew of Cornish men shipped here from becoming disorderly.
44.	State— a. At what period. b. Of what duration. c. And the alleged causes.	c. The alleged causes of dissatisfaction chiefly are leaky ships, tyranny, drunkedness; on the other hand, particularly on outward-bound voyages, the crews having had a month's advance, at other ports raise objections, real or imaginary, if putting in here to get free of their agreements, while perhaps they have worked but one week, thereby taking advantage of the owners.
45.	By what means, and on what conditions, where they terminated?	1. By the crews running from their ships, 2. By the master's allowing them to walk over the ships' sides, 3. By the interference of the police and the magistrates. 4. By the discharging the crews to the ships' loss.

47.	Has the establishment given rise to hostile combinations among the manufacturers or workpeople of the locality?	The crimps [612] and runners are hostile, and were ever so; so are other low vagabonds who prey on sailors about the landing-places; to meet which, the Home at first kept a boat and two men to board every ship coming in to port. The superintendent now pays 1s per head to boatmen for each seaman who may remain an inmate 48 hours, brought by their means.
51.	What is its gross annual income, and whence derived?	The tabular form supplied will exemplify.
52.	What are the annual expenses of management? a. And of collection, where subscriptions are paid?	The secretary and superintendent £40 per annum, for his entire services of supervision, correspondence (almost endless), and the collection of donations and subscriptions.
53.	What is the number of paid officers?	Two, the secretary and superintendent, and the purveyor.
54.	And their salaries?	The secretary and superintendent (see 52) the purveyor, refer to the abstract of agreement furnished.
55.	The conditions on which the inmates are commonly received, and the average duration of their stay in the institution? [613]	All as a rule are received who are not deserters from ships, or known bad characters, or pronounced by the doctor to be infected with contagious disease. Their average stay. See question 8.
56.	The weekly cost of the inmate per head. If entirely, or in what proportion, it is defrayed from the funds of the institution, or in what other way?	The weekly cost in 1886 was £1 2s. 7¼d., of which 7s. was defrayed from the donation and subscription fund.
57.	Is any, and what, money allowance made to the inmates, and any, and what gratuity given to them on leaving the institution?	Sick and destitute men have from 3s. to 5s. given them in money and food, when leaving the Home for a distance and passage by steam through the influence of the chairman of the directors, are gratuitously allowed by the London and Irish steam companies; the Home receiving from time to time sick and hurt from their crews.
58.	State what has been the total yearly cost during the last five years.	In 1862, £171 11s 3d; 1863, £438 4s 2d; 1864, £561 17s 10d; 1865, £647 19s 2d; 1866, £594 1s 7d. These sums do not show "the expenditure" in each year, from the circumstances, that in some of them there were extraordinary payments, such as in 1865 and 1866, for purchasing the new premises, repairing the old on quittance, and in building the new hospital but they express what appears to be required, the "cost" of working the establishment.
59.	Is there any provision made to provide for, or encourage— a. Sickness. b. Education. c. Religious teaching.	a. 1862, £60 10s; 1863, £61 8s 8d. 1864, £2 6s 8d.; 1865, £54 3s, 1866, £37 18s (see medical officer's agreement). The doctor is paid 6s., or what amount for a fracture it may be, if the inmate has the means of payment. b. A well furnished library which the inmates have to

---

[612] Kidnapping or 'crimping,'– the role of crimps and the spread of the practice of shanghaiing resulted from a combination of laws, economic conditions, and the shortage of experienced sailors on the American West Coast in the mid-19th century. Some crimps made as much as $9,500 per year in 1890s dollars, equivalent to about $220,000 in 2007 dollars.—*WikiPedia.*

[613] The Swansea Home states that: 'Simply that they are seamen, of whatever nation or religious creed'. This suggests that there was no colour discrimination in place but that was not the case. The "Coloured Sailors' Home" (officially the "The Strangers' Home") was opened on 1857, in West India Dock Road, Limehouse, London, and this supports the assumption, that discrimination was a factor here.

d.   Recreation.

e.   Temperance.[614]

command, containing books in almost every known language, and comprising nautical, historical, geographical, arithmetical (elementary) books; likewise religious (approved) works, and select light literature

c. The visiting clergyman, when in attendance on the inmates, affords instruction in writing and in arithmetic, which enables those confined in bed to pass advantageously many an otherwise dreary hour, and cause their ailments to be partially relieved by mental exercise. The Home is open to all ministers of religion to attend to the members of their own flock. The bishop of the diocese has licensed a clergyman to attend. The Roman Catholic clergyman is very constant. The seaman's missionary visits daily. Several ladies and gentlemen also attend the bedside of the sick, and read portions of the Holy Scriptures in various languages.

d. Backgammon, draughts and chessboards; the library as referred to. Seamen do not care for exertion in physical strength on shore as a rule.

e. By the allowance of a half-pint of beer or porter to each with his dinner, the directors had in view to keep the inmates from the public houses, as a promotion of temperance, and this quantity of beer, as a rule (small as it is) is not requested to be exceeded.

60.   What has been the average sum spent, under each of the heads (ref: 59 a – e), during each of the last five years?

For "sickness" hurts (including broken limbs) £36 11s 9d. The clergy and ministers attending voluntarily, and without fee and reward, to instruct and afford religious consolation, and do so likewise do lay gentlemen and ladies. They also often bring fruit or other luxuries for the sick. Books are presented. The institution has an excellent library thus accumulated.

61.   By whom and, and, under what control, are funds managed?

By the directory. By having submitted to them, at their meetings, requisitions; possible for these, contracts may be issued; the bills on being turned in are examined and attested by the superintendent, and if approved by the board are signed by two members, after which the superintendents pays them, or draws a check on the treasurer; which check must be crossed by two directors before being cashed by the treasurer.

62.   Have you any other information to offer on this subject, or in regard specially to your establishment.[615]

From the situation of the port of Falmouth, its noble harbour is open to receive ships of ALL flags, and not a few enter the port in consequence of some matter in relation to their crews. Often vessels have sickness aboard through hard weather at sea, bad water for drinking, long passages, or want of anti-scorbutics.[616] This Home there from is subject to serious drawbacks, to which other homes are not exposed; because 1st. from its geographical position; 2ndly, from the large number of sick and hurt shipwrecked and destitute inmates it receives; 3rdly, it benefits those (foreigners as well as British) who do not themselves or their governments pay towards its expenses.

---

[614] The Swansea response, felt it necessary to include: 'The master of the home is a temperance man, and has signed the pledge'.

[615] The Liverpool Home reported that: 'We are comparatively empty at present, through the prevalence of easterly winds'. Proof indeed, that this was the age of sail.

[616] This relates to the treatment of scurvy—from the New Latin "scorbutus" meaning scurvy.

64.	Names of the persons, with their officers, by whom the affairs of the society are managed.	William Carne (Chairman), J. Baynard, Wm. Broad, A. L. Fox, J. Freeman, W. H. Bond, Esquires, and Major M. V. Bull are the directors; R. M. Tweedy, Esq., treasurer; Alfred B. Duckham, Esq., secretary and superintendent.
68.	What special means are adopted for scouring [617] the object of its formation? [618]	Good seamen (not bereft of their senses) need no special means to draw them to this establishment. The sick and the destitute are sure to seek the Samaritan-like care of this home. The home at first had a boat to induce seamen while on board their ships to come to it; its cost of £22 per annum was substituted by a payment £3 3s. to the coxswain of a ship agent's boat for dispensing cards. But this payment is now saved from the directors' conviction that those that have been inmates tell others and in fact because sailors' homes have attained a standing. The directors, however, encourage watermen to bring inmates (see line 47) in continuance by the payment of a small gratuity.
69.	Give a short sketch, with statistics of its progress, development, and present prosperity. [Copies of earliest and latest reports (including the balance sheets) should be filed with this form.	Enclosed last year's report. To prevent sailors going into bad lodgings, being robbed. The home is very prosperous. Building costs about £4,000 and fittings up. Now all free, no debt. Deposited by sailors about £900, and sent to friends. This home formed Sept. 1, 1851 in the first five months realized in annual subscriptions £61 5s 6d., donations £256 19s 1d. On May 17, 1853 the amount obtained was £494 10s 9d., which included £81 13s 9d. by collecting cards. During 1853 the sum of £3 3s. was deposited in the savings bank to form a nucleus around which to gather a fund for a hospital in connexion [sic]; this small commencement bore fruit so rapidly that in ten years notwithstanding many a struggle, the home became in a position to purchase commodious premises, and in its rear to build a splendid hospital. The future *fixed* outlay now chiefly only being fire and life insurances in addition to rates to the local authorities. In 1854 a ladies' bazaar realized £206 net. The annual donations and subscriptions have each averaged £150, equal to £300 per annum.
70.	In what respect does the society fulfill the condition on which a claim can be submitted on its behalf to the international jury, in accordance with the principles laid down at their first meeting?	1st. The institution originated from the, "spirit of charity and beneficence". 2ndly. The Home was a consequence of a "free and spontaneous initiative," which had been led to a magnificent result. 3rdly. The "praiseworthiness" of this institution. 4thly. The up-hill work this institution has successfully borne the brunt of truthfully illustrates that its prosperity has been energetically sustained and progressive. 5thly. The seamen benefited (of every clime) reckon beyond 10,800, whilst the institution is possessed of, and occupies a splendid property which cost a £1,000, but is worth much more. The success

[617] Scouring: To ferret out, find, or go over with a fine-tooth comb.

[618] The Liverpool Home stated: ' … that, besides the good effect of temperate habits produced in the men who frequent this Home, its good results are felt throughout the land in the amount of money saved from the grasp of the worst of both sexes, and sent to spend at home by the men in the bosoms of their families.'

attending the home is a constant source of wonder even to the directors themselves.

80. Are there any relief funds, asylums, or life assurances connected with the society and is any provision secured in case of future need?

The whole system of this home is one of "relief" more particularly the hospital provision.

The report also contained the following financial information, as well statistics for its hotel business:

I. The Royal Cornwall Sailors' Home and Infirmary for Seamen of All Nations, at Falmouth, opened in 1852 for 20 boarders,[619] now has accommodation for 54 officers and seamen. Commodious premises have been purchased, and a house built in the rear for a hospital.

II. In 1866 the number of boarders was 792, of whom 267 were foreigners. The average stay of the sick is 13 days. Since the opening of the Institution there have been 10,322 boarders, of whom one-third were foreigners. The weekly charge is 14s. for officers and men; if sick, 16s. (including nurses' attendance); 10s. 6d. for boys and apprentices.

In 1866 —

The number of	rations issued	—	11,257
The number of	beds occupied	—	3,970
The number of	casual beds supplied	—	175
The number of	casual meals supplied	—	163
The number of	shipwrecked seamen received	—	125

III

	£.	s.	d.
The gross income for 1866 was	794	1	4
Of which inmates paid (including medical fees)	295	10	0
Donations and subscriptions , &c. yielded	455	11	4
The gross expenditure was	850	2	10

nearly £200, of which went towards cost of building the hospital, and for the doctors' fees £13. 8s.
For the sick occupant the average cost to the establishment in 1866 per diem was 3s 2¾d; of convalescence the cost was 2s. 2d.
The outlay as salary to secretary and superintendent was £40.
The purveyor receives 14s. weekly, and sundry allowances.

IV.

	In 1866	Since the opening.
		£
The deposits by seamen	£. s d. 1,048 0 9	1,000 annual average.

V. There is a library in connection with the Home and also a hospital.

VI. Alfred B. Duckham, Esq., is the superintendent and secretary of the Institution. He has continued the Secretary from the first meeting of its originators.

The seaport towns in which Sailors' Homes have been established [1867] are:—

---

[619] This was later increased to a capacity for 54 boarders.

IN ENGLAND, 16, viz.:—

1. London, Dock Street, E.
2. London, Poplar, E.
3. Bristol.

4. Devonport.
5. Dover.
6. Cornwall (Falmouth).
7. Gloucester.
8. Great Yarmouth.
9. Hull.
10 Liverpool.
11. North Shields.
12. Plymouth.
13. Portsmouth.
14. Ramsgate.
15. Southampton.
16. Sunderland.

IN WALES, 3, viz.:—

17. Cardiff.
18. Milford.
19. Swansea.

IN SCOTLAND, 5, viz.:—

20. Aberdeen.
21. Glasgow.
22. Greenock.
23. Leith.
24. Stornaway.

IN IRELAND, 5, viz.:—

25. Belfast.
26. Cork.
27. Dublin.
28. Limerick.
29. Queenstown.

Homes have also been established,—

IN THE COLONIES, 11, viz.:—

Sydney.
Melbourne.
Calcutta.
Bombay.
Madras.
Cape of Good Hope.
Mauritius.
Hong Kong.
Shanghai.
St. John's, Newfoundland.
St. John's, New Brunswick.

IN FOREIGN PORTS, 9, viz.:—

New York.
Boston.
San Francisco.
Marseilles.
Havre.
Amsterdam.
Rotterdam..
Hamburg.
Callao.[620]

The 1854 *Merchant Shipping Act* further provided that the engagement of seamen for foreign trade voyages, must take place before a Superintendent, and laid down rules (based on observation of the Home's practice) to ensure that at the end of a voyage wages were properly accounted for and received:

> After the vessel had docked, the crew are paid off in the presence of a Board of Trade officer as soon as convenient and now-a-days are at once signed on again for the next voyage.[621]

---

[620] Callao is situated in Peru, and provided a rich source of guano, that was very important to the Peruvian economy in the 19th century. During the 1840s, the use of guano as a fertilizer, and with its Chile saltpetre content, was a key ingredient in explosives; making the area strategically valuable.

[621] Magginis, John, *The Atlantic Ferry: Its Ships, Men, And Working*; London, UK: Whitaker & Co.1893, 113.

A fool and his money are soon parted.

A seaman was able to place his pay in the safekeeping of the Home, through its internal banking system. Hitherto, a seaman had suffered the perils of the sea, the risk of being shanghaied,[622] cheated out his pay, suffering injuries on board, and fleeced of his hard-earned money—by the so-called 'land-sharks'—now at least, there would be a universal organisation that would offer care, security and sanctuary whilst ashore.

One religion is as true as another.

The London Sailors' Home had an all-embracing religious policy, as regards its approach to its patrons:

DOCK STREET AND QUEEN'S QUAY SAILORS' INSTITUTES

The report added—"No destitute seaman is ever refused help, be he Protestant or Roman Catholic, Mohammedan or pagan". [623]

An indication of the varied work accomplished by the Falmouth Home is conveniently recorded in the annual general meeting for the year 1886:

ANNUAL GENERAL MEETING

The house expenditure for the year amounted at £597 2s. 7d. Receipts, including £157 1s. 5d. contributions, were £557 9s 7d, shewing a debit balance of £12 4s. 9d. During the year there had been received—British 344, French 43, Norwegians 55, Swedes 49, Italians 25, Danes 7, Germans 39, Belgians 3, Portugese 3, Spaniards 4, Greeks 3, West Indians 4, Russians 3, Dutch, 3 Finlanders and 1 American. There had been 8 deaths. Money deposited for safekeeping or for remittance to inmates' friends amounted to £1,026 9s.[624] There were 105 inmates destitute, to whom half third-class railway fares were conferred. The period of occupation by healthy sailors was 780 days, and in the hospital by sick and hurt men 1,519 days. In addition, 148 breakfasts, 88 dinners, 153 teas, 147 nights' lodgings were supplied.[625]

This report truly conveys the mix of nationalities of the seamen, turning up on the doorstep. No surprise, given the thousands of ships from all nations that wended their way up and down the English Channel, and with some of their number calling at Falmouth Port.

Another service offered by the Home, was the holding of monies on behalf of the sailors, and with a safe distribution network to their 'inmates' and 'friends'. As can be seen above, large sums of money were handled on their behalf.

---

[622] Kidnapping or 'crimping,'– the role of crimps and the spread of the practice of shanghaiing resulted from a combination of laws, economic conditions, and the shortage of experienced sailors on the American West Coast in the mid-19th century. Some crimps made as much as $9,500 per year in 1890s dollars, equivalent to about $220,000 dollars in the year 2007.—*WikiPedia*.

[623] *The Belfast News-Letter* (Belfast, Ireland); Thursday, January 26th 1899.

[624] £61,507 is the equivalent in modern currency.

[625] *The Royal Cornwall Gazette Falmouth Packet, Cornish Weekly News, & General Advertiser;* Friday, 26th March 1886.

The ups and downs of life.

As with all charitable organizations (to this day), their fortune and opportunities fluctuate over time. The Royal Cornwall Sailors' Home was not immune to the ups and downs of the economic cycle, as expressed here in the record of the 1859 annual general meeting:

ROYAL CORNWALL SAILORS' HOME

It will be found on reference to the several reports that the funds of the institution have gradually diminished for the past two years, so that the reserve fund alone remains. It will be therefore evident that unless some very energetic measures are speedily adopted, such as a strong appeal to the county (this being the only establishment offering similar refuge to the mariner in Cornwall), and to the public generally, the decline of this philanthropic institution must unhappily result.—The directors regret also that their efforts to obtain funds for building or purchasing a Home have been responded to with so little success, that they have been deemed it prudent to secure a renewal of their present lease. Brighter prospects however seem not distant. The national value of this port, situated so advantageously at the entrance of the British Channel, is at length likely to be acknowledged. The commercial marine of the world evinces an increasing appreciation of its geographical position and should the proposed docks be completed (of which there is now but little doubt) a Sailors' Home will hardly fail to be recognised as the first indispensable provision.—Your directors, therefore, indulge a sanguine expectation that, before long, public support will enable them to afford considerably increased advantages, and a more convenient Home to that brave and hardy race of men who contribute to our individual comfort and luxuries, and constitute the strength and security. The wealth and glory, of the kingdom.[626]

The year of 1893 saw an unprecedented economic depression develop in the USA, dubbed the 'Panic of 1893.'[627] This undoubtedly led to a reduction in transatlantic maritime traffic, which would have had an adverse economic impact on trade and the UK economy (see Appendix 15: p. 462):

The depression set off by the Panic of 1893 was the greatest depression America had known, and was only surpassed by the Great Depression of the 1930s. In early May 1893 the New York stock market dropped sharply, and in late June panic selling caused the stock market to crash. A severe credit crisis resulted, and more than 16,000 businesses had failed by the end of 1893. Included in the failed businesses were 156 railroads and nearly 500 banks. Unemployment spread until one in six American men lost their jobs. The depression caused by the Panic of 1893 lasted for about four years, ending in 1897.[628]

A kind offer by one of the institution's directors realized additional financial savings for the Home:

---

[626] *The Royal Cornwall Gazette, Falmouth Packet, and General Advertiser;* Friday, 18th February 1859.

[627] In the United States history, the Gilded Age was the period following the Civil War, running from 1877 to 1893 and was a time of widespread economic growth as the United States jumped to the lead in industrialisation ahead of Britain. It heralded enormous growth that attracted millions from Europe and railroads were the major industry. This was followed by the Progressive Era, in which two 'Panics" occurred—1873 and 1893.

[628] See http://history1800s.about.com/od/thegildedage/a/financialpanics.htm.

Mr. H. Fooks, collector of customs, and a director of the Royal Cornwall Sailors' Home and Hospital, Falmouth, has been appointed honorary secretary of the institution, vice Mr. W. S. Bonham, resigned. This new voluntary service on the part of Mr. Fooks will be a saving to the funds.[629]

At the end of the 1898 year, the Home's balance sheet showed a reduced balance, from the previous year; notwithstanding a generous donation from the Miss Fox's legacy. This being the year of the *Mohegan* disaster, there would have been an exceptional draw on funds:

RECEIPTS				EXPENDITURE			
	£	s	d		£	s	d
Balance 1st January, 1898	97	4	8	Boarding	224	7	0
Home Boarding	318	5	5	Superintendent	110	1	8
Subscriptions and Donations	177	9	0	Repairs to House, etc.	33	1	6
Dividend on Investments	24	7	5	Fuel	20	0	0
Doctors' Fees	34	4	0	Rates	12	9	0
Mortuary Fees	6	16	6	Charity Cases	29	6	0
Miss Fox's Legacy [630]	20	0	0	Night Nursing	16	15	0
Sundries		2	6	Stationery, Printing, and Postage	5	13	0
				Bringing Seamen	1	0	0
				Secretary	30	0	0
				Doctors' Fees	39	12	0
				Life and Fire Insurance	12	1	0
				Purchase of Consols [631]	111	9	0
				Sundries		11	4
				Balance	31	4	0
	678	9	6		678	9	6

Table 11: The Royal Cornwall Sailors' Home: The Balance Sheet for 1899.

The business of the 1898 annual general meeting commenced:

---

[629] *The Royal Cornwall Gazette Falmouth Packet, Cornish Weekly News, & General Advertiser;* Thursday, 22nd February 1900.

[630] Anna Maria Fox (21 February 1816 – 18 November 1897—BMD: 18th November 1897, Falmouth 5c 103) was a promoter of the Royal Cornwall Polytechnic Society and the artistic and cultural development of Falmouth in Cornwall, UK. In 1896, Anna Maria Fox was elected as Vice-Patroness of the Polytechnic, sharing this role with the Prince of Wales—*WikiPedia.*

[631] Consols (originally short for consolidated annuities, but can now be taken to mean consolidated stock) are a form of British government bond (gilt), dating originally from the 18th century – *WikiPedia.*

THE ROYAL CORNWALL SAILORS' HOME

AND

INFIRMARY FOR SEAMEN OF ALL NATIONS

THE ANNUAL MEETING of the subscribers of the Royal Cornwall Sailors' Home was held on Tuesday, 9th May, 1899.

Those who attended had the pleasure of hearing an interesting and thoughtful speech in support of the claims of the Home by Mr. J. C. Williams, who presided over the meeting. Among others present were, Messrs. G. G. Pender, G. H. Fox,[632] H. Fooks (Directors of the Home), General Aylmer, Major Gibney, Rev, H. C. Deson, Messrs. Robert Fox, Howard Fox, Barclay Fox, J. Cole (Mawnan), R. N. Rogers, J. H. S. Burder, RN., F. J. Bowles, A. H. Lord, J. W. Buckley, and several ladies; Mr. and Mrs. Toulson (Superintendent and Matron of the Home), and Mr. Bonham (Secretary).

Letters for apology for non-attendance were received from Colonel Horsford, Messrs. T. R. and W. M. Grylls, T. Webber, and G. E. Marcon.

Mr. Pender, in opening the proceedings, said they had been most fortunate in securing the attendance of a gentleman so well-known and appreciated in the county as Mr. J. C. Williams—(applause).

Mr. Bonham, the Secretary of the Home, then read the following

———ooo REPORT ooo———

The Directors have much pleasure in presenting their 47th report. The year 1898 was eventful for the Home in many ways and more particularly in the case of the wreck of the "*Mohegan*" on the Manacle Rocks in October last. The Home was a veritable "House of Refuge" to the survivors of the crew and friends and relatives seeking the remains of their lost ones. Five of the crew who were injured were received, medically attended and nursed until they were fit to take their discharge. Although the number of survivors (including the injured) who were brought to the Home was 37 and the corpses of nine were also brought, these being all (with exception of four which were taken to the Town Mortuary) that were brought into Falmouth. These nine were prepared for identification by their friends. As often before in the course of its long and splendid history the Home again justified its existence and a Home which could in an emergency so terrible in its suddenness render such really practical help deserves all the kind words and support which sympathetic people can afford. The warmest thanks of the Atlantic Transport Company, to whom ill-fated "*Mohegan*" belonged, were personally conveyed by Mr. Williams, one of the managing owners, to Mr. and Mrs. Toulson for their many acts of kindness and sympathy so freely given to the rescued and the friends of those who perished. This terrible disaster brought before your Directors the need for increased mortuary accommodation upon sanitary and up-to-date lines, and plans have been submitted for consideration with a view to the erection of a mortuary to meet the demands of the Home, and other improvements such as the erection of a bathroom, and the remodelling of the pantry and out-offices of the Institution are contemplated, the total cost of which will entail a considerable outlay. Your Directors venture to appeal to all who are interested in the comfort of the toilers of the deep and the extension of the usefulness of the House at this the first and last port in the English Channel for financial support to enable these improvements to be carried out without touching the funds of the Institution.

The Boys of the *H.M.S.* "*Ganges*" [633] make use of the Home in large numbers on Thursday and Saturday afternoons, and much appreciate the privilege. Your Directors gratefully acknowledge the receipt of a communication from the Lords

---

[632] The Fox family of Falmouth, Cornwall, was very influential in the development of the town of Falmouth in the 19th Century, and of the Cornish Industrial Revolution. In the 18th and 19th centuries, many of them were members of the Religious Society of Friends (Quakers).

[633] The *HMS Ganges* was built in Bombay and was launched on 10th November 1821, subsequently arriving at Portsmouth in October 1822. After various commissions *HMS Ganges* was commissioned as the flag-ship of Rear Admiral R. L. Bayes on the Pacific Station and left for the Pacific in September 1857. On return to England in 1861 *HMS Ganges* entered the history book as being the last sailing ship to be a sea going flag-ship. In 1866 *H.M.S. Ganges* became the boys' training ship—anchored off Mylor, Carrick Roads Falmouth—where she remained until August 1899, leaving in-tow for Plymouth on Tuesday, 29th August, 1899. In November 1899 *H.M.S. Ganges* was transferred to Harwich harbour in Suffolk. It had accommodation aboard for up to 600 boys. The *H.M.S. 'Ganges'* memorial in Mylor churchyard commemorates the 53 boys, training for a service career, who died whilst training on the *H.M.S. 'Ganges'* during the 33 year period at Falmouth. (see Figs. 70-72).

of the Admiralty to the effect that they had been pleased to make a grant of periodicals, &c., to the amount of £ 12 per annum, which will bring the Reading Room of the Home more into line with the accommodation usually found at Sailors' Homes at larger ports. The Institution has sustained a great loss through the resignation, owing to ill-health and infirmity of age, of Mr. L. L. Haslope, who for a period of a quarter of a century has given the Home the benefit of his invaluable advice, and has, as Chairman, steered it through many vicissitudes, till it is, as your Directors are fully persuaded, one of the best managed Institutions in the Country. They have prevailed upon Mr. G. G. Pender, who has been connected with the work of the Home for some years past, to accept the post of Chairman in his stead, and for the vacancy thus created have been fortunate in the securing the co-operation and the support of Mr. Fooks of H.M. Custom. Captain Anson R.N., *H.M.S. Ganges*, succeeds to a seat at the Board in virtue of his command.

During the year 1898 there were received at the Home 181 English men, 24 Norwegians, 5 Swedes, 11 Germans, 3 French men, 14 Italians, 10 Americans, 4 Russians, 2 Danes, 1 Austrian, 1 Greek, 1 Spaniard, 1 Maltese, making a total of 258 (independent of the considerable number who came or were brought from the "*Mohegan*" and are referred to above).[634] Of these 32 were shipwrecked, and 55 were afforded treatment in the Hospital. After careful nursing and medical attention 51 of these were cured and 4 died. Owing to the seriousness of many of the Hospital cases, several patients having been landed with broken limbs, the aggregate number of days on which the Hospital was occupied reached the unusually large number of 2,147 shewing the average number of days to each case to be 39. The Home was occupied by healthy seamen for 427 days. 83 of the seamen referred to above received assistance to enable them to get to their homes. Your Directors desire to thank those charitable ladies and gentlemen who by their subscriptions and donations have made the grand work of the Home possible and through whose generosity such material assistance has been rendered to many toilers of the deep who have sought the shelter and the rest of the Home, of have been brought to be medically attended and nursed there until fit to resume their work, or go home to friends; also the Consular Authorities,[635] of the Port, the Great Western Railway Company, Mr. F. L. Earle (the local agent of the Shipwrecked Mariners' Society) are thanked for their ungrudging assistance to seamen, also the proprietors of the "Western Morning News," the "Western Daily Mercury," the "Cornish Echo" for gifts of their valuable papers. Thanks are also offered for gifts of flowers, fruit, vegetables, newspapers, periodicals, magazines, books, &c., &c. to the following ladies and gentlemen…[a list of the great and good of Falmouth and surrounding area, appears here].

Three Letters of Gratitude

The Secretary said he would like to read one or two letters which he had received. The first was from one of the survivors of the crew of the *Mohegan*, who wrote that he could not find words sufficient to express his heartfelt gratitude for the kindness bestowed not only to upon himself, but upon others of the ill-fated *Mohegan* at the Sailors' Home. He was sure that everything that could be done was done for the comfort and welfare of the survivors, and such a home as the Royal Cornwall he firmly believed for homely comforts and cheerful attendants could not be excelled,

---

[634] From the *Mohegan* wreck, 37 survivors were accommodated at the home. In addition, there were 12 dead, who were placed in the Home's mortuary for identification and with subsequent arrangements made for burial, by the officials of the institution.

[635] The title of 'Consul' is used for the official representatives through the hearing of the government of one state and in the territory of another, normally acting to assist and protect the citizens of the consul's own country, and to facilitate trade and friendship between the people of the country to whom he or she is accredited and the country of which he or she is a representative. Consul is not similar to an Ambassador and the duty of the consul is different than the duties of an ambassador. This distinguishes the consul from the ambassador, who is, technically, a representative from one head of state to another. While there can be but one ambassador of a given country in another country, representing the first country's head of state to that of the second, and his or her duties revolve around diplomatic relations between the two countries, there may be several consuls, one in each of several main cities, providing assistance with bureaucratic issues to both the citizens of the consul's own country travelling or living abroad, and to the citizens of the country the consul resides in who wish to travel to or trade with the consul's country. Their seamen, arriving at a port, were paid wages by the consul office.

Mr. A. E. Williams, one of the Managing Owners of the Atlantic Transport Company, wrote acknowledging the services rendered to the sufferers of the *Mohegan* catastrophe by the Home and the kindness and hospitality shown to the surviving members of the crew.

Mr. J. Barnes, whose son [William Barnes] lost his life in the *Mohegan* catastrophe wrote stating that he and his family wished to express how deeply indebted they were to the officers at the Home for the kindness shewn them. As an expression of their gratitude he enclosed £1 for the purchase of books for use at the Sailors' Home.

The Funds

The balance sheet read by the Secretary showed that the year was begun with a balance in hand of £97 4*s* 8*d*. and this with the income during the year made a total of £678 9*s.* 6*d*. After meeting the expenditure and purchasing £100 in Consols there was a balance in hand of £31 4*s*. 1*d*.

Mr. Pender moved the adoption of the report and accounts.

The Chairman, who was heartily applauded on rising to second this, said that those present were intimately concerned with the work it was not at all likely that he could add anything to the report, but there some remarks he would like to address more particularly, not to the Falmouth people, but to their fellow Cornishmen in other neighbourhoods. He had had evidence of the excellent character of the work the Home was doing, but in going over the Home he had been a good deal struck by the disadvantages they experienced in carrying on the work, more particularly in the buildings at the back, and he really thought they could fairly claim from their fellow Cornishmen and neighbours—and even from a larger, a wider circle than Cornishmen, but certainly from Cornishmen who had an intimate knowledge of the excellent character of the work—some assistance in re-modeling the building—(applause). He ventured to appeal to outsiders, because he was an outsider himself, and therefore came there with an impartial mind. It was quite plain to an ordinary observer that a seaport such as Falmouth at the entrance to the Channel must have thrown on it, by the very nature of its position, a quantity of work arising from the adversities of those engaged in shipping out of all proportion to its standing in the shipping world. That no doubt was the case here. So he thought he was justified in asking for some little assistance from our neighbours. There was some £150 necessary for rebuilding some of the back premises and putting them in a more suitable condition for the work. Personally, he would be very glad to contribute to the same, and it was important that the claims of the Home should be recognised by the man, he hoped others would contribute towards the sum. It did not need a great deal of argument to drive home to the minds of everybody the claim on them to assist in such work. Our forefathers were taught to pray against the, "terrible visitations plague, pestilence, and famine". That might now be revised or improved into a prayer against fire and shipwreck, for they were the two great disasters which hang over our heads in a more immediate ways than plague, pestilence and famine. And if they were to turn their mind to it for a moment they would have no difficulty in raising the sum required and he felt sure their neighbours would also gladly respond to the little appeal he made. (applause) Unless he was personally acquainted with the work he would not venture to appeal for support from his fellows elsewhere. (applause)

A Hint to Cornish Philanthropists

Mr. H. Fooks, in supporting, remarked that since the *Mohegan* disaster the Directors of the Institution had thought it necessary to provide improved mortuary accommodation, and with a view of carrying this into effect they had sought the services of Mr. Swift, architect, of Truro. There were very few ports where homes of this kind existed and when he came into Cornwall and found the Royal Cornwall Sailors' Home it greatly relieved his mind, knowing he would have a place where he could advise shipping men to go if they were sick or injured. The Institution was a home to seamen of any nation of the world; a place of refuge for the destitute, more valuable in the extreme, and there were many who felt the need of a home and comfort such as the Royal Cornwall Sailors' Home provided. It was peculiar that some of the Cornish philanthropists had not seen their way to perpetuate their memory in this way.[636] If they only saw the necessity for doing something for the poor sailor this Home would be in a very much better condition. (applause)

Thanks to the Directors.

The report and balance sheet were then adopted.

Mr. J. Cole said that though a comparatively new resident and subscriber he knew much of the good work of the Home. The success of such a Home depended on the prudence of the Directors and they knew the work was in very good hands. He proposed that the Directors be thanked for their services and that they are asked to continue in office. He was sorry they lost the valued services of Mr. Haslope, but was glad to find there were people ready to step into the breach and to work with the same ability and on the same lines as their predecessors.

Mr. Robert Fox seconded the resolution. He thought one of the reasons they had for being grateful to the Directors was because they were so successful in the choice of their officers. Their thanks were especially due to Mr. and Mrs. Toulson (applause) who had managed the Home so successfully and with such kindly spirit, and to their efforts the success of the Home was largely due. He congratulated the Directors on having obtained the services of Mr. Bonham as Secretary. (applause) They missed the face of Mr. George Carter, who was for many years the Secretary of the Home. He heartedly congratulated the Directors on their successful management, and they could not do better than leave the works in the hands of the same gentlemen. He felt that not only the County and England generally, but the whole of Europe owed them a debt of gratitude.

Mr. Pender then moved a vote of thanks to Mr. Williams for presiding, and in Mr. Bowles in seconding, remarked that they always appreciated the visit of Mr. Williams to Falmouth. They cordially thanked him for the impetus he had given the movement for the improvement and enlargement of the Home. (applause)—The motion was carried very heartily.

The Chairman, in reply, remarked that we were living in a time when everybody rather hugs himself in the Imperialism, and that form of patriotism which calls itself Imperial. He was afraid he took a rather exaggerated view of Imperialism, but he did not think they might fairly call upon those persons who held these views to give evidence of the faith that is in them. There was no doubt that there was no better way of showing the nature of the faith than in supporting Institutions such as the Royal Cornwall Sailors' Home (applause). The ordinary civilian in England stayed at home. And when he felt in the temper he shouted more or less vigorously as an ardent Imperialist but in the sailors they had the men who did the principal part in relation to that very Imperialism. (hear, hear). Their life was rough, and they necessarily could not afford to suffer from exaggerated refinements, but they were manly at any rate, and as far as people in England were concerned they could try, when misfortune overtook them, to drown like men, and not save themselves at the expense of the women and children (applause). When they read these narratives they felt a thrill of satisfaction that they were members of the same race, and there was more or less a reflected glory on those that stayed at home. Perhaps the glory would be more really reflected if they helped those who survived and suffered from their misfortunes, and they could not help them more directly than supporting such an Institution as this. (applause) [637]

The meeting ended, amid much bonhomie and buoyed up by their achievements attained in the previous difficult year, in spite of an unusually large draw on the establishment's funds.

Several incumbent superintendents were mentioned in the Press reports, since the inauguration of the institution. These included: Mr Richard J. Head (1856); Mr William J. Robinson (1860) and Commander

---

[636] Was this a thinly-veiled criticism of Mr Passmore Edwards who had offered to erect a lighthouse on Manacle Point, but never seemed minded to contribute to the Falmouth Sailors' Home itself?

[637] *The Royal Cornwall Gazette Falmouth Packet, Cornish Weekly News, & General Advertiser;* Thursday, 11th May 1899.

George Pooley R.N. The first record for Mr Harry M. Toulson, as the new purveyor for the Sailors' Home, is a report of an accident (or possibly an affray) from the year 1893:

WOUNDED SAILOR FOUND.—On Sunday morning the Falmouth police found a sailor named Gjertsen, belonging to the steamer *Shakespear*, lying on the dock with a large scalp wound about six inches long. He was immediately conveyed to the Sailors' Home, and kindly attended to by Mr. Toulson, the purveyor.[638]

Mr and Mrs Toulson were in place (as fate had intended) for the *Mohegan* catastrophe. He and his wife played a significant role in that event.

It is not the disease but neglect of the remedy which generally destroys life.

Each week, a local newspaper would give an account of the business, undertaken by the Home, in that period. Here is a representative example for such an account:

Royal Cornwall Sailors' Home.

Weekly Report from 1st to 7th Oct. inclusive.

Remaining by last Report	6
Admitted since	14–20
Discharged	7
Remaining	13

Of these, in the Sick Ward:—

Remaining by last Report	0
Admitted since	7
Cared	2
Died	0
Remaining	5

Of this number:—

Compound Fractures	0
Internal Disease	2
Sea Scurvy	3
Average number victualied daily	18

Amount received from inmates and remitted to their friends Or remaining in the Superintendent's hands £61 17s. 2d.

RICHARD J. HEAD, R.N., Superintendent.[639]

Table 12: Royal Cornwall Sailors' Home: Weekly Report (1856).

---

[638] *The Royal Cornwall Gazette Falmouth Packet, Cornish Weekly News, & General Advertiser;* Thursday, 20th July 1893.

[639] *The Royal Cornwall Gazette, Falmouth Packet, and General Advertiser;* Friday, 10th October 1856.

The reports give us an insight to the common conditions and ailments, encountered by the seamen of the day. Scurvy, a disease resulting from a deficiency of vitamin-C, was a common occurrence among sailors and others aboard ships at sea, for longer periods than perishable fruits and vegetables could be stored for (subsisting instead only on cured and salted meats, and dried grains).[640] The cause of scurvy was not known until 1932, and treatment was inconsistent, with many ineffective therapies surviving into the 20th century.

Such was the prevalence of scurvy in the British seamen, that it was proposed, at the annual general meeting (1859) of the Royal Cornwall Sailors' Home that, "Communication be made with other Sailors' Homes, with a view of making a combined effort with the Board of Trade and the Ship-owners' Societies to remedy so great an evil in the Merchant Service, and which happily no longer prevails in the Royal Navy." [641]

If two doctors visit a sick man, the sexton rings the bells.

Another common ailment, caused by another vitamin deficiency, was beri beri.[642] In the years 1897–1900, 35 Norwegian, 8 Germans, and 2 Italians had been treated for this ailment, in the Royal Cornwall Home. The Norwegian Government had been trying to find the cause for this disease, and had given orders to their vessels that water, should always be boiled before use. Not in itself a bad idea, given the state of general hygiene aboard ships, but of no use whatever in the prevention of this disease. In the year 1899, a German ship was found to have several crew suffering from this affliction:

More Beri Beri at Falmouth

The German ship *Rigel, Captain Leopold*, arrived at Falmouth on Sunday for orders from Rangoon with rice. Almost eight or nine of the crew are suffering from beri beri. On arriving in port the vessel was boarded by the Custom House officials, who immediately communicated with Dr. W. King Bullmore, the medical officer of the Falmouth and Truro Port Sanitary Authority. His deputy (Dr. C. C. Bullmore) boarded the vessel and ordered one man to be removed to the hospital of the Royal Cornwall Sailors' Home. The remainder are not suffering severely from the disease, and their removal to the hospital was not deemed necessary.[643]

And again, in the following year:

Eight survivors and the dead body of one of the crew of the Norwegian barque *Homewood*, from Ship Island,[644] were landed at Falmouth yesterday from the barque *Brilliante*. The *Homewood* became waterlogged, and nine out of sixteen of

---

[640] A good account of this malady aboard 19th c. Merchant and Royal Naval ships is found here; http://pmj.bmj.com/content/80/942/224.full.

[641] *The Royal Cornwall Gazette, Falmouth Packet, and General Advertiser*; Friday, 18th February 1859. The Navy carried lime-juice for the crew, and that accounted for the lack of scurvy aboard their ships.

[642] Beriberi is an ailment, affecting the nervous system, caused by a thiamine deficiency (Vitamin B1) in the diet. The name of the disease comes from a Sinhalese phrase meaning "I can't, I can't," a reference to the debilitating symptoms of advanced beriberi – *WikiPedia*.

[643] *The Royal Cornwall Gazette Falmouth Packet, Cornish Weekly News, & General Advertiser*; Thursday, 28th September 1899.

[644] Ship Island is the name for the island off the Gulf Coast of Mississippi, part of Gulf Islands National Seashore.

the crew fell sick with beri-beri. The *Brilliante* arrived, but the captain and six of the crew refused to leave. One man died aboard the *Brilliante*.[645]

The doctor is often more to be feared than the disease.

Internal disease was a catch-all for conditions that were many and varied; most were never properly diagnosed, given the basic medicine of the time. In such cases, the Home could but offer only basic nursing care, a warm bed, and victuals. The rest was in the gift of Fortuna.

Typhoid was a constant scourge and a mass killer in an era lacking modern-day antibiotics. Such an outbreak is reported here:

> The remaining cases of typhoid were all at Mylor dockyard, and were among the boys landed at sick from *H.M.S. Ganges*. These cases were in the hospital at the dockyard, and it was uneceesary to say that every sanitary precaution had been adopted. . . . The twenty-two deaths in the district included eight which really had no connection with it [typhoid] , three of the boys landed sick from the *Ganges*, and five of persons whose bodies were washed in from the s.s. *Mohegan*.[646]

Not surprisingly, bone fractures were a significant hazard in a seaman's life and with no antibiotics, such accidents were ever prone to life-threatening infection; always an unwelcome spectre at the bedside for an unfortunate seamen who missed his footing, while about his business. Here, such an event proved fatal for an unfortunate seaman:

> ADVANTAGES OF THE ROYAL CORNWALL SAILORS' HOME − Some time since, a fine German lad was received into the Royal Cornwall Sailors' Home, having fallen from the mast-head of a vessel and crushed his instep. The utmost care and solicitude were evinced by the medical men and others, particularly the ladies, who frequently visited him; and after having been in the Home for a few weeks, amputation of his thigh took place. The poor boy lingered for about a week or ten days and then died, feeling assured (as he declared five minutes before his death) that he was going to Jesus Christ in Heaven. This happy end [*sic*] may be attributed to the kindness and unwearied attention of those who constantly visit the Sailors' Home for the purpose of administering spiritual comfort to its inmates, and affords a striking instance of God's blessing on their endeavours.

The Home's sick-ward was a welcome haven for incapacitated seamen, on returning to the UK:

ROYAL CORNWALL SAILORS' HOME

The Infirmary or Sick Ward, which eminently distinguishes the Royal Cornwall Sailors' Home from others of it size and class, had this last year proved extremely beneficial, not so much perhaps on account of the number of invalids as for the character of their complaints; out of 93 cases, some of the severe and lengthened sufferings, no less than 47, half the number, were afflicted with that dreadful scourge sea-scurvy, a disease now entirely unknown in the Royal Navy. From one

---

[645] *The Royal Cornwall Gazette Falmouth Packet, Cornish Weekly News, & General Advertiser;* Thursday, 18th October, 1900.

[646] *The Royal Cornwall Gazette Falmouth Packet, Cornish Weekly News, & General Advertiser;* Thursday, 10th November, 1898.

ship alone, the 'Star of the South,' of Liverpool, 16 men were sent to the Infirmary. One of whom died on his passage from the ship to the shore, a second about a week after his admission, and the others remained for some time more or less debilitated. By the assiduity and skill of the medical gentlemen attending them and after they had received the benefit of careful nursing and of every comfort the Home could administer, they were enabled ultimately to join their own or other ships. In stating this circumstance the directors feel it their duty, though not without some degree of shame and regret, to call the attention of the subscribers to the lamentable fact that the prevalence of this disorder exists in British ships to a greater extent than in foreign, evincing on the part of their captains and owners an indifference to the welfare of their crews deserving the strongest reprobation as a criminal evasion of the wholesome regulations established by the *Mercantile Marine Act* for the prevention of so dire and afflicting a malady.—Several cases of smallpox were admitted during the past year, but their reception operated so prejudicially on the minds of seamen that they avoided the Home for a time. The directors therefore, after much consideration, deemed it advisable not to admit contagious or infectious cases pending the pleasure of the general meeting. Your directors will be glad to receive and expression of your wishes on this important subject.[647]

An inhumane case came to light, whereby a seaman was left onboard his ship, despite having been injured. The captain of the vessel came ashore and was 'shopping-around' for the cheapest way of funding medical treatment for this crew member. The captain showed a quite callous disregard for his charge, and blamed the Sailors' Home for the delay in treatment for the man. The Home, anxious to safeguard its reputation, retaliated in the local press:

THE ROYAL CORNWALL SAILORS' HOME

To the Editor of the Royal Cornwall Gazette.

Falmouth, Aug, 18, 1857.

Sir, A letter having appeared in the *West Briton* of the 14th inst., with reference to the admission of a hurt seaman into the Home, signed, "Eye Witness," calculated by its falsehood and misrepresentation to prejudice the above Institution, the Directors will be obliged by your inserting the following particulars in relation to the case.

Immediately it became known to the Directors that the rumour so anxiously taken advantage of by "Eye Witness" was in wide circulation, two of them, with the acting Superintendent, repaired to the Home, and there instituted a strict enquiry into all the circumstances of the case. It appeared that the master of the vessel came to the Home about 6.0 p.m., (leaving the injured man on board), to bargain for his admission, offering the amount of the man's wages, about £1, for this expenses whilst there. The Purveyor, (the Superintendent not being on the spot), told him the terms and regulations of the Home, which are in print all over the establishment, and informed him that he had no power to vary these regulations and referred to him to myself as secretary. The master then came to see me and inquired if, under the circumstances, the man could be admitted? I replied in the affirmative, and in further conversation I explained to him that by the Marine Act the owners were liable to all the expenses. The master remarked that, "he could do it much cheaper and, as he was a rate payer, he should send him to the Union"; thus clearly determining not to bring the man to the Home and not because the Home had refused admission, but because, "it would be cheaper!" The master then went off to his vessel and brought the seaman to the Market Strand (a long way from the Home) where he kept him a considerable time to make arrangements for his

---

[647] *The Royal Cornwall Gazette, Falmouth Packet, and General Advertiser; Friday*, 18th February 1857.

conveyance to the Union telling the bystanders, in order to screen his own inhumanity, the Home had refused to take his seaman in.

The Home has no reason whatever for refusing admission to such cases, but on the contrary its interest in every way is to admit them in order to benefit the suffering seaman, and to shew the public the value of the Institution.

A little enquiry in the proper quarter by "Eye Witness" would have satisfied him that what the master stated was perhaps incorrect but such was not his object, nor could it be expected from an individual not having the manliness to attach his name to his letter, nor, it is thought the generosity even enable him to sign himself "a subscriber".

All the contributors are so fully acquainted with the expenditure as to know how far the state of the funds of the Institution will admit of sick or injured inmates being received gratuitously.

By the order of the Board.

I am, Sir, your obedient servant,

ALFRED B. DUCKHAM, Secretary.[648]

The scale of the Sailors' Home operation is shown here, where as well as the physical comforts on offer, a series of educational programmes were made available to improve the mind, and with a banking system that gave some financial security for a seaman:

UNIVERSITY INTELLIGENCE.

SAILORS' HOME, WELL-STREET, LONDON DOCKS

The annual meeting of the friends of this institution was held, yesterday, in the museum of the home—Admiral W. Bowles, C.B., M.P., in the chair. The chairman briefly opened the meeting, and called upon the secretary to read the report. It appeared that the Home is capable of receiving 300 boarders, giving every man a sleeping cabin to himself, and at the same time protecting them from the system of extortion and imposition, so notoriously well known, to which sailors ashore are constantly exposed. During the past year 4,745 boarders have been received and it was a gratifying circumstance to the directors to be able to state that of £30,557 of their money, which in the course of that period had passed through the cashier's hands, £7,984 17s. 6d. had been sent by the officers of the institution to the sailors themselves, or to their friends in different parts of the country. Since the opening of the Home, a period of 17 years, 55,371 seamen had passed through; of this number 15,409 were old or returned boarders, and during the time about £400,000 had been received from them, and disbursed under their own instructions. The total number of seamen who had become depositors in the savings bank was 1,040, and the aggregate amount of the sums invested reached £8,862, while at the present moment £3,392 11s. 5d. stands to the credit of 251 depositors. Many of the adult seamen had been assiduous in their attention at the evening school, where navigation, writing, and arithmetic, were taught without any additional expense. At the conclusion of the reading of the report, resolutions in support of the objects of the institution were agreed to, and, after the usual vote of thanks to the chairman, the meeting separated.[649]

In the above report, the Homes' savings banks are well described. It offered a safe, and well-managed, financial service, for a peripatetic sailor; where a seaman could place his earnings into the safe hands of the superintendent, or remove money for everyday essentials. Some quite large sums of money passed over the

---

[648] *The Royal Cornwall Gazette, Falmouth Packet, and General Advertiser;* Friday, 21st August 1857.

[649] *The Morning Post* (London, England); Friday 14th May 1852.

counter in the Homes and it afforded a valuable service for the seamen, who otherwise might be tempted to spend their hard-earned money on the dubious attractions that were on offer in all ports of call. The value of such an internal banking system is reflected here, in the London Home annual report of business for the year 1856:

The Directors invite the ladies and gentlemen of the county to visit and inspect the establishment, in order that they may be enabled to judge for themselves of its working and of the value of its operations. And as substantial evidence on the part of the seamen of its benefits, the large amount of £1,200 was deposited for safekeeping during the year 1853; £1,112 in 1854; £1,274 in 1855 and from January 1st to July 31st of this present year, £1,119 7s. 7d. the greater part of which, in all probability, would have been lost or squandered in profligacy, had not such an asylum existed.

N.B.—The following paper, published by the Director of the Home in Well Street, is printed here, for the purpose of showing the nature of the advantages offered by the Sailors' Homes to the class for whose benefit they are established, as well as some of the arrangements for the practical working of such an institution.

ADDRESS TO OFFICERS AND SEAMEN WHO FREQUENT THE PORT OF LONDON

The Director of the Sailors' Home are anxious that seamen should clearly understand that the Institution was designed for their sole benefit, and established with a view of protecting them from the systematic extortion of crimps, and other snares to which their circumstances and calling render them particularly liable and, above all, to promote their moral elevation, social improvement, and religious instruction.

The rules by which the Institution is governed are, as far as in practicable, adapted to meet the habits of all who participate in its benefits, and to further their best interests. It is conducted on principle of order, comfort, and liberality and no restraint is exercised beyond that which common prudence and mutual interests require. In the "Home" thus provided, which embraces security, freedom of action, and social enjoyment, the Directors desire to create and sustain mutual sympathy, trust and good will, and to employ those agencies which attend most to mature habits of frugality, self-respect, and the love of God.

Advantages of the Institution

Protection,—This embraces every possible arrangements for securing the persons and property of seamen, both before and after receiving their wages, from the imposition to which they are exposed.

Comfort,—Under this head are included medical attendance, a separate cabin, four good and substantial meals a day, with excellent attendance, at a fixed and moderate charge, and the best advice of the officers of the "Home" on all occasions.

Recreation,—In-door and out-door amusements such as chess, draughts, bagatelle, skittles, &c.; a good library, and a course of useful and entertaining lectures during the winter months.

Professional improvement,—This is provided for in a navigation school established on the spot, and conducted by an able and an experienced master, who prepares both officers and seamen for the examinations that are required by the Mercantile Marine Act.

Religious instruction,—Comprising domestic prayer morning and evening, in the "Home," and Divine service in the seamen's church immediately adjoining; the watchful care and good counsels of the chaplain and his staff at all times; together with the use of Bibles and religious publications, which may be purchased at the repository established on the premises.

Post Office,—A necessary and safe medium of communications between seamen and their families.

Slops,—Tradesmen are permitted to exhibit a list of their prices in the "Home" for the information and protection of seamen but no slop-seller [650] is allowed to press his solicitations for custom on the premises. Seamen have also the opportunity of submitting their tradesmen's bills to the secretary, cashier, or superintendent for examination, when there is any doubt as to the justice of the claim.

Mercantile Marine Office,—This is under the control of the Board of Trade, and forms part of the establishment. Here seamen may choose their ship and the voyage they wish to undertake and, when paid off, they may at once deposit their wages with the cashier. The Royal Naval Reserve Office being also attached to it, seamen may enroll themselves for that service.

Advanced Notes,—These, when issued, are dealt with on the most liberal terms, being either cashed at once or collected when due, and the amount remitted to the friends of the seamen. At the same time the Directors wish seamen clearly to understand that they deal with these notes solely to protect themselves from the extortions of discounters outside the building. And with no intention of countenancing a system of advances, so often fraught with injurious consequences both to the sailor and his employer. Nor can the Directors sufficiently deprecate the conduct of those men who, after receiving cash, or its equivalents in board, &c. for their notes, willfully fail to fulfill the engagements to which they have solemnly affixed their names, thus inflicting a pecuniary loss upon the holders of the notes, and wronging those who have engaged their services. The Directors are willing to believe that men guilty of this conduct have not seriously considered the enormity of their twofold offence, nor the material injury their own characters sustain by such fraudulent practices.

Allotment Notes,—These notes are intended for the support of the families of seamen, and when granted, will, if payable in London, be collected and remitted by the cashier to the persons in whose favour they are drawn.

Seamen's Savings' Bank,—This bank is established under the Board of Trade, for the purpose of encouraging habits of economy and prudence in seamen. Any sum, from 5*s.* to £200, may be deposited therein at 3% interest and withdrawn at any seaport in the United Kingdom.

Money Orders,—These are issued to seamen in order that they may remit their wages to any friend or relative, and, instead of carrying any unnecessary sums about their persons, may receive payment at the place of their destination.

Agents,—Persons are employed to attend the principal Mercantile Marine office in London to receive the wages of the seamen, with a view of protecting them from the depredation of crimps and others.

The directors carefully entreat seamen to take advantage of all these precautions and safeguards, which are solely organised to promote their interest and welfare.

Carman,—A man attends the various docks to disembark seamen and convey their chests, &c., to the "Home," at a fixed and reasonable charge. His services are also available for the conveyance of seamen and their luggage from the Home" to the railway stations, the docks, or elsewhere.

Since the opening of the institution in May 1835, to the 30th of April, 1866, 169,905 sailors have been received into the "Home," of which number 49,286 have been old or returned boarders and the sum of £1,358,704 has been deposited by sailors in the Institution, of which £766,018 has been drawn out by sailors, £496,301 has been remitted to their friends, and £50,062 invested in the Savings' Bank.

To Officers of the Mercantile Marine

The "Home" is now in a position to offer a separate mess-room and distinct sleeping accommodation to masters and mates, at a trifling additional charge.

Masters attending the Mercantile Marine Office and the friends of officers boarding at the "Home" may, with the permission of the Secretary, obtain an excellent dinner in the officer's mess-room at a moderate charge.

---

[650] A slopseller was an English merchant who sold slops; or rough working dress. Typically these would be butchers' aprons or similar clothing [a seaman's working dress]. The term slop is derived from an early form of hose—*WikiPedia.*

N.B.—Masters will find the most favourable opportunity of engaging picked men in the Mercantile Marine Office established in the "Home," and every facility for discharging their crews on their return.

Terms,—Officers of the Mercantile Marine availing themselves of the separate accommodation provided will be charged at the rate of 18*s. 6d.* per week, washing included.

Seamen, apprentices, and boys will have to pay at the rate of 15*s.* per week for board and accommodation, which will include a reasonable amount of washing.

Seamen arriving at the "Home" after being paid off will be expected to pay at least one week's board in advance.
Each boarder will have a separate account in the ledger, where every cash transaction will be duly recorded and the Institution will be responsible for all monies deposited by the boarders. Sextants and similar valuables, if lodged with the cashier or superintendent, will be considered in the care of the Institution but it must be understood, however, that the Institution is not liable for robbery, theft, of loss of any article from the cabin (whether kept or left locked or not) or dormitories, nor from the mess-rooms, recreation rooms, or any other part of the building.
After a boarder's chest or other luggage has been lodged in his cabin, and while he is waiting to receive his wages, the superintendent is authorised to advance him a sum of money not exceeding 20*s.*, porterage included. All private money transactions with the officers or servants of the Institution are strictly prohibited.

When a boarder's name is entered his charge for board will go, unless notice to the superintendent of accountant be given to the contrary at 4 p.m. on the previous day.

Any boarder wishing to deposit property, luggage, &c., in the care of the Institution, during his absence, must give the superintendent the necessary information thereof, when it will be placed in the safe custody of the storekeeper until his return.

Should a boarder, on quitting the "Home" leave any property in his cabin or in the hands of the washerman, without informing the superintendent, the Institution cannot be answerable and it will be sold at the expiration of two years as "unclaimed property".

If a boarder go away in debt of the Institution, leaving property, the latter will be sold at the expiration of two years, for the benefit of the "Home," unless the debtor communicate with the Secretary in the interval, holding out a reasonable prospect of redeeming the same.

Hours,—Morning and evening prayers will be held daily in the dining hall at 7.30 a.m. and 8.30 p.m., punctually and regularly throughout the year and it is earnestly hoped that the boarders will take part in the worship.

The street door is closed at 11.30 p.m. but boarders wishing to remain out after that hour are admitted by a pass from the superintendent.

Breakfast will be served at 8 a.m., dinner at 1 p.m., tea at 5.30 p.m., and supper at 9 p.m. Men unavoidably absent at the appointed meal times may be afterwards served in the steward's kitchen, on application to the superintendent. For the sake of regularity, and on account of the servants, it is hoped that the men will attend punctually at meals.

The officer's dinner will be served in their mess room at 1.15 p.m., or as late as 3 p.m. in another apartment.

Divine Service is held in the Seamen's Church adjoining the "Home" on Sundays at 11 a.m. and 6.30 p.m.; also on Thursdays at 7 p.m. A prayer meeting will also be held in the "Home" every Tuesday evening at 7 o'clock.

Conduct,—All swearing and improper language so unbecoming the character of a man, and so dishonouring to God, must be entirely avoided.

Drunkenness, that disgraceful vice which sinks a man to the level of the very beasts that perish, and which is so contrary to order and decency, the men must judge of themselves, cannot be permitted.

Smoking must be confined to the reception hall on the ground floor, and the courtyards and recreation rooms in the basement. In the library, dining hall, and dormitories, smoking is prohibited: and Lucifer matches,[651] also, are strictly forbidden.

Gravesend,—Three boatmen are paid to board all vessels on arrival at Gravesend, and to distribute cards setting forth the advantages of the Sailors' Home and whereas some boarding-house keeper and slop-dealers, by means of their runners, are in the habit of exhibiting cards purporting to come from the Sailors' Home, seamen are informed that all circulars, cards, &c., issued by the Directors will be signed by the Secretary, and bear the authenticated stamp or woodcut of the Institution.

By order of the Directors, W. H. Webb, Secretary.[652]

If more evidence for the good work provided by the Falmouth Home is required, one need go no further than this reference to the Home's accounts:

THE ROYAL CORNWALL SAILORS' HOME

The Rev. W. J. Coope, with his wonted eloquence, alluded to the formation and usefulness of Sailors' Homes, particularly alluding to the returns of the Well-street, (London) Home which presented that from 1835 to 1858 that institution had received 96,716 inmates and that in 1858 the sum of £75,968 had been deposited by seamen, of which there had been remitted home, £31,486, and £3,636 had been placed in the Seamen's Saving Bank. The total amount received as sailors' deposit being £726,534 since the Home's foundation.

Mr. Coope then called attention to the Royal Cornwall Sailors' Home, in relation to the operations of which that day met, The total number of men received since its opening was 5323; of which 347 were shipwrecked, and 760 were sick : the total money deposited £10,921 of which about one-half had been remitted to their friends and relations. The reverend speaker deemed this fact a significant proof of usefulness, not trusting to the emotions of a sick bed so much as to the virtuous principles of having due regard to the providing for the wife, the children, or the mother.[653]

Southampton, a much larger port than Falmouth, had a far greater throughput of clientele. It hosted 5,563 clients from January 1898 to December 1898.

The safeguarding of monies deposited in the Falmouth Sailors' Home was largely as a result of the growing confidence in the Institution:

The public will judge of the high estimation and confidence of Seamen in the Royal Cornwall Sailors' Home at Falmouth, from the following large amounts deposited by them for safe keeping, during the periods stated, which circumstance will prominently present itself to the consideration of the friends of seamen, as a valuable feature of the operations of this Home, an that an institution, affording to such an extent, a guardianship to the hard earnings of sailors, which otherwise would be squandered in profligacy, deserves their utmost individual support :—

---

[651] A match made of a sliver of wood tipped with a combustible substance, and ignited by friction—an obvious fire-risk.

[652] *The Royal Cornwall Gazette, Falmouth Packet, and General Advertiser;* Thursday, 29th August 1856.

[653] *The Royal Cornwall Gazette, Falmouth Packet, and General Advertiser;* Friday, 18th February 1859.

Deposited from Sept. 25th, to Sept. 30th.......... £234   0   0

Ditto, from October 1st, to Oct, 7th 61 17   2

Ditto, from October 18th, to Oct, 14th 208   0   0

£503 17   0 [654]

The value of the Sailors' Home institution, as an advocate for the seafarer, is shown here in a dispute over wages:

POLICE INTELLIGENCE

CLAIM FOR WAGES.—Richard Lloyd summoned the captain of the ship *Orleans* for the payment of £17 18s., being arrears of wages alleged to be due. The complainant had shipped as steward for a voyage to New Orleans and back, at £3 a month. The vessel sailed on the 1st of November last, and arrived back on the 30th of April. The complainant had been offered payment at the Sailors' Home, with certain deductions, which was refused. The defendant showed that, through the negligence of the complainant, a quantity of beef, valued at £1 16s. had been stolen from the vessel; other things were also missing and he (the complainant) had received an advance. The magistrate ordered that the sum of £14 15s. 7½d. should be paid to the steward.[655]

The network of Sailors' Home was an inspired concept. It was instigated at a time when the country relied on its mercantile marine service, to supply its growing industries with raw materials; as well as products that supported a rapidly expanding commercial market. It made sense to promote and protect the wellbeing of seamen, both physically and spiritually. The Homes were extremely well run, with a pride and dedication that we now associate with such a well-ordered society, indicative of the Victorian era: this being a time when life was both short in duration, and extreme, in terms of poverty and suffering.

A Sailors' Home was a beacon that shone its light far-and-wide, over hazardous shores; where an ever-present seaport low-life, was ready to entrap a mariner. He was assured of a welcoming Home, warm, well regulated, and with an engaging environment that offered a brief respite from the squalor of life aboard ship.[656]

The Royal Sailors' Home and Infirmary for Seamen of all Nations in Cornwall, embodied the same underlying concept of its larger sister institution, in Well Street, London. Falmouth was all the better for it.

Many shipwrecked crew passed through the Falmouth Home, during its long history. Some lucky ones availed themselves of its hotel comforts; some less lucky individuals, were obliged to be hospitalized; and the luckless were laid out in its mortuary.

Following the *Mohegan* disaster, the next major shipping incident on these shores, was that of the *SS Paris*.[657] This American liner ran aground on Lowland Point, within viewing distance of the *Mohegan*'s

---

[654] *The Royal Cornwall Gazette, Falmouth Packet, and General Advertiser;* Friday, October 17, 1856.

[655] *Liverpool Mercury etc.* (Liverpool, England); Friday 14th May 1852.

[656] An illustrative overview appeared in the *Hansard,* which is an account of a parliamentary debate around the Sailors' Homes and their inception A transcript can be found here; http://hansard.millbanksystems.com/commons/1861/apr/09/sailors-homes-resolution.

masts, on 2nd May 1899. Fortunately, no injuries or deaths occurred, and the ship was eventually pulled off the rocks. Again, the Falmouth Home played host to many members of the crew and passengers, whilst arrangements were made to relocate them.

Gone, but not forgotten.

A stalwart, Mr Alfred Benjamin Duckham, who will forever be associated with the Royal Cornwall Sailors' Home, passed away in the year of 1894:

DEATH OF MR. DUCKHAM OF FALMOUTH.

By the death of Mr. Alfred B. Duckham, which occurred on Thursday evening, Falmouth loses a well-known figure and one of its oldest inhabitants. From boyhood, Mr. Duckham has been almost continuously connected with the town. At the age of twenty he sailed for the Madras as layman on behalf of the Church Missionary Society, but, through failing health, was compelled to abandon this work and return to Cornwall. His subsequent usefulness in Falmouth will best be indicated by the fact that he was one of the promoters of the Royal Cornwall Sailors' Home and Hospital, and in the threefold capacity of superintendent, treasurer, and secretary, served that institution from its foundation in 1852. Mr. Duckham was not unfrequently spoken of as "the old shipping master," he having been at one time a recognised agent for supplying vessels with seamen. In addition to being collector of the rector's rate, he was for many years—and during the Rev. W. J. Coope's time, churchwarden. As he advanced in years his attention was for the most part devoted to the business of Admiralty chart agent, and his interest in this was maintained to the last. The deceased gentleman, who had reached his 84th birthday, has left a family of four daughters and five sons. One of the latter, Mr. Frederick E. Duckham, is chief engineer at Millwall Docks, and is widely known as the patentee of Duckham's weighing machine, dredging apparatus, &c. As a mark of respect the flag at the Sailors' Home is hoisted half-mast high.[658]

One volunteer is worth two pressed men.

As regards the ever-present danger of being shanghaied, a story appeared in a New Zealand newspaper that graphically reports the general indifference towards a casualty of this form of assault. Interestingly, a dramatic denouement for this story, as it ended at the Royal Cornwall Sailors' Home, Falmouth:

SWIM FOR LIBERTY.

"Shanghaied" Sailor's Long Story

Quite in the old style of romance was the narrative related by a Russian seaman named Gedart, after he had been admitted to the Royal Cornwall Sailors' Home at Falmouth. His adventures started in South America. He was staying in a boarding-house in Rossario,[659] and the proprietor gave him a glass of wine. It must have been drugged, for he lost consciousness, and on regaining his senses found himself on the high seas on board the Italian barque *Regina*, the captain of the vessel declared

---

[657] Following repairs, the *Paris* was renamed the *Philadelphia*, and resumed the North Atlantic passenger service in August 1901, finally being sold for scrap in 1923.

[658] *The Royal Cornwall Gazette Falmouth Packet, Cornish Weekly News, & General Advertiser*; Thursday, 15th February 1894.

[659] Rosario is the largest city in the province of Santa Fe, Argentina. It is located 300 km (187 miles) northwest of Buenos Aires, on the western shore of the Paraná River.

that he had paid the boarding-house proprietor a certain sum for a sailor. As matters turned out, Gedart found that he had been "Shanghaied"—a nautical term for being placed in a vessel by force.

Protests were of no avail, and Gedart tried to make the best of matters, making up his mind to leave the ship at the first opportunity. But when the *Regina* arrived in Falmouth Harbour the young Russian was not allowed to go on shore, and so, with the top of a small table and a couple of lifebuoys, he made a miniature raft. Watching his opportunity, at 9 o'clock one night he threw this frail craft into the sea and leaped after it.

To his great dismay, he found the raft would not bear his weight. It was impossible to get back to the *Regina* without being discovered, and he at once made up his mind to swim for his life, and struck out for the nearest vessel, which happened to be the French barque *Bidart*, anchored several thousand yards from the *Regina*.

For four hours the young sailor battled with a heavy swell which prevailed, but at last he reached the side of the *Bidart* and cried for assistance. A rope was thrown to him. And he was hauled on board in a terrible exhausted condition. The French crew treated him most hospitably, and, after particularly drying his clothes, launched their boat and took him ashore.

At the Sailors' Home the tale was investigated and found to be correct. He was provided with dry clothing, and soon recovered from the effects of his long immersion. He states that during the time he was in the water he experienced terrible sufferings from the cold, whilst he was greatly hampered by the strong tide that he had to battle against.

Mr. Howard Cox, the Russian Vice-Consul at Falmouth, when interviewed said that this Shanghaiing of sailors in South American ports was a common occurrence. If Gedart had completed the voyage to the port of destination he might have been able to claim his wages. Having broken the voyage, however, at Falmouth, he had no legal claim, nor did Mr. Cox think it possible to bring an action for damages against the captain of the vessel in an English court.

The Russian seaman had been supplied with money by charitable people, and his fare paid by the Shipwrecked Mariners' Society to Cardiff, where he hopes to get a berth on a ship. Gedart, however, is disappointed that he cannot get redress for having been "Shanghaied," or compel that captain to pay him any wages for three months' work. "In England," he remarked regretfully, "I thought people could get all wrongs righted". [660]

In the 1901 UK census, the Toulson couple (together with Mr Toulson's niece) is still resident at the Home:

Sailors' Home 3 Bank Place Falmouth Cornwall	Mr. Richard M. Toulson (Superintendent) Age 40 – Born: Carlton, Notts. Mrs. Emma Toulson (Wife/Matron) Age 44 years – Born: Pinxton, Notts. Cissie Toulson (Niece) Age 17 years (DoB: 1884) – General Servant

The UK census for the year 1911 shows that they had now left Falmouth and were running an apartment house in Bournemouth. Mr Toulson was registered as 'Own Account' that is, 'neither employing others nor working for a trade employer,' by which definition indicates that he was probably the owner and proprietor of the establishment:

[660] *Taranaki Herald*, Rōrahi LIV. Putanga; 13575, 5 Hakihea – 1907.

10 Cambridge Rd.	Mr. Richard Morris Toulson – Apartment Housekeeper
Bournemouth	Age 50 – Born: Heckington, Lincs.
	Mrs. Emma Toulson – Apartment Housekeeper
Dorset	Age 52 [*sic*] years – Born: Pinxton, Notts.
	and with 3 domestic servants in residence

The Toulson couple must have left the Falmouth Home sometime between 1901 and 1906, as in that latter year, a new superintendent was in post, named as Mr Randolph Dainty. [661] Rather surprisingly, no report of the Toulsons having left Falmouth is recorded, despite the couple's immense contribution to the Sailor's Home.

Bacchus has drowned more men than Neptune.

An exception is in the year 1899, when Falmouth played host to suprisingly huge numbers of abstemious seamen:

> It is calculated that about thirty thousand seafaring men, representing fifteen nationalities, were in Falmouth harbour last year. Of that number only six were convicted of drunkenness.[662]

The shipping activity for the Port of Falmouth, over a period of twelve years and ending in the year of the *Mohegan* disaster, is shown in the following table: [663]

FALMOUTH SHIPPING TRADE 1887 – 1898.		
Year	No. of Ships	Tonnage
1898	798	870,225
1897	791	723,909
1896	907	783,078
1895	1,103	971,017
1894	1,206	973,652
1893	1,082	864,173
1892	1,233	933,890
1891	1,218	792,925
1890	1,518	981,085
1889	1,484	924,126
1888	1,428	811,603
1887	1,357	840,603

Table 13: Falmouth Shipping Trade 1887–1898.

[661] *Kelly's Directory* for Falmouth; 1906. He is recorded as the Superintendent at the Home in the 1901 UK census.

[662] *The Royal Cornwall Gazette Falmouth Packet, Cornish Weekly News, & General Advertiser;* Thursday, September 6th 1900.

[663] *The Royal Cornwall Gazette Falmouth Packet, Cornish Weekly News, & General Advertiser;* Thursday, January 4th 1900.

The world's overall shipping in 1899, confirmed Britain and America as having the lion's share:

The entire fleet of the world in 1899 was, according to Lloyds Register, 28,180 steamers and sailing vessels, with a total tonnage of 27,673,528, of which 39 per cent, are British. There are 3,010 American vessels, with 2,465,387 tonnage; 1,676 German vessels, with 2,453,334 tonnage; 2,528 Norwegian vessels, with 1,694,230 tonnage; 1,408 Swedish vessels, with 605,991 tonnage; 1,218 Russian vessels, with 643,527 tonnage, 1,150 Italian, 1,182 French, 841 Japanese, 796 Danish, 701 Spanish vessels. One-half of the ship tonnage is British and American.[664]

For the year 1899, the distribution for ethnicity by visiting crew is shown in the following table: [665]

FALMOUTH SHIPPING VESSEL ARRIVALS – 1899.		
Nationality	No. of Ships	Tonnage
English	331	407,824
Norwegian	121	74,452
German	96	144,422
Danish	44	16,409
Italian	35	30,411
Russian	22	15,141
Swedish	20	9,360
French	16	18,176
Dutch	14	7,210
Greek	3	3,893
Spanish	3	2,148
Austrian	3	2,565
American	2	69,920
Portuguese	2	443
Brazilian	1	174
Peruvian	1	50
Belgian	1	176
Total	715	739,774

Table 14: Falmouth Shipping Vessel Arrivals (1899).

As to be expected, the main group of foreign crews came from Northern Europe, including the Baltic countries.

---

[664] Hoyt, John C.; *Old Ocean's Ferry; the Log of the Modern Mariner, the Trans-Atlantic Traveler, and Quaint Facts of Neptune's Realm*

[665] *The Royal Cornwall Gazette Falmouth Packet, Cornish Weekly News, & General Advertiser;* Thursday, January 4th 1900.

With a vibrant economy and an empire to service and maintain, it was not surprising that ships employed foreigners as members of the crew. Such a racial mix would not be seen above decks on a transatlantic liner, but the merchant service vessels were much more attracted to hiring foreign crew, with the added commercial advantage of cheaper labour costs.

> With respect to crews there was no requirement in 1898 for a British ship to carry British nationals, and ships could sail with all foreign-born crews, (I think including masters though certification had to be of UK. origin). However, polyglot crews were much more prevalent in sailing ships, though with eastern trades ships, the use of all Indian, Lascars [666] or Chinese crews was well established by that date (30,000 – 40, 000). There were 7,000 Germans placed in British ships in 1914.[667]

However, less tolerance was given to black persons, by the shipping lines and their crew. Their role was in areas of: cleaning; stoking coal and heavy manual duties on the docks. Non-whites were not well received in the Sailors' Homes and this eventually led to purpose-built establishments, for their exclusive use.[668] The Home for Asiatics in the West India Docks was in place by the year 1900.[669]

The Royal Cornwall Sailors' Home was still in operation in the year 1930, as a substantial legacy made to that charity confirms:

> WILLS AND BEQUESTS
>
> GIFTS TO CHARITY
>
> Mrs Annie Davey, of Holyrood, Falmouth and of Ardmore, Torquay, who died on December 30, aged 77, widow of R. Davey, left unsettled property in her disposition of the gross value of £319, 232 … She left:—£1,000 to the Falmouth Sailors' Home and Hospital … and £100 to John Knowles, of Falmouth, formerly Captain of her late husband's yacht.[670]

And again, another bequest, made to the Home in 1940:

> Mrs. Eliza Maude Beatson, of Purley who died on December 23, widow of Major-General Finlay Compton Beatson (retd.), C.B., left £32,007, with net personality £31,791. She left:—£100 to the Royal Cornwall Sailors' Home and Hospital, £100 to the Royal Cornwall Home for Destitute Little Girls.[671]

---

[666] Lascar (local crew members from South East Asia or East Africa) is a term rarely used now but was once the name used to describe a sailor or militiaman from the Indian subcontinent or other countries east of the Cape of Good Hope, employed on European ships from the 16th century until the beginning of the 20th century.

[667] Personal communication: Mr Alston Kennerley–Plymouth University (2011).

[668] Even less hospitality was the norm for the American blacks, and as early as 1839, "Homes for Colored Seamen" were erected in New York's sailortown—Seamen's Missions: Their Origin and Early Growth: Roald Kverndal.

[669] The Royal Cornwall Gazette Falmouth Packet, Cornish Weekly News, & General Advertiser; Thursday, July 20th 1900.

[670] The Times; Friday, February 21st 1930.

[671] The Times; Monday, March 25th 1940.

In passing, during a personal tour of the building, by this author, a foundation-stone was discovered at the rear of the premises, with the following inscription:

Admiral Sir Lewis A. Beaumont KCB, CMG. [672]

August 23rd 1905.

It is not known for sure why this foundation-stone was laid and its connection with the Royal Cornwall Sailors' Home; however, there is reference to a new hospital wing being attached to the home and opened in 1906 and it is likely that this is the inscribed foundation-stone for that building, and was unveiled by the Admiral, in the previous year:

> A new hospital is being erected in connection with the Royal Cornwall Sailors' Home at Falmouth, at a cost of £2,000. The home does a good work among British as well as foreign sailors, and is maintained by voluntary effort. Mr. John Charles Williams of Cearhayes Castle,[673] who has contributed £100 to the fund, is to open the new hospital.[674]

As appropriate for a hospital-wing, a professional staff replaced the unskilled and highly dedicated workers, who had established the Home's pre-eminent reputation both here in the UK and internationally:

> Royal Cornwall Sailors' Hospital, Falmouth—Miss Helm Mair has been appointed Sister. She was trained at the Royal Infirmary, Edinburgh, and was called up for duty with the Territorial Force Nursing Service in 1914, and served for six years in this capacity. She was Sister-in-Charge of Surgical Wards in a Casualty Clearing Station in France, and later was with the British Army on the Rhine.[675]

The End of the Line.

In the year 1956, the Royal Cornwall Sailors' Home announced its closure:

> The Royal Cornwall Sailors' Home—A chapter covering just over a century in Falmouth's proud sea history ends on Saturday, when the Royal Cornwall Sailors' Home at Bank will be closed. It will no longer be available for the accommodation of seaman of all nations.
>
> So concludes an association with some of the most memorable and thrilling sea episodes off the Cornish coast and in the Atlantic approaches.[676]

---

[672] Admiral Sir Lewis Anthony Beaumont was also the Commander-in-Chief at Plymouth (1902);
http://fleetorganization.com/1906rnadmirals.html. / www.dreadnoughtproject.org/tfs/index.../Lewis_Anthony_Beaumont

[673] John Charles Williams was born at Caerhays Castle on September 30th 1861. The Castle had been bought in 1854 with all the land in the parish, by his grandfather, Michael Williams, Sheriff of Glamorganshire 1839, MP for West Cornwall 1853 - 1858, and chairman of the Cornwall railway, who renovated the building and developed its grounds His son, John Michael Williams, the father of John Charles was a very busy man; he was Sheriff of Cornwall 1865, and took a leading part in finance and banking in the county. The estate with its castle is located in a sheltered valley overlooking Porthluney Cove on the South Cornish Coast equidistant from Truro and St Austell.

[674] *The British Journal of Nursing;* 3rd November, 1906.

[675] *British Journal of Nursing*, Vol. LXVI; 1st January, 1921.

[676] *West Briton;* April 19th 1956.

This last reference to the Falmouth Home announced the end of an illustrious period in maritime history. The changes in shipping practice and the superior hotel accommodation, now routinely available on modern ships, meant that such facilities ashore became less attractive. This, coupled with a more secular attitude adopted by society, was the death knell for a now rather dated organisation, based on a Victorian Christian model—the core ethos for the Sailors' Home movement.

Its role as a hospital diminished, with the development of a national health service. In 1939, an emergency medical service, as the country came under command and control because of the Second World War. In his report on social welfare systems Beveridge [677] had little to say about the precise nature or funding of a health service, though seeing one as essential to a satisfactory system of social security (1942).[678]

The Royal Cornwall Sailors' Home and Infirmary for Seamen of All Nations, closed its doors on Saturday, April 14th 1956.

The premises now serve as individual apartments and offices, and the grounds at the rear have been converted to a storage facility, for a chain of a British department store operating in the West Country.[679]

The Sailors' Home and Red Ensign Club in Dock Street, London.

The fore-runner for the inauguration in 1827 of the national Sailors' Home network finally followed in closing its doors, signalling an end for the movement. It had survived for a further eighteen years after the demise of its sister organisation in Falmouth; in part, due to the huge maritime infrastructure—it being the engine-room of Britain's mercantile Empire—located on its own doorstep. But as the Empire ebbed away, so did the mercantile ships and its crews; a rather sad end of an era:

Seamen say farewell to their shore berth

The home from home for sailors stranded in the Port of London is closing its hospitable doors. For a century and a half the Sailors' Home and Red Ensign Club in Dock Street E1, has been a haven between voyages for seamen; for some of them the only home in England, or even on dry land, that they had. The changed pattern of the shipping industry in the past 10 years and inflation have created such losses for it that it can no longer continue.

---

[677] William Henry Beveridge, 1st Baron Beveridge KCB (5 March 1879 – 16 March 1963) was a British economist and social reformer. He is perhaps best known for his 1942 report Social Insurance and Allied Services (known as the Beveridge Report) which served as the basis for the post-World War II Welfare State put in place by the Labour government – *WikiPedia*.

[678] Rivett G. C.: *National Health Service History* n.d. retrieved 8 July 2009 from; www.nhshistory.net.

[679] A recent visit by this author to the site revealed obvious links with the Sailors' Home organisation. Original features still exist with the hospital and possible mortuary facilities being still recognisable. Current anecdotal reference allude to coffins being transported from the rear of the premises to the front of the building, through the storage area, presumably following death and post-mortem examinations, and then on to burial. The building is referred to as Chy An Mor—"House by the Sea".

The charity began as the Destitute Sailors' Asylum in 1827. From this evolved the Home "for reception, lodging, and protection of all persons and property of sailors, the improvement of their morals, saving them from the crimps (two-legged land sharks) of London, and regularly shipping them on outward bound vessels to all parts of the world". In those days London was a perilous sea for sailors who had just been paid off. The notorious streets around the docks were infested with brothels, clip-joints, and cheap boarding-houses, where many a poor seaman was shipwrecked, rolled and skinned alive.

Montague Williams, an East End magistrate, described it in the 1860s: "If the sailors were not entirely fleeced inside the saloons, the process was completed by the bullies and fighting men when they staggered out into the streets". The Home kept vans drawn by horses and in charge of tough drivers to meet ships at the docks and bring seamen and their kit safe home past the parasites and tarts. It also taught navigation and other seamanly skills. These educative functions have now gone to other institutions, except for nautical cookery. The only place in London where you can train for your ticket as a ship's cook.

It still provides a cheap non-profit-making hotel and residential club, without any denominational axe to grind, for seafarers. Bed and breakfast costs £1.70. Bedrooms are called cabins, and the kitchen, the galley. The bar is filled with faces of every colour and racial idiosyncrasy under the sun, but all with the watchful eyes of seamen spying a landlubber on board. Somalis off a giant tanker just in at Thames Haven book in; Pakistanis book out to catch a flight to join a ship at Abu Dhabi.

Various changes have been made the old Home no longer viable. Automation and increased wages have reduced the numbers employed in the British merchant fleet from 150,000 before the seaman's strike of 1967 to less than half that number. Voyages take less time these days, and seamen are less feckless; when they reach London they go home to their families and wait to be telephoned by their companies. All seamen are now under contract either directly to a shipping company or, to the British Shipping Federation. So it is no longer possible for a sailor to lodge at the Home, while going down to the docks each day in the hope of making a pier-head jump on an outward bound ship. The docks, in any case, have moved downstream from Stepney.

The Secretary of the Home, Wing Commander Bill Fleming, known to his sailor-guests as "Wings", can remember days only a decade ago when a seaman would stay for a fortnight and spend £400 on booze, the local betting-shops, and the dingy local rooms that supplied seamen with other traditional sailors' comforts after a long voyage. He says: "This place used to be a home. Now it has become a place of transit. Old seamen who have been coming here for 20 years and more feel our closure very painfully". Seamen seldom stay for longer than a night or two now, before being flown home to Karachi or Hong Kong or some other landfall to join a ship.

The Home, whose chief-stone was laid by Palmerston [680] and which was opened by the Prince of Wales, had accommodation for 200, and is never more than half full. The charitable trust that runs it has been amalgamated with the Marine Society, and there were enterprising and practicable plans to redevelop the Home as a Marine Centre, with fewer rooms and modern accommodation for the new type of seaman. Inflation and the economic crisis have scuppered these plans, temporarily at least. When the old billet for sailors up the London River closes, something of value and honourable history will vanish from dockland.

Philip Howard.[681]

---

[680] Lord Palmerston, the British statesman who served twice as Prime Minister of the United Kingdom in the mid-19th century.

[681] *The Times;* December 14th 1974.

We shall never again see the like of such an organisation. The wealthy and privileged few saw it as their duty to subscribe to the wellbeing of those disadvantaged members of society: unable to fend for themselves and many living in abject poverty.

From the pitiful ranks of the poor were drawn the foot soldiers for the greatest maritime service ever seen in human history. The Victorian era was indeed the golden age for this country. Such advances in technology and in its innovative application thereof, the maritime industry equipped itself to become the workhorse, for a supply of materials and resources from the world over. An expanded empire and its dominions that required protection, rule, and harvesting, demanded a comensurate shipping fleet, and so provided a service of unparalleled size and complexity.

The Sailors' Home movement was of its time. It acted as a safety net for those engaged in the peripatetic nature of seafaring activities. In this role, it served brilliantly: as a welcoming beacon, in an otherwise indifferent world.

The Royal Cornwall Sailors' Home - Falmouth.

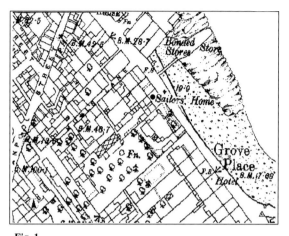

Fig. 1

Royal Cornwall Sailors' Home – 1880 © Crown copyright.

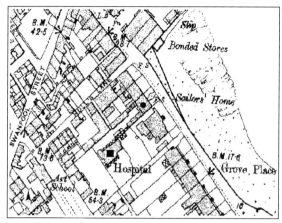

Fig. 2

Royal Cornwall Sailors' Home – 1907 © Crown copyright.

The two ordnance survey sheets with a 27 year gap between them, shows the development undertaken on site. The later map reveals an apparent appropriation of land next door, on which has been erected a hospital – 1905 (■). This is clearly labelled in the 1907 map, the year the hospital was completed. The address of the Home was and remains 3 Bank Place (●). The building stands to this day; however, not as the Sailors' Home, which closed its doors in 1956. It now comprises offices and living accommodation.

Fig. 3   Royal Cornwall Sailors' Home
3 Bank Place, Falmouth; c. 2013.

Fig. 4 The rear of the Royal Cornwall Sailors' Home
looking down Hull's Lane; c. 1898.

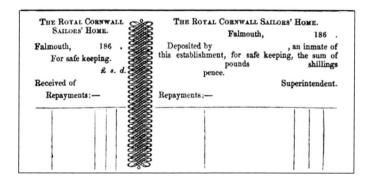

Fig. 5   A Paying-in slip for the Royal Cornwall Sailors' Home
used by a ship's member of crew c. 1867

Fig. 6 A deck-chair from the *Mohegan.*

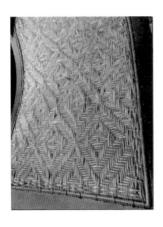

Fig. 7 The deck-chair fabric.

Fig. 8 A rare example of an intact dinner plate, retrieved from the wreck.

Fig. 9 The main staircase from the *Mohegan* installed at Parc Behan, Coverack.

Fig. 10 General wreckage from the *Mohegan,* on the shoreline.
(Gibson, Penzance)

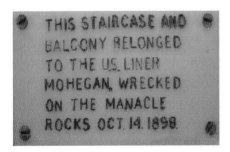

Fig. 11

A plate attached to the newel post at the end of the 19th century. It would appear to be made of ivory.

Fig. 12

The ship's bell showing the original name, before becoming the *Mohegan.*

Fig. 13

The *Mohegan's* mast base deck-plate, in pierced bronze. and showing the ship builder's imprint.

Fig. 14
Mr. Bernard Nadal Baker

Fig. 15
Mr John Llewellyn. Couch
(Photo: Bostwick - New York)

Fig. 16
Mr Ernest Benjamin Cole.
(Photo: Matthews - Philadelphia)

Fig. 17
Capt. Richard Griffith
(Photo: Hargrave - New York)

Fig. 18
Quartermaster John William
Juddery

Fig. 19
Katherine Bell Noble.

Fig. 20
William Kinley – Assistant Engineer.

Fig. 21
Mr Edmund Laurence Carlyon
c. 1939.

Fig. 22

Canon Diggens, his wife and son. Photograph taken
in Australia c. 1890, based on apparent age of the boy.

Courtesy: John Oxley Library, State Library of
Queensland, Image No.14097.

Fig. 23

Rev. W. A. Diggens with his wife and sister
c. 1912.

Fig. 24

Dr. Edward James Leverton-Spry.
(1844-1912)
Courtesy : Harry Spry-Leverton

Fig. 25   The *S.S. Mohegan.*

Fig. 26 Posing as passengers stranded in the rigging of the *S.S. Mohegan.*

Fig. 27   A silhouette of the steamship *Mohegan.*

Fig. 28 The Falmouth-built tug *Penguin.*

Fig. 29   A view of (from left to right) the *SS Paris*, Manacle Rocks, *SS Mohegan,* (funnel stack now missing) and the Manacle Buoy. Note the St. Keverne church spire on the horizon

Fig. 30   The *Mohegan's* last resting place amongst the Manacles.

Fig. 31   A battered metal lifeboat from the *Mohegan.*
(Gibson, Penzance)

Fig. 32   Transporting a coffin across the square in St. Keverne, 1898. The large white cottage no longer stands in the square.

The five local men who helped dig the mass grave are, from left to right: Jim Perrow, Thomas John Joyce, William John Tripp, Johnny Ben Tripcony, Jack Nicholas, and Dudley Peters. The photograph was most likely taken just after the burial service, with the mourners still present.

Fig. 33   The burial service at the mass grave at St. Keverne Church.

Fig. 34   The hard work of the grave-diggers is admired by onlookers.

Fig. 35   St. Akeveranus Church, St. Keverne.

Fig. 36   The mass grave at St. Keverne and the curious.

Fig. 37 Onlookers gather at yet another body taken from the sea.

Fig. 38 Coffins are stacked in St. Keverne Church.

Fig 39   This is a controversial photograph of some of the victims, taken in the nave of the St. Keverne Church. They are clearly laid out on a bed of brush-wood, awaiting identification. The matter of an image being sold to members of the general public was raised at the Board of Trade inquiry, causing some general disquiet.

Fig. 40 The memorial window in the St. Keverne Church.

Fig. 41 The memorial cross at the *Mohegan* Mass Grave, in the St. Keverne churchyard – Courtesy: Terry Moyle.

Fig. 42 St. Keverne Schoolhouse – Venue for the Coroner's Inquest.

Fig. 43 The base of the memorial cross With its simple inscription.

A Selection of Rocks from The Manacles.

Fig. 44   Inner Manacles.*

Fig. 45   The Cormorants stand guard on a Manacle Rock.*

Fig. 46   The Voces (Varses) Rock.*

Fig. 47   The Shark's Fin - Site of the *Andola* wreck.*

Fig. 48   Manacle Point - looking out over the *Mohegan* wreck. Note the people using this vantage point - 1898.
(Photo: Major and Darker, Falmouth).

* Photographs taken by this author, on a low Spring Tide.

Fig. 49
Depicted in this Paul Gustave *Doré* engraving is a typical East end of
London scene of the period, a home to many of the ship's crew.

Fig. 51   The Falmouth Lifeboat crew of the *Bob Newbon,*
who attended the *Mohegan* disaster.

Fig. 50   The vessel *Danmark* – *"And Every Soul was Saved"*
By the Royal Academician – Mr. Thomas M. M. Hemy

Fig. 52

A state room on the *Mohegan's* sister ship *Mesaba*, from1909 (Kinghorn)

Fig. 53   The *S.S. Paris* stranded on Lowland Point - 1899.

Fig. 54   Supplement to *The Graphic*, October 22, 1898. The Wreck of the liner *Mohegan* on the Manacle Rocks:
The Porthoustock Lifeboat is rescuing the Crew stranded in the ship's rigging.
Drawn by J. Nash, R.A.

Fig. 55

A view of Porthoustock Beach with the Lifeboat Station
on the left. The sea almost reached the building at the
time of the *Mohegan* disaster.

(Copyright The Francis Frith Collection)

Fig. 56   Greasing the runners in front of the
Porthoustock Lifeboat Station c. 1898.

Fig. 57 James Hill outside the lifeboat station,
Porthoustock, c. 1898.

Fig. 58   Falmouth Lifeboat Station and slipway.

Fig. 59   The Porthoustock Lifeboat '*Charlotte*' with the crew aboard c. 1898.

Fig. 61 James Hill - Coxswain.
Photo taken by Rev. W. Diggens

Fig. 6   Porthoustock Lifeboat Station and Crew c. 1898:

Alfred Roberts, George Dalley, William John Tripconey, William Hill, Frank Tripconey, Joe James, Henry Roberts, Unknown.

Tom Roskruge, James Hill, John Williams, George Martin Tripconey, Dick Sobey, William Rashleigh, Dudley Peters, W.J. Bastain, J. H. Cliff (2nd Cox.).
Note: The Tripconey family names, appended to this photograph, hanging in the Porthoustock village hall, appears at odds with the list as seen in fig. 92.

Fig. 62 Lizard Head, from the old lifeboat
Station and slipway at Polpeor Cove.

Fig. 63 The Watch-house, Manacle Point c. 1900, no longer in place.
Note the Manacles in the distance.

Fig. 64 St. Anthony's Lighthouse
Copyright: The Francis Frith Collection

Fig. 65 The Lizard Lighthouse.

Fig. 66 The Lloyds Signal Station, Lizard Head.

Fig. 67 The Manacle Buoy c. 1898.
(Photo: A.W.T. Channell)

Fig. 68 The Manacle Buoy c. 2011.
(Photo: Chris Holwill)

Fig. 69 The Eddystone Lighthouse.
Note the stump of the Smeaton Tower.

The *HMS Ganges* Training Ship − Royal Naval Dockyard at Mylor, upstream from Falmouth, Cornwall.

Fig. 70 The Boy sailors aboard the *HMS Ganges* Training ship (c. 1898). The wistful expressions on their faces (many of them being orphans) perhaps reveals the harsh conditions aboard.

Fig. 71 The full ship's company - crew and boy apprentices aboard the *HMS Ganges* Training ship (c. 1898).

Fig. 72 The *HMS Ganges* Training ship, built in Bombay in the early 19th century.

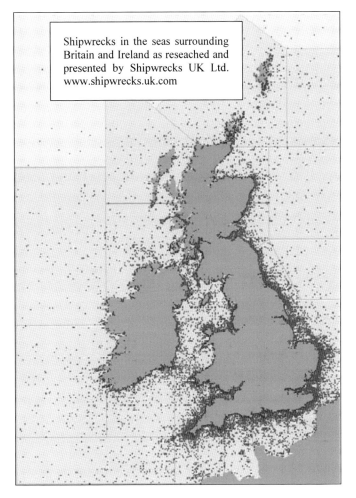

Fig. 73   The distribution of known shipwreck sites in the UK.

(Courtesy of Shipwrecks UK Ltd.)

Shipwrecks in the seas surrounding Britain and Ireland as reseached and presented by Shipwrecks UK Ltd. www.shipwrecks.uk.com

Fig. 74   A button from an officer's tunic, showing the Atlantic Transport Line logo.

Fig. 75 Memorial Tablet for Capt. Griffith – Bwlch Cemetery, Abersoch, North Wales.

Fig. 76   The Falmouth Lifeboat crew of the *Bob Newbon,* who attended the *Mohegan* disaster, attract many well-wishers – c. 1898.

Fig. 77   The Rogers family at Rosenithon. Katie Bell Noble initially stayed with this family, following the disaster.

Fig. 78 Daniel Gallaway and wife Emma with their son Norman on her lap c. 1918. This photograph could be to commemorate the Christening of the young boy Norman.

Fig. 79
Mr George Pottie - Superintendent to the London Agent for Atlantic Transport Line.
Courtesy: Jonathan Kinghorn.

Fig. 80 John Horniman, Esq., M.P.

Fig. 81 Norman Gallaway, as a young man.

Fig. 82 A cottage in Porthoustock with the upturned *Charlotte* lifeboat acting as the roof. It was home for Mrs Julia Jenkin, who is seen here.

Fig. 83

Fig. 84 The backing-card to the photograph in **Fig.** 83

Capt. Griffith's children; Walter (Wally) Hugh and Selina May.
Their apparent ages are 10 years and five years respectively, and
the year in which this photograph was taken being c.1895.

Fig. 85   Capt. Richard Griffith (see **Fig. 88**). The
ship is unknown but the date is certainly post-1894.

Fig. 86   Capt. Richard Griffith (see **Fig**. 87) - ship unknown. Note the Atlantic
Transport logo on his cap-band so, the date would be post-1890.

Fig. 87   *Our Captain at home on the Atlantic.*
Capt. Richard Griffith relaxing in his sleeping quarters: the ship and date are unknown.
Note his bed on the left and a china plate hanging on the wall, featuring a dog

Fig. 88

Capt. Richard Griffith (standing second from left) and his four officers. The person on the far left is the third officer in his working clothes and the ambiguous figure seated in the middle is the fourth officer and is dressed in an undercoat and a thick raglan overcoat. He also has a large empty sack around his waist (on the land, a ploughman was sent out with a bag of bags to keep him dry). and he would have been employed on outside duties, in all weathers. The date for this image is thought to be c.1897.

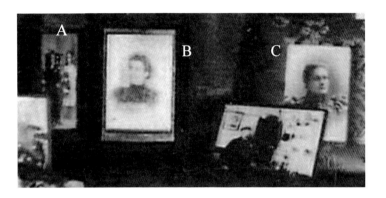

Fig. 89   Personal photographs displayed on the Captain's bureau secretaire in his sleeping quarters (see Fig. 87).

An intriguing glimpse of the Captain's domestic life, appearing in three of the

above photographs (see Fig. 87).

 A speculation is made here as to the identity of the persons featured in the images:

A. Wedding scene showing the bride holding a floral bouquet (2nd marriage) ?

B. The Captain's wife - from his second marriage?

C. Perhaps his mother - Mary Griffith?

Note: Figs. 83 to 89 are courtesy of Mr Edward Prettejohn: grandson to Capt. Richard Griffith.

Fig. 90   The *Queen of the Fal:* a popular Falmouth pleasure-boat; c. 1900.

Note the overcrowding on board and with just two life-belts adding a decorative feature up front (clearly Health and Safety was not an issue at this time) and with the belching funnel acting as an early contributor to global-warming. Pendennis Castle can be seen on the land, in a vertical line with the bow of the vessel.

Fig. 91

The original board, that traditionally appeared in all RNLI Lifeboat Stations, recording the operational history of its Lifeboats, though its history abruptly ends in the year 1931; whereas, the station continued operationally until 1945. The board still hangs in the Porthoustock Village Hall. Courtesy: Porthoustock Village hall Committee.

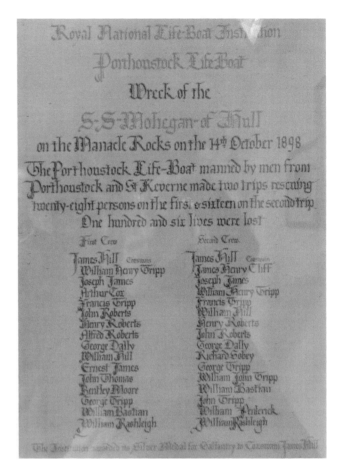

Fig. 92

This inscription currently takes pride of place on the wall of the Porthoustock Village Hall - previously the Porthoustock lifeboat station. For a more legible list, see Appendix 20. Courtesy: Porthoustock Village hall Committee.

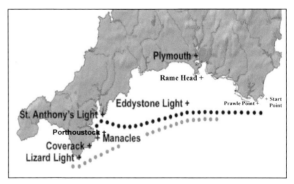

Fig. 93 The track for the *Mohegan* from Start Point to the Manacle Rocks. The grey track shows the approximate route the ship should have taken.

Fig. 94   A launching of the Porthoustock lifeboat, *Mary Ann Storey;* (1869-1886).
This was obviously a staged event, and the woman in the foreground could well
be a visiting dignitary, given her dress and prominent position in the photo.

Fig. 95   A launching of the Porthoustock lifeboat, *Mary Ann Storey;* 1869-1886).
A remarkably high-quality photograph for the time. Note the woman in
the foreground, knitting a woollen cap for a lifeboat crewman, and in the
background the local village policeman - the adult standing man on the left.

CHAPTER 18

Captain Richard Griffith: Master of the *SS Mohegan*

Richard Griffith was born in Llanengan,[682] in the county of Carnarvonshire, in the year 1852.[683]

His immediate family appeared in the UK census for the year 1861.[684] In the Llanengan census for 1881, Richard Griffiths does not appear on the roll. However, his siblings, Griffith Griffith,[685] aged 40, remained as a farm labourer, and Catherine Griffith, now aged 27, remains as a 'daughter of the household.' His other siblings, Mary and Elizabeth Griffith, appear to have left the family home. At this time, the household had a housekeeper and two female servants, as well as two male farm labourers. The census also records that the language used at home by the family was Welsh.

His mother Mary died on January 2nd 1883, aged 76 years and was buried in the family plot at Bwlch Cemetery, Abersoch North Wales.[686]

His father Hugh died on the 11th January, 1888, aged 83 years and was also buried in the Bwlch Cemetery. His estate was valued at £149 15s.[687]

Griffith Griffith, his eldest son, sought Probate for his father's will:

> On 24th February, 1888—The Will with a Codicil of Hugh Griffith, late of Creigir Uchaf in the Parish of Llanengan in the County of Carnarvon. Farmer who died 11 January 1888 at Creigir Uchaf was proved at the Principal Registry by Griffith Griffith of Creigir Uchaf—Farmer; the Son of sole Executor.

The absent one will not be the heir.

Interestingly, his father, Hugh Griffith, had added a codicil to his will in 1883 (the same year as Richard Griffith's marriage to the sister of his first wife) in which he appeared to have 'disinherited' his son. Whether this was as a result of Richard Griffith's second marriage, or that his eldest son and heir, Griffith Griffith, still being at home and perhaps having the greater claim to the estate, is not known.

---

[682] Llanengan is a hamlet in North West Wales, just over a mile from Cardigan Bay, and near the small town of Pwllheli.

[683] GRO/BMD: 1852 Q2; Pwllheli 11b 454.

[684] See http://rhiw.com/census_1861/llanengan_census_1861_01.htm (see page 450).
In the 1841 UK census, the Griffith family were resident at Creigir Engan and in the 1851 UK census, were then resident at the Creigir Uchaf farmstead.

[685] This unusual double name is a Welsh convention and is only ever given to a first-born. Gryffydd Gryffydd—translation:'The Lion of Lions'—and as such, is also heir-apparent to the Chief of the local tribe; courtesy of Mr Edward Prettejohn.

[686] Bwlch chapel, Llanengan is a Calvinistic Methodist chapel. The Calvinistic Methodists represent the largest religious group in Wales. Its members are intensely national in sentiment and aspirations and are staunch loyalists. They take a great interest in social, political and educational matters, and are much represented onvarious public bodies.

[687] This equates to £8,850 in today's currency value.

Richard Griffith started his maritime career as a seventeen year old man, in Hull 1869. There is tentative evidence that he worked in Chester, and the UK census for 1871 [688] could well link him to that town. He gained a practical knowledge of navigation and seamanship in the coasting trade and in voyages to the Baltic. He served nine years in sailing vessels, and obtained his master's certificate on July 22nd, 1887, and had spent twelve years in the employ of the Atlantic Transport Line, commencing as a second-mate and ending as the master of the ill-fated *Mohegan*.

Captain Richard Griffith was the senior captain in the Atlantic Transport Line's service, and the organisation had the greatest confidence in him, awarding him the title 'commodore' of the fleet. Nothing against him had been recorded during his lifetime. That would change.

A brief review of his maritime career listed in the Welsh Mariners log,[689] shows an initial entry as first mate on the vessel *Sunrise,* in 1882. He then became captain, on the vessel *Surrey* between 1886 and 1888. He was also the master of the vessel *Michigan* [690] in 1888 and then became the master of the *Cleopatra* in 1898 and finally, as master of the *Mohegan* [691] later that same year.

Griffith also commanded the Atlantic Transport liner *Massachusetts* [692] and letters to her captain, published with the record of the Board of Trade inquiry into the loss of the *Mohegan*, show that in September 1894 and February 1895 he was then in command of the *Manitoba*.[693] He also captained the *Maine* and the *Minnewaska* [694] in June of 1898, immediately before her sale to the U.S. government.

Following the *Mohegan* disaster, this short biography for Capt. Griffith was reported in the press:

He was a self made man, and was a typical British seaman, who had done so much to establish our supremacy of the seas. When quite a young man, Griffith entered the service of a shipping firm at Hull, and gained a practical knowledge of navigation and seamanship in the coasting trade, and in voyages to the Baltic. After being several years at sea, he obtained a mate's certificate, and received an appointment as mate in the Atlantic Transport Company's service, about 15 years ago. He made his first journey to New York on board a steamer commanded by Captain Robinson, now the marine superintendent of the line. After a short time, Griffith was appointed to the command of the *Maine*. From that time his promotion was rapid

---

[688] He is recorded as a lodger at Handbridge, Westminster Terrace St. Mary in Chester and as being born in 1852 in Caernarvonshire.

[689] See http://welshmariners.org.uk/search.php.

[690] In 1888 *Surrey* was renamed *Michigan* to comply with the shipping line's in-house practice of naming its ships beginning with the letter 'M'. The following year she was handed over to Williams, Torrey & Feild's Bernard Steamship Company and in 1889 was sold on to Christopher Furness.

[691] The vessel was originally named as the *Cleopatra* and later renamed as the *Mohegan.*

[692] The *Massachusetts* is recorded as having made 61 voyages to New York between May 1892 and July of 1898 under the ATL flag.

[693] The *Manitoba* was built for the Atlantic Transport Line's new London to New York passenger service, making 62 voyages to New York between April 1892 and June of 1898.

[694] The *Minnewaska* was built as the *Persia* for the Hamburg America Line's service to New York. She was bought by the Atlantic Transport Line in 1897, for $660,000 [£138,600], because she was "practically a sister" to the Massachusetts class of ships already purchased. The ship was promptly renamed *Minnewaska* (which means "clear water") and employed on the ATL's New York service. She is recorded as making just three voyages to New York for the ATL; Tuesday, March, 8, 1898, Tuesday, April, 12, 1898, and Monday, May, 16, 1898. In June of 1898, immediately before her sale, *Minnewaska* was under the command of Captain Richard Griffiths. An article in the *New York Times* records that her consumption of coal was 60 tons per day: an indication of the daily workload for a fireman, having to shift this load from a coal-bunker to the boiler's firebox.

and he successively became captain of the *Manitoba*,[695] the *Minnewaska*,[696] and the *Mohegan*. It is computed that he had crossed and re-crossed the Atlantic about three hundred times.[697]

A report in the *Baltimore Sun;* 1891, referred to him as, "the pleasant-natured Captain Griffiths of the *Minnesota*". There is an interesting piece recorded here, that further supports this view of the Captain's pleasing personality and demeanour:

PERILS OF THE SEA.

Further Particulars Concerning the Mohegan.

The loss of the ship *Mohegan* of the American Transpot Line, on last Friday, has proven a source of sadness to several Stauntonians. On the 11th of September, 1897, Mrs. R. S. Turk, wife of the editor of the SPECTATOR, and Miss Glen Atkinson, of this city took passage on the *Manitoba* of that line for London. Capt. R. Griffiths [*sic*] was the commander, and they soon made his acquaintance and that of his crew. He was a burly Welshman, weighing about two hundred pounds of florid complexion, about 50 years of age, and with apparently rough exterior, but of most kindly disposition, as they soon learned, and a perfect master of his work. He had been on the sea during his life, and was devoted to it. He constantly showed his thoughtfulness of his passengers by attentions generally unexpected when they came, and which were not apparently consistent with the exterior of the man of the seafaring man, but told that he was a diamond in the rough. These ladies were placed by him at his own table, and before the ten day voyage was ended they and he had become well acquainted, and when London was reached which was done in perfect company and safety they parted with regrets, at least on the part of the ladies. When Mrs. Turk returned in April [1898] last, she took passage on the *Minnewaska* of the same line, and what was her surprise and delight on reaching her ship to find Capt. Griffiths in command with most of the crew she had parted with some months before on the *Manitoba.* On the return trip she was most kindly and politely treated by the Captain. He had with him on this trip his son, a lad of fourteen, who was visiting for the first time the United States. This little fellow became a favourite with all, so handsome, polite and gentlemanly was he found to be (see fig. 83). The *Manitoba* and the *Minnewaska* were both sold to the government, when the Spanish war began, and the company bought other ships.[698]

There is also recorded here, a hitherto little known fact, which may have contributed to the contrary navigation of the *Mohegan,* under Griffith's command:

GOSSIP OF THE WEEK

CAPTAIN GRIFFITHS

I have just been speaking (writes a correspondent of the *Daily* News) with two ladies [699] who crossed the Atlantic last year [1897] in a ship under the command of Captain Griffiths, of the *Mohegan*. They tell me that the captain, although reserved

---

[695] Letters to her captain published with the official record of the Board of Trade's inquiry into the loss of *Mohegan* indicate that in September 1894 and February 1895 *Manitoba* was commanded by Richard Griffiths.

[696] The *Minnewaska* of the Atlantic Transport Line was sunk on November, 29th 1917, off one of the Greek islands after striking a mine, with 1,600 Troops aboard, bound for Saloniki, who were all saved. Capt. Richard Griffith was her master in September 1894 and in February 1895.

[697] *Western Mail* (Cardiff, Wales), Tuesday, October 18, 1898.

[698] *The Daily Staunton Spectator;* Staunton, V.A. Tuesday Morning, October 18, 1898.

[699] *The Royal Cornwall Gazette Falmouth Packet, Cornish Weekly News, & General Advertiser* (Truro, England), Thursday, November 10th 1898.

272

and somewhat taciturn, was a very winning personality, and inspired implicit confidence. He was a man of dauntless courage and iron will. He had lost an eye in an attack made upon him many years ago by the ringleaders of a mutinous crew of a sailing ship, whose turbulence, however, he succeeded by force of character and fearlessness in completely quelling.[700]

This unfortunate incident could account for the odd pose adopted by Capt. Griffith, in the only photograph that (until now) seemed to exist for the man  (see fig. 17). His upper body is three-quarters inclined towards the viewer, but his head is in complete profile; a rather unnatural pose, it must be said. But, now we know of his eye-injury, the adopted pose speaks for itself; we may deduce that he had lost his right eye. Certainly, the images of Capt. Griffith that appeared in the newspapers bore no resemblance to him whatsoever, and were entirely fictitious; as seen in this posthumous image in the year 1898.[701] However, this author has located two, hitherto unpublished images of the Captain (see Figs. 84 – 87).

As the company's commodore captain, he was regarded as a safe pair of hands. His role over the last few years was that of the company's trouble-shooter; indeed, he appeared to have been given a free hand, when it came to choosing a ship to sail as her master. As new boats were built for the company, he would have the pick of the finest and the biggest.

There is a time to speak and a time to be silent.

He was described as a martinet; a rigid disciplinarian. A revealing insight as to the captain's demeanour is suggested here:

THE MOHEGAN DISASTER

Some important new facts about the wreck of the *Mohegan* are given by "Scuratator" elsewhere, and the following somewhat extraordinary letter has been addressed to the *Daily Mail* by G E.D.L—

Early last year I sailed from London to New York with Captain Griffiths, of the unfortunate *Mohegan*, in charge. We were late getting out of the Thames, and it was dark before we passed the Eddystone Lighthouse. Some hours after we had retired I awoke, and noticed that the ship was not moving.

In the morning as we were seating ourselves at the captain's table for breakfast, an elderly gentleman from Toronto turned to the captain, and said, "That was quite a delay we had last night captain"; the captain gruffly replied, "We had no delay last night". "Oh I mean when the ship stopped," was the reply. "The ship didn't stop," was the captain's answer in still gruffer tones. "Why," remarked the passenger, "I noticed that the machinery was not going, and when I looked out of my port-hole I saw several lights, dressed myself and went on deck, noticed many shore lights and the light of the lighthouse". Several others during these remarks had also put in a few words to the effect that they too had noticed the shore lights.

---

[700] *Nottinghamshire Guardian* (London, England); Saturday, 22nd October 1898.

[701] *Manchester Times* (Manchester, England) Friday, October 21st 1898.

The captain scarcely allowed the last remark to be finished, but most angrily turned upon the passenger, and told him that the ship did not stop that night, and that he saw no lights. The captain's tone was such that the subject was instantly dropped, and there was little conversation during that breakfast at our table.

When the captain left the room at least six or eight of the passengers declared positively that they had noticed that the machinery has stopped, and remained so for one or two hours and those who had seen the lights either through the portholes or from the deck declared the land was very close.

Considering the hour it now appears to me that we were in the neighbourhood of the Manacles; and more than one passenger of the *Manitoba*[702] on that trip, now believes I am confident, that we might easily have shared the same fate as the *Mohegan,* and that we were preferably waiting for tide or something of the sort. It would be interesting to know whether the ship's log makes any reference to that stoppage, and at what point the ship lay during these hours.[703]

What had the captain to hide from his passengers? Their description of the events strongly suggests they were off Falmouth, and the lighthouse referred to as being St. Anthony's. Whether this was coincidental or by design, we do not know. Either way, it suggests a rather strange fixation with this port and in placing his vessel here, for no good reason. One has to question his judgment: particularly with the subsequent events involving the *Mohegan.* Was there some planned rendezvous with someone (or some other vessel) at Falmouth; or was it another example of the captain's questionable navigation? It would indeed be of great interest to examine the ship's log for this trip.[704]

Capt. Griffith's confrontation at the breakfast table with his passengers, perhaps illustrates another side to his character, and not necessarily as the "pleasant-natured" individual, referred to earlier. He could so easily have come up with an excuse, as to the reason for the ship's delay in transit. Instead, he chose to vehemently deny it and to suggest his passengers were mistaken in their observations. Little wonder then that the conversation at the breakfast table fell away at that point.

A safe pair of hands.

Griffith was sent to Hull in July 1898 to superintend the completion of the steamship *Cleopatra* and to oversee tasks completed by the builders, which he regarded as necessary. He officially took command of the *Cleopatra* on the 20th July 1898.[705] What followed was an unhappy maiden voyage for Griffith and his crew. The vessel returned to the UK and underwent extensive remedial work on her boilers and leaking plates.

There are suggestions that he had been ordered to set sail with the *Mohegan* against his wishes, and that in the ensuing standoff he had been stripped of his title of commodore of the fleet. This helped fuel the ensuing

---

[702] *SS Manitoba;* Arrived in New York on 17th June, 1897; its final trip being on 7th July 1898 and then sold on to the US Government.

[703] *The Royal Cornwall Gazette Falmouth Packet, Cornish Weekly News, & General Advertiser;* Thursday, 27th October 1898.

[704] The ship's log books are not included in either the National Archives at Kew or the Memorial University of Newfoundland (MUN) records.

[705] As recorded in the *Agreement and Account of Crew* documentation—Courtesy of: Maritime History Archive, Memorial University of Newfoundland.

conspiracy theory: in that, Griffith having a grievance against the company led him to wreak a terrible revenge, in his bringing about the subsequent disaster. As unlikely as this was, Griffith was undoubtedly a proud man and would have been sorely tested by these events.

On the first day of sailing, it was reported that he had been looking very ill all day, and had taken to lying down.[706] This could have a simple explanation: perhaps he was just taken ill—a case of seasickness for example: having no respect, even for a ship's 'commodore' commander.

Every drunken skipper trusts to Providence. But one of the ways
of Providence with drunken skippers is to run them on the rocks.

Another possible cause for his illness could have been brought on by the pre-voyage celebration at Tilbury, on the eve of the day she sailed on her fateful trip. One passenger noted, in an interview with the *New York Times* on her return to America, that there had been, "dancing that evening" and that the passenger had been, "disgusted at seeing crew members drinking". Another passenger – Mr A. E. L. Smith – had noted that Capt. Griffith had appeared, "morose, preoccupied, pale, and worried".

Was it possible that Griffith had taken, against his better judgment and despite his declared abstemiousness, imbibed a little too much alcoholic beverage? If indeed he was not one for drinking, a small amount could have had a disproportionate after-effect. Mr A. S. Williams, a representative of the shipping line, at the Board of Trade investigation said that, he had bade farewell to the captain just as he left the docks, and that he had, "appeared perfectly well". The chief steward later testified at the Board of Trade inquiry that he had served Griffith with a half-glass of champagne topped up with soda-water.

Loneliness is the penalty of leadership.

Capt. Griffith had a reputation to maintain and his elevated position in the company must have pressurised him greatly: having a wife and three young children, and with long periods away from home. He was also rumoured to be in debt.[707] As the commander of the ship, he was not able to mix socially with the crew, having to maintain a strictly professional demeanour, with no quality time in which to relax. In such a closeted society, forever alert to the safety of his ship and the wellbeing of his passengers, what seemed to an outsider as a rather envious position, was in fact, more a gilded cage.

Here was a man from a relatively lowly background, reaching an exalted status, in a remarkably short time. Mixing with rich and influential people, was he perhaps socially ill-at-ease? He was said not to use two

---

[706] The passengers Mr Arthur Ernest Leeson Smith, was quoted as making this observation, in *The Belfast News–Letter* (Belfast, Ireland), Monday, October 17, 1898. Both he and another passenger, Mr W. J. Bloomingdale, confirmed that the captain did not come down to dinner on the evening of the disaster.

[707] On the 7th December, 1898, application for probate was lodged by Martha Wickham Clark, Griffiths' widow, with the estate valued at £4,839, the current modern day value being £230,000. Not an insubstantial sum of money, though of rumoured debts (if any) he had, at the time of his death, nothing is known.

words, where one would do. Was this for fear of revealing his imagined (or actual) social shortcomings? He must have been a complex character, and one would imagine his being a rather insular man, not given to revealing too much about his personal life or background—with good reason, as we shall see later.

Whom the gods would destroy they first make mad.

In a disparaging account given to the *New York Times,* by the passenger Miss Kate Noble, she was of the belief that Capt. Griffith was:

> . . . "Mentally unbalanced", and she stated that: "It seems singular, that he permitted to direct three sane men to steer the Mohegan on to the rocks—such was the fact, however, and a lack of discipline was responsible for the terrible loss of life. It was suppertime; Capt. Griffiths was not in the [dining] saloon. My seat was next to his and was empty. I was told that he was in another cabin with some woman". [708]

Mr A. S. Williams, the head of the firm Williams, Torrey and Field, stongly denied such accusations, at the subsequent Board of Trade investigation.

A passenger, Miss Roudebush, told the same newspaper that:

> "If Capt. Griffith was responsible for the wreck he had certainly gone out of his mind". She continued: "As I remember it, he [Griffith] at 4 o'clock left the chief officer [Llewllyn Couch] in command. The chief officer was relieved at 6 o'clock by the third officer [Hindmarsh], who I understand, was young and inexperienced. The fact remains the boat went on the rock, and despite the fact that those on shore saw her course of danger, and sent up rockets of warning, I saw no officers who were apparently in authority during the excitement". [709]

Miss Roudebush seemed well acquainted with the ship's officer personnel, their shipboard duties, and timetable. All the officers referred to, in her view of the events leading up to the disaster, perished and so were not able to refute those accusations.

Hell hath no fury than a woman scorned.

Of course, all this could be so much shipboard tittle-tattle: a result of bored passengers, amusing themselves with rather outlandish stories designed to shock and titillate. Later, these stories would take on a greater significance, particularly in the ensuing aftermath, following the disaster. The accusations made were never offered as evidence at either the coroner's inquest, or at the Board of Trade investigation, and so, they had never been legally challenged. It is probably mere hearsay; however, hell hath no fury than that of a woman scorned—particularly at a captain's table. Miss Noble would perhaps have been somewhat piqued at a rather

---

[708] *New York Times;* 20th November 1898.

[709] Ibid.

public rejection by the captain on the previous evening at the dinner table,[710] and here again on the following evening, by his total absence. Perhaps this was her revenge: in concocting the story, that of the captain's alleged dalliance with another woman, in his or the woman's cabin.

He who hesitates is lost.

With the *Mohegan* finding itself within the confines of Falmouth Bay, the crew eventually realised the danger the vessel was in. The ship's wheel was abruptly turned about, as they desperately made for open water. As the ship swung over hard to port, Griffith, if indeed he had been in a cabin at that point, would have instinctively sensed a problem, requiring his immediate presence on the bridge. As the disaster unfolded, the captain was now placed on the ship's bridge, and in controlling events. His heroism and firm command of the situation was later much commented on, and enthusiastically promoted by the Atlantic Transport Line management.

The last visual report of him aboard was that of his going down with his ship. His body was not recovered locally. There were several bodies recovered over the next three months, which, understandably, were not able to be positively identified and were officially designated by the coroner as 'Unknown' in the GRO/BMD register. It is conceivable that one such body was that of Capt. Griffith and if his jacket had been removed by its finder, then that item of clothing would have not been present, enabling a means of positive identification for him.

His loss in the *Mohegan* tragedy was reported in a Welsh newspaper:

> The captain of the *Mohegan*, the vessel which recently foundered between Falmouth and the Lizard Head was a native of Llanengan, son of the late Hugh Griffiths, Creigiruchaf,[711] brother of Griffith Griffiths [712] the present occupier, and to Miss Griffiths, who resides at Devonald Street, Holyhead.[713] Captain Griffiths whose home is at Leytonstone Essex,[714] left a widow and three children. [715]

---

[710] See reference to this incident in Chapter 24; Miss Katherine Bell Noble; A Passenger's Account.

[711] The name of the family farm translates to English as: *creigir* – a stony place, and *uchaf* – upper.

[712] The captain's brother, Griffith Griffiths (1841–1925), was at this time aged 57 years, and with both his parents now deceased. In the 1901 UK census he was described as head of the household and as an employer; living at the same family home, now with his wife Judith Griffith, 13 years his junior.

[713] Catherine Griffith: 1901 UK census: 11, Board School House Devonald Street Holyhead Anglesey. Relation: Head / Condition: Single.
1911 UK census: Bryn Llanfeog Ty Croes, Holyhead, Anglesey / Relation: Head / Marital State: Single / Occupation: Lodging House Keeper. Death: Aged 72 years, January, March 1915, Holyhead, Anglsey; GRO/BMD; 11b 846.

[714] 'Manhattan' Queens Road, Leytonstone, Essex London. It is likely that, due to the numerous trips made by Capt. Griffiths to New York, he named his house with this unusual soubriquet, *Manhattan*. His eldest son; Walter Hugh Griffith, (14 years of age at the time of the disaster); had made the voyage across the Atlantic with his father, in April, in the year of the disaster. He also had a daughter Selina May Griffith aged 9 years, and another son, Victor, aged about 12 months. The earliest electoral register at the Vestry House Museum, Waltamstow, London, is for 1893. It has no entry for Griffith(s) in Queens Road (which was in the Leytonstone Polling District) nor in the 1894 register; however, the 1895 electoral register has the entry: Griffiths, Richard; *Manhattan*, Queens Road, Leytonstone. The 1899 electoral register has this entry: Griffiths, Richard—26, Queens Road, Leytonstone. By this time Capt. Griffith was supposedly deceased but his widow continued to live at this address; however, there is no entry for her at that address in the 1900 electoral register. The Kelly's street directories gave the same overall picture but records his name as 'Griffith' and the house name as 'Manhathan' [*sic*] until it was eventually numbered as 26. The 1886 Kelly's only shows 4 houses in Queen's Road. Capt. Wm. Fife was living at

The popular account for the demise of Griffith was that his headless body was said to have been found, three months after the disaster, in Caernarvon Bay, Anglesey. The body was tentatively identified by means of its clothing: a captain's uniform jacket, together with the appropriate insignia, and with its brass buttons, on which were embossed the ATL company logo.

This author has been unable to find any such report in a contemporaneous newspaper, on either side of the Atlantic, or as a report arising from a local coroner's inquest. If the story was true, then astonishingly the event was not mentioned in the Welsh newspapers, despite his being a local man and with a report of his loss having previously been published. It is implausible that the arrival of his body, on home turf, would not have attracted some considerable interest. One could imagine a newspaper headline, pandering to a Victorian obsession in such morbid matters:

Horror from Mohegan Shipwreck: Captain's Headless Body Returns Home to Wales.

Yet, such an eye-catching headline failed to appear. If the headless corpse of Captain Griffith had washed ashore in Caernarvon Bay, this would have proclaimed that the sea had finally finished with the *Mohegan,* and with its master.[716] But that was not to be.[717]

The distance between the scene of the disaster and his eventual 'appearance' is 250 nautical miles. In a review of the *Mohegan* victims' bodies retrieved, not one was reported as having been recovered west of the Lizard. That the body should have navigated its way, around Land's End, and eventually arriving at its final resting place in Caernarvon Bay, ranges from the bizarre to the incredulous. If so, then he showed a quite unerring sense of navigation, which seemed to have eluded him on his last voyage as master of the *Mohegan.* On the surface, the story suggests a rather contrived ending to the affair of the *Mohegan* disaster.

There is little other reference to Capt. Griffith, in the newspapers; apart from the reporting of the Board of Trade inquiry and the support given him by his employer and this piece recalling his standing in the town of Swansea:

THE CAPTAIN WELL KNOWN IN SWANSEA

Captain Griffith, who had command of the vessel, was (says the Swansea "*Leader*") very well known in Swansea. He had commanded many of Messrs. Williams, Torrey, and Field's boats, which traded to Swansea, before he took charge of the *Mohegan,* and was looked up to in shipping circles as an experienced and capable man.[718]

'Meta House.' The 1894/5 Kelly's Directory shows Capt. Jas. Gray at 'The Sisters' sharing with George Morgan, and next door to Richard Griffith. The street itself would seem to be a popular residential area for ships' captains. Courtesy: David Boote; Leyton and Leytonstone Historical Society.

[715] *Caernarfon and Denbeigh Herald;* 29th October 1898. Note that the family name was reported in the newspaper as 'Griffiths' (a common misspelling) whereas the 1861 and 1881 UK census had recorded the true family name as 'Griffith'.

[716] A research undertaken by the Archive, Museums and Arts Service – Gwynedd Council, failed to find any reference to this event in the local Welsh newspapers, for the period January, 1899 to December 1900. A search for a coroner's report was not successful.

[717] Depending on the temperature of the seawater, a body could well remain relatively intact over a prolonged period. From the wreck of the *HMS Weazle,* in North Devon (1799), Lt. W. C. Butler's body was said to be, apart from some damage to the face, in "as perfect a state as if he had only just drowned". Interestingly, that wreck occurred at about the same time of the year as with the *Mohegan* and Butler's body was immersed in water for 3 months: as was Griffith—allegedly. Kendall McDonald; *Great British Wrecks: The Wreck Diver's Logbook, Vol. 3* (Underwater Publications Ltd.), 116.

A Cornish author, Mr Frank Strike, has revealed an interesting find that gives an interesting insight by the way in which affected individuals viewed the *Mohegan* event:

Quite recently, during alterations to an old cottage in Gweek,[719] a letter was found above a ceiling. Written from the United States to Mr. James,[720] of St. Keverne, it advances an unusual theory, as to the loss of the *Mohegan*, which has, to the best of the author's [Frank Strike] belief, not been published before.

To: Mr. H. James   From: Thomas Oakes and Co,
St. Keverne.   Successors to D. Oakes,
                                                    Woollen Manufacturers,
                                                    Bloomfield,
                                                    N.J.

My Dear Sir,

I was very pleased to hear from you and to receive your photograph, which I think very good indeed, and thank you sincerely for it.

I am of the same opinion as you in regard to the *Mohegan* that she was run ashore purposely by—although I don't know if it was done for insurance or not.

When I first made up my mind she was run ashore, I thought it was for the insurance, but now I think perhaps the company knew nothing of it and that the Captain did it for spite. Because some of the Captain's relatives, or intimate friends living in Ohio, told a friend of Mr. Firing's [721] that the Captain of the *Mohegan* had had quite a row with the Company before sailing. He had been given the *Mohegan* when he did not want that ship and the position of Commander [*sic*] of the Line had been taken away from him. From what these Ohio people said it was thought that the Captain has done this out of anger and to spite the Company. But this is only guess work, and from what you said in your letter it would look as if it were done for the insurance and that the Company did not want anyone saved to tell the story.

I think it very strange that nothing had been said about the Captain and Officers in the papers, I have seen no mention of their bodies having been recorded or anything said about them, which makes me think that perhaps they might have escaped somehow in a boat and landed in disguise on some distant point from St. Keverne. Do you think such a thing possible or probable? Whatever the notion for doing this, I believe she was run on the rocks purposely. Did you hear from the survivors if there had been any trouble between the Captain and Officers before she struck?

I think if Mr. Firing is in good health next summer, you will see him at St. Keverne; at least he talks that way.

I will appreciate a letter from you when you have time and feel like writing me very much.

---

[718] *Western Mail* (Cardiff, Wales); Monday, 17th October 1898.

[719] Gweek is a small port, 3½ miles from Helston. The pilchard-fishery is carried on extensively, 200 boats being employed in taking the fish, which are cured in the various creeks and coves within the limits of the port. In addition to the fishery, the chief trade consists in the exportation of copper-ore, corn, moorstone, and oysters, and the importation of timber, coal, and limestone; Lewis's Topographical Dictionary of England published in 1848.

[720] Most probably Hannibal James, in the opinion of Terry Moyle. UK census 1891: Hannibal, JAMES / Son / Single / Age:29 / Farmer's Son / Churchtown, St. Keverne.

[721] The remains for Mrs E. V. Firing, the wife of John Phelps Firing—chief clerk to the Paymaster of the US Navy—were cremated at Woking, Surrey. The ashes were accompanied back to America by Mr Firing, and in the company of Mr George Oakes, both of whom had made a special journey from America, following the foundering of the *Mohegan*. It was probable that both men had visited the scene of the disaster and so struck up an acquaintance with Mr H. James, resulting in a subsequent letter that was later discovered in Gweek.

With kind regards for all friends at St. Keverne, and many thanks for your picture.

Believe me.

Very truly, Geo. A. Oakes. February 6th, 1899.[722]

The letter is quite explicit, as regards a criminal intent on the part of the captain, and possibly in collusion with his officers; however, it is really not feasible. Yet, the letter does contain an interesting remark: that of the Captain's relatives or intimate friends living in Ohio. Again, there is no proof for this, but it does raise the possibility that, had Capt. Griffith indeed survived the wrecking and was the man seen running up the beach at Porthoustock, then he could well have established a new life for himself, in Ohio, aided by those same people—or so the argument goes.

At the subsequent Board of Trade inquiry, and at the coroner's inquest in Cornwall, Mr Williams, head of the firm Williams, Torrey and Feild, giving evidence on behalf of the shipping-line, lavished fulsome praise on Griffith's character and professional ability, and was at pains to comment on his abstemiousness. Mr Frank Nicklin, a steward who had survived the *Mohegan* disaster, gave evidence, in which he said that the only time he saw Capt. Griffith partake of alcoholic beverage, was during the reception aboard the *Mohegan*, before her sailing, and that consisted of a glass of champagne transferred to a tumbler and topped up with soda-water. So, not entirely abstemious, as earlier remarks would have suggested.

Mr. Philip Franklin, the company's agent of the line in New York, issued the following statement, when asked about a report that the Griffith was not in a suitable condition to manage the ship, he said:

Capt. Griffiths was a one of our most competent men. He was the commodore of the fleet and an officer in which we had the utmost confidence. On several occasions I have crossed the Atlantic with Capt. Griffiths, and I cannot use too strong language in contradicting the insinuation that he was in any way unfit for duty when the ship struck. Capt. Griffiths has been in the service of the company for thirteen years, and in all these years of service I have never known him to use intoxicating liquors in any shape. [723]

Capt. Griffith was described as a brave and gallant officer, and with his character beyond reproach. Again, Mr A. S. Williams, at the coroner's inquest held in Cornwall, stated that the captain was, "A perfectly sober man. I made a voyage with him to America and have seen him [on] every voyage for the last twelve years. He was a man of good nerve. You would never see him in the least degree excited: a strict disciplinarian and a most capable commander."

---

[722] Frank Strike, B.E.M.; *Cornish Shipwrecks* (Published by F. L. Strike, Porthleven, Cornwall 1965).

[723] *New York Times;* 18th October 1898.

Why need I volumes, if one word suffice.

Asked if Griffith was a morose man Williams replied: "No, he was a self contained man. He did not speak two words if one would do. He was fairly sociable, but if there was business to be done he did not waste a word."

Quite obviously, during the run up to the formal investigation, the rumour that Griffith was intoxicated, during the trip, had made the rounds. This could account for the rather robust defence on his behalf at the hearings, coupled with a firm rebuttal as to his being incapable of professional judgment, due to alcohol impairment. Mr A. S. Williams had bade farewell to the captain, as he left the docks on his fateful journey, and to him he appeared perfectly well.

Little strokes fell great oaks.

There is a possibility that Captain Griffith was suffering a medical condition, affecting his brain and leading to an impairment of his cognitive function. A series of mini-strokes, a medical condition known as Transient Ischaemic Attacks (TIA),[724] could have had a bearing on events.

The symptoms of stroke and TIA are the same and depend upon the particular region of the brain that is affected. But while a stroke is permanent, a TIA, by definition, resolves itself within 24 hours or even a few minutes. The usual symptoms, which can vary in severity, are:

- a neurologic deficit appearing suddenly and affecting the ability to move or feel on one side of the body
- it may cause sudden dimming or loss of vision, aphasia, slurred speech and mental confusion
- an afflicted person may experience confusion, difficulty saying words, or an inability to follow commands (or give them).

Those who cannot themselves observe can at least acquire the observation of others.

Griffith was said to have looked ill and taken to lying down throughout the day of the disaster. The proximity of the Eddystone Light and the coast line thereafter could well have been not apparent to Capt. Griffith, because of this medical condition, and bearing in mind he had only one good eye.[725] His officers being disinclined to question their Captain regarding the positioning of the vessel, had inevitably led to the disaster

---

[724] TIAs, like a stroke, may have large, obvious neurologic defects such as paralysis. However, the symptoms may also be subtle, such as numbness or burning [sensation] of a limb or clumsiness with the use of hand or while walking. If the cerebellum is affected because of issues with the vertebral arteries, the symptoms are much different. Symptoms of posterior circulation stroke or cerebrovascular accident include: dizziness; loss of balance and coordination, and trouble walking. Drop attacks, in which the patient falls suddenly without warning, with or without losing consciousness, occur as a result of a TIA to the base of the brain. Amaurosis Fugax is a specific type of TIA where there is sudden loss of vision in one eye that resolves spontaneously. It occurs when debris from the carotid artery on the same side occludes one of the ophthalmic arteries and stops blood supply to the retina (the nerve complex in the back of the eye that interprets light and visual signals). http://emedicinehealth.com/transient_ischemic_attack_mini-stroke/page2_em.htm.

[725] His loss of an eye was as a result of a mutiny and a fracas aboard a ship of his command, some years previously.

later that day. If indeed TIA was the problem, it is certain that Captain Griffith would not have confided his condition to his officers, including his ship's medical officer, and would have desperately tried to maintain his standing and authority, despite his affliction.

The comments made by Miss Noble, relating to the events at dinner on the previous evening, where she stated that Capt. Griffith failed totally to respond to her attempted conversation with him, could well be attributed to this same medical condition.

The question that remains unanswered is, was his medical condition (or at least its manifestation) apparent to the managers of his shipping company, or the crew? The altercation between the captain and his manager, at the point of sailing, could have had some significance, in the circumstance. It is perhaps telling, that the ATL managers and the ship's doctor were as one, in attesting as to the robust health of their captain, at the subsequent Board of Trade inquiry.

Men pass away, but their deeds abide.

Griffith's apparent demise went on to reveal a rather complicated domestic life and it may help here to establish a timeline for his significant lifetime events, to help clarify the family relationships:

Party:	Event:	Date:	Notes:
Mary Ann Clark	Birth	1855	Poplar, Limehouse, London
	Marriage	Sept 25th 1879	Spouse: Richard Griffith
Martha Wickham Clark	Birth	1862	Poplar, Limehouse, London
	Marriage	18th Aug 1883	Spouse: Richard Griffith
	Probate Application	1898	December 1898, following her husband's death
	Death	1958	Tregawne, Withiel Cornwall
Hugh Griffith	Legal Transaction	16th Aug 1883	Father to Richard Griffith —Last Will and Testament
	Legal Transaction	12th Sept 1887	Codicil to his 1883 Will
	Death	11th Jan 1888	Bwlch Cemetery, Abersoch North Wales
Richard Griffith	Birth	1852	Llanengan, Carnarvonshire
	Marriage	Sept 25th 1879	Spouse: Mary Ann Clark
	Marriage [*sic*]	August 18th 1883	Spouse: Martha Clark
	Legal Transaction	June 1889	Last Will and Testament

Party:	Event:	Date:	Notes:
Selina May Griffith	Birth	1889	Stepney, London
	Marriage	Dec 12th 1915	Spouse: Ernest Prettejohn
	Death	1989	GRO/BMD; Q3 1989 Truro; 21 650
Victor Richard Griffith	Birth	1897	Son to Richard and Martha Griffith
	Marriage	August 9th 1924	Spouse: Helen Hilda Head
	Death	1978	Chelmsford, Essex
Walter Hugh Griffith[726]	Birth	1885	Son to Richard and Martha Griffith
	Marriage	June 8th 1912	Spouse: Ada Elizabeth Brown
	Death	1920	Romford, Essex

Table 15: Griffith / Clark Families: A Genealogical Report.

Richard Griffith had prepared a will in 1889 and a transcript follows:

> **THIS IS THE LAST WILL** of me Richard Griffith of No 54 Turners Road E.[727] Shipmaster in the employ of The Atlantic Transport Line. I devise and bequeath all my real and personal Estate of every description whatever to my present wife formerly known as Martha Wickham Clark (and now as Martha Wickham Griffith) of the same place to the exclusion of my former wife whether I am lawfully married to the said Martha Wickham Griffith or not. And I appoint the said Martha Wickham Griffith to be the sole EXECUTRIX of this my Will In WITNESS whereof I have set my hand to this my WILL the first day of June One thousand eight hundred and eighty nine [728]
>
> RICHARD GRIFFITH; SIGNED by the above named Richard Griffith as his last Will in the presence of us both being present at the same time who in his presence and in the presence of each other have hereunto subscribed our names as Witnesses; J. WHEATLEY 23 Leadenhall Street E.C.   Solicitor; P.W. KNIGHT Managing Clerk to J. Wheatley.

Following the disaster, his wife Martha Wickham Griffith made an application for Probate, and it was granted accordingly:

> On the 7th day Probate of this Will was granted to Martha Wickham Clark otherwise Griffith, Spinster the sole Executrix.
>
>   BE IT KNOWN, that at the date hereunder written, the last Will and Testament of *Richard Griffith*
>
> Of *Manhattan Queen's Road Leytonstone in the County of Essex Master Mariner formerly of N^O. 54 Turner's Road in the said County* deceased, who died on the *14th* day of *October* 189 *8* at *sea in the wreck of the* S.S. *Mohegan*
>
> was proved and registered in the Principal Probate Registry of Her Majesty's High Court of Justice, and that administration of all the estate which by law devolves to and vests in the personal representative of the said deceased was granted by the aforesaid Court to *Martha Wickham Clark otherwise Griffith of Manhattan aforesaid Spinster the sole Executrix* [729]
>
> Named in the said *Will Re-sworn Oct; 1901 £4989-7-0*
>
> Dated the *7th.* day of *December* 189 *8*
>
> Gross value of Estate ... *£ 4389-7-9*.

---

[726] The family nickname for Walter Griffith was 'Wally'—Courtesy: Edward Prettejohn.

[727] Turners Road is situated in Limehouse, Tower Hamlets, East London, and was his in-law's home. At the time of death, the Griffith family had moved to 'Manhattan', Queens Road, Leytonstone.

[728] The will was made six years after his 'marriage' to Martha Clark and in the same year as the arrival of his first child.

[729] EXECUTRIX is the term that describes a woman who has been appointed by a will to execute such will or testament.

The gross value of the estate was £ 250,000 in modern terms—a large sum of money. One assumes that this must have included the Leytonstone family home and possible life insurance payments. There was rumour that Capt. Griffith was in debt. That might well have been the case during his lifetime, but in death, his wife would have certainly benefited from this consolidation of funds—enough to later install herself in a new family home, situated in a rather pleasant area of north London.

The probate document records that: '... *was granted by the aforesaid Court to Martha Wickham Clark otherwise Griffith of Manhattan aforesaid Spinster the sole Executrix*'.

This rather unexpected wording in both the will and the Probate documents, can only lead to the conclusion that the second marriage was bigamous.[730] The will, written in 1889, implied his first wife as being still alive, as she is expressly excluded as a beneficiary of his estate.

The legal terminology of 'spinster' is defined as, 'a woman who had never married.' This is clearly at odds with her marriage certificate details (see page 441) and this same certificate shows Richard Griffith described as being a, 'bachelor', which again is a total fabrication.

Martha Wickham Griffith's true marital status was revealed to the Principal Probate Registry authority as a matter of course, by the very terms of the will. This accounts for the, 'spinster' title, used in the Probate document. The will was accepted as valid, despite the circumstances surrounding Richard Griffith's death, and so there was no good reason to rake over old coals. The mystery remains however, over the whereabouts of Griffith's first wife, through all this.

Given the public attitude towards bigamous marriages, and with a male dominance within the marital union, it is perhaps not surprising that Richard Griffith was prepared to risk undertaking such a step.[731] At the second marriage, neither of the two sets of witnesses was from their respective family; whereas, at the first marriage, two members of the Clark family were recorded in that role. The possibility here is that the second marriage was a secret affair and unknown to the families, until some time after the event. It is generally known that such bigamous marriages were relatively common in the 19th century and were tacitly accepted by society and the families involved.

---

[730] In the 19th century, there was in fact a shortage of available and eligible men. UK census figures for the period reveal there were far more women than men. By 1861 there were 10,380,285 women living in England and Wales but only 9,825,246 men. The laws in Britain were based on the idea that women would get married and that their husbands would take care of them. Before the passing of the 1882 Married Property Act, when a woman got married her wealth was passed to her husband. If a woman worked after marriage, her earnings also belonged to her husband. Based on 221 bigamy cases between 1830 and 1900, it is argued that many couples, particularly in the working class, entered bigamous unions throughout the nineteenth century. Most communities accepted these unions if they followed certain norms. The bigamist had to have a good reason to have left his or her spouse, had to have been honest with the second spouse, and had to be able to support multiple families. Within these parameters, neighbours and friends accepted illegal marriages, following in a long tradition of self-marriage and self-divorce. In fact, by the end of the century, judges followed community standards in their sentencing and often gave nominal punishment to both male and female bigamists. In the 1880s and 1890s, law enforcement officials were reluctant in bringing bigamy charges because pressure from below had so compromised prosecutions—Courtesy: Ginger Frost; *Living in Sin: Cohabiting as Husband and Wife in Nineteenth-Century England.*

[731] *The Offences Against The Person Act 1861*, Section 57; Bigamy. This section creates the offence of bigamy. It replaces section-22 of *The Offences Against The Person Act 1828.*—'Whosoever, being married, shall marry any other person during the life of the former husband or wife, whether the second marriage shall have taken place in England or Ireland or elsewhere, shall be guilty of felony, and being convicted thereof shall be liable to be kept in penal servitude for any term not exceeding seven years'—*WikiPedia.*

There is no record of a divorce for Richard Griffith from his first wife, Mary Ann Griffith.[732] Even had a divorce taken place, another equally serious impediment for the second marriage, was the situation regarding a marriage between a man and his first wife's sister. This was prohibited in law, and not changed until the *Deceased Wife's Sister's Marriage Act 1907*[733] had been placed on the statute book: allowing a man, if his wife had died, to marry her sister. Had this event become known to the authorities, Griffith would almost certainly have faced criminal charges and a custodial sentence, particularly as he had been both married bigamously *and* to his wife's sister. Until the passing of the Act, even the death of a first wife still barred a subsequent marriage by her husband, to the first wife's sibling.

In the UK census for 1901, Martha Wickham Griffith was once again in residence at her parents' address—54 Turners Road, Limehouse—together with her two sisters, Caroline and Sarah. This being two years after the death of Richard Griffith, and before she moved to a new home: Wanstead Park Avenue, Redbridge Essex, where the UK 1911 census, show the same two sisters now living with her and her children (see page 451).

This rather complicated affair would suggest that at some stage during 1879 and 1883, either: Richard Griffith had parted from his first wife; she had died at some point; or had become a long-term inmate of some institution or other.

There is a formal burial record which could explain the reason for her apparent disappearance. This was an interment in the burial ground of the Lunatic Asylum in the County of Essex, which took place on December 28th 1889.[734] Her age was recorded as 27 years; some three or four years younger than her actual age, based on the year of birth as 1858. Also, the surname was 'Griffiths' but this was a common misspelling seen throughout the official records for this family.[735]

---

[732] 1858–1937 Divorce records—The National Archives, Kew: Catalogue (J77). Divorce was a very rare event, in the UK and was almost an exclusive preserve of the rich and for the aristocracy. It was unheard of for an ordinary family to consider a divorce. In 1857 the *Matrimonial Causes Act* went through which made it possible to obtain a divorce in England, other than by Act of Parliament. Before this, a few hundred cases had gone through. Only six of these had been by suit of the wife who was legally disadvantaged, even if her husband had committed adultery. This situation continued until women had a right to their property. In fact many people separated informally and in some cases married bigamously. This might explain a situation where husbands and wives sometimes did not live under the same roof during the UK census recording in the Nineteenth Century, and were living with other people. In 1923 Women were allowed a divorce on grounds of adultery alone. The 1937 Divorce Act allowed that desertion and insanity could be grounds for divorce. Courtesy: Timothy J. Owston, York, UK.

[733] The desire of widowed men to marry the sister of their deceased wife became the subject for particular agitation from the 1860s onwards and strong feelings were roused on both sides. However, it was to be nearly 50 years before the campaign for a change in the law was successful, despite the introduction of draft legislation in Parliament on many occasions. This Act removed the prohibition (although it allowed individual clergy, if they chose, to refuse to conduct marriages which would previously have been prohibited), but the Act did exactly what it said and no more so, for example, it was not until 1921 that the Deceased Brother's Widow's Marriage Act 1921 was passed. *The Marriage (Prohibited Degrees) Relationship Act 1931* extended the operation of the 1907 Act to allow the marriages of nieces and nephews by marriage as well. *WikiPedia*

[734] Her death was six years after his 'marriage' to Martha Clark and in the same year as the arrival of his second child, and in the year in which he made his will.

[735] Experience has shown that, when a person goes into a mental institution and dies there, it is the institution that registers the death, so the patient's name and age might not be given exactly, especially if they had been in the institution for some years. They are also sometimes difficult to spot on UK census as often their full names are not given, just initials—Moderator "Valda": Rootschat.com

No. 1781

Burial Registry for the Lunatic Asylum – County of Essex.[736]

If this was not the person in question, then she might well have left her husband for another man, having adopted *his* name and lived as his common-law wife, or having bigamously married him. Either way, a change in name would explain the absence of Mary Ann Griffith(s) / Clark, in any subsequent GRO/BMD records.

An untoward incident on Porthoustock Beach.

Returning to the events of that fateful night of the disaster, when a man was seen to run up the beach after alighting from the lifeboat: who was this man? Local villagers insist that this person was Captain Griffith, despite the conflicting statements as to his dress, at the time. Some said he was attired in evening dress; others, an engineer's boiler suit. In the confusion of that night, it was perhaps not surprising to hear such disparate views. In the darkness, the captain's uniform (without his cap) may well have been mistaken for evening-dress.[737]

A rather condescending report in the local Press tells of the villagers' continued insistence on the survival of the captain:

LOCAL GOSSIP.

Cornwall is the home of strange beliefs and superstitions. Of one thing many peasants and fishers in the neighbourhood of the Manacles are quite convinced and that is the captain of the *Mohegan* came ashore somehow from the wreck. To this belief they cling, in spite of all that has been said, "down upon the paper" about his death. It is enough for them, says "Country Life," [738] that some people say he came ashore with them,[739] that cottagers speak of a mysterious visitor that night who looked in, ate and drank, and then passed on and that no one identified his body. Fishermen of the locality have declared to a representative of the *Royal Cornwall Gazette* that the captain did come ashore, and that it is a well-known fact in the district.[740]

---

[736] Courtesy of the Seax; Essex Archives Online, Essex Record Office. http://seax.essexcc.gov.uk/Images.Net.

[737] At the centenary remembrance service held at St. Keverne, in the year 1998, a woman approached Mr Russell Hocking and introduced herself as the sister [*sic*] of the man who had ran up the beach that night. She says that, the family believed him to be lost in the disaster, but he turned up at their home on the Sunday, whilst dinner was being served. Regrettably, Mr Hocking had neglected to take the woman's details, for which he says, "I could kick myself". Personal communication: Mr Russell Hocking; St. Keverne—a local historian.

[738] *Country Life* was launched in 1897, incorporating *Racing Illustrated*. At this time it was owned by Edward Hudson, the owner of Lindisfarne Castle and various Lutyens-designed houses including The Deanery in Sonning. At that time golf and racing served as its main content, as well as the property coverage, initially of manorial estates, that has become its mainstay—*WikiPedia*.

[739] This would have been aboard the first run of the *Charlotte* lifeboat (in darkness), as the second trip only consisted of the 16 persons from the *Mohegan*'s rigging, and his presence here would have been confirmed absolutely: as by this time, it would have been in daylight.

[740] *The Royal Cornwall Gazette Falmouth Packet, Cornish Weekly News, & General Advertiser*; Thursday, 30th November 1899.

It is worth noting that this report came out in December 1899 and this being 11 months after his body was purported to have been found in Caernarfon Bay. It further supports the view that his body was never 'officially' recovered at the scene of the disaster.

Local stories tell that on the day following the disaster, a man was seen taking a boat and rowing it across the Helford River estuary. This could well have been the same man who ran up the beach the previous evening, making for the port of Falmouth. It is quite feasible for a man to walk the distance from Porthoustock beach to the Helford River by the morning, albeit at night and over difficult terrain.

In Capt. Griffith's thirty-year long maritime career, it is almost certain that he would several times have been on a vessel that put into Falmouth Harbour. The relative position of the Manacles to Falmouth and with the Helford Passage sited between the two locations, would have been well known to him. Did he plan this escape on the spur of the moment, on reaching the beach that night, and then to lose himself in the busy port of Falmouth?

Apart from Captain Griffith, who else might have needed to make good his escape up the beach that night? It could simply have been an individual so traumatised by events, that he felt an overriding need to escape the horror surrounding him. It is also feasible that this same individual may well have returned later that night, or the next morning, and that the boat incident on the Helford River estuary, was entirely coincidental.[741]

Moving on is simple, it's what you leave behind that makes it so difficult.

Let us consider that Capt. Griffith, having survived the disaster, was indeed the man in a hurry to leave the beach, that night.

On arrival in Falmouth, he would not have sought help at the Royal Cornwall Sailors' Home, as he would undoubtedly have been recognised by other members of the crew. He may well have carried money with him and this would have enabled him to catch a train from Falmouth, making his way back to London, or his family home in Wales. Whatever the course of events, and with the newspapers full of the story of the wreck, he knew things would have become uncomfortable for him, had he broken cover at this point. Unlike modern newspapers, photographic images were not routinely published, and so recognition by a member of the public would have been almost impossible.[742]

---

[741] There was no official report made of a boat being commandeered at the Helston estuary, at around this time.

[742] LITHOGRAPHY (surface printing) - introduced c. 1880. Although this process was invented at the end of the 18th century, it did not see common use until the latter part of the 19th century, when it was adapted to mechanisation. The design was drawn on to a flat stone surface, using a greasy ink, which was then 'fixed' chemically. A new field of photography was emerging in 1910; newspapers wanted photographs to replace sketches and drawings for the news events they were going to print. The era of news photography was just beginning. Indeed, the newspapers used sketches of Capt. Griffith in their copy, based on this technology (see page. 273).

Had he eventually been exposed, Capt. Griffith would have been made to account for his role in the event and would have faced a charge of criminally negligent manslaughter. It is possible that Griffith would have, at some stage, contacted his previous employer, the Atlantic Transport Line. They would have been horrified at a re-emergence of Griffith, causing immense publicity and returning the *Mohegan* story to the front-page of every newspaper. The true story might well then be exposed: Griffith's confrontation with the company, the alleged stripping him of the title of commodore of the fleet and, not least, any conflicting evidence given by its own directors and employees, at the Board of Trade inquiry or at the coroner's inquest in Cornwall. In this unlikely situation, the company, in connivance with Griffith, would have spirited him out of the country, away from a public scrutiny. The *Cleopatra / Mohegan* saga had already dented their reputation, and further revelations could have provoked public outrage and damaged future business prospects for the company. With Griffith surreptitiously removed from the scene, he could have settled in America and kept a low profile there. But this is pure conjecture.

No death certificate has been found for Richard Griffith, in the UK. Had his body surfaced in Caernarfon Bay, three months later, it would be expected that the Welsh coroner would have formally recorded that event; here again, there is no reference of such an outcome. The story of his having survived the disaster is, at this point, unproven.

In an American newspaper, a question of Griffith's nauturalistion status arose:

> Captain Griffiths leaves a wife and three children in London. He was a naturalized citizen of the United States, and had his certificate of master in the merchant marine of this country.[743]

The Griffith family grave is located in *Plot b. 138* in Bwlch Cemetery, on the Llanengan Road, Abersoch North Wales. The grave contains the remains of his father, and mother. Also present here, is a memorial tablet (see fig. 75) to Capt. Richard Griffith, which is inscribed:

In affectionate remembrance of
Richard Griffith
(the youngest son of the above Hugh and Mary Griffith)
Master of the ill-fated s.s. *Mohegan*
Who lost his life, with 105 others
On the Manacle Rocks, off Cornwall
October 14th, 1898 aged 46 years.

"In the midst of life we are in death"

---

[743] The Baltimore *Sun* (1837; 1985); Oct 18th 1898.
Capt. Thomas F. Gates was made a naturalised American citizen, as a result of the purchase of ATL ships by the USA Government on the 29th July, 1898: Jonathan Kinghorn; *The Atlantic Transport Line, 1881–1931: A History with Details on All Ships.*
It is possible that Richard Griffith attained a similar status at this same time, and for the same reason.

This unequivocally informs us that Griffith perished in the wreck, but it does not confirm that his remains are interred here. Indeed, it could merely be a memorial plaque, and with having no more relevance than that. There had been a suggestion that his body had been taken to London for burial, following its discovery. Again, there is no evidence come to light that this had occurred, and no such interment in London has, to this date, been uncovered (see Appendix 10, p. 453).

Whatever the outcome had been for Capt. Griffith, his second wife appeared in the UK 1911 census, as resident at, 26 Wanstead Park Avenue, Manor Park, North London.

His son, Walter Hugh Griffith was married to Ada Elizabeth Brown, in the year 1912 (see page 442). He died on the 24th March, 1920 (see page 448), from influenzal pneumonia, contracted during the terrifying worldwide pandemic known as the Spanish Flu.[744] His wife re-married on April 24th 1921, to a sailor (see page 441). It is not known if there were any children by the first marriage. A year before his marriage he was employed in Falmouth, residing there in a boarding house (see page 452). From Cliff Road, a popular Falmouth promenade, he would have been able to see the Manacle Rocks in the far distance, at low tide.

Walter's sister, Selina May Griffith, married in the year 1915 (see page 442). Her husband, Ernest J. Prettejohn, was a sapper [745] in the Royal Engineers.[746]

Richard Griffith's youngest son, Victor Richard Griffiths, was married in 1924 (see page 442) and his mother, Martha W. Griffith, was recorded as, 'in the presence of' on the marriage certificate. He died in the year 1978 (see page 448).

It is noted that all three siblings' marriage certificates listed their father as Richard Griffith and formally declared him as being a, 'mariner – deceased'.

Martha Griffith, in her later years, lived at her daughter Selina Prettejohn's home at Tregawne, Withiel, Cornwall, and died here in the year 1958 at the age of 96 years.[747] Her 'occupation' was recorded on the death certificate as 'Widow of Richard Griffith, Master Mariner'.[748] She never re-married.

Selina May Prettejohn, the last of the Griffith siblings, died in the year 1989 at the remarkable age of 100 years,[749] her husband having predeceased her at the age of 79 years, in 1972.

---

[744] The 1918 flu pandemic (the Spanish Flu) was an unusually severe and deadly form of the illness. Most victims were healthy young adults, and the pandemic lasted from June 1918 to December 1920 and between 50 and 100 million died of the illness, making it one of the deadliest natural disasters in human history.

[745] A sapper, pioneer or combat engineer is a combatant soldier who performs a wide variety of combat engineering duties, typically including, but not limited to, bridge-building, laying or clearing minefields, demolitions, field defences, general construction and building.

[746] The Prettejohn couple appeared on the electoral rolls for 1924–1927 as resident at Martha Griffith's abode; 26 Wanstead Road. From 1932 they were now residing at an address: 11 Roehampton Lane, London SW 15. The 1946–1950 electoral rolls show them at this same address and now with their son, Edward Prettejohn – (GRO/BMD; Q3 1924 West Ham; 4a 517).

[747] GRO/BMD; Q4 1958 Bodmin; 7a 15 (see page 446).

[748] Administration (with Will) Bodmin 13th February—Midland Bank Executor & Trustee Co. Ltd. Effects to a value of £4,209 13s. 10d. (no probate records found; most likely, her estate being of little value and so' informally' disbursed by her exexcutors).

[749] GRO/BMD; Q3 1989 Truro; 21 650 (see page 448).

Capt. Griffith's daughter, Selina May Prettejohn, was mother to both Edward and Richard Prettejohn. Both gentlemen still live in Cornwall at the same family home and are currently aged 88 and 93 years, respectively. Edward Prettejohn kindly responded with a most informative series of letters communicating some interesting family anecdotes, that have much developed the *Mohegan* story. There follows a summary of his fascinating letters, in which Mr Prettejohn's words, style and emphasis are retained, where they appear as direct quotations.

Edward Prettejohn confirms the family tree, as described earlier in this chapter, though he is totally unaware of Capt. Griffith's first marriage. He describes Martha Griffith's (his grandmother) sisters; Caroline Clark and Sarah Jane Clark, "as wonderful cooks: Aunt Carrie for bread and toffee and Aunt Jane for her pastry; both spoiling Edward and my brother rotten." They also, "made glorious chutneys to go with cold meats; as our grandfather had been on the Far-East run for years before being made Commodore of the Line, and put on the North America run."

Of the steamship *Cleopatra,* he says that, "My grandfather found it a hopeless ship; the compass was completely unreliable; and he said, the whole ship did not sail in a seaman fashion. He refused to take any passengers on the return voyage to England, told the Company of its faults, and his crew; that, 'they were sailors and were obliged to man the ship properly for the journey home.'"

Edward Prettejohn then describes the duty of a transatlantic captain as to, "wine and dine with the passengers, and to invite them into his own home between voyages; hence Aunts Carrie and Jane being made 'top operatives' of the family ménage and hence, the largish house for the Captain and his family." [750]

Mr Prettejohn's parents' house (11 Roehampton Lane, London) had, "all the glass blown out and everything else survived,[751] including the piano which was an iron-framed upright, tuned to concert pitch, and used in the days of the *Mohegan*, for the Captain's soirees, at 26 Wanstead Park Avenue, London. After my [Edward Prettejohn] wife's death it was sold, as no one else could play it, and enjoy playing it. Grandma Griffith's house took a direct hit, on the kitchen, and the whole house had to be demolished.[752] She was staying in Cornwall at the time."

Regarding a malfunctioning compass aboard the *Mohegan* and with external magnetic fields being blamed for the disaster, Mr Prettejohn makes some interesting observations on this point: "After the loss of the *Cleopatra/Mohegan*, the same shipbuilders finished a 'sister' ship, alike in all details, except they did the electrics properly . . . the ship's lights were put on (I believe she [*Mohegan*] was 'dressed overall'; with a string of lights from bow to stern, and secured to to the mast-tops in between). That string of electric light

---

[750] This would have been the 'Manhattan', Queens Road, Leytonstone residence.

[751] Presumably, this refers to the bomb-damage sustained during the Second World War.

[752] The 26 Wanstead Park Avenue residence.

bulbs, presumably with old-fashioned innards (black carbon wires) would each have been chucking out a magnetic field all over the ship, and from varying angles; enough to give sheer hell to any compass and all altering in magnetic value, according to whatever electrical equipment was operating at any particular moment, and so affecting the load on the ship's generator, and the quality of electricity produced. Hence, all electrical wires concerned are now shielded with woven metal sheaths around them. Just like the cables connecting things to the scart sockets on your television set." [753]

He continues with a revealing account of the dinner, on the eve of the disaster, " . . . everyone was at dinner—the main social gathering of the day—with most of the main officers present, including the Captain [*sic*], the first, second and third officers, and with just the fourth officer left on the bridge in charge. And he did NOT have a Master's Certificate; the others did.

"My grandfather was known to be good swimmer,[754] so I guess that grandad really did swim back [to the shore] and then lay doggo[755] through a sheer horror of what had happened, and blamed himself (quite rightly in my opinion) for leaving the 4th officer in charge. Even the 2nd Officer would have seen what the coastguard saw, and [would have] reacted promptly. Grandad then dissapeared from the scene. Grandma was approached by an elderly seaman saying that he had seen Captain Griffith in New York (he had a remarkable head of bright ginger hair) and was absolutely unmissable. That must have surprised her. The Company paid a good amount to Grandma as compensation (£10,000 I believe) for his death.[756] [In the circumstances] I would imagine she said nothing and kept the money. She had three kids to think of; also her two sisters who were dependent on her, and a large house to keep up.

"My father and mother both visited grandad's parents[757] at their farm in North Wales [Cregir Uchaf, Llanengan]; and thought that they were troubled by something, and that something was not quite right.

"Capt. Richard's first son, Walter Hugh, accompanied his father on a voyage to New York,[758] at the age of 14 years. His son was also involved in an incident on the River Thames, in which he had capsized in a rowing-boat, downstream from London itself, and in a thick fog. He managed to swim to shore and was found unconcious on a mud-bank."

[753] Mr Prettejohn speaks here with some authority; he was a radar-operative in the Second World War.

[754] Both Edward and Dick Prettejohn exhibit this family trait, by both swimming in later life; his older brother still swimming regularly to this day.

[755] *Doggo* – concealment; out of sight.

[756] An improbable sum that equates to £570,000 in today's currency and is more likely to be the equivalent sum of £10,000 in today's currency.

[757] As both the Richard Griffith's parents had died before 1888 and Mr Prettejohn's parents having been married in the year 1915, it must have been Richard Griffith's brother, Griffith Griffith and his wife that they had in fact visited. This would have been sometime between 1915 and 1925.

[758] SS Minnewaska April 1898.

Dropping a bombshell.

Edward Prettejohn then gives an account the start of which is both strange and intriguing: "There is a special place, almost anywhere, that attracts the suicidal; Arch Hill Bridge in Truro; the Clifton Suspension Bridge, in Bristol; Vortigern's Leap,[759] near the 'The Rivals'[760] in North Wales, fairly close to Caernarvon and not too far from Bryn Celyn at Abersoch, about a day's walk for a *one-way trip.* The local newspaper at Caernarvon mentioned that, a body was found by a local fisherman, which was dressed in a captain's uniform of the America Line [*sic*] (now the United States Line); it was headless and and was interred at Caernarvon. I do not know the name of the newspaper, or its date, or any further details, and I do not speak or read Welsh."

Mr Prettejohn was in Wales engaged in training as an RAF Leading Aircraftman radar-operator in 1943 (see addendum below: A secret war-time mission), and had an opportunity to take a trip by lorry from Nevin[761] on a weekly ration run, on his day off: providing he had helped with the unloading of the provisions, at its destination. He continues: ". . . I went; it was dry overhead, but there had been a storm, force-7 at least, and there was a fair sea running. The main road [most probably the B 417] passed close enough to *The Rivals* to see what things were like; the cliff is 800 feet high, and the waves were thudding against the cliff and the top of the white part of the wave was a quarter the way up the cliffs, as it reached the top of its travel. I imagine even if Grandad's head was not knocked off by striking some rocky portion of the cliff as he threw himself down, the waves would have done so, when he reached the sea."

This astonishing family disclosure clearly indicates that Capt. Griffith had survived the disaster and had sought sanctuary at his old family home, at Llanengan. In a state of despair and overwhelming depression, he eventually took his life by leaping off a cliff, that was within walking distance from his brother's home.

Do your homework!

On a final note, Mr Prettejohn urges this author to make sure that his research is thorough.[762] In his own words, "If you make any use of this letter; please research this well. Don't do as the shipbuilder did and gloss things over; they managed to do it OK, after the loss of the *Cleopatra/Mohegan*; they COULD have done it when Grandad brought her back from New York by the sun and the stars, and I would have had Grandad

---

[759] Named as Vortigern's Valley (Trwyn-y-Gorlech) on the Bartholomew's Revised Half-Inch Map (c. 1930). However, this location is not now listed on the modern Landranger Map (Lleyn Peninsula c. 2011) – 1¼ inches to the mile.
Western Mail (Cardiff, Wales), Friday, July 13, 1900; Vertigern's Valley lies between the peaks of the triple-headed [Yr] Eifl and the beauty of the spot makes a visit to it from Pwllheli a thing to be long treasured in the memory.

[760] *The Rivals*, is the highest point on the Llyn Peninsula in North Wales and has three summits. *Garn Ganol*, the central summit, is the highest at 564m, followed by *Tre'r Ceiri* (485m) and *Garn For* (444m). Though clouded by legend it seems likely that during the early post-Roman period of the mid fifth century a Brythonic warlord rose to prominence; a man known to later centuries as Gwrtheyrn or Vortigern: http://celtnet.org.uk/gods_g/gwrtheyrn.

[761] Nevin is situated on the northern flank of the Lleyn Peninsula.

[762] On that point, Mr Prettejohn can be rest assured: at least 3,000 hours of research have been undertaken in the preparation of this publication.

properly. I never saw Richard Griffith; he was already dead before I was born." It is they [ATL] who are responsible for the loss of the ship and over 100 people – NOT my grandfather, his suicide should never have been necessary, and his wife and children allowed to grow up normally as a complete family. I never even saw my grandfather.

"Out of the whole sorry story – to my mind, the occurrence of the most note is NOT of my grandfather's suicide – BUT the hopeless inadequacy of the attention given to my grandfather's complaint that the ship's compass was giving incorrect readings that <u>varied</u> in inaccuracy."

Edward Prettejohn

Clearly, the family remain indignant at the way in which Capt. Griffith had been treated by ATL,[763] and no doubt by the reports in the UK newspapers of the time. There is a suspicion (voiced elsewhere in this publication) that ATL was at pains to cover-up certain facts, concerning the disaster: not least, that there was an argument between the Captain and the company and resulting in the removal of his 'Commodore' title, which was strongly denied at the subsequent Board of Trade inquiry. In view of the Captain's serious concerns over the state of the ship's compasses, then it would strongly suggest that such an altercation could have in fact taken place. Indeed, in those circumstances, it would be surprising if this was not the case.

Well!

What are we to make of these astonishing facts?

This unexpected development comes from a branch of the family, close to Capt. Griffith, and no doubt there is an essential truth in the story. But, as with the Gallaway family anecdotes (see elsewhere in this publication) 'caution' has to be the watchword. A story often changes as it is passed down the successive family generations, by an unintended distortion in its re-telling.

However, this story is nonetheless compelling, in that:

Captain Richard Griffith did survive the wrecking of the *SS Mohegan*.

Taken at face value.

The generally accepted story—that Griffith perished on the Manacles and with his body then transporting itself to Caernarvon Bay—was an obvious conclusion made by the Welsh authorities: as the Griffith family never revealed that the Captain had survived and had returned to Wales. Their silence ensured that the

---

[763] Nonetheless, Mr Prettejohn did note that, "The America Line [*sic*] behaved properly throughout; they accepted that one of their vessels had been found faulty and paid out compensation generously to my grandmother, and to everyone else as well."

unpalatable fact that he had committed suicide never became public and their discredited member of the family would suffer no further ignominy, as a consequence of making it known that the man had taken his own life.

The attitude of Victorian society, regarding suicide within the family, was one of shame and dishonour,[764] and so a cover-up is entirely understandable, in the circumstance. Did Capt. Griffith have a Christian burial? His body almost certainly now rests in Wales. But where, still remains a mystery.

Give the Devil his due.

The revelations now made by his family, one hundred and fourteen years after the disaster, brings some closure to the unhappy story of the wrecking of the *SS Mohegan*. Richard Griffith had left behind a grieving family, his reputation destroyed and now, with further disclosure of deceit and a failure to face up to his responsibility. Despite this, one has to retain a shred of humanity towards the man. Notwithstanding his reckless acts, aboard the *Mohegan* and in subsequent events, we have here a broken man being unable to live with himself, and so choosing to make an ultimate sacrifice: his *own* life.

Death is the last line of the chapter.

As this troubled man stood atop the vertiginous cliff face at Vortigern's Leap, already mentally destroyed, he would now destroy himself physically and have the sea, that had rewarded him a remarkable career, now afford him a final act of kindness.

The pieces have fallen into place: a member of the crew in stating that Capt. Griffith was aboard the *Charlotte* lifeboat; the man who ran up the Porthoustock beach, on the night of the disaster; the man who took a rowing-boat and crossed the Helston River estuary; and with Capt. Griffith's body being found in Caernarvon Bay; all those events now take on a greater significance.

Did Martha Griffith know that her husband had survived the disaster? She applied for and was granted Probate for her husband's will, receiving the disbursement of proceeds two months after the disaster. One assumes the story must have come from Martha Griffith through her daughter Selina May and mother to the current informant, Edward Prettejohn. Did she visit her husband, following an astonishing and revelatory telegram from Wales, or did he perhaps go to his family home in London directly from the scene of the disaster, and then having relocated himself to Wales?

---

[764] In the 19th century, suicide was regarded as a lethal form of mental disease as well as a criminal act, and with the church denouncing the act of suicide, automatically condemning the soul to everlasting hell and with no hope for a Christian burial. Even in 1900 the Revd J. Gurnhill in *The Morals of Suicide* still deplored suicide as 'this deadly sin'. In later Victorian Britain a secular view of suicide gained support, explaining suicide either as a result of mental influence or as a rational choice based on socio-economic circumstances. These perspectives had been developed since the Enlightenment, but has been less influential while the Evangelical movement was powerful.—Pat Galland; *Death in the Victorian Family*, 71. Oxford University Press, 1996.
Little wonder then that it remained a major taboo for society.

These are questions that will likely never be answered, and Edward Prettejohn was not prepared to speculate further on these issues. But they are of little consequence now, when one has instead the answer to the enigma that was Captain Richard Griffith, the Master of the ill-fated steamship.

Finally laid to rest.

In conclusion, it would seem the good people of St. Keverne and Porthoustock are now vindicated. They were correct and fully justified in what they said at the time (and believe to this day) that the Captain came ashore that night and had made good a hasty departure from the scene, amid the confusion and the horror of the affair, for which he was plainly responsible.

Addendum: A secret war-time mission.

The subject of the following item is most likely connected with Mr Edward Prettejohn's RAF involvement in North Wales, during his wartime career:

> At the height of World War II, Rhiw[765] played an important and secret part in the forthcoming invasion of France in 1944. A team of electronic engineers led by Frank Bott set up an experimental Ultra High Frequency radio station on the Clip (now the site of the MOD radar station). From there they developed a viable radio system operating on a wavelength of 5cm. (The frequency now used by mobile phones and microwave ovens) They were able make a direct link with a radio station at Fishguard and with another station on the Great Orme at Llandudno. Having proved the system it was used at the Normandy landings as a reliable link on a frequency which the German Forces could not monitor nor jam. The valve used known as a magnetron was tested to be working by the scientists placing their hands near it. If they felt their skin warming up and reddening (like cooking in a microwave oven) then they knew the valve was working. None of the team ever suffered any ill effects from this, even years after; a point which should be considered by those people who think that the extremely low power radiation from mobile phone masts has a detrimental effect on their health. [766]

---

[765] At its northern end Mynydd Rhiw rises to 1,000 feet (300 m), the outcrop of Clip y Gylfinhir (English: *Curlew's Crag*) looming above the village of Y Rhiw Mynydd.

[766] http://www.rhiw.com/website_maps/history_of_rhiw.htm [snippets IV].

CHAPTER 19

Mr. Llewellyn Couch: Chief Officer

The crew of the *Mohegan* comprised men and women of the highest calibre, and who had received much deserved praise for their bravery: not only in confronting their own deaths, but also in previous encounters of gallantry at sea, in which they had participated. Messrs. Couch, Cole, Hindmarsh, Browning, Sennington and Cruickshank (John Grant) were an exemplar of men who show that admirable British Victorian ethos:

'Greater love has no one than this: that he lay down his life – for those who endure the perils of the sea.'

Mr. Llewellyn Couch was born November 2nd 1868 in Swansea, Glamorgan South Wales.[767] He was the son of Dr James Couch[768] of Swansea, and brother to both Thomas Henry Couch, the Swansea manager for the Atlantic Transport Line, and Mr Kynaston Couch, also a doctor in Swansea. Llewellyn Couch had married Louise Marie Frost Sweet in his home town of Swansea, in the year 1894.[769] His marriage certificate described him as a 'Master Mariner'.

He was recorded as second-mate in 1888, first mate in 1891 and as an OC in 1893. He attained a commission on the *Mohawk* (1897), and as first-officer aboard the *Cleopatra* (1898).[770] He had been in the employ of the Atlantic Transport Line company for eight years, commencing in 1890 as a fourth officer.

He was kept on the payroll during the ship's refurbishment; being first mate aboard the *Cleopatra* and and remained in post, following her maiden voyage. That same ship was then re-named as the *Mohegan* and he sailed as its first officer, on that fateful voyage in October 1898.

An interesting reference, relating to Mr Couch, is this report in a Welsh newspaper; which seemed to infer that he had misgivings over his last ship:

SWANSEA MAN ON BOARD.

[Lloyd's agent at Falmouth telegraphs several messages on the evening of Sunday 17th October, including] . . . The Mr. Llewellyn Couch referred to in a previous telegram is the senior chief officer of the line, and would shortly attain a command. He belongs to a well known Swansea family, being a son of an old Swansea medical practitioner at Swansea. His brother, Dr. Kynaston Couch, also practices in the town, whilst another brother is the Swansea agent for the American Transport Line. Mr. Couch in a letter to his brother at Swansea last week sounded a note of dissatisfaction about the vessel

---

[767] GRO/BMD: 1868 Q1 – Swansea 11a 574.

[768] He was a general practitioner in Swansea.

[769] GRO/BMD: 1894 Q2 – Swansea 11a 574; St. Paul's Parish Church, Sketty Swansea, Glamorgan.

[770] His crew-card number was recorded as 022382—Dr Reginald Davies; Welsh Mariners (1800 – 1945).

[*Mohegan*]. The re-naming was not lucky, and she only did thirteen knots on her trial. Mr. Couch had distinguished himself by acts of gallantry at sea.[771]

Another source seems to corroborate the story of the vessel's perceived shortcomings:

For the past weeks the steamer has been in dock undergoing repairs, and the manager says she was in perfect condition when she left port on this, her first voyage under her own name. The friends of the crew state, however, that in a 24-hour trial last week, her performances were very unsatisfactory and the crew did not wish to go on her account of the change of name and the previous defect in her engines. The assumption here is that her engines broke down and also that owing to her weak boilers, the vessel, in the rough sea and heavy gale which prevailed, drifted helplessly on the [Manacle] rocks.[772]

Brave deeds are the monuments of brave men.

A dramatic account of a prior shipping drama, in which Llewellyn Couch played a leading role, is recorded here:

LOSS OF A NORWEGIAN BARQUE

TWO OF THE CREW DROWNED

A TERRIBLE VOYAGE

QUEENSTOWN, Friday.—The Cunard liner *Lucania*, that arrived to-day, brings particulars of the abandonment of the *Persia* and the loss of two of her crew 500 miles off the [Newfoundland, Grand] Banks, in latitude 46.40 west and longitude 44.14 north. Rudderless, leaking, and foundering, the Norwegian barque *Persia* fought her last battle with the North Atlantic storms one week ago yesterday, after forty-four years of active service upon the sea. The storm was the victor in the struggle, and the old packet ship went down beneath the waves which she had been crossing and re-crossing for the last forty-four years. The Atlantic transport line steamer *Mohawk*, which came into port early yesterday morning, brought the *Persia*'s captain and crew of seventeen men. The *Mohawk* had rescued them at two o'clock on a black ocean night, after they had resigned themselves to sharing the same fate as the ship, they all fought to save. The *Persia* left Cardiff, Wales, on January 3, in ballast for St. John, N.B. Almost as soon as the barque was out of sight of the Cornish coast, winds from the west began to drive her back. On the night of February 17 the cold steady west wind, changed to a hurricane and later into a cyclone. "I am twenty years at sea," said Captain Gjersten yesterday, "I never saw or heard of such a sea. A hurricane was rolling up from the west, but there were gusts from the south and the north. They chopped the banks of waves into small mountains, which kept smashing down on us, tearing away our bulwarks and rigging piece by piece. Early in the morning of the 18th, as I stood at the wheel, looking over the stern, I saw what I could only describe as a mountain range of waves concentrating under our rudder. Before I had time to take a second look the *Persia* was buried under a mass of water. Several of the crew were at the time repairing the mizzen boom. A part of the cabin-house was smashed into kindling woods, and the men were literally strewn about the deck. When the wave finally passed over the starboard bow we found that seaman Alfred Petersen was missing. He had been washed overboard. He must have been drowned before he left the deck. Then, with a sudden lurch, the sand ballast of the *Persia* shifted to the starboard, and she listed painfully. For a while

---

[771] *Western Mail* (Cardiff, Wales); Monday 17th, October 1898. If the first officer had qualms over his vessel, then Capt. Griffith must have had similar misgivings, which could have been a basis for his altercation with the company, prior to sailing on October 14th.

[772] *Democrat Chronicle;* Sunday, 16th October, 1898.

the steam pump kept her free, but the ballast finally choked the pump, and made it useless. The lashed rudder split. The three reserve sets of sails were torn into shreds almost as quickly as they were put into place, and the *Persia* lay in the trough of the sea. In the remnants of the twisted rigging the crew took refuge, peering out through the darkness for the light of some craft. 'Steamer's light three miles to leeward,' cried Mate Bulkstrom shortly before midnight, Captain Gjertsen sprang into the rigging. Sure enough the light was there. Improvised torches, made of rags soaked in petroleum, were waved from the struggling *Persia*. The steamer saw them. She changed her course, and came to the *Persia*'s relief. The steamer was the *Mohawk*. One of the *Mohawk*'s boats, manned by a crew of six men, in charge of First Officer [Llewellyn] Couch, rowed to within thirty feet of the *Persia*'s bow. A line was thrown from her deck, and made fast to the stern of the lifeboat. "Give way," cried Couch. The order was obeyed. The line became as taut as a rod of iron. Down it one by one, hand over hand, went the *Persia*'s crew. It was two o'clock on Saturday morning before the seventeen half drowned sailors stood on the deck of the *Mohawk*". The *Persia* was one of the last survivors of the Black Ball line [773] of clipper ships, which fifty years ago used to leave the foot of Beekmen Street [New York] twice a month for Liverpool.[774]

Fortune favours the brave.

A Royal resolution of November 1897, No. 144 from the *Indredepartementet, Konsulatkontoret* (Ministry of the Interior, Consulates Office) [775] concerning the awards made to members of the crew, involved in this rescue, was issued. The resolution shows that Captain Thomas Francis Gates [776] was awarded a pair of navy binoculars, Couch received the 2nd class rescue medal, and five others the 3rd class rescue medal.[777]

In due course, and in recognition of the bravery of Couch and other members of the crew, the Norwegian Government made the appropriate awards:

SAVING LFE AT SEA

The Board of Trade have received through the Consul-General for Sweden and Norway a binocular glass for Mr. Thomas Frederick Gates, master, a silver medal of the second class and diploma for Mr. Llewellyn Couch, first mate, and silver medals of the third class and diplomas for John Schuster and John Grant Cruikshank,[778] boatswains, and William Henry

---

[773] The Black Ball Line sailed a fleet of packet ships running between Liverpool and New York; the first scheduled trans-Atlantic service, which was founded in 1817.

[774] *The Belfast News-Letter* (Belfast, Ireland); Saturday, 6th March 1897.

[775] RefLeif Thingsrud, Archivist for *Riksarkivet*; The National Archives of Norway.

[776] Capt. Thomas F. Gates spent fifty-eight years in service, forty-five of them as a Master. He joined the Atlantic Transport Line in 1883 and had commanded 18 of their vessels. He was master of the Atlantic Transport liner *Minnetonka* since she came out in 1924 and dean of the shipmasters of the seven seas. He celebrated his seventy-second birthday on January 5th, 1934, but did not look a day over fifty-five years and carried himself as erect as any seagoing officer half his age. He was a naturalised American citizen, as a result of the purchase of ATL ships by the USA Government; *New York Times*, July 1934.

[777] A Royal resolution of November 1897, No. 144 from the *Indredepartementet, Konsulatkontoret* (Ministry of the Interior, Consulates Office) concerning the awards made to members of the crew, involved in this rescue. *Western Morning News;* 4th August, 1990. The 2nd class medal has the full Norwegian name: *Medaljen for edel dåd* ('Medal for Heroism'). Ref: Leif Thingsrud; Archivist for *Riksarkivet*—The National Archives of Norway.
The medal was suspended from a ribbon with the Norwegian national colors, where two wide stripes of red distinguishes three groups of narrow stripes in white-blue-white. The Medal for Heroism was instituted by King Oscar II by royal decree dated 19 August 1885. Originally the medal constituted three classes: gold crown, silver crown and silver.—WikiPedia.

[778] Cruikshank was subsequently a boatswain aboard the *Mohegan* and his life was saved in that disaster.

Holmes, Geo. Roaches and James Seager, seamen of the steamship *Mohawk*, of London, which have been awarded to them by the Norwegian Government in recognition of their services to the shipwrecked crew of the Norwegian barque *Persia*.[779]

The photograph of Llewellyn Couch in this publication (see fig. 18) shows what is almost certainly the beribboned Norwegian medal pinned to his chest. Mr Couch had been bestowed the medal in January of the year of the *Mohegan* disaster. It is not surprising that he would wish to have this photograph as a personal memento—most probably taken in New York, during the *Cleopatra* episode. Naturally, the shipping company would have been be pleased to promote the admirable quality of its officer class and a photograph of one of their commended officers would communicate a positive public-relations message, that would help instil confidence in their passengers.

Fate, an unavoidable destination and the journey of a life.

Following the drowning in the *Mohegan* disaster, Llewellyn Couch's two brothers travelled to Falmouth. There they identified his body and arranged for its return to Swansea, for burial:[780]

> His body was found at Maenporth, Falmouth, and brought ashore by a boatman named Pascoe. His place of birth was Swansea, Wales, where he was returned for burial, in St. Mary's church, Dan-y-graig Cemetery. He was the son of Dr. James Couch of Swansea, and brother to Mr. T. H. Couch, the Swansea manager for the Atlantic Transport Line. The latter together with another brother, Mr. Kynaston Couch,[781] have been to Falmouth, following the incident.[782]

There was an outpouring of sympathy from the people of Swansea for his bereaved wife; who was at that time expecting their second child (Dorothy Couch). This was reflected over the 18 months following the disaster, by the inauguration of a fund to help financially support Mrs Couch and her family, and to meet the cost of a memorial tablet. The unveiling of the memorial stone was recorded in a local newspaper:

> At Swansea Parish Church on Monday afternoon, Miss Watkins, Mayoress, in the presence of a large assemblage of friends, unveiled a suitable tablet to the memory of Llewellyn Couch, a native of the town, and chief officer of the steamer *Mohegan*, which was wrecked on the Manacle Rocks on October 14, 1898. In addition to the cost of the tablet it was stated that £105[783] had been realised by local efforts for the benefit of the young widow and family.[784]

---

[779] *Daily News* (London, England); Monday, 17th January 1898.

[780] Dan-y-graig Cemetery, Danygraig Road, Port Tennant, Swansea, SA1 8NB; *Grave No. 555, Section–Q*: the church here was severely damaged by bombing, during the Second World War. As a consequence, the memorial tablet for Llewllyn Couch, placed on the church wall, is now missing. Personal communication: Elsey, Lyndon; Asst. Registrar of Cemeteries and Crematorium, Swansea.
Danygraig was the first Municipal Cemetery in Swansea, intended to replace the overcrowded and potentially unsanitary graveyards in the town centre. It is situated above the Port Tennant area of Swansea, east of the district of St. Thomas, in a moderately elevated position on the side of Kilvey Hill.

[781] Kynaston Couch, M.R.C.S., L.R.C.P.: Assistant Surgeon, Swansea General and Eye Hospital.

[782] *Leicester Chronicle and the Leicestershire Mercury* (Leicester, England); Saturday, 25th November 1898.

[783] This sum of £105 converts to approximately £6,000 in today's money.

[784] *The Royal Cornwall Gazette Falmouth Packet, Cornish Weekly News, & General Advertiser*; Thursday 29th March 1900.

The funeral for Llewellyn Couch was most appropriate for a brave and well-respected man:

FUNERAL OF CHIEF OFFICER COUCH AT SWANSEA.

The funeral of the late Mr. Ll[ewellyn] Couch, chief mate of the steamship *Mohegan,* which was lost on the Manacle Rocks, took place at Swansea on Wednesday morning, amid every token of respect amongst the inhabitants, by whom deceased and his family were well known and respected. There was a large attendance of friends of the deceased, representatives the local agency for Williams, Torrey, and Field, &c. The body was taken to the grave in a glass hearse and the coffin was covered with wreaths from Swansea and other friends. The Rev. Thom. Morris, curate of St. Mary's officiated at the grave.[785]

His grave still remains in the churchyard, and its headstone reads:

In loving memory of
LLEWELLYN COUCH CHIEF OFFICER OF THE s.s. MOHEGAN
WHO LOST HIS LIFE OCT. 14th 1898. AGED 30 YEARS.
_____

MARIE LOUISE FROST
HIS WIFE WHO DIED FEB. 9th 1952. AGED 83 YEARS.[786]
_____

Beloved Parents of Arthur and Dorothy
_____

ARTHUR COUCH THEIR DEAR SON
WHO DIED NOV. 21st 1981. AGED 86 YEARS.

Every picture tells a story.

The following news item is interesting, in that it records a marine auction that was said to include a part of Mr Llewellyn Couch's estate—including a painting. From the details known of the artist responsible, it is assumed that Mr Couch had commissioned the picture, in New York and probably while a member of crew of the actual ship, featured in this painting:

At a marine auction, held in Plymouth, one lot was a painting of the *ss Mississipi,*[787] by the artist Antonio Jacobson [*sic*].[788]

This, and certain other items, once belonged to the *Mississipi*'s first mate, who was Mr. Llewellyn Couch. He had been

---

[785] *Western Mail* (Cardiff, Wales); Thursday, November 3rd 1898.

[786] GRO/BMD: 1952 Q1 – Swansea 8b 704.

[787] The picture was entitled, "*SS Mississipi in An Open Sea*" and was an item in an auction held at Saltram House, Plymouth (UK) on Wednesday 8th August, 1990. The guide price was £7,000 – 10,000. There were other personal items included in the sale under the hammer of the Phillips Auctioneers, London—*Western Morning News;* 4th August 1990.

[788] Jacobsen was born in Copenhagen, Denmark. Jacobsen attended the Royal Academy of Design before heading across the Atlantic Ocean. He came to the United States in 1871, and settled in West Hoboken, New Jersey (now Union City, New Jersey), across the Hudson River from Manhattan and New York Harbour, its port filled with ships from America and around the world. Jacobsen got his start painting pictures of ships on safes, and as his reputation grew, he was asked to do portraits of ships by their owners, captains and crew members, with many of his works sold for five dollars. Jacobsen painted over 6,000 portraits of sail and steam vessels, making him "the most prolific of marine artists". Many of his commissions came from sea captains, and Jacobsen was chosen both for the accuracy of his work and the low fees he commanded.—*WikiPedia.*

awarded a commendation by the Norwegian Government, in 1897, for rescuing the crew of the *Persia*, a Norwegian barque. He was married and lived in London, and was in the employ of the Atlantic Transport Line company for eight years, commencing in 1890 as fourth officer, and had worked his way up to the position of chief officer. He held a master's certificate. He was on watch duty, on the bridge, at the time of the disaster. His widow and three children, one of whom was born after the disaster, had received £75 [£4,300 in today's currency] and £5 was received to erect a tablet to his memory, in the church.[789]

The UK census for the year 1901 shows his wife, Marie Louise Couch along with her two children, living with her widowed mother, Charlotte Sweet. Again, the 1911 UK census (see page 452) describes a similar domestic arrangement. It would appear that Marie Louise Frost Couch never married again. She died on February 9th 1952 at the age of 83 years, and was buried alongside her husband in the Dan-y-graig cemetery.

---

[789] *Leicester Chronicle and the Leicestershire Mercury* (Leicester, England); Saturday, 25th November 1898.

CHAPTER 20

Mr Edward Colston Sennington: Chief Steward

He was the chief steward on the *Mohegan,* and had perished in the disaster. He had also taken part in a sea-rescue, whilst acting as a steward, aboard the steamship *Missouri,* in 1889.

The stricken vessel was the steamship *Danmark*.[790] She was found abandoned, with no crew or passengers aboard, by the vessel *City of Chester*, and the very worst outcome was suspected. The master telegrammed this stark account of their find:

DISASTERS AT SEA
A DERELICT EMIGRANT VESSEL

The Inman Steamer *City of Chester* arrived at Queenstown on Friday morning from New York, and reported that on the 8th inst. when in lat. 45N. Long. 37W. she passed a large steamer called the *Danmark* derelict. Her decks were under water, her sails torn to pieces, and she appeared to have been recently abandoned, evidently having encountered terrific weather. The vessel had a cream coloured funnel, with a black top and broad white band in the centre, with a black star. There was no appearance of the crew in the vicinity. The steamer is believed to be the *Danmark,* of Copenhagen, 2,262 tons register, which sailed from Swinemunde [Poland] on the 19th March, and cleared at Christiania[791] [also known as Freetown Christiania] on the 23rd of the same month, bound for New York. She is believed to have on board a large number of Scandinavian emigrants.[792]

Anxious families and a dismayed public held on to the slim hope, that previous reports had raised; that all were saved and the good news would be heard soon:

COPENHAGEN, SUNDAY NIGHT

Nothing has yet been heard of the steamer *Danmark*. The *Island*, belonging to the same Company, which left four days later than the *Danmark*, arrived at New York yesterday. The *Danmark* was of two thousand four hundred and eighty-four tons register. She was built in 1880 by Messrs. Mitchell and Co., of Newcastle. She conveyed six hundred and sixty-seven passengers, and had a crew of fifty-four. Hope is still is still entertained that the passengers and crew have been rescued by some passing vessel.[793]

General alarm was raised on both sides of the Atlantic, over a suspected tragedy of the greatest enormity:

---

[790] 'The *Danmark* was an iron vessel of tonnage of 3,414 tons gross and 2,547 tons net. She is 340 feet long, of 40 feet beam, and of 26 feet depth of hold. She was built at Newcastle, England, in 1880, by C. Mitchell and Co., for the White Cross Line and was first called the *Jan Breydel*. She was a three master, with three decks and an awning deck, and had five water-tight bulkheads. Her engines were the old compound cylinder engines, with a piston stroke of 48 inches. She was regarded as a first-class seaworthy vessel, and is ranked in British Lloyd's as 100 A1 – the highest rating.'— *New York Times*, 1899.

[791] The city was named as Christiania in 1624. It was then known as Kristiania from 1877 to 1925, whereafter it was named as Oslo.

[792] *The Morning Post* (London, England); Saturday, April 13rd 1889.

[793] *The Standard* (London, England); Monday, 15th April 1889.

No further intelligence has been received by Lloyd's respecting the derelict steamer *Danmark*, passed in the Atlantic. Should she prove to be the steamer *Danmark*, bound from Christiania to New York, it is feared there has been a large loss of life. This vessel had 623 passengers.

Lloyd's correspondent at Liverpool telegraphs that the master of the *City of Chester* states he is of the opinion that the crew and passengers of the steamer *Danmark* had been rescued, as the vessel appeared to have no boats, and a cable chain was hanging over the bow, which looked as if she had been in tow. He can give no further particulars.[794]

Unknown to the world at this point, the *Danmark* had providentially been encountered by the *SS Missouri,* and an extraordinary rescue had already taken place:

THE LOSS OF THE DANMARK.

A BRITISH CAPTAIN THROWS HIS CARGO OVERBOARD
AND SAVES 800 EMIGRANTS

The Central News has been furnished with the following information by the chairman of the Eastern Telegraph Company in reference to the rescue of the crew and passengers of the derelict steamer *Danmark.* The information was obtained by their representative from Mr. Peter Rabsen, third mate of the *Danmark,* on board the Portuguese mail boat *Acor,* at Lisbon. He states that all the passengers were saved with the exception of the chief engineer, Kaur, who was found dead in the engine-room at the time of the accident. On the 4th of April the steamer broke down about 800 miles from Newfoundland. On the 5th of April they met the English steamer *Missouri*, of London bound to Philadelphia, which took them in tow till the morning of the 6th, when the *Danmark* could no longer keep afloat. They asked the *Missouri* to take the passengers on board. The *Missouri* had accommodation for only 20 passengers but she threw part of her cargo overboard, and made room for them—800 odd. The *Missouri* came back to the Azores, where she landed part of them, and proceeded afterwards on her voyage to Philadelphia, taking 340 passengers of the *Danmark,* and some of the crew to assist them. The *Danmark* captain and three engineers left the Azores for London on board an English steamer *Demerara,* bound for London. The chief and second mates are still at the Azores and the remaining passengers, 42 in all, are on board the *Acor,* in charge of Mr. Rabsen, the third mate.

The news of the safety of the passengers and crew of the emigrant steamship *Danmark* was received in London yesterday afternoon with the liveliest satisfaction. When it became apparent beyond reasonable doubt that the *Danmark* had been abandoned, the greatest anxiety prevailed as to the fate that had overtaken her passengers and crew. The circumstances that there were somewhere about 800 people on board the steamer was enough to account for the anxiety, even if it had to be remembered that few of them, if indeed, any, were English. The *Danmark* would have taken from Copenhagen to New York is so frequented by all kinds of ships that anxiety as to the safety of all those who were in her had almost grown to despair. Indeed, the long absence of the barest tidings had driven some to the conclusion that, in addition to the loss of the vessel, there must have been a terrible loss of life. Others, however, who were well qualified to judge, continued to believe that though the *Danmark* had certainly been abandoned the people whom she carried had contrived to get away in safety. This belief they in a large measure built upon the fact that none of the wreckage which betokens a disaster to human life had been met on the seas. If, they argued, the passengers and crew had been lost, there would have been some evidence of their unfortunate fate while, as a matter of fact, all that had been made out was that the *Danmark* had been abandoned. On one or two occasions there were gleams of news confirmatory of this position, and most confirmatory of all was the story

---

[794] *The North-Eastern Daily Gazette* (Middlesbrough, England); Monday, 15th April 1889.

brought to London by the captain of the ship *Minnesota,* from Baltimore to London. Captain Blacklin, of the *Minnesota,* arrived at Tilbury early on Saturday morning, bringing the information that on Thursday week he passed a derelict lifeboat. The *Minnesota* was then about 1500 miles from England, sailing in a sea made somewhat choppy by a strong breeze. The watch made out some object flowing away on the bow, and Captain Blacklin said that the boat had belonged to some large passenger ship, and on a closer inspection discovered the word "*Danmar*" flanked by the figure five painted on the bows of the little craft. That there had been passengers in the boat there was no reason to doubt, and the orderly condition in which the oars and whole gearing had been left indicated pretty conclusively that it had not been left hurriedly. Captain Blacklin felt perfectly satisfied that whoever had been in the boat had been taken off by a vessel, and so he did not delay to pick up the tiny derelict. The news that the *Minnesota* brought was eagerly fastened upon as proof that of the many souls on the *Danmark* few, if any, had perished. The barely 24 hours after the *Minnesota* had brought up at Tilbury, there came the welcome news that, although the *Danmark* had been lost, those whom she carried had been saved. No mention is made in the telegrams of how the ship became unseaworthy, but the general belief is that an explosion must have taken place in the engine room. Doubtless, it was through this explosion that one of the engineers lost his life, and if his death was attest of its violence, the fittings of the engine room must have been fairly wrecked, or an effort would have been made to patch up the damaged machinery and keep the water from making its way through the holes made in the sides of the vessel by the force of the explosion. One can quite understand, however, how abortive these attempts were in a rough sea and the imagination pictures the scene when the emigrants had to be told that the ship was at the mercy of the elements. Being a first class passenger steamer, the *Danmark* was fitted with powerful pumping machinery, but the strongest of pumps could do little against the incessant inroads of the waves. The *Danmark* was in a pitiful plight of a practically unmanageable craft when the *Missouri* hove in sight, saw the signals of distress flying, and bore down to her assistance. The boats of both ships were used in removing the passengers which circumstance accounts very likely for the seeing of one of the *Danmark* boats by the *Minnesota*. The *Missouri* was too small a boat almost to carry the passengers, much less to take on board the boats of the *Danmark*. It is likely to be some little time before the crew of the *Danmark* can return to Europe, but it is certain that they will touch at England before going on to Copenhagen. A telegram dated Lisbon, Sunday, says the *Danmark* on April 4th had her shaft broken.[795]

Mr Sennington was one of the *Missouri* crew who had been engaged in this brave act of gallantry:

The young man was for a long time in the service of Messrs. Mark Whitwill and Son,[796] and had crossed the Atlantic in *Bristol* and other steamers a number of times. He was chief steward of the ill-fated *Mohegan*, in which he was making his first voyage at the time of the distressing accident. Mr. Sennington was aboard the steamship *Missouri* when the vessel under sensational circumstances rescued the officers and crew of the steamer *Danmark* in mid-ocean, an incident that has been immortalized in the painting "*And every Soul was Saved*". Mr. Sennington's portrait appears in that picture. For his services on that occasion, in which conspicuous gallantry was shown by all aboard the *Missouri*, he received a gold watch and a medal.[797]

The *Missouri* was one of four freighters built for the Atlantic Transport Line to carry cargo; cattle, other goods between London, Swansea, Philadelphia, and Baltimore; and was 2,845 tons, manned by a crew

---

[795] *The Sheffield & Rotherham Independent* (Sheffield, England); Monday, April 22nd 1889.

[796] Mark Whitwill & Son, Ship-Owners (Bristol).

[797] *The Bristol Mercury and Daily Post* (Bristol, England); Wednesday, 19th October 1889.

numbering thirty-seven. Because it was a freighter and had insufficient quarters for people and supplies, it could only accommodate an additional 20 persons. However, as its cargo hold was constructed to haul cattle, it had a large fresh water condenser capable of condensing 8,000 gallons of water per day. A fortunate arrangement, as it turned out.

The good seaman is known in bad weather.

The *Missouri*'s Captain Hamilton Murrell, bound from London to Philadelphia, upon seeing the distress flags of the *Danmark*, ordered his crew to set a course and steered as close as possible to the disabled steamship. A startling signal was seen by the *Missouri,* sent from the stricken ship: "I have 735 passengers on board, and that is too many lives to be lost from one vessel."

A line was established between the two vessels which at once took hold of the *Danmark* and towed her through the long night; but the next morning it was seen that the vessel was hopelessly sinking, and that the passengers must now be transferred. The lifeboats were launched, and a mid-ocean transportation of the passengers began. They behaved nobly under the circumstances, the women especially preserving a wonderful coolness under the trying ordeal. The heavy swell running all day made the work dangerous and difficult to prevent the swamping of the lifeboats. Five hours were taken in the transfer, without a single accident: the women and children taken off first, and then the men. As the *Missouri* was not a passenger ship, the captain was hard pushed to accommodate his big load, but as fast as a boat laden with its human freight came alongside, a corresponding load of the cargo was unhesitatingly thrown overboard to make room for the passengers.

With an overwhelming sense of gratitude, the master and crew of the *Missouri* were lauded with accolades from the highest quarters, and appropriate awards were made, on both sides of the Atlantic, for their outstanding bravery and charitable action.

The rescuing officers were received at Washington by the President, and publicly thanked. A further fund was raised in England, and on May 24th 1889 in the Hall of the Mansion House, the Lord Mayor presented the testimonials and cheques. Edward Sennington was referred to as the *Mohegan*'s "commodore steward".

In Copenhagen on April 27, 1889, Capt. Murrell was appointed a knight of the *Order of the Dannebrog* by King Christian of Denmark, in recognition of his role in the rescue of the *Danmark.*

A picture speaks a thousand words.

Such was the excitement, generated by this outstanding rescue, that a picture was commissioned, to capture the event. It not only depicted the drama at sea, but used actual participants in portrait sittings (including the Chief Steward, Sennington) and was painted, by no less than a Royal Academician, Mr Thomas Maria Madawaska Hemy (1852–1937):

"AND EVERY SOUL WAS SAVED"

CAPT. MURRELL'S RESCUE OF THE *DANMARK*'S PASSENGERS ON CANVAS.

BALTIMORE, March 14.—Chief Engineer Arthur N. Cross[798] of the Atlantic Transport Line steamship *Missouri* writes to the *American* that a picture is being painted by Mr. J. M. Henry [*sic*], R.A., for the Royal Academy, London, in commemoration of the rescue of the *Danmark*'s Passengers by Capt. Murrell of the *Missouri*. It is the intention of the artist to exhibit it in the principal cities of the United States before it is finally placed in the Academy.

The title of the painting is "*And Every Soul Was Saved*". The picture will be 9 by 15 feet, and the artist has taken every possible means to get it exact in every detail, even procuring tracings from the builders of the two ships. Upwards of one hundred living models were selected, and all the prominent faces on the two ships and in the small boats are taken from life, even to the babies. Capt. Murrell and the others of the *Missouri* have given the artist sittings.

The Captain stands on the bridge with outstretched arm directing to movements of the small boats coming alongside with their living freight. The *Missouri* arrived in Philadelphia yesterday, and Capt. Murrell will rejoin his ship, having laid off two trips on account of an affection of the eyes and heart. He will be married soon in Baltimore.[799]

The maritime rescue captured the world's headlines, as far afield as New Zealand.[800] The mammoth-sized picture was valued at $12,000, and caught the imagination of the public (see fig. 50).[801]

Mr. Bernard Nadal Baker, the President of the Baltimore Storage and Lighterage Company presented, on behalf of the Life-Saving Benevolent Association of New York, a gold medal to Captain Murrell, on June 22nd 1889. It would further seem that the first, second and third officers of the *Missouri* (viz. Gates, Forsyth, and Lucas) were similarly honoured. Captain Murrell was also to receive a painting of the rescue by Lewis Muller and it was presented to him in appreciation for his efforts—a gift from Danish residents of Baltimore and Washington.

The following item appeared in a Baltimore newspaper the day after Captain Murrell died (aged 54 years – 1916) and refers to the renowned painting: [802]

This painting was brought to Baltimore by the late David Bendann, and it is said that 40,000 people viewed it when it was first put on exhibition. It was purchased by Bernard N. Baker, bought back by the Bendanns and sold again to Dr. R. J. Slater for the Ocean Club of Long Branch. Later it was repurchased for the second time by Mr. Bendann and finally sold to the late James L. Kernan, who hung it in the art gallery of the Kernan Hotel,[803] where it may still be seen. The rope that

---

[798] His son was to have lost his life in the *Mohegan* disaster.

[799] *The New York Times*, 15th March 1890.

[800] *Otago Witness;* 1892.

[801] *And Every Soul Was Saved;* the title of an oil painting by Thomas M. M. Hemy (1852–1937), celebrated the rescue of the *Danmark*'s passengers. The painting was widely exhibited, and was briefly owned by Bernard N. Baker, the owner of the Atlantic Transport Line. A detailed account of the event, the artist and his picture is seen here: http://searlecanada.org/hemy/thomashemydata10.html.

[802] Two excellent websites have much more background to this story, for those so interested; http://searlecanada.org/hemy/thomashemydata11.html; http://norwayheritage.com/articles/templates/great-disasters.asp?articleid=114&zoneid=1.

[803] The Hotel Kernan was built in 1906 by its namesake, James L. Kernan, a performing arts impresario. The hotel was part of a three-building complex that was once a prime destination for famous performers and artists including Will Rogers, the Marx Brothers, Bob Hope, Jack Benny, Al Jolson, Sophie Tucker, W.C. Fields and Charlie Chaplin, to name a few. Zelda and F. Scott Fitzgerald were patrons of the theatre, staying at the luxurious

appears on the frame is a piece of the original tow line that was flung from the Danmark to the Missouri. The price of the painting is said to have gone up with each sale, the sum paid by Mr. Kernan having been $10,000.[804]

A rather sad and poignant ending for Mr Sennington, in that he lost his life in his own personal disaster, aboard the *Mohegan*:

> The thrilling story of the rescue of the passengers and crew, 735 all told, of the ill-fated Danish emigrant ship *Danmark* by the West Hartlepool built steamer *Missouri*, is recalled by the sad fate which has befallen Mr. Edward Sennington who had just lost his life through the disaster to the steamer *Mohegan*, wrecked near Falmouth. Mr. Sennington, who was one of the victims of that terrible disaster, was chief steward of the *Mohegan* and held a similar position on board the *Missouri*, when in April 1889 the world-famed rescue was effected. He took an active part in that gallant feat, which was especially interesting to the Hartlepools from the fact that Captain Murrell, who conducted it, was locally connected. For his services on that occasion Captain Murrell received from the hands of the Lord Mayor of London a silver salver bearing a suitable inscription and a cheque for £500, whilst Mr. Sennington, in addition to a gold watch and two month's pay, received a large silver medal from the Danish Government, a medal of virgin gold from the people of Baltimore, and a handsome gold medal and clasp from the people of Philadelphia. Though unknown to the people of the Hartlepools Mr. Sennington's loss will none the less be deplored by them, for he was one of the brave men of the sea.[805]

The announcement of the funeral for Mr Sennington provoked a wave of sympathy in his home city and in prompting his old school friends to respond to the sad news:

> The Old School Croft's Society … the members learnt with much regret of the death of Mr. Sennington in the accident that befell the *Mohegan*, he being educated at the Old School.[806]

Such was the admiration expressed at the heroism displayed in the *Danmark* rescue that some observer noted that:

> "It was an indomitable courage and daring, greater and more heroic than any which have ever earned the distinction of the Victoria Cross amid the clash of arms, because they have been effected under more thrilling circumstances, and in a higher and nobler cause". [807]

Mr. Sennington's burial was recorded in the local newspaper and yet again, a lightly-veiled accusation of appropriated valuables from a victim of the disaster, came to light:

---

rococo style Hotel Kernan. The hotel was purchased on March 22 1938 by M. J. Firey, and was renamed The Congress Hotel. The Marble Bar hosted Fred Astaire and Ginger Rogers in dancing exhibitions.

[804] *Sun;* Baltimore, September 7th, 1916.

[805] *The North-Eastern Daily Gazette* (Middlesbrough, England); Thursday, 20th October 1898.

[806] *The Bristol Mercury and Daily Post* (Bristol, England); Friday, 21st October 1898.

[807] Magginis, John, *The Atlantic Ferry: Its Ships, Men, And Working* (London, UK: Whitaker & Co.1893), 102.

On Saturday, at the Unitarian burial ground, Berkley Square [*sic*], the remains of Mr. Edward Colston Sennington; chief steward of the *Mohegan*, were interred. There was a large number of people present in the Square, but only those who attended the funeral were admitted to the burial ground. The service was very impressively conducted by the Rev. A. N. Blatchford, who in the course of a touching address spoke of his many year's acquaintance with the deceased; whose simple, brave, and unpretentious manhood he bore testimony to. There were many floral tributes, including a wreath from the surviving members of the crew of the *Mohegan*, The mourners present were:— his widow and three daughters. Mr. Frank Sennington (brother), Mrs. N. Revie (sister), Mr. N. Revie (brother-in-law), and other relatives. Mr. C. Harris was present representing the Atlantic Transport Line; the owners of the *Mohegan*. There were representatives from the Croft School Old Boys' Society, of which the deceased was a member. The deceased was a Freemason and the following members attended :—Brothers Harford. J. Owner, W. G. Courtnay, S. G. Moxey, W. Ireland, F. Owen, W. James H. B. Stone, J. Stoates, and G. Longford. It is stated that two valuable rings were missing from the deceased's fingers. This is somewhat singular, as they were exceptionally tight and could not have fallen off. In fact they were so difficult to get over the knuckles that the deceased wore them continuously. The late Mr. Sennington received his education at the Stokes Croft School, and his family have been attendants, for generations, at Lewins's Mead [808] meeting.[809]

Cowards die many times before their deaths; the valiant never taste death but once.

The Reverend Blatchford's funeral oratory was particularly eloquent, that it deserves repeating here. It captures the moment and articulates an appropriate eulogy for the everyman:

"Who would not desire that every scene of peril and every wave-washed deck, all might, without exception, come safe to land, and no home might be darkened by sorrow for some true-hearted one that would come thither never again! Not only with the saved are in our thought today. With gratitude to God, we have to remember that this race of ours numbers others, aye, and multitudes of heroic spirits, who we believe, find, and ever will find, "heaven as near by sea, as land". For, it will surely ever be, that even be amid the wildest scene of wreck and fate, instance after instance shall be found of simple and devoted souls who follow that Master whose image the very storm-cloud cannot darken. For, they, like him, could save others, but could not, and in their noble yet tender manhood, would not save themselves. Blessed are all those who could claim the memory of such a spirit, and such there are among us today. Are the sea's vast depths rich with sunken gold and gem? But what treasure that ocean claims from wind and cloud shall compare with the remembrance of those brave hearts, who, being dead, yet speak to tell us of self-denying duty instantly done even in the dark hour of swift and unlooked for catastrophe. No single one of such can be counted as lost—for in our hearts they live forever and by their grand, their implicit self embandonment to the call of simple duty, they lift us ever to better and to higher life. Faith in the Great Father who loveth all, and forgetteth not the least prompts the beautiful and comforting assurance that, "They shall be mine," saith

---

[808] The reference to the Lewin's Mead Meeting is interesting, as it ties all the strands of Mr Sennington's life together, that ended here at his funeral. This organisation was established as a Presbyterian society in the early 1690's. Early meetings were held in the room of a private house, but by 1706 a meeting house and Young Men's meeting room were in existence. The Old Meeting House was demolished in 1787, and the present building (the 1898 building in question) erected the following year. The Meeting remained Presbyterian until the late eighteenth century, but by the beginning of the nineteenth century had changed to Unitarianism. In 1722 the Stokes Croft Unitarian school (Sennington's alma mater) was established by the Lewin's Mead Society, for the education of 30 boys, together. with an Almshouse for twelve people. The Burial Ground in Brunswick Square was purchased by the Society in 1768. The last burial took place here in 1963.

[809] *The Bristol Mercury and Daily Post* (Bristol, England); Monday 24th October 1898. The funeral arrangements were carried out by Lewis & Co., of Stokes croft (a road in the north of Bristol).

the Lord, "in that day when I make up my jewels!" It may be, that all God's "waves and billows" have gone over them but, though tears bedim our trust, let us patiently wait a little longer, for the solemn legend shall find fulfilment yet—"The sea shall give up its dead," then at last in all its glory shall be unrolled the record of every simple life that flashed into true greatness, at fate's supremest hour — then shall we see the beauty of that thought of others before self, which by its quiet devotion shed amid the scene of calamity that peace which surely flows from the sight of constancy amid suffering and before approaching doom, and proves the true brotherhood to Him who said in words forever true that, "Greater love hath no man than this, that a man lay down his life for his friends". [810]

Such was the public feeling, generated by the *Mohegan* disaster, that no less a figure than the Archbishop of Canterbury, preaching at St Mary's Church, Dover,[811] was moved to say:

"All things that received honour from mankind self-sacrifice stood at the head, and we saw how men admired it in great battle or in the deep admiration felt for those who on a stormy night went out at the risk of their lives to a sinking ship, as was the case near Falmouth. Self-sacrifice was in reality the fountain of all the highest honour". [812]

No doubt, churches the length and breadth of the land echoed those sentiments, in reference to the bravery of the few and with the loss of many, in the *Mohegan* tragedy that had touched the hearts of the multitudes.

---

[810] *The Bristol Mercury and Daily Post* (Bristol, England); Monday 24th October 1898.

[811] This address was on Sunday, October 17th, 1898 at the St Mary in Castro, or St Mary de Castro, a church in the grounds of Dover Castle, Kent. It is still a thriving church serving the Army and local people, and is the Dover Garrison Church.

[812] *The Ipswich Journal* (Ipswich, England); Saturday, October 22, 1898.

CHAPTER 21

Mrs. Agnes Maud Piggott: Assistant Stewardess

Worse things happen at sea.

A vivid account from the only woman who spent a precarious night in the ship's rigging is well recorded in this newspaper article. What makes it the more interesting is that it is a personal and self-penned description of that horrifying night of the *Mohegan* disaster:

WRECK OF THE MOHEGAN

STORY OF THE STEWARDESS

(WRITTEN BY HERSELF)

I was engaged as a stewardess on the steamship *Mohegan,* of the Atlantic Transport Company, and joined at Tilbury Docks on Oct. 13. All went well until about 6.45 p.m. on Friday, the 14th ult., at which time most of the passengers were seated at dinner, we being far down Channel. I had just served poor Mrs. Grandin with a jug of hot water, and was waiting at the saloon entrance when I heard and felt a terrific crash beneath my feet, and the vessel at once listed to one side, which upset three big piles of plates that were standing on a table, from which soup was being served. The passengers all became alarmed, and rushed out, seeking what was the matter. One lady turned to me and inquired if it was anything serious. I advised her to keep cool and collected, and she would all right. Most of the people rushed on deck, and I went, to my cabin and disposed about my person the few valuables I had. Mrs. Bowles, the other stewardess did likewise. She inquired of me if I felt afraid, I hesitatingly replied, "No," and she told me not be.

I then secured a life-belt with which each cabin was provided, and returned to the companions-way to see if I could render any assistance and on coming out of my cabin I fell in with a stream of passengers who had evidently also been to their cabins to secure lifebelts and their valuables. Just then one of the stewards, Gray [William C. Henry], I think, came rushing down the companion stairs calling out: "Ladies and children to the boats!" We made direct for the companion-way, and as we reached it the electric suddenly went out, because the engines stopped or were choked by the sea. A thought struck me that, I should require a cloak, and getting a box of matches from one of the stewards, I made my way back and secured one for myself and Mrs. Bowles. On leaving the cabin again I heard someone in the corridor, and called out, "Who is there?" I was answered by a gentleman whom I afterwards found out to be Dr. Fellowes [*sic*]. He told me he was in search of another lifebelt. I struck one of my matches, and we got some out of cabin 35. We then made our way back.

On arriving at, the head of the stairs, Robb [David], one of the stewards, who, with several of his fellows, had been busy in equipping passengers with belts, and rendering what aid they could, called out for matches. I replied, "I have some". He said to me, "Come stewardess, let us find some more belts," and we made our way to the cabins nearest the saloon", where we found several, which Robb placed on passengers. Just then I noticed that the water was coming into the companion-way and felt it, cold round my ankles. I then joined the stream of passengers who were making their way in an orderly fashion, without any crowding, to the deck, where they were at once helped to the upper side, where the lifeboats were situated. I heard the agonizing cry of a little boy, who had been snatched from his berth by his mother and simply wrapped in a blanket, calling out, "Papa, papa, I don't want to die. Don't let me die!" It was terrible to hear him. The officers and crew were already there, working bravely to get the passengers in and launch the boats, one passenger,

310

Miss Saunders, with Mrs. Bowles and myself, left. I afterwards found myself standing by Miss Saunders at the foot of the mizzen-mast, with the terrible cries of someone calling for help, and on looking round, I found a man—one of the passengers, I believe—hanging by one foot from the rigging, his head and shoulders being on deck, which of course, was very much aslant. I aided him to get free. He righted himself, with the intention, no doubt, of climbing again, when I grieve to say, he missed his hold, and slid down the deck into the sea before my eyes—a sight I shall *not* soon forget. I then turned to the lady at my side, and found her lifebelt had somehow got entangled in the ratlins.[813] I freed it and tied it round her. We then both sat at the foot of the rigging and waited—I praying to God to help us—and this lady comforting me all she could. The next thing I realised was being suddenly under water, washed there by a great incoming wave. I seemed to stay down a long time, but I had the presence of mind to keep my mouth closed, and tried to float myself. In doing this my left hand came in contact with a rope, which I clutched and held to for dear life, my feet also touching some other ropes, and I succeeded in getting on to the rigging, where the first thing I did was to loosen the heavy golf cloak I was wearing, and which was helping to pull me back. I then looked round and saw a boat at my feet. I cried out, "Can I come in? Let her come in!" A man answered, "Jump!" This I did, and found myself in the stern, the boat being full of people and filled also with water, the sea swamping it at every wave and nearly washing me out. I had to hold on very tightly to keep my place. I heard someone calling out for a knife to cut the ropes which were entangling the boat and preventing her getting away from the wreck. Having one in my pocket, I passed it along, but, feeling certain there was very little chance of being saved by this boat, I looked up and saw the rigging still above my head.

Waiting for a wave to carry the boat high, I jumped with all my strength, and luckily caught the rigging with my hands, and hung full length, crying out for "Help, help". Soon I saw a figure coming down the rigging quickly, calling out, "It's a woman," "It's a woman," and I felt myself caught by the wrists and hauled up into safety. I was by this time terribly exhausted. I and my preserver seated ourselves as best we could in the rigging. We then had time to look round, and start a little conversation, asking each other's names, and what we were. I found out that my preserver was Quartermaster Butt. He told me then that his head was terribly cut, and one of his fingers smashed. He wished he had something to tie around his head, and I said, "Here, take my apron," and between us we tore it from the band, and he fastened it around his head. By this time I was beginning to feel frightfully cold, and, to make matters worse, the wind was rather high. The waves every now and again washed over the bottom of my dress and feet. We sat there for hours, seeing lights and signals on shore, but no help at hand. Once or twice I became very drowsy, and was inclined to go to sleep, but, luckily, did not succeed. So to try and get my hands warm, which were becoming numbed, I placed them inside the tops of Quartermaster Butt's sea-boots. While on the rigging Butt told me he saw the captain at his post to the last, giving his orders clearly and calmly.

At length, after what seemed ages, though really only a few hours, we saw to our great joy, a lifeboat making for the wreck. As they dared not approach within 50ft of us, Quartermaster Juddery bravely jumped into the sea, and by swimming to the boat secured a rope, and brought it back to the rigging, where it was passed over to Quartermaster Butt, who tied it safely round me, and, with the help of a second rope, I was let down into the sea and hauled through the waves to the lifeboat, where I was fished up, soaked and cold, like a bale of goods. My first words were, "Thank God" and, "Oh, you brave men!" The work of the rescue went on until twelve more were saved from the mizzen rigging. Then the lifeboat, with great difficulty, made her way forward and rescued two men from the mainmast, then back again to the jiggermast, from which one man was taken. At this juncture a little dispute arose as to whether there was anyone clinging to the funnel, some saying there was, and some saying there was not but Coxswain Hill of the lifeboat declared he would not leave until he was quite certain there was no one left on the wreck. After calling several times, they came to the conclusion there was someone on the funnel, and with great risk, making their way as close as they dared to the spot, they

[813] Ratlines (rattlins) - a series of small ropes fastened across a sailing ship's shrouds like the rungs of a ladder, used for climbing the rigging.

found a man—Ferguson, the third. Engineer—clinging to the funnel by one hand—the other being injured—and up to his waist in water.[814] A rope was thrown to him, and he was rescued. While this was going on I was lying in the bottom of the boat near the coxswain, and was dosed with brandy, as was each survivor when he was rescued. I cannot speak highly enough of the splendid fellows who manned the lifeboat. Coxswain Hill must have been hoarse for several days after, as he did not seem able to get his orders out loud or quick enough, for he kept calling out, "Pull blue," "Pull white," [815] and encouraging his men all the time. One thing I must not omit, that when the last survivor was taken from the wreck into the lifeboat we all gave three as hearty cheers as we were able for the lifeboat crew, and the remainder of the two bottles of brandy was divided amongst those brave men, as this was their second trip during the night, having saved twenty-eight in the first trip and sixteen in the second. We then started on our journey to the blessed shore, and landed in the little bay of Porthoustock. As the boat touched ground I saw a scene I shall not easily forget—in the background the dim outline of the whitewashed cottages with their thatched roofs, and the crowd of people on the beach lighting up the scene with their lanterns, and anxious survivors peering into our faces to see if they could recognise any of their friends. On landing I was immediately taken possession of by three kind women, who helped me to their home close by and gave me every possible attention. It is simply impossible for me to relate the great kindness I received from everyone in that little village or rather hamlet, as it contains only thirteen cottages, and the lifeboat house. The inhabitants are working people, with only one or two pensioners, a stone quarry on the cliffs nearby occupying the men during the day. I am sure none of those dear people had any rest, for days and nights, as they were so busy in attending to the survivors and making them comfortable in every way. One may perhaps wonder how, in such a tiny out-of-the-way place, food was found to supply us all. Luckily they had just had their monthly supplies sent in from Helston, and the women, while waiting for the lifeboat to come in a second time, had employed themselves in baking batches of bread. Many of the survivors as they were landed made their way or were taken to the village of St. Keverne, which is a mile inland from Porthoustock, over a rough and hilly road. Here, again, all was kindness.

Dr. Leverton-Spry was in demand in every direction, binding up fractured and broken limbs, attending to hurts and bruises. I myself saw two doctors, Dr. Liverton [*sic*] Spry and Dr. Bushall and I believe they went round to all. Canon Diggins, [*sic*] the rector of St. Keverne, was also at hand relieving and comforting all, and giving what aid he could.

Mrs. [Harriet Maria] Leverton Spry and Mrs. [Annie Scott] Diggens, with many other ladies, were busy with clothes of all sorts and sizes—and it must have pretty well have emptied their wardrobes to meet the demand. I myself was clad by Mrs. Biggs, of Coverack, who sent me more than I could wear, and the rector even brought me a warm blouse and petticoat from his wife's store. Mrs. Leverton-Spry had most, if not all (men included) supplied with a new rig-out later on, and these were provided by the Shipwrecked Mariners' Society at their own cost, and very good clothes they were. Most of the crew were sent off to the Sailors' Home at Falmouth, which is under the care of Mr. and Mrs. Toulson. Whose acquaintance I made later on, and found them to be just as good and kind as the rest, although they are not Cornish people. When my dear old preserver, Quartermaster Butt, came to my room to say, "Good-bye" before being sent to Falmouth, I felt very downhearted, and was half afraid I was going to be left behind but he and some others of the crew cheered me up and said I should be all right and well looked after. And so I was by everyone, not forgetting my two hostesses and their daughter, Miss [Beatrice M.] Jordan, to whom the cottage belongs, Mrs. [Elizabeth S.] Hocking, her

---

[814] From Mrs Piggot's report, the total saved appears to be 17—a mistake, as later in the same report she confirms the true number as 16.

[815] These commands were instructions to the independent lines of oarsmen on the port and starboard sides of a lifeboat. Each line assigned as the 'whites' or the 'blues' and their relevant response, on command, would steer the boat in the direction the coxswain desired.

widow sister, with her three children, Bessie, Will, and Sidney, doing their level best for us all.[816] God bless them all and prosper all their works!

One of the crew, Farlane, [*sic*] a lad of seventeen years, had his legs broken in three places. He is at the little general shop (the only shop in the hamlet), which has to answer the purpose of a kitchen as well, and is kept by an old couple named Matthew,[817] who are both over eighty years of age. These good people even gave up their bed to those requiring rest and warmth. These old people are aided by their daughter, Mrs. West, who looks after things generally. The boy is well taken care of and receives every attention. The firm of Messrs. Williams, Torry and Field has been most kind in looking after every individual. Messrs. Fox, their agents, have had a free hand to do all in their power for everyone, and they have both had their full complement of work, night and day.

The identification of the killed was a protracted and painful business. Many of the friends had their dead embalmed, to be sent to a distance to be buried in their family vaults, or conveyed over the sea to New York. Here again the firm rendered every assistance possible and did all in their power to make things as easy as possible for all. This was no light task. It must be remembered how far we were—twenty-five miles—from the two nearest [railway] stations, Helston or Falmouth.

On the Tuesday [October 19th] the funeral took place amid a downpour of rain. The vicar's wife with the doctor's wife had made many wreaths and crosses to place on each coffin. Not one was forgotten. The next day, being Wednesday, two nice boys, Alfred Roberts and his cousin, who are only waiting vacancies to join the lifeboat crew, rowed me out to the wreck, where we came across the Trinity boat,[818] from which some officers and sailors were examining the wreck and coast. One of the sailors put his boat-hook deep into the water and pulled up a part of a blue and red flag, which I think is one of the signal flags. We rowed to meet them, and when near enough I asked for a piece of the flag, telling them I was one of the survivors, and they very kindly tore it in half and passed it to me. I have it now, and shall always keep it.

The inquest was adjourned, and I wanted badly to see my friends. Mr. Weight, one of the firm's solicitors, made arrangements for me to come to London on Monday—so after Sunday [Oct 24th] after the memorial service (which completely unnerved me)—I went to lunch at the doctor's house and the carriage came round at 2.30 with Mr. Weight, who kindly escorted me all the way to London. We had a long drive of 25 miles to Falmouth, and on arrival at the Sailors' Home I was met in the passage by Quartermaster Butt [819] and Mr. and Mrs. Toulson. The master and matron came forward at once and gave me a hearty greeting.

After a long journey, and being well looked after by Mr. Weight, who had rendered me kindness previously, we arrived at Paddington next day, and were soon being greeted by loving friends.

One more word, which is an appeal to the public. A subscription is being got up for the widows and orphans of those brave men who went down in that ship. The president of the company, Mr. Baker, has headed the list with £2,000 [820] —a grand beginning—and I hope the people of England who have hearts in their breasts will help liberally. As for myself, I may gratefully mention that I have been offered a post in another company, but I prefer to keep my present employers.

---

[816]. The head of the household was a widow, Elizabeth Jane Hocking (38 years), her son William (13 years), second son John Sidney (12 years) and daughter Bessie (15 years). In the 1901 UK census, Elizabeth and Bessie were described as 'laundresses;' John Sidney, as an office-boy in the local stone quarry and William as a farm servant.

[817] Census 1901: William Matthews / Age 75 years / Naval Pensioner / Lost an eye / Daughters: Grace Jane Matthews / Grocer, shop-keeper; Mary Matthews / Housekeeper.

[818] By not mentioning it here, Mrs Piggott obviously missed an incident that occurred on the same day, that of Capt. Robert M. Robinson and others on examining the wreck in a rowing-boat, holed their boat and had to escape by climbing into the *Mohegan*'s rigging. It would have been ironic if she and her companions had saved those gentlemen in the same circumstance, as she had experienced five days previously.

[819] By this time, most of the crew had returned to London. Quartermaster Butt had remained at the Sailor's Home, to have his injuries tended to.

[820] This sum of £2,000 is the equivalent of £115,000 in today's currency.

One can't help drawing comparisons when I think of the splendid treatment we shipwrecked English received from everyone, and then read of the other poor creatures who have had to do with selfish, brutal crews and unkind people on other shores. I have wanted to write all this principally to say, with tears and thanks, that I did not see a single exception all that dreadful night to the manhood of all, from the captain to the ship's boys.—A. M. Piggott.[821]

Mrs Piggot was quite obviously a brave and a good soul. That she ventured to visit the wreck, in the company of two young lads who volunteered to row her out to the site, speaks volumes. Not many would have accepted the offer, having almost lost their life, and having seen many others losing theirs, on that horrendous night.

[821] *The Telegraph;* Thursday, November 10th 1898.

CHAPTER 22

Miss Katherine Bell Noble: A Passenger

That which does not kill us makes us stronger.

Miss Noble was the daughter of Mr Horace W. Noble and Mrs Mary Spencer Harrison Noble, of Baltimore and a niece to a previous Secretary of State, Mr Oswald Tilghman.[822] She was an only child (a brother had died in infancy) and was from a well-to-do family: a member out of the top-drawer of Baltimore society.

Having holidayed in the UK she had the misfortune in returning home on the vessel *Mohegan*. A report on her adventure appeared in the New York Press:

MISS NOBLE A GOOD SWIMMER

Miss Katherine Noble, who is reported to have made a plucky and successful fight for life, is a resident of Baltimore, where she is known as Miss Katy Bell Noble, and has a reputation as a swimmer. Her father is Horace W. Noble, a retired capitalist, who lives on West North Avenue, and she is his only child. In June Miss Noble went to England, where she has a great many friends. After the close of the London season she attended quite a number of house parties, which delayed her departure for home. She was accompanied on the *Mohegan* by a young English woman, who was to be her guest in Baltimore. The name of this lady is not known. Miss Noble is not unknown in the social circles of this city. One of her most intimate friends is Miss Verona Spencer, daughter of Samuel Spencer, the representative of J. Pierpoint Morgan's interests in all Southern railroad enterprises. Two Winters ago, whilst a guest of Miss Spencer, Miss Noble attended a cotillion [823] at Sherry's [824] and her beauty was much remarked. Henry Noble, a lawyer of 141 Broadway, is a relative of Miss Noble. Upon learning late yesterday afternoon that his cousin was among the rescued he sent her a cablegram of congratulation.[825]

Opportunities come but do not linger.

She would have lost her life, but for a fortuitous encounter with the Porthoustock lifeboat, whilst it was returning to base, having picked up twenty-eight persons on the first of two lifesaving trips. She was later referred to as, 'Miss Noble, the plucky American lady who was rescued after clinging four hours to an oar'. Her no-nonsense approach to life and a lack of fear for her own safety, was apparent in her exchange with the coxswain of the lifeboat *Charlotte:* "Just chuck me a line" she said. On being helped aboard, she sat among the rescued alive, the dead, and the dying; brushing herself down, and showing little regard for her own

---

[822] Colonel Oswald Tilghman (1841–1932) played an active role in the American Civil War. He was a member of the Maryland Senate, Talbot County, 1894 – 96. As a personal friend of Governor Warfield, and in 1904–1908; the latter appointed him secretary of state under his administration. Miss Katherine Noble visited his wife on August 24, 1899, at Foxley Hall.

[823] A *cotillon* is a formal ball, which offered an opportunity to present young women to society.

[824] A venue used by the wealthy families of Baltimore, to present their daughters on to the social and marriage market. The young girls were known as debutantes and were taking part in the annual 'season'.

[825] *The New York Times;* October 16th 1898.

remarkable experience. Quite obviously, her talent for swimming and with the removal of her outer-clothing before entering the sea, had paid dividends.

After the disaster, she was cared for that night by Mr William Rogers and his wife Margaret Ann, at Rosenithon, less than a mile from St. Keverne. As can be seen in the accompanying photograph, (see fig. 77) showing the Rogers family, posing outside their primitive farmhouse with ten family members sharing this home, it must have been something of a culture shock for a young upper-class lady from Baltimore. But as revealed in this disaster and in the events of later life, she was made of stronger stuff: taking this setback well in her stride, and probably finding the whole post-disaster period a novel experience.

A villager stated that, "It was with great sadness that the villagers in St. Keverne said goodbye to the person they had taken to their hearts." Miss Noble later sent a personal photograph (see fig. 19) to the Rogers family, as a memento of the event. The following morning, Dr Leverton-Spry's wife attended and took Miss Noble back to her the family home, and comforted her there. Later on the following Sunday, friends arrived to take her back to their home in London.

Her dramatic account, as relayed to a Baltimore newspaper, is worth including here:

MISS NOBLE'S RESCUE

Graphically Told In A Letter To Her Parents From London

BATTLED WITH THE WAVES

Home in The Water After The Sinking Of The Mohegan

Picked Up By A Lifeboat Numb And Stiff From Exposure
She Was Tenderly Nursed Back To Strength And Is In London.

Mr. and Mrs. Horace Noble, 8 West North avenue, received a letter yesterday morning from their daughter, Miss Katherine Noble, who is in London, England, and who was one of the passengers saved from the wreck of the steamer *Mohegan*, on the Atlantic Transport Line, off the coast of Cornwall, at 7 o'clock Friday evening, October 14. It was the first letter received from her since her awful experience on the ill-fated steamer, cablegrams only being received before, assuring them she was saved and recovering from the ordeal through which she had gone.

The letter was written at 11 Mornington avenue, Kensington, Saturday, October 22, and mailed the same day. Miss Noble wrote that she had about recovered from the shock and exposure in the water.

The letter, which was directed to Mrs. Noble, is in part as follows:

"Ever since arrival in London I have been besieged by reporters, telegrams, letters and visitors until I should have lost my mind, except by direction of the doctor, who would not allow me to see any one until yesterday, when I saw two of my best friends. Even now I do not realize what I have been through, as the doctor will not allow me to talk of it. However, I suppose you are anxious to know the particulars. Everything on the trip promised to be so pleasant, for we had such a friendly set of passengers.

At Dinner When The Crash Came.

"All went well until Friday night at 7 o'clock, when I was at dinner. I sat next to the captain,[826] with Mr. and Mrs. King opposite, all of whom were lost. Suddenly there was a crash, which I first thought was the machinery breaking down, and went on deck to see what was the matter. I was, as usual, first to reach the deck to see what was the matter.

"—when I reached the deck I saw at once there was to be a struggle for our lives—"

"The ship was fast sinking, and the waves washing over the deck, and the fourth officer [Browning] came and said: 'Miss Noble, you must jump on the deck and try to get to the rigging.' So I took off my shoes so that I could climb better and jumped. The wave knocked us both down, but I held on until he could get off his coat and boots; then we tried to get to the rigging. But could not : so I asked him to help me over the railings and I would stay there, which he did.

Washed Off By A Wave.

"The ship was breaking up, and just as I was about to brace myself for a shock, a wave washed over us, and my next sensation was of going down, down, down. Not for an instant did I lose my presence of mind. I waited until it was time to come up and began to tread water. The few moments I shall never forget: the shrieks and screams of those poor people drowning around me.

"I soon found some wreckage, and many of us drifted around together, the waves knocking us in every conceivable direction and breaking over us. The fourth officer came up on a hatch cover, and told me not to struggle, and help would surely come, as he was sure we were near land. He was with me some time, when a wave broke over us and he has not been seen since.

Alone In The Water.

"Towards the last I was entirely alone, all my fellow-passengers having gone down one by one. After having been in that awful ocean I was rescued by the life-boat, so numb and stiff that I could not get in the boat, but, as the papers say, 'still cheerful.'

"To this day I cannot understand how I managed to be saved. Not a soul who was in the water or went over with me ever survived. Even the men were worn out and exhausted by the strength of the waves. The crew who were saved were taken from the rigging and lifeboats that were washed overboard. The wave that sent me overboard probably saved my life. The most of those poor creatures went down with the ship. I am, too, thankful that I was with no one, for I should probably have followed them, but as it was I did just as my sense dictated.

Picked Up By A Life Crew.

"After being taken into the lifeboat I was laid across the laps of two seamen, who rubbed my limbs and poured brandy down my throat, which made me deathly sick and relieved me of a quantity of salt water I had swallowed. One poor man took off his coat and covered me. The money, &c., which I had placed in my dress, had been washed out; how, I do not know.

"I could not move when I was put on shore, and my idea that I was in for a case of inflammatory rheumatism. I was then taken into a poor fisherman's house, where I received every care and attention. The daughters rubbed me down, rolled me in hot blankets, water bottles around me and dosed me with hot water and whisky. The doctor came at once and said I would be all right. I never saw such good, kind people in all, my life. They were up with me all night, and, of course, no one had any sleep.

"The next morning the doctor's wife and friends came bright and early to bring me some clothes, and I was driven to the doctor's house,[827] where I remained until Sunday evening, when Mr. and Mrs. Silo [828] came for me.

---

[826] Miss Noble had confused the two evenings, as it was the previous evening where she sat next to the captain. He failed to arrive at the dinner table on the night of the disaster and was accused by her, as being in a cabin with another woman.

[827] Dr Leverton-Spry's residence and combined surgery being at Churchtown, St. Keverne.

"Before leaving the little fishing village I went around to see the men and crew who had been saved, and their appreciation was most touching. One poor man who had his fingers cut off, came up and kissed me: said he had a family at home.

"This little village [Porthoustock] is a mile from where the doctor lived. When I reached him I was put to bed and well cared for. Sunday morning, though, I got up and went to the little church, and it was only then I realized what I had been through and from what I had been saved. One part of the church was curtained off to conceal the bodies of those that had been lost and were waiting to be identified.

"Mrs. Leverton-Spry, the doctor's wife, has an only child. So you know they did everything for me. Telegrams poured in from all directions, and I never knew before I had so many friends over here. Everyone wanted me to come direct to their house, but Sunday afternoon I was dumbfounded to see Mr and Mrs. Silo. They had travelled all night [by railway] and had then driven twenty miles [from Falmouth] to get to me. Of course, we had a grand weeping match. Jane had brought all necessary clothing. Even to a veil and a purse of gold sent by a friend, for they knew I had lost everything. They are, indeed, true friends.

"After they had changed horses they drove me back to Falmouth, another twenty miles, where we had a fine dinner, but I could eat nothing, so went to bed. I was sorry to leave all those good, kind people behind me.

"Monday we came over to London, a ten hour's trip where I was put to bed, and the doctor sent for Tuesday, who gave me something to make me sleep and quiet my nerves. He kept me in bed two days, which weakened me considerably, but I knew it was best.

"I have kept all my letters and telegrams for you to read, which still continue to come. This morning I had a nice note and photograph from the young woman who was saved from the *Elbe,* and also a letter with clippings from the French papers. Why people are making such a fuss over me I do not know.

"Capt. John Findlay, of the steamer *Massachusetts,* has just called, and I told him I would not return on any steamer of the Atlantic Transport Line except with him. The crew of the *Mohegan* were exceedingly brave and active in their efforts to save passengers, particularly women and children, even at the cost of their own lives".

The letter contained clippings from the London Daily Telegraph of October 18, giving an account of the wreck.

J. H. James, one of the *Mohegan* saved,[829] is quoted as saying: "On our way to land passengers we had in a lifeboat we picked up a lady about two miles from the wreck, the pluckiest lady I ever saw—Miss Noble, of Baltimore. She was going along a plank, to which she was holding like grim death".

Miss Noble's letter also contained the letter and photograph she had received from Miss Anna Bocker of England, who was rescued after the steamer *Elbe* foundered some years ago.

A number of friends called to see Mr. and Mrs. Noble yesterday, to whom the letter was read.

Miss Noble did not say when she will start for home.[830]

She returned to New York, arriving November 19th on the liner *Lucania,* generating much interest both there and in her home town of Baltimore. Her first-hand report captures the drama of the moment:

[828] Mr Piero and Jane (Jeannie) Silo had arrived from Kensington, London. Piero was a stockbroker agent by profession, and was an Italian and a naturalised British subject.

[829] Joseph H. James was a member of the lifeboat crew, as there was no such named member on the *Mohegan* crew/passenger lists.

[830] *The Sun;* Baltimore (1837–1985); Oct 31st 1898

MISS NOBLE HOME.

Heroine of The *Mohegan* Disaster Warmly Greeted in Baltimore.

Sailors Tried To Do Their Best, But There Was No Head.

A Scene of Confusion When The Steamer Struck The Rocks—

Reported That Captain Griffiths Did Not Go Down With His Ship.

Miss Katherine Bell Noble, who was one of the passengers saved from the wreck of the wreck of the Atlantic Transport Liner *Mohegan*, off the coast of Cornwall, on the night of the October 14, is safe at the house of her father, Mr. Horace Noble, 8 West North Avenue, She arrived there from New York Saturday night, and was welcomed by a member of her intimate friends, who had gathered to meet her,

The parlors of the house had been transformed into a veritable flower bower. While her friends felt hesitancy about discussing with her the wreck and the subsequent experiences, she seemed not at all loath to tell them the story.

The Cunard Line steamer *Lucania*, upon which Miss Noble crossed the ocean, was due in New York on Friday, but had a very rough passage, and did not dock until about 10 o'clock Saturday morning. Mr. and Mrs. Noble were at the Hoffman House [831] Thursday night waiting for the ship. They were accompanied by Mr. Joseph Whitney, of Baltimore, and by Mr. and Mrs. Robert Patterson, of Philadelphia, who chaperoned Miss Noble when, several years ago, she made a fourteen month's tour through Europe. A representative of THE SUN also went to New York to meet the steamer, and a few minutes after her arrival had a lengthy interview with Miss Noble at the Hoffman House. He also talked with her at her home, on North Avenue, yesterday afternoon.

The *Lucania* was sighted late Friday night and, after anchoring, started for her dock at daybreak Saturday. Mr. Noble, through the influences of Collector of the Port Stone of Baltimore, had secured permission to go aboard the United States revenue cutter, which was to take the boarding officers to the ship. He left the Barge Office at the Battery at 7 o'clock and met his daughter on the vessel at quarantine. Mrs. Noble and the rest of the party awaited her arrival at the dock on the North river.

The Sun's Tidings Were First.

"I want to thank THE SUN for its great kindness to me and my parents since the wreck," was one of the first things Miss Noble said. "Not only has its accounts been accurate, but when my father was trying in vain to learn whether I had been saved or not, it was from THE SUN's office that the first tidings came to him that I was still in the land of the living.

"I scarcely know what to tell you about my experiences in the wreck," she said to the SUN's representative. "The letter which I wrote to my father, and which was published exclusively in the SUN, told about all there was to be told. It seems like a dream to me now. I can never forget the sight of those poor people drowning like rats before my eyes, and nobody able to help them.

"As to the cause of the wreck, I know nothing. I have an opinion, of course, and I am at liberty to express it. In what purports to be an interview with me sent from New York by telegraph on Saturday I was quoted as saying that Captain Griffiths was undoubtedly insane. I would like to have this corrected in THE SUN. I said nothing of the kind. In my testimony before the Board of Trade which is investigating the wreck. I was asked about the captain's physical condition

---

[831] The Hoffman House is a Dutch Colonial style stone house built about 1679 and the building has remained basically unchanged since its initial construction, and the Hoffman family occupied the house for 201 years, until the late 19th century. Hoffman House is located in the Stockade Historic District at 94 North Front Street, at the corner of Green Street.

and I told that board that I knew absolutely nothing about his health, as he had not confided in me and I had asked him no questions.

Captain Griffiths' Peculiarities.

"I do not know whether he was sane or insane, whether he was ill or well, but I do not know that it was a most remarkable thing for him to take the *Mohegan* ten or twelve miles out of her course on a calm, fogless night, and run her upon the rocks inside of the warning bell buoy, which rocked and rang at the seaward edge of the ledge. If he had tried to wreck the boat he could not have done it any better.

"I really did not know Captain Griffiths, although I sat next to him at the table. I tried to chat with him, but could not get a word out of him. When I spoke to him he would say nothing, and stare at me as if he thought I had not a ray of sense.[832] I told some of my friends on the boat that he was absolutely the most disagreeable man I ever saw, and they quite agreed with me".

One of Two Causes.

"Is there any way in which you, personally, can account for the wreck?"

"Well, yes and no. I cannot tell exactly what caused it, but I think that it was either because the officers were incompetent or that the ship was unseaworthy. We sailed on Thursday, you know, and Thursday night something got wrong with the dynamos, and there was not an electric light on board. All day Friday the ship had a decided list to port, which no one seemed able to account for. The cargo had not shifted it was said, and the list was still on her when she struck the rock.

"If Captain Griffiths was temporarily insane he was certainly so when we passed the Eddystone light several hours before the wreck. He was miles out of his course then, and a passenger who had passed the light a dozen times said to me that he had never known a steamer to be so close to it.

"Granting even that Captain Griffiths was insane, were all the officers insane? Did they not know that the vessel's course was west, one quarter north, when it should have been west by north? And if they knew the captain had laid the wrong course for the men at the wheel, ought not they have told him of his error and had it corrected? You see, the whole thing is entirely incomprehensible. It looks more as if all the officers were incompetent than the captain was insane".

Proper Discipline Lacking.

"We have heard both the officers and the members of the crew acted with great bravery after the vessel struck," remarked THE SUN's representative.

"Yes, I have heard so, too. The captain was on the bridge shouting to the sailors when I went upon deck, and the second officer was one of the first to jump overboard. I do not know what became of the third officer. The fourth officer was a brave man. He was the one who floated near me in the water for so long. He had no life belt and was clinging to a hatch cover. He tried to keep up my courage, and then a wave washed him off the hatch and he was drowned.

"Had there been proper discipline there is no reason in the world why every passenger should not have been saved. In the first place, when the captain found where he was he turned the ship just exactly the wrong way. The result was that she went grinding upon the rocks. If he had turned her the other way he could have grounded her, and we could all have walked to shore.

"I was at dinner when we struck. There was no shock or jar worth mentioning. We just stopped suddenly. The list, which had been on the boat all day long, disappeared and she righted. Some friends who sat opposite to me thought that they had shifted the water ballast. The gentleman turned to his wife and said, laughingly: 'That's the way they run you down upon the rocks!' They were both drowned.

---

[832] This incident is alluded to earlier, as a possible manifestation of a medical condition—Transient Ischaemic Attacks (see page 281).

No Head To Anything.

"Finally I became somewhat anxious and went upon the deck. An officer said to me: 'It's all right; we will go on in a minute.' But I knew better, I could see the position, and I knew she was lost. Then the captain began ordering out the life-boats. I hurried below, put on a life-belt and got out my rug and my cloak, so as to be ready to get into a boat. I put my money inside my dress. My jewelry was left in my trunk in the stateroom.

"When I got upon the deck again the scene of confusion surpassed anything I ever saw. I dropped my rug, my cape and the satin skirt which I wore and got into a boat, but there seemed to be nobody who knew how to launch it, and I got out again. The captain was shouting, 'Get the boats out men,' 'It's our only chance.' 'Why can't you men work there?' and other encouraging things. But the results were painfully lacking. The sailors seemed to be doing the best they could, but there was no head to anything and no systematic organized effort.

"They could not launch the boats at all. The tackle or something was all out of order, and the men were calling for razors or knives or anything to cut the ropes.

"It was disgraceful, and the loss of many lives is attributable to this unnecessary delay, I really believe.

"The stewards and the sailors gave the passengers all the help they could as individuals, tying on life-preservers and helping the women and the children to get into the boats, which the sailors were still trying to launch.

"When the ship was fast sinking and the waves were breaking over the deck the fourth officer approached and advised me to try and get into the rigging. We took off our shoes, so that we could climb better, and both tried to reach the rigging, but we could not do so. The waves were too strong and kept knocking us down. He then helped me over the railing, and I stayed there until a giant wave came along and washed me overboard. I went under the water, but soon came up again, and at once struck out to get away from the people who were clutching at me, and also from the sinking ship.

Drifting Out To Sea.

"I got hold of a board and rested my arms upon it. This with the lifebelt, just kept my head out of water, and the waves kept curling up like mountains and breaking over me. The fourth officer had no lifebelt, and he was washed overboard by the same wave that took me off. He got upon a hatch cover near me and did the best to encourage me. He said that we were near land and he was sure we would be saved.

"After a pause," continued Miss Noble, "I asked the fourth officer how it had happened. His only answer was: 'That man ought to be shot!'"

"Who did he mean by that man?'"

"It was my impression that he meant Captain Griffiths, We kept drifting out to sea, as the current was running out when we struck. The officer and I were keeping our eyes open for a lifebelt for him. It is strange that all through this I did not lose my presence of mind and did not get a bit excited. It was bitter cold in the water, though, and my teeth were chattering so that I could hardly talk. There was even something amusing in the situation. I reminded myself of Mrs. Lecks and Mrs. Aleshine in Stockton's amusing story.[833]

"At last I got hold of another lifebelt, and just as I told the officer that I found one a wave washed him off the hatch and that was the last of him. He was not three feet from me when he disappeared. In fact I had hold of the hatch with one hand. Then I drifted out, out to sea.

"I did not think much about anything. Was I lonesome? No, it did not seem to occur to me to be lonesome. Then I heard someone calling and I answered as loud as I could. It was one of the life-saving boats. They were looking for the wreck and happened to run across me. I was over two miles from the vessel then and had been in the water nearly four hours.

---

[833] Frank R. Stockton, *The Casting Away of Mrs. Lecks and Mrs. Aleshine* (1886); it tells of two middle-aged women on a sea voyage to Japan who become castaways on a deserted island.

Wanted A Rope, Not An Oar.

The boat was twenty feet from me when I first saw it. I am very near-sighted, and I had lost my lorgnette [834] when I was washed overboard. The men in the boat say that the first thing I said to them was: 'Don't shove me an oar; chuck me a rope!' Possibly I did say this, but not exactly in this language, as my hands were so numb that I could not have taken hold of the oar. [835]

"They came up near me and crossed two oars behind my back. A wave pushed me alongside and the men lifted me in. There were some other passengers in the boat, who had been picked up. Some women were lying in the bottom and I thought they were dead, but they revived. I sat up and talked to the men. I was deathly sick, on account of having swallowed so much sea water. It seemed to me that I had swallowed the whole ocean, but I guess I didn't". What happened to me after I was landed has already been told in the letter from me to my father, which appeared in THE SUN. I stayed in a fisherman's hut at Porthoustock that night, and the next day I was taken to the little village of St. Keverne, where I remained until some friends came for me on Sunday night. They had sent me, in care of the company, a number of letters and telegrams and were trying to find out where I was, but some of these messages the company delivered to me. After that I visited some of the friends whom I had already visited last summer. I wanted to come home right away, but the doctor would not consent to it for several weeks, and then I had to wait for and testify before the Board of Trade".

Nervous On The Trip Home.

Miss Noble went abroad in June and has been a guest at many house parties during the summer. She was for a time at Egford Park, Burton-on-the-Water, Gloucestershire, the country seat of the Hon. Mr. Chatham, a member of Parliament, and at Judge King's, in Somerset.

"Were you nervous while coming home on the *Lucania*?" she was asked.

"Nervous? I should say I was. I was so nervous that I made almost everybody on board nervous. It was a very rough voyage, and every time a wave would hit the ship I would think we had struck a rock. I was continually on the jump. I remember one day a friend came down from the deck and I asked how many officers were on the bridge. 'Five', he said. 'What,' cried another gentleman who was sitting near, 'did you say fire?' 'No.' I answered, 'he said five—five officers on the bridge.' 'Oh,' he said in a relieved tone. Then he added: 'My condition is all due to your nervousness.'

Meeting of Mother And Daughter.

It was raining in torrents when the *Lucania* reached her dock on Saturday, and Mrs. Noble had been waiting on the dismal pier, listening to the dreary patter of the raindrops, for nearly three hours, when the big liner hove in sight. It had been a trying time upon the mother, and an equally trying one on the daughter, who had been at anchor off Sandy Hook [836] all night.

The scene when Mrs. Noble and Miss Noble met was an effecting one, and many on the pier who did not know who they were turned away with moist eyes. Not a word was said by either of them for several minutes. They simply fled to each other's arms and let the silent tears give mute testimony of their joy at being reunited.

All of the clothes which Miss Noble had were lost with the *Mohegan*. She had also lost all her money, it having been washed out of her dress. She had to purchase a new outfit to come home in. When she landed she wore a light gray cloth gown, English made, trimmed with white braid. A purple scarf was about her neck, and a picture hat, with black plumes, adorned her head.

---

[834] A pair of glasses or opera glasses held by a single long handle on one side.

[835] Katie Bell Noble also told her family that, when she had encountered the *Charlotte* lifeboat, some of the saved persons already aboard urged the coxswain to ignore her cries, lest one more person might capsize the already filled lifeboat. Terry Moyle; *The Mohegan – 1898 – 1998*, 30.

[836] Sandy Hook is a large sand spit or barrier spit, the extension of a barrier peninsula along the coast of New Jersey, separated from the mainland by the estuary of the Shrewsbury River. Historically, Sandy Hook has been a convenient anchorage for ships before proceeding into Upper New York Harbour 15½ miles distance–*WikiPedia*.

She said she had made an inventory of what she had lost—clothing and jewellery—and found she could not replace her wardrobe for less than $1,975. The Atlantic Transport Line, she said, had offered her $100 and her passage home upon any steamer which she might select.

"Is The Captain Alive?"

"What was the last you saw of Captain Griffiths?" Miss Noble was asked.

"The last time I saw him he was standing on the bridge. A sailor, however, told me a few days later that the captain was in a life-boat with him and that he wore two life belts. There were many persons in London who are not quite sure that Captain Griffiths is dead, and I myself would not be surprised if he should turn up some day. You know his body was never found".

Miss Noble is the only child of Mr. and Mrs. Horace Noble. Her mother was Miss. Mary Spencer Harrison, a sister of the wife of Col. Oswald Tilghman, of Easton. Miss Noble made her debut into Baltimore society six years ago, and she has a host of friends. She is a pronounced brunette, of medium height, with brilliant dark brown eyes. She speaks French and German fluently, and this was her third trip abroad.

"Father and mother say that I shall never go again," she said yesterday, "but I think I shall".

Since the wreck of the *Mohegan* Miss Noble has lost twelve pounds and the change is rather becoming to her. The remarkable self-control which she exhibits while discussing the details of an affair which must be harrowing to her has been wondered at by all who have talked to her. She evinces no nervousness and modestly deprecates any allusions to her nerve and bravery.

"All I did was to hang on to a plank until they picked me up," she says". [837]

In the modern parlance, she would have been described as a 'tough cookie' and probably somewhat pushy and with a confident personality. Those enduring qualities helped her during the disaster, and in later life; however, such characteristics would have no doubt failed to impress the rather brusque Captain Griffith. One supposes that a brash American female with a mind of her own, was not to the Captain's taste, at the dinner table.

What is interesting in her personal report, is that Miss Noble unequivocally places Capt. Griffith at the dinner table, seated next to her on the night before the disaster, and his absence on the night of the disaster. Another point of interest, raised by Miss Noble, was her reference to the continuous list to port, adopted by the *Mohegan* throughout the day of travel down the Channel. She was told there was no shift in cargo that could have accounted for this, in which case, what could have been its cause? No mention was made of this situation by a witness at any subsequent inquiry, so one must assume it was of no real significance.

A bittersweet moment.

An American confectionery company produced a chewing-gum product, named the, "Katie Bell",[838] in order to capitalise on her moment of fame; this in spite of one hundred and five deaths that accompanied Miss

---

[837] *The Sun;* Baltimore – November 21st 1898.

[838] This information came from John Fraser (Jnr.), a resident of Annapolis, Maryland, USA, whose mother was a first cousin to Miss Noble and who passed on this information to the author; Terry Moyle – *The Mohegan 1898 – 1998,* 30.

Noble's adventure. It is not known whether this commercial enterprise improved the company's market share.[839]

In the meantime, Miss Noble wasted no time in suing the shipping company for substantial damages:

MISS NOBLE'S SUIT

———

She Claims $30,000 For Injury In The Wreck Of The Mohegan

———

GROSS NEGLIGENCE ALLEGED

———

Atlantic Transport Company The Only Defendant.

The suit of Miss Katherine Bells Noble, for personal injury sustained by her in the wreck of the steamship *Mohegan* on the 14th of last October, was instituted yesterday, as THE SUN stated it would be. It was filed in the [Baltimore] City Court by Thomas G. Hayes, James P. Gorter and H. Arthur Stump, attorneys for Miss Noble. The claim is for $30,000 [840] damages.

The Atlantic Transport Company is the only defendant in the case and is sued as the character of the steamship. This company was incorporated in West Virginia. Its president is Mr. B. N. Baker, of Baltimore, and has its principal office here. A number of other survivors of the wreck have sued for damages in the Admiralty Court in New York, the suits in such cases being against the vessel and its owners. Miss Noble's suit is in a State court.

Miss Noble is the daughter of Mr. and Mrs. Horace Noble, 8 West North avenue. An account of her fearful experience has been given to THE SUN. "The officers, agents, servants and employees of the defendant company," the declaration states, "on the first day out negligently ran the steamship down the English Channel without her lifeboats swung out and without proper precautions for the of passengers in the event of disaster. They negligently and carelessly, in the daytime and in fair weather, did take the vessel miles to the westward of the well-known and established course down said channel, and negligently and carelessly sunk the said ship upon the well-known and dangerous Manacle Rocks, off the Cornish coast".

While Miss Noble lost all her effects, valued at about $1,000,[841] in the wreck, no claim for these is made in the suit. A jury trial is asked.[842]

On another legal matter, there was a difficulty in fulfilling the provisions of the will for the deceased, Mr Thomas Worthington King, a passenger on the *Mohegan*. Miss Noble was called to give evidence:

TO SHOW WHICH DIED FIRST

———

A Survivor of the Mohegan Helps to
Clear Up the Provisions of a Will.

(Kansas City Star)

Upon a unique question which involved the settlement of the estate of Rufus King of Columbus, Ohio. Miss Katherine Noble of this city, one of the survivors of the wreck of the steamer *Mohegan*, on the English coast, two years ago, has given testimony which is intended to determine whether Mr. King or his little son Rufus, died first, as both were lost.

---

[839] The American chewing-gum market was valued at $6,000,000 annually – *The Yorkshire and The York Herald;* April 19th 1899.

[840] This sum converts to £6,300 in today's currency.

[841] This sum converts to £210 in today's currency.

[842] The Evening Times (Washington, D.C.) March 28, 1899,

The will of Mr. King bequeathed the greater portion of his large estate to his son, with the proviso that if the father should survive the son, the son's share should revert to another member of the family. Mr. King's wife and her mother also perished in the disaster. The whole family, together with Miss Noble and others, were swept from the deck of the steamer together. In her testimony, given at the request of the executors, Miss Noble says that she and the members of the King family were among the last to leave the ship. When a big wave washed them overboard and she came to the surface, she caught hold of a plank, and little Rufus King, about a minute afterward, rose and caught hold of the same plank. She tried to help him, but could not. He clung on for some time, but finally dropped off exhausted. The child was the only member of the King family she saw after they were swept into the sea in the dark.[843]

In the meanwhile, Miss Katie Noble continued to fascinate the American public:

Lucius J. Cornwell, A Salesman, Expires of Apoplexy.

His Three Brothers were notified.

Lucius J. Cornwell, aged fifty-eight years, was found dead yesterday afternoon on the floor of his room, in the house of Henry Krause, 519 West Mulberry street. Coroner Grempler, of the Western district, decided that Mr. Cornwell's death was due to apoplexy [cerebral hemorrhage; a stroke].

The deceased had been employed as a salesman by August Mencken & Bro. 600 West Pratt street. He was unmarried and has three brothers—B. E. Cornwell, of Urbana, Va., John S. Cornwell, of Vienna, Md., and a third brother is a member of the firm of Cornwell, Bodle & Co. of Cambridge, Md. They have been notified.

In looking over Mr. Cornwell's effect, Coroner Grempler found certificates for ten shares of stock of the Consolidated Gas Company, fifteen share of stock of the Baltimore Cider and Vinegar Company, bank deposit books showing credits amounting to $441.54, and a promissory note for $500, with interest, dated June 30, 1886. A number of newspaper clippings were found in his possession, one of which was a picture of Miss Katherine B. Noble, the heroine of the *Mohegan* disaster.[844]

Despite Miss Noble's bad experience at sea, this did not deter her from further travelling abroad. This later trip seemed to have been planned to coincide with a nostalgic visit to the scene of her near-death experience:

MISS NOBLE GOING ABROAD

To Visit Fisher Folk Who Rescued
Her When Shipwrecked.

Miss Katherine Noble will sail August 3 [1907] for Italy, going by the Mediterranean route and travelling through Italy into Germany. She will spend the Autumn visiting friends in England, and while there will run down to see her old fishing folk friends at St. Keverne, the little seacoast hamlet off Manacle Rocks, where she was rescued from shipwreck several years ago.

Miss Noble has kept in touch with her fishermen rescuers, and a number of them have written to her expressing a desire to have her revisit in their humble homes.[845]

---

[843] *The New York Times;* 1890.

[844] *The Sun (VA) Newspaper;* 3rd December 1898.

[845] *Sun;* Maryland – June 30th 1907.

It is not known if Miss Noble kept the promise to her friends in St. Keverne;[846] however, she and her travelling companion, Miss Jennie Stone of Washington, left that same city for a three month tour of Canada in 1906: spending some time in the mountains near Lake St. John and returning by way of Montreal and Quebec.[847] The much travelled Miss Noble again embarked on a European tour, with her same companion. They both set sail on the vessel *SS Koenig Albert* [848] from New York, on August 11, 1907. The voyage was to include Munich for the opera, and visiting Gibraltar, Touraine, Rome, Naples and Paris.

Blest is the bride the sun shines on.

In 1908, Miss Noble became engaged to Mr Ernesto Trevi-Simondetti, formerly of Turin, Italy and now of Mexico.[849] He was a newspaper publisher and an importer:

HEROINE OF DISASTER AT SEA IS TO WED

Katherine Noble, Whose Bravery at Time Mohegan Sank in Channel Gave her Wide Fame, Will Marry

BALTIMORE, Jan 3 – The engagement of Miss Katherine Noble, the heroine of the *Mohegan* disaster, is announced. She will wed Ernesto Trouvi-Simondetti of Mexico.

Miss Noble was a passenger on board the steamer *Mohegan* when it sank in the English Channel, October 15, 1898. She placed a lifebelt around her and clung to a plank in the water for five hours before she was rescued.

Sailors tried to take her into the lifeboats, but she refused, saying that they were overcrowded and the addition of her weight would lessen the chances of those already in the boats [*sic*]. The sailors said she was the pluckiest girl they had ever seen. She was one of eleven passengers saved out of ninety-seven.[850]

Quite obviously, the *Mohegan* story becomes the more enhanced, in subsequent tellings.

Her husband-to-be was from a prominent Italian family and was the nephew of Tancredi Canonica, President of the Roman Senate, as well as being related to many other Italians of distinction.

Following the wedding, the couple was to take up residence in Mexico City, occupying one of its most beautiful houses there.

It was during the year of 1910 that Mr Simondetti was awarded the *Chevalier of the Legion of Honor of the Crown of Italy*, by the King of Italy.[851] The honour was resulting from Mr Simondetti supporting the Italian

---

[846] Most likely not: as there was no reference to any such visit, which in itself, would have generated a great deal of interest and so being reported in the local newspapers.

[847] *Washington Times;* July 15th 1906.

[848] *SS Koenig Albert*—shipping-line: Nord-Deutrscher Lloyd Bremen, Baltimore.

[849] Among the guests present from out-of-town were Sĕnor Don Jose T. Godey, Charge d'affaires of the Mexican Embassy at Washington.

[850] *Los Angeles Herald;* January 4th 1908.

[851] *Sun;* Maryland - February 10th 1910.

colony in Mexico City. The previous year, he and his wife had visited Italy and had had a private audience with the King.[852]

The couple lived for three years in Mexico City, and it was during this period that her husband became embroiled in the murky world of Mexican politics, following the election of a new president, as reported here:

SAME OLD PRESS CENSORSHIP RULES

American Asks For Protection From Maderistas in Mexico

Baltimore, Md. Nov. 30.—Mrs. Simondetti who was formerly Miss Katherine Noble, of this city, arrived here today from Mexico a refugee. Her husband, who is the publisher of *El Diaro,* a newspaper in Mexico City, stopped in Washington to consult with friends and lawyers concerning his case.

El Diaro supported de la Barra in the campaign which resulted in the election of Madero as president of Mexico and for this reason, she declared, Mr. Simondetti had been persecuted by the Maderistas. Believing they could not get justice or protection from the Madero government, they have come to this country for assistance.

Mrs. Simondetti said her husband had been subjected to the bitterest criticism, their home had been watched, and their mail opened. Finally a criminal accusation was laid against him and, at her pleading he left the country, going to San Antonio while she remained behind to endeavor to clear his name. In this she was successful, Mrs. Simondetti added, but she was afraid to permit her husband to return. The paper, she said, was now in the hands of their enemies, the Maderistas.[853]

Interesting to note that Mrs Simondetti remained in Mexico (at no doubt with some considerable risk to herself) in order to clear her husband's name. Another example of her indomitable spirit, that seems to have carried her through all life's travails.

Mr Simondetti continued to flirt with the Mexican authorities (though safely operating on the American-side of the border) being employed on an American-led project. This seemingly innocent investigation and with the various interested parties involved, one would have to suspect an ulterior motive or two:

EL DIARO MAN HERE

E. T. Simondetti, of *El Diaro,* Mexico City, is here on a tour of the Mexican border to study conditions. He is writing a series of stories for the Hearst publications in Mexico. He came here from San Antonio and will be here several days. He was in Mexico City during the bombardment.[854]

If more evidence is needed, as to the drive and a sense of purpose for Mrs Simodetti, this correspondent's piece should dispel any futher doubt:

---

[852] Vittorio Emmanuel III, King of Italy (1900–1946).

[853] *El Paso Herald;* November 30th 1911.

[854] *El Paso Herald;* July 5th 1913.

YEARS TO WHIP MEXICO
Mrs. Simondetti Also Thinks Huerta[855]
Will Seek War And Calls
Hale Anti-Mexican.

Mrs. Ernesto Simondetti, wife of the publisher of the *El Diaro*, a daily newspaper of Mexico City, and formerly Miss Katherine Noble, of 8 West North avenue Baltimoe, will deliver her first public speech next Tuesday morning before the Washington Club, an organisation of prominent society women of the national capital. Her topic will be, "The Mexican Situation from an American Woman's Viewpoint".

Mr. and Mrs. Simondetti are making their home in New York, awaiting a favourable opportunity to return to Mexico.

"But we are going back," Mrs. Simondetti informed the *Sun*'s New York correspondent, "revolution or no revolution I'm anxious to get back as soon as I can. Our friends in Mexico City write that things are not half as bad as reported there and that the capital is gayer and quieter than ever. Huerta, they say, goes about town as though nothing had ever happened and dines with friends at the cafes as though he didn't know what trouble was".

She spent five years in Mexico and left two years ago when, she says, the Maderistas confiscated her husband's newspaper after he had escaped across the American border and after they had imprisoned two other adverse editors. For five years after her husband's departure Mrs. Simondetti herself edited and published the paper, She is strongly opposed to the suggestion that the United States permit the rebels to obtain arms in this country.

"It would have been the same had every negro in the South here been armed during the Civil War," she said.

"The rebels are largely uncivilised. There are 27 bands of them, none of which would recognise as President any but one of their number, and to arm them would mean havoc. Villa, one of the rebel leaders, has captured a town. As the spoils of war he took the ammunition and the women of the town.

"I approve of course, of any effort on the part of the United States to assist Mexico, but I think President Wilson is misguided by advisers who are not familiar with the real conditions. William Reynard Hale, for instance, has always been an anti Latin-American. If the Mexicans were far advanced as any people here we would expect honest elections and good goverment, but there are 12,000,000 Indians in the country who don't care who is at the head of Government and only 13,000,000 persons there altogether,"

Asked if she thought intervention would be necessary, Mrs. Simondetti said that she fears Huerta may be pressed into late frenzied aggression if the United States continues its present policy and that he may send troops across the American border to precipitate conflict. It would take 10 years, she says, for this country to whip Mexico.[856]

In leaving Mexico, they lived for many years in Stamford Connecticut, where her husband continued with his import business interest. They then, returned to New York and eventually moved to Florence, Italy, where due to the war and with the occupation by the Nazis, she was obliged to go into hiding. It was in this same city that her mother, Mary Spencer Noble died at her daughter's home in 1943.

In later life, and now resident again in New York, Mrs Katherine Simondetti was actively engaged in the charitable organization, the *League for Animals*. She served on its committee, both as director and

---

[855] In early 1913, Gen. Victoriano Huerta, who commanded the armed forces, conspired with U.S. Ambassador Henry Lane Wilson and Mexican politicians Félix Díaz and Bernardo Reyes to remove Madero from power. Huerta, Félix Díaz and Henry Lane Wilson met and signed the "Embassy Pact" in which they agreed to move against Madero and install Huerta as president.—WikiPedia.

[856] *Sun;* Maryland – November 29th 1913.

chairwoman for the organisation. She also supported the, *Seeing Eye Foundation,*[857] a charitable organization that trained dogs to guide the blind.

She died in 1950, at her home in the city of Florence.[858] Her husband and two cousins survived her. There was no mention of any children by the marriage.

---

[857] The *Seeing Eye Foundation* was founded on January 29, 1929. *The Seeing Eye, Inc.* is the now the oldest existing guide-dog school in the world.

[858] *New York Times;* May 11th 1950.

C H A P T E R   23

The Rev. Canon William Alfred Diggens

The man was born in Newport Salop, in 1852 [859] and was baptised on January 2nd 1853. He came from a scholarly family and his father, William Diggens, was a schoolmaster.[860] He had five sisters and the family lived in Lilleshall, Shropshire.[861] His mother, Emma Diggens, a school mistress, had died by the time the 1861 UK census had been compiled, at which point her son William was 8 years of age. He was educated in the University of Cambridge—St. John's College (non-collegiate)—and attained his Batchelor of Arts degree in the year 1877. He married at the age of 25 years to Annie Scott Thompson.[862] The marriage took place in the year 1878 in the church of St. Stephen at Stockport, Cheshire.[863]

There follows a list of his clerical appointments:

September 24th 1876–1878	Curate – St. Stephen, Hulme diocese, Manchester.
January 30th 1878–1879	Curate – St. Thomas Stockport and as Chaplain to the Barnes convalescent home, Cheadle, Manchester.
February 1st 1879 to December 1890	Rector – Rockhampton,[864] Australia.
January 28th 1891–1896	Incumbent at the St. John Roslyn diocese, Dunedin, N.Z.
1894–1896	Canon at Dunedin, N.Z.
September 28th 1896–1913	Rector in the St. Keverne diocese, Truro, Cornwall.
May to August 1899	In charge at St. James the Apostle, Wardle Lancashire.
September 1899	Re-instated as the Canon at the St. Keverne diocese.
1903–1913	Chaplain to the High Sheriff of Cornwall.
1907–1913	Appointed as the rural Dean of Kerrier.[865]
1913–1916	Vicar at St. Stephen-by-Saltash.

Table 16: Canon W. A. Diggens: List of Clerical Appointments.

---

[859] GRO/BMD: 1852 Q4 – Newport Salop, Shropshire, Staffordshire 6a 611

[860] He was born c1820 Hambledon Hampshire and was registered in 1851 as a school master; in 1861 as a National schoolmaster in Lilleshall and again as a schoolmaster in 1871.

[861] UK census report for 1861 (see page 449).

[862] His wife was born in Greater Manchester. GRO/BMD: 1857 Q4 – Chorlton 8c 477. Her father was a chemical manufacturer, employing 18 men [UK census 1881].

[863] GRO/BMD: Q4 1878 – Stockport, Cheshire 8a 111. He was a curate at this church, at the time of his marriage ceremony.

[864] Rockhampton is a city and local government area in Queensland, Australia. The city sits on the Fitzroy River, approximately 40 kilometres (25 miles) from the river mouth, and some 600 kilometres (370 miles) north of the state capital, Brisbane—*WikiPedia*.

[865] *Auckland Star;* 6th June, 1916.

Following his two ministries in the North Country, he embarked on a seventeen year missionary period in both Australia and New Zealand.[866]

A useful indicator of the Rev. Diggens' character is hinted at here, in the recording of his arrival in Australia:

The arrival of the Reverend W.A. Diggens, in 1879, "a young man fresh from Oxford – the hot-bed and cradle of "Ritualism", as the correspondent of the *Evangelical Standard* described him, signalled fresh upheavals among the Anglicans themselves. Some disaffected parishioners petitioned Bishop Hale, but the Bishop's investigations revealed that Diggens was not as extreme as his detractors claimed, though his advanced churchmanship did provoke a temporary manifestation of 'Free Church of England' activity under the leadership of Dr Hughes. Nevertheless, Diggens displayed great zeal in his work and the disaffection died away, and for more than a decade throughout the eighties he ministered in Rockhampton and the district far around. For years he visited Gladstone for two weeks every second month, and with his assistant even extended his ministrations as far as Springsure. Considering the distance of the latter centre from Rockhampton however, it is suprising that the Springsure church committee wrote to the Bishop Webber pleading for a 'division of the said 'Parish' which is far too large to be satisfactorily worked from one centre". It was under Diggen's energetic, if controversial, leadership that the fine stone church of St. Paul was built in Rockhampton at a cost of £8,300 for the building and and fittings – a very notable achievement for a town of this size. The building was consecrated in 1883.[867]

It was during his tenure at Queensland and shortly after his arrival, that he became involved with a faction within his church. The following correspondence clearly highlights the issue and the overwhelming support given to him by his bishop and congregation:

Rockhampton, Queensland Australia Anglican Church.

In a recent number of the *Evangelical Standard*, published in Brisbane, there appeared a long communication and correspondence evidently intended to show that, in the new church of St. Paul's, now being erected in Rockhampton, the Rev. Mr. Diggens was having effect given to his alleged ritualistic proclivities by the introduction of crosses among the carved stone work. It was also represented that this was being done against the wishes of members of St. Paul's congregation. In connection with this matter, we have been requested to publish the following correspondence, which explains itself:

Rockhampton, November 18, 1880. Rev. W. A. DIGGENS, B.A.

Dear Sir,—I have much pleasure in handing you the enclosed testimonial signed by 111 males, members, and shareholders, of Saint Paul's Church—nearly double the number of signatures could have been obtained had time permitted.

    I remain, yours faithfully, Richard Sexton.

Rockhampton, November 15, 1880.

---

[866] At this time, the convict settlements and the Maori wars of the early nineteenth Century were matters of ancient history.

[867] Keith Rayner; *The History of the Church of England in Queensland* – A Thesis Submitted to The University of Queensland; December, 1962.

The Rev. W. A. DIGGENS, M.A., Rector of St. Paul's Church, Rockhampton.

Reverend and Dear Sir,—We, the under-signed members and adherents of Saint Paul's Church, Rockhampton, desire to express our indignation at the unwarrantable attack made on you by an anonymous correspondent in the columns of *Queensland Evangelical Standard* [868] of 6th instant, and to record our testimony as to its being a tissue of misrepresentations and distortion of facts and we further desire to express the full confidence, esteem, and respect in which you are held by us as our pastor.

Signed [by] 111 Gentlemen.

The Rectory, Rockhampton, November 18, 1880
To R. Sexton, Esq.

My Dear Sir,—I have to acknowledge the receipt of your letter and the enclosed memorial. And I must sincerely thank the gentlemen of my congregation for their prompt and hearty expression of goodwill at a time when I have been most unjustly attacked.

Our Bishop agrees with me that after such abundant proof of the good feeling that exists between the pastor and people of St. Paul's Church there is no necessity for holding a public meeting.

Believe me, my dear Sirs,

Yours very faithfully,

W. A. DIGGENS. [869]

In the year 1890, his ministry in Rockhampton came to an end. His congregation much regretted his departure, after having worked with them for over 11 years and achieving much good during that time. Noel, his first and only child, was born in Queensland, Australia c. 1881. A family photograph [870] (see fig. 22) taken in Australia, shows Canon Diggens, his wife and son. Based on a probable age of nine years for the boy, this would date the photograph to c. 1890: the year he left Queensland for New Zealand. This photograph could well have been taken as a parting memento to commemorate his 12–year ministry with that parish.

A report in the local newspaper illustrated his career, including his vocation in Australia:

THE REV. W. A. DIGGENS.

Reference has already been made to the early departure of the Rev. W. A. Diggens, B.A., Rector of St. Paul's Anglican Church, Rockhampton,[871] for New Zealand, and it will not be without interest to his many friends to learn a little of his career in the ministry.

Mr. Diggens is a native of Shropshire, and was educated at the Newport Grammar School. Thence he passed on to Cambridge University; where he graduated Bachelor of Arts in 1876. The same year he was ordained, at Manchester, by the Bishop of that See, and the following year in Cheshire a priest by the Bishop of Chester. During the first year of his

---

[868] The *Queensland Evangelical Standard* was regarded as one of the liveliest newspapers in Brisbane and North Queensland respectively and kept anti-Irish and anti-Catholic sentiment alive, well into the 1880s.

[869] *Morning Bulletin;* Friday 19th November 1880 – Rockhampton, Queensland, Australia.

[870] Courtesy of the John Oxley library, State Library of Queensland (Image no. 14097).

[871] The cathedral is situated at 89 William Street, Rockhampton, Queensland. Canon Diggens and his family resided in Denison Street, which abuts to William Street.

ministry Mr. Diggens was a curate in Manchester, and in 1877 and 1878 he had charge of a mission church in Cheshire. In the latter part of 1878 Mr. Diggers came out to Queensland, accompanied by Mrs. Diggens, at the invitation of the then Bishop of Brisbane (Dr. Hale), landing in that city about Christmas, so that he has now been a resident of this colony for twelve years. For a few weeks Mr. Diggens was a temporary charge of the church at Toowong, when he was appointed to Rockhampton, reaching this town about the end of January, 1879 and here he has remained ever since, with the exception of about six months in 1887, when, in company with Mrs. Diggens, be paid a visit to the old country. Mr. Diggens's ministry here has been very successful, and he has gathered around him a large circle of friends, who all greatly regret his departure, and is a clergyman of a stamp of which we have too few. Outspoken in the pulpit, he has never swerved from what he deemed to be his duty, whether to the church, to the country, or to himself. In his connection with various public movements—and these notably of a charitable nature—Mr. Diggens has also been one to speak his mind very plainly, and whatever omission may be laid to his charge, it cannot be said that at any time has he been actuated by a feeling other than that of the public good. In charitable acts he has, with Mrs. Diggens, always been foremost, and there are many of the poor among our community who will greatly miss both. At the time of Mr. Diggens's arrival in Rockhampton the services were held in the old church in front of The Rectory—the building that is now used as a Sunday school-room. The foundations of a new stone edifice, on the site of the present place of worship, had been laid years before but there its building stopped. The funds had run short and no one bad the energy to institute a fresh and vigorous canvass. This task fell to Mr. Diggens's lot, and, heavy though it was, he undertook it and carried it out with the determination that is one of his chief characteristics. And in 1883 the new church, a structure which has not its equal in the town among the many church buildings that Rockhampton possesses—and not in the colony among Anglican churches—and which cost altogether between £9,000 and £10,000, was opened with a debt of only £1,700. This debt, it may be mentioned, was wiped off two or three years later by the liberality of several prominent residents, and the church now stands as a monument to Mr. Diggens's labours amongst us. At the time the Rector of St Paul's first settled here church work was confined almost exclusively to Rockhampton; little was being done in the surrounding districts. For hundreds of miles, in almost every direction, there were people who had never seen a minister of the Anglican Church for years, and then only when they chanced to come into Rockhampton for a day or two. Mr. Diggens early took this matter into his consideration, and, thanks to his untiring exertions, there are now clergy permanently stationed at Gladstone, Springsure, Clermont, Mount Morgan, and North Rockhampton, and latterly Emu Park has been created a parochial district. With the aid of a curate, Mr. Diggens for many years ministered regularly to the spiritual wants of the people in these places, as well as in many others, including Yeppoon, St. Lawrence, Cawarral, and the coast settlements between Rockhampton and Yeppoon. Financial aid was also given towards the support of a separate clergyman in at least one case for two or three years. It will thus be seen that mission work has formed no small part in Mr. Diggens's ministrations in Rockhampton. As to the congregation to which he has personally ministered, it has progressed in a way that few thought possible, it is scarcely necessary to say that we need only point to the handsome edifice in which the congregation worships every Sunday. To enter into particulars, the number, in each week who attend Holy Communion is larger than the number who attended monthly when Mr. Diggens came to Rockhampton; the revenue has almost doubled; the Sunday School has increased to such an extent that a branch school has had to be opened at Allenstown, which has now an average attendance of between sixty and seventy and though the finances at the present moment are not in quite as satisfactory a condition as could be wished, a circumstance which may be attributed to the dull times that have prevailed of late, there is every hope that they will improve in the near future. Mr. Diggens has been instrumental in starting a Guild in connection with the church, which has done excellent work in ministering to the comforts of the sick in our hospitals and other benevolent institutions, and in providing social amusement for the parishoners; a branch of the Girls' Friendly Society, a work in which Mrs. Diggens took a keen interest and a branch of the Church of England Temperance Society. There is little more to be told regarding the Mr. Diggen's labours in Rockhampton, but our notice would not be complete did we omit mention of the fact that three years ago he was appointed Rural Dean of the Central Division, and was quite recently reappointed to that office for a further period of three years. Mr. Diggens has been appointed Rector of St. Johns Church, Rosslyn Dunedin, New Zealand. Rosslyn is the fashionable suburb of Dunedin, and a place of some importance. It is situated some 600ft. above the sea level and from the church and parsonage a fine view is to be obtained of the harbour and shipping. It is approached by a cable tramway from the city. Mr Diggens will leave here on Tuesday evening next by the *SS Arawatta* for Sydney, where he will remain for a few days, and then take a steamer for Dunedin, which he expects to reach about the end of January. On Sunday he will preach his farewell sermons, and take final leave of the congregation in the church on Tuesday evening, when an organ recital is to be given by the new organist, Mr. T. C. Webb.[872]

In another report (not included here) it seems the move to New Zealand was, in part, brought on by Mrs Diggens' health problems. This next ministry was to last from 1891–1896.

He returned to the 'old country' and became the vicar at St. Keverne, in the year 1896. He was, by a stroke of fate, in place for that next momentous event in his clerical life.

Although the world is full of suffering, it is also full of the overcoming of it.

Following the *Mohegan* disaster, this story appeared in a New Zealand newspaper, related to his having been a previous appointee at St. John's Church, Dunedin:

> With reference to the disastrous wreck of the American steamer *Mohegan* on the Manacle Rocks, Cornwall, it will interest many New Zealand friends of the Vicar of St. Keverne, who was benevolently active both in the case of the survivors and in providing reverently for the care and solemn interment of the remains of those who perished, to learn that he is the Rev. Canon Diggens, formerly of Dunedin, New Zealand. A spectator writes to me: "He and his wife rendered right royal service night and day". Those who had the pleasure of knowing Mr. and Mrs. Diggens in New Zealand will not be surprised to hear of this.
>
> The Rev. Thomas Flavell happened to be at St. Keverne, as representing S.P.G.[873] on the Sunday when that terrible array of 36 corpses lay in the church during all the services, and it fell to him to make reference in the pulpit to the deplorable disaster. I feel sure that his comments were, as is always the case with him, made with deep feeling and appropriateness. Mr Flavell writes to me: "It was truly a most mournful sight to see those 36 corpses lying in the church, and to observe the grief of friends and relatives as they came to identify those whom they has lost". [874]

A letter, including some pertinent remarks as to the identification of disaster victims, was written by an expert, who was best placed to comment on the difficulty in managing the aftermath of any such disaster. That man was Canon Diggens. As vicar of St. Keverne and with the nearness of his parish to the Manacles, he drew considerable attention to this disaster, and opened his pulpit up to a far wider congregation, as this newspaper piece illustrates:

---

[872] *Morning Bulletin;* Rockhampton, Queensland, Australia - Friday 26th December 1890.

[873] This was most probably the *Society for the Propagation of the Gospel — in Foreign Parts.*

[874] *Otago Witness;* (Issue 2337) 15th December 1898 - New Zealand.

Permit me to say a word as to the identification of the bodies of the drowned. It is the practice—at least in these parts—when the body is recovered, the finder, be he police officer, Coastguardsman, or private individual—to remove at once, all rings, chains, watches, purses, papers, and even artificial teeth [875] from the deceased. It follows when a body is brought to a central place, as for instance, to the church of St. Keverne, there is the greatest difficulty experienced in its identification. The features are probably battered and swollen out of recognition, and the trinkets that would provide an infallible clue to identify are nowhere to be found. Even in cases where, after much enquiry, they are produced, the discoverers of the bodies are often unable to assert positively from which bodies they removed the goods. I would suggest in the case of a wreck the local staff of coastguardsmen should be immediately and largely augmented by drafts upon neighbouring stations; that one of the staff should accompany each body to the place where the dead are laid out; that police constables be on watch at the said place to guard the bodies and property and that personal effects should be untouched until after identification. Such a plan should be of easy execution, and would, besides preventing pilfering, enormously increase the facilities for deciding the names of the deceased. Much trouble and labour have been experienced here for lack of such a plan.

I am Sir. W.A. Diggens,

Vicar of St. Keverne. [876]

In his own hand, Diggens wrote, as a preamble to the *Mohegan* victims' entries in the St. Keverne burial register, the following transcript:

October 14th. 1898 about 7 o'clock in the evening, the steamship, an American liner belonging to the Atlantic Transport Company, ran at great speed on to the Manacle Rocks. The Porthoustock lifeboat succeeded in saving 44 persons and 3 or 4 more were saved in other ways. 107 lost their lives. Forty bodies are laid out in the church at one time. Of these many were bruised. Some were removed by friends and others were embalmed and sent to America. Memorial services attended by a very large number of people were held in the parish church on Tuesday Oct. 18th. The vicar preached in the morning and the Archdeacon of Cornwall in the evening. I, the vicar, having seen much of the suffering of the rescued and the sorrows of the bereaved, earnestly pray that effectual steps made be taken to warn vessels of the position of the dread rocks, which have been the scenes of many terrible disasters.

W. A. Diggens.

The Rev. Canon Diggens, driven by the enormity of this event, again set his pen to paper, making his views known to the highest authority:

To the Solicitor of the Board of Trade.

Wreck of the ss *Mohegan*.

I, William Alfred Diggens, Vicar of St. Keverne in the County of Cornwall, having made many voyages at sea, and having been most intimately acquainted with the events that occurred immediately subsequent to the wreck of the ss *Mohegan,* beg to make the following observations based on the experience thus acquired:

[875] Dentures were a valuable commodity: as newspapers of the time carried advertisements inviting redundant dentures to be forwarded for cash payment. These would be then sold on to grateful recipients!

[876] *The Times;* 23rd December 1898.

1) That in all human probability if a lighthouse had been in existence at the Manacles, the above valuable ship with more than a hundred still more valuable lives, would not have been lost.

2) That such a light would have prevented a very large number of the casualties that have unfortunately taken place in this locality.

3) That if such a light is not provided, measures much more ample and efficient for the saving of life and property than those existing in this neighborhood, should be adopted. For instance:

   a) Since lifeboats from distance places cannot work safely and effectually in these (to them) strange and dangerous waters, a second lifeboat should be placed at Coverack. The fishermen at this village are familiar with the Manacles and the boat could be launched in all weathers.

   b) There should be a life saving apparatus at St. Keverne from which an easy descent could be made to any part of the adjacent coast. If the Coverack Rocket carriage is employed on the shore near the Manacles, it has first to be brought (probably pushed) up a long, steep hill, a mile in length, before it can be conveyed to its ultimate destination. The delay thus occasioned has proved disastrous in at least one instance.

   c) The Coastguard station, instead of being established (as seems to be the intention) in Porthoustock Cove, should be established at or near the old Watch House on Manacle Point. Vessels approaching the dangerous rocks might then perhaps be warned off in time to avert a disaster.

4) Lifeboats in search of wrecks and survivors should on dark nights carry powerful lights. Possibly more lives might have been saved, if this had been done on the night of the *Mohegan* wreck.

5) There should be some system of signals by which people ashore can convey messages to lifeboats at sea. Such a system would have been of great value on the night of the wreck.

6) That the mast-head and side-lights on ships should be altogether independent of any general lighting system of illumination.

7) That a scheme for rendering each separate iron deck a horizontal watertight bulkhead, might prevent such losses as that of the *Mohegan*.

8) That practical tests of the boat lowering of vessels should be made at frequent intervals in the presence of Officers of the Board of Trade, and that weekly boat drills on ships should be made compulsory. I have only to add that I should like to have given evidence at the Board of Trade Enquiry, as I think that my evidence might have been of some value, especially in the matter of life-saving.

William A. Diggens – November 2nd, 1898.[877]

Cometh the moment, cometh the man.

A phrase that exactly describes the Rev. Canon William Alfred Diggens. Amid the confusion, the suffering, and the appalling disruption to lives, not only of the survivors but also the local population, Canon Diggens served his community well: by giving solace, charity, and in offering balm to the bereaved. This would have so endeared him to all those who encountered this man. In such a testing time, he would have been seen as a hospitable rock amid a swirling tide of human emotion.

---

[877] Courtesy of the St. Keverne Local History Society.

His reputation was by now spreading far and wide. Quick to capitalise on such a high-profile event, a workers' organization approached the Rev. Diggens with a proposal for a national fund, no doubt allied to their own dangerous working lives, while in service to the general public:

ODD FACTS

The vicar of St. Keverne has been requested by the Bootle Branch of the National Sailor's and Firemen's Union to draw attention, at the adjourned inquest, to the necessity for the establishment of a national fund by the Government for the purpose of maintaining the widows, orphans, and aged parents of men who lost their lives in the performance of dangerous duties.[878]

Such an undertaking would have greatly taxed the Rev. Diggens in those difficult times, and in any event, the *Mohegan* appeal for charitable funds was eventually taken up by the commercial fraternity and bankers, in London, to good effect (see page 219).

A memorial Window at St. Keverne Church.

The Atlantic Transport Line company made a very generous donation to the people of St. Keverne (following the advice given by Canon Diggens) in the form of a memorial window, installed in the church above the altar piece:

THE MOHEGAN DISASTER
Memorial Window at St. Keverne

In the parish church of St. Keverne the memory of those whose lives were sacrificed in the wreck of the steamship, *Mohegan*, off Falmouth, has been perpetuated by the placing of a stained glass window in the east end of the edifice. It bears the following explanatory inscription :—"To the glory of God, and in memory of the 106 persons who perished in the wreck of the *SS Mohegan*, on the Manacle Rocks, October 14, 1898., this window was dedicated by the Atlantic Transport Company, owners of the vessel". The ceremony of dedication was performed on Wednesday evening [April 26th,1899], when the church was crowded by the inhabitants and visitors from the district. The surpliced clergy in attendance were Archdeacon Cornish, the Revs. C. F. Rogers (Rural Dean), Canon W. A. Diggens (vicar of St. Keverne), Dr. Eager (Manaccan), F. R. Sell (St. Martin), C. Vyvyan (Ruan Minor), and C. H. Scholefield (Mullion). The Rev. Sir Vyell Vyvyan was amongst others present. The hymns "Lead, kindly light," Eternal Father, strong to save," and, "Peace, perfect peace," were sung. Mr. A. S. Williams, manager of the Atlantic Transport Company, unveiled the window, and the customary form of dedication was observed. The Archdeacon, in his sermon, observed that the window was being offered to God's service as a very solemn thing. It conveyed to them a special message, an undying message: "Be ye ready, for as such time as ye know not the Son of Man cometh". The dead were preaching to them, and the dead, by that window, would preach to their children. The victims of the *Mohegan* would not have delivered such a message had they died one by one. The offertory, amounting to over £20, will be devoted to the cost of erecting a Cornish cross over the large grave in the churchyard, containing many of the *Mohegan*'s dead.

[878] *The Royal Cornwall Gazette Falmouth Packet, Cornish Weekly News, & General Advertiser*; Thursday, 27th October 1898.

Subsequently, at a large gathering of the parishioners Dr. Leverton-Spry moved that that a telegram be sent to Mr. and Mrs. P. D. Williams,[879] expressing congratulations and good wishes on the occasion of their wedding,—Mr. E. P. Roskruge seconded, remarking that Mr. Williams had always shown the greatest interest in the affairs of St. Keverne.—The motion was cordially assented to.

The vicar proposed hearty thanks to the Atlantic Transport Company for their gift of the window. Following the foundering of the *Mohegan*, the company did their very best to make every possible provision for the care of the dead and the comfort of the living. In many instances of similar disaster the trouble was greatly intensified by the lack of that ready assistance which ought to be forthcoming. The Atlantic Transport Company, however, met all reasonable demands most handsomely (applause). He desired to mention the diligence of the local agents (Messrs. Fox & Co.) in supplying all possible information to the friends of the lost and, and in caring for the survivors (hear, hear).—Mr. J. BOADE, in seconding, observed that a gathering of that description had not been held in the parish previously. Their coast had been strewn with wrecks, but in no case had a company behaved in the magnificent manner of the Atlantic Transport Line. In spite of their great loss, the company had made a very handsome gift to the parish (applause).—Mr. W. James supporting, said he was glad to recognise the kindness manifested towards St. Keverne by the owners of the *Mohegan*, in return for the consideration with which the inhabitants treated the survivors (hear, hear).—The proposition was unanimously agreed to.

Mr. A. S. WILLIAMS said Mr. Baker, chairman of the company, had found it impossible to come over for the purpose of unveiling the window, much to the regret of all. Therefore it devolved upon him (Mr. Williams) to acknowledge their generous vote of thanks. He was glad to be among men who did not hesitate to expose their lives to the utmost danger to save their fellow creatures. The *Mohegan* calamity illustrated not only the bravery of those who manned the lifeboat on that coast, but also the charity of the people on shore. Nothing could have been better than the feeling shown by the whole neighbourhood to the poor people who landed after exposure to terrible suffering. He wished the company could have done more. One speaker had referred to the heavy loss, which the company had experienced, and he was bound to confirm that statement. But for that loss, he should be delighted to have arranged for the more liberal remuneration by the company of those who place their lives in jeopardy. The giving of the window was the idea of the chairman and it gave himself and his colleagues in London much pleasure to carry out the suggestion. He wished heartily to echo the expression of thanks to Messrs, Fox and Co. Long might Cornwall possess brave men like those went to the rescue of those on board the *Mohegan* (applause).

The VICAR said the company had spared no expense to make their gift as handsome as possible, and all would agree that it was a magnificent work of art.

Mr. WILLIAMS mentioned that the fund for the relief of the families of the crew amounted to about £4,000, and had been expended in donations for immediate relief and small annuities to the widows, and making provision for the children (applause).

Mr. G. H. FOX remarked that at the time of the wreck his chief anxiety was that Cornishmen should do their duty to the living and the dead in the right spirit, and he was glad to say that everything was so done. In some cases the owners of wrecked vessels allowed the parish to pay the expense of burial, but the Atlantic Transport Company behaved magnificently (hear, hear).

Mr. T. J. JOYCE alluded with regret to the forthcoming departure of the vicar. During his short stay at St. Keverne he had made himself one with his people, who would be exceedingly sorry to lose him and his wife.—Dr. LEVERTON-SPRY[880]

---

[879] Mr Percival Dacres Williams (1865–1935) had long been a Justice of the Peace and had held the honourable position of High Sheriff of Cornwall. He was the Squire of Lanarth and was a notable daffodil and narcissus horticulturalist. He had married Ada Beatrice Dixon; GRO/BMD: 1899 Q2 – Middlesboro' 9d 961.

[880] A resident of Churchtown, St. Keverne and he was a Surgeon, General Practitioner and was employed by Kenwyn [a settlement and civil parish and a suburb of the city of Truro. It gives its name to one of three rivers that flow through the city] as recorded in the 1891 UK census for Cornwall.

spoke of Mr. Diggens as an excellent preacher and a hard working clergyman. On the occasion of the wreck of the *Mohegan* he was of the greatest value, and volunteered to take an oar in a shore boat which it was intended to send off to the Manacles. That boat, however, proved unseaworthy, and could not be floated. To the vicar and his wife the parishioners wished God-speed.—Messrs. E. P. Roskruge,[881] C. H. Fox, W. Roskruge,[882] Clatworthy, Jeffers and Martin (Coverack), and E[dwin] Rule [883] (representing the Nonconformists) alluded in complimentary terms to the vicar, who said it was with sorrow that he left a people with whom he had laboured so happily (applause).[884]

Even though Canon Diggens and his wife were warmly wished *bon-voyage* for their new venture in Lancashire, the Canon (rather strangely) returned to the parish of St. Keverne in the same year. He then remained here, as its incumbent vicar, for a further fifteen years. The Canon gave, what was thought, his final sermon to his flock at St. Keverne on a Sunday during April 1899, before handing over the incumbency to the Rev. Henry Baugh, MA. But the move to Lancashire seemed to have been temporary, and altogether mysterious.

There is, however, an interesting piece of additional information that has come to light—a list of the vicars for the church in question; St, James the Apostle, Wardle Lancashire:

The Rev. John Ducker, M.A.	—	1858 – 1892
The Rev. Arthur Dimock	—	1892 – 1896
The Rev. Henry Baugh	—	1896 – 1903
The Rev. Canon W.A. Diggens in charge May to August 1899 [885]		
The Rev. Christopher Norton Wright	—	1903 – 1920 [886]

The reason for Canon Diggens' rather short period 'in charge' is accounted for here:

A St. Keverne Ecclesiastical Difficulty.

A remarkable state of affairs exists in regard to the vicarage of Wardle, near Rochdale. Rev. H. Baugh went to the parish from Bedfordshire about two years ago, having exchanged livings with with the former vicar. Mr. Baugh soon made up his mind to leave Wardle, and effected an exchange with Canon Diggens, incumbent of St. Keverne. Canon Diggens went to Wardle some months ago, and was duly inducted to the living. Mr. Baugh, however, will not settle at St. Keverne, refuses to be inducted there, and insists that he is still the vicar of Wardle. In these circumstances the Bishop of Truro has recalled Canon Diggens to Cornwall. Canon Diggens worded his resignation at St. Keverne so that it would not take effect

---

[881] A resident of Churchtown, St. Keverne: a local grocer, by trade – 1891 UK census.

[882] A resident of Churchtown, St. Keverne: a local ironmonger, by trade – 1891 UK census.

[883] Edwin Rule – Census 1901: Grocer and draper, Churchtown, St. Keverne (see fig. 32 – his shop appears in the image).

[884] *The Royal Cornwall Gazette Falmouth Packet, Cornish Weekly News, & General Advertiser;* Thursday, April 27th 1899.

[885] *The Royal Cornwall Gazette Falmouth Packet, Cornish Weekly News, & General Advertiser;* Thursday, April 27th 1899—There will be universal regret in the parish when Canon Diggens leaves us, for by his geniality and sweet reasonalbeness has endeared himself to the hearts of all broadminded people. It is understood that he has accepted a living in East Lancashire.

[886] *Souvenir Centenary Handbook 1858 – 1958;* courtesy of the Wardle and Smallbridge History Group.

unless the exchange of livings was completed, but Mr. Baugh so framed his resignation that it would not take effect unless he was instituted at St. Keverne. Mr. Baugh has not been instituted, and therefore claims to be the vicar of Wardle. A meeting of the Wardle parishioners has been held, and the Bishop of Manchester has been approached with a view of seeing whether matters can be arranged for Canon Diggens to remain at Wardle. The good folk of St. Keverne have been hoping to have their Canon back.[887]

The truth will out.

The whole story was now played out in public:

VICARS AT VARIANCE

In the Nisi Prius Court [888] at the Manchester Assizes, on Wednesday, before Mr. Justice Phillimore, a peculiar action, resulting from an exchange of the livings of Wardle, near Rochdale, and St. Keverne, Cornwall, was heard, in which the plantiff, the Rev. Canon Diggins [sic], claimed damages for breach of agreement and for libel. Mr. Pickford, Q.C., and Mr. Langdon represented plaintiff, and Mr. C. R. Russell, Q.C., and Mr. Acton represented defendant, the Rev. Henry Baugh, vicar of Wardle.

Mr. Pickford said that the plaintiff was the vicar of St. Keverne, Cornwall, the advocation of which was held by a gentleman named Thompson, living in Whalley Range.[889] Canon Diggens was son-in-law of Mr. Thompson, and his wife was desirous to live near her family, negotiations were entered into with the Rev. H. Baugh, who desired to exchange his parish at Wardle for one in the South in consequence of health considerations. Canon Diggins and Mr. Baugh had several interviews, and considerable correspondence took place. The net income of St. Keverne was stated to be £306 9s 8d., or £282 if the vicarage was not let for a month in the year, as had been customary. Mr. Baugh asked for a financial consideration, as he considered that to exchange the livings would not be a fair to himself, having regard to the difficult circumstances of the two parishes as [it included Coverack]. Mr. Baugh asked for £300, and alleged that it was agreed that the sum should be paid to him when the exchange was effected. It was decided to exchange livings, and Canon Diggins was inducted to the living of Wardle. Mr. Baugh, however, refused to carry out the agreement or to be inducted at St. Keverne, alleging that Canon Diggins had misrepresented the amount of work and the condition of the vicarage. Canon Diggins claimed £120 for breach of the agreement and expenses incurred in travelling to Wardle from St. Keverne, and in being inducted to the living at Wardle. The dispute created considerable interest in Wardle and St. Keverne. At Wardle a meeting of parishioners was held to consider the question. At that time Canon Diggins had not gone back to St. Keverne, and there was consequently a question as to who was really vicar of Wardle. The question was eventually settled by Mr. Kemp, an eminent gentleman in ecclesiastical law, who decided that Mr. Baugh, not having been instituted or inducted to the living of St. Keverne, was still vicar of Wardle, and that Canon Diggins, although he had been inducted to the living to the living of Wardle was still the vicar of St. Keverne. Reports of the speeches made by Canon Diggins, Mr. Thompson, the patron of St. Keverne, and Mr. Peters, the patron of Wardle, were published in the Rochdale newspapers, and in order that his version of the case should be presented to the public Mr. Baugh granted an interview to the representatives of two Rochdale newspapers. In the account published of the interview Mr. Baugh had been reported to have said that whereas Canon Diggins appeared to have been well satisfied with everthing at Wardle, he [Mr. Baugh] had been grieviously

---

[887] *The Royal Cornwall Gazette Falmouth Packet, Cornish Weekly News, & General Advertiser*, Thursday, September 28, 1899.

[888] Nisi prius is a Latin term, meaning "unless the first". A nisi prius court is a court in which as case is first heard by as judge and jury, as opposed to an appellate level court. A nisi prius court is also called the "court of original jurisdiction".

[889] UK census 1901: William Goulden Thompson – Brookfield Road, Manchester. This gentleman was the Rev. Diggens' father-in-law.

disappointed by what he found at St. Keverne. The furniture was not what he had expected; the supply of kitchen articles was of the most meager character, locks and keys were out of order, panes of glass were broken, and generally speaking considerable repairs were necessary at the vicarage. There was no drinking water on the premises, as had been represented with the exception of a well in the yard, and there was a coach house and stable, which were so dilapidated that they ought to be pulled down. Mr. Baugh, in the report, was also stated to have said that the work of the parish of St. Keverne had not been correctedly set forth. The consequence must be that the exchange of livings must fall through, as nothing could induce him to become Vicar of St. Keverne. Canon Diggle [*sic*] denied these allegations, and contended that there was no reason why the agreement as to the exchange should not have been effected. Canon Diggins had been put to very considerable expense in travelling to and from St. Keverne, but he did not mind that so much as the slur on his character. What Canon Diggins desired as a result of that action was that he should be freed from the imputation of any such misrepresentation as Mr. Baugh had alleged.

Canon Diggins corroborated counsel's statement remarking that everything he had said to Mr. Baugh relative to the parish of St. Keverne had been perfectly true.

After plaintiff's evidence had concluded, Mr. Pickford said he was glad to say they would not have to fight a painful case any further. Neither Canon Diggins nor himself were anxious to fight the matter to the bitter end, all they wanted was that any imputation upon Canon Diggins should be removed. There had been misunderstandings which were to be greatly regretted, and it was much better that a fair and honourable settlement should be arrived at. What any misunderstnding might be unfortunately have arisen in Mr. Baugh's mind as to whether the income of St. Keverne was not what had been represented, he entirely acquitted Canon Diggins of having willfully made any representation, and also wished to say that the statement he made in the Rochdale papers was not made with the intention of reflecting upon Canon Diggins but for the purpose of defending himself against the statement made at the parshioners' meeting at Wardle. The aspersion made by Mr. Baugh had been considered so serious by Canon Diggins as to necessitate that action, but Canon Diggins was quite willing to accept Mr. Baugh's statement that he did not intend to make any reflection of his character in the matter. Under those circumstances he would ask for a juror to be withdrawn.

His Lordship, in accepting the withdrawl of a juror, said he did not consider it entirely in the interests of the Church that that case should not have been thrashed out to the bottom. So far as he could see, he did not think that Canon Diggins' conduct needed further inquiry. He did not say in the least that there was anything against Mr. Baugh, but, so far as he had read the papers in the action, he was not at all satisfied that it would not be very much to the public advantage that Mr. Baugh's conduct should have been enquired into.

Mr Russell: I desire to say that I am perfectly prepared and desirous now that the matter be fought out.

His Lordship: Very well. Call the next case.[890]

This was a fractious and unsettling time for Canon Diggens. However, he had put all that behind him and had returned to a welcoming parish that had embraced him with open arms.

---

[890] *Manchester Times* (Manchester, England), Friday, April 27, 1900.

Life is like the moon: now full, now dark.

It must have been a huge shock and given much sorrow when his only child, Alfred Noel Diggens, died at the St. Keverne vicarage, on October 15th 1905.[891] His father was present at the bedside, when the young man's life ended.

His son was a qualified dental surgeon, and had appeared as a dental student in the UK 1901 census.[892] He was born in 1880 in Queensland, Australia, on the morning of Christmas Day—which would explain the forename of 'Noel'. His last resting place is alongside the *Mohegan* mass grave, and has the following epitaph:

"Take now thy Son, thine only Son, whom thou lovest and offer him". GEN, XXII

Alfred Noel Diggens L.D.S., R.C.S.
The only child of THE VICAR and Annie Scott Diggens,
Born Christmas Morning 1880, Died Sunday Morning Oct. 15th, 1905, Aged 24.

"Make him to be numbered with thy Saints in glory everlasting".

When you live next to the cemetery, you cannot weep for everyone.

A devastating blow for his parents; being as he was their only child, on the threshold of a new career and adulthood. After coming to terms with the deaths of the many victims from the *Mohegan* and in the everyday lifecycle events of the village, it must have crushed the Diggens' spirits, and to have sorely tested their faith—this deeply personal tragedy. But the indomitability of the human spirit prevailed and he continued his ministry at St. Keverne for a further seven years or so.

During his tenure at St. Keverne (1896–1913) he compiled extensive notes on the history, origins, and the folk ways of the parish. His papers extend to some 200 pages and the subjects range from the occurrence of asbestos, with fanciful speculation on its use in antiquity, to listings from the Court Rolls of the 14th and 15th centuries.[893]

On completing his ministry at St. Keverne in 1913, a report records his move to the St. Stephen-by-Saltash Church,[894] in the same year:

---

[891] GRO/BMD: 1905 Q4 – Helston 5c 119 (see page 444). This date is on the anniversary weekend of the *Mohegan* disaster.

[892] The UK census: 1901 (see page 450)

[893] Some of his papers he had extended in essay form and are, in part, included on the St. Keverne Local History website. The group intend to deposit a full text copy with the Cornish Studies Library in Redruth, at some future date.

[894] Saltash town is on the Cornish side of the River Tamar (which marks the Devon/Cornwall boundary).

Canon W. A. Diggens, vicar of St. Keverne, has been appointed to the vicarage of the St. Stephen-by-Saltash, Cornwall—patrons, the Dean and Chapter of Windsor.[895]

Love life and life will love you back. Love people and they will love you back.

In April 1916, the Rev. Canon Diggens died, and an obituary for the man appeared in a national newspaper:

Canon W. A. Diggens, vicar of St. Stephen-by-Saltash, Cornwall, whose death is announced, was at one time the only Church of England clergyman in the whole of Central Queensland [Australia]. He raised £13,000 [£910,000 in modern currency] to build the Cathedral of the diocese of Rockhampton. Soon after, he became the vicar of St. Keverne, Cornwall. The *Mohegan* was wrecked on the Manacles, and owing to his exertions, a light was placed on those rocks and a second lifeboat given to the parish [Coverack].[896]

He was buried in a lone grave, in the churchyard at St. Stephen-by-Saltash. It is a further measure of the esteem for the man, whereby his St. Stephen-by-Saltash parishioners saw fit to have added his wife's epitaph to his headstone, even though she outlived him by a further twenty-one years. Her death was recorded in Fylde, in the county of Lancashire.[897]

Engraved on the three sides of the base of a simple stone cross, are the following epitaphs.

Also Annie Scott Diggens Died Aug. 23rd 1937 Aged 79 Years	Sacred To The Memory Of William A. Diggens. B.A. Vicar of this Parish. Who fell asleep April 15th. 1916 Aged 63 Years. His last words were "Praise Ye the Lord" This monument was erected as a token of love and esteem by his parishioners and friends.	Also Alfred Noel Diggens Their beloved son died Oct. 15th 1905, aged 24 years and was interred at St. Keverne.

His life story affirmed him as a good man, who lived through many trials and tribulations, in his varied ministries. His name will always be associated with St. Keverne and the *Mohegan* disaster in particular. But there was much more for which he will be warmly remembered: not only in this country, but also in the Antipodes.

---

[895] *The Times;* Wednesday, 7th May 1913

[896] *The Times;* 25th April 1916 – death certificate (see page 444).

[897] GRO/BMD: 1937 Q4 – Fylde, Lancashire 8e 669.

C H A P T E R 24

Mr Bernard Nadal Baker: President of the ATL Company

Mr. Baker, a confirmed anglophile, had crossed the Atlantic 120 times and supposedly had known England almost as well as his home at Maryland, USA. When in London in the year 1901 he was presented to the Prince of Wales (shortly to become King Edward VII). He was well connected with the upper echelons of the English establishment:

> Mr. Baker was a very wealthy businessman, and his elevated position in the international shipping circles gave both him and his family access to highly placed English families; with invitations to English country estates, as a matter of course. The loan of his company's vessel, the *SS Maine*, for use as a hospital ship during the Boer War, was much appreciated by the British Government, and brought him to the attention of Lady Randolph Churchill,[898] and with members of the British royal family. He was rewarded with teas at Kensington Palace, races at Ascot, and finally, his daughter was presented at court, to Queen Victoria.[899]

The enormous loss of life on the *Mohegan* prompted Mr Baker in not wasting any time making for England. No expense was spared in this task, as this report records:

HURRY WORK BY MR. BAKER.

Record-Breaking Trip of the Transport Line's President to Catch the Campania.

BALTIMORE, OCT. 15.—President B. N. Baker of the Atlantic Transport line broke all records to-day by making the trip from Baltimore to New York in 3 hours and 30 minutes. He was notified by telephone direct to his house from New York at 1 o'clock this morning. He is now bound from New York on the Cunard line steamship *Campania* for the scene of the wreck.

In order to catch the *Campania* Mr. Baker had to do a great deal of hustling, which included an early morning carriage ride to the city and a trip to New York on a special train. His small cabin trunk and satchel were hastily packed, and about 3:30 o'clock he took leave of his family and entered the family carriage, to which a pair of fast horses had been harnessed. The coachman had orders to drive as quickly as possible to the Union Station [Baltimore]. The team covered the distance at a pace that would have done credit to a racing rig.

The train despatcher was in charge and blandly informed Mr. Baker that the last train for New York had left at midnight, and there was no other train for that place until 8 o'clock. That train would not arrive in New York in time to enable him to catch the *Campania,* so he ordered a special train at once. Engineer Askew, one of the best men in the service, and Conductor Ritterbush, who holds a record on fast trips, happened to be in reserve and were detailed for the run.

---

[898] Lady Randolph Churchill (1854–1921), born Jeanette Jerome, was the American-born wife of Lord Randolph Churchill and the mother of British Prime Minister Winston Churchill. She became well-known for chartering a hospital ship to care for those wounded in the Boer War. It is tempting to imagine a close compatriotic link here, between Mr Baker and Lady Randolph.

[899] Elizabeth Fagg Olds; *Women of the Four Winds.* © Mariner Books.

At exactly one minute after 5 o'clock Mr. Baker, the solitary passenger boarded the car and the train pulled out. It passed Biddle street and Bayview junctions like a skyrocket, and at 6:43, or just about 1 hour and 42 minutes later, whisked past Gray's Ferry, ninety-two miles distant from Union Station and three miles distant from Broad street station, Philadelphia to change engines and train crews, the special passed round the city and sped onward toward Jersey City, where it arrived at 8:31, making the run of 184 miles in 3 hours and thirty minutes. Mr. Baker caught a ferryboat upon the arrival of the train, and a few minutes later he was in New York.

Prior to leaving Baltimore Mr. Baker said he could not understand the great loss of life, as he knew Capt. Griffiths of the ill-fated steamer to be a most competent shipmaster and alert at all times in the hour of danger or emergency.[900]

Mr Baker was a typical example of the entrepreneurial American with a spirit of optimism and with a 'can-do' attitude to life. His political antennae were activated over the *Mohegan* affair and he felt his presence at the company's internal inquiry warranted the dash across the Atlantic, with no hesitation over the cost of the trip.

On arrival in London he would have immediately engaged in urgent discussions with his senior management and legal teams. It needed a firm control on events and Mr Baker was the man for that task.

He would have used his authority to sanction payments made to survivors, the overseeing of onward transportation of American citizens to their destinations and, importantly, in minimizing any long-term damage to his company and to his own reputation.

On his return from the UK, he conveniently had as his travelling companion, a representative from his local newspaper, THE SUN (Baltimore)*,* who obliged Mr Baker with a graphic and sympathetic account of his trip, in the newspaper:

A MYSTERY OF THE SEA

———————

Mr. Bernard N. Baker Returns From Investigating The *Mohegan* Disaster

———————

NO CAUSE CAN BE ASSIGNED

———————

For Loss Of The Steamship And 101 Passengers And Crew

———————

The Vessel Was Considered The Best Of The Atlantic Transport Line Fleet—
Her Captain Was Reliable And Her Compasses Had Just Been Adjusted.

Mr. Bernard N. Baker, president of the Atlantic Transport Line, returned to Baltimore early yesterday morning from London. He had been away from this city just three weeks and one day, the object of this hurried trip being to investigate the steamship *Mohegan,* of Mr. Baker's line. The vessel went ashore on the night of October 14th, in the vicinity of the Lizard, off the coast of England, between the Manacles and Lowlands.

The wreck was one of the most disastrous in the recent history of the sea, only fourteen out of fifty-three passengers being saved. Of the officers and crew there were 31 saved and 62 drowned, making a total of 101 lives lost. The list of the dead was published in THE SUN shortly after the accident. The ship, a new one, and one of the best in the Atlantic Transport Line's fleet, was totally wrecked and went to pieces.

---

[900] *The Sun;* Baltimore, October 16th 1898.

Mr Baker's trip to New York on a special train over the Pennsylvania Railroad was one of the quickest on record. He heard of the loss of the *Mohegan* about 2.30 o'clock in the morning of October 15, the news having been telephoned to him at his country house, near Catonsville. He prepared for his voyage with the utmost dispatch and was driven to Union Station. He wanted to catch the Cunarder *Campania* for Liverpool, which was to sail at 1 P. M. that day, and no regular train would get him to New York on time. He caught the boat, however, and returned to America on the same vessel.

The special train which Mr. Baker chartered, left Baltimore at 5.01 A. M. and arrived at Jersey City at 8.31 A. M., having covered the distance of 184 miles in three hours and a half, the average speed of the train, which consisted only of a locomotive and a coach, being 52.57 miles an hour.

Mr. Baker was due in New York on his return trip last Friday morning, but the *Campania* was not sighted until after 11 o'clock that night. It was announced that she would dock at 7.30 A. M. Saturday, but a very heavy fog prevailed in the lower bay and it was 2 P. M. when Mr. Baker reached the Waldorf-Astoria, where his wife and daughter were awaiting his arrival. He left New York at midnight Saturday, his wife remaining there with Miss Baker, and he reached home yesterday morning.

A representative of THE SUN met Mr. Baker at the Waldorf on Saturday and came to Baltimore on the train with him. Mr. Baker told in detail of the investigations which he had made into the wreck during his brief stay in England and it was well into Sunday morning when he retired to his berth on the sleeper.

The Cause is a Mystery.

"Of course," said he, "the cause of the wreck's what we would all like to ascertain, but I fear it will have to be classed with many other mysteries of the sea. After most careful examination of surviving witnesses, both among the passengers and the crew, there can be no tangible version devolved why Captain Griffiths ever got so far out of his course as to run upon the fatal Manacles. He was more than familiarly acquainted with the very foot of the Cornish coast and none of the survivors had any idea that anything was wrong until the ship actually struck upon the rocks.

I was confident at first that the ship's engines must have become deranged and that she had been blown ashore, but the engineers who survived declare that the engines were never working better than they were at the minute of the accident. They had just been put through a speed test and there was not the slightest trace of friction in their action. Again it suggested itself to me that the compasses might have been slightly off, but it has developed that that was practically impossible. They had been adjusted but a few days before and no variation was found in them. What it was that cause the wreck God only knows and I am sure that no one on this earth will ever know. Had there been one officer saved he might have thrown light upon the mystery, but every single officer was drowned, and, as I have said, others who survive can offer no explanation whatever.

Confidence in Captain Griffiths.

"As for Captain Griffiths, I never knew a man for whom I had higher regard. He was the commodore of our fleet and a man in whom the officers of the company placed the greatest confidence. He never drank intoxicating liquors aboard his ship and was devoted to the performance of his full duty. This was our newest ship, having been constructed less than a year ago, and we considered it our best one. It was for that reason, Captain Griffiths being the commodore of the fleet, that he was placed in her command.

"It is likely that this would have been Captain Griffiths' last trip on the *Mohegan*, for he would probably have been put in charge of a fine twin-screw steamer which we are now building. It is customary for us to give our best ship to our best Captain and he would have left the *Mohegan* to look at the construction of the new vessel. Our captains are given opportunity to know every bolt and every rivet that is being put in the vessel which they are to command, and the engineers, too, have a chance to supervise the construction of the engines before they are placed in the vessel's hold.

"The seaworthiness and safety of the vessel cannot be questioned. She was absolutely safe when we bought her, a new boat, but we spent over $25,000 in making her what we consider safer. Alterations were made which convinced us would preclude any accidents through faults of the steering apparatus or engines, and there wasn't a safer vessel ploughing the waves".

Mr. Baker said that he believed that something must have happened to Captain Griffiths which, for a moment, made him irresponsible.

"There are incidents in history," he said, "when the sudden seemingly insane action of an otherwise rational man has changed the destinies of entire nations. Soldiers have been known to betray their plans to the enemy at a critical point in the battle and there are on record events which show that the captains of ships must have been seized with some mad freak of mind which resulted in a disaster. It is suggested that he might have had a stroke or apoplexy or that his brain was affected in some way so that he missed his bearings and at a point which he knew so well sent his vessel upon the rocks. I can see no other way to account for it.[901] All we know is that the vessel's course when she struck was west, one-quarter north, when it should have been west by north [*sic*].

Crashed Upon A Rock.

Statements made after the wreck prove conclusively that there was no fog at the time and that the wind was not blowing with any great violence. There was a heavy swell on, there being nothing to break it between that place and the equator, but it did not seriously inconvenience the passengers, according to Mr. Baker. Daylight had lasted until long after the Eddystone was passed and when twilight arrived and deepened the Lizard light ought either to have been in sight or its absence should have created suspicion. The fact remains that the boat was six or seven miles north of the course she should have taken to pass safely around Lizard Head. Dinner was just over and the passengers were betaking themselves to various pastimes and occupations when the ship suddenly struck on a rock, which ripped open her plates and sent a terrible shock through her frames. An hour would have sufficed to save all on board, for the officers and crew worked manfully, but it was not to be. Four life-boats, Mr. Baker declares—in spite of contrary statements—were launched in twenty minutes, and life belts were tied about the women and children. Three of the boats were launched and loaded and the fourth was swamped and sank.

"More boats could have been launched," continued the president of the company, "had the water not be pouring like an avalanche into the ship causing her to settle down so rapidly as to render further organized effort impossible. First she lurched over to the left side, which made the launching of boats on one side of the vessel unfeasible, and then she lurched to the other side as the swells struck her, finally plunging and settling rapidly until only her masts and funnel were visible. She was running at a rate of thirteen knots an hour when she struck. This fact proves that the officers believed themselves to be perfectly well assured of her course. After the wreck she lay with her head seaward and her stern towards the land.

Rocket Of Warning.

The coast guards, Mr. Baker says, had noticed the strange course of the vessel and a rocket was sent up to warn it of her impending danger. It was unavailing, and when the ship struck the news was telephoned from station to station. The Porthoustock boat, the nearest, had about two miles to pull against a heavy swell. She made good time, though, and rescued many of those who were swarming in the water. Some were hanging on to the keels of upturned boats; others were clinging to spars, while the hope of many lay in their own strength to keep afloat by swimming.

The boat picked up nearly thirty and landed them, immediately returning to the wreck. People were discovered clinging to the mast, but it was impossible to get the boat near enough to the wreck to take them off. One of the crew jumped from the rigging and swam to the lifeboat from which he obtained a line and fastened it to one of the masts, establishing the desired communication. It was an act of exceptional bravery and nobleness.

---

[901] A suspicion here that Capt. Griffith had some brain malfunction could support a possibility for TIA attacks (see page 281).

"Nothing I heard from the passengers while on the other side," said Mr. Baker, "had anything but praise for the officers and crew. All of the survivors say that the employees of the company worked like demons to save the passengers, often clearly sacrificing their own lives in the effort. That this is true is shown in the death list. Not an officer lived to tell the tale of the catastrophe. Of the firemen, nine were saved and nineteen were drowned. Of the sailors, eleven were saved and nine were drowned, this proportion being probably accounted for by fact that the sailors are usually better swimmers than the other members of the crew, and probably saved themselves by that means after they had been swept from the ship. The poor stewards suffered most, and the passengers who got ashore have nothing but praise for them. They never lost their heads for a moment, but went to work with a will in getting out the life belts and placing them about the passengers. Seven of them were saved and twenty-two of them were drowned. Of the engineers six were saved and seven were drowned".

"Did you go to the scene of the wreck?" he was asked. "No, it was too late when I arrived in London. There was then nothing to be seen there and nothing to be done. I stayed in London and looked after the comforts of the survivors and the welfare of those who were left destitute by the death of some of those who were drowned. Every passenger who was saved will be fully recompensed by the company for the baggage and other property he had lost in the wreck and will be furnished transportation to America by any ship he may elect. The saved members of the crew are being well taken care of as are the families of the crew who were lost. There has been little complaint upon the part of those who were saved. They know no way of account for the accident and simply call it a horrible mystery.

Saving Women And Children.

The fact that the women and children were first looked out for has been clearly brought out. Captain Griffiths, who is declared to have been on the bridge with the third officer [Hindmarsh] when the ship struck, immediately ordered out the boats and the life belts, shouting at the top of his voice: "Save the women and children first!" So well was these orders carried out that some of the boats were said to have been so crowded with women and children that there were not enough men in them to man them. Of the truth of this, however, I can say nothing, not having been there to see".[902]

"The company will also see that the life guardsmen who worked so heroically at saving the lives of those who were struggling in the water will be well rewarded by the company and there are many others who cared for the survivors after they were sent ashore and who took part in the work of rescue and succour who will not be forgotten".

On November 10, unless the date has been changed since Mr. Baker's departure from England, the Board of Trade of Great Britain will fully investigate the cause of the wreck of the *Mohegan* and endeavour to place the responsibility.[903] A large number of witnesses will be called, most of whom have already indicated their line of testimony. Not one has any plausible theory of the cause of the accident to advance and almost all speak with emphasis of the good discipline which prevailed on board after the vessel struck and of the good conduct of the officers and the crew. The lifeboats are said by many to have been in good working order, with the falls working well. There was no panic and the stewards were all placing lifebelts upon the women and children. Agnes Maud Liggott, [*sic*] one of the rescued stewardesses, is especially commended for the heroism which she displayed.

The Captains's Last Words.

One of the crew gives a graphic description of the scene on deck as the vessel went down. "As the ship struck," he says, "she heeled over to the starboard side, where all the passengers and crew congregated. The captain was on the bridge and behaved with perfect calmness. When the orders were given to man the boats all the people rushed to the leeward side,

---

[902] There is more than a hint of 'public relations' here, and as Mr Baker was not there to corroborate the fact, then he was at liberty to construe events, that supported the company's objective. But that was his role and he played it impeccably.

[903] Mr Baker, having expended a small fortune on legal support, was perhaps well advised to leave the UK three days before the Board of Trade inquiry commenced: a question of, 'don't keep a dog and bark yourself.'

having only five or six of us on the other side. After two or three attempts we launched one of the boats and got five passengers into her. The work was most difficult, and it was nothing short of a miracle that she was not swamped. The captain saw our difficulty and shouted: 'For God's sake, boys, get clear if you can.' Those were the last words he spoke. The ship disappeared a moment afterwards".

While in London, Mr. Baker saw Miss Katherine B. Noble of Baltimore, who was one of the passengers rescued. The story of her heroism and the trials through which she went has already been told fully in THE SUN. Mr. Baker communicated with Miss Noble's father, in Baltimore, Mr. Horace Noble, and will furnish the young lady with transportation home and indemnify her for the loss of her wardrobe and valuables.

Visited Miss Noble.

"Miss Noble looked quite well," said Mr. Baker, "considering what she had been through, but she certainly had an awful experience. However, the people of Baltimore probably knew the details of her rescue before I did. I do not know how long she will remain abroad, she had not decided, when I left, when she would start for home, but I imagine it will be before long. She was somewhat nervous, naturally, and will be for some time, but she has acted with great fortitude.

"She told me that she never would have been saved had it not been for the words of encouragement of an officer, who was clinging to a spar near where she was floating. 'He kept cheering me up.' She said, 'and recalling cases where women have been rescued after floating for hours and nearly giving up all hope. I promised I would hold on as long as I possibly could, and then suddenly the sound of his voice came to me no more across the water. The brave man had been swept from the spar by a wave and disappeared for ever. I owe my life primarily to the efforts of that brave man to keep me from losing my heart and dropping back into the sea.'"

The Fatal Rocks.

The Manacle Rocks, upon which the *Mohegan* struck, are about a mile from the coast, nearly due southeast from Manacles Point. The Cornish coast runs southward from Falmouth bay to the deeply projecting spur called the Lizard. The Manacles lay half way between Falmouth and the southern promontory forming the most easterly point along the shore. It would be fatally easy for any vessel a little out of her reckoning, as the *Mohegan* doubtless was, and endeavoring to shape her course for the Lizard, to run afoul of these perilous reefs.

A most unenviable reputation among mariners has this spot, and some years ago a large emigrant ship [*John* – 1855] sank in the same waters with the loss of 200 lives. There is no lighthouse on the rocks, but there is a bell-buoy, and experienced captains always give it a wide berth. The British papers are loud in their demands to know why such a place should not be better protected, and why the responsible authorities have persistently refused, as they are said to have done, to place a lightship on the Manacles and so prevent the recurrence of such catastrophe as have occurred there again and again.

Mr. Baker brought with him from England several photographs of the wreck of the *Mohegan* taken on the morning after the accident. In these the rocks which tore holes in the ship and sent her to the bottom are clearly discernible.[904]

Mr. Baker later dictated a new regime to be adopted aboard his ships, to prevent any repeat of the *Mohegan* disaster. This involved a shared responsibility for a ship's navigation, between a captain and his senior officers. This had already been suggested by the passenger, Mr John Hyslop some two months previously. Mr Baker's proposal was given a high profile cover in the American press:

NEWS OF THE SHIPPING

Atlantic Transport's Company's

---

[904] *The Sun;* Baltimore (1837–1985) November 7th 1898.

New Order to Captains.

The Atlantic Transport Company, Mr. Bernard N. Baker, president, has adopted a maritime innovation by which it is expected to minimize the chances of disasters at sea. The plan is explained in the following order, which has been sent to all captains of the line:

Dear Sir.—Will you be good enough to note the following instructions upon this subject:

That the courses to be persued shall be set by the junior officer on the watch; then each course shall be approved or altered by the senior officer on watch, and finally by yourself. This of course, leaves the responsibility upon you and the object of the change is to prevent there being any hesitation in regard to an alteration of a course which is observed to be wrong. Where the course is now set by a junior officer there can be no hesitation on the part of his seniors on pointing out or rectifying an error. Where the course is set by the captain there may be hesitation in this rectification which may end in casualty.

It was stated at the office of the Atlantic Transport Company yesterday that the captains had received the instructions, which would go into effect at once. The company's officials had been considering the plan for some time, it was stated. The idea of establishing a system of checks on commanding officers was thought to be a good one. Under the old system a subordinate might hesitate to call his superior's attention to what might seem an error of judgment, but if the course is set by a junior, his seniors would at once correct any errors.

The *New York Evening Telegraph* of yesterday said:

"Interest in the accident which sent the *Paris* aground has been revived by the unexpected floating of the hapless liner. This with the not wholly unexpected suspension of Captain [Frederic] Watkins and the radical action of the Atlantic Transport Company in establishing a system of checks on commanding officers, by which it is sought to minimize the chances of such disaster as befell the *Paris,* are now topics which are being discussed with great interest.

"So far as a canvass of local steamship agencies could discover, none of the other lines are disposed to follow the lead of the Atlantic Transport in this matter.

"Clement A. Griscom, of the American Line, would not discuss it further than to say that the rule would not be adopted by his company. In his opinion there is nothing to be gained by it. Moreover, he could see no room for improvement in the system now in vogue with the American Line.

"James A. Wright, vice-president of the line, was more reticent, refusing to discuss the matter at all, 'You can say that we will take all needful precautions,' Mr, Wright said, and refused to say anything further on the subject.

"Vernon H. Brown, agent of the Cunard Line, was equally non-committal. 'Any order that tends to minimize the dangers of navigation is desirable,' said Mr. Brown.' 'The Cunard Line takes every precaution that tends to that end.'

"John Lea, agent of the White Star Line, was not, he said, prepared to express an opinion on the new rule of The Atlantic Transport Line.

"To Gustav H. Schwab, local manager of the North German Lloyd Company, it seemed like reversing the natural order of things.

"Mr. Boss, of the Hamburg American Line, would not discuss the matter. He explained that with his company it was the rule to hold the chief officer jointly responsible with the captain. In case of disagreement the captain's orders were to be obeyed always and the subordinate was resulted to enter his objection in the log". [905]

---

[905] *The Sun;* Baltimore (1837–1985) July 14th 1899.

A Brief history of the Atlantic Transport Line:

There is some little confusion over the name of the shipping company that features in this story: it being either the Atlantic Transport Company, or the Atlantic Transport Line. Here, an expert in the company's history helps unravel a rather complex business evolution:

> The 'Atlantic Transport Line' was the popular name given to the service inaugurated by the Baltimore Lighterage & Storage Company in 1881. The service was operated for them by agents in London (Hooper, Murrell & Williams) who set up and managed on their behalf single ship companies, one to own each vessel in the fleet—each vessel then being chartered to the Baltimore Lighterage & Storage Co. These single ship companies were named after their ships: the Suffolk Steamship Company etc., except that the very first was christened the Atlantic Transport Company.
>
> In 1886 this arrangement changed, with a new firm of agents set up (Williams, Torrey & Feild) with two American directors (Torrey & Feild), established to take over the management of the operation in London. This continued with single ship companies until 1889, when a limited liability company was incorporated in London (The Atlantic Transport Company Ltd.) and the single ship companies (including the Atlantic Transport Company) were wound up and incorporated into it.
>
> In 1898 the Atlantic Transport Company of West Virginia was incorporated in the USA to replace the Baltimore Storage & Lighterage Company (whose name had become a misnomer by then) and so assert American ownership of the line's British assets, including all of the shares of the Atlantic Transport Company Ltd.
>
> At the time of the *Mohegan* disaster the service was being operated by Atlantic Transport Company Ltd. of London (managed by Williams, Torrey & Feild) on behalf of the American parent company. It is likely that the Atlantic Transport Company of West Virginia had been incorporated by October that year, but that is conjecture, at this time.
>
> In short, the 'Atlantic Transport Line' was the public face of the service, the name that the service was marketed by the various companies and agents.[906]

With money you can build a road in the sea.

> Formed in 1881 by Bernard Baker of the Baltimore Storage & Lighterage Co, he found it economical to operate his ships under the British flag. Although American owned, the Atlantic Transport Line operated out of Britain, with British registered and manned vessels, most of which were British built. Initial voyages were between Barrow and New York and the following year, between Amsterdam and New York under charter to the Royal Netherlands Steamship Co. In 1883, regular London to Baltimore voyages commenced and a London to New York service started in 1890. Occasional voyages were also made to New York from Swansea and Belfast.
>
> General cargo, live cattle, and small numbers of passengers were carried to British ports and the line developed an excellent reputation for shipping valuable horses. A full-scale regular passenger service to New York commenced in 1892 and today the line is best known for its first class only direct London to New York passenger/cargo service operated by its four 'Minne' class ships – *Minneapolis, Minnehaha, Minnetonka* and *Minnewaska* from 1900 to 1915.
>
> In 1896, Atlantic Transport Line took over the fleet and assets of National Line. The Atlantic Transport Line was an American company, but was effectively British operated. The solution to this in America was to form the Atlantic Transport Company of West Virginia in 1898 to acquire the assets and ships of Atlantic Transport Line and to build and

---

[906] Personal communication: Jonathan Kinghorn, *The Atlantic Transport Line, 1881–1931: A History with Details on All Ships.*

own their own American flagged ships. For economical reasons, the current fleet continued under the British flag, but was American controlled. In 1904, the company, together with many others came under the control of the newly formed International Mercantile Marine Company (IMMC).[907]

The shipping-line was well known as a reliable means of transporting horse and cattle. Many thoroughbred horses were so transported back and forth, across the Atlantic. Typically, ALT had chartered the ship, *Massachusetts*, to bring the bulk of Barnum & Bailey's Circus to London in November of 1897. Animals carried included 22 elephants, 11 camels, 136 trained circus horses, 240 draught horses, 4 tigers, 6 lions, 6 zebras, 30 different kinds of antelopes, several wild boars, a pelican, a female gorilla ("the gem of the zoological collection"), an adjutant bird (a large wading bird in the stork family), an ostrich, an emu, a cassowary, a rhea, "and other animals and birds too numerous to mention". A giraffe named Daisy evidently fell during rough weather and died. Other casualties of the voyage were 3 draught horses, 2 monkeys, and the black stallion *Eagle*, 36 years old, "an accomplished dancer—buried in British waters". Besides the livestock, *Massachusetts* carried as passengers, 240 employees connected with the show.[908] One must be thankful that the *Mohegan* did not have onboad such an astonishing menagerie of exotic animals.

What goes up must come down.

The Atlantic Transport Line fell victim to the economic disaster – the Wall Street Crash[909]:

> Much of the line's fleet was sunk during the First World War. After the war the freight business was rebuilt and four huge replacements for the *Minne*-class ships were planned. Only two of these were built however and the passenger service, which recommenced in 1923, never matched pre-war successes. With first class travel declining the ATL introduced a tourist third class ship in 1925 and for two seasons operated another. But the line was faltering even before the Wall Street Crash and with the recession of 1931 its remaining ships were laid up or transferred to other IMMC lines, and it effectively ceased to exist. The depression of 1931 caused IMM to commence selling Atlantic Transport Line's passenger fleet and by 1936 their last ship, *Columbia* was scrapped and both companies (American and British) ceased to exist. The *SS Minnewaska* was the last ship the Atlantic Transport Line operated.[910]

Mr Bernard Nadal Baker (1854–1918).

[907] Ibid.

[908] The *Era;* November 27th 1897.

[909] The Wall Street Crash in October 1929, created the worst depression in American history.

[910] *WikiPedia*

CHAPTER 25

Mr John William Henry Juddery: Quartermaster

Do what is right, come what may.

He was born in1869 in Leyton, Essex[911] and had lost his father, John William Juddery,[912] at an early age. He was the eldest of five children, three of whom died young. His mother Alice (née Peterkin) re-married Charles King, and John and his sister Alice lived with them and their two half-siblings in Billinghurst.

There is no record of him in the UK census for 1891, 1901, or 1911 which suggests that he went to sea at quite a young age. He was awarded his Certificate of Compentency by the Board of Trade, as first mate of a foreign-going ship, on the 14th March, 1895 and he eventually became a quartermaster and then a captain. He married Bertha Ann Crosby in Islington, London on August 27th 1898, in the year of the *Mohegan* disaster. Through the ensuing years, he and his wife had eleven children, though three died at a young age. His final posting was as Master of the Surrey Docks.

Following his retirement, he moved to Ditchling (Hassocks, East Sussex) and lived at the *'Anchorage'* in East End Lane. It was here that he met and befriended the reclusive artist Sir Frank Brangwyn,[913] who lived close by, through a mutual love of sailing and the sea. Juddery's early retirement was not to his liking and he became a lay-preacher for the Mission to Seamen organization. He and his wife Bertha then left Ditchling and spent some years in Northumberland, spreading the gospel.

Brangwyn promised to build a house in Ditchling, for renting by his friend, if he were to return there to live, which he duly did. He then retired to *'Letterewe'* in Beacon Road, where he remained until his death in 1946. His wife Bertha died in the year 1948.

His headstone at St. Margaret's Church, Ditchling, East Sussex, reads:

In loving memory of John William Henry Juddery
Died 28th October 1946 aged 76 years.
'Resting'

Also of Bertha Ann Juddery died 14th December 1948 Aged 71 years.
'Reunited'

---

[911] GRO/BMD: 1869 Q1 – W. Ham 4a 7.

[912] GRO/BMD: 1875 Q3 – W. Ham 4a 9.

[913] Sir Frank William Brangwyn RA. RWS. RBA. (12th May 1867 – 11th June 1956) was an Anglo-Welsh artist, painter, water-colourist, virtuoso engraver, illustrator, and progressive designer. He was born in Bruges, Belgium, and his mother (Elenor) was born in Wales.

In 1943, the *Mid Sussex Times* recorded that he, 'gave a talk about sailors and recounted his own experiences of sailing ships in his young days'. He also raised funds for the Mission to Seamen, a cause very dear to his heart. A local lad, Dick Morley, recounts in his book [914] the time he received a New Testament, signed by Captain Juddery and with an inscribed script in his hand, bidding him to, "Search the Scriptures".

His moment of glory.

Though holding the certificate of a first mate, he served on the *Mohegan* as a quartermaster; having never served on a liner before. On the day of the *Mohegan* calamity, Juddery was on the chief officer's (Llewellyn Couch) watch, and on duty from 8 a.m. to noon. It was during the period 10 a.m. to noon that the course was set at west three-quarters north. The Board of Trade inquiry established that Juddery was helmsman on the wheel and steered the *Mohegan* between the Isle of Wight and Portland, on that same heading.[915]

Following the stranding, Juddery was in the ship's mizzen-rigging overnight with other survivors. The next morning, on sighting that the *Charlotte* lifeboat could not approach any nearer to the wreck, owing to a strong tidal current, he plunged into the sea and swam towards the lifeboat. Taking a line, he returned again to the wreck, and through this prompt and brave action, he helped to save the other fifteen people in the rigging. He was justly awarded a silver medal for his gallantry:

> The committee at Lloyd's later decided to bestow the silver medal of the Society of Lloyd's upon Quartermaster J. W. H Juddery, of the steamship Mohegan, as an honorary acknowledgment of his extraordinary exertions in contributing to the saving of life on the occasion of the loss of that vessel.[916]

He was also awarded the silver *Sea Gallantry Medal* for bravery, by the Board of Trade, on the 8th April, 1899: [917]

> William Juddery, quartermaster aboard the *Mohegan*, was, on the 8th inst., at Stratford, publicly presented with the silver medal of the Board of Trade,[918] in recognition of his gallantry on the occasion of the wreck of that vessel on the Manacle Rocks, Cornwall. It was stated that Juddery, who is now third officer of the *Manhattan*, belonging to the same owners, on the occasion of the disaster of the *Mohegan* clung to a mast for seven hours, and that although half dead with cold he dived into the sea repeatedly and succeeded in saving twelve lives. Mr Juddery, in acknowledging the presentation, said he only performed a duty which any sailor would have done in similar circumstances.[919]

---

[914] Dick Morley; *No Ordinary Place;* The Ditchling Society May 2003, 51.

[915] *The Pall Mall Gazette* (London, England); Thursday, 24th November 1898.

[916] *The Royal Cornwall Gazette Falmouth Packet, Cornish Weekly News, & General Advertiser*; Wednesday 29th December 1898.

[917] *Liverpool Mercury* (Liverpool, England); Tuesday, 11th April 1899.

[918] The usual monthly meeting of the Royal Humane Society, presided over by Colonel Horace Montagu, treasurer, was held yesterday at the office, at 4 Trafalgar-square, when several cases of heroism in saving or attempting to save life were investigated and rewarded, including that of J. W. Juddery.

[919] *The Belfast News-Letter* (Belfast, Ireland); Tuesday, 11th April 1899.

At this time (February, 2011) Captain Juddery's daughter, Millicent, still lives in the village of Ditchling, at the age of 95 years and along with her extended family.

Such deeds as thine are registered in Heaven.

It would be churlish not to mention the American cattleman, Mr Thomas Mitchell, who bravely followed the example of Quartermaster Juddery, in taking a second rope between the *Charlotte* lifeboat and the *Mohegan*'s mast, to retrieve the remainder of the personnel stranded there. There is no record of recognition for his brave act, and apparently, Quartermaster Juddery had swum off with all the honours:

CONSPICUOUS BRAVERY.

HOW PEOPLE IN THE RIGGING WERE SAVED.

The special correspondent of the *Star* says:—The lifeboat from Porthoustock (with fifteen noble fellows under command of James Hill, coxswain) came in with the ship's lifeboat No. 4, and took off its sad cargo of dead, dying and living. The Porthoustock lifeboat put out to sea again, and succeeded in approaching the wreck. Benumbed with cold, drenched with surf, hoarse and tired with shouting, the sixteen poor creatures were praying for daylight. The darkness was so inky that it was only by shouting from one mast to the other that comrades could ascertain that a friend had not given up the struggle and slipped out of sight for ever. "Afraid I can't get near enough," shouted Coxswain Hill. Then his command, "Pull blues, pull whites," [920] grew faintly audible in the night, but again they were heard in another direction. Some body high up in the rigging offered to swim to the lifeboat with a line, but he was so high up and so numb that he would have fallen had he released his grip. "By God, boys," shouted Quartermaster Judbery [*sic*]—(There were many others in that terrible night, but they were not blasphemous)—"By God, boys, I'll swim to them from a rope end". Then he plunged from the rigging into the sea, and he was lost sight of. Minutes passed. They seemed like hours. Coxswain Hill's voice could still be heard. Then came the splash of waves. Judbery had succeeded, and was coming back with a rope tied round his body. This was made fast to the mast and a bowline rope passed along. Women first. It was tied around Mrs. Piggott. "She leapt into the water like a retriever," said Dr. Trevor, "and was the first to be dragged into the Porthoustock lifeboat". After the fifth rescue the line broke. All hope of speedy rescue for the remaining eleven seemed gone, but what Judbery had done, Cattleman Mitchell volunteered to attempt.[921] He succeeded and the refugees on the mizzen were all rescued. After that came a two hour's struggle. The lifeboat in safety could not approach the mainmast. Time after time were the recuers baffled. Thrice the boat got close enough to throw a rope; thrice the cord slipped out of the benumbed fingers of the boatswain; but at length he and his companions were got safely on board, and Ferguson, the last officer to leave the ship alive, was taken from his perilous perch on the funnel.[922]

His heroic effort is further alluded to by the American Press, when Mr Thomas Mitchell arrived in New York:

[920] The oars on the port side were painted white in colour and those on the starboard side were painted blue. The coxswain's commands, "Pull blues … pull whites" were used to control the lifeboat's direction of travel, and in allowing a co-ordinated manoeuvring of the vessel.

[921] The remaining four, still stranded in the rigging, were saved by one of their party—Thomas Mitchell, the American cattleman—in an identical manoeuvre, that had been adopted by Juddery.

[922] *The Royal Cornwall Gazette Falmouth Packet, Cornish Weekly News, & General Advertiser;* Thursday, October 20th 1898.

Thomas Mitchell and James Ward Arrive on the *Marquette*.

Two survivors of the *Mohegan* disaster arrived here yesterday on the Atlantic Transport Line steamship *Marquette*. They are Thomas Mitchell of Boston and James Ward of Jersey City, both of whom went to London on the *Mohegan* [as the Cleopatra] as cattlemen, and were returning when the steamer ran on to the rocks at the Manacles. Mitchell was instrumental in saving eleven lives. He was modest about his achievement, however, and declined to talk, rushing off as soon as the *Marquette* docked to catch a train for Boston.

Ward said: "I am still unable to understand why the *Mohegan* was permitted to go on the rocks. It was a clear evening and the shore was visible. The officers on the bridge paid no attention to the rockets fired on shore to warn the vessel off the coast". Ward said that there were twenty-seven others in the lifeboat in which he escaped from the steamer, but all of them would have been lost had not the coast guard [*sic*] come out and taken them into the surfboat.[923] There was no plug in the *Mohegan*'s boat, and she was filling rapidly. The men used their shoes to bail her with, and Mrs. Pemberton gave her hat for the same purpose. Capt. Griffith was on the bridge when the port lifeboat drifted away from the steamer. The starboard lifeboat was overloaded and capsized.[924]

Penny Worth, a local researcher and member of the Ditchling History Project [2012] , was engaged in a detailed recording of the inscriptions on the gravestones in the St. Margaret's Church, Ditchling. This project led to a publication of a book[925] and quartermaster Juddery's story quite figuratively rose from the grave.[926]

The Juddery family history report was sent to Karen Richards of the St. Keverne Local History Society (because of its association with the *Mohegan*) who, in turn, passed it on to this author.

I am deeply indebted to each of them, for this very interesting background to one of the true heroes of the *Mohegan* disaster, and (as far as I am aware) this is the only published photograph of the man, (see fig. 18).

The sharing of information demonstrates the valuable role for local history societies in a preservation of ephemeral material, that urgently needs recording for future generations. The parlous state of many of the UK graveyards, and with their insecure future, only serves to emphasise this need for a secure preservation of their full record for interments.

Mr John William Henry Juddery (1869–1946).

---

[923] One of the old traditions of the 19th-century American Lifesaving Service was certifying surfboat coxswains, who captained rescue boats through the pounding waves to rescue those lost at sea, as Surfmen operating in surfboats (lifeboats).

[924] *The New York Times*; 2nd November, 1898.

[925] Ditchling History Society, *In Memoriam: History and Design in a Village Churchyard. Life's Work Well Done: A Collection of Life Stories.*

[926] Grave site – plot reference: AC-5-27.

CHAPTER 26

Daniel Christopher Gallaway: A Second Stowaway

Never a ship sails out of bay but carries my heart as a stowaway.

At some point, during the *Mohegan*'s voyage, a stowaway was found aboard the vessel. It is likely that he had remained hidden until the pilot was put ashore at Dover, and with the *Mohegan* well on its way to New York. The name of this individual is not known, but he was mentioned during the Board of Trade inquiry, that followed the foundering of the *Mohegan*. He was, supposedly, a partner of a Hungarian woman already living in New York with their child, and that he was on his way to reunite with them there. His body was recovered from the sea off Porthallow and recognised by a member of the crew as the stowaway. The poor unfortunate was buried in the mass grave, in the St. Keverne churchyard. It is not known whether his wife in New York, awaiting his arrival, ever knew the fate of her husband and his unfortunate association with the *Mohegan*.

According to information in the public domain, there are claims that another stowaway was aboard the *Mohegan* named Daniel Christopher Gallaway.[927] This assertion is made by the modern day Gallaways, who are engaged in a genealogical study for their family. It is as a result of their investigation that an apparent link with the *Mohegan* has come to light. It is, therefore, necessary to record these events as a part of this story, and to attempt to uphold the family's claim.

Daniel Gallaway was a black American, born on the 18th March, 1876 in the town of Boston, New York State. The UK marriage certificate (1910) for Daniel Gallaway (see page 440) recorded his father as Frank Gallaway and his occupation as a 'colt-breaker'[928] and as having been deceased at the time of the marriage.[929]

There is conflicting evidence as to his true birthplace:[930] other locations include St. Lucia and Trinidad. It is quite possible that his earlier family was from the Caribbean and were unfortunately caught up in the slave trade. If so, Daniel Gallaway was undoubtedly a freeborn at birth.[931] His family tells of his having had a sister who lived in St. Lucia.; in which case, if this was his birthplace, he could have made his way to America,

---

[927] He is also recorded elsewhere as 'Galloway'.

[928] Full details are found in his UK marriage certificate (see page 440). His father was referred to in the same document as: 'Frank Gallaway / occupation: colt-breaker / deceased'. His father was also thought to have lived in Alabama, prior to moving to Boston, where the 1860 census records show that enslaved Africans comprised 45% of the state's total population. The name of his mother is not known. The UK census report for 1911 also records Boston, USA as Daniel Gallaway's birthplace.

[929] His life story, recorded here, arises as a result of having made contact with his current family and I am indebted to his great-granddaughter (Paula Bate) for this information. Nothing more substantial is known at this time, for Daniel Gallaway's father or birth family.

[930] See Appendix 12, p. 459.

[931] Freeborn (not born into slavery) as having being born after the ending of slavery, following the American Civil war in 1865.

either as a stowaway, a member of a ship's crew, or as a migrant (illegal or otherwise). It is not known at this time if he had ever been a naturalised American.

An anecdotal story told by the family, suggests he had worked on fishing boats in the USA and during this time had been, put in touch with the owners of a luxury American passenger shipping line, this being the American Transport Line, who were about to send the stricken *Cleopatra* back to the UK in August 1898. As a result of this introduction, he was apparently hired as a crewman, working in the ship's catering division.[932]

The family record that, "the vessel had a lot of navigational troubles, on the way". There was also an account that he had employed a bugle to announce meal-times to the wealthy American passengers. He might well have employed his talent on that instrument, but there would have been no passengers aboard to enjoy his early morning reveille, as the *Cleopatra* had returned to the UK with just the crew and a number of unappreciative livestock. The cancellation of the passengers' bookings was as a consequence of the vessel's technical problems: which could have compromised their comfort and safety.

An examination of the *Agreement and Account of Crew*[933] documentation, for the return voyage of the *Cleopatra*, reveals no record for Mr Gallaway as a member of that crew. Given the meticulous nature of the recordings made within this document, it would be almost unthinkable that his contract (had it existed) would have been overlooked. But, these were extraordinary times: the ship was distressed, passenger lists were cancelled and the company would have been engaged in a huge administrative task in informing and arranging alternative passage, for their inconvenienced passengers. In addition to this, several of the outward-bound crew had jumped ship in New York. It is not impossible that, in the general confusion, Gallaway may have been taken on at the very last moment, and with an uncustomary lapse in the formal contractual proceedings.

There is no record of his arrival in the United Kingdom , or of any official payment made by the Atlantic Transport Line, as recompense for his service. Assuming that the story is true, we now need to track his subsequent movements within the UK.

It is not known if he remained on the company's payroll, or if he had jumped ship to become an itinerant worker, here. It is quite possible, during the four months the *Cleopatra* was laid up, that he had gained employment in the local docks, or even travelled back and forth across the Atlantic as a crew member on other ships. There was a sufficient time period to have completed more than one such trip before his eventual encounter with the *Mohegan*. Whatever this resourceful man did during that period, he had now decided to return to the United States.

As to Gallaway becoming a stowaway aboard the *Mohegan*, it was quite feasible. He would have been familiar with the ship's layout and so he would have known where to hide, until it was safe to reveal himself

---

[932] If Daniel Gallaway was an American, then he must have either arrived in the UK as a crew member, or as a stowaway. He would certainly not have been a paying passenger. One is intrigued, why he wished to come to the UK in the first place.

[933] Courtesy of the Memorial University, Newfoundland (MUN)—Maritime Archives.

to the ship's company, and then with no possibility of being put ashore.[934] As the captain was also the master aboard the *Cleopatra*, he might have been recognised as a previous member of that crew, and put to task, in order to work his passage home. An investigation would certainly have taken place, and a record made by the officer in the ship's event log. The log-books were never recovered.

There is no record of a black man having been on board the *Mohegan*; no record of such a person alighting from the lifeboat, following the disaster; or appearing in any newspaper report. One is a little thoughtful as to why such an exotic figure as an American black man, would not have attracted comment—either in the local folklore, by the surviving crew, or in the newspaper reports of the time.

There is no doubt that Daniel Gallaway was used to having to live on his wits. Life was not easy for the working class in Victorian times, and even harder for a black man, who had to endure the daily insults and rejections meted out to foreigners, in those more intolerant times. He was no doubt skilled in recognising opportunities and with using his gift of the gab, remained one step ahead of those who would deny him. As we shall see later in this story, those skills would enable him to forge a new life for himself in the UK and against all odds. As a man already burdened with disadvantage, he was not easily deterred by untoward events; always having an eye for the main chance. That included a convenient shipwrecking.

O God thy sea is so great and my boat is so small.

Fate, however, had other plans for him. For whatever reason, Gallaway found himself aboard the *Mohegan* and was now on his way home; that is, until the vessel unexpectedly struck the Manacle Rocks. Filled with terror, and imploring for deliverance by his Lord God, he would have quickly made his way to the deck, where he found the crew were having great difficulty in launching the lifeboats.

The ship was listing to port, and with the rough sea breaking over the rails, reminding them all of the peril they were in. The captain was shouting above the din, urging his crew to, "Get the boats away lads." Capt. Griffith knew in his heart, that it was becoming increasingly futile. Looking down from the wheelhouse at the chaos below him, he knew they were doomed. The low growling noise from the grinding of the ship's plates on her rocky deathbed signalled her imminent demise. With a sudden lurch, the ship slid off the rocks and slipped beneath the waves.

A collective cry went up from the poor souls gathered on the sloping deck, at a sudden realisation that this was now the end. The sea had usurped the captain's authority and left him shouting useless orders into the wind. The Manacles had claimed its prize.

---

[934] There were strict rules concerning the well-being of the apprehended stowaway, on board a ship (see page 367).

He that would learn to pray let him go to sea.

For Daniel Gallaway, this was to be his greatest test of endurance. But he was not yet destined for a pine-box. He fell headlong into the cold dark water and struck out in desperation to save his own life, surrounded by screaming passengers, and with the waves crashing against the nearby rocks, drawing them all towards their cruel razor sharpness. The acrid smell of oil, paraffin, and the contents of the quenched fireboxes and ship's heads, was overpowering and the tainted water was choking him, as he gasped for breath.

Dodging the grasping hands of those who would cling and hold him imploring for his help, his sole intent now was his own survival. He struck out, and vowed that, if he were to get through this nightmare, he would forever dedicate himself to the good Lord and his Church. Amen!

Commitment got Daniel thrown into the lion's den: faith got him out.

His family states that Daniel Gallaway managed to swim to the harbour of Coverack, some three miles southwest of the Manacles. Indeed, two crew members did manage to reach Coverack, but Gallaway was not one of their number.[935] His saviour was a crew member aboard the lifeboat *Charlotte*, and so would have encountered Daniel Gallaway in the vicinity of the wreck some hour or so after the *Mohegan*'s foundering. Another story is that he had been snatched from the sea by Henry Tripconey.[936] His pleadings to his Lord were answered and this lucky man was chosen by Him to survive this catastrophe.

It is possible that Daniel Gallaway was the man who, on arrival at Porthoustock beach, had alighted from the lifeboat and run up through the valley, disappearing from the scene. What is not disputed is that a person did indeed make a desperate dash up the beach and that the next morning—according to a local story—a boat was apparently commandeered from the south bank of the Helford River and rowed across to the other side of the estuary. Certainly, Gallaway would have been resourceful enough to take this action, in an attempt to place some miles between him and the scene of the disaster. Fearful of the outcome of his having been a stowaway and as an alien in the UK, he had every reason to remove himself from the area.

On reaching the far shore and pulling the boat up above the tide-line, he would then have made his way towards Falmouth. Arriving in the town, tired, wet and exhausted, he would again have relied on his remarkable talent for survival, by turning every event to his own advantage. Perhaps, in telling his audience of his good fortune in surviving the wreck of the *Mohegan*, he would have been directed towards the Falmouth Sailors' Home, where many other surviving crew-members would be staying over the next few days. He would have avoided that establishment, for obvious reasons.

---

[935] The men who swam ashore were: Arthur Ernest Leeson Smith (a passenger) and Robert Barrow (a greaser).

[936] Mr Tripconey was not a member of the *Charlotte* crew in attendance for the *Mohegan*; a member of the Tripp family is the more likely candidate here. However, Tripconey had taken part in the rescue of the *John*, in 1855. On Thursday 3rd May, 1855, the *John* left Plymouth bound for Quebec, captained by Edward Rawle. She carried 268 passengers and 19 crew members. Later that night she foundered on the Manacle Rocks, St. Keverne Cornwall. 194 passengers drowned, while the crew all survived..

With such a epic disaster on their doorstep, the good folk of Falmouth had pulled out all the stops, in giving charitable help and succour to the poor unfortunates, who came their way. Daniel Gallaway would have readily availed himself of all the help on offer. But he was already ahead of the game. He was going nowhere. He would see what was available to him, here, in Cornwall.

The man who has experienced shipwreck shudders even at a calm sea.

He told all who would listen, of his fear at venturing to sea again, and that he was now obliged to remain in the UK. Taking pity on him, he would perhaps have been offered casual employment and given rudimentary accommodation by some kindly people: perhaps the religious institutions with which he would now have a close bond.

It was during this 'golden' period that apparently he made a happy encounter and an employment with a Mr Gay. There are two prospective candidates for this particular Mr Gay in the 1901 UK census, and these are:

(i)

Giles Gay—(Head of household, age 58 years—Cattleman on a farm in Ruan, Lanihorne, Cornwall)

Elizabeth A. Gay (Wife, age 66 years)

Samuel Henry Gay (Son, age 34 years—horseman on the same farm).

(ii)

Samuel Gay—(Head of household, age 71 years—Farmer: Trescobeas, Budock Cornwall)

Mary Gay (Wife, age 74 years)

Thomas Gay (Son, age 34 years—Milk Carrier on the same farm).

John Jordin (Servant. Age 27 years—Carter and Driver on Farm)

Note that there is a particular link on both farms with horses, and Daniel Gallaway's father's occupation had been described as a 'colt-breaker.' This skill could well have passed from father to son. But even if that was not the case, Daniel Gallaway would no doubt have quickly claimed a talent for horsemanship, which would have been of some value, especially for the Gay (i) household, who kept and reared racehorses. Again, displaying a knack for thinking on his feet, and in exploiting any opportunity that came his way, he possibly gained employed by the one or other Gay family.[937] According to a family anecdote, the son of the Gay family taught Daniel Gallaway the art of Cornish wrestling.[938]

There is no record for Daniel Gallaway in the UK census for 1901.

The next significant event in his life was a meeting with his future wife, almost nine years after the *Mohegan* incident. This chance encounter took place in an unknown village church (most probably in the

---

[937] There is no substantive proof that Gallaway had any contact with either of the two families; we can only take note of what his modern day family believes to be the case.

[938] Cornish wrestling is Cornwall's oldest sport, and has been established in Cornwall (in South West England) for several centuries.

village of Probus or Perranzabuloe). He met the widow, Harriet Emma Burt (née Lean), whilst singing in church. She had been married to a labourer, Frederick George Burt, in the year of 1899. That union produced two children. Sadly, her husband was killed at the age of twenty-four years, in 1901, whilst working for the railway company, on the Perran and Newquay Railway Works project.[939]

His wife was left with a raising of her one-year old son (Frederick Burt) and was expecting a second child at the time of the death of her husband. She struggled on as a lone parent; until the fortuitous meeting in church with Daniel Christopher Gallaway, probably at around the year 1909.

The family you come from isn't as important as the family you're going to have.

The relationship evidently blossomed, as they married on the 13th August 1910, at the Register Office in Truro. Coincidentally, the same Registrar and Superintendent Registrar officiated as at Harriet Lean's first marriage ceremony, eleven years previously.

In the following year, the 1911 UK census records the Gallaway [940] family as in residence at Trevorva Cottage, Nancemabyn Probus (see page 450). Interestingly, at the same address lived a Mr George Gay with his own family, and he was also a farm labourer. It is likely that the aforementioned Gay family households had nothing whatever to do with Daniel Gallaway, and that the association with a Mr Gay was in fact, his working relationship with his neighbour, on Trevorva Farm.

One can but only imagine the attitude of a local community towards a mixed marriage in the Victorian era, and particularly in a small rural village in the depths of Cornwall It must have generated a lot of talk, and indeed outright hostility in some quarters; however, the marriage went ahead, despite the sensitivities of some of their neighbours.

The children from the first marriage must also have become the target of cruel jibes, from other children: particularly Frederick Burt, who at this time, seemed to be the only child attending the local school, in 1911. Notwithstanding the social attitudes of the day, the marriage proved to be a success—at least in producing a large family:[941]

---

[939] The accident took place in the Hendrawna cutting, close to Perranporth, on the route of the new railway line (Truro to Newquay). Burt sustained shocking injuries to his head; another team member, Bert Gilbert had a severely crushed leg and foot. Gilbert was taken to the Royal Cornwall Infirmary, at Truro, where he was reported as being: "in a very critical condition". The exact location of the accident was in a field belonging to Mr Harlan Mitchell—*Western Morning News;* Wednesday, September 24th 1901.

[940] Note, the family name is recorded as 'Galaway'; whereas, the previous marriage certificate was in the name of 'Gallaway.'—Another example of the inconsistent approach to name spelling, which can bedevil researchers of a family history.

[941] Courtesy of Paula Bate: great-granddaughter to Daniel Gallaway.

Name:	Birth	Death:	Relationship:	Birthplace:
Frank Christopher Gallaway	1912	—	Son	Probus, Cornwall
Norman Gallaway	1917	—	Son	Probus, Cornwall
Alfred Gallaway	1921	1992	Son	Probus, Cornwall
Violet Gallaway	1924	—	Daughter	Probus, Cornwall

That this family survived financially, on Daniel Gallaway's low wage as an agricultural labourer,[942] is quite remarkable. He must have worked hard all the hours God gave him. But, coupled with his gift of the gab, his personality, and go-getting (typically American) attitude, this undoubtedly helped the family survive. He must have quickly assimilated himself into that small rural society, and had become a popular neighbour (though remaining an exotic figure) in the daily village life. The Gallaway family photograph (see fig. 78) bears testament to a well-nourished and cared for family group.

The birth certificate for his son Frank Christopher (1912) [943] shows his father's occupation as a 'clay labourer' and the family residence was now at Trelion Downs, St Stephens Grampound.[944]

His Methodist church and his God, to whom he swore allegiance on that fearful night in 1898, would serve him well over the intervening years. He must have been exceedingly proud of his family and achievements, here in the UK. All was well with the world, and his life in America seemed a far-off memory, and no longer of great attraction for him.

All good things must come to an end.

Disaster struck for Daniel Gallaway (sometime after the birth of his son Norman in 1917) in a bicycling accident, resulting in a serious head injury. He remained in a coma for two weeks. This was a huge blow, both physically and metaphorically, for him and his family. His luck, that had served him well all these years, had now deserted him.

Those who suffer severe head injury, are often predisposed to a later development of a psychotic condition.[945] Indeed, Daniel Gallaway most likely fell victim to this unfortunate outcome, as personality change, coupled with a tendency towards anger and violent behaviour, led to a general decline in his wellbeing: such that his wife became afraid of him and eventually they parted company. Over the next few years, Daniel Gallaway was in and out of the Redruth Union Workhouse.[946] He did, from time to time, return

---

[942] The average wage for an agricultural worker, at the time, was 60*d.* per week, at a time when £1 = 240*d.*

[943] GRO/BMD: 1912 Q2 – Grampound 5c 195

[944] There were many China clay labourers listed as living in the St Stephens Grampound in the UK census for 1861; http://freepages.genealogy.rootsweb.ancestry.com/~kayhin/61551a.html.

[945] *Schizophrenia-Like Psychosis Following Traumatic Brain Injury*—PERMINDER SACHDEV, M.D., PH.D., FRANZCP, School of Psychiatry, University of New South Wales, Sydney, Australia—*J. Neuropsychiatry Clin. Neurosci.* 13:533—534, November 2001 © 2001 American Psychiatric Press, Inc.

[946] Workhouse Asylums and Lunatic Wards: Several workhouses, however, contained wards exclusively used for lunatics and in some places a separate building (belonging to and administered by the local Poor Law authority) was used exclusively for the lunatics, or as a general hospital with lunatic wards. There was such a ward at the Redruth Union Home. Redruth Poor Law Union was officially formed on 10th June 1837. Its operation was

home, but these reunions were transient and he routinely returned to the workhouse. An examination of Daniel Christopher Gallaway's record for *Admissions and Discharges for the Redruth Poor Union Workhouse* reveals a detailed account of Gallaway's progressive illness, and social interactions (see Appendix 11, p. 456).

He eventually died there in 1939, at the age of sixty-three years.[947] By all accounts, the only family mourner at his funeral was his son Norman.

Daniel Gallaway had had a colourful, eventful, and a mainly charmed life. Were it not for the *Mohegan* disaster, and a claimed association with that event, we would never have been aware of his existence. He would have returned to the USA, and who knows what fate would had in store for him there. Whatever it had to offer, he would have no doubt used all his social skills, upbeat personality, and unfailing opportunism, to get the best out of life for both himself and for those who surrounded him. A sad end for this indefatigable man, whose story we are privileged to share.

His wife, Harriet Emma Gallaway, died nine years later, in the year 1948.[948]

A Daniel Come to Judgment.

While Gallaway's adventures makes for a good storyline, it has to be viewed with a degree of scepticism. Not least that, only one stowaway was ever acknowledged by the representatives for the Atlantic Transport Line, at the Board of Trade enquiry.[949] At no time was any mention made of a black man being encountered on board, or alighting from a lifeboat at Porthoustock beach. Despite the confusion and heightened emotions of that night, such an unusual encounter (for this out-of-the-way hamlet) would surely have remained in the collective memory. It didn't.

Now we have all the known facts, together with the family history, we need to come to a conclusion, as to the association between Daniel Gallaway and the *Mohegan* shipwreck.

The elements of the overall story which can be verified are: the actual shipwreck itself; the eventual appearance of Daniel Gallaway in the county of Cornwall; his marriage to Harriet Emma Burt; his workhouse attendances; and finally, his death. What lacks verification (and conviction), are the events leading up to his marriage.

---

overseen by an elected Board of Guardians, 29 in number, representing its 8 constituent parishes as listed below (figures in brackets indicate numbers of Guardians if more than one): Cornwall: Camborne (5), Gwennap (6), Gwinear (2), Gwithian, Illogan (4), Phillack (3), Redruth (6), Stythians (2). The population falling within the Union at the 1831 UK census had been 38,695 with parishes ranging in size from Gwithian (population 539) to Gwennap (8,539) and Redruth itself (8,191). The average annual poor-rate expenditure for the period 1834—36 had been £8,485 or 4s.5d. per head of the population. The Redruth Union workhouse was built in 1838 at Carn Brea near Redruth. It was designed by George Gilbert Scott and his partner William Bonython Moffatt who were also the architects for other Cornish workhouses in Liskeard, Penzance, St Austell, and St Columb Major. Intended to accommodate 450 inmates, the Poor Law Commissioners authorised the sum of £6,000 on its construction; http://www.workhouses.org.uk/.

[947] Registered during the period Q4 1939 [GRO Ref. No. 5c 589] (see page 444).

[948] Registered during the period Q4 1948 [GRO Ref. No. 7a 231] (see page 444).

[949] The inclusion as a 'crew member' was (in this context) an administrative term; as clearly a stowaway was not a bona-fide passenger, but almost certainly would have be assigned crewing duties, for the duration of the voyage.

Notwithstanding the Gallaway family belief that he was born in America, that remains equivocal. He could well have been born in the UK, and taken on the persona of an American citizen, simply to support a fictitious account of his *Mohegan* adventure. How he appeared in Falmouth still remains a mystery. But, if he had been employed aboard UK ships, then he could well have turned up in Falmouth, *and* at the time of the *Mohegan* incident. Perhaps, he used this opportunity to construct the story of his miraculous redemption, and in declaring his vow never to go to sea again. There were a variety of means a beggar could adopt in persuading a gullible public in helping him. A well-known ploy, at the time, was to pose as a shipwrecked mariner:[950] this could well have been Gallaway's tactic in the circumstance.

There is no official record of Gallaway ever having been associated with either the *Cleopatra* or the *Mohegan* vessels. One has to conclude that Daniel Gallaway was not a crew member aboard either ship. His birthplace could well have been in the UK, and not in America. By chance, he had found himself in Falmouth at around the time of the *Mohegan* disaster, and this being a major event, remained a talking point for some time afterwards. Gallaway would have quickly picked up on this and could have used it to construct a story around his 'association' with that ship. By the time the genuine crew members had left Falmouth (within days of the disaster) Gallaway would have had an exclusive on the story. An opportunist no doubt, but desperate times needed desperate measures. One must have a sneaking regard for the audacity of a disadvantaged man, who against all odds was, nonetheless, able to recognise an opportunity and in promoting his own prospects.

There is the slight possibility of there having been two stowaways aboard the *Mohegan* and with Gallaway, not having been exposed, as such. Naturally, he would have left his hiding place at the time of the disaster and made for the open deck with the others. In the darkness and confusion, it was quite possible that a black man in their presence went entirely unnoticed—there were other more important matters to hand.[951] A quick exit from the scene at Porthoustock beach would have ensured his anonymity to this day.

A Person of colour.

Another point has to be raised here; the ATL organisation was almost certainly operating a colour-bar in a selection for their travelling passengers, though not explicitly so. A passenger, who was a relative of the distinguished and dominant figure in the African-American community (Booker T. Washington [952]) and his family, was refused passage because of his colour. Sadly, given this institutional intolerance, Daniel Gallaway

---

[950] Henry Mayhew and Others. *The London Underworld in the Victorian Period; Authentic First-Person Accounts by Beggars, Thieves and Prostitutes* (Dover Publications, Inc. Minolca, New York, 2005) 368.

[951] Daniel Simons and Christopher Chabris; *The Invisible Gorilla: And Other Ways Our Intuition Deceives Us.* The accompanying video; http://youtube.com/watch?v=vJG698U2Mvo conveys the point; that one sees selectively, and can be totally oblivious to other competing distractions. This is known as inattentional or perceptual blindness and it typically occurs as humans are easily be overloaded with competing stimuli.

[952] Personal communication: Jonathan Kinghorn, *The Atlantic Transport Line, 1881 1931: A History with Details on All Ships.*
Booker T. Washington (1856–1915) was an African-American educator, author, orator, and advisor to Republican presidents. He was the dominant leader in the African-American community in the United States from 1890 to 1915—WikiPedia.

would unlikely have been taken on the crew list by ATL—in case he was encountered by a member of the exclusively white (and mainly racist) passenger list, let alone some equally racist crew members.

A shadowy figure.

On balance, the story of Daniel Gallaway and his association with the *Mohegan* disaster is, at most, tenuous, and while it makes for a good story line, there are considerable misgivings as to its authenticity. A story often changes as it is passed down the successive family generations: misinterpretation, embellishments and with dates, names, and events, all being subject to a distortion in the re-telling. Perhaps Daniel Gallaway wanted his life to be remembered in a more flamboyant way, or that he used the story merely to amuse and captivate an audience. He remains a shadowy figure, particularly in his earlier years, prior to his marriage in 1910.

On reflection, his family must look back at Daniel Galloway's life and achievements with pride—and with some justification. Notwithstanding this author's rather more sceptical view of his story, it is hoped that the family continue to research their colourful relative and perhaps reveal further evidence that supports his version of events.

What can't be cured must be endured.

The whole question of stowaways much exercised the minds of shipping-lines and their sea captains; and it was always exasperating when one (or more) came to light. It was a public declaration of a security failure, on the part of the ship's authorities, and always encumbered them with an additional administration and an unwelcome additional cost pressure for the company. A report here explains the predicament for the authorities, on encountering a stowaway:

> There's a common family myth, or fable, concerning those distant family members who had arrived in countries (foreign to them) as stowaways, aboard a ship Almost all stowaways were detected, identified and recorded either at sea or on arrival at the port destination.
>
> Stowaways have existed since the beginning of sea travel, and over time, rules and regulations have been introduced, in order to formally deal with the situation. When they are found on the high sea, the maritime description is as a "frustrated stowaway". If they are found in territorial waters, they could be escorted ashore and delivered to the requisite authority. Outside territorial waters, the situation becomes the responsibility for the shipping company and that liability, must cover the expense of: transportation, disembarkation and any medical attention, as is necessary, during the trip and on arrival at the port of destination. During the travel it's completely forbidden for a ship to deviate from its route, with the intention of putting a stowaway ashore. Usually, on the discovery of a stowaway, that person was put to work, in order to recompense for the cost of having him on board. After apprehension, the individual is identified, and any documents were then verified. If the documentation is validated, they were registered in the passenger-list, usually as the bottom line, thus designating

their status onboard. A further option was to set them to work the duration of the voyage; in this case the individual is recorded as a "steam crew member". [953]

Since the foundation of the first maritime insurance company (Lloyd's of London, in 1688) an insurance claim made by a shipping company, for the expense incurred by the presence of a stowaway, resulted in rising insurance costs for the industry. This was a powerful incentive for ships' masters to carefully avoid the presence of any stowaway and led to a close watch being made of all valid embarkations and of attendant visitors aboard a ship. Routine searches were made in all the likely places that a stowaway would be obliged to use:

The traditional stowaway techniques adopted were: to hide one's self in a dark place; or obtain a visitor's pass, board the vessel, and neglect to return ashore; or, hidden in a closet, possibly protected by a passenger accomplice. In the case where the stowaway is not protected by a person aboard the ship, the stowaway may be obliged to remain hidden for the duration of the voyage. That would mean enduring many days without food and water, and arriving at the destination in a poor state of health. In this case, before embarking on legal and administrative steps, the authorities must send him to get medical assistance, with all expenses to be covered by the shipping company.

It would have been difficult for a stowaway to arrive at the destination and to leave the ship, without being apprehended. Invariably, ports were carefully monitored, and the passenger/crew arrivals very well controlled. If captains could let them go without being observed by anybody, no doubt they would do it, in order to not incur further cost to the company. Once on dry land, stowaways can formally apply for refuge or asylum, by reason of war, political persecution, or extreme necessity. Frequently, in those cases, the stowaway was accepted by almost all countries, provided that their personal documentation is validated. In the absence of the correct documentation, they would most likely have been repatriated, on the next available ship, of the same shipping line that had brought them to the port.

Almost all the stowaways were male; very few such women were encountered. During the 19th and at the beginning of the 20th century, female stowaways were placed in the custody of a man—either being a relative or a family friend—at the port of destination. Women were never left alone, once apprehended and if pregnant, deportation was not an option.

It is well documented that some of our ancestors (not as much as is generally thought) arrived in foreign ports as stowaways. In America, the Ellis Island database has many instances of stowaways, recorded on their passenger arrival lists, as they were formally regarded as a "passenger".

Nevertheless, the myth of the stowaway is a common occurrence in family histories; almost as common as the myth of the noble ancestor, or of being related with some famous character in history, of the same family name. [954]

Here is an account of a typical exasperation, caused by the discovery of a stowaway aboard ship:

[953] Pablo Briand; GENBRIAND – 25th July 2009.

[954] Ibid.

"I am not given to losing my temper". said one captain to a writer in "Cassell's Magazine" [955] for March, "but I confess that when on one voyage we found that no fewer than fourteen men had managed to stow themselves away below, I felt inclined to give them all a ducking, and said so".

This was a captain of an American liner, a man to whom a stowaway is a perpetual nuisance. Though the strictest watch is kept to his getting on board, it is rare for a trip to be made without one or two specimens of the dead-head fraternity being carried, willy-nilly, free. Of course, this is not done entirely without connivance on the part of somebody on board the ship.

The stokers are not infrequently the guilty parties. With their or others' aid the stowaway gets down into the hold and finds a dark corner in which to secrete himself until the vessel is at sea. If then he is discovered and set to work he does not mind. It is not work he is afraid of, but the being without work, and the bread that accompanies it.

When it is considered what an enormous thing an Atlantic liner is, and how many dark places there are in her vast interior, it is not surprising to hear that scores of men during the course of a year get free passages across the herring-pond in one ship or another—and this though a steamer never leaves a port without a search being made to see that no unauthorised person is on board.

Many are discovered in bunkers and other such places, and, of course, carefully conducted on shore: but not a few manage to elude detection. And, of course, once away from land little is to be feared from discovery.

There is a curious notion prevalent among some sailors; it is that a stowaway is a lucky passenger to carry. Asked once why it was, an old salt answered that he never heard of a ship being lost that had a stowaway on board. Of course, he had an instance in point to relate. It was to the effect that a stowaway was discovered in hiding on an outgoing vessel at the last moment and ejected. Shaking his fist at the captain, the would-be voyager cried: "I'm glad you've turned me out of your rotten ship: neither she nor you will live to see Christmas Day, while I shall". The prophecy proved a true one. The vessel went down within a week of sailing, and only the second officer and a few men were saved.

One wonders how such a superstition arose, if superstition it can be called. Does it arise from the notion—old as the hills—that the unfortunate are ever under the special protection of heaven, and that it is particularly displeasing to the providence that watches over such waifs if anything be done to thwart their wishes? The foolish, the blind, children, and drunkards are proverbially said to be under such peculiar guardianship and care. Perhaps, henceforth, we must add the stowaway to the list.[956]

As to the benefits of having a stowaway aboard one's vessel, one has only to refer to the stowaway aboard the *Mohegan,* and the catastrophe that befell both that unfortunate and the other unlucky victims of that disaster. Perhaps it is this particular exception that proves the rule—though that is not much comfort to those involved.

---

[955] *Cassell's Magazine* was the successor to *Cassell's Illustrated Family Paper*, which was published from 1853 to 1867, becoming *Cassell's Family Magazine* in 1874 and *Cassell's Magazine* in 1897—*WikiPedia.*

[956] *The Weekly Standard and Express* (Blackburn, England); Saturday, 4th March 1899.

CHAPTER 27

The Passenger/Crew Lists for the Steamship *Mohegan*

Better poor on land than rich at sea.

The members of the ship's company and the passengers, usually appear as mere names in a list, with little or no accompanying information relating to their lives and personal histories. Their story continues to speak to us from the 19th century and deserve a voice and a place in the archives of maritime history.:

Baxter, Robert Arthur, Mr

Resident of: Surrey, England.
Outcome: Drowned
GRO/BMD: 1898 Q4 – Helston 5c 119

He was aged 41 years, and a surgeon. His body was taken to Trythance Farm, near St. Keverne. He was the son to the late Robert Gordy Baxter of Hethersett, Reigate, Surrey – in his time a well known architect – and of the late Catherine Jane Baxter, who was the daughter of Manthorpe Daniel Folkard, founder of the famous jeweler and silversmith firm of Folkard & Son, of 29a King's Road, Brighton, England, and who had been the first mayor of that town. At the time of his death he was on his way to Mrs Katherine Dix Lawrence, at Plainfield, N.J., whose son L. P. Lawrence was one his most intimate friends. He was widely travelled and had a reputation as a musician and a linguist. Mr Baxter has paid a visit every autumn to the Lawrences, and on this occasion he took the *Mohegan*, as he desired to avail himself of the longer ocean voyage. Unwittingly, he had contracted himself to a voyage lasting an eternity. He had left a wife and twelve-year-old daughter in England. From papers, found in his possession, he had been living in London, and had a Barclays Bank account.

Blackey, M. James

Resident of: Toronto, Canada
Outcome: Drowned
GRO/BMD: 1898 Q4 – Helston 5c 120

About 42 years of age (recorded as aged 35 years on the death certificate). His body was taken to St. Keverne Church. A buyer, by trade, he worked for MacDonald and Company, the largest dry goods house in Canada, for nineteen years and was held in high esteem by his employer. Mr John MacDonald received a cable message from the Steamship's representative at Falmouth announcing that Mr Blackey's body had been recovered, and asking for instructions. Mr MacDonald immediately contacted Mr Blackey's two brothers, and instructions were wired, 'to return the body to Toronto, Canada.' His embalmed body was so returned. He was married with two children, who with his wife, all of whom survive him. He had been a member of the Erskine Presbyterian Church, and was the leader of the young men's Bible Class.[957]

Bloomingdale, W. J. Mr (also reported as Blowingdale and Bloomberg)

 Resident of: Brooklyn, NY.
Outcome: Saved.

He described the first intimation of the grounding as a 'slight grating noise' and so he went below to continue his dinner. It soon became apparent to him, that the vessel was sinking, and so he made his way to the rigging and climbed up to safety. Making himself comfortable, he remained there until the lifeboat took him aboard, at about 3.00 p.m. the next morning. He was a member of the firm of W. C. Bloomingdale, of No. 95 Broad Street, New York.

---

[957] *The Toronto Star;* 17th October 1898.

Bushnell, Elverda, Miss

Resident of: Mansfield, Ohio
Outcome: Drowned
GRO/BMD: 1898 Q4 – St. Germans 5c 25

She was aged 24 years. Her body was found and eventually returned to America [arriving on November 19th] in the ship *SS Paris*, which itself ran aground on the Lowland rocks, within sight of the *Mohegan*, in the following year of 1899. The casket was accompanied by her brother, Dr William S. Bushnell, from Mansfield, Ohio, who had travelled to Falmouth to search for his sister.

> The recovery of Miss Bushnell's Body—the body of a lady was recovered on Thursday from the sea at Portwrinkle [east of Looe, and in Whitsand Bay]. At about half past six o'clock in the morning, a local fisherman saw the body floating close inshore, and having drawn it in to the beach he called the coastguardsmen, who promptly advised P.C. Davey at Anthony [a nearby village]. The latter examined the deceased and found under the waistband of her dress a gold watch, bearing the name, "Elverda Bushnell". The body was fully dressed, but the features were unrecognisable. In a small bag suspended round the neck by a cord were eighteen American notes, two for 100 dollars each, four for five dollars, nine for two dollars, and three for one dollar. There were three gold and diamond rings on her fingers. The silver clasps of the garters bore a monogram "E.B". The deceased is that of Dr Bushnell's sister, who was a passenger on the ill-fated *Mohegan*, and for the recovery of whose body a reward of £20 has been offered. Superintendent Philp, to whom the matter was reported, at once telegraphed particulars to Messrs. Fox and Co., at Falmouth. On the body of the lady found at Portwrinkle were discovered in a bag on her breast 242 dollars in green-backs, six unset stones, and three gold rings, also a gold double-case watch, which stopped at 8.10 p.m. She also had a gold brooch, on which was the word, "Seymore". [958]

An announcement of the death of Miss Bushnell appeared in her hometown newspapers:

> Bushnell, Elverda—The body of Miss Elverda Bushnell, daughter of Mr & Mrs M. B. Bushnell, has been found after many days. During the past 48 hours Mr Bushnell has been in receipt of cable messages from his son, Dr William S. Bushnell and also dispatches from Dr Albert Shunk, of New York, which were preparatory in a measure to the one received by Mr Bushnell at 7:30 o'clock this morning. The cable explains itself and reads as follows:
>
> > "Lizard, Nov. 4—Elverda been identified. / Will take time to arrange matters. / Start for home next week. / May not get her to Southampton for several days."–*Mansfield Semi-Weekly News;* 08 November 1898.
>
> Bushnell, Elverda—M. B. Bushnell is in receipt of a cablegram from his son, D. William Bushnell, dated at Southampton, England, in which he says that he will sail for home on the "City of Paris" of the American line, Saturday, Nov. 12, bringing with him the body of his sister, Miss Elverda Bushnell. The "City of Paris" [959] is due to arrive in New York, Nov. 19, and Dr. Bushnell will bring the body direct from New York home.–*Mansfield Semi-Weekly News;* 11 November 1898.
>
> The remains of Miss Elverda Bushnell arrived here Monday evening, accompanied by her brother, Dr William Bushnell. Miss Bushnell was one of the many unfortunates who went down with the ship *Mohegan,* which was wrecked not far from Falmouth, England, October 13th [*sic*]. Miss Bushnell is the daughter of Mr and Mrs. Martin B. Bushnell. She leaves besides her parents, brothers William, Fred and Charles. Her sister, Irene died January 17, 1890. – *Richland Shield and Banner* – November 22nd 1898.
>
> She was buried in her hometown on the 21st November, 1898.

Cordary, Mr (also reported as Cordery and Cardery)

Resident of: Not known
Outcome: Drowned

Cowan, Helena Mary, Miss (also reported as Cohen, Miss)

Resident of: Westburn Drive, Cambuslang, Glasgow.
Outcome: Drowned
GRO/BMD: 1898 Q4 – Helston 5c 120

She was aged 27 years and the sister to Mr Herbert Francis Cowan [q.v.]. She was buried anongside him at Budock Church, Cornwall.

---

[958] *Royal Cornwall Gazette;* 10th November 1898.

[959] The *City of Paris* was herself grounded near the Manacles the following year. She was eventually dragged off the rocks by tugs and survived.

Cowan, Herbert Francis, Mr

Resident of: 28, Adamson Road, Hampstead, NW3.
Outcome: Drowned
GRO/BMD: 1898 Q4 – Helston 5c 133

He was the brother to Miss Helena Mary Cowan [q.v.] and was aged 24 years. His body was landed at Porthoustock, and later buried at Budock Church, on the 19th October. The funeral was taken by Rev. C. A. Walker, Chaplain to the Seaman's Mission, Falmouth. He was the second son to Thomas W. and Fanny Cowan [960] – Hampstead, London.[961] Herbert and his sister Helena were on the way to their brother Alexander, who was a fruit farmer [962] in Loomis, Placer County, California. Their parents also planned to leave for Loomis—via New York—by ship from Liverpool, as a permanent move to California, and their two children had sailed from London, as they were anxious to go ahead of their parents. The *Mohegan* was their ship of choice. Following the funeral at St. Budock, the parents returned to Liverpool to embark on the *ss Etruria* for California. Thomas Cowan, his wife and Edith their unmarried daughter, returned in 1906 to their retirement in Taunton, Somerset.

Herbert and Helena Cowan's gravestone has the following epitaph:

"Death is Swallowed up in Victory"

Sacred to the memory of Helena Mary Cowan

Aged 27 years
And
Herbert Francis Cowan Aged 24 years
Both Born at Horsham Sussex

Who were the taken home in the wreck of the Mohegan on Oct[R] 14TH 1898 On the Manacles Near this spot.

"Underneath Are the Everlasting Arms"

"This is the Victory that Overcometh The World Even Our Faith"

Their parents donated a boat, in memory of their lost children:

The sailing boat *Victoria,* belonging to the Mission to Seamen [963] at Falmouth, has been replaced by one a little larger, given by Mr T. W. Cowan in memory of Helena Mary, and Herbert Francis Cowan, drowned in the wreck of the *Mohegan* on the Manacle Rocks, October 14th 1898. The boat has been named the *Victory*, to commemorate the victorious faith of the departed ones. The vessel is clinker built, copper fastened, and yawl rigged, and has several large lockers for the storage of Bibles, prayer-books, and literature.[964]

---

[960] Thomas W. Cowan F.L.S., F.G.S., F.R.M.S., F.E.S., D.Sc., Ph.D. (Hon.), was born in Russia. The family returned to England at the outbreak of the Crimean war. He was a wealthy individual (married to Fanny, who had the poet Percy Bysshe Shelley as a member in her family-tree) and was a leading figure in the *British BeeKeeping Association* (BBKA) for fifty years. He was both proprietor and editor of the *British Bee Journal*. His practical knowledge, influence and sheer drive, coupled with financial means and leisure time, were instrumental in enabling him to move the craft forward; not only in the UK., but also in the new world. Courtesy: David Charles, Editor of *BBK News*.

[961] *The Morning Post* – London, 20th October 1898.

[962] In the early part of the 20th century, Loomis was the second largest fruit-shipping station in Placer County.

[963] The Mission to Seafarers (formerly, The Mission to Seamen) is an international not-for-profit charity serving sailors in over 230 ports around the world. It is supported entirely by donations from the public, whose generosity has funded its work for more than a century and a half. Its formal creation was in 1856 through the Church of England although the Mission had its roots in the earlier work of an Anglican priest, John Ashley, who in 1835 was on the shore at Clevedon with his son who asked him how the people on Flat Holm (an island lying in the Bristol Channel) could go to church. For the next three months Ashley voluntarily ministered to the population of the island. From there he recognised the needs of the seafarers on the four hundred sailing vessels in the Bristol Channel and created the Bristol Channel Mission. He raised funds and in 1839 a specially designed mission cutter was built with a main cabin which could be converted into a chapel for 100 people—*WikiPedia*.

[964] *The Royal Cornwall Gazette Falmouth Packet, Cornish Weekly News, & General Advertiser*; Thursday, 20th July 1899.

Crane, Sophie Cass, Mrs (also reported as Sophia Cass Hall—her maiden name)

Resident of: Detroit, MI. (and also reported as California, Santa Cruz)
Outcome: Drowned

Her body was embalmed and returned to New York. She was the wealthy widow of Mr Alfred C. Crane. She was also the brother to the Revd. F. A. Hall, a clergyman of Westfield New York. He stated that he had left his sister in London, four weeks ago and at this time, he was in no doubt that she was aboard the *Mohegan,* as she was to have sailed at about that time. Both brother and sister had been travelling together in England since July 1st. He had left England and she was to have stayed a further four weeks and was bound for her home in San Francisco—*The San Francisco Call;* October 17th, 1898.

She was mother to Mrs Wallace R. Farrington, a newspaper editor in Honolula.
Mrs Crane's death announcement appeared in her local newspaper:

> . . . friends are invited to attend the funeral services at the residence of her sister, Mrs. Stephen G. Nye, 692 Twenty-fourth street, Oakland, this day (Sunday) at 3 o'clock. Interment at Santa Cruz Monday, November 14, at 12 o'clock, on the arrival of the narrow-gauge train. Friends are also invited to the burial service.[965]

Duncan, Charles Joseph, Mr.

Resident of: Sacramento, CA. c/o Messrs. Allen Bros. Co. (address unknown).
Outcome: Drowned
GRO/BMD: 1898 Q4 – Helston 5c 120

He was aged 70 years and had been variously described as a financier, mining engineer, and as an accused swindler. Duncan was at the head of the San Francisco's Safe Deposit Savings and Loans Society, in early days when that institution failed, after accumulating several million dollars from credulous depositors. He played an integral part in this 1877 banking collapse. After the failure of the bank, Duncan dabbled in mines and later went to Los Angeles, where he made $100,000 in real estate deals. He lost this in other speculations and again entered the mining business, in which business he was engaged at the time of his death. He was reputed to be very wealthy.[966]

He was the father to Isadora Duncan, the famous, avant-garde dancer. His body was recovered on 18th October and was buried at the St. Keverne churchyard, in the mass grave on the same day.

Duncan, Mary, Mrs

Resident of: Sacramento, CA.
Outcome: Drowned
GRO/BMD: 1898 Q4 – Helston 5c 120

She was the third wife of Mr Charles Duncan [q.v.]. Her body was recovered on 18th October and buried at St. Keverne churchyard, in the mass grave, on the same day.

Duncan, Rosa, Miss (also reported as Duncan, Roza)

Resident of: Sacramento, CA.
Outcome: Drowned
GRO/BMD: 1898 Q4 – Helston 5c 120
She was aged 12 years and daughter to Mr and Mrs Charles Duncan [q.v.]. Her body was recovered on 18th October and buried on the same day at St. Keverne churchyard, in the mass grave.

Elliott, Ellen, Miss

Resident of: Elstree, Hertsfordshire, England
Last Place of Abode: Alfriston, Sussex
Outcome: Drowned
GRO/BMD: 1898 Q4 – Falmouth 5c 102

---

[965] The *San Francisco Call*; November 13th 1898.

[966] *The Herald* (Los Angeles – Calif.); October 21st 1898.

She was aged 21 years and the maid in Mrs Thomas Worthington King's service. She was reported as the only British passenger on board. Her body was recovered on the 18th October at Maenporth, Falmouth, and her funeral took place at Budock, in Cornwall. Her parents, from Hertsfordshire, and Mr Thomas Worthington King's valet, Mr Joseph O'Rourke, were in attendance. The cortege started from the premises of Mr H. Liddicoat, who with Mr Valentine Coryn and others attended the interment. The Rev. W. H. Hodge, vicar at Budock, officiated.

Fallows, John S., Dr

Resident of: Columbus, GA.
Outcome: Drowned
GRO/BMD: 1898 Q4 – Falmouth 5c 101

He was aged 35 years and was unmarried. He was the son of Mr Joseph S. Fallows of London, Ontario. He came from a medical family in the Midlands and first studied in Queens College, Birmingham, and then passed on to the Middlesex Hospital and completed his education at the Edinburgh University, where he received his diploma in 1890. He commenced practice in London (England), at 2, Princes Mansion, 66, Victoria Street. Mr Fallows was late clinical assistant in the Eye Department (out-patients) at the German Hospital; he was the extra-mural house-surgeon at the Ear Hospital, Soho Square, and was a Licentiate of the Society of Apothecaries. He was the personal doctor to another passenger, Mrs Compton Swift, and he was attending her on the voyage to New York. He had been resident in London for the past 10 years, having spent his early years in Woodstock [Ontario], and travelled extensively in South America, before settling in London, to practice medicine. He was a specialist in skin diseases, and had patients in St. Petersburgh, New York, and elsewhere.

His body was recovered at Durgan, at the entrance to the Helford River, on the 16th October, and he was buried in his grandfather's vault at Kensal, London, England. Both his and Mrs Compton Swift's voyage tickets were found on his body.

The Woodstock Sentinel Review reported that:

A gloom has been cast over the vicinity in learning of the very sad drowning. Much sympathy is felt throughout the community for the bereaved parents, and his only brother Howard S. Fallows.

The Fallows' family, recorded in the Cemetery Index for the West Missouri Township in Middlesex County, Ontario, refers to the family tombstone and an inscription contained thereon reads:

In Memory of John Fallows, aged 35 years, who was lost in the wreck of the S.S. *Mohegan off Cornwall, England, November [sic] 14th 1898. Interred at Kensal, England.*

During the month following his death, his effects were put up for auction in London:

Sales During the Current Week.

Mr. J. C. STEVENS will SELL BY AUCTION, at his Great Rooms, 38, King-street,

Covent Gardens, as follows, at Half-past Twelve precisely each day :—

Friday.—Surgical Apparatus, Household Furniture, and other Effects of the late Dr.

Fallow: also Cameras and Lenses, Lanterns and Slides. &c.

On view mornings of sale and catalogues had.[967]

Fenton, Florence Maria, Mrs

Resident of: Not known
Last Place of Abode: 6 Woodlands Rd., Ilford, Essex.
Outcome: Drowned
GRO/BMD: 1898 Q4 – Helston 5c 119

Buried at the Falmouth (Old) Cemetery, Swanpool, Cornwall (Plot No. J C 39). The inscription on the headstone reads:

---

[967] *The Standard* (London, England); Monday, 28th November 1898.

IHS [968]

In Loving Memory of

Florence Marie Fenton

Who lost her life in Wreck of Mohegan

Oct 14 1898 Aged 41 Years

Thy Will Be Done

Fireng, Bessie May, Miss (also reported as Fireing and Firing)

Resident of: Boston, MA.
Outcome: Drowned
GRO/BMD: 1898 Q4 – Helston 5c 121

She was aged 25 years and was holidaying in Europe with her mother, Mrs E.V. Fireng [q.v.]. Because of a delay in receiving some articles of clothing they had purchased, they had cancelled their tickcts on the steamer *La Bourgogne*, deciding to return home later, on the *Mohegan.* Their remains were cremated at Woking, Surrey.[969]

Fireng, E. V., Mrs (also reported as Mr J. H. Fireing and Firing)

Resident of: New York, NJ.
Outcome: Drowned
GRO/BMD: 1898 Q4 – Falmouth 5c 102

She was aged 55 years, the wife of John Phelps Fireng, chief clerk to the Paymaster of the US Navy, and of Glen Ridge, New Jersey, who was given 30 days leave of absence and permission to leave America, by the USA Secretary Long. Her remains were cremated at Woking, Surrey. The ashes of both mother and daughter were accompanied back to America by the husband of the deceased, and by Mr G. Oakes; both of whom had made a special journey from America, after the foundering of the *Mohegan*. Her husband later made a donation of £50 to the Royal Sailors' Home, Falmouth, as a contribution to its improvement-fund.[970]

Fraser, Mary, Mrs (also reported as Frazer)

Resident of: Marion, IA.
Last Place of Abode: c/o G. W. Wheatley & Co., London.
Outcome: Drowned
GRO/BMD: 1898 Q4 – Falmouth 5c 102

She was aged about 34 years and her death occurred on returning from a holiday in England with her niece, Miss Susan Shepherd [q.v.], who also perished. Her body was recovered on the 19th October. She was buried at St. Mary's, Biscovey, near St. Blazey, Cornwall, on the Sunday afternoon, of 23rd October, 1898, where the churchyard was crowded with mourners. The body had been brought from Falmouth by train. The funeral was attended by Mr and Mrs F. Lukes, from Par, and Miss Lukes, all friends of the deceased lady. The service was assisted by the Rev. D. R. Vaughan, assisted by the Rev. A. H. Cook, of Redruth. The coffin was borne to the grave by the employees of Mr Frederick W. Lukes, at the Beaver Mills, Par (UK census 1901–Par Green, Tywardreath, Cornwall). It would be sadly ironic had Miss Fraser visited her friends in Par; indeed, even had worshiped here in St. Mary's church, only to find herself buried there, in a short while. No headstone has been found for her in this churchyard.

She once resided in Woodstock Ontario, where her father was the dispatcher of for the Grand Trunk railway station, and she was the sister to Mr. S. W. Fraser.[971]

---

[968] The inscription *Iesus Hominum Salvator;* translates as *Jesus Saviour of men.*

[969] The first crematoria in Europe were built in 1878 in Woking, England and in Gotha, Germany.

[970] Information derived from the Home's Annual Statement of Accounts, for the year 1898, held by the Cornish Records Office (Ref J/2187).

[971] *The San Francisco Call;* October 17, 1898. "Toledo, Oct., 16. Her brother, Mr S. W. Fraser, a well-known Toledo attorney, had received word that his sister, Mrs. Mary Fraser of Marion, Ind., was aboard the ill-fated steamer *Mohegan.* "

Fuller, Benjamin Franklin, Mr

Resident of: Boston, MA.
Outcome: Drowned
GRO/BMD: 1898 Q4 – Helston 5c 120

He was aged 76 years and was an importer by trade. His body was recovered at Coverack and buried, separately to the mass burial site, at St. Keverne on the 19th October. His headstone reads:

In Loving memory of Benjamin Franklin Fuller of Boston Massachusetts, USA. Born March 25th. 1823.

Drowned at the wreck of the s.s. Mohegan October 14th. 1898.

Hopeful, Loving and Faithful.

He had been engaged on business in London, England for forty years. He was described as an American importer, in the St. Keverne burial register. He was found to have in his possession, some valuable bonds. His favourite sports were hunting and fishing, and was probably returning to participate in these activities, in the forests of Maine. In the 1860 Boston Census, he was recorded as a lumber merchant, and living with his wife Mary, and three children.

Grandin, Lizzie Small, Mrs

Resident of: Jamestown, New York
Outcome: Died of an accidental axe injury, shock and massive haemorrhage.
GRO/BMD: 1898 Q4 – Helston 5c 119

She was aged 52 years (?) (1842–1898) and was Maude Small Roudebush's [q.v.] mother and the widow of Samuel Grandin, an oil merchant. She had broken both legs and had fallen overboard. The life-boatman, named Tripp, at once jumped from the lifeboat and succeeded in saving the lady. This act of heroism was unfortunately fruitless, for the lady died of shock before reaching the shore: following an accidental axe injury, during its use in the release of an adjacent passenger in the boat, Amelia Compton Swift [q.v.]. This incident was not listed as a contributory factor on the death certificate; even though it was the most likely cause of death. She was embalmed and returned to New York.

The remains of Mrs. L. S. Grandin, who lost her life in the wreck of the Mohegan, arrived in Meadville from New York today. Interment took place immediately in Greendale Cemetery.[972]

Grumbrecht, Amelia (Millie), Mrs (also reported as Gumbrecht)

Resident of: Stamford, CT.
Outcome: Her death was recorded in the Account of Crew document as, 'from shock after being rescued.'
GRO/BMD: 1898 Q4 – Helston 5c 121

She was aged 35 years. Her body was recovered on the 19th October. She was the daughter of another passenger, Mr F. W. Lockwood [q.v.]. Her finger rings had been taken by persons unknown.

Harrington, A. H., Mr (also reported as Harrington, Mr A. W.)

Resident of: Germantown, PA.
Outcome: Drowned
GRO/BMD: 1898 Q4 – Helston 5c 119

Hart, Hannah (Anne), Mrs (also reported as Miss Hannah F. Hart)

Resident of: New York, NJ.
Outcome: Drowned

She was aged about 48 years. G. C. Fox & Co. shipping agent for the Atlantic Transport Company had issued a bounty of a £10 reward to the finder of the body of Miss Hannah Hart. She was the daughter of the late Henry L. Hart of New York, and the step-daughter to another victim, Mr Henry Morrison Jr. [q.v.]. She was well known for her missionary work among the poor of New York.

---

[972] *Advance Argus;* 10th November 1898; Greendale Cemetery, Meadville, Crawford County, Pennsylvania, USA. Plot: Sec. 4; Lot 15

Hyslop, John S. (also reported as Hislop, John)

Nationality/Birth Place: Wigan Lancashire.
Resident of: New York, NJ.
Outcome: Saved

He was aged 64 years. He managed to climb into the ship's rigging, where he was saved by the lifeboat, the following morning. He had emigrated earlier in his life, to live in New York and became a renowned Yacht Measurer: a role he played for 19 years, 17 years of which were with the New York Yacht Club.

At a meeting of the Society of Naval Architects Rold's Annual Session, Mr John Hyslop presented a paper, entitled: *Suggestions as to Improved Appliances for Launching Ships' Boats.*[973] No doubt his paper arose from his terrifying experience aboard the *Mohegan* and with his personally witnessing the debacle surrounding the launch of her lifeboats, on the night of the disaster.

He had taken part in many international yacht races for many years, and died in his adopted New York, in the year 1919. He left a deposition, as evidence for the Board of Trade inquiry, before a justice of the peace in Lancashire. It was declared inadmissible by the inquiry and was never made public.

Kelly, Richard, Mr (also reported as Kelley, Mr Richard)

Resident of: Not known
Outcome: Saved

Mr. Kelly attended the initial coroner's inquest and at the following Board of Trade inquiry as a witness. He failed to attend the resumption of the coroner's inquest. He had survived the catastrophe by climbing into the rigging and later saved by the Porthoustock lifeboat, *Charlotte*.

King, Thomas Worthington, Mr

Resident of: Saratoga, New York
Outcome: Drowned
GRO/BMD: 1898 Q4 – Helston 5c 119

He was aged 47 years His wife and sons Rufus and Anthony [q.v.] were also drowned. The family had a summer residence at Carbis, North Cornwall, where they had befriended their neighbours, Mr and Mrs Cornish. The description, in the London dispatch of T. W. King as [being] a newspaper proprietor[974] at Nantucket, Mass., is probably erroneous. Inquiry shows that the proprietors of the local papers in Nantucket and its vicinity bear other names.[975] In Boston newspaper circles Mr King's name is unfamiliar. Probably he was a wealthy summer resident at Nantucket (Siasconset).[976]

Mr Thomas Worthington King was the grandson of the celebrated Govenor of Ohio, Thomas Worthington, and the great-grandson of Rufus King, twice Minister to England [*Envoy Extraordinary and Minister Plenipotentiary;* May 1825] and first appointed by Washington.[977]

In St. Keverne Church, the bell No, 7 was placed in the tower by William Neil King of Ohio. It was donated in memory of his brother, Thomas Worthington King, and the inscription reads:

> *In Memory Of The Family Of Thomas Worthington King. Formerly Of Cincinnati Ohio U.S.A.*
> *All Lost On The Mohegan. October 14, 1898. "God's Word Receive, His Truth Believe".*

There is a memorial plaque for the family, placed at the Spring Grove Cemetery Ohio, and reads:[978]

---

[973] *Duluth News-Tribune;* May 27th 1899.

[974] Charles G. Rich, a Boston theatrical manager, said today that T. W. King, was a well-known summer resident of Siasconset, Nantucket. Mr Rich was a neighbour of Mr King on that island and knew him well. Mr King had one of the finest places on the Siasconset section of the island. The family usually spent the winters at the Fifth Avenue Hotel, New York. He inherited a large legacy from his mother and had no regular business. He employed himself occasionally in writing short stories, and exciting novels of Western life. This, Mr Rich thinks, accounts for the statement that he was a newspaper man. The family spent the last two seasons in England. Mr Rich supposes that Mr King must have been called to this country [USA] by some business in connection with his mother's estate.

[975] Mr King was associated with newspapers as he was a former Chillicothe (Missouri, USA) newspaper man. *The News-Herald.*, October 20, 1898.

[976] *Democrat Chronicle; –* Rochester N.Y., 17th October 1898.

[977] *The New York Times;* 19th October 1898.

IN MEMORIAM
THOMAS WORTHINGTON KING,
BORN DECEMBER 9, 1850;
HIS WIFE GERTUDE WELLER KING,
BORN JANUARY 27, 1865;
AND THEIR TWO SONS,
RUFUS BORN OCTOBER 12, 1887;
AND WORTHINGTON, BORN JUNE 25, 1893;
WERE ALL LOST IN THE WRECK OF
THE STEAMSHIP MOHEGAN AT
THE MANACLES, OFF
CORNWALL ENGLAND,
OCTOBER 14, 1898.

King, Gertrude Weller, Mrs

Resident of: Saratoga, New York
Outcome: Drowned

She was aged 33 years. Mrs King's body, and those of her mother, Mrs Weller and little boy, had been embalmed and were lying at the Masonic-Hall, Penzance, awaiting return to America.

King, Rufus, Master

Resident of: Saratoga, New York
Outcome: Drowned

He was aged 11 years and was the eldest son to the King couple [q.v.]. The body of one or other of the sons was recovered, embalmed and returned to America.

King, Anthony, Master

Resident of: Saratoga, New York
Outcome: Drowned
GRO/BMD: 1898 Q4 – Helston 5c 119

He was aged 7 years and was the younger son to the King couple [q.v.]. The body of one or other of the sons was recovered, embalmed and returned to America.

Kipling, Richard A. Mr

Resident of: Paris, France
Outcome: Drowned
GRO/BMD: 1898 Q4 – Falmouth

He was aged 50 years. His body was found in Falmouth Bay On Thursday evening [20th October] by a boatman named Scantlebury.[979] A diamond merchant, he had left the town of Elizabeth, New Jersey, some 50 years before. He had left his wife and family in France and was visiting his elderly parents (his father was Mr Richard Kipling), in Roselle – a suburb of Elizabeth NJ. At first there was a suggestion that he was the author, Rudyard Kipling, but it was later denied.

Le Lacheur, John Guille, Master

Resident of: Guernsey
Outcome: Drowned

[978] Spring Grove Cemetery: 4521 Spring Grove Avenue Cincinnati, Ohio 45232, United States. A photograph of the memorial and of the two headstones may be seen here; http://flickr.com/photos/professormassa/5670989720/. The two graves mark the family plot for the extended King family.

[979] *Royal Cornwall Gazette;* 10th November, 1898.

GRO/BMD: 1898 Q4 – Falmouth 5c 102.

He was aged 7 years. The bodies of Mrs Le Lacheur and her little boy were dispatched from the Falmouth Sailors' Home to Jersey, via Weymouth. Lloyd's Gazette reported on the 19th October that: the body of a little boy Le Lacheur was identified by the Sheriff of Guernsey, Mr. H. C. Manger.

Le Lacheur, John Guille, Mr

Resident of: Guernsey
Outcome: Drowned
GRO/BMD: 1898 Q4 – Kingsbridge 5b 121

He was aged 46 years and the Managing Director for the Gilly-Alles Library, Guernsey. He formerly lived in Mount Vernon, New York. The family was on its way to visit his nephew, at Grandview on the Hudson River. The Mr D. S. Hubbell and his wife of 238 South Sixth Avenue, Mount Vernon, called at the New York company office to enquire after the Lacheur family. His body was recovered at Kingsbridge, South Devon.

Le Lacheur, Alice Maria, Mrs

Resident of: Guernsey
Outcome: Drowned
GRO/BMD: 1898 Q4 – Helston 5c 121

The bodies of Mrs Le Lacheur and her little boy were dispatched from the Sailors' Home [Falmouth] to Jersey, via Weymouth. The headstone at the Foulon cemetery, St. Peter Port, Guernsey reads:

> *In loving memory of John Isaac Le Lacheur, managing director of the Guille Alles Library aged 46 years. Also his wife Alice*
> *M. Renier aged 43 and their only child John Guille aged 6 who all perished off the Cornish coast on the 14th. of October 1898.*
> *John Le Lacheur, father of the aforesaid, was master of the America who died at sea on 19th. October 1857 aged 41 years.*

Lockwood, Frederick W., Mr (also reported as Lockwood, Frederick Weed)

Resident of: Stamford, CT.
Last Place of Abode: Royal Hotel, Blackfriars, London. EC.
Outcome: Drowned

He was aged about 65 years and was employed as the foreign representative of the Standard Oil Corporation, and was an inventor of many valuable aids for the transportation of oils in tropical countries and was said to be worth $500,000.[980] His office was at 81 New Street, Stamford, and had been in business with his brother George Lockwood. He was an excellent sailor, the owner of a schooner yacht *Nera* and a member of the New York Yacht Club. He was the father of another passenger, Mrs Amelia Grumbretch [q.v.]. His body was found six or seven weeks after the disaster, by a St. Keverne man – Billy Matthews.

Mr Lockwood's residence was sold to a tobacco company magnate:

> STAMFORD, Conn., June 8,—J. B. Cobb, First Vice President of the American Tobacco Company, has just purchased at a
> sum said to be about $75,000, of a handsome mansion of the late Frederick Lockwood, a Standard Oil magnate, who was
> drowned a few years ago while making a translantic trip. The residence is on Strawberry Hill, the fashionable section of
> the town, and is one of the finest in the vicinity. It is understood that Mr. Cobb is to make it his permanent home.[981]

Luke, Loren M., Mr (also reported as Fluke, Mrs Loren M.)

Resident of: Wyoming Avenue, Kingston, PA.
Outcome: Drowned
GRO/BMD: 1898 Q4 – Helston 5c 121

---

[980] This sum of $500,000 converts to £105,000 in today's currency.

[981] *The New York Times;* 9th June 1901

He was aged 26 years and had been a graduate of Princeton University in the class of '93. A newspaper report describes the arrival of his body in the USA:

> The bodies of Mr & Mrs Loren M. LUKE, of Kingston, who perished at sea while returning on the *Mohegan* from a European trip, arrived in Wilkes Barre Tuesday night on the Lehigh Valley train. The remains were accompanied from NY by Peter MILLS, of Nanticoke, an uncle of Mr LUKE and Robert P. BRODHEAD, Mrs LUKE's brother-in-law.[982]

An obituary appeared in *The Daily Princetonian;* October 19th, 1898:

> Princton has lost a well-known aluminus Loren M. Luke. Mr. Luke and his wife went abroad last August, immediately following the death of their only son. Mr. Luke was born in Nanticoke, Pa., about thirty years ago and entered Princton in 1890. After graduation, Mr. Luke (Attorney) studied law in Kingston, Pa., and was admitted to the Bar in December, 1894. Two years later, in November, he was married to Miss Emily Loveland. They leave a host of sorrowing friends and relatives in Wyoming Valley.

Luke, Emily, Mrs

Resident of: Kingston, PA.
Outcome: Drowned

She was the wife of Mr Loren M. Luke (q.v.).

Merryweather, E. M., Miss

Resident of: Cincinnati, OH
Last Place of Abode: 38, Mayfield Road, Hansworth, Birmingham.
Outcome: Drowned

Morrison, Henry, Jr., Mr

Resident of: New York New Jersey
Outcome: Drowned

He was aged 42 years. G. C. Fox & Co., agents of the Atlantic Transport Company, had issued a bounty of £10 reward to the finder of the body of Henry Morrison – there was no taker He was the son of Mr Henry Morrison, a well-known lawyer of 223, West 78th. Street, New York and was himself a retired lawyer and was unmarried.

Noble, Katherine (also recorded as Noble, Katie Bell)

Resident of: Baltimore MD.
Outcome: Saved

O'Neill, David J., Rev. (also reported as Mr W. J. O'Neill)

Resident of: Germantown, PA.
Outcome: Drowned

He was a Presbyterian minister of Germantown, aged about 35 years, and had been ordained for about 4 years. He had been on a three month vacation with a friend, probably M. A. H. Harrington [q.v.]. He was unmarried and lived with his mother.

O'Rorke, Joseph, Mr (also reported as Mr Joseph O'Rourke)

Resident of: Saratoga, NY.
Outcome: Saved

He was Mr Thomas Worthington King's valet. O'Rorke was on deck with the two King boys, who were told to look out for Penzance, where Mr Cornish lived (the family had stayed at his summer home in Carbis Bay, Cornwall).

As the ship struck, he heard Mr King telling his family, in the salon, to "keep cool". [983] The family all perished. O'Rourke stayed in the ship's rigging, until plucked to safety at 8.00 p.m., the next day. He was despatched to St. Keverne, to identify the King family, and to accompany their bodies back to the USA.

---

[982] Newspaper Extractions: Meshoppen Enterprise, Wyoming County, PA – 1st October 1897–30th May 1901.

[983] *The Bristol Mercury and Daily Post;* Friday, 11th November 1898.

Pemberton, Francis W., Mr

Resident of: New York, NY.
Outcome: Saved

He was saved from a almost swamped ship's lifeboat by the Porthoustock lifeboat. He was a banker son of the Confederate General, John C. Pemberton. He met William Gibb McAdoo and together they formed a firm, Pemberton and McAdoo, to sell investment securities, based in Wall Street NY. He later sent a £50 donation to the Porthoustock Lifeboat crew. The family lived at 24, West Eighty-fifth Street, New York. He left a deposition with the United States Consulate in Southampton, as evidence for the Board of Trade inquiry. It was declared inadmissible by the inquiry and was never made public.

Pemberton, F. W., Mrs

Resident of: New York, NY.
Outcome: Saved.

She was the wife of Mr Francis W. Pemberton [q.v.] and she was saved from a *Mohegan*'s lifeboat.

Pemberton, Francis R., Master

Resident of: New York, NY.
Outcome: Saved

He was aged 5 years and was a son to the Pemberton family [q.v.] and he was saved from a *Mohegan*'s lifeboat

Pemberton, Clifford John, Master

Resident of: New York, NY.
Outcome: Saved

He was aged 4 years and was a son to the Pemberton family [q.v.] and he was saved from a *Mohegan*'s lifeboat

Reyen, Miss (also reported as Regan and Ryan)

Resident of: New York, NY.
Outcome: Saved

She was a French governess (also referred to as a 'nurse') to the Pemberton family [q.v.].

Roudebush, Maude Small, Miss (also reported as Miss Maud Rounds)

Resident of: Meadville, PA.
Outcome: Saved

She was a professional singer (soprano) whose stage name was Maude Roudez. Her father died and her mother married Mr J. J. Grandin. She had been in the UK for six years. She studied at the Paris Conservatoire and sang in the Metropolitan Opera House, New York, Paris, and London. She was returning to the Metropolitan Opera House to take up a new engagement. A relative received a telegram from, Miss Roudebush, stating: "*Ship wrecked / Mother* [*Grandin, Lizzie Small*] *dead / I am alrig*ht".

She was saved from under the upturned ship's lifeboat. Following the disaster, she returned to New York from Liverpool, on the ship *Etruria*, leaving the UK on October 22nd, 1898. The death certificate for her mother recorded a drowning, as the cause of death. She more likely died of trauma, following an accidental axe injury, sustained during her recovery by the lifeboat crew. Miss Roudebush's address was recorded on the certificate as: 34 Trebovir Road, Earles [*sic*] Court, London.

Mrs. Maud Roudebush Barling, an 1887 graduate of Allegheny College, studied music in Paris and sang there in Grand Opera. She was engaged for a time in concert work in New York. She was married in 1907 to Wilard W. Barling.[984] She died in Oct. 1946.

---

[984] Smith, Ernest Ashton, Allegheny: A Century of Education, 1815–1915, Meadville, Pa., 1916.

Saunders, Emily Mogg, Miss

Resident of: 22 Belsize Road, South Hampstead, London
Outcome: Drowned
GRO/BMD: 1898 Q1 – Helston 5c 136

She was aged 54 year and was the 'grey-haired lady' who was taken to St. Keverne Church. She was identified by the initials *E. S.* on her vest. She was buried at the St. Keverne churchyard on the 20th October and her grave is alongside the path, directly opposite the North door of the church. The headstone reads:

> "In loving memory of Emily M. Saunders who passed away in the
> wreck of the Mohegan on the night of October, 14th. 1898 aged 53 years.
> *"My trust is in the tender mercy of the Lord for ever and ever"*.

The Revd. H. Newton, Bedford, who was conducting a fortnight's mission, for the parish church at Matlock, Bath, left there on Monday for Falmouth, in consequence of his sister-in-law, Miss Saunders, being one of the passengers lost in the *Mohegan* disaster. The mission, as a result, has been abandoned.[985]

At the following anniversary of her death, the same in-memoriam piece appeared in a newspaper: [986]

Her *In Memoriam* card showed that she was a religious lady, who was greatly respected:

IN MEMORIAM
───────

Drowned upon October 14th, 1898, in the wreck of the Steamship "Mohegan,"
upon the Manacles Reef, near Falmouth, and buried in the adjacent churchyard of St. Keverne,

EMILY M. SAUNDERS,

for years a worshipper in St. Luke's Church, And a loving friend to many poor in this and other, parishs.

───────

> "We bow our heads before the mystery of this sudden and grievous loss.
> Miss Saunders was upon her way to America to visit and solace friends.
> She had been recommended to this special vessel on which to make the journey.
> She was overheard at the last amid the darkness and confusion of that night, encouraging
> those around her to trust in God. This was in full accord with the unselfish courage of her
> whole life of helpfulness. Her will, when opened, was found to contain the words,

> *"Let me be buried wherever it is most convenient, and with as little trouble as possible to*
> *anyone, and if a stone be put up, though it is quite unnecessary, let*
> *these words be placed upon it—My trust is in his tender mercy of God forever and ever.*

> We ought to be the better Christians for having had such a sweet nature among us". [987]

In memory of Miss Saunders, a memorial fund was set up:

"THE EMILY SAUNDERS MEMORIAL FUND"

The Committee in closing the above fund, desire to thank the many friends of MISS SAUNDERS who have so cordially responded to their appeal sent out in November last. They also desire to say how much they have been touched by the warmth of feeling expressed in many of the letters, showing what tender remembereance

[985] *Western Mail*—(Cardiff, Wales), Tuesday, October 18th 1898.

[986] *The Standard*—Saturday, 13th October 1899.

[987] Extract from St. Luke's Parish Magazine, December, 1898.

their friend is held. The Committee have given £180, the balance of the Fund, which has reached the sum of £183 6s. 6d., in equal parts to St. Luke's Parish and to the Marylebone Committee of the Charity Organisation Society, with both of which organizations MISS SAUNDERS was so long connected.

No condition has been imposed upon these Associations as regards the distribution of money except that the Fund shall be called, "The Emily Saunders Memorial Pension Fund". [988]

Emily Saunders – Probate details:

London 18th November 1898 to the Rev. Clement Morgan Saunders, clerk, and William Henry Williams Esq. – Effects £ 2,528 3s. 5d

Seymour, George, Claude, Mr

Resident of: 168 Cromwell Rd., So. Kensington, London W.
Outcome: Drowned
GRO/BMD: 1898 Q4 – Helston 5c 119

Shepherd, Susan, Miss

Last Place of Abode: c/o G. W. Wheatley & Co., London.
Resident of: Woodstock, Ontario.
Outcome: Drowned

The aunt to another passenger, Miss Mary Frazer [q.v.] and was aged about 34 years. She had been studying music in Germany. She was the sister of Beaumont Shepherd of Montreal. Miss Shepherd, who is missing, is thought to be the only sister of Beaumont Shepherd, a prominent citizen of Montreal, where he is manager for Greenshields and Greenshields. Miss Shepherd had been in Germany for some time studying music, in which she had taken many honours.[989]

Smith, Arthur Ernest Leeson, Mr (also reported as Smith, Mr A. G. L.)

Resident of: Lena, Morrow Oregon.
Outcome: Saved

He was aged 32 years and had migrated to the USA in 1891. He had been a farmer in Oregon, USA for ten years as a "sheep grower' – USA census, 1900. He had been holidaying in the UK staying at Staverton Grange, Guildford. This was his second visit to the old country, having come over on the Atlantic Transport Line's ship, the *Boadicea.* Initially he managed to get aboard a life raft, but kindly surrendered it to a woman passenger. Her name was reported as Miss Webb; however, no such name appears on the company list. He was in the water for one hour and attempted to scramble up on to a rock, but was swept off by a wave. Eventually he managed to swim ashore, at Coverack.[990] According to the *The Times* (Washington DC), Mr Smith stated that: "All day Friday Capt. Griffiths appeared to be morose, preoccupied, pale, and worried". He also added that he was a jockey and had often ridden against Mr. Tod Sloan.[991]

Swift, Amelia Compton, Mrs

Resident of: Columbus, Georgia.
Outcome: Saved

She had been an invalid for several years and was accompanied on this trip by her personal doctor, John Fallows [q.v.], who drowned in the disaster. She was the wife of William A. Swift and they had a daughter Amelia. Sadly, this daughter died in April 1896 and five

---

[988] Bristol Records Office: Ref No.20535/221 Red House, Aldeburgh – 21st October 1898.

[989] *The Qu'Appelle Progress;* (Saskatchewan); – 20th October 1898.

[990] *Democrat Chronicle;* Rochester N.Y. 17th October 1898.

[991] *The Times;* Washington DC, October 17th 1898:
James Forman "Tod" Sloan (August 10, 1874 - December 21, 1933) was an American thoroughbred horse racing jockey. He was elected to the National Museum of Racing and Hall of Fame in 1955. After retiring he eventually went to Paris, France, where in 1911 he converted a small bistro into what became the famous *Harry's New York Bar.* The name of Tod Sloan left a mark on the English language. His name was already famous in London because he rode many winners in England where his first name was adopted into the rhyming slang used by the Cockneys of the East end of London to mean 'own' as in 'on his own' (from Tod Sl'oan'). Hence, someone 'on his tod' is alone – *WikiPedia.*

days later her father died of a broken heart. Mrs Compton Swift had experienced great sadness, having lost both her husband and daughter within a very short period.

According to the *Chicago Times-Herald*, Mrs Compton had a great deal of acting ability and spent a considerable time in studying Shakespear [*sic*]. Her niece, daughter of her brother Shelley, had enjoyed a measure of success as an actress on the London stage, under the name of Juliette Compton.[992] She was described as a beautiful American woman who was well known in Chicago society. Mrs Swift's life has been full of romance and was nearly ended by this tragedy of the sea. She was the great granddaughter of General Isaac Shelby of Kentucky and a cousin of General Joe Shelby, the hero of the Mexican War. While in Chicago a year ago, Mrs Compton Swift read before Mrs Milward Adams,[993] who advised her to go upon the stage but she was against it. Her readings given in the drawing rooms of fashionable friends in Boston were enthusiastically received and in London, where she went a little later, she responded to invitations to read and met with flattering success. The romance in her early life continued in her widowhood for she was miraculously saved by a noted physician of London who was a warm friend and admirer and who lost his life in saving hers.

Mrs. Compton Swift had previously travelled on six transatlantic voyages; so was well experienced enough to make cogent comments at the Board of Trade inquiry: on the nearness of the Eddystone Lighthouse, as well as the close proximity of the shore. She had received praise for the lucidity in which she gave her evidence at the inquiry. She managed to get into the ship's lifeboat and was saved from under that upturned ship's lifeboat. She died in 1901.

Warner, Louisa H., Miss

Resident of: Columbus, GA.
Last Place of Abode: c/o C.P.R.R. Co., Cockspur Street W.
Outcome: Drowned
GRO/BMD: 1898 Q4 – Helston 5c 121

This person was probably Louise Warner of New York City, aged about 36 years, and the niece of Miss L. H. Mershon [34 West Thirty-Second Street, New York]. Her embalmed body was returned to America on the steamship *Marquette*, which arrived at New York on November 1st. It was immediately sent to her home in Eirie, Pa., and was buried two days later. She was a member of a prominent family in Eirie. She left a mother, a brother, and two sisters.

Weller, Mrs.

Resident of: Saratoga, GA.
Outcome: Drowned
GRO/BMD: 1898 Q4 – Helston 5c 123

Mother to Mrs Gertrude King [q.v.] and was aged about 65 years. Her body was recovered on the 18th October and was embalmed and returned to Saratoga CA.

---

[992] Juliette Compton (May 3rd 1899–March 19th 1989) was an American actress whose career began in the silent film era and concluded with *That Hamilton Woman*, in 1941 – *WikiPedia*.

[993] Wife of Milward Adams (January 6th 1857 - January 18th 1923) was born in Lexington, Kentucky. Mr Adams rose to prominence as the first manager of the Chicago Symphony Orchestra and the Auditorium Theater. Adams worked his way up in the performing arts world, beginning as a janitor at various theatres and ending as a theater manager with many connections in the Chicago arts scene.—WikiPedia.

The Crew List for the Steamship *Mohegan* [994]

Good men must die, but death cannot kill their names.

Adams, John

Nationality/Birth Place: Woolwich
Age: 25 years
Position: Greaser
Home Address: 17? Road, Custom House, London.
Previous Ship: *Columbian*
Outcome: Saved

Adams, W.

Nationality/Birth Place: London
Age: 15 years
Position: Cattlemen's Steward
Home Address: 198 Cable Street, London.
Previous Ship: *Exmouth T.S.* [Training Ship]
Outcome: Drowned

This person appeared to be the youngest crew-member, aboard the ship

W. Adams

Ainsworth, E.

Nationality/Birth Place: Liverpool
Age: 39 years
Position: Steward
Home Address: 2 Robert Road, Woolwich, London.
Previous Ship: *Mobile*
Outcome: Drowned

E. Ainsworth

Anderson, Alex

Nationality/Birth Place: Philadelphia
Age: 44 years
Position: Fireman
Home Address: 1 Gautrey Road, Custom House, London.
Previous Ship: *Star of Victoria*
Outcome: Saved

S. Anderson

August, George Ernest

Nationality/Birth Place: Suffolk
Age: 21 years
Position: Able Seaman Quartermaster
Previous Ship: *Mohawk*

---

[994] Where available, a crew member's signature is appended to each record here. Some were unable to write their name and so signed with an 'X' and was then validated by the superintendent officer with '*his*' written alongside that individual's moniker

Home Address: 54 Turners Road, Limehouse, London
Outcome: Drowned

He was on duty at the time of the disaster, after taking the ship's wheel from Quartermaster Butt at 6.00 pm.

[signature: G August]

Bailey, J. (also reported as Bailey, W.)

Nationality/Birth Place: London
Age: 28 years
Position: Fireman
Home Address: 41 Sydney Street, Tidal Basin, London.
Previous Ship: *Winifreda*
Outcome: Drowned

[signature: JS Bailey]

Barnes, William

Nationality/Birth Place: East Ham
Age: 32 years
Position: Assistant Steward
Home Address: Railway Station, Plaistow, London.
Previous Ship: *Cleopatra*
Outcome: Drowned
GRO/BMD: 1898 Q4 – Falmouth 5c 101

He was buried at Falmouth (Old) Cemetery, Swanpool, Cornwall, on the 18th. October (*Plot No. E C 24* – no headstone found). The Lloyd's Gazette records:

> A steward, Barnes, was buried yesterday at Falmouth Cemetery in the presence of thousands of townspeople. The deceased's father, Mr E. L. Barnes, and brother and [George] Maule, one of the survivors, a New York cattleman, was the principal mourner. In accordance with the Mayor's request, the Falmouth shops were partially closed for several hours.

His father had sent a letter to the undertaker, Mr E. H. Moss which read, "Mr Barnes and family are deeply moved at the respectful tokens of sympathy which the inhabitants of Falmouth have expressed at the sad bereavement which had overtaken them in conjunction with others at the sad disaster". Mr Barnes later sent a contribution [£1] to the Falmouth Sailors' Home, as a practical expression of thanks.

[signature: W Barnes]

Barrow, Robert (also reported as Barron)

Nationality/Birth Place: London
Age: 28 years
Position: Greaser
Home Address: 80 Burrard Road, Custom House, London.
Previous Ship: *Culgoa*
Outcome: Saved

He managed to swim from the wreck to Coverack, some two and a half miles, where he was found totally exhausted on the cliff top the following day at two in the morning, by a search party. He accomplished this "wonderful feat dressed only in his drawers and a singlet".

[signature: R Barrow]

Bennett, Joseph

Nationality/Birth Place: London
Age: 20 years
Position: Ordinary Seaman
Home Address: 29 Leys Road, Custom House, London.
Previous Ship: *Clyde,* Whitstable
Outcome: Drowned
GRO/BMD: 1898 Q4 – Helston 5c 122

He was aged 21 years and was buried at St. Keverne churchyard, October 18th 1898.

[signature: J. Bennett]

Blake, Leslie Aston

Nationality/Birth Place: Suffolk
Age: 22 years
Position: Able Seaman Quartermaster
Home Address: "Hill View" Victoria Road, Woodbridge, Suffolk
Previous Ship: *Lord Rosebery*
Outcome: Drowned
GRO/BMD: 1898 Q4 – Falmouth 5c 103

In the 1891 UK census, he was recorded as having been born in "Perrim Porth" [Perranporth], Cornwall in 1877, his mother (Emily Blake) was described as a widow and 'living on her own means'.

His body was recovered in the mouth of Falmouth Harbour on Friday, the 29th October, 1898, and he was placed in a shell [casket] and taken to Mawnan, where it rested at Mrs Houghton's Roscarrick-Villas. His features were entirely unrecognizable and he was identified by tattoo marks, clothing, and other evidence, by his brother, Mr Maxwell Blake. He was the son of Mrs Emily Blake of Woodbridge, and was well known in the [River] Deben boating circles as a fearless and competent sailor. He was buried at Mawnan Parish Church, in a grave site, chosen by his brother, in sight of the wreck.

> The service was performed by the Rev. H. L. Leverton, rector of Mawnan, assisted by the Rev. Campion. The mourners were: Mr. Maxwell Blake (brother), Miss Powell of Woodbridge, Suffolk, Mrs. Campion, Mr and Miss Rogers of Carwinion; Mr. W. Houghton, Nurse Houghton, Mr. J. Houghton, Mr. Dell, chief coastguard, Mrs. Dell, Mrs. Sara, Mrs. Nicklos, Miss Houghton, Miss Pascoe, Mr. Sadler, Mr. Terymaine, and many other sympathisers in the neighbourhood attended. The coffin was carried to the grave by the coastguards of Helston and Mainporth, Mr. Dell and his men volunteering their assistance. There were twenty beautiful wreaths and crosses, from his mother and brothers, his sweetheart; also Miss Rogers, Mrs. Backhouse, Mr. Houghton, Mrs. Houghton, Nurse Houghton, Mrs. Dell, anchor of flowers from the coastguards, and many other wreaths from unknown friends. [995]

His headstone reads:

In Loving Memory of Leslie Aston Blake

Lost on the Wreck of the Mohegan

Oct. 14th 1898.

Aged 22.

"Love Is Strong As Death"

[signature: L. A. Blake]

Bourne, Hugh

Nationality/Birth Place: Greenwich
Age: 21 years
Position: Scullion [employed to perform menial kitchen chores]

---

[995] *Royal Cornwall Gazette;* 18th November 1898.

Home Address: 8 Thorpe Road, East Ham, London.
Previous Ship: First ship
Outcome: Drowned

H. Bowne

Bowles, Emily

Nationality/Birth Place: London
Age: 42 years
Position: Chief Stewardess
Home Address: 59 Percy Road, Upton Park, London
Previous Ship: *Minnewaska*
Outcome: Drowned
GRO/BMD: 1898 Q4 – Helston 5c 122

She was buried at St. Keverne, in the mass grave. A short time later, either her friends or family expressed a wish to exhume her body, and re-locate her to another grave site. It is not known if this had taken place.

E. Bowles.

Bravery, Henry

Nationality/Birth Place: Brighton
Age: 24 years
Position: Assistant Steward
Previous Ship: *Mohawk*
Outcome: Drowned
GRO/BMD: 1898 Q4 – Helston 5c 135

He was buried at St. Keverne, in the mass grave.

H Bravery

Bredenberg, William (also recorded as **Branderbury,** William)

Nationality/Birth Place: Genoa
Position: Boatswain's Mate
Previous Ship: *Cleopatra*
Home Address: 64 St. Lukes Square, Tidal Basin, London.
Outcome: Saved

William x Bradenbury

Brown, Percival Francis

Nationality/Birth Place: Chelsea
Age: 21 years
Position: Assistant Steward
Home Address: 50 Fairland Road, Stratford, London.
Outcome: Drowned
Previous Ship: *Harwardin Castle*
GRO/BMD: 1898 Q4 – Helston 5c 122

He was buried at St. Keverne, in the mass grave.

P. Brown

Browning, Stanley

Nationality/Birth Place: Helensburgh, Scotland
Age: 33 years
Position: Fourth Officer
Home Address: 17 Sydenham Avenue, Liverpool.
Previous Ship: *Cleopatra*
Outcome: Drowned

He discharged three rockets from the port-hand side of the *Mohegan*, before she sank.. He also helped Miss Noble on to a plank, but he himself eventually drifted away from her. He had joined the company in 1898 and held a second-mate's certificate. He was referred to in the Board of Trade inquiry by Mr A. S. Williams as "a nice smart lad!" His family UK census report for 1891 is included (see page 449).

[signature: S. Browning]

Brownjohn, Charles Cyril

Nationality/Birth Place: London
Age: 22 years
Position: Assistant Deck Steward
Home Address: 39 Cambridge Street, S.W., London.
Previous Ship: First ship
Outcome: Drowned
GRO/BMD: 1898 Q4 – Helston 5c 133

He lived in London. The poignant epitaph on his grave, in St. Keverne churchyard reads:

> *"In Loving Memory of Charles Cyril Brownjohn, London S.W., England aged 23 who went down in the wreck of the* S.S.
> *Mohegan October 14th. Interred October 18th. 1898. The devoted and only son of a widowed mother.*
> *"He never said an unkind word to her in his life"*

[signature: C. C. Brownjohn]

Buck, Emil Raymond (also reported as Buck, Emil Raimund)

Nationality/Birth Place: Hobart
Age: 41 years
Position: Second Engineer
Home Address: 543 Romford Road, Forest Gate, London.
Previous Ship: *Massachusetts*
Outcome: Drowned
GRO/BMD: 1898 Q4 – Helston 5c 120

He was buried at St. Keverne churchyard, Oct. 19th 1898.

Butt, Frederick

Nationality/Birth Place: Bristol
Age: 50 years
Position: Able Seaman / Quartermaster
Previous Ship: *Cleopatra*
Home Address: 216 Gloucester Road, Bristol
Outcome: Saved

A Bristolian man and brother to Mr William Butt, a well know resident of Horfield. He was one of the persons saved from the ship's mizzen rigging, from where he pulled the stewardess Mrs Agnes Piggott into the rigging, together with him and others. Butt had sustained a bad head injury and a crushed finger, on his left hand. Mrs Piggott had torn up her apron and used it to make a head-bandage for him. He gave evidence at the Board of Trade inquiry.

Frederick Batt [signature]

Campbell, Neil (also reported as Campbell, V.)

Nationality/Birth Place: Glasgow
Age: 29 years
Position: Fireman
Home Address: 278 Victoria Road, Victoria Docks, London.
Previous Ship: *Hawarden Castle*
Outcome: Drowned

Cavanagh, Matthew (also reported as Kavanagh)

Nationality/Birth Place: Wexford
Age: 39
Position: Fireman
Home Address: 97 Forty Acre Lane, Canning Town, London.
Previous Ship: *Georgian*
Outcome: Saved

M Cavanagh [signature]

Chaffey, George

Nationality/Birth Place: Sussex
Age: 43 years
Position: Fireman
Previous Ship: *Sussex*
Home Address: 4? Street, Poplar, London.
Outcome: Drowned

Chapman, Edward

Nationality/Birth Place: New Brompton
Age: 40 years
Position: Greaser
Home Address: 70 Martin Road, Tidal Basin, London
Previous Ship: *Missouri*
Outcome: Drowned
GRO/BMD: 1898 Q4 – Devonport 5b 215

The body of a man was picked up by the torpedo destroyer *Bat* (3rd. November), whilst at exercise in the Channel, and was landed at Devonport. The body was terribly disfigured and had evidently been in the water for some time. On the clothes being searched, several discharge papers from the Shipping Federation (No: 15184) were found, and these gave the name of Chapman, a fireman, and lived at 70 Martin Road, London. The Borough Coroner, Mr J. A. Pearce, held an inquiry at the Clarence Hotel, Morice Town [Devonport] on Saturday, November 5th 1898. The coroner had his officer, Mr Irish telegraph London, and a reply had been received that the wife would attend on the 4th, but for some reason she had not arrived. The coroner was satisfied that the body was that of Mr Chapman, and in view of the impending Board of Trade enquiry, and with the adjourned inquest by the County Coroner, Mr Carlyon, it was only necessary to return a formal verdict, and the jury brought in a verdict of "found drowned".

Chappell, Murdock

Nationality/Birth Place: Jersey
Age: 42 years
Position: Storekeeper
Home Address: 70 Martin Road, Tidal Basin, London
Previous Ship: *Rosse*
Outcome: Saved

Childs, Harry Robert

Nationality/Birth Place: Portsea, Hants.
Age: 30 years
Position: Assistant Steward
Home Address: 1 Hack Road, Tidal Basin, London
Previous Ship: *Chickahominy*
Outcome: Drowned
GRO/BMD: 1898 Q4 – Helston 5c 121

He was buried at St. Keverne, in the mass grave.

H. Childs

Cleux, John

Nationality/Birth Place: London
Age: 24 years
Position: Fireman
Home Address: 33 High Street, Tidal Basin, London.
Previous Ship: *Jumna*
Outcome: Drowned

Cole, Ernest Benjamin

Position: Second Officer
Nationality/Birth Place: Wivenhoe
Age: 30 years
Home Address: Park Road, Wivenhoe, Essex
Previous Ship: *Cleopatra*
Outcome: Drowned
GRO/BMD: 1898 Q4 – Falmouth 5c 103

He was born 1868 in Wivenhoe, Essex. He entered in service to the company in 1890, commencing as fourth officer. He held a master's certificate. His body was found two miles off the St. Anthony Lighthouse. He married Annie Elizabeth Howling in 1897.[996] His father was Capt. Benjamin Cole, who died, at sea, between Port Said and Calcutta, 29th July, 1881, aged 47 years.

E. B. Cole.

Cotter, John

Nationality/Birth Place: Hants.
Age: 35 years
Position: Greaser
Home Address: 113 Hermit Road, Plaistow, London.
Previous Ship: *Minnewaska*
Outcome: Drowned

Couch, Llewellyn (also reported as Couch, Llewelyn)

Nationality/Birth Place: Swansea
Age: 30 years
Position: Senior Chief Officer
Home Address: 170 Neville Road, Upton Park
Previous Ship: *Cleopatra*
Outcome: Drowned

---

[996] Mr Cole, the second officer, resided at Wivenhoe near Colchester. He was married about twelve months ago, and the news of the shipwreck has proved a terrible shock to his young wife, who will presently become a mother.—*The Pall Mall* Gazette (London, England), Monday, October 17th 1898.

Lt Couch

Crawley, J.

Nationality/Birth Place: London
Age: 22 years
Position: Fireman
Home Address: 28 Charlotte Street, Tidal Basin, London
Previous Ship: *Georgian*
Outcome: Drowned

Cross, Arthur M.

Nationality/Birth Place: Durham
Age: 21 years
Position: Sixth Engineer
Home Address: 15 Sydney Road, Forest Gate, London.
Previous Ship: First ship
Outcome: Drowned

He was the son of the shipping line's superintending engineer in New York, Mr N. A. Cross, and on his first voyage as an engineer. The body, supposed to be that of Arthur Cross, was buried at Coverack, on Sunday, 30th October, 1898.

Cruickshank, F.

Nationality/Birth Place: Aberdeen
Age: 18
Position: Captain's Servant
Previous Ship: Mohawk
Home Address: 6 St Lukes Sq.
Outcome: Drowned

It is not known whether or not this individual was related to John Grant Cruikshank [q.v.] as they were both born in Aberdeen.

Cruickshank, John Grant (also reported as Cruikshank, J. R.)

Nationality/Birth Place: Aberdeen
Age: 21 years
Position: Boatswain
Previous Ship: *Cleopatra*
Home Address: 68 St. Lukes Street, Tidal Basin
Outcome: Saved

He was five years in the service of the Company. He was in his bunk at the time of the disaster. His life was saved by clinging to the ship's main mast. He was also involved with Llewellyn Couch in the rescue of the crew of the Norwegian barque, *Persia,* for which he was awarded a silver medal of the third class and a diploma from the Norwegian Government.

J. Cruickshank

Dalton, Henry J. (also reported as Dalton, Harry T.)

Nationality/Birth Place: Yorkshire
Age: 22 years
Position: Carpenter and Second Mate
Previous Ship: *Cleopatra*
Home Address: 14 Cambridge Terrace, Gateshead
Outcome: Drowned

He was one of two crew members from Hull who died in this disaster. His Bible was contained in his locker-box, which was found floating in the sea. It was returned to his family, in the keepsake of his cousin, J. H. Pearson. In 1983, a Rabone carpenter's rule was found by a diver on the wreck site and this would certainly have belonged to either Henry Pinfold [q.v.] or Henry J. Dalton, the carpenters aboard the *Mohegan*.

Daniels, William (also reported as **Daniel** – A.B.)

Nationality/Birth Place: Dover, Kent
Age: 33 years
Position: Able Seaman (Royal Naval Reserve)
Home Address: 10 Hill Street, Hastings
Previous Ship: *Brittania*
Outcome: Drowned
GRO/BMD: 1898 Helston Q4 – 5c 120

He was buried at St. Keverne in the mass grave, on October, 18th. Daniels was alleged by J. G. Cruikshank (boatswain) to have been in the crow's nest, at the time of the wrecking. Shortly after six o'clock in the evening, he rang the bell from the crow's nest and hailed, "Light about two points to the starboard bow" – this being his last formal pronouncement.

Davies, E. L.

Position: Cattleman
Outcome: Drowned
GRO/BMD: 1898 Q4 – Falmouth 5c 115

He was aged 59 years. His body was recovered. No relatives were present, but Mr and Mrs Toulson [997] accompanied the body.

Davis, Mr.

Position: Engineer
Outcome: Drowned

His body was found by a 6-oared gig, the property of Mr Chard that had been towed out from Falmouth by the tugboat, *S.S. Telephone*. The party, consisting of Messrs. R. Toms, J. Dunstone, J. Carbis, G. Fittock, J. Rusden, W. Fenton, F. Thomas, carried with them gear for decently covering any remains they might find. They skirted the coast from Coverack to Falmouth, and brought back the body. A watch, found on the body, was stopped at ten minutes to twelve. The name of this so-called crew member is not recorded on the official list for crew.

De Grouchy, William T. W. (also reported as Gruchy)

Nationality/Birth Place: Newfoundland
Age: 36 years
Position: Fireman
Home Address: 93 Princes Road, Bermondsey, London.
Previous Ship: *Cairngorm*
Outcome: Drowned
GRO/BMD: 1898 Q4 – Helston 5c 122

Dinnair, Ernest (also reported as Dunnair)

Nationality/Birth Place: Liverpool
Age: 22 years

---

[997] Mr Toulson was the superintendent and working with his wife, at the Royal Cornwall Sailors' Home, Falmouth. This establishment played a major role in caring for the victims of the disaster. They also attended to the crew from the *SS. Paris*, which went aground in 1899.

Position: Cattlemens' Steward
Previous Ship: *Mohawk*
Home Address: 116 Argyll Road, Custom House, London.
Previous Ship: *Mohawk*
Outcome: Drowned
GRO/BMD: 1899 Q4 – Helston 5c 135

He was buried at St. Keverne and was the son of Frederick Dinnair, who also lost his life in the disaster [q.v.].

[signature: E Dinnair]

Dinnair, Frederick (also reported as Dunnair)

Nationality/Birth Place: Falmouth
Age: 55 years
Position: Night Watchman
Home Address: 106 Argyll Road, Customs House
Previous Ship: *Minnewaska*
Outcome: Drowned
GRO/BMD: 1898 Q4 – Helston 5c 134

He was aged 50 years and buried at St. Keverne. He was father to Ernest Dunnair, who also lost his life in this disaster [q.v.].

Edge, John

Nationality/Birth Place: Birkenhead
Age: 36 years
Position: Chief Cook
Home Address: Benson Avenue, East Ham, London.
Previous Ship: *Minnewaska*
Outcome: Saved

He was saved from the ship's rigging.

[signature: John Edge]

Feehan, Edward

Nationality/Birth Place: Tipperary
Age: 25 years
Position: Fireman
Home Address: 23 Phillip Street, Kingsland, Shoreditch, London.
Previous Ship: First ship
Outcome: Drowned

[signature: E Feehan]

Ferguson, William

Nationality/Birth Place: Belfast
Age: 32 years
Position: Second Auxiliary Engineer
Home Address: 220 Beckton Road, Forest Gate, London
Previous Ship: *Cleopatra*
Outcome: Saved

He was on engine-room duty at the time of the disaster and rushed to his cabin to get his lifejacket. His hand was badly crushed, in attempting to launch a lifeboat, aboard the *Mohegan*. He climbed to safety on the ship's funnel, from where he was later rescued. He had been in the employ of the American Transport Line for 7 years, working his way up from fifth engineer to his current position.

[signature: W Ferguson]

Fieldhouse, E.

Nationality/Birth Place: London
Age: 20 years
Position: Assistant Steward
Previous Ship: First ship
Home Address: 111 Amity Road, Stratford, London.
Outcome: Drowned
GRO/BMD: 1898 Q4 – Falmouth 5c 111

[signature: E. Fieldhouse]

Foster, George

Nationality/Birth Place: Bucks.
Age: 37 years
Position: Pantry Boy
Home Address: 22 St. Leonards Road, Poplar, London.
Previous Ship: *Minnewaska*
Outcome: Drowned

[signature: Geo. Foster]

Gray, M. Ewan

Nationality/Birth Place: Dundee
Age: 35 years
Position: Fourth Engineer
Previous Ship: *Cleopatra*
Home Address: 14 Randolph Road [?London or Glasgow]
Outcome: Saved

He was on duty at the time of the disaster and was one of the fortunate few, saved from the ship's mizzen rigging.

[signature: M.E.Gray.]

Gray, William C. Henry

Nationality/Birth Place: Newhaven
Age: 43 years
Position: Steward
Home Address: 188 East India Dock Road, London.
Previous Ship: *Cleopatra*
Outcome: Drowned

He was on duty at the time of the disaster.

[signature: H.Gray.]

Griffith, Richard (also recorded as Griffiths, Richard)

Nationality/Birth Place: Carnarvon
Age: 46 years
Position: Master of the *Mohegan*. [011891]
Home Address: 'Manhattan', Queens Road, Leytonstone, Essex, London.

Previous Ship: *Cleopatra*
Outcome: Alleged to have been drowned

Hammond, William

Nationality/Birth Place: Victoria, Australia
Age: 36 years
Position: Fireman
Home Address: 33? Street, Tidal Basin, London.
Previous Ship: *Fitzpatrick*
Outcome: Drowned
GRO/BMD: 1899 Q1 – Plymouth 6b 180

Hamper, Hubert William

Nationality/Birth Place: Newcastle
Age: 34 years
Position: Second Steward
Home Address: 19 Cottage Grove, Bow E., London.
Previous Ship: *Minnewaska*
Outcome: Drowned
GRO/BMD: 1898 Q4 – Helston 5c 121

Harris, John.

Nationality/Birth Place: Liverpool
Age: 26 years
Position: Fireman
Home Address: 32 Durham Road, Canning Town, London.
Previous Ship: *Chickahominy*
Outcome: Saved

Hill, George

Nationality/Birth Place: Liverpool
Age: 50 years
Position: Able Seaman
Home Address: Peter Street, Hackney, London
Previous Ship: *Missouri*
Character for Conduct: 'Very Good'—as stamped on the *Certificate Of Discharge*
Character for Ability: 'Very Good'—as stamped on the *Certificate Of Discharge*
Outcome: Saved

He sustained a broken collar-bone. His name Hillson in the Account of Crew was amended to that of Hill. He and his shipmate, William Moore, managed to get into an empty ship's lifeboat and eventually landed on Lowland where they were picked up by ashore-party and taken by cart to St. Keverne.

Hindmarsh, William Logan

Nationality/Birth Place: Glasgow
Age: 30 years
Position: Third Officer (Aux. 2nd Mate)
Home Address: 50 Heathwood Gdns, Old Charlton, London.
Previous Ship: *Binnie*
Outcome: Drowned
GRO/BMD: 1898 Q4 – Helston 5c 123

He had held a master's certificate. He was on watch duty with the captain on the bridge, at the time of the disaster. He had been employed by the company for two years and was in Baltimore in 1897 as third officer aboard the *SS Montana*, with Capt. Sidney Watkins as its master. He was buried at the St. Peter's Church, Coverack. The church register reads: "*30 October 1898 unknown male person drowned in S.S. Mohegan landed at Coverack, aged about 35*". The name "*Hindmarsh*" had been added in the margin; obviously in the following of a later recognition and confirmation. There is a headstone in the churchyard, which reads:

> *In Loving Remembrance of William Logan Hindmarsh, Third Officer of the S.S. Mohegan which*
>
> *was wrecked on the Manacle Rocks on October 14th. 1898.*
>
> *Interred October 29th, 1898.*
>
> *He sent from above, He took me. He drew me out of many waters. (2 Sam., XXII 17).*
>
> *This stone was erected by the people of Coverack, assisted by the owners of the ship.*

W Hindmarsh [signature]

Horne, Alexander

Nationality: Not known
Age: 45 years
Position: On a/c [?associate contractor] Weir Pumps (Engineer)
Home Address: 14 Cambridge Terrace, Gateshead
Outcome: Drowned
GRO/BMD: 1898 Q4 – Falmouth 5c 102

His body was taken to the Falmouth Sailors' Home, from whence he was conveyed to the Falmouth (Old) Cemetery, Swanpool (*Plot No. E C 2* – no headstone was found). His coffin was draped with the Union Jack flag, and many wreaths, supplied by local people. The Rev. C. A. Walker conducted the service and surviving members of the crew, waiting at Falmouth for the re-commencement of the inquest, were there to see their colleague off, on the 20th October. No relatives were present, but Mr and Mrs Toulson, from the Home, accompanied the body to the graveside. He was aboard the ship to observe the pumps, of his own patent. He was employed by the company – Messrs. Clarke, Chapman, and Co., Gateshead. He was well known in this area as an inventor and patentee. He leaves a widow and five children.

Huntley, Frank

Nationality/Birth Place: Dover
Age: 27 years
Position: Able Seaman
Previous Ship: *Maryland*
Home Address: 6 St. Lukes Square, Tidal Basin, London
Outcome: Saved:
He was picked off the *Mohegan*'s fore-rigging by the crew of the lifeboat *Charlotte*.

F Huntley [signature]

Isherwood, James

Nationality/Birth Place: Glasgow
Age: 25 years
Position: Fireman
Home Address: 21 Union Street, Banring
Previous Ship: *Victoria*
Outcome: Drowned

Juddery, John William Henry

Nationality/Birth Place: London
Age: 29 years [1869 – 1946]
Position: Quartermaster
Home Address: 33 St. George Avenue, Forest Gate
Previous Ship: *Port Albert*
Outcome: Saved

He was awarded medals for swimming from the *Mohegan*'s mast to the *Charlotte* lifeboat, and returning with a rope. He was instrumental in saving some persons, stranded in the ship's rigging.

[signature: Joh. William Henry Juddery]

Kemp, G. (also reported as Kempt)

Position: Cattleman
Outcome: Saved

Kinley, William

Nationality/Birth Place: Isle-of-Man
Age: 45 years
Position: Assistant Engineer
Home Address: 167 Charles St., N. York
Previous Ship: *Minnewaska*
Outcome: Drowned
GRO/BMD: 1898 Q4 – Helston 5c 120

The body was dispatched from the Falmouth Sailors' Home to Upton Park (an area in the modern London Borough of Newham) for burial. He was a Manx man, and he and his family were well known in Castletown, Isle of Man. He was an engineer aboard the ill-fated American warship *Maine*, prior to his joining the equally ill-fated *Mohegan*.[998]

Legg, James

Nationality/Birth Place: London
Age: 29 years
Position: Fireman
Home Address: 25 York Street, Canning Town, London.
Previous Ship: *Columbian*
Outcome: Drowned

MacFarlane, John M. (also reported as Farlane and McFarlane)[999]

Nationality/Birth Place: 7 Stainby Road, Limehouse, London
Age: 16 years

---

[998] *The Standard* (London); Monday, 17th October 1898.

[999] MacFarlane might well have been John Miles McFarlane, born in the year 1882, in South Shields, and if so he would have been aged about 15 years, at the time of the disaster. [GRO/BMD 10a, 767]

Position: Able Seaman
Date of Engagement: 12.10.98
Home Address: London
Previous Ship: *Exmouth T.S.* [Training ship]
Character for Conduct: 'Very Good'—as stamped on the *Certificate Of Discharge*
Character for Ability: 'Very Good'—as stamped on the *Certificate Of Discharge*
Outcome: Saved

He broke both legs in the disaster, and stayed at Porthoustock, in the care of Mrs Cogar's mother [for 6 months].[1000]
At the end of December 1898—The boy MacFarlane, whose legs were broken, still remains in the locality. He is now sufficiently recovered to get about on crutches. When sufficiently well he will proceed to his home in London.[1001] He was much remembered in the village for his whistling and swearing! His previous maritime experience was aboard the training-ship, *Exmouth*.[1002] His pay aboard the *Mohegan* was eight pence a day.

[signature: J M Farlane]

Mansell, Richard (also reported as Mansen and Mensell)

Nationality/Birth Place: London
Age: 27 years
Position: Water Tender Fireman
Home Address: 15 Newman Road, Plaistow, London.
Previous Ship: *Walton Belle*
Outcome: Saved

[signature: R Mansell]

Marshall, John

Nationality/Birth Place: London
Age: 23 years
Position: Third Engineer
Home Address: 43 Solent Road, Forest Gate, London.
Previous Ship: *Mobile*
Outcome: Drowned
GRO/BMD: 1898 Q4 – Helston 5c 132

He was buried at St. Keverne churchyard on October 19th. His grave was separate from the mass grave and his headstone inscription reads:

In Loving Memory of our Beloved Son
John Marshall Aged 24 Years. Third Engineer of "S.S. Mohegan"

Which Foundered On the Manacle Rocks, Oct. 14th 1898. Interred Oct. 17th

"SLEEP ON BELOVED, SLEEP AND TAKE THY REST".

[1000] *The Times;* 17th October 1898.

[1001] *The Royal Cornwall Gazette Falmouth Packet, Cornish Weekly News, & General Advertiser;* Wednesday, 29th December 1898.

[1002] Commissioned in 1876, and moored in the River Thames, London. The ship's low headroom common in such ships made her impractical for any other activity below decks other than eating or sleeping. She lost her spars, doghouses were built on her decks, and stoves were installed to prevent the boys freezing to death in the depths of winter. They slept all year round in hammocks and the wind whistled through the old badly fitting gun ports; http://bibulousbibliophiles.com/training_ship.php.

Private grave of W. & E. Marshall, Serbert Rd. Forest Gate, London E. [1003]

Richards & Spargo — Stithians & Helston. [1004]

Mr Marshall had an interesting history:

> Mr. John Marshall was a member of the Stratford Presbyterian Church, of which the Rev. Alexander Jeffery is pastor. Mr. Marshall had only just returned from Cuba, where he had served on a transport which had conveyed the Spanish soldiers from the island after the recent blockade. The church at Stratford is largely composed of men in the shipping world, and by the wreck of the *Drummond Castle* no less than 26 persons connected with the church were drowned. [1005]

J. Marshall

Maule, George (also reported as Moule and Maul)

Position: Cattleman/Assistant horseman
Outcome: Saved

He was a Texan operating from New York. He was taking tea in his cabin, when the disaster occurred and was saved after spending seven hours immersed in the sea. Rescued by the Falmouth tug *Penguin*, he was taken to the Falmouth Sailors' Home. He was employed by the Atlantic Transport Line for many years as a cattleman, and knows every horse of consequence, and was known by all English horsemen. He rather pretentiously described himself as a 'shipper of horses.'

McHugh, J.

Position: Cattleman
Home Address: America
Outcome: Drowned

He was listed as: 'Cattleman, returning to New York, – free passage.'

McKechnie, John (also reported as McTechnie, J. and Mackechnie, J.)

Nationality/Birth Place: Glasgow
Age: 47 years
Position: Greaser
Home Address: 54 Gray Street, Silvertown, London.
Previous Ship: *Alexandra*
Outcome: Saved

McKechnie

McLaren, Robert (also reported as Maclaren, R.)

Nationality/Birth Place: Glasgow
Age: 57 years
Position: Chief Engineer
Home Address: 280 Boulevard Hull, North Humberside.
Previous Ship: *Cleopatra*
Outcome: Drowned
GRO/BMD: 1898 Q4 – Falmouth 5c 102

[1003] William S. Marshall and his wife E. Marshall were resident at 43, Serbert Road. There were two other sons, aged 13 and 11 years [UK census 1901]. The Marshall couple seemed to have made a point that their son's grave was independent of the mass grave and separately funded by themselves.

[1004] John Spargo, Address: 19, Chapel Row, Mabe, Cornwall [UK census 1861]. He was aged: 40 years. Occupation: stonemason.

[1005] *The Royal Cornwall Gazette Falmouth Packet, Cornish Weekly News, & General Advertiser*; Thursday, October 27th 1898.

He was buried at Falmouth (Old) Cemetery, Swanpool, Cornwall, on the 19th. October, 1898 (*Plot No. E E 25*).

The Lloyd's Gazette reported that, "The funeral of Mr McLaren took place yesterday afternoon at Falmouth Cemetery and was attended by a large number of people". His headstone reads:

"In Loving Memory of Robert McLaren of Hull, Yorkshire,
who lost his life in the S.S. Mohegan October 14 1898 aged 57 years"

R. Mc Laren

McWhirter, A. (also reported as MacWhirter, A. N.)

Nationality/Birth Place: Glasgow
Age: 30 years
Position: Second Cook
Home Address: 468 East India Dock Road, London.
Previous Ship: *Mobile*
Outcome: Saved

A. Mc Whirter

Mitchell, Thomas (also reported as Mitchel, F.)

Position: Cattleman
Home Address: Boston, America – 274 West Street, New York.
Outcome: Saved

He was said to have also swam to the lifeboat, after Juddery's brave accomplishment, and taken a line back to those remaining in the rigging in the *Mohegan*. If so, then he was overlooked in the awarding of a medal for bravery.[1006] A report in *The New York Times* confirmed Mitchell's brave act, in an interview with him, on returning home to America. He was said to have been very modest about his achievement and wanted to leave immediately for home, declining any further discourse on the matter.

T. Mitchell

Molyneux, J.

Position: Able Seaman
Nationality/Birth Place: Montserrat
Age: 25 years
Date of Joining: 13th Oct 1898
Previous Ship: *Winfreda*
Home Address: 14 Merrow Street, Camberwell, London.
Outcome: Drowned

J Molyneux

Moore, Thomas (also reported as More, T.)

Nationality/Birth Place: Galway
Age: 30 years
Position: Fireman
Previous Ship: *Cambrian*
Home Address: 44 Martin Road, Custom House
Outcome: Saved

Thos Moore

[1006] *The Graphic* (London, England); Saturday, 22nd October 1898.

Moore, William (also reported as Moore, W. Hilsen)

Nationality/Birth Place: London
Age: 24 years
Position: Able Seaman
Previous Ship: *Duchess*
Home Address: 10 West road, Leyes road, Victoria Docks, London.
Outcome: Saved

After being thrown into the sea, he managed to pull himself aboard an empty lifeboat, almost filled with water. He also pulled aboard a shipmate [George Hill] who was exhausted, and clinging to a spar. They managed to get the boat ashore, where they were assisted by a coastguard-man, and taken to St. Keverne by cart.[1007]

W Moore

Murrell, Samuel

Nationality/Birth Place: London
Age: 36 years
Position: Greaser
Home Address: 4 Charlotte Street, Custom House, London.
Previous Ship: *Victoria*
Outcome: Drowned

He was buried at St. Keverne, in the mass grave. He was known as 'Sam' by his colleagues.

Nichols, Thomas

Nationality/Birth Place: Norfolk
Age: 33 years
Position: Able Seaman
Previous Ship: *Oporto*
Outcome: Saved

J Nichols

Nicklin, Frank (also reported as Nicklan, J., Necklin, F., Micklin, and Mikling, Frank)

Age: 28 years
Nationality/Birth Place: Liverpool
Position: Chief Steward
Home Address: 17 Malham Grove, East Dulwich, London.
Previous Ship: *Chickahominy*
Outcome: Saved

He had sailed on the vessel's maiden voyage, as the *Cleopatra*. He managed to get into the ship's lifeboat and was eventually saved by the Porthoustock lifeboat. His discharge paper, at the end of the *Mohegan* voyage, was recorded as 'very good' for both ability and conduct. Two years after the disaster, Mr Nicklan was once again mentioned in a newspaper; this time, in not so happy a circumstance:

> POLICE INTELLIGENCE—Frank Nicklan [*sic*], 34, a steward on the *ss Dunottar Castle*,[1008] was charged with violently assaulting Robert Joy and Ernest Mist, officials of the South-Western Railway Company—Mr. Dutton defended—it was stated that on Saturday night on the arrival of a Southampton train at Vauxhall [London], the Prisoner slept in a carriage. On being awakened and asked for his ticket, the Prisoner struck the Inspector a violent blow in the mouth, which cut his

---

[1007] *Belfast Newsletter;* 17th October 1898.

[1008] The *RMS Dunottar Castle* was built at Govan Shipyards in 1889 by the Fairfield Ship Building & Engineering Co. for the Castle Line, passing to the Union Castle Line in 1900. This steam ship became famous in the 1890s for reducing the voyage time from Southampton, England, to Cape Town, South Africa, from 42 days to 17 days and 20 hours. In 1894 the *Dunottar Castle* came very close to being wrecked, she must be one of the very few vessels to actually run aground on the Eddystone Rocks and live to tell the tale.

lip open. He also kicked the Inspector in the stomach. Other officials were summoned, and Prisoner hit out right and left, acting as they said, like a madman; he had to be held down all the way to Waterloo, and there, after being got out on to one of the platforms, he threw down Inspector Mist, hurting his back by contact with a footboard of a carriage. Mr Dutton said he could only appeal for a fine instead of imprisonment. Defendant had undoubtedly too much to drink. He left the *Dunottar Castle* on Saturday to come to town, and hardly knew what he was about when he was aroused by the ticket collector. As a matter of fact, Defendant had been unstrung by his terrible experience on the *Mohegan* when she foundered two years ago on the Cornish coast.—Witnesses to character were called, and for the two assaults Mr. Horace Smith fined Defendant £10 in all or two months hard labour. Defendant thanked the Magistrate, and immediately paid the fine.[1009]

F. Nickolls

Nickolls, Charles

Position: Water Tender Fireman
Outcome: Saved

He managed to get into the ship's lifeboat and was saved by the Porthoustock lifeboat.

Nobes, F. (also reported as Nobles, Nobas and Nobis)

Nationality/Birth Place: London
Age: 26 years
Position: Assistant Donkeyman
Previous Ship: *Victoria*
Home Address: 70 Argyll Road, Tidal Basin, London
Outcome: Drowned

F. Nobes

Piggott, Agnes Maude (also reported as Pigott)

Nationality/Birth Place: Lancashire
Age: 34 years
Position: Assistant Stewardess
Home Address: 24 Harrington Road, S. Kensington
Previous Ship: First ship
Outcome: Saved

She was the only woman who managed to reach the safety of the mizzen mast rigging, from where she was saved by the Porthoustock lifeboat *Charlotte*.

A. M. Piggott

Pinfold, Henry

Nationality/Birth Place: Kent
Age: 28 years
Position: Carpenter's Mate
Home Address: 11 Peter St., Gravesend
Previous Ship: *Cleopatra*

[1009] *The Standard* (London, England); Tuesday 11th December 1900.
It is quite possible that this outburst was as a result of his experience aboard the *Mohegan*. At a time when counseling and help with post-traumatic stress disorder (PTSD), was virtually absent (or even recognised as such) an individual was expected to cope alone with his "demons". In fourteen years hence, 306 British and Commonwealth soldiers were shot on the orders of military top brass and senior officers. The pretext for the execution of British soldiers had a common theme: many were suffering shell shock (also called, "war neurosis" or "combat stress") and is now, of course, recognised as PTSD.

Outcome: Drowned
GRO/BMD: 1898 Q4 – Falmouth 5c 111

In 1983, a Rabone carpenter's rule was found by a diver on the wreck site and this would certainly have belonged to either Henry J. Dalton [q.v.], or Henry Pinfold, the carpenters aboard the *Mohegan*.

His body was interred in the Mawnan Parish Church, and his headstone reads:

In Loving Memory Of our Dear Brother
Henry Pinfold Aged 29.
Wrecked on the Mohegan
Off the Manacles
Oct. 14. 1898. R.I.P.

H Pinfold

Rainour, G.

Position: Cattleman
Outcome: Drowned

Rawlings, Victor (also reported as Rawlins, Victor)

Nationality Barmouth
Age: 18 years
Position: Officers' Steward/Servant
Home Address: ? Road, Brixton
Previous Ship: *Europe*
Outcome: Saved

V Rawlings

Roach, Jerrard Joseph J. (also reported as Roach, R.)

Nationality/Birth Place: Essex
Age: 24 years
Position: Fireman
Home Address: 30 Sydney S. Tidal Basin, London
Previous Ship: *Australasian*
Outcome: Drowned

Robb, David

Nationality/Birth Place: Dundee
Age: 37 years
Position: Assistant Steward/Chief Bedroom Steward
Home Address: 13 Winston Road, Custom House, London.
Previous Ship: *Cleopatra*
Outcome: Drowned
GRO/BMD: 1898 Q4 – Helston 5c 122

He was buried at St. Keverne, in the mass grave. His death was recorded in *The Dundee Courier & Argus* (Dundee, Scotland), Monday, January 30, 1899.

D. Robb

Sennington, Edward Colston (also reported as Fennington and Senington, E.)

Nationality/Birth Place: Gloucestershire, 1856
Age: 42 years
Position: Chief Steward

Home Address: 11 Victoria Avenue, East Ham, London.
Previous Ship: *Minnewaska*
Outcome: Drowned
GRO/BMD: 1898 Q4 – Helston 5c 119

He was the son of the late Mr G. Sennington of St. Pauls, who for many years was the secretary of the Liberal Operatives' Association. He was buried on Saturday 22nd October, 1898 at the Unitarian burial ground in Brunswick Square, Bristol.[1010] The owners of the vessel sent a magnificent floral anchor, and they were represented at the funeral by Mr C. Harris. The Freemasons and the Old Croft Schoolboys' Society were also numerously represented. He was involved in a brave rescue at sea and the full story of that incident is contained elsewhere in this book.

[signature: E Sennington]

Simmonds, Howard (also reported as Simmons, Howard)

Nationality/Birth Place: Surrey
Age: 29 years
Position: Third Cook and Butcher
Home Address: 33 Braemar Road, Plaistow London
Previous Ship: *SS Ovingdean Grange*
Outcome: Drowned
GRO/BMD: 1898 Q4 – Helston 5c 120

His body was taken to St. Keverne Church.

[signature: H Simmonds]

Smith, John C. (also reported as Smith, J. E.)

Nationality/Birth Place: Spain (B.S.) [1011]
Age: 22 years
Position: Fifth Engineer
Home Address: 39 Scowen Road, Deptford, London
Previous Ship: First ship
Outcome: Saved

He was on watch-duty at the time of the disaster. A strong swimmer; he was in the water for three and a half hours before reaching the shore, supported by a plank.

[signature: John C. Smith]

Smithers, Joseph John

Nationality/Birth Place: London
Age: 29 years
Position: Fireman
Home Address: 64 Martindale Road, Customs House, London.
Previous Ship: *Lloyd*
Outcome: Drowned

[1010] The current Unitarian congregations in Bristol state that there was no Unitarian Burial Ground in Berkley Square . In fact, he was interred in the Unitarian Burial Ground in Brunswick Square, St. Pauls, Bristol. The newspapers, of the time, mistakenly thought otherwise–Courtesy: Carla Contractor; a Unitarian, a local historian, and Trustee of the Arnos Vale Cemetery.

[1011] B.S. indicates his being a **B**ritish **S**ubject.

Stevens, Alex

Nationality/Birth Place: Barking
Age: 16 years
Position: Second Pantry Boy
Home Address: 106 Terrace Road, Plaistow, London.
Previous Ship: *Minnewaska*
Outcome: Drowned

Alex Stevens.

Stott, J. (also reported as Stubbs, J.)

Nationality/Birth Place: London
Age: 27 years
Position: Fireman
Home Address: ?? Road. Barking Road
Previous Ship: *Ariel*
Outcome: Drowned

Stuart, Joseph

Nationality/Birth Place: London
Age: 32 years
Position: Fireman
Home Address: 21 Wellington Street, Poplar, London.
Previous Ship: *Georgian*
Outcome: Drowned

Thurlow, George W. (also reported as J. M. Thurlowe, and Thulrow)

Nationality/Birth Place: London
Age: 21 years
Position: Fireman
Home Address: 2 Quay Road, Poplar, London.
Previous Ship: *Boadicea*
Outcome: Saved

J. W. Thurlow

Toppin, J. P.[1012] (also reported as Topin, Topham, Topping and Topsham)

Position: Cattleman
Home Address: America
Outcome: Drowned
GRO/BMD: 1898 Q4 – Falmouth 5c 102

He is believed to be a Texan. His body was taken to the Falmouth Sailors' Home, from whence he was conveyed to the Falmouth (Old) Cemetery, Swanpool, Cornwall (*Plot No. E D 26* – no headstone found). His coffin was draped with the Union Jack flag, and many wreaths, supplied by local people. The Rev. C. A. Walker conducted the service and surviving members of the crew, waiting at Falmouth for the re-commencement of the inquest, were there to see their colleague off. He was listed as 'Cattleman, returning to New York – free passage.'

Trevaskis, John (also reported as Trevaskie)

Nationality/Birth Place: Liverpool
Age: 31 years
Position: Fireman

[1012] A surname 'Topping' appeared in the Account of Crew document where the name was amended, and countersigned, as 'Toppin.'

Home Address: 39 Hack Road, Custom House, London.
Previous Ship: *Inchdoon*
Outcome: Drowned
GRO/BMD: 1899 Q1 – Helston 5c 122

Body recovered and buried at St. Keverne, in the mass grave.

Trevor, Arthur Herbert, Dr

Position: Ship's Medical Officer (1896-Surgeon)
Nationality/Birth Place: London
Age: 28 years
Home Address: 48 Queens Gdns. Hyde Park, London.
Previous Ship: *Cleopatra*
Date of Discharge: 20th October, 1898
Character for Conduct: 'Very Good'—as stamped on the *Certificate Of Discharge*
Character for Ability: 'Very Good'—as stamped on the *Certificate Of Discharge*
Outcome: Saved

He had been on the *Mohegan*'s maiden voyage (then named as the *Cleopatra*). He knew Capt. Griffith well. He was one of the lucky few, saved from the ship's rigging.

Triphor, P. (also reported as Tripton and Treptow) [1013]

Nationality/Birth Place: Danlzic [1014]
Age: 29 years
Position: Able Seaman
Previous Ship: *Georgian*
Home Address: 12 Ferry Road, Tidal Basin
Outcome: Drowned

Underwood, James (also reported as Isherwood and Esherwood)

Nationality/Birth Place: Dundee
Age: 42 years
Position: Fireman
Home Address: 49 Cundy, Custom Home, London.
Previous Ship: *Brazilian*
Outcome: Drowned
GRO/BMD: 1899 Q1 – Helston 5c 134

He was buried at St. Keverne Church, in the mass grave. His death was recorded in *The Dundee Courier & Argus* (Dundee, Scotland), Monday, January 30, 1899.

Unknown Male – assumed crew member

Position: Greaser
Outcome: Drowned

[1013] The original surname on the official 'Account of Crew List' was recorded as 'Tripton.' This was later crossed out and amended to 'Triphor 2/12/98' and initialled.

[1014] Danzig, one of the great Baltic ports situated at the mouth of the Vistula (Weichsel), and now, as Gdańsk, included in Poland.

He was aged about 40 years. He sported a tattoo—"J.M.H". and was buried at St. Keverne Church on October 18th in the mass grave.

Unknown Male – assumed crew member

He was aged about 35 years. Buried at St. Keverne Church on November 5th in the mass grave

Unknown Male – assumed crew member

He was aged about 45 years and buried at St. Keverne Churchyard on October 18th in the mass grave

Unknown Male – assumed crew member

Aged about 25 years and buried at St. Keverne Church on October 18th in the mass grave.

Unknown Male – assumed crew member – buried at St. Keverne Churchyard in the mass grave.

Unknown Male – assumed crew member of the *Mohegan.*

Outcome: Drowned
GRO/BMD: 1898 Q4 – Kingsbridge

Mr. Kellock, County Coroner, held an inquest at Rickham Farm, Portlemouth, yesterday, relative to the death of a man whose body was found at Limebury Point,[1015] on Sunday [November 13th]. There is a strong belief that the man was one of the victims of the *Mohegan.*[1016] Messrs. Fox and Co. have, on behalf of the owners, agreed to pay the expenses for the burial of the supposed *Mohegan* victim.

Unknown Male – assumed crew member

Aged about 45 years and buried at St. Keverne Churchyard on October 29th in the mass grave.

Unknown Male – assumed crew member

Aged about 28 years and buried at St. Keverne Churchyard on November 1st in the mass grave

Unknown Male – assumed crew member

Aged about 50 years and buried at St. Keverne Churchyard on November 9th in the mass grave

Unknown Male, Stowaway (male)

This body was found at Porthallow and recognised as the stowaway, by another member of the crew. The stowaway was allegedly en-route for New York, to meet up with his Hungarian wife and child. He was buried at St. Keverne Churchyard in the mass grave

Waite, Percy Curtis

Nationality Sussex
Age: 23 years
Position: Printer
Home Address: Langdal[e], Cromwell Road, Bexhill-on-Sea, Sussex
Previous Ship: *Marquette*
Outcome: Drowned
GRO/BMD: 1898 Q4 – Falmouth 5c 103

He was aged 22 years and a printer by trade. His body was found two miles off the Manacles, by the tug *Dragon*. Mr T. Waite, his father, said he should have known him by his clothes. The funeral took place on Monday, 31st October. The deceased's money (in notes), gold watch and ring are missing. His father had taken the 5.20 p.m. Falmouth train for Truro, immediately following his son's funeral, when the train ran off the track and careered down an embankment:

[1015] Limebury Point is located on the eastern side of the mouth of the Salcombe estuary, South Devon.

[1016] *The Royal Cornwall Gazette Falmouth Packet, Cornish Weekly News, & General Advertiser;* Thursday, 17th November 1898.

. . . one or two gentlemen who were wearing top hats emerged with their headgear telescoped. Among the passengers was a wedding party, en route for Plymouth, and also Mr. Wait [*sic*], of Bexhill-on-Sea, who had been staying at Falmouth since the wreck of the *Mohegan* awaiting the recovery of his son's body, and that morning had attended the funeral. The additional misfortune of the railway accident affected him very greatly after his sad mission to Falmouth. It was his intention to proceed on Monday night by the mail train, as it was impossible for him to get through.[1017]

Ward, James

Position: Cattleman
Home Address: Jersey City, America.
Previous Ship: *Cleopatra*
Outcome: Saved

He was listed as a 'Cattleman, returning to New York, – free passage.' He was one of twenty-eight persons aboard the port-side lifeboat that was successfully launched. It had no plug in its bottom and rapidly filled with water, necessitating urgent bailing with the men's shoes and Mrs Pemberton's [a passenger] hat.

J. Ward.

Warren, Alfred

Nationality/Birth Place: London
Age: 24 years
Position: Donkeyman (Fifth Engineer)
Home Address: 33 Liverpool Road, Canning Town, London
Previous Ship: *Mobile*
Outcome: Saved

A. Warren

Wassell, Charles

Nationality/Birth Place: Portsmouth
Age: 26 years
Position: Second Saloon Steward
Home Address: 158 Malmesbury Road, Canning Town, London.
Previous Ship: *Cleopatra*
Outcome: Drowned
GRO/BMD: 1898 Q4 – Falmouth 5c 111

He was buried at Mawnan Parish Church. His headstone reads:

> *In Loving Memory of Charles Wassell Who was Drowned in the Wreck of the Mohegan on the* Manacles *14th. Oct. 1898. His Body was Found in the Helford River Oct 16th And Interred In This Churchyard On Oct, 23rd.*

C. Wassell

Watson, Robert

Nationality/Birth Place: Glasgow
Age: 42 years
Position: Water Tender Fireman
Home Address: 13 Coolfin Road, Tidal Basin, London.

[1017] *The Royal Cornwall Gazette Falmouth Packet, Cornish Weekly News, & General Advertiser;* Thursday, 3rd November 1898.
The engine driver and stoker were both killed in the accident. The coroner for their inquests was the same coroner as for the *Mohegan,* and he recalled that this [the Mohegan] was one of his most notable inquiries during his long career–*West Briton;* January 18th 1940.

Previous Ship: *Bishopgate*
Outcome: Saved

White, William C.

Age: 25 years
Nationality/Birth Place: Kent
Position: Stewards' Storekeeper and the barkeeper
Home Address: 18 Rain Road, Peckham, London.
Previous Ship: *Chickahominy*
Outcome: Drowned
GRO/BMD: 1898 Q4 – Helston 5c 122
He was buried at St. Keverne, in the mass grave.

W. C. White [signature]

Whitehead, Walter

Age: 38 years
Nationality/Birth Place: Norfolk
Position: Able Seaman
Previous Ship: *Aotea*
Home Address: 7 Bickton Rd. Plaistow
Outcome: Saved

In the year 1937, Mr Whitehead was living in Australia.[1018] A small news item appeared in the local newspaper,[1019] under the heading: 'Survivor of wreck of *Mohegan*.' The story went on to reveal that: 'he was anxious to learn of any other survivor of the wreck who might now be living in Australia.' It is not known if his appeal was successful.

Walter Whitehead [signature]

Whitehead, Richard Edward

Nationality/Birth Place: Bolton
Age: 31 years
Position: Fireman
Home Address: 9a High Street, North Woolwich, London.
Previous Ship: *Aotea*
Outcome: Saved

R Whitehead [signature]

Wiggington, S. J. (also reported as Wiggenton, J.)

Nationality/Birth Place: London
Age: 29 years
Position: Ship's (Stewards') Cook
Home Address: 3 Moness Street, Poplar, London.
Previous Ship: *Larne*
Outcome: Saved

J Wigington [signature]

[1018] Mr Whitehead's address: Sydney Road, North Coburg, Melbourne.

[1019] *The Argus* (Melbourne, Victoria, Australia); Wednesday 24th November 1937.

Wood, George (also reported as Woods, Geo.)

Nationality/Birth Place: London
Age: 38 years
Position: Able Seaman
Home Address: 61 Blackstrick Road, Tewksbury
Previous Ship: *Kaikoura*
Outcome: Saved

He was taken off the ship's mizzen rigging at 3 o'clock in the morning.

[signature: Geo. Woods]

Yeaxlee, Nelson (also reported as Yexhill, Yearlie, and Yealie)

Nationality/Birth Place: Southampton
Age: 26 years
Position: Baker
Home Address: 168 New Barn Street, Plaistow, London.
Previous Ship: *S.Y. Victoria*
Outcome: Drowned

His body was recovered 20th October. He was supposedly buried in the mass grave, at St. Keverne. However, the church had maintained a record of those buried whose name could be determined, but Yeaxlee's is not amongst them.
There is a memorial to Yeaxlee at the Highland Road Cemetery, Portsmouth. The inscription unequivocally establishes his name as Yeaxlee,[1020] and his signature below would appear to confirm this:

In Loving Memory of
CLARENCE YEAXLEE
WHO FELL ASLEEP MAY 25th 1901
AGED 69 YEARS
ALSO
SARAH ANNE, HIS WIFE
WHO FELL ASLEEP MARCH 13th 1901
AGED 72 YEARS

Also
NELSON, THEIR SON
WHO PERISHED IN THE FOUNDERING OF THE "MOHEGAN"
ON THE MANACLE ROCKS, OFF FALMOUTH
OCTOBER 14th 1898
AGED 26 YEARS.

[signature: N. Yeaxlee]

A further six *Unknown* persons were recorded in the GRO/BMD registers for 1898 (Q4) and 1899 (Q1). It is assumed that most (or all) were on account of the *Mohegan* shipwreck. Subjects' ages ranged between 25 and 45 years. Of the crew members who perished, twenty-eight bodies were never found. Eight unknown persons were buried at St. Keverne, five of whom were definitely crew members.

One of the unknown persons would have been the official stowaway,[1021] who was never named. To the credit of the shipping company, they arranged a burial for him, in the mass grave.

[1020] There is a photograph of his gravestone here; http://www.memorials.inportsmouth.co.uk/.

[1021] His body was found at Porthallow and subsequently recognised by a crew member as the stowaway.

During the period leading up to the *Mohegan*'s embarkation, the shipping line administration had to sign-up a full crew complement. There were seven crew posts where the individuals were categorized as: 'seamen who have failed to join,' and in addition, one person was transferred to the *SS. Victoria*. In their place, nine individuals were hurriedly recruited, and so unwittingly joined those who found themselves as crew on the final voyage of the *Mohegan* and for most of this group, their final voyage. The nine persons, who were recruited at the last minute, were:

J. Crawley	Fireman	Drowned
A. M. Cross	Sixth Engineer	Drowned
F. Dinnair	Night Watchman	Drowned
W. Kinley	Asst. Engineer	Drowned
A. M. Piggot	Stewardess	Saved
V. Rawlings	Steward	Saved
J. Stott	Fireman	Drowned
J. Smithers	Fireman	Drowned
P. C. Waite	Printer	Drowned

Table 17: Last Minute Recruitement for the *Mohegan* Crew.

THE DEATH ROLL.		
The complete death-roll was as under:		
Total officers and crew	....	103
Total Passengers	....	53
Total number on board	....	156
Passengers drowned	....	42
Officers and crew drowned	....	64
Total drowned	....	106
Passengers saved	....	11
Officers and crew saved	....	39
Total saved	....	50

Table 18: *Mohegan*: Passenger / Crew Survival Outcomes. [1022]

The numbers who perished and those saved, across the various groups of ship's crew:

[1022] *The Royal Cornwall Gazette Falmouth Packet, Cornish Weekly News, & General Advertiser*; Thursday, 20th October 1898.

Class	Died	Percentage	Saved	Percentage
Cattlemen	4	50	4	50
Engineers	6	46	7	54
Firemen	9	32	19	68
Officers	3	75	1	25
Sailors	11	55	9	45
Stewards	7	24	22	76

Table 19: *Mohegan*: Survival for Crew by Class Groups.

An account given by Mrs Agnes Maud Piggot (see Chapter 23) unequivocally lists 16 fortunate individuals, saved from the ship's rigging:

Bloomingdale, W. J.	Ferguson, William	Juddery, J. W. H.	Piggott, Agnes Maud
Butt, Frederick	Gray, Ewan M.	Kelly, Richard	Smith, Ernest Leeson (?) [1023]
Cruickshank, John G.	Huntley, Frank	Mitchell, Thomas	Trevor, Arthur Herbert
Edge, John	Hyslop, John	O'Rorke, Joseph	Wood, George

Table 20: Passengers / Crew List: Saved from the *Mohegan*'s Rigging.

The mass grave was the last resting place for the following victims:

Bennett, Joseph	Daniels, William	Fuller, Benjamin Frank	Unknown greaser
Bowles, Emily	Duncan, Charles	Marshall, John	Unknown stowaway
Brownjohn, Charles Cyril	Duncan, Mary	Murrel, Samuel	Unknown others x 8
Bravery, Henry	Duncan, Rosa	Robb, David	White, William C.
Brown, Percival Francis	Dunnair, Ernest	Trevaskis, John	—
Buck, Emil Raymond	Dunnair, Frederick	Underwood, James	—
Childs, Harry Robert	De-Grouchy, W.T.H	Unknown fireman	—

Table 21: *Mohegan* Passengers / Crew List: Interment in Mass Grave.

Further unknown crew members were buried in the mass grave on 29th October and 1st November and with other unknown persons on the 5th, 9th and 11th November 1898.

Though they sink through the sea they shall rise again.

Meanwhile, the gruesome job of picking up the victims at sea continued over the ensuing weeks and months. Some of the victims had poignant personal items about them that could have identified them to their loved

---

[1023] This individual was also reported as having come ashore at Coverack, after swimming from the wreck.

ones, had the information been passed on. Unfortunately, the usual outcome was for a news item to be published in local newspapers and not necessarily syndicated to the national newspapers. Even if this was not the case, almost all those who would have an interest (and living mainly in London), were probably illiterate. Here are typical newspaper reports of such grisly incidents:

- The bodies of several of the persons drowned through the wreck of the *Mohegan* have been picked up along the south coast of Cornwall. They include those of Mr. Couch, the first officer, of Swansea, and Mr. P. C. Waite, printer, of Bexhill-on-Sea, with one believed to be that of the sixth engineer and those of two who may have been members of the crew. Two of the bodies were found as far to the eastward as Par and Polperro. Forty-three of the dead are still unaccounted for, including several bodies for the recovery of which rewards have been offered.[1024]
- The body of the chief officer of the ill-fated *Mohegan*, Mr. L. Couch, was interred at Swansea, on Monday. Like all other bodies recently recovered, that of Couch was difficult of identification. At Porthoustock, on Monday, Mr. J. Cliffe recovered the body of a man, supposed to be a greaser of the *Mohegan*. There are still forty-two bodies in the sea.[1025]
- The body of a man, presumably a stoker or seaman of the *Mohegan*, was found by John Puckey, fisherman of Polperro, on Saturday morning [30th October, 1898], in the water about two miles to the west of Polperro. The body measures about 5 feet eight inches in height, and is clad in a white shirt, grey jacket, black and white plaid trousers, and one red stocking on left foot, and is much decomposed. It was landed near the spot where found, and carefully moved by the coastguard to an outbuilding of Coombe Farm, near by, to await identification and inquest.[1026]
- One body was that of a lady and was discovered by the coastguard at Portwrinkle (3rd November). Jewelry and a considerable sum of money, mostly in dollars, were found on her.[1027]
- Body Washed Ashore Near Par.—About one o'clock on Friday afternoon [29th October, 1898] the body of a man, apparently a seaman, or belonging to the engineering department of a steamer, was picked up on Crinnis Beach,[1028] Par. Deceased must have been about 6 ft. in height, and the little hair that remained on the head was black. He was tattooed with a bracelet around the right wrist, and dressed in a new serge trousers and flannel. A purse in the trousers pocket contained about 5*s*. The buttons on the trousers bear the name of a Poplar [district in the East End of London] maker. The age of the deceased is estimated at between thirty and forty, but the face was so disfigured that recognition thereby would be impossible.[1029]
- While the crew of the Plymouth *Goshawk* [also reported as the *Gorhawk*] were engaged in fishing about two miles off Rame Head on Thursday morning, [3rd November, 1898] they picked up the body of a man in a very advanced state of decomposition. The *Goshawk* was making easy progress and the men were busy superintending the trawl, when the second hand, Thomas Langdon, observed a body floating immediately ahead of the boat. He at once communicated the news to his mates. The first hand, William Langdon, took steps to secure the body. The *Goshawk* was steered within a

---

[1024] *The Royal Cornwall Gazette Falmouth Packet, Cornish Weekly News, & General Advertiser;* Thursday, 20th October 1898.

[1025] *The Royal Cornwall Gazette Falmouth Packet, Cornish Weekly News, & General Advertiser;* Thursday, 3rd November 1898.

[1026] Ibid.

[1027] *The Times*, 4th November, 1898.

[1028] Crinnis Beach is popularly known today as Carlyon Bay.

[1029] *The Royal Cornwall Gazette Falmouth Packet, Cornish Weekly News, & General Advertiser;* 3rd November, 1898.

short distance of it, and a successful attempt was made to throw a rope over it in such a manner that it could be drawn in without anyone leaving the boat. When the boat had drawn sufficiently near to admit of a closer examination, the crew learnt that it was that of a man dressed in seafaring clothes. Considering the decomposed condition of the body, the skipper directed it to be slung to the side of his boat. The *Goshawk* then bore up for Plymouth where information was given to the police. Skipper Langdon moored up off Lambhay [in the Barbican area of Plymouth] was conveyed by way of Sutton Pool to the Vauxhall Street mortuary, and P.C. Rule, with a stretcher from the Barbican Police-station proceeded to the *Goshawk*, the body having been transferred to the stretcher. It was not handled from the time it was picked up until it was placed in position at the mortuary, preparatory to an inquest. The body is that of a man in middle height, attired in a blue serge suit and lace-up boots, and is evidently that of a merchant seaman. In some quarters it is conjectured that it is one of the crew of the ill-fated *Mohegan*, but there is little possibility of identification. No man engaged in the local fishing industry has been lost for a considerable time, and in all probability, will prove no addition to the mysteries of the sea.[1030]

- Cast Ashore Near Veryan.—A body of a man in a very advanced state of decomposition was cast ashore at Veryan (Porla Beach) on Thursday [8th November]. It was supposed to be that of one of the *Mohegan* victims.[1031] There was a silver watch (bought in Philadelphia) and silver coins in the pockets. There is not likely to be much difficulty in identification, as one leg is shorter that the other and a double-heeled boot was worn.[1032]

- On Thursday evening another body from the wreck of the *Mohegan* was recovered, that of Mr. Kipling, a passenger. It was found in Falmouth Bay by a boatman named Scantlebury.[1033]

- Floating In Paradoe Cove.—A body was picked up from the wreck of the *Mohegan*, at Paradoe Cove, near the Nave [Nare Head].[1034]

- A body, bearing several tattoo marks was washed ashore at Lowlands Point, Coverack, on Thursday [24th November]. Though not identified the remains are presumed to be those of one of the *Mohegan* victims.[1035]

- The dead body of a man, apparently about 45 years of age, and six feet high, was washed ashore [on Berbain Beach] near Portloe, Veryan, on Saturday evening. It had on a knitted jersey, lifebelt, and silver ring on the third finger with Freemason's emblem. The body was taken in charge by the overseer, Mr Trudgian, who with help wrapped it carefully up, and took it into a house kindly lent by Mr T. Langdon, Treviskey.[1036]

- A *Mohegan* Victim.—On Sunday [11th June, 1899] the body of a sailor was found in the surf not far from the liner *Paris* and about a mile from the wreck of the *Mohegan*. It was that of a strongly-built man of 5ft 10in, in a frightfully decomposed state, being only held together by clothing, which as follows :—Short black jacket, blue knitted guernsey, red flannel singlet with the name, "Andre" worked in white cotton on the breast, blue knitted scarf around the neck, oilskin trousers, dungaree pants, grey trousers with white stripe, red flannel drawers, brown knitted socks, and lined leather slippers. It was thought that the blasting operations in connection with the *Mohegan* and the *Paris*, and also the anchoring of vessels in the sand, have tended to disturb the bottom, thus causing the body to rise to the surface. The

---

[1030] *West Briton;* 7th November 1898.

[1031] The body was found by Mr John Johns, on the 8th November and thought to be a fireman from the *Mohegan*, The body was placed in a coffin made by Mr Blamey, of Portloe. The burial took place at Veryan, on the 10th November.

[1032] *Royal Cornwall Gazette;* 10th November 1898.

[1033] Ibid.

[1034] Ibid.

[1035] Ibid

[1036] Ibid.

coroner did not think it necessary to hold an inquest, and the burial took place on Monday [12th June, 1899]. Eight months after the wreck of the *John* [1855] the body of one of the victims was recovered.[1037]

- Dead Bodies Washed Up.—In Saturday afternoon boys bathing on Pentewan beach [1038] observed a dead body in the water. Coastguards Tregido and Menhennet, securing a door, took a corpse about one hundred yards above high water. The police searched the body, but found nothing to lead to its identity. Both feet and hands were gone, and also the lower jaw, the remainder being in a very decomposed condition. Mr. E. G. Hamley, county coroner, held an inquest at Pentewan on Monday relative to the body of an unknown man. Coastguard R. Menhennet stated that he received information from Mevagissey that a body was floating near Pentewan. Going on the beach he saw the body close to the water's edge. With assistance it was taken above the high-water mark. On the body was a dark blue jacket, black cloth trousers, over which were oilskin trousers; blue shirt with red and white stripe, flannel drawers with red stripe, and a grey scarf. In a pocket was a white handkerchief with a fancy "*L*" worked in one corner with white silk. The body was decomposed beyond all recognition.—The Jury (Captain James Prettyman, foreman) returned a verdict of "Washed ashore". [1039]

- Discovery of a Lady's Body.—During the passage of the Great Western Railways Company's Steamer *Sir Richard Grenville* from Plymouth to the Manacles on Monday two bodies were passed. The first was seen off Dodman and Gull Rock, and was that of a lady attired only in a nightdress. It appeared to have been in the water a comparatively short time. The other body was passed in Falmouth Bay on the passage from the Manacles to Falmouth. It was that of a merchant seaman clothed in duck overalls, and had been in the water a long time, the extremities having been eaten away. On the journey back to Plymouth a lifeboat tank was passed off Whitsand Bay.[1040]

- Notes at St. Keverne.—At Porthoustock on Monday Oct. 31st Mr. J. Cliffe recovered a body of a man, thought to be a greaser of the *Mohegan.* There are still forty-two bodies at sea.[1041]

The hand-sewn insignias, found on various items of either clothing or handkerchiefs, did not necessarily represent the victim's name. In most such cases it probably denoted a loved one, who wished to provide an affectionate reminder of their relationship.

Six feet of earth makes us all equal.

The eventual distribution of graves, including the mass grave in the St. Keverne churchyard, was reported thus:

Those interred in the big grave at St. Keverne are:—Mr. B. F. Fuller [not correct—he was buried separately, alongside the mass grave], Mr. and Mrs. C. Duncan and Miss Rosa Duncan – passengers : two greasers (tattooed respectively, "J.M.H". and, "W.T.J".) Underwood or J. Isherwood [Underwood], D. Robb, C. Brown, John T. Bennett, Fred and Ernest Dinnair, P[ercival] Brown, Mrs. Bowles, H. Bravery, S. Murrell, W. Daniels, W. C. White, H. R. Childs, J. Trevaskis, R. Yeaela

---

[1037] *Royal Cornwall Gazette Falmouth Packet, Cornish Weekly News, & General Advertiser*; Thursday, 15th June 1899.

[1038] Pentewan beach is just west of Mevagissey, South Cornwall.

[1039] *Royal Cornwall Gazette Falmouth Packet, Cornish Weekly News, & General Advertiser*; Thursday, 15th June 1899.

[1040] Ibid.

[1041] *The Royal Cornwall Gazette Falmouth Packet, Cornish Weekly News, & General Advertiser*), Thursday, November 03, 1898

[N. Yeaxlee], and a fireman, name unknown. Single graves are distributed throughout the churchyard containing the remains of Miss Saunders, Mr. Marshall, and Mr. E. R. Back [Buck].[1042]

Several Americans were embalmed and returned to the USA. This was undertaken in strict secrecy, as it was considered bad luck by the crew in having a corpse aboard a ship:

Some of the bodies of the *Mohegan* dead [1043] are well on their way across the Atlantic–carried, too, by a sister ship of the *Mohegan* belonging to the Atlantic Transport Line, and starting from the same dock as the ill-fated *Mohegan*, which these very passengers, then living, left a week before. They are in mid-ocean, and the sailors who are taking them are quite unaware of their grim cargo or—it is hardly too much to say—the *Marquette* would never have raised a crew to take her out of dock. The bodies that are being taken back to rest in American soil are those of Miss Warner and Mr. J. P. Blackley, and great were the precautions taken lest the dread secret should get wind and the superstitious fears of the typical sailor should be aroused. The coffins were carefully disguised by being enclosed in a square outer packing-case, and as they were handed on from one official to another, they were verbally described as two boxes of machinery. "Good reason, too," said one of the foreman leaders. "Why if they ever got to know there was a corpse aboard, not a man jack of them would have set sail in that boat: ay. ay. sir, if you want to see the good old sort of superstition still—go among the sailors". [1044]

The cattlemen (exclusively American) aboard the *Mohegan* were not spared in the tragedy, with a significant loss of life within their ranks:

Name:	Outcome:
Davies, E. L.	Drowned
Kemp, G.	Saved
Maule, George	Saved
McHugh, J.	Drowned
Mitchell, Thomas	Saved
Raynour, G.	Drowned
Toppin, J. P.	Drowned
Ward, James	Saved

Table 22: Cattlemen aboard the *SS Mohegan.*

[1042] *Royal Cornwall Gazette Falmouth Packet, Cornish Weekly News, & General Advertiser*; Thursday, 27th October 1898.

[1043] These were the bodies of: Mrs. T. W. King and one of her sons; Mrs. Weller; L. M. Luke; Mrs. A. B. Grumbrecht; Mrs. L. S. Grandin and Mrs. Sophia C. Crane. The hermetically sealed caskets, containing the bodies, were labelled as 'machinery parts', so as not to trouble the ship's crew.

[1044] *The North-Eastern Daily Gazette* (Middlesbrough, England); Tuesday, 25th October 1898.

CHAPTER 28

The Manacles

The Manacle reef is an outcrop of rocks, a mile from its nearest access point, that of Porthoustock Cove and is five and a half miles south of Falmouth and are known colloquially as the *Manacles*. The reef, a perpetual menace to shipping, consists of a square mile of barely submerged rocks and over the years have claimed a staggering amount of shipping (with some saying as many as 3,000) and with a countless number of lives lost.

The coordinates[1045] for the Manacles are:

50° 2' 40" N 5° 2' 46" W

The name Manacles has nothing to do with fetters: rather, it is possibly derived from the word Meneage (Managhek) [1046] and this would relate to both the rocks and the headland, named Manacle Point, in the parish of St. Keverne. An alternative name derivation is from the old Cornish words *Maen Eglos* (meaning Church Stones) an obvious reference to the church at St. Keverne that can be seen at sea, from just beyond the Manacle Rocks, and is still used to this day as a navigational mark.

Of the Manacles and surrounding area, Sir John Killigrew stated, in the year 1620:

"Neither is yet possible to get parfett notice of the whence and what the ships are that yearly do suffer on and near The Lizard, for yet is seldom that any man escapes, and the ships split in small pieces".

As its name suggests, these rocks have an evil reputation, since some 110 known ships and over a thousand lives have been lost in this relatively small area. Not without good reason has it has been said that, the Manacle Rocks is the 'graveyard of a thousand ships'.

There is no comparable reef on the entire south coast of Britain that has caused such a loss to shipping. Its proximity to Falmouth, lying as it does on its southern approaches, has been the direct cause of the majority of losses. But even large ships, which should have been many miles offshore, seem to have become entangled with this sprawling and quite lethal mass of rock.

[1045] All Latitude/Longitude and Grid Reference coordinates are published in good faith and no responsibility is taken for an individual in using these for the purpose of visiting their assumed location and local knowledge is the preferred source for reliable information.

[1046] Meneage means "Land of the Monks", and is given to the land north east of the Lizard peninsula, including the parishes of St Anthony, Manaccan, St. Keverne, St Martin and part of Mawgan. There is evidence to show long before the Norman Conquest the district was possessed by an ill-assorted confederacy of small monasteries, founded perhaps by immigrants from Brittany. Among other interpretations of the word Meneage, was 'Meanake'—the deaf stone—the reason given for this rendering being that though there are several mineral lodes or veins in this district, they are 'deaf' or barren. What greater punishment could be inflicted on Cornishmen than depriving their native soil of the precious ore which gives employment to some and fortunes to others? This did St. Keveran: for the irreligion of the inhabitants and for their disrespect, he pronounced a curse against them, and caused the mineral veins to be unproductive. Hence the local proverb, "No metal will run, within the sound of St. Keverne Bells".

The Gods had not made life easy for sailors: having just made a safe rounding of the hazardous Lizard, the next hurdle is the Manacle Rocks, so cruelly positioned between them and the safety of Falmouth harbour. Unfortunately, a greater part of this reef is submerged at all states of tide, and although two and a half miles wide, and jutting out a mile and a half from the shore, all but one, the Carn Du rock,[1047] are covered by the highest tides, which of course renders them the more treacherous.

A sailing vessel would naturally give these rocks a wide berth but with only primitive navigational aids, fog, or with a running tide and a deadly onshore wind, a vessel could easily find itself embayed, and at the mercy of this unforgiving coastline.

In what seems to be a straight run for the safety of Falmouth, many masters have misjudged their position, or have been powerless to stop their vessel being drawn on to the Manacle Rocks. One can only imagine the horror for the crew, knowing what fate awaited them, as the rocks loomed up ahead, ensuring almost certain disaster. In the hours of darkness, the only indication for their fate is the white water that shows itself in the fleeting moonlight, or the sound of the breakers as they crash against the base of the Carn-du, or the useless buoy bell needlessly heralding their imminent disaster.

In a very few recorded cases, the crew, manage against all odds, to climb into the ship's rigging, still showing above the waves. From their vantage point, the waves menacingly beckon from below: heralding their intent by sending ominous shudders through the masts, as the ship is relentlessly dashed against the reef, in its death throes. Some unfortunates have been found frozen to the rigging, either dead or simply unable to muster the strength or the courage to leave their insecure perch.[1048]

By morning light, the drama has unfolded, most crew swept to their death, their vessel smashed to pieces, and the only evidence for that night's terrible event, had been the flotsam, and jetsam found in the nearby small coves, and on the beaches. And with the presence of those poor victims of this tragedy, crushed and disfigured by the awesome forces that nature inflicts, and with no mercy. The pathetic remains being picked over by grateful Cornishmen, who know full well of the terrible events that had led to this, their momentary good fortune, and yet is tempered by the thought that, "But for the grace of God, there go I".

A boat trip to the rocks is at first beguiling as a sweeping arc denoting the inner and the outer Manacles, unfolds itself. It is when we are among the rocks themselves, we feel a certain foreboding; knowing that there is at one moment but a few feet of water beneath us, and then, a sudden drop-off; suspended over a precipitous underwater chasm. A diver here, in the gloom that is the Manacle Rocks, can but imagine some of the horror that this place has inflicted on seafarers, over the ages. Hopes, dreams, and ambitions, dashed on these rocks,

---

[1047] The southernmost rock in the Manacles is the *Carn du*. At low tide it is the largest rock, though it does have a striking similarity to *Maen Voes*, and at high tide it is the only one to break the surface, by some three metres. An alternative old-stye spelling for this rock is *Carn Dhu*.

[1048] The most famous such wreck was that of the *Bay of Panama* – 1891, where the crew found a precarious safety in the ship's rigging. With the bitterly cold winter weather, and snow storms, many were found the following morning, frozen to death, where they had sought safety. On that day, the headmistress of the Girl's School at Coverack had recorded that, "Terrible snowstorm—only four [pupils] present, so could not keep school". Fortuitously, the *Mohegan* wreck offered 16 persons a lifesaving opportunity, as the masts and rigging remained jutting above the surface, after her sinking and settling on the seabed.

which forever stand as a testament to the bravery and to the fragility of man. Standing off the Manacle Rocks in rough weather, you will witness a shoreline that great seascape painters used to depict as the, *'Gates of Hell'*.

That lonely bell set in the rushing shoals / To warn us from the place of jeopardy.

A simple warning is posted to the east of the outer Manacle Rocks: the only close navigational marker that warns ships away from this place: the Manacle bell-buoy.[1049] An evocative view of this forbidding place is well captured in this descriptive piece:

> On Friday evening, in fairly good weather, an appalling disaster occurred off the Cornish coast, where many a time before the blue waters from the Atlantic which roll down the English Channel have swallowed up hundreds of human beings, and cast their whitened corpses upon the rugged shore. About six or eight miles across the beautiful bay, west of Falmouth harbour, lie, as is well known to the Cornish folk, The Manacle Rocks. Jutting out from the mainland, topped by the spire of St. Keverne Church, is a beetling chain of treacherous rocks—treacherous, sharp, insidious. When weather is fair and light is clear, no mariner needs run his craft into the jaws of death which here may await him, for at all states of the tide one or more of the treacherous fangs rise ghaunt [*sic*] and steep out of the waves. But in stress of weather, and in darksome nights, there is no light to warn him of his danger. South-westward are the Lizard lights, south-eastward the revolving light of St. Anthony. The only warning monitor that haunts the lonely, rock-strewn place is the solitary buoy which, swaying with the wind and the tide, keeps up a perpetual tolling, from its bell-top. Years has this warning voice sounded over the restless deep, many times has its message of mercy been turned into a death knell of scores of hapless men, women, and children as they struggled and fought for life, where mercy has no ear.[1050]

Following the *Mohegan* disaster, again much criticism was made against this ineffectual alarm:

> We have the un-contradicted statements of seamen of all classes, that the bell-buoy, fixed to one of the outer Manacle Rocks, is utterly inadequate to warn vessels of their nearness to danger. And when the sounds of that bell came in the landward breeze to where I stood looking across the reef, they seemed not a message of warning to those who cross the deep, but as the death-knell of the hundreds of men, women, and children who have breathed their last in the sea around the Manacle Rocks.[1051]

[1049] According to the Trinity House Buoy Book of 1927, a buoy had been placed near the Manacles in the year 1838, by Trinity House. It had received some criticism (particularly in the aftermath of the *Mohegan* disaster) as with an onshore wind, the bell is not heard by vessels immediately outside the buoy, and so does not offer adequate warning of danger. This view still prevails today. The Roskilly family of St. Keverne tells this author that the sound of the bell can clearly be heard at their farm, when the wind is in that direction. Four years after the *Mohegan* wreck, a larger bell buoy was placed at a distance of 112 yards, south east of the sunken rock [probably the Penwin] at the eastern extremity of the Manacles, at a reputed cost of £1,100. The buoy was black in colour, and had the dreaded word **MANACLE** painted in white (see fig. 67). To this day, no additional safety measure has been installed, in the form of a lighthouse or light-ship. The modern buoy has a flashing light that is powered by solar photovoltaic panels (see fig. 68).

[1050] *The Royal Cornwall Gazette Falmouth Packet, Cornish Weekly News, & General* Advertiser; Thursday, 20th October 1898.

[1051] Albert Bluett, *The Cornish Magazine 'The Riviera'*; 1898. The bell-buoy is not fixed to a rock, but is attached by chain, to a sinker on the seabed.

The buoy itself is located in deep water, some 60 metres (200 feet) depth. To this day, it still has a bell which tolls by wave action; a mournful sound that seems to exactly complement this sad place, over which it stands guard.

While many ships have come to grief on the Manacles, a small number manage to find clear water, and make for safety. Many others over the years have not been so lucky. Once caught, the fearsome Manacles rarely lose its grip and a ship pays the price, with its human coinage. Such a vessel was a south Wales steamer the *Gwentland*. Land's End radio station picked up an SOS from the *Gwentland* at 2.45 p.m. on August 6, 1927. The ship radioed, "*SOS / On Manacle Rocks / Want lifeboat"*. The ship later sent a message saying, "*Struck rocks in thick fog near Manacle Rocks / Making water in number one hold / Contacted Falmouth for tugs."* The 2,000 ton vessel, bound for Newport from Antwerp with a cargo of steel, had encountered fog in the Channel making navigation difficult for her master, Captain Lewis.

Falmouth boatman, Henry Morrison, was out fishing in his boat when he saw the *Gwentland* steam out of the fog close by. He shouted up to the bridge warning of the impending danger, but the vessel struck the Maen Garrick rocks. Falmouth, Coverack and Porthoustock rowing lifeboats were launched on service to assist the *Gwentland*. The Porthoustock self-righting lifeboat *Queen Victoria*, closest to the shipwreck, was first to reach the ship and stood by, along with some local fishing boats, until the Falmouth tugs *Lynch* and *Victor* arrived. On a rising tide in calm conditions, the *Lynch* managed to pull the ship from the rocks. Both tugs towed the vessel to Falmouth where the salvage ship *Restorer* went alongside with pumps and divers.

If a seaman was familiar with the Manacles and with their geography, this could be used to his advantage, as illustrated here:

THE DREAD OF THE MANACLES

The name of this grim line of rocks is the sign of the dread which they inspired in the breast of the bold smugglers and small traders of early days, with whom it was a saying: "Once inside the Manacle Rocks, you never get free again". Only one [such vessel] was known to get out of the Manacle Rocks, and curiously enough, its master did it deliberately. It was early in the last 18th Century. Captain John Bull, of the famous packet *Marlborough*, having fought his way across the Atlantic, encountered a [enemy] frigate off the Lizard. Knowing the coast from boyhood, he deliberately went inside the Manacle Rocks, and the Frenchman followed. Bull, owing to his matchless seamanship and knowledge, got through, but the Frenchman lost his ship.[1052]

A miss is as good as a mile.

There are other anecdotal accounts of near misses, as are referred to here:

"The narrow and miraculous escapes from among this tangle of reefs have been many. *The Cornish Magazine*, now extinct, once published an article, in which the writer spoke of a Porthoustock fisherman telling him, from memory, the names of

---

[1052] *Royal Cornwall Gazette;* 20th October 1898.

420

thirty vessels of all kinds, from steamships down to ketches that had been totally lost here. He told a thrilling tale of a ship drifting inshore in a fog, and of the captain anchoring until the fog cleared away, when he sailed off in safety, to the astonishment of the many who had collected on the cliffs. There was also the story of the steamship which came so close to the cliffs that the noise of her engines could be distinctly heard on shore, but she, too, got away. Many have been the ships among the Manacles, and no word ever said about it; their captains even going the length of covering over the name of their vessels with a sail, lest their mistake in navigation should be published to the world". [1053]

Countless numbers of unfortunate vessels having dashed themselves upon these rocks, for this is no place for the ill-prepared, or novice boatman. Tides and sudden changes in wind direction, or a sea-mist rolling in and cloaking the Manacles, all pose potential disaster for those unwary mariners caught out by events. The Manacles now imposes itself and reminds the interlopers that they stray into these forbidding waters, at their peril.[1054]

Previous attempts had been made to have a more substantial warning to mariners, at this most dangerous point and yet again, the Trinity House Brethren had been reluctant to act on these requests:

Following the *Mohegan* disaster, there was cause for the bitterest regret that the offer which was made by Mr Passmore Edwards to erect a lighthouse on the Manacle Rocks was refused by the Trinity House authorities, who could not see their way clear to bear the burden of the expense of the maintenance. This offer of a lighthouse for this dangerous reef of rocks met with hearty public approval, and at the time the Trinity House were severely criticised for not taking advantage of it.[1055]

The middle Manacles in the north, consist of: Maen Chynoweth (or Morah), Chyronos, Maen Gerrick and the Gwinges; the eastern group has, Vase Rock and Pen Vin; the large group in the centre include the Mistrel Rock, Carn-dhu, Maen Voes (the Voices) and the Quants; and Maen Land is in the south-west.

The second half of the ebbing tide will have many rocks increasingly exposed, during this period.

Many of the well-known wrecks are in the central group where depths, in parts, are less than 6 metres for an area of 300 metres by 200 metres. These wrecks include:

H.M.S. Primrose, an 18-gun Cruiser class brig-sloop, sank on 21 June 1809, with only 1 of the 126 on board, surviving – 17 year old John Meaghen. The Mistrel Rock is the site of this wreck.[1056]

SS *Mohegan* sank on the Voices rock [50 02 38; 05 02 26W].

[1053] Harper Charles G.: *The Cornish Coast, South, and The Isles of Scilly;* 1863–1943; Publisher: London Chapman & Hall, 1910.

[1054] There are two deaths every year on average, for divers who dive on the Manacles. Diving here should only be attempted 5 hours before and 1 hour after HW, with 1 hour after neaps giving the best window of opportunity: that of 2 hours with 2 knots flow. Fearsome tides will be encountered outside these windows of opportunity.

[1055] *Royal Cornwall Gazette;* 20th October 1898.

[1056] The gudgeon-pin for the *Primrose* was coincidentally found by fishermen operating over the wreck site. It is now on display on the St. Keverne Church belfry wall.

Spyridon Vagliano, a Greek steamer carrying grain from Novorossijsk to Falmouth sank in the near vicinity of the *Mohegan* wreck site, on 8th February 1890.[1057] [50 02 48; 05 02 41W]

The barque, *John*, carrying 263 emigrants to Canada, sank on the Maen Land rocks in May 1855; only 86 survived. The captain and his crew were all saved and their drunkedness and lack of concern for their passengers was a shameful incident, still remarked on to this day.

Individual Rocks that Constitute the Manacles:

Carag Luz (also known as *Carrag Luz*; *Carrag Luze*; *Carracklooze*; *Grey Rock*)

Carn-du (also known as *Carn-dhu*)

Chyronos
Description: part of the middle Manacles group.

Foam Rock
Description: situated off Lowland Point.

Great Wrea
Description: situated off Lowland Point.

Gwinges

Description: part of the middle Manacles group. On a big spring tide it shows on a low water. On an ebbing tide, particularly the bigger tides, this can cause overfalls that produce waves of up to 2m on a flat calm day.

Little Wrea

Description: Dries 5.2 metres (17 feet) – situated off Lowland Point.

Maen Garrick

Description: The rocks are due east of Manacle Point with steep rock faces from 17 to 24 metres below sea level. On an ebbing tide, particularly the bigger tides, this can cause overfalls that produce waves of up to 2m on a flat calm day.

Maen Land Rock

Description: Lies off the Dean Quarries, Porthoustock, and comprises four peaks that partially dry at low water springs. The general depth is 12 metres in between the rock gullies. The vessel *John* carrying 263 emigrants to Canada sank on the Maen Land in May 1855.

[1057] She was carrying 10,666 quarters of grain from the Black Sea [Novorossijsk] for discharge at Falmouth for Messrs. S. & T. Trounson of Redruth. It is believed her reckoning was at fault after passing the Lizard since there was no pilot on board and she struck the Manacles before those on board knew where they were. The boats were got out but owing to the darkness and heavy seas there was considerable difficulty and danger in launching them. The captain [Capt. Cambitys] was drowned whilst trying to land through heavy seas at midnight at a local beach. Eight Greek sailors groped their way across the fields to Rosenithon, where they found the house of Mr William Eddy, a local farmer. A boat containing 13 other members of the crew was still missing up to a late hour on the Monday evening. She sank in deep water and completely disappeared, a total loss. The body of the Captain was buried in St. Keverne churchyard. Of her total crew of 22,14 were lost.

Maen-Chynoweth (also known as: *Morah Rock*)

Description: Dries 1.2 metres (4 feet). On an ebbing tide, particularly the bigger tides, this can cause overfalls that produce waves of up to 2m on a flat calm day.

Maen Voes (also known as: *The Voices*)

Lat/Long: 50° 02 72N, 5° 02 60W

Description: Consists of three peaks and dries 1.2 metres (4 feet). They are the first to ebb up

Mistrel Rock

Description: This is the site for the wreck of *HMS Primrose*.

The Oar

Description: Dries 4.34 metres.

Pencra Reef

Lat/Long: 50° 03 420N; 5° 03 29 W

Description: The shallow reef here extends a good half a mile out to sea, but there is also a wall from 20 or 25 metres to past 30 metres on the east and south-east sides of the reef.

Pen win (also known as:the Penvin).

Lat/Long: 50° 02 58; 05° 03 21W

Description: Pinnacles with sheer drop-offs 2–50 metres and a minimum of 12 feet of water covering the rock itself. The *Mohegan*'s rudder is said to rest here. On a big spring tide it shows on a low water and on an ebbing tide, particularly the bigger tides, can cause overfalls that produce waves of up to 2 metres on a flat calm day.

The Raglans

Lat/Long: at 50° 02 35; 05° 02 27W

Description: A series of pinnacles coming to within 7 metres of the surface as a pinnacle, and drops to 44m on the seaward side. The current is very strong here, so dive only on slack tide. Note, the slack water period is the shortest on this particular rock. No wreckage found here, but a very scenic dive.

Shark's *Fin*

Description: A most distinctively shaped rock that fully justifies its name. It is positioned just off Porthoustock beach.

Vase Rock (also known as: Varses; Voces)

Lat/Long: 50°03 00N; 50 02 38; 05 02 26W

Description: Between 15 and 40 metres (50 - 130 feet) depth and is just awash at low springs. The *Mohegan* shipwreck is situated here (50 02 38; 05 02 26W). Slack water on the *Mohegan* is 2 hours after high water at Porthoustock Beach. The Vase Rock was once said to have stood several metres proud of the surface until the *SS Mohegan*, struck her. On a big spring tide it shows on a low water and and on an ebbing tide, particularly the bigger tides, can cause overfalls that produce waves of up to 2 metres on a flat calm day.

Vervan Rocks

Description: Dries 5.2 metres (17 feet) and situated off the village of Porthoustock.

Woodford's Wall

Description: about 6 to 45 metres (20 – 170 feet) and consists of a sheer wall and with drop-offs covered in marine life.

Whatever the geological constitution of the Manacle Rocks, Nature's handiwork was of little interest to those who found themselves unintentionally close enough for examination. However, an inquisitive member of the Royal Geological Society of Cornwall put aside all fears to report his findings, thus:

> I landed on the Manacle Rocks and found it composed of fine syenite, consisting of violet feldspar, dillage, and common horneblend, and traversed by nearly vertical veins of greenstone, from 15 inches to five feet wide, and dipping east. In the middle of some of the veins are small veins of saussurite running parallel with the greenstone.[1058]

The entire Manacles reef is a continuation in the sea of a large dyke of green stone which traverses St. Keverne, and gives to it its extraordinary fertility. In its course, this dyke is studded by boulders which become more numerous as the coast is neared. Beneath the surface of the water they are very unevenly distributed, and in some places wide enough set apart for a vessel to pass through, but these channels are only navigable to those who know them well [1059]

[1058] *Transactions of the Royal Geological Society of Cornwall, Volumes 1–2;* By Royal Geological Society of Cornwal: *On the Serpentine District of Cornwall*: By the Rev. John Rogers (Member of the Society) October 1822.

[1059] Courtesy of: St. Keverne Local History Society.

ENDPIECE

Quite clearly, the ship's course was wrongly set and Captain Griffith stands accused of placing his vessel in a dangerous position, which ultimately cost the lives of 105 persons. Unfortunately, his navigating bridge officers all perished in the disaster and the Captain failed to attend the subsequent inquiries, whose members had to rely on the anecdotal evidence given by the surviving crew members and passengers:

Had the captain attended and his officers been available at the inquiry, the following list of questions would have been most pertinent:

To the Captain:

- Did you have any alcohol at the evening reception, prior to sailing?
- Was this a factor in your being incapacitated the following day?
- Were you suffering from any medical condition at this time?
- Why did the *Mohegan* accompany the vessel, *Scottish King* (travelling at a much slower speed), at the early stage of the voyage, down the Channel?
- Why was the ship, arbitrarily sent to Prawle Point, to relay a signal to the shipping company?
- Were you solely responsible for the navigation and computations, at all stages of the vessel's progress down the Channel, or was it in collaboration with your senior officer?
- Were the navigational charts supplied by the company, or were they your personal items?
- Were the navigational charts the current versions available to mariners?
- What was the method of conveying any change in heading, top-down to the helmsman?
- What validation checks were made, as to the confirmation of any change to the ships' heading?
- Having suffered a loss of your right eye, in an incident some years previously, was the vision in your remaining eye adequate for reading charts, as well as having sufficient long-distance viewing capability?
- Did you wear spectacles? If not, had you been subject to any recent eye-test?
- What is the shipping company's policy, in checking a captain and an officer's medical state, as being fit for service?
- Were you on the bridge, at this time of the incident?
- Were you aware of the onshore warning flares, just prior to the disaster happening?

And To the Officers:

- Did the captain show any signs, during the voyage, of illness or incapacity?
- Was the captain approachable; willing to share navigational matters and enable you to confirm his computations?
- Did you have unfettered access to the charts and navigational equipment?
- Either way, were the charts up-to-date, and in good condition?
- At any time, did any one of the officers (or indeed, the helmsman) have misgivings, when the heading of 'west by north' was given, after passing the Eddystone Light?
- Did the vessel pass seaward of the Eddystone, or landward of that position?
- Did the proximity of the Cornish coast, to the ship's position, raise any comment or concern, among the crew?
- What were the sea and atmospheric conditions, during the latter part of the voyage, particularly just prior to the ship's foundering?
- At which point in the voyage, were the electric lights (other than navigational lights) switched on?
- Was it a factor that these lights were apt to cause glare and so compromise all round vision from the ship's bridge, at night?
- Was an absence of a clear and unambiguous light signal emanating from the direction of the Lizard, a cause for concern?
- When a light *was* noted on the starboard side, by the man in the crows-nest, was this taken to be the Lizard, or that of the St. Anthony light?
- Was evasive action taken; by steering the vessel hard to port, in order to avoid the looming land ahead and who had sanctioned this action?
- If and until this evasive action was taken, did any one of the officers sense that the vessel had been in any danger?
- If the captain was absent on the bridge, at what point did he eventually appear, prior to the disaster?
- Were the blue flares sent aloft from the shore noticed by you, and if so, what interpretation was made of this event by the officers on the bridge?
- Was evasive action taken before or after the blue fares were noticed?

And a final question to both the captain and each of his officers in turn:

And in your view, why did the *Mohegan* find itself among the Manacle Rocks?

Conclusion:

Why the *Mohegan* came to grief will probably never be fully explained. This only increases the allure of this story, for those who have an interest in the sea and our maritime history.

Those magnificent days of steamship travel, are now relegated to that of cruise-ships: plying their trade as floating hotels, casinos, shopping malls, and entertainment palaces. That more leisurely time when twelve days were taken in sailing between the old and the new countries, and with a service that reflected the more leisured classes, afforded by money and social standing, epitomized a bygone age: the *Belle Époque*. The *Mohegan* and its players in that tragedy, all unwittingly brought together for that terrible event, have now found their voice in the pages of this book.

The astonishing fact that Capt. Griffith did indeed survive the disaster and had reached the shore, absolutely transforms the *Mohegan* story, and coming to light after one hundred and fourteen years, as it does, is quite remarkable.

The revelations made to this author, by his family members, are responsible for this outcome. I feel privileged, and cannot thank them enough in allowing me to be the spokesperson in making public this sensitive family matter. However, I am mindful that the family were under no obligation to respond to my initial approach, and seemed quite appreciative in having an opportunity in putting the story straight. I know they will forgive me in calling them elderly, but I feel that this is perhaps their motivation: in a need to close a chapter in their family book.

We are fortunate in having those records from the newspapers of the day, and without which, we would not have had such detailed account of a moving human drama that is, and always will always be, the *Mohegan* story.

Appendices

Appendix 1

A Graphological Assessment for Capt. Richard Griffith:

The spoken word perishes, the written words remain.

The study of Griffith's handwriting was undertaken, in an attempt to assess his character and his motivation in life. It was hoped it would reveal hidden traits that could help explain his seemingly irrational behaviour, aboard the *Mohegan*.

But first, an overview for the science of graphology is recounted here:

Graphology is the study of handwriting and handwriting analysis is now an accepted and increasingly used technique for assessment of people within organizations. Handwriting analysis is an effective and reliable indicator of personality and behaviour, and so is a useful tool for many organizational processes, for example: recruitment, interviewing and selection, team-building, counselling, and career-planning.

Graphology has been described as 'brainwriting' – the handwriting comes directly from the writer in a uniquely personal and individual way, irrespective of how the person has been taught to write: an expert graphologist understands the styles of the different countries and languages and makes allowances for 'taught' influences. Also largely irrelevant to the actual analysis is the content of the written text.

The science of graphology uses at least 300 different handwriting features in its investigative approach. The graphologist's interpretation skill is in the psychological art of understanding the particular blend of handwriting features - an expert is able to see the writer 'step off the page.' [1060]

A detailed report on Capt. Griffith's graphology analysis follows:

The dominance in the writing is very clear, as is the perfectionist approach. Second best would never have been tolerated.

This is indicated by the firmness of the rightward slant, the balance of the zones and angularity of the letters, combined with the over-emphasised **t**-bars.

However, he didn't go into things with a target that was set in stone. The mixture of joined and un-joined letters within words shows he used both logic and intuition, which helped him to 'read' people, even though the knowledge he gained didn't deter him from doing what he believed was right. He wanted to be fair, but wasn't sentimental. The angularity of the letter forms shows the analyst he didn't do anything lightly. Not a man to make judgments spontaneously, all his actions would be the result of observation, investigation, planning and experience.

Definitely a shrewd operator, but he wasn't vindictive and in fact his rationale was to give his energy for the public benefit. The lower case '**y**' in the word 'probably' is curved open to the right, which tends to appear in the scripts of those who work in senior positions with others. A sense of public accountability is usually indicated by this, though it may mean that the writer's interpretation is from a personal standpoint. In his case I believe he is genuine and wanted to fulfill his responsibilities honorably.

[1060] See here for a more detailed account of the techniques employed; http://businessballs.com/graphologyhandwritinganalysis.htm.

The fact that the letters slant further rightwards on the right hand side of the page (the area of other people and the future), does show his ability to react strongly when he is upset or thwarted by what he sees as insubordination. He will have had a low boiling-point at such times and his reputation as a hard person would have been justified. The **i**-dots which are very firm reflect this also, and the signature with a hook at the end of the **t**-bar shows that he didn't let go when he believed he was right.

In contrast, the curved finals at the ends of some words show that he wasn't just a hard man, but could be pleasant when the pressure was off. The perfectionist streak and sense of tradition would have been dominant when he was on duty, but he did have another side to him that could emerge when he wasn't on duty.

The layout of the piece of script shows his ability to stay in control of the action and keep focused when under pressure. He could judge his actions finely and avoid being overtaken by events, while still operating close to the edge. Obviously these skills would be valuable in his career and no doubt why he was so respected.[1061]

The above report is based on the following handwriting samples: [1062]

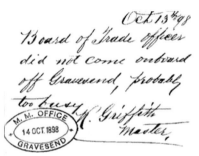

Specimen (1) Richard Griffith's hand-writing and his signature.

Specimen (2) Richard Griffith's signature

The report is most useful as it is possible to compare each observed attribute with Capt. Griffith's character, achievements, and other events throughout his career. He is described as a perfectionist and this he undoubtedly was: a man does not reach the top of the tree without an eye to detail, with a thoroughness, to the point of nit-picking. His colleagues seem to support this trait, though putting it in a more generalized form, "He was something of a martinet."

[1061] Personal communication: Elaine Quigley B.A. Hons. M.BIG (Dip) – Past Chairman of, *The British Institute of Graphologists* and is currently the Administrator and Journal Editor (2011).

[1062] Courtesy of the Memorial University, Newfoundland – Maritime History Archives.

The report assesses him as a shrewd operator. This would have helped his rise through the ranks, to reach the exalted position of commodore captain, at a relatively early age. Clearly, the overall attributes revealed in this report, leave us in no doubt that Griffith was a man with a mission; a born team leader, with an ability to accurately assess a person's worth and to capitalize on that.

He was generally well-liked by his crew. Again, the report shows he was a fair man, not given to rash decisions and with a sense of underlying public duty. Indeed, a genuine and honorable man. However, he would not tolerate indiscipline or insubordination. He was the captain and no one was going to forget that fact in a hurry.

The report goes on to say that, "[it] shows his ability to stay in control of the action and keep focused when under pressure. He could judge his actions finely and avoid being overtaken by events, while still operating close to the edge." This is well reflected in his actions, during the final moments of the *Mohegan* catastrophe. He was described, during that event as, cool, giving orders to his crew members, from the ship's bridge; urging them on in the launching of the lifeboats, even though he must have realised that the end was inevitable. The doomed ship would sink, taking his career with it. His own life was in the balance and yet his professionalism and cool-under-fire attitude to life, gave him some small credit, notwithstanding his terrible blunder, that was so out of character for the man.

Had he revealed himself, following the disaster, the burden of his action would have been unbearable; a proud man, undone by a moment of madness. A spectacular fall from grace awarded him an unenviable legacy, that of the man responsible for the loss of 105 lives, through a monumental misjudgment.

His misfortune is, as revealed in his handwriting, that he would not have countenanced any interference from his officers, in the management of his ship. Though surrounded by able officers who must have inwardly questioned the ship's course, they were not so inclined to raise this with their captain.

It would appear one can run a tight ship a little *too* tightly.

Appendix 2

A Graphological Assessment for Capt. Robins Purdy:

What are striking are the uneven pressure and the intensity of the rightward stroke. When the stroke is very firmly rightward, there is underlying hysteria in the thinking of the writer. The way the page is filled indicates obsession with a topic or a person to the extent that rationality and objectivity are not part of the approach to it. This wasn't a man to do things by halves and the consistently joined letters within words reflect the single-mindedness that would have characterised his attack on any activity that he wanted to complete. It would also indicate lack of patience with alternative options. Having invested his energy in what he believed in firmly, he wouldn't be willing to be flexible and concede ground, because that would indicate that he could have been wrong in his judgment and that wouldn't fit in with his way of thinking.

There is no real violence shown in the script, but the tension indicated by uneven pressure, could have produced emotional violence in the guise of impatience and irritation. It is like someone with a bee-in-his-bonnet, rather than a dangerous attacker. However, he is likely to have been irascible and difficult to deal with. The curved end strokes of the words usually show a pleasant interactive style, so it is more than likely that he was suffering from a form of mental disturbance that prevented him from being rational and tolerant. It is as though he has wound himself up and is now on a treadmill that he cannot leave. Many of the lower zones of the letters show a lighter pressure, as though he hasn't the strength to pull himself out of this and get back onto a more balanced thinking pattern.[1063]

The above report is based on the handwriting sample that follows, and it speaks for itself: [1064]

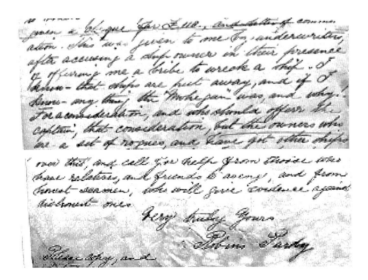

[1063] Personal communication: Elaine Quigley B.A. Hons. M.BIG (Dip) – Past Chairman of: *The British Institute of Graphologists* and is currently its Administrator and Journal Editor (2012).

[1064] Courtesy of the London Metropolitan Archives.

Appendix 3

A Board of Trade Ship Inspection – 19th Century:

There are instances for a Board of Trade inspection, mentioned in this publication; not least, the two inspections, one for the *Cleopatra* and the other for the *Mohegan*.

With typical thoroughness, the Victorian approach was a careful and systematic one; no doubt (in part) designed to instil confidence in a sea-faring public. Here is a description of a Board of Trade survey for a vessel, which appeared in a publication from the late nineteenth century. It would certainly have been the basis for each Board of Trade survey, in our ship of interest:

> In order to show the excellence of this annual inspection which invariably carried out by the Board's own Officials (men of tried experience), it will not be out of place to briefly describe the routine and conditions necessary to obtain the renewal of the passenger certificate. The first thing is to pay into a mercantile marine office the necessary fees, which vary in amount according to tonnage, at the same time giving notice of where the vessel is lying, and also the hour she will ready in a graving dock for the purpose of allowing the surver to "sight," otherwise carefully survey the bottom, propeller, and all other fittings not visible afloat, which must be done before any painting or exterior work is affected. This is looked upon as the most vital point of the survey, the passenger certificate always dating from the day of the sighting.
>
> Other matters examined by the surveyors are the deck and other fittings and gear; the holds and the hand and bilge-pumps, which must have all the parts shipped in place, and the valves and interiors open for examination; in addition as many of the bilge strainer boxes as possible must be exposed, together with as many of the limbers,[1065] in order to examine the state of the cement in bilges and to note any signs of working of the ship itself. The bulkhead sluices [1066] must also be turned, the water-tight doors closed and opened the handles and fittings for these being permanently attached or suspended in convenient position alongside. The fire-hose must be connected to the water service, and be stretched out for inspection with projecting nozzles attached, and connecting keys in place.
>
> The elaborate equipment of boats has to receive careful attention; each must be uncovered and actually have on board the necessary sails, masts, yards, oars, thole-pins, and rowlocks attached with strong chains; rudder and tiller ready in place, plugs, bailers, two fresh-water breakers or casks, bread-tank, life-belts, and axe, so that each article can be thoroughly inspected,
>
> The capacities and lowering arrangements of the boats—which are strictly defined, not only by the British but also the United States authorities—must be up to standard, and a complete list of their sizes and capacities, when required, must be handed to the surveyor; the boats must be lowered into the water to test the gear and their water-tightness.
>
> All the scheduled signal and spare lamps must be cleaned and open for survey, the various fog-horns, rockets, etc., for night signalling, and the sounding leads, must be submitted to inspection.
>
> The anchors must also be cleaned and scraped, with the official and proof numbers distinctly visible, and, in dry dock, the whole of the cables must be run out in the bottom of the dock and have the shackle-pins all backed out, so that the numbers may be verified with the certificates of tests.

[1065] *Limbers*; is the space between the frames of the vessel in the bottom under the ceiling.

[1066] *Bulkhead sluices*; are the valves in the bulkhead, running through the bulkheads.

A still more extensive survey has to be gone through in the machinery departments; the whole of the working-parts, such as cylinders, valves, pistons, pumps, crank-pins, bearings, safety-valves, fresh-water condensers and other portions must be opened up for inspection, also the boilers both in the steam and on the fire sides; it is also necessary at stated intervals to take off the propellers and draw in the stern shafts for examination. This precaution is now generally taken every twelve months by most of the leading lines, a practice strongly to be commended.

In addition to these requirements all the official papers of the ship, namely ship's register, the various certificates relating to the compasses, chains, and anchors, and also those of the captain, chief and second officers, and chief and second engineers, have to be presented for notification.

After all these steps have been completed the Board's surveyor has to send to the principal office in Whitehall, London, a declaration made by him stating that the ship is complete in all requirements. On receipt of this the certificate is forwarded to the owners, which allows her to carry passengers for a stated period.

When it is remembered that, in addition to all these requirements, very extensive rules and regulations of the Board of Trade have to be complied with by the builders of the ship and machinery previous to the vessel's obtaining a certificate, it is evident that but little is left to be desired in the thoroughness of the protection afforded to the marine travelling public by the British Legislature; and when the enactments are carried out by the surveying staff with much ability, intelligence, and willingness to help at all times, as the author has experienced over fifteen years, there is no doubt they prove a strong incentive to all concerned to aim at and achieve a higher grade of perfection in the safe and perfect working of high-speed passenger vessels even than that now reached.

True it is that now and again murmurs of discontent arise from some enterprising builder or engineer, or from some far-seeing shipowner, who finds a restriction placed on some new untried advance; but if a successful trial proves a new idea to be satisfactory and safe so far as human life is concerned, which is the Board of Trade's first requirement, then ready acceptance may be obtained, even if outside the usual authorized forms.

In addition to this annual inspection in the home ports, another has now-a-days to be undergone by the surveying staff of the United States Government, who, some twelve years ago, enacted a law which rendered it compulsory for all vessels carrying passengers from the ports of that country to have a certificate, granted on somewhat similar conditions to the British regulations.

Returning now to the direct working of the ship: as soon as the advertised date for sailing draws near, the "Outside" section having had the work on board completed and all departments in order, steam raised and engines tried, and everything ready to receive passengers, while the "Inside" section has transacted all its portions of the work, definite dates are announced for the embarkation of first the steerage, then the second class, and finally the saloon passengers, This may take place at the loading berth in the company's dock, but more generally from the landing-stage, a notice of these hours being widely circulated. At a certain specified hour the official clearance takes place on board, which means the passing of the ship by the Health and Emigration officers, as well as by the Board of Trade, the Custom clearance having been arranged previously, so that the vessel may go out of dock into the river and await the passengers and mails.

The form of clearing a vessel is carried out by two Government officers, one being a sea-going officer of tried experience from either the Royal Navy or Mercantile Marine, and the other a fully qualified medical man; these two gentlemen upon arrival proceed to examine the steerage passengers accommodation as to the sleeping, lavatories, exits, ventilation, and other necessaries; afterwards each individual steerage passenger, adult or child, has to pass the medical officer, to provide against the chance of any infectious disease on the passage. The medical outfit is subjected to examination, and the entire crew has to be mustered and pass the inspection of both officials, so as to ensure their being fit and able men for their respective duties. A careful examination is also made of the lifeboats, some being lowered into the water, and often an inspection of other details, such as night signals and rockets, the supply of fresh water, freeboard, etc.

The necessary papers being filled in and signed, the vessel is cleared, and ready to proceed to sea as soon as the saloon passengers and perhaps mails are on board.

The embarkation of the saloon passengers, which, as a rule, is the final scene, takes place from the dock or landing-stage at a convenient time shortly preceding that at which the vessels gets under weigh, and is accompanied with much bustle and stir but no confusion, everything being done systematically.

The celebrated landing-stage, which plays so useful a part in the coming and going of the Liverpool Transatlantic liners, is one of the most important appurtenances of the great port of the Mersey. Notwithstanding its close proximity to the surface of the water, it was completely destroyed by fire on July 28th, 1874. This disaster was occasioned by some workmen, who were working near the embayment in the stage, allowing a naked light to set fire to some of the creosoted wooden beams then existing below the deck of the stage, and owing to the inflammable nature of the material and to its inaccessibility, no effectual means could be found to extinguish it, so that whole structure, extending nearly half a mile was totally destroyed. No lives were lost, but the reconstruction of the stage occupied a considerable period, and entailed a cost of over £250,000.

Upon the arrival of the tender with the saloon passengers alongside the ship, the commander and officers are in attendance at the gangway to receive them, and all the stewards ranged ready, under the purser and chief steward, to direct them to their different rooms and berths, and attend to the removal of the smaller baggage; the larger baggage (which is despatched by another tender) being stowed by the deck department in quarters specially set apart for it. After a short period, the whole of the passengers and their baggage being on board, and all ready for sailing, the tender leaves and returns to the stage with the owners or representatives, and officials of the company, and, if the state of tide permits, the vessel gets under weigh at once under the supreme charge of the captain, whose station is on the navigating bridge. With him is also the pilot, whose duty it is to navigate the vessel through the channels and passages for which he is duly licensed. There is also on the bridge, alongside the captain and the pilot, the fourth officer, whose duty is to transmit the engine-room and steering orders.

The chief officer's position when leaving or entering port is in the bow of the ship, to attend to the working of the anchor, and other duties in that quarter; to attend to the stern, the second officer takes up his position in the poop; the third officer give special attention to the prompt carrying out of the orders given to the quartermaster at the wheel, and so on, each officer having a proper station and duty assigned to him.

In the engine department, also, the duties of each of the staff are distinctly defined for the time of leaving and entering port; so that nothing is left undone to secure systematic working throughout.

After the vessel has got fairly under weigh and cleared the channel the "stand-by," as it is technically termed, is dispensed with, and the duties are changed for the regular watches at sea, not to be changed again until the arrival off New York, except in event of foggy weather coming on at sea.[1067]

[1067] Magginis, John; *The Atlantic Ferry: Its Ships, Men, And Working* (London, UK: Whitaker & Co.1893), 116.

Appendix 4

DISCIPLINE STANDARDS ABOARD THE STEAMSHIP *CLEOPATRA* / *MOHEGAN:*

<table>
<tr><td colspan="3" align="center">REGULATIONS FOR MAINTAINING DISCIPLINE,
SANCTIONED BY THE BOARD OF TRADE IN PURSUANCE OF S. 114 (2) OF THE MERCHANT SHIPPING ACT, 1894.</td></tr>
</table>

Three regulations are distinct from, and in addition to, those contained in the Act, and are sanctioned but not universally required by Law. All or any of them may be adopted by agreement between a Master and his Crew, and thereupon the offences specified in such of them as are so adopted will be legally punishable by the appropriate Fines or Punishments. These regulations, however, are not to apply to Certificated Officers.

These regulations are all numbered, and the numbers of such of them as are adopted must be inserted in the space left for that purpose in the Agreement, page 1, and the following copy of these Regulations must be made to correspond with the Agreement by erasing such of the Regulations as are not adopted. The signatures or initials of the Superintendent of a Mercantile Marine Office, Consular of other Officer before whom the agreement is made, must be placed opposite such of the Regulations as are adopted.

For the purpose of legally enforcing any of the following penalties, the same steps must be adopted as in the case of other Offences punishable under the Act; that is to say, a statement of the Offence must, immediately after its commission, be entered in the Official Log Book by the direction of the Master, and must be at the same time be attested to be true by the signatures of the Master and the Mate, or one of the Crew and a copy of such entry must be furnished, or the same must be read over to the Offender, before the ship reaches any Port or departs from the Port at which she is and an entry that the same has been so furnished or read over, and of the reply, if any, of the Offender, must be made and signed in the same manner as the entry of the Offence. These entries must, upon discharge of the Offender, be shewn to the Superintendent of a Mercantile Marine Office before whom the Offender is discharged and if he is satisfied that the Offence is proved, and that the entries have been properly made, the Fine must be deducted from the Offender's wages and paid over to the Superintendent.

If, in consequence of subsequent Good Conduct, the Master thinks fit to remit or reduce any Fine upon any Member of his Crew which has been entered in the Official Log, and signifies the same to the Superintendent, the fine shall be remitted or reduced accordingly. If wages are contracted for by the Voyage or by Share, the amount of the Fines is to be ascertained in the matter in which the Amount of Forfeiture is ascertained in similar cases under Sect, 234.

No	OFFENCE	Fine / Punishment
1	Striking or assaulting any person on Board or belonging to the Ship (if not otherwise prosecuted)	Five shillings.
2	Bringing or having on Board spirituous liquors	Five shillings.
3	Drunkenness. First Offence Drunkenness. Second and for each subsequent Offence	Five shillings. Ten shillings.
4	Taking on Board and keeping possession of any fire-arms, knuckle-duster, loaded cane, slung-shot, sword-stick, bowie knife, dagger, or any other offensive weapon or offensive instrument, without the concurrence of the Master, for every day during which a seaman retains such weapon or instrument.	Five shillings.

Appendix 5

AGREEMENT AND ACCOUNT OF CREW
FOREIGN–GOING SHIP

The term "Foreign-going Ship" means every Ship employed in trading or, going between some place or places in The United Kingdom and some place or places situated beyond Coasts of the United Kingdom, The Isles of Guernsey, Jersey, Sark, Alderney, and Man, and the continent of Europe, between the River Elbe and Brest inclusive.

The Several Persons whose names are hereto subscribed and whose descriptions are contained on page 4 hereof, and of whom *13* are engaged as Sailors, hereby agree to serve on board the said Ship in the several capacities expressed against their respective Names on a Voyage from

London to New York and/or any ports or places within the limits of 70 degrees North and 70 degrees South latitude, trading to and from, for any period not exceeding twelve months, and back to the port of final discharge in the United Kingdom.

And the Crew agree to conduct themselves in an orderly, faithful, honest, and sober manner, and to be at all times diligent in their respective duties, and to be obedient to the lawful commands of the said Master, or of any Person who shall lawfully succeed him, and of their Superior Officers, in everything relating to the said Ship and the stores and cargo thereof, whether on board, in boats, or on the shore. In considerations of which Services to be duly performed, the said Master hereby agrees to pay to the said Crew as Wages the sums against their Names respectively expressed, and to supply them with Provisions according to the Scale on the other side hereof.

And it is hereby agreed that any Embezzlement or wilful or negligent Destruction of any part of the Ship's Cargo or Stores shall be made good to the Owner out the Wages of the Persons guilty of the same.

And if any Persons enters himself as qualified for a duty which he proves incompetent to perform, his Wages shall be reduced in proportion to his incompetency : And it is also agreed, That the Regulations authorized by the Board of Trade, which are printed herein and numbered *1 2 3* and *4* are adopted by the parties hereto, and shall be considered as embodied in this Agreement : And it is also agreed, That if any Member of the Crew considers himself to be aggrieved by any breach of the Agreement or otherwise, he shall represent the same to the Master or Officer in charge of the Ship in a quiet and orderly manner, who shall thereupon take such steps as the case may require : and it is also stipulated that the Seaman shall receive the advances of wages entered herein against their names.

AND IT IS ALSO AGREED that the said master shall be entitled to deduct from the wages of the said crew respectively the following amount, viz., for not joining in the time specified in col. 10, 2 days' pay or any expenses which have been properly incurred in hiring a substitute, and for absence from the ship at any time without leave, a sum not exceeding 2 weeks' pay and it is hereby mutually agreed that any dispute arising on the subject of these deductions shall be settled by the superintendent of a mercantile marine office, consular office or shipping master abroad, and that his decision shall be final. AND IT IS ALSO AGREED that any member of the crew swearing or using blasphemous language shall be fined 5/– for each offence; that no cash be advanced or liberty granted abroad and that the seamen and firemen assist each other in the general duties of the ship and clean out their quarters at least three times a week or more often if required, and leave their quarters in a clean and sanitary condition to the satisfaction of the master at the end of the voyage, under a penalty 5s. each for each offence. That in the event of any member of the crew failing to join at the time specified, the master may engage a substitute at once for the voyage, and that the crew shall muster for inspection, wearing the Company's uniform, and attend boat and fire drill whenever called upon, either night or day, under a penalty of 5s. for each omission. AND IT IS ALSO AGREED that the crew shall attend divine service every Sunday morning. It is also agreed that the seamen and stewards shall appear clean and in uniform on arrival and departure at and from each port, attending to embarkation and disembarkation of passengers.[1068]

[1068] Courtesy: Memorial University, Newfoundland; Maritime History Archives.

Appendix 6

REGISTRATION FOR BIRTHS: [1069]

CLARK, Mary Ann Maria

Sex: Female
Registration District: POPLAR UNION Sub-District: POPLAR – County of Middlesex
Date of Birth: 18th May, 1855
Name of Father: Samuel Clark
Occupation of Father: Rigger Journeyman
Surname and Maiden Name of Mother: Martha Clark – formerly Wickham
Place of Birth: 2 William Street
When Registered: 2nd June, 1858
Informant and Residence: Martha Clark – 2 William Street

CLARK, Martha Wickham

Sex: Girl
Registration District: POPLAR UNION Sub-District: POPLAR – County of Middlesex
Date of Birth: 25th May, 1862
Name of Father: Samuel Clark
Occupation of Father: Rigger Journeyman
Surname and Maiden Name of Mother: Martha Clark (formerly Wickham)
Place of Birth: 2 William Street
When Registered: 30th January, 1852
Informant and Residence: S. Clark (father) – 2 William Street Poplar

GRIFFITH, Walter Hugh

Sex: Male
Registration District: STEPNEY Sub-District: LIMEHOUSE – County of Middlesex
Date of Birth: 5th March, 1885
Name of Father: Richard Griffiths
Occupation of Father: Mariner (deceased)
Surname and Maiden Name of Mother: Martha Griffith—formerly Clark
Place of Birth: 135 Narrow Street
When Registered: 14th April, 1885
Informant and Residence: M. Griffiths (Mother) 135 Narrow Street, Limehouse

GALLAWAY, Frank Christopher

Sex: Male
Registration District: ST. AUSTELL Sub-District: GRAMPOUND – County of Cornwall
Date of Birth: 18th April, 1912
Name of Father: Daniel Christopher Gallaway
Occupation of Father: Clay Labourer
Surname and Maiden Name of Mother: Harriet Emma Gallaway; late Burt; formerly Lean.
Place of Birth: Trelion Downs, St. Stephens
When Registered: 25th May, 1912
Informant and Residence: D. C. Gallaway. Father

[1069] Courtesy: General Records Office.

Appendix 7

BURT, Frederick George
Sex: Male
Age: 21 Years
Condition: Bachelor
Occupation: Labourer
Residence at time of marriage:
  Rejirrah, Newlyn East
Name of Father: William Burt
Occupation of Father: Labourer

LEAN, Harriet Emma
Sex: Female
Age: 22 Years
Condition: Spinster
Residence at time of marriage:
  Reen Farm, Perranzabuloe
Name of Father: John Lean
Occupation of Father: Labourer

Registration District: Register Office, District of Truro, County of Cornwall
Married In: Register Office by Certificate
Date of Marriage: 5th August, 1899
In the Presence of: John Lean / Christ. Harris Jnr
Registrar: Jno. Chas. Mill
Superintendent Registrar: Frank Truscott

DIGGENS, William Alfred
Sex: Male
Age: 25 Years
Condition: Bachelor
Residence at time of marriage:
  Gatley [Cheadley, Stockport]
Name of Father: William Diggens
Occupation of Father: Tutor

THOMPSON, Annie Scott
Sex: Female
Age: 21 Years
Condition: Spinster
Residence at time of marriage:
  Cornbrook Abbey, Stockport
Name of Father: William Goulden Thompson
Occupation of Father: Merchant

Registration District: Chester
Married Solemnized at: Parish Church in the parish of St. Thomas' Stockport
Married By: B. Bradshaw – Rector of St. Stephens, Hulme
Date of Marriage: 4th October, 1878
In the Presence of: William Goulon Thompson [Father] / Emily Duckworth

---

GALLOWAY, Daniel Christopher
Sex: Male
Age: 34 Years
Condition: Bachelor
Occupation: Agricultural Labourer
Residence at time of marriage:
  Rose, Perranzabuloe
Name of Father: Frank Galloway (Deceased)
Occupation of Father: Colt Breaker

BURT, Harriet Emma
Sex: Female
Age: 32 Years
Condition: Widow
Residence at time of marriage:
  Rose Perranzabuloe
Name of Father: John Lean
Occupation of Father: Labourer

Registration District: Register Office, District of Truro, County of Cornwall
Married In: Register Office by Certificate
Date of Marriage: 13th August, 1910
In the Presence of: Bessie Cleave / E. Carnall
Registrar: Jno. Chas. Mill
Superintendent Registrar: Frank Truscott

[1070] Courtesy: General Records Office.

GRIFFITH, Ada Elizabeth
Sex: Female
Age: 33 Years
Condition: Widow
Residence at time of marriage:
   123 Thorold Road, Ilford
Name of Father: Joseph Brown
Occupation of Father: Grocer's Assistant

HENDERSON John
Sex: Male
Age: 42 Years
Condition: Bachelor
Occupation: Sailor
Residence at time of marriage:
   Holy Trinity , Brompton Kent
Name of Father: William Henderson
Occupation of Father: Railway Officer

Registration District: Parish Church
Married Solemnized at: Parish Church, Gt. Ilford, Essex
Married By: By License by A. Wyndam Ottoway – Vicar
Date of Marriage: 24th April, 1921
In the Presence of: W. J. Monkton / Elizabeth Brown

GRIFFITH, Richard
Sex: Male
Age: Full [Adult – 27 years]
Condition: Bachelor
Occupation: Mariner
Residence at time of marriage:
   Bromley
Name of Father: Hugh Griffith
Occupation of Father: Farmer

CLARK, Mary Ann
Sex: Female
Age: Full [24 years]
Condition: Spinster
Residence at time of marriage: Bromley
Name of Father: Samuel Clark
Occupation of Father: Rigger
Residence at time of marriage:
   Bromley

Married Solemnized at: Parish Church in the parish of Bromley St. Leonards, Middlesex
Married By: By License
Date of Marriage: 25th September, 1879
In the Presence of: Henry W. Clark / Caroline Clark
By Me: John G. Griffiths

GRIFFITH, Richard
Sex: Male
Age: 31 Years
Condition: Bachelor
Occupation: Seaman Merchant Service
Residence at time of marriage:
   135 Narrow Street, Limehouse
Name of Father: Hugh Griffith
Occupation of Father: Farmer

CLARK, Martha Wickham
Sex: Female
Age: 21 Years
Condition: Spinster
Residence at time of marriage:
   135 Narrow Street, Limehouse
Name of Father: Samuel Clark
Occupation of Father: Rigger

Registration District: Register Office, District of Stepney
Married Solemnized at: Register Office
Married By: By License
Date of Marriage: 18th August, 1883
In the Presence of: F. E. Bennett / T. G. Stacey
Registrar: S. E. Lewis
Deputy Superintendent Registrar: M. Archer

GRIFFITH, Selina May
Age: 26 Years
Condition: Spinster
Occupation:—
Residence at time of marriage:
  26 Wanstead Park Avenue
Name of Father: Richard Griffith
Occupation of Father: Captain MS (deceased)

PRETTEJOHN, Ernest
Age: 30 Years
Condition: Bachelor
Occupation: Sapper RE
Residence at time of marriage:
  Chatham
Name of Father: Edward James Prettejohn (deceased)
Occupation of Father: Merchant

Registration District: West Ham, Essex
Married Solemnized at: St. Gabriels Church, Aldersbrook [Wanstead]
Married By: W. H. Holdsworth – Asst. Curate
Date of Marriage: December 12th 1915
In the Presence of: Edith Prettejohn / Walter H. Griffith

GRIFFITH, Victor Richard
Sex: Male
Age: 27 Years
Registration:
Condition: Bachelor
Occupation: Motor Mechanic
Residence at time of marriage:
  26 Wanstead Park Avenue, Manor Park
Name of Father: Richard Griffith
Occupation of Father: Master Mariner (Deceased)

HEAD, Helen Hilda
Sex: Female
Age: 25 Years
Condition: Spinster
Residence at time of marriage:
  46 Guildford Road Seven Kings
Name of Father: Harry Head
Occupation of Father: Provisions Manager

Married in the: Register Office
In the District of: West Ham
Married By: After Banns by Charles G D LaLouche – Rector
In the Counties of: Essex, Ham C.B. & West Ham C.B.
Date of Marriage: 9th August, 1924
In the Presence of: Harry Head; Martha W. Griffith
Registrar: Alfred Scott, Deputy Registrar / Alfred Hall – Superintendent Registrar

---

GRIFFITH, Walter Hugh
Sex: Male
Age: 27 Years
Registration: Q2 1912, Medway, Volume No. 2a;
Page No. 1406.
Condition: Bachelor
Occupation: Commercial Clerk
Residence at time of marriage:
  26 Wanstead Park Avenue, Little Ilford
Name of Father: Richard Griffith
Occupation of Father: Master Mariner (Deceased)

BROWN, Ada Elizabeth
Sex: Female
Age: 24 Years
Condition: Spinster
Residence at time of marriage:
  30 Wyndham Road Chatham
Name of Father: Joseph Brown
Occupation of Father: Grocer's Assistant

Married Solemnized at: Parish Church in the parish of St. John's Chatham in the County of Kent
Registration District: Register Office, District of Romford, County of Essex
Married By: After Banns by Charles G. D. LaLouche – Rector
Date of Marriage: 8th June, 1912
In the Presence of: Joseph Brown / Ernest Rhymes Mitchell

POTTER, Mary Elizabeth [1071]
Age: 37 Years
Condition: Spinster
Residence at time of marriage:
   The Vicarage, St. Keverne
Name of Father: Richard Potter
Occupation of Father: Fisherman

MILDREN, William
Age: 44 Years
Condition: Bachelor
Residence at time of marriage:
   Roskerwell [St. Keverne]
Name of Father: John Mildren
Occupation of Father: Farmer

Registration District: Helston
Married Solemnized at: The Wesleyan Chapel, St. Keverne
Married By: Joseph Higham, Wesleyan Minister
Date of Marriage: January 2nd 1906
In the Presence of: Henry Benney / Joseph Hendy James.

[1071] The connection with Canon Diggens is that Elizabeth Potter came to St. Keverne with the Canon and Mrs Diggens from Lancashire, when he took up his ministry at St. Keverne church in 1896. In the 1891 UK census, it is recorded that she had worked as a housekeeper for John H. Gillet – a handkerchief printer, in Gravel Lane, Wilmslow, Cheshire. Courtesy of Alan Potter; Lancashire, who claims she was his great-great-Aunt.

Appendix 8

BURT, Frederick

Age: 24 Years   Sex: Male
Registration District: TRURO
Sub-District: St. Agnes – County of Cornwall
Date of Death: 23rd September, 1901
Place of Death: Perranporth, Perranzabuloe R.D.
Occupation: General Labourer
Cause of Death: Killed by a fall of ground whilst at work on the Perran and Newquay Railway Works
Certified by: E. Lawrence Carlyon, Coroner for Cornwall
Description and residence of informant: Inquest held 24th September 1901
When Registered: 25th September, 1901   **Registrar:** Christr. Harris

DIGGENS, Alfred Noel

Age: 24 Years   Sex: Male
Registration District: HELSTON
Sub-District: St. Keverne – County of Cornwall
Date of Death: 15th October, 1905
Place of Death: The Vicarage, St. Keverne, R.D.
Occupation: Dental Surgeon
Cause of Death: Albuminuria 12 months; Hypertrophy; Dilation of Heart
Certified by: E. J. L. Spry M.R.C.S. [Dr Leverton-Spry]
Description and residence of informant: W. A. Diggens (Father) Present at the death—The Vicarage, St. Keverne
When Registered: 16th October, 1905   Registrar: S. Joyce

DIGGENS, William Alfred

Age: 63 Years   Sex: Male
Registration District: St. GERMANS
Sub-District: St. Saltash – County of Cornwall
Date of Death: 15th April, 1916
Place of Death: The Vicarage, St. Stephens, R.D.
Occupation: Clerk in Holy Orders
Cause of Death: (1) Double Pneumonia; (2) Syncope
Certified by: E. W. Lewis M.R.C.S.
Description and residence of informant: S. Diggens (Sister) Present at the death—9 Beatrice Ave., St. Stephens
When Registered: 18th April, 1916   Registrar: S. Joyce

GALLOWAY, Daniel Christopher

Age: 67 Years   Sex: Male
Registration District: REDRUTH
Sub-District: Redruth – County of Cornwall
Date of Death: 22rd November, 1939
Place of Death: 1 Barncoose Place Illogan Camborne Redruth [1073]
Occupation: Back Lane West Redruth, Camborne Redruth U.D. General Labourer
Cause of Death: Cerebral Thombosis
Certified by: D. Clahane M.B.
Description and residence of informant: R. Cockshoot—Present at the death – 1 Barncoose Place Redruth (Workhouse)
When Registered: 25th November, 1939   Registrar: Charles Thomas

GALLOWAY, Harriet Emma

Age: 67 Years   Sex: Female
Registration District: TRURO

[1072] Courtesy: General Records Office.

[1073] This is the postal address for the Redruth Union Workhouse.

Sub-District: Truro – County of Cornwall
Date of Death: 24th December, 1948
Place of Death: 10 Council Houses, Probus, R.D.
Occupation: Widow of Daniel Gallaway
Cause of Death: 1. (a) Myocarditis (b) Bronchial Asthma
Certified by: Edwin H. Eastcott L.R.C.P.
Description and residence of informant: Catherine Commons (Sister) – 42, Fairmantle Street, Truro.
When Registered: 27th December, 1948   Registrar: A. E. Buzza

GAY, Elizabeth Ann

Age: 77 Years   Sex: Female
Registration District: TRURO
Sub-District: St. Just – County of Cornwall
Date of Death: 15th October, 1911
Place of Death: Churchtown, Ruanlanihorne, R.D.
Occupation: Wife of Giles Gay – A farm Labourer
Cause of Death: Chronic Bronchitis; Exhaustion; Cardiac Failure
Certified by: Martin Glover M.R.C.S.
Description and residence of informant: *X* The mark of Giles Gay (Widower) Present at the death –
Churchtown, Ruanlanihorne
When Registered: 16th October, 1911   Registrar: John Lobb

GAY, Giles

Age: 78 Years   Sex: Male
Registration District: TRURO
Sub-District: St. Just – County of Cornwall
Date of Death: 27th April, 1922
Place of Death: Ruan, Lanihorne, R.D.
Occupation: Farm Labourer
Cause of Death: Senile Decay; Cardiac Failure
Certified by: Frank S. Scott M.R.C.S.
Description and residence of informant: Giles M. Burgess (Daughter) Present at the death
58 Roberts Road, Larkbear, Exeter
When Registered: 27th October, 1922   Registrar: A. W. Perry

GAY, Samuel Henry

Age: 42 Years   Sex: Male
Registration District: REDRUTH
Sub-District: Redruth – County of Cornwall
Date of Death: 12th July, 1907
Place of Death: Churchtown, Lanihorne, R.D.
Occupation: Farm Labourer
Cause of Death: Cerebral Haemorrhage
Certified by: Martin Clover M.R.C.S.
Description and residence of informant: Giles Gay (Father) Present at the death—Churchtown, Lanihorne
When Registered: 13th July, 1907   Registrar: John Lobb

GRANDIN, Lizzie Small

Age: 52 Years   Sex: Female
Registration District: HELSTON
Sub-District: St. Keverne – County of Cornwall
Date of Death: 14th October, 1898
Place of Death: In the Manacle Rocks in the Parish of St. Keverne
Occupation: Widow of Samuel Grandin an oil merchant
Cause of Death: Drowned on the Manacle Rocks from the Wreck of the S. Ship *Mohegan*
Certified by:
Description and residence of informant: Maud Small Roudebush, Daughter – causing the body to be
buried. 34 Trebovir Road Earles [*sic*] Court London
When Registered: 16th October 1898   Registrar: Thomas S. Joyce

GRIFFITH, Griffith

Age: 84 Years   Sex: Male
Registration District: PWLLHELI
Sub-District: Ilford – Aberdaron County of Canarvon
Date of Death: 21st April, 1925
Place of Death: Caereglwys Llanengan
Occupation: Retired Farmer
Cause of Death: (1) Bronchitis 1 year (2) Pulmonary Oedema No P.M.
Certified by: R. H. Parry M.B.
Description and residence of informant: R. J. Griffith; Brother-in-law – Belle Vue, Sarn, Meillteyrn.
When Registered: 23rd April, 1925   Registrar: Robert Roberts.

GRIFFITH, Hugh [father to Capt. Richard Griffith]

Age: 83 Years   Sex: Male
Registration District: PWLLHELI UNION
Sub-District: Pwllheli – County of Canarvon
Date of Death: 11th January, 1888
Place of Death: Creigiruchaf, Llanengan, R. S. D.
Occupation: Farmer
Cause of Death: Disease of the Heart; Mortification of the Foot 5 months
Certified by: Theo. Hunter Hughes M.R.C.S.
Description and residence of informant: Griffith Griffith (Son) In attendance—Creigiruchaf, Llanengan
When Registered: 13th January, 1888   Registrar: Evan Thoˢ Griffith

GRIFFITH, Martha Wickham

Age: 96 Years   Sex: Female
Registration District: BODMIN In the: County of Cornwall
Date of Death: 27 December, 1958
Place of Death: Tregawne, Withiel
Occupation: Widow of Richard Griffith
Cause of Death: 1 (a) Senility
Certified by: Alexander M. Killock M.B.
Description and residence of informant: E. Prettejohn; Son-in-law, Tregawne, Withiel
When Registered: 27 December, 1958   Registrar: F.A. Sanders

GRIFFITH, Mary [mother to Capt. Richard Griffith]

Age: 76 Years   Sex: Female
Registration District: PWLLHELI UNION
Sub-District: Pwllheli – County of Canarvon
Date of Death: 1st February, 1883
Place of Death: Creigiruchaf, Llanengan, R. S. D.
Occupation: Wife of Hugh Griffith—Farmer
Cause of Death: Chronic Bronchitis
Certified by: I. Edmund Jones M.B. & C.M.
Description and residence of informant: Griffith Griffith (Son). In attendance—Creigiruchaf, Llanengan
When Registered: 9th January, 1883. Registrar: Evan Thoˢ Griffith

GRIFFITH, Mary [not related]

Age: 21 Years   Sex: Female
Registration District: PWLLHELI UNION
Sub-District: Aberdaron – County of Carnarvon
Date of Death: 20th June, 1880
Place of Death: Cefn Treuddyn Penllech
Occupation: Daughter of John Griffith Farmer (Deceased)
Cause of Death: Consumption many years
Certified by: R. H. Clusen – Surgeon
Description and residence of informant: Richard Hughes (Father in Law)
Present at the death, at Cefn Treuddyn, Penllech
When Registered: Twenty fifth June 1880.
Registrar: Thomas Griffith

GRIFFITH, Mary [not related]

Age: 23 Years   Sex: Female
Registration District: HEREFORD
Sub-District: Hereford City – County of Hereford
Date of Death: 14th October, 1882
Place of Death: Belle Vue Terrace. Parish of St Owen U S D
Occupation: Spinster
Cause of Death: Disease of the Brain
Certified by: John Lambe – Coroner for Hereford
Description and residence of informant: Certificate received from Inquest, 17th October, 1882
When Registered: 18th October, 1882   Registrar: Henry Griffith

GRIFFITH, Mary Ann:[not related]

Age: 53 Years   Sex: Female
Registration District: EDMONTON
Sub-District: Enfield – County of Middlesex
Date of Death: 2nd March, 1908
Place of Death: 37 Seaford Road, Enfield U. D.
Occupation: Wife of William Reuben Griffith a Musical Instrument Maker
Cause of Death: Valvular Heart disease, Dropsy, Cellulitis of leg
Certified by: R. J. Gardiner MB
Description and residence of informant: Pauline Griffith Daughter
Present at the death – 37 Seaford Road, Enfield
When Registered: 3rd March, 1908   Registrar: Wm James Matthews

GRIFFITH, Mary Ann [not related]

Age: 22 Years   Sex: Female
Registration District: SWANSEA
Sub-District: Llansamlet – County of Glamorgan
Date of Death: 27th April, 1880
Place of Death: Birchgrove, Llansamlet, Higher
Occupation: Wife of Edward Griffiths, Coal miner
Cause of Death: Phthisis Pulmonalis [pulmonary tuberculosis]
Certified by: D. L. Davies M. B.
Description and residence of informant: Thomas Davies (Stepfather)
Present at the death at Birchgrove, Llansamlet, Higher
When Registered: 29th April. 1880   Registrar: John Rees

GRIFFITHS, Mary Anne [not related]

Age: 23 Years   Sex: Female
Registration District: CAMARTHEN
Sub-District: Llangendeirne – County of Camarthen
Date of Death: 22nd July, 1882
Place of Death: Birchgrove, Llansamlet, Higher
Occupation: Daughter of Jacob Griffiths (a Labourer, deceased)
Cause of Death: Heart Disease Dropsy
Certified by: N. L. Jones L.R.C.P.
Description and residence of informant: Thomas Williams
Present at the death at Heol fawr Mill, Llanarthney, R.S.D.
When Registered: 18th October, 1882   Registrar: Henry Griffith

GRIFFITHS, Mary Ann [? related]

Age: 27 Years   Sex: Female
Registration District: BILLERICAY
Sub-District: Brentwood, Essex
Date of Death: 24th December, 1889
Place of Death: Essex Lunatic Asylum, South Weald
Occupation: No occupation. From Wansdworth Asylum
Cause of Death: Pneumonia
Certified by: John Turner M.B.

Description and residence of informant: E. Hubbard present at the Death. Essex Lunatic Asylum, South Weald
When Registered: 28th December 1889   Registrar: E. W. Cottee

GRIFFITH, Victor Richard

Age: 81 Years   Sex: Male
Date of Birth: Wanstead Park, Redbridge.
Place of birth: 3rd June, 1897
Usual Address: 139, Glaster Avenue, Chelmsford, Essex.
Registration District: CHELMSFORD
Sub-District: Ilford – County of Essex
Date of Death: 4th July, 1978
Place of Death: Broomfield Hospital, Broomfield
Occupation: Insurance Agent / Clerical Worker (retired)
Cause of Death: a. Left Ventricular Failure
                   b. Atrial Fibrillation
                   c. Ischaemic Heart Disease
Certified by: D. R. Edwards, MB
Description and residence of informant: Eugenie Victoria KITCHEN (daughter)
45 Juniper Drive, Chelmsford Essex.
When Registered: 4th July, 1978. Registrar (Deputy): J. R.

GRIFFITH, Walter Hugh

Age: 35 Years   Sex: Male
Registration District: ROMFORD
Sub-District: Ilford – County of Essex
Date of Death: 24th March, 1920
Place of Death: 123 Thorold Road U.D.
Occupation: Provision Merchants Manager
Cause of Death: Influenza; Influenzal Pneumonia
Certified by: J. E. Price Watts M.R.C.S.
Description and residence of informant: A.E. Griffith – Widow of deceased Present at the death
123 Thorold Road, Ilford
When Registered: 24th March, 1920   Registrar: Jno. Farrow

HINDMARSH, William Logan

Age: 35 Years   Sex: Male
Registration District: HELSTON
Sub-District: St. Keverne – County of Cornwall
Date of Death: 14th October, 1898
Place of Death: On the Manacle Rocks in the Parish of St. Keverne
Occupation: Third Officer – *SS Mohegan*
Cause of Death: Drowned on the Manacle Rocks from the Wreck of the *S.S. Mohegan*
Certified by: H. O. Fox – Causing the Body to be Buried – Falmouth
Description and residence of informant: H. O. Fox – Causing the Body to be Buried, Falmouth
When Registered: 29th October, 1898   Registrar: Thomas S. Joyce

PRETTEJOHN, Selina, May

Age: 100 Years   Sex: Female
Registration District: TRURO
Sub-District: Truro – County of Cornwall
Date and place of birth: 6th April 1899 – Limehouse, London
Date of Death: 5th September, 1989
Place of Death: Henly House Nursing Home, Mount Hawke, Truro
Occupation: Widow of Ernest PRETTEJOHN – Tourist Agent (Retired)
Cause of Death: ███████████
Certified by: H. Whitwoth, M.B.
Description and residence of informant: Edward PRETTEJOHN (Son) ███████████
When Registered: 6th September, 1989
Registrar: S. Anderson

Appendix 9

UK CENSUS REPORTS: [1074]

1891

Address: 28 Jermyn Street, Toxeth Park, Lancashire [Stanley Browning – 4th Officer, *Mohegan:* family members]

Name:	Relation	Condition	Sex	Age	Birth Year	Occupation Disability	Where Born
BROWNING, Thomas	Head	Married	M	58		Merchant Captain	Edingburgh Scotland
BROWNING, Mary	Wife	Married	F	48			Lancashire
BROWNING, Nancy	Daughter	Single	F	19	1872		Helensburgh Scotland
BROWNING, Mabel	Daughter	Single	F	17	1874		Dunoon Scotland
BROWNING, Stanley	Son		M	13	1878		Helensburgh Scotland
REID, Marion	Grandmother	Widow	F	78	1847		Carshoall Glasgow
CORLESS, Agnes	Servant	Single	F	18	1	General Servant (domestic)	Liverpool

1861

Address: 2 William Street, All Saints, Poplar

Name:	Relation	Condition	Sex	Age	Birth Year	Occupation Disability	Where Born
CLARK, Samuel	Head	Married	M	35	1826	Journeyman Rigger	Greater Burstead Essex
CLARK, Martha	Wife	Married	F	37	1824		Stepney Middlesex
CLARK, Henry	Son	Unmarried	M	12	1849	Scholar	Barking Essex
CLARK, Martha	Daughter		F	11	1850	Scholar	Barking Essex
CLARK, William E.	Son		M	7	1854	Scholar	Barking Essex
CLARK, Caroline	Daughter		F	5	1856	Scholar	Poplar Middlesex
CLARK, Mary Ann	Daughter		F	2	1859		Poplar Middlesex
CLARK, Keith	Son		M	1	1860		Poplar Middlesex

1861

Address: Lilleshall Village, Lilleshall

Name:	Relation	Condition	Sex	Age	Birth Year	Occupation Disability	Where Born
DIGGENS, William	Head	Widower	M	41	1820	National Schoolmaster	Hambledon Hampshire
DIGGENS, Emily	Daughter		F	14	1847	Scholar	Lilleshall Shropshire
DIGGENS, Martha Elizabeth	Daughter		F	12	1849	Scholar	Lilleshall Shropshire
DIGGENS, Mary Jane	Daughter		F	11	1850	Scholar	Lilleshall Shropshire
DIGGENS, William Alfred	Son		M	8	1853	Scholar	Lilleshall Shropshire
DIGGENS, Sarah Emma	Daughter		F	6	1855	Scholar	Lilleshall Shropshire
HALES, Jane	Niece	Unmarried	F	27	1834	House Servant	Woodcote Shropshire

1901

Address: The Vicarage, Church Town, St. Keverne, Cornwall

Name:	Relation	Condition	Sex	Age	Birth Year	Occupation Disability	Where Born
DIGGENS, William A	Head	Married	M	48	1853	Clergyman (Ch. of E.)	Newport Salop
DIGGENS, Annie S	Wife	Married	F	42	1859		Manchester Yorkshire
GIBSON, Susanna A	Visitor	Widow	F	40	1861	NK	St. Ives Huntingdonshire
POTTER, Mary Elizabeth[1075]	Servant	Single	F	35	1866	Gen Servant Domestic	York Fishwick

[1074] Courtesy: General Records Office.

1901

Address: 19, Albert Street, St Pancras

Name:	Relation	Condition	Sex	Age	Birth Year	Occupation Disability	Where Born
DIGGENS, Alfred Noel	Head	Single	M	20	1881	Dental Student	Queensland Australia

1911

Address: Church Town, St. Keverne, Cornwall.

Name:	Relation	Condition	Sex	Age	Birth Year	Occupation Disability	Where Born
DIGGENS, William Alfred	Head	Married	M	57	1854	Clerk On Holy Orders	Newport Salop
DIGGENS, Annie Scott	Wife	Married	F	51	1860		Greenhayes Manchester

1911

Address: Nancemabyn, Probus, Cornwall

Name:	Relation	Condition	Sex	Age	Birth Year	Occupation Disability	Where Born
GALAWAY [sic], Daniel	Head	Married	M	33	1878	Farm Labourer	Boston, New York
GALAWAY, Harriet	Wife	Married	M	28	1873		Perranporth, Cornwa
BURT, Frederick	Stepson	Single	M	11	1900	School	Rejerrah, Cornwall
BURT, Florence	Stepdaughter	Single	F	9	1902		Perranporth, Cornwall
BURT, Jack	Stepson	Single	M	7	1904		Perranporth, Cornwall
BURT, Samuel	Stepson	Single	M	5	906		Perranporth, Cornwall

1861

Address: Creigir Uchaf, Hendy, Llanengan

Name:	Relation	Condition	Sex	Age	Birth Year	Occupation Disability	Where Born
GRIFFITH, Hugh	Head	Married	M	57	1804	Farmer of 74 acres Employing 3 labourers	Penellech
GRIFFITH, Mary	Wife	Married	F	54	1807		Aberdaron
GRIFFITH, Griffith	Son	Unmarried	M	20	1841		Llanengan
GRIFFITH, Catherine	Daughter	Single	F	17	1844		Llanengan
GRIFFITH, Mary	Daughter	Scholar	F	15	1846		Llanengan
GRIFFITH, Margaret	Daughter	Scholar	F	13	1848		Llanengan
GRIFFITH, Richard	Son	Scholar	M	9	1852		Llanengan

1871

Address: Creigir Uchaf, Hendy, Llanengan

Name:	Relation	Condition	Sex	Age	Birth Year	Occupation Disability	Where Born
GRIFFITH, Hugh	Head	Married	M	57	1804	Farmer of 74 acres Employing 3 labourers	Penellech
GRIFFITH, Mary	Wife	Married	F	54	1807		Aberdaron
GRIFFITH, Griffith	Son	Unmarried	M	20	1841		Llanengan
GRIFFITH, Catherine	Daughter	Single	F	17	1844		Llanengan
GRIFFITH, Mary	Daughter	Scholar	F	15	1846		Llanengan
GRIFFITH, Margaret	Daughter	Scholar	F	13	1848		Llanengan
GRIFFITH, Richard	Son	Scholar	M	9	1852		Llanengan

[1075] POTTER, Mary Elizabeth – came to St. Keverne from Lancashire with Canon Diggens and his wife. She married a St. Keverne man (MILDREN, William – GRO/BMD: 1906 Q1 – Helston 5c 281). The couple married in the Wesleyan (Methodist) Chapel in St. Keverne; not in the main St. Keverne church. Canon Diggens' name did not appear at all on the marriage certificate.

1881

Address: Cregir Uchaf, Llanengan

Name:	Relation	Condition	Sex	Age	Birth Year	Occupation Disability	Where Born
GRIFFITH, Hugh	Head	Married	M	76		Farmer of 75 Acres	Penllech, Caernarvon
GRIFFITH, Mary	Wife	Married	F	72			Aberdaron, Caernarvon
GRIFFITH, Griffith	Son	Single	M	40	1842	Farm Labourer	Llanengan, Caernarvon
GRIFFITH, Catherine	Daughter	Unmarried	F	37		General Servant and Housekeeper	Llanengan, Caernarvon

1891

Address: 54 Turner's Road, Limehouse London

Name:	Relation	Condition	Sex	Age	Birth Year	Occupation Disability	Where Born
GRIFFITH, Martha	Head	Married	F	49	1862		Poplar, London
GRIFFITH, Selina	Daughter	Single	F	21	1890	School Teacher	Limehouse
GRIFFITH, Walter H.	Son	Single	M	6	1885		Limehouse
CLARK, Caroline	Sister	Single	F	55	1850	Dressmaker	Poplar E
CLARK, Sarah Jane	Sister	Single	F	47	1853	Dressmaker	Poplar E

1901

Address: 54 Turner's Road, Limehouse London

Name:	Relation	Condition	Sex	Age	Birth Year	Occupation Disability	Where Born
GRIFFITH, Martha	Head	Widow	F	49	1862	Living on own means	Poplar, London
GRIFFITH, Selina	Daughter	Single	F	21	1890	School Teacher	Limehouse E
GRIFFITH, Victor	Son		M	13	1897	School	Leytonstone
CLARK, Samuel	Head	Married	M	35	1826	Journeyman Rigger	Greater Burstead Essex
CLARK, Martha	Wife	Married	F	37	1824		Stepney Middlesex
CLARK, Caroline	Sister	Single	F	55	1850	Dressmaker	Poplar E
CLARK, Sarah Jane	Sister	Single	F	47	1853	Dressmaker	Poplar E

1911

Address: 26 Wanstead Park Avenue, East Ham, Essex.

Name:	Relation	Condition	Sex	Age	Birth Year	Occupation Disability	Where Born
GRIFFITH, Martha	Head	Widow	F	49	1862	Living on own means	Poplar, London
GRIFFITH, Selina	Daughter	Single	F	21	1890	School Teacher	Limehouse E
GRIFFITH, Victor	Son	Single	M	4	1897		Leytonstone
CLARK, Caroline	Sister	Single	F	55	1850	Dressmaker	Poplar E
CLARK, Sarah Jane	Sister	Single	F	47	1853	Dressmaker	Poplar E

1911

Address: 10 Berkeley Vale, Falmouth

Name:	Relation	Condition	Sex	Age	Birth Year	Occupation Disability	Where Born
PELLOW, Edwin	Head	Married	M	48		Butcher	Falmouth
PELLOW. Emma Mary	Wife	Married	F	46			Perran
PELLOW, Arthur Edward	Son	Single	M	20		Blacksmith	Falmouth
PELLOW, Mary Blanche	Daughter	Single	F	18		Dressmaker	Falmouth
PELLOW, Dorothy Pellow	Daughter	Single	F	13			Falmouth
MORTON, Frederick Charles	Boarder	Married	M	32		Grocer	Wandsworth
GRIFFITH, Walter Hugh	Boarder	Single	M	26		Clerk	Stepney

1851

Address: Fullers Hill, Norfolk

Name:	Relation	Condition	Sex	Age	Birth Year	Occupation Disability	Where Born
PURDY, Thomas	Head	Married	M	39		Spirit Merchant	Yarmouth
PURDY. Charlotte	Wife	Married	F	35			Yarmouth
PURDY, Charlotte	Daughter	Single	M	11			Yarmouth
PURDY, Ann	Daughter	Single	F	10			Yarmouth
PURDY, Ellen	Daughter	Single	F	7			Yarmouth
PURDY, Robins	Son	Married	M	5			Yarmouth
PURDY, Mary Ann	Daughter	Single	M	6			Yarmouth

1901

Address: 24 Kensington Avenue, Little Ilford, East Ham.

Name:	Relation	Condition	Sex	Age	Birth Year	Occupation Disability	Where Born
PURDY, Robins	**Head**	**Single**	**M**	**56**	**1845**	Master Mariner Ship Owner (Employer) [1076]	Norfolk, Gt. Yarmouth

1911

Address: 24, Kensington Avenue, Little Ilford, East Ham.

Name:	Relation	Condition	Sex	Age	Birth Year	Occupation Disability	Where Born
PURDY, Robins	Head	Single	M	66	1845	Master Mariner Ship Owner (Employer) Teaching Navigation. Working at home. [1077]	Norfolk, Gt. Yarmouth

1911

Address: 16 Trafalgar Place, Swansea, Wales

Name:	Relation	Condition	Sex	Age	Birth Year	Occupation Disability	Where Born
SWEET, Charlotte	Head	Widow	F	67	1844		Bristol Gloucestershire
SWEET, Edwin Ernest Fair	Son	Single	M	49	1862	Solicitor's Clerk	Manchester Lancashire
COUCH, Mary Louise	Daughter	Widow	F	42	1869		Durham
COUCH, Arthur Llewelyn	Nephew	Single	M	16	1895	Student	Kent Woolwich
COUCH, Dorothy Louisa	Niece		F	12	1899	School	Essex Upton Park

---

[1076] The UK census also recorded him as aboard the vessel *Gamecock* in the South Dock, London.

[1077] Ibid.

Appendix 10

POSSIBLE LOCATIONS FOR THE INTERMENT OF CAPT. RICHARD GRIFFITH:

CEMETERIES IN LONDON

Chingford, St. Peter and St Paul

The Green, Chingford E4
Location of Burial Registers: Waltham Forest Archives*
Year when Registers Begin: 1813—Parish Clerk's fee books from 1790

Chingford, All Saints Church

Old Church Road, Chingford E4
Location of Burial Registers: Waltham Forest Archives*
Year when Registers Begin: 1617

Leyton, St. Mary the Virgin

Church Road, Leyton E10
Location of Burial Registers: Waltham Forest Archives*
Year when Registers Begin: 1617

Leytonstone, St. John the Baptist

Church Road, Leyton E11
Location of Burial Registers: Waltham Forest Archives*
Year when Registers Begin: 1834

Walthamstow, St. Mary the Virgin

Church Lane, Walthamstow E17
Location of Burial Registers: Waltham Forest Archives*
Year when Registers Begin: 1645

Walthamstow, St. Peter

Woodford New Road, Walthamstow E17
Location of Burial Registers: Waltham Forest Archives*
Year when Registers Begin: 1845

CEMETERIES IN WALTHAM FOREST:

Chingford Mount Cemetery

121 Old Church Road, Chingford E4 6ST – Tel: 020 8524 5030

Location of Burial Registers: Registers 1884—1952 at Waltham Forest Archives *

Year when Registers Begin: 1886

St. Patrick's Roman Catholic Cemetery

Langthorne Road, Leytonstone E11 4HL. Tel: 020 8539 2451

Location of Burial Registers: At the cemetery

Year when Registers Begin: 1861

Walthamstow Cemetery [1078]

Queen's Road, Walthamstow E17 8QP – Tel: 020 8520 1131

Chingford Mount Cemetery**

Location of Burial Registers: Chingford Mount Cemetery **

Year when Registers Begin: 1872

West Ham Cemetery

Cemetery Road

Forest Gate E7 9DG

Location of Burial Registers: At the cemetery

Year when Registers Begin: 1854

Barkingside Cemetery

Ockendon Road, Corbet Tey, Upminster, RM14 2UY – Tel: 01708 434 433

Location of Burial Registers: Internet listing; http://findagrave.com/.

Year when Registers Begin: Not known

Corbets Tey Cemetery

Ockendon Road, Corbet Tey, Upminster, RM14 2UY – Tel: 01708 434 433

Location of Burial Registers: Internet listing; http://findagrave.com/.

Year when Registers Begin: Not known

CEMETERIES NEAR WALTHAM FOREST:

City of London Cemetery

Aldersbrook Road, Manor Park E12 5DQ – Tel: 020 8530 2151

Location of Burial Registers: At the cemetery – copies 1856–1915 at Guildhall Library[+]

Year when Registers Begin: 1856

East London Cemetery

Grange Road, Plaistow E13 0HB – Tel: 020 7476 5109

Location of Burial Registers: At the cemetery

Year when Registers Begin: 1874

Manor Park Cemetery

Sebert Road, Manor Park E7 0NP – Tel: 020 8534 1486

Location of Burial Registers: At the cemetery

Year when Registers Begin: 1875

[1078] No interment found from verbal communication: Mr Peter Wilson.

Woodgrange Park Cemetery

540 Romford Road, London E7 8AF – Tel: 01375 891440

Location of Burial Registers: Badgehurst Ltd., Fen Lane, Orsett, Grays, Essex RM16 3LT

Year when Registers Begin: 1889

* Waltham Forest Archives	** Chingford Mount Cemetery	+ Guildhall Library
Vestry House Museum		
Vestry Road	121 Old Church Road	Aldermanbury
Walthamstow	Chingford, London E4 6ST	London EC2P 2EJ
London E17 9NH	cemeteries@walthamforest.gov.uk	
vhm.enquiries@walthamforest.gov.uk		

Despite a meticulous search, carried out in the above London cemetery registers, a grave and last resting place for Capt. Richard Griffith was not found. This supports the premise that his body was never transferred from Wales to London.

Appendix 11

Admissions and Discharges at the Redruth Poor Union Workhouse:

Daniel Christopher Gallaway; 1936–1939

Date of Admission: Monday, September 7th 1936

Name: Gallaway, Daniel C,

Religion: Meth[odist]

Occupation: Labourer

Next Meal: D[inner] [1079]

By Whose Order Admitted: U Bath [1080]

Date of Discharge: Thursday, September 17th 1936

_____

Name: Gallaway, Daniel C,

Last Meal Before Discharge: B[reakfast]

How Discharged and if by Order, by Whose Order.

In case of death, say "Dead": At own request

_____

Date of Admission: Monday, October 5th 1936

Name: Gallaway, Daniel C,

Religion: Meth[odist]

Occupation: Labourer

Next Meal: D[inner]

By Whose Order Admitted: *U* Bath

No Discharge Record found, following this Admission.

_____

Date of Admission: Monday, November 23rd 1936

Name: Gallaway, Daniel C,

Religion: Meth[odist]

Occupation: Labourer

Next Meal: D[inner]

By Whose Order Admitted: *U* Marks

Date of Discharge: Wednesday, December 9th 1936

Name: Gallaway, Daniel C,

Last Meal Before Discharge: B[reakfast]

_____

[1079] A preoccupation with the meals taken, following an admission and before a discharge of an inmate, was probably a part of the institution's detailed record of expenditure.

[1080] The "U" appears to be some sort of code, as various names in this particular field of the general records, are prefixed with this letter. The name "Bath" is listed as an administrator.

How Discharged and if by Order, by Whose Order.

In case of death, say "Dead": At own request

_____

Date of Admission: Tuesday, April 6th 1937

Name: Gallaway, Daniel C,

Religion: Meth[odist]

Occupation: Labourer

Next Meal: S[upper]

_____

By Whose Order Admitted: *U* Bath

Date of Discharge: Monday, May 10th 1937

Name: Gallaway, Daniel C,

Last Meal Before Discharge: B[reakfast]

How Discharged and if by Order, by Whose Order.

In case of death, say "Dead": At own request

_____

Date of Admission: Sunday, February 5th 1939

Name: Gallaway, Daniel C,

Religion: Meth[odist]

Occupation: Labourer

Next Meal: S[upper]

_____

By Whose Order Admitted: Master's [Master of the workhouse?]

No Discharge Record, following this Admission. It is possible that Gallaway was discharged from one ward to another, within this particular episode.

_____

Date of Admission: Monday, March 27th 1939

Name: Gallaway, Daniel C,

Religion: Meth[odist]

Occupation: Labourer

Next Meal: B[reakfast]

By Date of Discharge: Monday, March 27th 1939

_____

Name: Gallaway, Daniel C,

Last Meal Before Discharge: B[reakfast]

How Discharged and if by Order, by Whose Order.

In case of death, say "Dead": At own request

No Record of an Admission, before this next Discharge.

Date of Discharge: Monday, April 17th 1939

Name: Gallaway, Daniel C,

Last Meal Before Discharge: B[reakfast]

How Discharged and if by Order, by Whose Order: At own request

_____

457

Date of Admission: Monday, October 28th 1939

Name: Gallaway, Daniel C,

Religion: Meth[odist]

Occupation: Labourer

Next Meal: D[inner]

By Whose Order Admitted: *U* Bath

Date of Discharge: Monday, November 23rd 1939

———————————————

Name: Gallaway, Daniel C,

Last Meal Before Discharge: D[inner]

How Discharged and if by Order, by Whose Order.

In case of death, say "Dead": Dead.

———————————————

Appendix 12

The Gallaway Bible contains a folded note.

A folded note, found in Daniel Christopher Gallaway's personal bible, shows an informal hand-written listing of his significant (presumed) family events between the years, 1783–1852. It is not known who the author is but most likely was Daniel Gallaway himself.[1081]

This list is included here in order to complement the known records for the Gallaway family and may help, eventually, to unravel the mystery surrounding the life of Daniel Christopher Gallaway.

It is possible that his father (Frank) was not born during the period that this list covers, as no reference is made of him.

<u>Grandfather</u>

John Gallaway was born July 4th 1783.

Died august 1853 age 70y – 1m – 25days

John Gallaway and Catherine Kempf [?Kemph]

was married January 19th 1808

George Gallaway Born Nov 16th 1808.

Died January 16th 1885, age 76-2months

John G. Born august 3rd 1810.

Mathias Born Dec 22nd 1813

Died Febuary [sic] 8th 1877. 66y.6m.5days.

Elizabeth Born Sept. 1st 1811

Joseph Born Nov 9th 1812

Nancy Born March 12th 1815

William Born March 29th 1817

Polly Born may 17th 1818

Catherine Born may 2nd 1820

David Born July 17th 1823

Catherine Kempf [?Keinpf] Born Nov 26th 1787

Died Dec. 25th 1827.

John Gallaway and Sarah Seighman was

married Sept 11th 1828.

Sarah Died January 13th 1835

John Gallaway and Sophiah Prout [?]

was married August 31st 1835.

Elijah was born May 31st 1836,

Cyrus Born April 19th 1838.

Sophiah Born March 15th 1840.

Christ Born May 7th 1842

Adaline Born August 8th 1827 [?]

Maggie Born April 11th 1848

Jacob Born April 15th 1852

that is all of guess there

was some go away no

wonder Dad was a *****

Have not heard from Dave for

a long time. If all goes well

I want to go to *****[1082] in

December latter part of it.

I got the note all right, I send

you <u>Johns</u> oldest Boy. John

and I set after while ****

around Saturday John said

he was to [sic] tired on sat. nite [sic]

Soon give me all the news But

is well I saw him today, he thinks

he will be closer there in

the Spring G. Elijah [?]

[Daniel Christopher Gallaway Born 18th March 1876]

[1081] Courtesy: Paula Bate – the Gallaway family.

[1082] Rather tantalisingly, the only place name in the list is indecipherable.

Appendix 13

The 19th Century Medical Treatment for Victims of Drowning:

Help to the drowning should comprise stimulation to the nervous system to restore sensation and artificial movements to set the breathing going again. The circulation should be quickened, heat and air introduced into the lungs.

As soon as the victim has been taken from the water he should be placed on his back with his head well down, all clothing cut away from his neck, his mouth opened widely and kept so, his throat freed from any liquid it may contain and the "tongue process" be put into execution as quickly as possible. The tongue should be seized firmly between the fingers, covered with a piece of linen to prevent its slipping. It should then be drawn forward and allowed to go back fifteen times a minute in regular movements. It is absolutely necessary that the rescuer should be sure that these tractions affect the base of the tongue and not the point only. At the beginning of the process, for the first two or three tractions, it is useful to run a finger down the throat in the hope of producing vomiting.[1083]

At the same time two other persons should execute artificial respiration by employing energetic and rhythmical pressure, one in a concentric direction on both sides of the chest, the other from below upward on the abdomen. The former should be made fifteen times a minute and should be followed each time by sudden and simultaneous release. Pressure on the abdomen and chest should alternate with traction on the tongue. This should be kept up for at least a quarter of an hour, during which period everything possible should be done to warm the patient.

When this has been methodically done the victim should be rapidly transported to the nearest shelter, all clothing removed, the body dried and wrapped in flannel and put to bed with the head low. If then breathing does not go on, artificial respiration should be renewed, using the process of drawing the elbows as far out as possible. A roll of clothes should be passed under the small of the back so as to throw the chest forward, the mouth kept open and the tongue drawn forward, and the rescuer, kneeling at the head, should seize the elbows, press them against the chest, draw them horizontally until they are at right angles, raise them vertically by the head, bringing them back to the wall of the chest fifteen times a minute for ten minutes.

After this for another quarter of an hour the tongue process should be again resorted to, combined as before with the pressure process of artificial respiration, and the two methods should be alternated in this way for an hour at least. While this is being done still other persons can help in restoring circulation and heat by the following means: Rubbing the entire body, the soles of the feet and palms of the hands with hair gloves, coarse towels, hot cloths, etc.; massage and kneading of the limbs; beating the surface of the body; hot water bottles, warmed irons or bricks, care being taken not to get them too hot.

If any attempt to breathe appears, ammonia or any object should be held before the nose or mouth. If there are symptoms of vomiting, put a finger into the throat. Nothing should be given to drink until consciousness has returned, except a few drops of cognac or vinegar for the purpose of bringing the drowned man back to his senses.

It should never be forgotten that an attempt should always be made to help a man who appears to be drowned, no matter how hopeless the case may seem; and such efforts should be kept up for a long time. If a person has been under water for five minutes he can almost always be rescued and some have been saved after half an hour's submersion. Success depends on rapid and intelligent action in the presence of such an accident [1084]

[1083] The preoccupation was for the removal of ingested/inhaled water. Mouth-to-mouth resuscitation and external cardiac massage, employed today, did not appear to feature at that time. Vomiting, while placed in this position, could have led to a life-threatening event, by its inhalation.

[1084] Hoyt, John C.; *Old Ocean's Ferry; the Log of the Modern Mariner, the Transatlantic Travel, and Quaint Facts of Neptune's Realm.*

Appendix 14

Ship's Bell – in regulating a sailor's watch.

A typical pattern for a system of a Ship's Watch:

For the purpose of discipline on shipboard and to divide the watch fairly, the crew is mustered in two divisions: the Starboard (right side, looking toward the head), and the Port (left). The day commences at noon, and is thus divided: Afternoon Watch, noon to 4 p.m.; First Dog Watch, 4 p.m. to 6 p.m.; Second Dog Watch, 6 p.m. to 8 p.m.; First Watch, 8 p.m. to midnight; Middle Watch, 12 a.m. to 4 a.m.; Morning Watch, 4 a.m. to 8 a.m.; Forenoon Watch, 8 a.m. to noon. This makes seven Watches, which enables the crew to keep them alternately, as the Watch which comes on duty at noon one day has the afternoon next day, and the men who have only four hours' rest one night have eight hours the next. This is the reason for having Dog Watches, which are made by dividing the hours between 4 p.m. and 8 p.m. into two Watches.[1085]

Number of bells	Bell pattern	Middle watch	Morning watch	Forenoon watch	Afternoon watch	First dog watch	Last dog watch	First watch
One bell	.	0:30	4:30	8:30	12:30	16:30	18:30†	20:30
Two bells	..	1:00	5:00	9:00	13:00	17:00	19:00†	21:00
Three bells	.. .	1:30	5:30	9:30	13:30	17:30	19:30†	21:30
Four bells	.. ..	2:00	6:00	10:00	14:00	18:00		22:00
Five bells	.. .. .	2:30	6:30	10:30	14:30		18:30	22:30
Six bells	.. .. ..	3:00	7:00	11:00	15:00		19:00	23:00
Seven bells	.. ..	3:30	7:30	11:30	15:30		19:30	23:30
Eight bells	.. ..	4:00	8:00	12:00‡	16:00		20:00	0:00

Table 23: Ship's Bells – in regulating a sailors' watch.   .

† *British usage after the Nore mutiny* (1797).

‡ *Before the introduction of time zones* (GMT-1847) *noon was not struck by the glass, but when the captain or officer of the deck confirmed local noon by the sun, using a sextant.*

At midnight on New Year's Eve sixteen bells would be struck – eight bells for the old year and eight bells for the new.

Most of the crew of a ship would be divided up into between two and four groups called watches. Each watch would take its turn with the essential activities of manning the helm, navigating, trimming sails, and keeping a lookout.

The hours between 16:00 and 20:00 are so arranged because that watch (the "dog-watch") was divided into two. The odd number of watches aimed to give each man a different watch each day. It also allows the entire crew of a vessel to eat an evening meal, the normal time being at 17:00 with First Dog watchmen eating at 18:00.

[1085] Ships and Shipping; Edited by: Francis Miltoun. Copyright, Kellscraft Studio1999–2007; http://kellscraft.com/ShipsandShipping/ShipsandShippingCh05.html.

Appendix 15

Merchant Vessels launched in the UK 1888–1901:

YEAR	STEAM		SAIL		TOTAL	
	N o.	Gross Tonnage	No.	Gross Tonnage	No.	Gross Tonnage
1888	458	757,081	81	80,959	539	838,040
1889	595	1,083,793	95	125,568	690	1,209,361
1890	651	1,061,619	92	133,086	743	1,194,705
1891	641	878,353	181	252,463	822	1,130,816
1892	512	841,356	169	268,594	681	1,109,950
1893	438	718,277	98	118,106	536	836,383
1894	549	964,926	65	81,582	614	1,046,508
1895	526	904,991	53	45,976	579	950,967
1896	628	1,113,831	68	45,920	696	1,159,751
1897	545	924,382	46	28,104	591	952,486
1898	744	1,363,318	17	4,252	761	1,367,570
1899	714	1,414,774	12	2,017	726	1,416,791
1900	664	1,432,600	28	9,871	692	1,442,471
1901	591	1,501,078	48	23,661	639	1,524,739

Table 24: Merchant Vessels: Launched in the UK: 1888–1901[1086]

The latter half of the 19th century was marked by *The Panic of 1873* (this was a result of the Coinage Act of 1873, which greatly depressed the value of silver). The *Panic* lead us right into what was called *The Long Depression,* throughout the USA and Europe between 1873–1896.

[1086] Courtesy: *Lloyds of London*

Appendix 16

A History of the Falmouth Lifeboat.[1087]

1867–1887

City of Gloucester

Operational Number: 118

In total, the lifeboat that had been funded by the people of Gloucester had been launched ten times on separate services but was not credited with saving any lives – unless one counts those souls who fell in during her launch ceremony at the Docks.

1887–1894

Jane Whittingham

Operational Number: —?

Legacy of Mrs J.P. Whittingham of London. On 9th August 1887 the RNLI lifeboat, the Jane Whittingham arrived at Falmouth to replace the Gloucester, which was withdrawn from active service. The *Whittingham* ended up with a similar career history, only making two unsuccessful services in her seven-year placement at the port .[1088] After being stood down, the *Gloucester* was returned to Forrestt of Limehouse who broke her up, probably re-using her timbers in other craft.

1894–1922

Bob Newbon

Operational Number: 372

Legacy of Mr Robert Alger Newbon.[1089] This lifeboat attended the *Mohegan* disaster.

1922–1928

Jane Anne

Operational Number: 417

Legacy of Mr G.Nicholls of London.

1928–1931

Herbert Sturmy

Operational Number: 664

Legacy of Mrs Herbert Sturmy of Blackheath.

1931–1934

The Brothers

Operational Number: 671

Gift of Mesdames Eddy, Torquay.

[1087] Courtesy of the Falmouth Lifeboat Service – RNLI: http://falmouthlifeboat.co.uk.

[1088] By John Putley, © 2007 – Gloucestershire Archives: Learning and Outreach Officer..

[1089] Robert Alger Newbon (1822–1891) was a very successful London auctioneer in Islington and a very wealthy man. He made a lengthy will, with numerous charitable bequests. Among the major beneficiaries were the Great Northern Central Hospital, Holloway Road (where his bequest of £15,000 went towards a 'Newbon Ward') and the National Lifeboat Institution. He left £20,000 towards five Newbon boats, which were thereafter in operation at the Selsey Lifeboat Station: the Ann Newbon (named after his mother), the Lucy Newbon (after his wife), the Betsey Newbon (after one of his sisters), the Nancy Newbon (after his other sister) and the Bob Newbon (after himself); http://newbonfamilyhistory.com/page34.html.

1934–1940

B.A.S.P.

Operational Number: 687

Amalgamation of legacies.

1940–1968

Crawford and Constance Coneybeare

Operational Number: 829

Gift of Mrs Coneybeare of London.

1968–1974

Lilla Marras [1090] (Watson class)

Operational Number: 928

Douglas and Will Legacies Mrs J Marra

Mr J Douglas Mr W Kennedy. She is now a luxury, floating hotel-suite in Harlingen (the Netherlands).

1974–1979

Rotary Service (Thames class)

Operational Number: 1031

Gift of Rotary International Great Britain and Ireland and legacies of Mr D I Craig, Mary Ann Redgate and Mary Conbronge Fowkes

1979–1997

Elizabeth Ann (Arun class)

Operational Number: 1058

Gift of John Slater Foundation, Sir Kirby Laing Foundation and a number of other gifts and legacies.

1997–2001

The Will (Severn class)

Operational Number: 1201

The Will was funded by The Will Charitable Trust.

2001–

Richard Cox Scott (Severn class)

Operational Number: 1256

It was principally funded by a bequest from Mrs Ruth Marygold Dix Scott, who passed away in May 1998, bequeathing her residuary estate to the RNLI. Mrs Scott had a love for the sea since her childhood and had lived in Cornwall for many years. The Lifeboat is named after her late husband.

[1090] Previously stationed at Cromarty where she was called-out on 24 occasions and saved 10 lives.

1867 - 1873	John Hurley	1947 - 1960	Charles Brown
1873 - 1875	Thomas Medlin	1960 - 1972	Bert West
1875 - 1882	John Roberts	1972 - 1975	Walter Brown
1882 - 1898	Edwin Hall	1975 - 1980	Arthur West
1898 - 1901	Francis Jose[1091]	1980 - 1989	Vivian Pentecost
1901 - 1919	Samuel Hingston	1989 - 1991	John Barton
1919 - 1921	William Tonkin	1991 - 2005	Alan Barnes
1921 - 1930	John Dunstone	2005 –	Mark Pollard
1930 - 1947	John Snell		

Table 25: Coxswains: Falmouth Lifeboat Service

[1091] The Coxswain on the night of the *Mohegan* disaster.

Appendix 17

Witnesses who gave evidence given at the *Mohegan* Board of Trade Inquiry.

Name:	Occupation:	Status:*
Williams, Mr Benjamin	Master of the tug *Penguin*	ANC
Butt, Mr Frederick	Quartermaster, *Mohegan*	ATL
Cruikshank, Mr John	Boatswain, *Mohegan*	ATL
Ferguson, Mr William	Second Engineer, *Mohegan*	ATL
Gray, Mr M. E.	Fourth Engineer, *Mohegan*	ATL
Nicklin, Mr Frank	Chief Steward, *Mohegan*	ATL
Juddery, Mr John W. H.	Quartermaster, *Mohegan*	ATL
Pollard, Mr William	Third Officer on the *Cleopatra*	ATL
Smith, Mr John C.	Fifth Engineer, *Mohegan*	ATL
Trevor, Dr Arthur Herbert	Resident doctor, *Mohegan*	ATL
Jeffery, Mr A. J.	Chief Coastguard officer at Coverack	CG
May, Mr Charles John	Boatman of the Coastguard station at Coverack	CG
Ross, Mr James	Chief Officer at the Lizard Coastguard station	CG
Snell, Mr Charles Robert	Boatman of the Coastguard station at Falmouth	CG
Burnfield, Mr Joseph	Signalman at Rame Head	CG
Dashwood, Mr George L.	Passenger on the *Mohegan*	PASS
Noble, Miss Katherine	Passenger on the *Mohegan*	PASS
Swift, Mrs Amelia Compton	Passenger on the *Mohegan*	PASS
Foote, Lt. Keppel	District Inspector for the RNLI.	RNLI
Hill, Mr James	Coxswain of the lifeboat, Porthoustock, *Charlotte*	RNLI
Jane, Mr Thomas	Coxswain of the Cadgwith lifeboat, *Minnie Moon*	RNLI
Jose, Mr Francis	Coxswain of the Falmouth lifeboat, *Bob Newbon*	RNLI
Matthews, Mr E.	Coxswain of the Lizard lifeboat	RNLI
Fooks, Mr Henry	Collector of Customs and Receiver of Wrecks at Falmouth	ROW
Mulley, Mr David Thomas	Trinity House Pilot, London Gravesend – Dover	TH

*Status:	Description:	Total:
ANC	Ancillary support	1
ATL	Atlantic Transport Line Employee	9
CG	Coastguard	5
PASS	*Mohegan* passenger	3
RNLI	Royal National Lifeboat Institution	5
ROW	Receiver of Wrecks	1
TH	Trinity House	1

Of the 25 witnesses that gave evidence, only three passengers were selected and two of those were female. Given the period in which this event took place, those two witnesses would have been subjected to the usual male-dominated societal pressures; though to be fair, Miss Katherine Noble was a feisty young woman and seemed well able to hold her own. The two male passengers who had left written depositions for inclusion at the inquiry, had them deemed as inadmissible, as their absence in court did not allow for a cross-examination of the evidence (see page 132).[1092] One imagines their reports were not what ATL would have wished to make public.

[1092] The two gentlemen being, Messrs. Francis Pemberton and John Hyslop.

Appendix 18

The Wreck of the Steamer *"Mohegan"*

Good people of high and low degree,
I pray ye all to list to me,
And I'll relate a terrible tale of the sea
Concerning the unfortunate steamer, Mohegan,
That against the Manacles Rocks, ran.

'Twas on Friday, the 14th of October, in the year of ninety-eight,
Which alas! must have been a dreadful sight;
She sailed out of the river Thames on Thursday,
While the hearts of the passengers felt light and gay.

And on board there were 133 passengers and crew,
And each one happier than another seemingly to view;
When suddenly the ship received some terrible shocks,
Until at last she ran against the Manacles Rocks.

Dinner was just over when the shock took place,
Which caused fear to be depicted in every face;
Because the ship was ripped open, and the water rushed in,
It was most dreadful to hear, it much such a terrific din.

Then the cries of children and women did rend the air,
And in despair many of them tore their hair
As they clung to their babies in wild despair,
While some of them cried - 'Oh, God, do Thou my babies spare!'

The disaster occurred between seven and eight o'clock at night,
Which caused some of the passengers to faint with fright;
As she struck on the Manacles Rocks between Falmouth and Lizard Head,
Which filled many of the passengers' hearts with dread.

Then the scene that followed was awful to behold,
As the captain hurried to the bridge like a hero bold;
And the seamen rushed manfully to their posts,
While many of the passengers with fear looked as pale as ghosts.

And the poor women and children were chilled to the heart,
And crying aloud for their husbands to come and take their part;
While the officers and crew did their duty manfully,
By launching the boats immediately into the sea.

Then lifebelts were tied round the women and children
By the brave officers and gallant seamen;
While the storm fiend did laugh and angry did roar,
When he saw the boats filled with passengers going towards the shore.

One of the boats, alas! unfortunately was swamped,
Which caused the officers and seamens' courage to be a little damped;
But they were thankful the other boats got safely away,
And tried hard to save the passengers without dismay.

Then a shriek of despair arose as the ship is sinking beneath the wave,
While some of the passengers cried to God their lives to save;
But the angry waves buffetted the breath out of them,
Alas, poor sickly children, also women and men.

Oh, heaven, it was most heartrending to see
A little girl crying and imploring most piteously,
For some one to save her as she didn't want to die,
But, alas, no one seemed to hear her agonizing cry.

For God's sake, boys, get clear, if ye can,
Were the captain's last words spoken like a brave man;
Then he and the officers sank with the ship in the briny deep,
Oh what a pitiful sight, 'tis enough to make one weep.

Oh think of the passengers that have been tempest tossed,
Besides, 100 souls and more, that have been lost;
Also, think of the mariner while on the briny deep,
And pray to God to protect him at night before ye sleep.

William Topaz McGonagall
(1830–1902) [1093]

[1093] See http://www.poemhunter.com/william-topaz-mcgonagall/.

Appendix 19

The Corporation of Trinity House: An American Perspective.

TRINITY HOUSE

A QUEER OLD INSTITUTION WHICH ADMINISTERS ENGLAND'S LIGHTHOUSE SYSTEM

IN 1617 IT REJECTED THE MAYFLOWER AS UNFIT FOR GOVERNMENT SERVICE. [1094]

In view of the disposition which prevails on both sides of the Atlantic to ascribe the stranding of the *Paris* on Sunday, as also the loss of the *Mohegan* last autumn, to the neglect of Trinity House to provide for the proper lighting and buoying of the most dangerous portion of the Cornish coast, a good many enquiries are being made as to what the Trinity House really is. It is in response to these demands for information on the subject and for the benefit for landsmen that the following brief sketch is given of an institution the name of which for at least two hundred years has been familiar to every seafaring man.

Trinity House is one of the oldest of those departments of the British Government which are virtually independent both of the National Treasury and of the Crown, and which manages its finances without the interference or supervision of Parliament. As the College of Heralds is permitted to maintain itself in existence by means of charging heavy fees for the registration of titles, for the grants of armorial bearings, for genealogical researches and for the management of State functions, so has the Trinity House been allowed during more than three centuries to raise an enormous revenue by levying pilotage and lighthouse dues on all vessels enttering British ports. In return for this Trinity House has undertaken, ever since its foundation, to maintain and erect lighthouses, to place buoys, and to furnish efficient pilots in all British ports and British waters, whether at home or abroad.

FOUNDED BY HENRY VIII

The origin of Trinity House must be ascribed to King Henry VIII. True, there are traditions to show that the institution was in existence before his day, under a different name, but it was he who first granted the charter of incorporation to what was then a guild of pilots, seamen and mariners at Deptford Stroud in the County of Kent. The deed of incorporation incites that it was granted by Henry VIII in sign of "the sincere and entire love, and likewise devotion, which we bear and have towards the most glorious and undividabale Trinty," and as a further sign of the royal favor the monarch placed under the direct control of the guild all the royal dockyards and arsenals then in existence. The corporation narrowly escaped dissolution during the two successive reigns, but developed when Elizabeth came to the throne [1559], the powers of the corporation being considerably enlarged by the Virgin Queen.

Its importance may be gathered from the fact that it undertook in the early part of the seventeenth century to put down piracy, while it was entrusted with the direction of the construction and designing of ships, as well as with the responsibilty of surveying them when built, hired or purchased by the Government. It determined the size and equipment of every fleet that left British shores, and, in the words of an historian of those days, "not a gun, not a charge of powder nor a round of shot was placed on board any vessel, whether belonging to the Government or not, without a Trinity House certificate".

Incidentally, it may be mentioned that in 1617 a vessel called the *Mayflower* was offered for sale to the Government, but was rejected as unfit for the public service by direction and on the report of the brethren of the Trinity House. While

---

[1094] The ship *Mayflower* that carried the Pilgrims from England to Plymouth, Massachusetts, where they established the first permanent New England colony in 1620.

there is nothing positively known on the subject, yet there is much circumstantial evidence to show that it was this very same ship thus rejected by the Crown which subsequently brought the Pigrim Fathers to this country.

In those days Trinity House likewise had charge of the victualling of the navy, had control of the navy stores at Deptford, its brethren sat as judges in all admiralty cases and the corporation as such even had the right of dealing directly with foreign rulers in the appointment of consuls at seaports.

It was during the reign of Queen Bess that Trinity House first undertook the lighting of the British coast, the earliest lighthouse which it built being that at Caistor, in Norfolk. The lighthouses and beacons which had existed until that time owed their existence and maintenance to private munificence, the majority of them having been kept up by great nobles, abbeys situated along the sea coast, and by the minicipalities of seaport towns. In fact, it was not until 1836—that is, just a year before Queen Victoria came to the throne—that Trinity House was authorised by Parliament to effect a compulsory purchase of all the lighthouses on British coasts, it being rightly held that private oenership of these beacons was detrimental to efficient service, and that the control of the entire system of lighting and buoying should be vested in the hands of one responsible department.

PENSIONS FOR SEAFARING MEN.

Curiously enough, Oliver Cromwell[1095] fell foul of the corporation and deprived it of most of its preogratives, which were only restored and enlarged after the restoration by King Charles II, thanks to the influence of Samuel Pepys, who, as a reward for his services in the matter, was admitted to the ranks of a younger brother of the guild. King Charles likewise gave the right to the corporation of levying shipping dues additional to those which it had until then imposed, "for the relief of poor mariners and seafaring men, with accounting to the Crown". That the corporation fulfilled the obligations thus imposed upon it is shown by the fact that in the early portion of the present reign it had on its books about ten thousand pensioners, besides three thousand children, the latter being the offspring of men who had lost in the service of their country either their lives or the power of earning their daily bread. In 1854, however, when by the Merchant Shipping act the constitution of Trinity House was placed upon a new footing, it was relieved of a good deal of its charitable work, while the sphere of its operations was restricted to a great extent to the all-important task of lighting and buoying the British coasts and waters. Trinity House still maintains some interesting old almshouses in the Mile End Road, where a limited number of pensioners are lodged and maintained.

How vast are the present responsibilties of Trinty House in connection with the lighting and buoying of British waters in various parts of the world may be gathered from the fact that there are close upon nine hundred lights along the coasts of the British Isles alone. In addition to these there is a large fleet of lightships, no less that four of these lonely craft being anchored on the Goodwin Sands.[1096] Then there are a sufficient number of sirens to form a concert loud enough to deafen an entire metropolis. Besides these, there are several thousand buoys of great variety of form and color, some of them furnishd with automatic whistles, other merely with bells, as in the olden days of the famous Abbot of Aberbrothock.[1097] It is largely owing to the fact that the buoy on the Manacle Rocks was merely provided with an antiquated bell, and devoid of any of the modern systems of automatic flashlights, that the *Paris*, like the *Mohegan* has been wrecked just at that particular point.

[1095] Oliver Cromwell (1599–1658) was an English military and political leader and later Lord Protector of the Commonwealth of England, Scotland and Ireland.

[1096] The notorious Goodwin Sands is a 10-mile-long sand-bank in the English Channel, lying six miles east of Deal in Kent, England.

[1097] Robert Stevenson, Engineer to the Board, stated "There is a tradition that an Abbot of Aberbrothock directed a bell to be erected on the Rock, so connected with a floating apparatus, that the winds and sea acted upon it, and tolled the bell, thus giving warning to the mariner of his approaching danger. Upon similar authority, the bell, it is said, was afterwards carried off by pirates and the humane intentions of the Abbot thus frustrated". http://www.nlb.org.uk/LighthouseLibrary/Lighthouse/Bell-Rock/.

The headquarters of the corporation, Trinity House as it styled, adjoin the Tower of London, and were built in 1795 from designs by Samuel Wyatt, being the third house erected for the corporation. The first was destroyed by the Great Fire in 1506 [*sic*],[1098] and the second building was situated in Water Lane, Deptford. The courtroom of the present home of the Trinity Brethren is a magnificent chamber richly decorated, while the walls of this, as of the other apartments of the building, are adorned with rare old portraits, with flags taken by Francis Drake and other celebrated English commanders from the enemy, and with relics of the Spanish Armada.

The brethren include among their members a few of the most experienced seamen of the world, mostly former officers of the mercantile navy, while the remainder are made up of distinuished statesmen, many of whom are not even acquainted with the sea as yachtsmen. Among the non-professional brethren are Lord Salisbury, Lord Roseberry, the Duke of Argyll and the Duke of Cambridge, who occupy the places formerly held by the great Duke of Wellington, Lord Liverpool, Lord Palmerston and Pitt. Mr. Gladstone was likewise and elder brother of the Trinity House, and it was the uniform of this office which he invariably wore at Court and state functions. It looks something like that of an admiral, and foreigners unacquainted with the Grand Old Man's connection with the Trinity House used to be at a loss to account for the decidely seafaring character of his gold-epualetted and anchor emdroidered garb.

These lay brethren, if I may be permitted to use the expression in order to distinguish them from the professional members of the corporation, are merely honoray, and have no part in the work of the institution, save to partake of the banquets, several of which are given each year, and which have been the cause a good deal of criticism; for, whereas the Trinity House constantly declines to erect lighthouses, or to even establish buoys at dangerous points on the coast, basing its refusal on the score of expense, and on the lack of funds, no such paltry considerations are ever permitted to interfere with the magnificent Trinity House banquets, which surpass in the excellence of the fare and in the perfection of the grand old wines those of most of the City Companies. The chair at these banquets is invariably taken by the master who to-day, as in times past, is a prince of the blood, the present head of of the institution being Duke of York, who succeeded his sailor uncle, The Duke of Edingburgh, when the latter ascended the German throne of Coburg and Gotha.

The real administrative power and responsibilty rests in the hands of of the deputy master, George Vivian, who is to-day a former merchant captain, belonging to the Royal Naval Reserve, his predecessor having been the late Sir Sidney Welsh. The latter, a fine old fellow, in discussing on one occasion that particular part of the Cornish coast where the *Paris* had gone on the rocks, happen to mention that, in his opinion, there were some mysterious magnetic influences at work there which impaired at times the reliability of the compass and were accountable for so many vessels going out of their courses just at that point. He talked of instigating a careful investigation of the matter, but as far as I know nothing has ever been done in the affair. His theory, however, would account for such experienced navigators as the skippers of the *Paris* and of the *Mohegan* steering the liners which they commanded straight on the rocks.

Captain Vivian, like Sir Sidney, draws a salary of $7,500 a year, while the Duke of York is supposed to enjoy emoluments to the extent of $15,000 a year for his purely honorary services as master. The professional members of the Board of Elder Brethren receive salaries ranging from $2,000 to $3,000, which they well earn; for, in addition to controlling and administering the entire British lighthouse system, they likewise are intrusted with the duty of directing the examinations of the navigating lieutenants of the Royal Navy and of acting as assessors and assistants to the presiding judge of the Admiralty Court. [1099]

EX-ATTACHE.

[1098] The Great Fire of London began on the night of September 2nd, 1666, as a small fire on Pudding Lane, in the bakeshop of Thomas Farynor, baker to King Charles II. Some 80% of the city proper was destroyed, including 13,000 homes, 52 Guild Halls and 89 churches.

[1099] *New-York Tribune* (Illustrated Supplement) May 28th 1899.

Every land has its own law.

An organization with such pedigree and with an astonishing degree of autonomy would perhaps, not surprisingly, become overly bureaucratic and self-serving. Clearly, there is a palpable exasperation shown in this unsympathetic news item. The Americans failed to understand the British way of doing things, and so were dismissive and remained unimpressed by the Trinity House's indulgence; not helped by its imperviousness and (dare one say) more than a whiff of corruption within its corporate ranks.

Having tragically lost a number of their own citizens in the *Mohegan* disaster, and with no clear reason for this calamity having come about, the Trinity House provided a convenient scapegoat for the Americans. It had not escaped their notice that this authority had received a great deal of criticism, over a perceived lack of warning signals erected on and around the Manacle Rocks.

In fairness, the Trinity House had produced a first class maritime service, much envied and admired in equal measure, and in prompting the rest of the world to follow in its wake. To this day, this venerable organisation remains the standard by which all others are measured.

Appendix 20

The Crew Lists for the Porthoustock Lifeboat attending the *Mohegan*.

Royal National Lifeboat Institution
Porthoustock Lifeboat
Wreck of the
S.S. Mohegan of Hull
On the Manacle Rocks on the 14th October 1898
The Porthoustock Life-Boat manned by men from
Porthoustock and St. Keverne made two trips rescuing
twenty-eight persons on the first & sixteen on the second trip
One hundred and six lives were lost

First Crew	Second Crew
James Hill coxswain	James Hill coxswain
William Henry Tripp	James Henry Cliff
Joseph James	Joseph James
Arthur Cox	William Henry Tripp
Francis Tripp	Francis Tripp
John Roberts	William Hill
Henry Roberts	Henry Roberts
Alfred Roberts	John Roberts
George Dally	George Dally
William Hill	Richard Sobey
Ernest James	George Tripp
John Thomas	William John Tripp
Bentley Moore	William Bastian
George Tripp	John Tripp
William Bastian	William Penlerick
William Rashleigh	William Rashleigh

The Institution awarded the Silver Medal for Gallantry to

Coxswain James Hill

This inscription is based on an original, currently taking pride of place on the wall of the Porthoustock village-hall: previously the Porthoustock lifeboat station (see fig. 92).[1100]

[1100] Courtesy: Mr Henry Bosustow; Chairman of the Porthoustock Village-hall Committee.

Bearing	Is the angle in degrees (clockwise) between North and the direction to a destination point [see **Course**, **Heading** and **Track**]
Bight	A curve or recess in a coastline, river, or other geographical feature.
Black Gang	So called because of their being covered by coal dust. They would be engaged in stoking [q.v.] and trimming [q.v.] duties in the engine room.
Bulkhead Sluices	These are the valves in the bulkhead, etc., running through the bulkheads themselves.
Captain	A largely honorary title, given to a ship's master. It is also used to honour anyone with a master's certificate, whether or not in command of their vessel.[1101]
Carpenter	Originally a woodworker. He would have responsibility for repairs, during the voyage. He may also be required to keep drinking-water from freezing and for sounding the bilges (the lowest inner part of a ship's hull).
Caulking	Caulking is used to make the seams in wooden boats or ships watertight, by driving fibrous materials into the wedge-shaped seams between planks. It is also the term to describe the process used to make riveted iron or steel ships and boilers watertight or steam-tight.
Course	The direction a vessel is actually moving in. [see **Bearing**, **Heading** and **Track**]
Crow's Nest	A lookout station positioned at the highest practical point on a ships mast. The origin of "nest" seems obvious, but why crows? One possibility is that Norse ships carried ravens in cages, which were hoisted aloft and released in order to find the direction to the nearest land.
Davit	A crane-like device (usually one of a pair) designed for suspending or lowering a lifeboat
Engineer	Assigned to service or maintain the ship's engines. The engineering team was headed by a Chief Engineer.
Falls	The ropes associated with a block and tackle, especially those attached to a lifeboat and used in their deployment.
Fireman	A crew member who has a variety of duties, around the fireboxes in the ship's boiler-rooms. He would have been a member of the *Black Gang*, which speaks for itself.
Flying Bridge	A flying bridge is a (usually open) area on top of, or at the side of, a ship's pilothouse, or closed bridge, that serves as an operating station for the ship's officers in good weather or when maneuvering in port, where good views along the ship sides are important.
Graving dock	A dry dock: a large dock from which water can be pumped out; used for building ships or for repairing a ship below its waterline.
Greaser	A member of the engine-room that lubricated the machinery moving parts, with grease.
Gunwale	The upper edge of the side of a vessel. So called because guns were mounted on it.
Heading	This is the direction in which a vessel is pointing but is not always the direction in which the vessel is moving; due to wind and tide. [see **Bearing**, **Course** and **Track**]
Knot	Until the 16th Century, seamen estimated their ship's speed through the water by noting the time it took a wood chip, or bubble, or piece of seaweed to pass along the length of their vessel and converting that distance and interval to velocity. Some time prior to 1578, the "log line" or "chip log" was invented to provide a more accurate measurement. It consisted of a triangular "chip" of wood attached to a light line by its three corners so that, when tossed overboard it "dug in" and pulled the line from its hand-held reel. Knots were tied in the line at intervals that equated to sea miles-per-hour. A half-minute sand glass was used as a timer. Once an hour in a Midshipman and Quartermaster of the Watch, together with a seaman helper, went aft to the taffrail and tossed the log. A taffrail log is an object dragged from the stern of the vessel to calculate the vessel's speed through the water. When the chip hit the water, the Quartermaster turned the glass. At his "Mark," the seaman would stop the run-out and as he reeled the line back in, the midshipman noted how many knots had run out and any fraction of distance between the reel and the last knot to run. This sea-speed, in "knots," was recorded on a slate kept near the ship's wheel for the purpose, together with a record of every change of direction (a new course set) and the time of change.[1102]
Limbers	The space between the frames of the vessel in the bottom under the ceiling.
Lookout	A crew member who is trained to report any untoward sightings or sounds, and to report these to the ship's command. By

---

[1101] Examples of such 'masters' in more lowly positions, for the *Mohegan* crew were: Llewellyn Couch, Ernest Benjamin Cole, and William Logan Hindmarsh.

[1102] See http://polkcounty.org/timonier/speaks/book18.html.

	law, they must not have any other duties assigned to them, which could interfere with their lookout duties.
Mizzen	Mizzenmast: third mast from the bow in a vessel having three or more masts.
Officer	Any member of the ship's crew that operates under an officer's license.
Purser	The clerical officer aboard a passenger or merchant ship. He is in charge of the vessel's accounts, documents, and payroll, and on most ships provides a safe for the passengers' valuables.
Ratlines	Ratlines, pronounced "rattlin's," are lengths of thin line tied between the shrouds of a sailing ship to form a ladder. Lower courses in a ratline are often made of slats of wood for support where the distance between shrouds is greatest.
Seamen	Any person who works on deck, with handling lines, steering the vessel, and stands lookout. Ordinary seamen are of a lower ranking that the able-body (AB) seaman.
Shrouds	1. Pieces of standing rigging which hold the mast up from side to side. 2. A sheet of cloth which is used to wrap a body for burial.
Standard Compass	This compass was designated as the standard for a vessel; it is located in a favorable position, that is, a position with a minimum magnetic aberration, and is accurately calibrated.
Stem	The very most forward part of a boat or ship's bow and is an extension of the keel itself and curves up to the wale of the boat. The stem is more often found on wooden boats or ships but not exclusively. The stem is part of the physical structure of a wooden boat or ship that gives it strength at the critical section of the structure, bringing together the port and starboard side planks of the hull.
Steward	A general term for any member of a ship's crew involved with commissary duties or personal services to passengers and/or crew. The term comes from an old Anglo-Saxon term: Styweard or Sty-warden, the keeper-of-the-pigs. Whether the pigs referred to here are the live animals once kept aboard as provisions on long voyages, or a commentary on the habits and personalities of some passengers is a matter of conjecture.
Stoker	Essentially, he shovels coal from a bunker into the firebox of the ship's furnaces. He would have been a member of the *Black Gang*, which speaks for itself.
Thwart	A seat or crossbeam in a small boat, from the Middle English *thwarte,* meaning "across".
Thole-pin	A wooden pin set vertically in the gunwale of a boat to serve as a fulcrum for an oar.
Track	Is the course over ground that a vessel takes, and is affected by wind and tide.
Tramp	A commercial steamer for hire; one having no regular schedule.
Trimmer	He rakes or 'trims' the burning coal in the boiler furnace, to enable maximum heat production and complete (efficient) combustion.
Well	Place in the ship's hold for pumps. To 'sound the wells' is to ascertain if the ship is taking in water.
Yard	A long, nearly cylindrical piece of timber, tapering toward the ends, used for supporting and extending a sail to the wind.

Bibliography:

Aberdeen Weekly Journal.

Advance Argus; Greenville, Pennsylvania.

And Now the Shipping Forecast; Peter Jefferson. Computer Bookshops.

Association of Royal Navy Officers; ARNO.

Auckland Star (New Zealand).

Barclay Fox's Journal 1832; 1854: Edited by R. L. Brett and Charles Fox. © Nielsen Book Services Limited.

The Belfast News-letter (Belfast, Ireland).

Blain Biographical Directory; Father Michael Blain; Wellington, NZ.

The Blizzard of '91; Clive Carter. David & Charles Publishers.

The Bristol Mercury and Daily Post (Bristol, England).

The British Institute of Graphologists

Byegone Falmouth; Sheila Bird. Phillimore & Co Ltd.

The Captain Speaks about "Old Ironsides" Her Crews; Her Times; A Timonier Publication, 1990, 1997, TGM.

Cassell's Magazine (UK).

Chicago Eagle.

The Cornish Magazine – "Around the Manacles" 1898, 414; Bluett, Albert.

Cornish Shipwrecks; Frank Strike.

Daily News (London, England).

Death in a Victorian Family; Oxford University Press. Pat Galland; Professor of History at the Australian National University.

Democrat Chronicle (Rochester, New York).

Down to the Sea in Ships, The Memoirs of James Henry Treloar Cliff; Dyllansow Truran – Truan Publications.

The Dundee Courier & Argus (Dundee, Scotland).

Ellesmere Guardian (New Zealand).

El Paso Herald.

The English Channel Pilot for the South and South West Coasts of England, the South Coast of Ireland and Part of the North Coast of France; Published by – Charles Wilson.

The Enigma That Was Thomas William Cowan; Robert J. Hawker. Northern Bee Books.

The Era (London England).

Evelyn Observer and Bourke East Record (Vic : 1902 - 1917); Australia.

The Evening Times (Washington, D.C.)

Falmouth Packet Archives & General Advertiser (Truro, England).

GENBRIAND; Briand, Pablo.

The Gippsland Times; Victoria, Australia.

Glasgow Herald (Glasgow, Scotland).

Good As Gold; Patten , Louise. Quercus Publishing Plc.

Great British Wrecks; Kendall McDonald. Underwater World Publications 1998.

Hampshire Telegraph and Sussex Chronicle etc. (Portsmouth, England).

Hansard; UK Parliament.

History of St.Keverne Church; Frank Curnow.

A History of the Church of England in Queensland;
    A Thesis Submitted to The University of Queensland, 1962 – Rayner, Keith.

The Invisible Gorilla: And Other Ways Our Intuition Deceives Us; Daniel Simons and Christopher Chabris.

Isadora; A Sensational Life; Peter Kurth. Little Brown and Company.

Illustrated London News.

L'Abeille, De La Nouvelle-Orleans.

Leicester Chronicle and the Leicestershire Mercury (UK).

The Lifeboat and its Story; Noel T. Methley. London Sidgwick & Jackson Ltd., 1912. [Project Gutenberg].

The Lifeboat Service – A History of the Royal National Life-boat Institution 1824–1974; Oliver Warner, Cassell – London.

Living in Sin: Cohabiting as Husband and Wife in Nineteenth-Century England; Ginger Frost. Indiana University Press.

The London Underworld in the Victorian Period; Henry Mayhew and Others. Dover Publications.

The Lower Fal in Old Photograph; Collected by Peter Gilson. History Press Limited.

The Manchester Times (Manchester, England).

Mansfield Semi-Weekly News (Ohio).

Merchant Fleets in Profile (*2*); Duncan Haws. Stephens, 1978.

The Mohegan 1898 – 1998; Terry Moyle.

Morning Bulletin; Rockhampton, Queensland, Australia.

The Morning Post (London, England).

National Health Service History; Mr Geoffrey Rivett.

The *New York Times*

No Ordinary Place; Dick Morley (The Ditchling Society May 2003).

The North-Eastern Daily Gazette (Middlesbrough, England).

Nottinghamshire Guardian (London, England).

Old Ocean's Ferry; the Log of the Modern Mariner, the Trans-Atlantic Traveler, and Quaint Facts of Neptune's Realm; John C. Hoyt – New York, Bonnell, Silver, 1900.

Otago Witness (New Zealand).

The Pall Mall Gazette (London, England).

The *Daily Princetonian* – Student newspaper, Princton University.

The *Professional Mariner Magazine* Marine Techniques Publishing, USA..

The Qu'Appelle Progress; Saskatchewan.

Richland Shield and Banner; Mansfield, Ohio, USA.

The Royal Cornwall Gazette Falmouth Packet, Cornish Weekly News.

The San Francisco Call.

Ships and Shipping; Edited by: Francis Miltoun.

A Short Cornish Dictionary (*Gerlyver Ber*); Christine Truran. Truran 2000.

The Standard (London, England).

The Star; New Zealand.

The Sun (VA) Newspaper.

Souvenir Centenary Handbook 1858 – 1958; Wardle and Smallbridge History Group.

The Toronto Star.

Trewman's Exeter Flying Post or Plymouth and Cornish Advertiser.

The Times (London, England).

Upon The Rolling Deep: 'The City of Gloucester Lifeboat'; John Putley.

The Vicar of Morwenstowe; S. Baring-Gould. Adamant Media Corporation 2002.

The Weekly Standard and Express (Blackburn, England).

Welsh Mariners (*1800 – 1945*); Dr Reginald Davies.

The West Briton.

Western Mail (Cardiff, Wales).

Western Morning News.

Women of the Four Winds; Elizabeth Fagg Olds – Mariner Books. Publisher: Houghton Mifflin, 1985.

Sources:

Badgehurst Ltd.
The British Beekeepers Association (BBKA).
Bristol Records Office.
The British Institute of Graphologists.
Charlestown Shipwreck and Heritage Centre; Charlestown, Cornwall.
Cornwall Records Office; Truro, Cornwall.
Cornish Studies Library; Redruth.
Essex Record Office.
Falmouth Municipal Library; Falmouth.
Falmouth Packet Archives.
Falmouth Harbour Commissioners; Lloyd Pond.
General Register Office; Southport, UK.
Gibsons of Scilly.
Google UK Ltd.
Gwynedd Council; Archives, Museums and Arts Service.
InfoRapid Knowledge Portal.
London Metropolitan Archives; City of London.
Memorial University, Newfoundland (MUN); Maritime History Archive.
The Music Hall and Theatre History; Arthur Lloyd
National Coastwatch Institution.
National Archives; Kew, London.
National Archives of Norway
National Coastwatch Institution.
National Library of Australia.
National Library of Wales, Aberystwyth.
National Maritime Museum, Cornwall.
Newquay Old Cornwall Society.
PIP Group Registrations; Chepstow, Monmouthshire.
Plymouth City Library; Reference Department.
Plymouth College of Art.
Plymouth and West Devon Record Office.
Porthkerris Divers; Porthkerris, Cornwall.
QuickPhase Pro—developed by CalculatorCat.com.
Royal National Lifeboat Institution.
Sheffield City Council; Local Studies Library.
Shipwreck UK Ltd.
St. Keverne Historical Society.
Vestry House Museum; Walthamstow, London.
WikiPedia.
Yahoo UK Ltd.

Websites:[1103]

Abbot of Aberbrothock and the Bell Rock bell.	http://www.nlb.org.uk/LighthouseLibrary/Lighthouse/Bell-Rock/
And Every Soul Was Saved - history of the painting (2).	http://norwayheritage.com/articles/templates/great-disasters.asp?articleid=114&zoneid=1
And Every Soul Was Saved - history of the painting (1).	http://searlecanada.org/hemy/thomashemydata10.html
Anglican parish of St George-in-the-East with St Paul.	http://stgite.org.uk/floatingchurch
Atlantic Transport Line – Night signals signature.	http://www.kellscraft.com
The Music Hall and Theatre History .	http:// arthurlloyd.co.uk
Beaumont, Admiral Sir Lewis Anthony; KCB, KCMG.	http://dreadnoughtproject.org/tfs/index.../Lewis_Anthony_Beaumont
Burial registers, location for.	http://findagrave.com/
Clark, Thomas; Magnetic rocks in West Cornwall	http://archive.org/stream/journalofroyalin11189193roya/journalofroyalin11189193roya_djvu.txt
Currency: US dollars to UK sterling conversion.	http://www.measuringworth.com/exchange/
Dysfunctional Bridge-Team Management.	http://maritimesun.com/portal/wp-content/uploads/2011/02/BTM-and-figures.pdf
Panic of 1893 – Economic cycles in the USA .	http://history1800s.about.com/od/thegildedage/a/financialpanics.htm.
Electronic oral recordings St. Keverne locals; source of.	http://st-keverne.com/History/mohegan/index
The *Exmouth* traning-ship, River Thames London.	http://bibulousbibliophiles.com/training_ship.php
Falmouth Lifeboat Service (R.N.L.I.).	http://falmouthlifeboat.co.uk
Fleet Organization website.	http://fleetorganization.com/1906rnadmirals
Graphology, an account of.	http://businessballs.com/graphologyhandwritinganalysis
Hansard account of a parliamentary debate around the Sailors' Homes and its inception.	http://hansard.millbanksystems.com/commons/1861/apr/09/sailors-homes-resolution.
Horniman, Frederick John. – M.P. Falmouth and Penryn.	http://www.horniman.ac.uk/media/_file/the_horniman_family_history.pdf
IMDB – Video for Porthoustock lifeboat, *SS Paris*, etc.	http://www.imdb.com/company/co0103009/
The Invisible Gorilla: And Other Ways Our Intuition Deceives Us.	http://youtube.com/watch?v=vJG698U2Mvo
King family; memorial at Spring Grove Cemetery, Ohio.	http://flickr.com/photos/professormassa/5670989720/
Kinghorn, Jonathan - website for.	http://atlantictransportline.us/index.htm
Leverton-Spry, Dr; family details.	http://yelland.info/LEVERTON/TNG/getperson.php?personID=I2836&tree=LEVERTON
Llanengan; 1861 UK census for	http://rhiw.com/census_1861/llanengan_census_1861_01.htm
Magnetic signatures in iron ships and effect on compasses.	http://myreckonings.com
McGonagall, William; Poet.	http://www.poemhunter.com/william-topaz-mcgonagall/
Mohegan memorial window – St. Keverne Church.	http://stkeverne.com/treleague/mohegan_window.php
The Music Hall and Theatre History	http://www.arthurlloyd.co.uk.
National Health Service History	http://nhshistory.net
Newbon family history	http://newbonfamilyhistory.com/page34.html
Porthoustock; *SS* Titanic survivor; Margaret Hold.	http://encyclopedia-titanica.org/family-information-11
QuickPhase Pro – Moon phase calculator	http://CalculatorCat.com
Royal Cornwall Sailors' Home; Paris Exhibition	http://pooleygates.co.uk/wp-content/uploads/2010/09/Sailorshomes.pdf
Royal Institution of Cornwall – Magnetism in rocks.	http://archive.org/stream/journalofroyalin11189193roya/journalofroyalin11189193roya_djvu.txt
Scurvy – a description of the disease.	http://pmj.bmj.com/content/80/942/224.full.
Essex Archives Online, Essex Record Office	http://seax.essexcc.gov.uk/Images.Net.
Situational Awareness Theory	http://maritimesun.com/portal/wp-content/uploads/2011/02/BTM-and-figures.pdf http://zonecours.hec.ca/documents/A2007-1-1399574.TheoricalUnderpinningsofSituationAwareness_ACriticalReview.pdf
St. Keverne Church and graveyard, panoramic view of.	http://panoramicearth.com/4697/Lizard_Peninsula/St_Akeveranus_GraveyardKeverne

---

[1103] These website addresses were legitimate at the time of publication of this book.

St. Keverne Church interior, panoramic view of.	http://www.panoramicearth.com/4698/Lizard_Peninsula/St_Akeveranus_Church
St. Keverne Local History Society.	http://st-keverne.com/History/mohegan/index
Ship's speed in knots, a description of.	http://polkcounty.org/timonier/speaks/book18
Ship's watch; a source for information.	http://kellscraft.com
Sound-mirrors; a forerunner for RADAR.	http://andrewgrantham.co.uk/soundmirrors/
Transient ischaemic attacks, description for.	http://emedicinehealth.com/transient_ischemic_attack_mini-stroke/page2_em.htm
Trinity House; official website.	http://trinityhouse.co.U.K
Ultra-High Frequency radio stations during WW2.	http://www.rhiw.com/website_maps/history_of_rhiw.htm
Vortigern (Gwrtheyrn) – a mythological figure who is associated with North Wales	http://celtnet.org.uk/gods_g/gwrtheyrn
Welsh Mariners Index	http://welshmariners.org.uk/search.php
Workhouses in the UK, history of.	http://workhouses.org.uk
Yeaxlee, Nelson – crew member's grave in Portsmouth.	http://www.memorials.inportsmouth.co.uk/

C

H

M

T